TAKING PUBLIC UNIVERSITIES SERIOUSLY

Taking Public Universities Seriously

Edited by

Frank Iacobucci and Carolyn Tuohy

UNIVERSITY OF TORONTO PRESS
Toronto Buffalo London

ISBN: 0-8020-9376-0 (paper)

∞

Printed on acid-free paper

Library and Archives Canada Cataloguing in Publication

Taking public universities seriously / edited by Frank Iacobucci and
Carolyn Tuohy.

Papers presented at a conference held at the University of Toronto,
Dec. 3–4, 2004.
Includes bibliographical references.
ISBN 0-8020-9376-0

1. Higher education and state – Congresses. 2. Education, Higher –
Finanace – Congresses. I. Iacobucci, Frank II. Tuohy, Carolyn J., 1945–

LC165.T34 2005   379.1'18   C2004-907261-7

University of Toronto Press acknowledges the financial assistance to
its publishing program of the Canada Council for the Arts and the
Ontario Arts Council.

University of Toronto Press acknowledges the financial support for
its publishing activities of the Government of Canada through the
Book Publishing Industry Development Program (BPIDP).

Contents

The Conference benefitted from the insightful comments of the following discussants. Some of these remarks may be found online at www.utoronto.ca/president/04conference/presentations.html

Part I

Professor Frank Milne
Bank of Montreal Professor of Economics & Finance, Economics Department, Queen's University

Dr. Ian D. Clark
President, Council of Ontario Universities

Part VI

Professor Frank Cunningham
Principal, Innis College, University of Toronto

Professor Sujit Choudhry
Faculty of Law, University of Toronto

Professor Mark Stabile
Department of Economics, University of Toronto

In addition, Mr. Michael Decter, Founding Chair, Health Council of Canada, gave an oral presentation at the conference.

Introduction

Public universities are central pillars of successful societies. Yet the public-policy framework that sustains them is under severe stress across nations. As university participation rates have increased, governments in virtually all countries have faced increasing expectations of access to post-secondary education. In a context of competing priorities, however, public funding for universities has not kept pace with expanding enrolments. An implicit public compact that prevailed when about 10 per cent or less of the 18-to-24-year age cohort attended university could not, apparently, be sustained when that rate more than doubled and promised to rise further. Some of the responsibility for funding has been shifted to students and their families, but judgments about the share to be borne privately, and the design of the appropriate tuition and financial aid policies, have been highly contested. Meanwhile, the quality of university education has been held hostage to the resolution of these disputes.

A major review of post-secondary education in the Canadian province of Ontario provided the occasion for the University of Toronto to convene an international symposium to address these common challenges and to explore the particular ways in which they are being addressed in different nations. The symposium, held at the University's Munk Centre for International Studies on December 3–4, 2004, brought together experts in the study and analysis of post-secondary education and related fields and university leaders from a range of jurisdictions. With different lenses – including considerations of justice, efficiency, and political feasibility – they analysed and weighed the experience with various policy options in several countries. Their presentations formed the basis for lively exchange with other conference participants – policy-makers, media commentators, and members of the university community. This book is the enduring record of that symposium. We believe that it has important messages, not only in the immediate context in which our symposium was convened, but well beyond.

Because each of these papers was prepared independently, there is some inevitable overlap across the set. Papers dealing with the same jurisdiction, for example, present different perspectives on a common experience. Nonetheless, while neither closely integrated nor exhaustive, the papers taken together encompass a broad range of experience, analysis, and reflection relevant to the key issues facing public universities, particularly in the Anglo-American nations.

What was most striking in the exchanges represented in these papers was the commonality across borders in the questions with which public universities, and the governments that support them, are wrestling.

- How do we recognize and evaluate both the private benefits that universities confer on those who attend and the public benefits that universities confer on society as a whole? And having recognized and evaluated these public and private benefits, what does that imply about how responsibility for funding should be balanced across governments, students and their families, and other private sources of support? How can this balance be established to ensure overall levels of funding as necessary for high-quality education and research, as well as broad accessibility to university education.
- To the extent that universities are publicly funded, they must compete with other public priorities for support within the fiscal framework of governments. What are the reasons for governments to invest in public universities? And within the university sector, how can public resources be most effectively invested? For example, can performance measures provide a guide for public investment in an area as complex and diverse as the university sector?
- What is the appropriate balance between centralization and decentralization in the governance of the public university sector? On the one hand, in the dynamic world of knowledge creation and dissemination, academic institutions need the flexibility and latitude to develop and pursue their own distinctive missions and strengths. On the other hand, the institutions that constitute the system of post-secondary education in a given jurisdiction should, taken together, provide a comprehensive range of options for a broad

population of students. How can this tension between institutional autonomy and system coordination best be reconciled in a publicly funded system? Is there a role for a body intermediate between universities and government in this regard?

These and related questions are being grappled with in each of the jurisdictions represented in this volume, and beyond. Moreover, in the Anglo-American countries represented here, they are being addressed in a context in which governments have been, on balance, progressively retreating from the support of university education, not only in terms of the relative share of the costs of university education borne by government, but also, in a number of cases, in terms of the absolute levels of funding per student. Bekhradnia notes that in the 1990s in England, public funding per student declined by 35 per cent. Parker indicates that the government share of university funding in Australia fell from 90 per cent in 1981 to 44 per cent 20 years later. Rosenstone reports that funding for higher education by American states declined, relative to personal income, by 36 per cent between the late 1970s and the early 2000s, while enrolment rose by about 30 per cent. While this withdrawal of the state is a cross-national phenomenon, there are persistent differences among countries in absolute funding levels. Daniels and Trebilcock, for example, point out that per-student public funding in Ontario continues to lag well behind that of peer jurisdictions among the American states.

As governments have reduced their funding to universities, they have in many cases sought to compensate in part by instituting or increasing tuition fees for students. A number of contributions to this volume make a compelling case for tuition fees as part of the overall financing package for universities, if those fees are accompanied by programs of financial aid designed to ensure equitable access (as further discussed below). Nonetheless, two observations on the experience reported here are striking. The first has to do with the substance of policy: it is critically important to get the details of the financial aid piece of the package right. As the American contributors to this volume lament, the policies and practices of government and public universities in the US have led to increased tuition and decreased need-based student aid, with the result that accessibility is widely threatened.

The second observation has to do with politics: while the slow but steady erosion of public funding for universities has in itself occasioned relatively little public outcry, governments have often encountered strong opposition to instituting or increasing tuition fees for students as part of the overall funding base for universities. The experience of the Blair government in England, as noted by Bekhradnia, provides a particularly notable case in point. In a number of other cases, political pressure has led governments in some jurisdictions to freeze (as in New Zealand and some Canadian provinces including Ontario) or indeed to abolish (as in Ireland) tuition increases instituted under predecessor governments of opposing partisan stripes. Universities have thus generally found themselves in a double bind – with declining levels of real public funding per student and tight constraints on the principal alternative source of funding, namely tuition fees.

Another striking observation of commonality of experience across nations has to do with the growing *differentiation* among universities, whether as a deliberate or as an indirect effect of public policy. China provides the most dramatic example of differentiation as a deliberate policy of the central government. As Hayhoe and Zha report, China's move to mass education at the post-secondary level in the 1990s as part of a strategy of economic progress was accomplished through massive public investment, tailored to support a hierarchy of institutions capped by a defined set of elite research-intensive universities. While China's expansion of higher education was accomplished in a political system very different from that of advanced democracies, it commands our attention given the growing geo-political and economic significance of this emerging giant on the international stage.

Elsewhere, differentiation has been less dramatic but nonetheless notable. In Britain, public policy has been deliberately designed to direct research funding to centres of high quality, as assessed by various measures of research performance, and also to reward universities that demonstrate high quality in teaching with increased funding. The result has been to increase greatly the differences across universities in the extent to which they are involved in graduate education and research, and in their disciplinary scope. In Australia, the degree of differentiation is increasing as individual universities enter into funding agreements incorporating various performance criteria with the Commonwealth (federal) government. (As one discussant, Frank Milne, pointed out, the policy framework that is driving this differentiation in Australia did not arise from a deliberate policy 'road map' – but the pragmatic responses of universities to prevailing policy will have no less a differentiating effect.) In the United States, the resource gap between historically public and private universities is growing wider, even as public universities themselves become more reliant on private sources of funding and are more or less successful in attracting private funds. In short, in many countries it is becoming less possible to speak of 'the' public university as a model of post-secondary education, and more important to think of the ways in which a set of publicly funded institutions together meet public goals for post-secondary education.

As governments and universities continue to grapple with these issues, what guidance can be drawn from experience in different nations, and indeed from the expertise that resides within academic disciplines themselves? It is an unfortunate irony that apart from institutional advocacy, universities themselves have been the source of less policy-relevant research and scholarship on higher education than they have for other areas of public policy. The present volume is one attempt to make up for that deficiency, and the contributions herein have some important suggestions to make.

As noted earlier, a theme common to many of the papers presented here is the necessity of recognizing both the public and the private benefits of higher education. Estimates of financial rates of 'return on investment' in higher education to individuals and to society as a whole suggest that the private and public pay-off is roughly equivalent (see the Dawkins and Williams and the Riddell contributions in particular). These financial models, however, do not capture the full benefits of university education either to the individual or to society. Riddell discusses the 'non-market' effects of higher education – such as benefits to health, social cohesion, and civic participation. Green argues that access to higher education is a fundamental condition for ensuring full equality of opportunity in a society. Dyzenhaus makes an eloquent case for university liberal education as engendering openness – to having one's ideas tested against experience and to understanding the experience of others – that underlies the capacity for mutual compromise on which societies depend. Gertler and Vinodrai, as well as Wolfe, describe universities as magnets in attracting talent to their local regions within a highly competitive global field, not only directly but also through their fostering of local communities of creativity.

One commentator – former University of Toronto president Rob Prichard – responded to such arguments with a question: How can it be that a case so compelling has failed to secure the level of resources, from both public and private sources, necessary for a flourishing public university sector? One response to this question may be that, in an increasing 'results-driven' agenda of competition for public resources, universities and their advocates have not be able to demonstrate in tangible ways the benefits of investment in universities (or, conversely, the harms of failure to invest). A second and related response is that in directing public funds to universities and in establishing the tuition and financial aid framework that governs the student contribution, *policy details matter*. Getting those details right is devilishly difficult, but poorly designed policies will either lock in perverse effects or prove unstable.

Both of these concerns come to bear in considering *performance-based* funding for universities. In the session devoted to this topic, and in several other papers presented at our conference, a number of points became clear. International experience is rife with cautionary tales regarding performance-based funding. As Lang demonstrates, performance-based funding schemes for higher education have proved to be unstable over time in most jurisdictions that have attempted them. In a number of cases, moreover, they have had unintended effects. In the competition for performance-based funds, for example, universities may be driven to adopt short-term strategies that are neither stable nor beneficial from a system perspective – such as the inter-university 'raiding' of faculty with high research profiles that has occurred in the UK. Such cautionary tales reinforce the message that it is important to get the details of performance-based funding right. In this regard, an important distinction emerged in our discussions.

On the one hand, funding can be tied directly to the achievement of certain objectives (such as degrees awarded), and it will drive institutions to comply with those objectives by meeting performance targets. Getting clarity on objectives, and on how best to measure them, is crucial in these circumstances. Attempts to incorporate measures of 'quality' in performance targets, as in the UK, have entailed very high transaction costs and, as noted, have led universities to attempt to 'game' the funding system as noted above (see Stein, and Green and Iacobucci, herein). In practice, however, as Lang points out, 'performance-based' funding in most jurisdictions has been little different from earlier volume-based funding formulae.

On the other hand, funding may be made conditional on the reporting of certain performance measures, while not being formulaically tied to those measures. This opens up a much broader range of possible measures, including signals of quality derived from peer-review processes (such as research grants and honours awarded to faculty) or from markets (such as the ability to attract excellent students according to standardized tests, often used in the assessment of professional schools).

Presenters from the health sector, where the reporting of performance measures has a longer recent history in several jurisdictions including Canada, made the point that the latter type of reporting can have a number of benefits – including improved communication about objectives and about the means of achieving them. (An understanding of the positive relationship between critical mass and quality in health-care facilities, for example, was greatly improved through the reporting of performance measures.) What matters, said Michael Decter, is 'who's keeping score,' whether the score-keepers are impartial, and whether they learn and improve over time.

This brings us to a key design issue for systems of higher education – namely, the potential role for intermediate or 'buffer' bodies between universities and governments. Such bodies, with varying mandates, exist or have existed in a number of jurisdictions. Some, such as the Commonwealth Tertiary Education Commission in Australia, and the Nova Scotia Council on Higher Education, have had executive authority. Others, such as the Ontario Council on University Affairs, have played an influential though formally advisory role. At their best, they have been impartial mediaries, negotiating agreements between universities and government funders, without being subject to directives from either party. (See Sossin on the potential for buffer bodies to advance the 'public interest' in this respect.)

The contributors to this volume differ as to the merits of buffer bodies, but they all acknowledge that in practice the record of such bodies for longevity is not strong – a common fate has been for the body to be abolished following a change in the government of the day. It may be, given the de facto limitations on the life of buffer bodies, that they are best established at key periods in the evolution of the post-secondary sector – for a defined period of time and with a specific mandate. There is nonetheless, as Gaskell argues, an important role to be played by an on-going organization with a mandate for research and analysis. Gaskell argues that such a research unit is best established within an academic setting, to guarantee the impartiality afforded by academic freedom independent of partisan politics or, for that matter, of institutional advocacy.

Turning to the private component of funding, our conference addressed one of the most contested sets of issues in public policy for post-secondary education: the relationship between tuition fees and accessibility, and the ways in which that relationship is conditioned by the availability and design of programs of financial support for students. Numerous contributors to our conference addressed this issue – not only in the final session dedicated to accessibility but throughout the two days of discussion. Several papers (Milway, Barr, and Alarie and Duff) review the Canadian and international evidence, which suggests that there is no evidence that higher levels of tuition result in lower participation rates. (In fact, Milway presents data indicating there may even be a positive association between the two, and suggests that this is because the increased revenues from tuition allow universities to expand the number of places for students.)

While these results may on their face seem counter-intuitive, they are understandable once systems of financial aid are taken into account. Tuition increases may indeed deter students from lower incomes and other disadvantaged backgrounds from attending university if appropriate needs-based programs of financial aid are not in place – as appears to be happening in the United States with the move away from needs-based to merit-based student support (see Rosenstone). However, data from the UK, Australia, New Zealand, and Canada show that increasing the availability of aid to low-income and disadvantaged students is associated with increased participation rates for those groups. Widely cited Canadian data for the 1990s, moreover, suggest that, while participation rates among the lowest income groups increased, there is a middle-income band of students, for whom aid is less available, whose participation rate began to decline. This finding was reinforced by more recent and as yet unpublished data reported by Stabile (based on work by Christine Neill) in his discussant's comments, available on the conference website.

Melissa Williams warns us about the political dynamics that may result from this interplay among levels of tuition, financial aid, and participation and may mean that there is a natural limit to the extent to which tuition can rise without compromising access for low-income and otherwise disadvantaged students. As Finnie argues, there is an important role for grants as well as for loans as mechanisms of student aid when there are incentive problems in the way of attitudinal barriers to access – as may well be the case for students from disadvantaged groups who have had little expectation of attending university. Grants, in effect, can give a 'boost' to students who would not otherwise choose to attend. But Williams cautions that as tuition fees rise to levels at which more middle-income students require aid, governments will increasingly direct financial aid to those programs that benefit middle-income groups – principally loan and tax benefits – at the expense of grant-based aid. Similar concerns were expressed by Cunningham as a discussant.

These warnings and others again underline the importance of getting the policy details right in designing programs of student aid. In this regard, there is much guidance to be gained from the contributions to this volume. In particular, much can be learned about the appropriate balance of grants and loans (see especially Finnie) and about the options for designing loan programs to take account of income after graduation. 'Income-contingent repayment programs' have been highly politically contested – in part because their introduction in Australia, New Zealand, and the United Kingdom was associated with introducing or increasing tuition fees. Yet there are strong arguments, on both equity and efficiency grounds, for such programs (see especially Barr, Alarie and Duff, and Ripstein) *if they are carefully designed*. Fortunately, experience with such programs, as well as the engagement of policymakers and analysts in a number of jurisdictions, is building up a stock of knowledge about the potential of this type of instrument.

We should point out that the papers presented at the conference and reproduced here were accompanied by insightful commentary by discussants which, because of space limitations, are not included in this volume. However, they can be obtained from our website: www.utoronto.ca/president/04conference/.

In conclusion, we wish to record our thanks to a number of individuals. First and foremost, to the contributors for this volume and the discussants at the conference, we are indebted not only for their contributions but also for their cooperation in meeting tight deadlines. We also wish to acknowledge the leadership of Dean Ron Daniels for his idea of convening the conference and publishing its work and for the initiation of the project with the great help of Nikki Gershbain and Jennifer Tam. We also would like to recognize the staffs of our offices who worked tirelessly to organize and produce what we believe was a most successful conference. Led by Bryn MacPherson-White, they include Brenda Ichikawa, Melanie Waring-Chapman, Zoe Steele, and Jessica Whiteside. Last but far from least, we should like to thank the team of the University of Toronto Press for their extraordinary efforts in mounting this publication under difficult time constraints and with so many chefs in the kitchen.

FRANK IACOBUCCI
CAROLYN TUOHY

TAKING PUBLIC UNIVERSITIES SERIOUSLY

PART I

The Challenges Confronting Public Universities

The Role of Public Universities in the Move to Mass Higher Education: Some Reflections on the Experience of Taiwan, Hong Kong, and China

RUTH HAYHOE AND QIANG ZHA*

The three higher education systems considered in this paper are all a part of what is often called 'Greater China.' All three can be seen as inheritors of a Confucian tradition which placed great value on higher education through a civil-service examination system going back to about 400 CE, and on the recognition and use of talent in public administration. Yet the pathways they chose in moving to mass higher education were somewhat different.

Under American influence Taiwan developed a vibrant economy in the 1960s and 1970s, and with the end of martial law in 1987 a multi-party democratic system emerged. There was an early recognition of the need for higher education to support economic development, and by 1970 14% of the eligible age cohort were able to participate in higher education, a figure which increased to 18% in 1980 and 34% in 1990. While public higher education played a leading role in this expansion, the development of private institutions in response to social demand was a vital strategy, with 64% of all students enrolled in the private sector in 1970, 69% in 1980, and 73% in 1990.[1] This pattern is very similar to that of Japan and Korea, societies with a shared Confucian heritage and strong familial support for higher education.

Both Hong Kong and Mainland China faced the challenge of a move to mass higher education much later – in the late 1980s in the case of Hong Kong, and the mid-1990s in the case of Mainland China. In striking contrast to Taiwan, both elected to carry out a dramatic and rapid expansion of the public higher education system, rather than depending upon the burgeoning of private institutions to achieve mass higher education. In 1981 Hong Kong had only two public universities and one polytechnic, and 2.2% of the age cohort enrolled in higher education.[2] By 1991, there were seven publicly funded higher institutions, including a newly established University of Science and Technology, two polytechnics which had been upgraded to university status, and two formerly private institutions which had been given public status and support. An eighth institution was added in 1994. While 8.6% of the age cohort was enrolled in degree-level higher education in 1989, this figure increased to 17.2% in 1995, and has remained close to this level up to the present, while sub-degree enrolments have continued to increase.[3]

For Mainland China the move to mass higher education has been even more dramatic, given the huge population. In 1990 China had a total enrolment of 2.1 million students in its public higher education system, with about 3.4% of the age cohort gaining access. By 1995 higher education enrolment had increased to 5.6 million, serving 7.2% of the age cohort, and by 2002 total enrolments reached 16 million, with 15% of the age cohort enrolled.[4] This was achieved by a massive expansion of the public system of higher education, and by huge increases in the size of major public institutions, in some cases involving large-scale mergers to achieve greater curricular breadth and teaching efficiency. While private higher education has been permitted to expand over this period, it has largely been at the sub-degree level, with only a handful of institutions recognized to offer degree programs.

In this paper we will focus on the experience of Hong Kong and Mainland China, and consider the differing reasons that led these two jurisdictions to give a parallel emphasis to public higher education in the massive expansion they undertook. The case of Taiwan stands as a comparative backdrop to the more recent experience of Hong Kong and Mainland China's transition to mass higher education. For political reasons there was virtually no consultation among these three societies, yet there are striking parallels in the policies chosen and development trajectories.

Taiwan has been completely isolated from both Hong Kong and Mainland China, and its early patterns of expansion depended heavily on the private sector, following the model of Japan and South Korea. After it achieved economic prosperity in the mid-1980s, however, considerable attention was given to the support of public higher education, and to its role in research for innovation in socio-political as well as economic areas of importance.

In the case of Hong Kong (HK), the stimulus for growth and change came with the Joint Agreement of Britain and China in 1984, which affirmed the end of colonial rule in 1997. This was followed by the Basic Law passed in 1990, which guaranteed the continuation of HK's legal system for at least 50 years under its status as a special administrative region of China. With this political-change agenda, it became clear that higher education would need to expand in face of a potential brain drain of talent. There were also pressing needs for the whole population to be educationally prepared for work in one of the world's most advanced knowledge societies. After China's opening to the world in 1978, the majority of HK's manufacturing jobs moved there, and a staggering 81.2% of GDP was coming from the service sector by 1993,[5] including sophisticated financial and management services, container shipping services, and many other service areas.

In the case of Mainland China, the major consideration affecting the expansion of public higher education has been an economic one. In 1978, when Deng Xiaoping declared a movement to open up and re-form in China, he set the goal of quadrupling China's gross economic product by the end of the century, and recognized that education would be a crucial factor in making this economic progress possible. While there had been considerable expansion of primary and secondary edu-cation during the decade of the Cultural Revolution (1966–76), higher education had been severely curtailed. Thus the rebuilding of China's university system was a key priority of the new pragmatic leadership. With the help of more than 1.2 billion US dollars in loans from the World Bank,[6] and a focused program of expansion and reorganization of the public higher education system, the dramatic expansion noted above has been achieved. There can be little doubt that China's remark-able economic achievements have owed a great deal to these educa-tional policies. It is also interesting to note some hesitation in the move to mass higher education arising from concern as to how it would affect China's political stability, with the tragic events surrounding the stu-dent movement of 1989 leading to a short-lived constraint on enrolment expansion in the early 1990s.[7]

In his influential analysis of the move to mass higher education, Martin Trow noted the importance of balancing considerations of equity and access with quality and the maintenance of standards of excellence.[8] He also noted how public higher education in a mass system becomes a major competitor for public expenditure, and thus needs justification in relation to economic, social, political, and cultural dimensions of a society's development.[9]

In looking at the role of public higher education in these three societies, we will thus concentrate on two interrelated questions, which may be of wider interest and relevance. The first is how issues of quality and equity have been balanced through an approach to expansion that has allowed a certain number of institutions to emerge as academic leaders, while the majority of public institutions have been expected to serve local, sectoral, or regional needs. The second is how government policies relating to the support of research in public higher education have shaped the public systems.

The Case of Taiwan

Taiwan's rapid and successful economic development from the 1960s to the 1980s earned it the title of one of the Four Little Dragons of Asia. Economically, it made a shift from basic industrial products to higher levels of technology and a greater emphasis on the service economy, as some of its manufacturing moved to Mainland China or other parts of Asia. This required the development of a sophisticated and highly trained workforce to keep up with changing technological demands. Politically, it made the transition from a one-party system to a multi-party democracy after martial law came to an end in 1987. In spite of the continuing sensitivity of its unresolved relationship with Mainland China, cultural, social, and economic ties with the Mainland have grown apace, and the Taiwan business community has been able to benefit from the many opportunities provided by China's dramatic economic development.

In higher education, we have noted already how massive expansion was achieved through encouragement of the private sector between the 1960s and the 1980s. There was also considerable attention given to short-cycle higher education through the expansion of junior colleges in both the private and public sectors. Table 1 shows how the number of junior colleges increased six-fold between 1960 and 1980, while the number of universities increased by less than two-fold. By contrast, in the period between 1985 and 2000 university-level institutions increased four-fold, while there was a steep decline in the number of junior colleges, as seen in Table 2. These changes reflect both the strong social demand for access to university-level higher education and the economy's need for a more highly educated workforce. They also reflect the shift from an approach to manpower planning that responded specifically to industrial development needs in the 1960s and 1970s to one that took into account plans for political and social democratization

Table 1   The Growth of Higher Education in Taiwan: 1960–1980

	1960	1970	1980	1980/1960
University & College	15	22	27	1.8
Public	9	10	14	1.6
Junior College	12	70	77	6.4
Public	5	20	21	4.2
Total	27	92	104	3.9
Public	14	30	35	2.5

Source: computed with data from Wang, Ru-Jer, 'From Elitism to Mass Higher Education in Taiwan: The Problems Faced,' Higher Education 46 (2003): 262, 264.

Table 2   The Growth of Higher Education in Taiwan: 1985–2000

	1985	1995	2000	2000/1985
University & College	28	60	127	4.5
Public	15	34	49	3.3
Junior College	77	74	23	0.3
Public	21	16	4	0.2
Total	105	134	139	1.3
Public	36	50	42	1.2

Source: computed with data from Wang, 'From Elitism to Mass Higher Education in Taiwan,' 264, 266.

in the 1980s. Government's commitment to public higher education can be seen in the increase from 15 public universities in 1985 to 49 in 2000, a more than three-fold expansion.

The government of Taiwan has thus given considerable importance to public higher education, while also nurturing the development of a highly diversified private higher education system. Government investment in public higher education has increased, significantly, as shown in Figure 1. The level of expenditure in private institutions has also increased, with the junior colleges being more and more dependent on private resources. However, Table 3 shows the gap that had emerged between public and private sectors by 1994, as measured by a number of resource indicators.

There has also been an increasing commitment to the provision of funds for university-based research in the public sector. In 1987, Taiwan's R&D appropriation was NT$30.3 billion, among which NT$2.0 billion

Figure 1   Higher Education Expenditure in Taiwan: 1980–1999

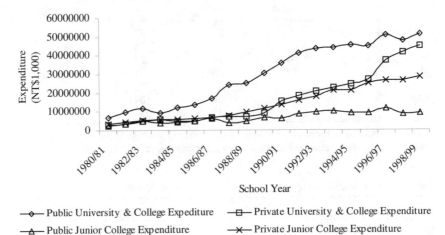

Source: computed with data from Ministry of Education, ed., *Education Statistics of the Republic of China 2003 Edition* (Taibei, Taiwan: Ministry of Education, 2003), 45–7.

Table 3   The Gap in Education Resources between Public and Private Institutions in Taiwan: 1994

Resource Item	Public Sector	Private Sector
Library Volume Per Student	66.63	28.81
Student/Teacher Ratio	11.83	20.70
Faculty with Ph.D.	57.83%	32.45%
Recurrent Funding Per Student	NT$162,370	NT$84,769
Capital Funding Per Student	NT$138,850	NT$46,232

Source: adapted from Wang, 'From Elitism to Mass Higher Education in Taiwan,' 282.

went to public universities, accounting for 86.2% of the total research funds appropriated to the higher education system.[10] Between 1991 and 1996 the annual budget of the National Research Council almost quadrupled, with more than half of this going to support research activities in public universities.[11]

Generally, there is a recognition of the importance of public higher education in ensuring a population that is able to take part responsibly in the country's democratic development and respond creatively to newly emerging social needs. This is evident in the policy change that puts 'equal emphasis on quality and quantity,' and stresses a balanced steady growth in the higher education population among humanities, social sciences, natural sciences, and technology.[12]

Taiwan remains in a kind of diplomatic limbo internationally, due to the unresolved tensions between those in its population who would like to see total independence from Mainland China and those who are seeking an acceptable way of acceding to Mainland China's insistence on sovereignty while promising autonomy over the island's internal affairs. In spite of this difficulty, Taiwan is respected as a prosperous and dynamic modern society which has been able to adapt successfully to the rapid changes around it in East Asia and contribute positively to Mainland China's remarkable economic resurgence. Politically, it is the only society in Greater China that has achieved a series of changes in government peacefully through a popular vote in which all citizens are able to participate. It is thus interesting to reflect on how far its system of public higher education, which has been greatly expanded in the last two decades, has contributed to these political, social, and economic achievements.

The Case of Hong Kong

Hong Kong's public higher education system consisted of two universities and one polytechnic in the early 1980s, with a University and Polytechnic Grants Committee (UPGC) responsible for the distribution of public funds to these three institutions. The University of Hong Kong has a history going back to 1911. It has been strongly influenced by a British university model, and its graduates dominated the colonial civil service. The Chinese University of Hong Kong was founded in the 1960s, through a merger of several colleges which had moved to HK from Mainland China after 1949. It developed along lines closer to the American model, while also stressing its Chinese identity through the use of the Chinese language in some of its teaching activities. The Hong Kong Polytechnic was founded in 1972 to provide for the economy's needs of more technically educated personnel. By the early 1980s, these three institutions functioned as an elite public system providing access to only 2.2% of the age cohort. None of them gave much attention to research, nor was this a significant part of their mandate.[13]

The 1980s were a kind of watershed in Hong Kong's development, for a number of reasons. Economically, with the opening up of Mainland China, most of the light industry that had provided employment for Hong Kong workers since the 1950s was moved to China, where wages were much lower. Meanwhile, property prices soared, as Hong Kong took up the role of a kind of 'middleman' for China's rapid industrialization, and new employment opportunities opened up in such areas as management, financial and legal services, and port services. Politically, it became clear that Hong Kong faced a major transition from its status as a colony of Britain since 1842 to a return to Mainland China when the 99-year lease on the New Territories came due in 1997. Discussions between Britain and China under the leadership of Margaret Thatcher and Deng Xiaoping resulted in the Sino-British Joint Agreement of 1984, in which both parties made a commitment to this transition. At the same time, it was made clear that Hong Kong would have the status of a special administration region with a high degree of autonomy over its internal affairs. This was followed by intensive efforts in drafting a Basic Law, which was adopted in 1990 and constitutes a kind of constitution for the Hong Kong Special Administrative Region. Culturally, Hong Kong had become quite a centre for the arts as its economic dynamism made possible many publicly supported cultural initiatives.

There were thus economic, political, social, and cultural factors that played into the demands for the reform of higher education and of the overall education system in the 1980s. A government-established Committee to Review Higher and Technical Education in 1980 recommended the expansion of the two universities and the establishment of a second polytechnic.[14] In the following year a high-level review of the education system was undertaken by a team of experts associated with the OECD, which reported 'tremendous social pressures from students, parents and industry ... for greater diversification of the educational opportunities available' in higher education.[15] In response, the government established the Education Commission as an influential advisory body to develop and oversee the implementation of needed educational reforms.[16]

The expansion of publicly funded higher education that followed can be described as no less than dramatic. In 1984 a second polytechnic was established, and a formerly private missionary college, the Baptist College, was brought into the public education sector and began to receive funding from the UPGC. In 1985 the two polytechnics were authorized to grant degrees, although degree students constituted only 30% of their student body in the initial years.[17] In 1986 plans were announced for the creation of an entirely new university of science and technology,

Table 4 Student Enrolment in UGC-Funded Institutions in Hong Kong: 1989–2000

	1989/90	1994/95	1999/00	Annual %
Student Enrolment (FTQ)				
Sub-degree	12,198	9,370	14,376	+1.8%
Undergraduate	24,027	41,782	45,489	+8.9%
Taught Postgraduate	2,250	4,236	6,320	+18.1%
Research Postgraduate	729	2,547	3,763	+41.6%
Total (FTQ)	39,205	57,935	69,948	+7.8%
Total (Headcount)	–	72,154	83,754	–
% of 17–20 Age Group Provided with First-Year First-Degree Places	8.6%	17.2%	16.4%	–

Source: computed with data from the University Grant Committee of Hong Kong, *General Statistics on Higher Education in Hong Kong* (June 2004), online at www.ugc.edu.hk/English/statistics/genstat.pdf; Rong, Wancheng, *Xianggang Gao Deng Jiao Yu: Zheng Ce Yu Li Nian* [Higher Education in Hong Kong: Policy and Conception] (Hong Kong: Joint Publishing (H.K.) Co., 2002), 23.

which would be part of the public system, and which opened its doors in 1991 as the Hong University of Science and Technology. In 1991 another private college, the Lingnan College, was brought into the public system and allowed to provide degree programs. In the subsequent years, all of these institutions took on the title of university, and the University and Polytechnic Grants Committee was renamed the University Grants Committee in 1994.[18] The final institution to come under its aegis was the Hong Kong Institute of Education, founded by the merger of five publicly funded teachers colleges in 1994. It achieved self-accrediting status as a degree-granting institution in 2003.

By the mid-1990s Hong Kong reached the level of a mass higher education system, with about 17.2% of the higher education age cohort in publicly funded degree programs (see table 4). There are no accurate statistics on the numbers enrolled in various forms of sub-degree higher education, though one scholar has estimated the overall higher education participation rate as 60% of the relevant age group in 2002.[19] There has also been a rapid expansion of postgraduate programs, as is evident in Table 4, with the majority of these programs being developed in the three most academically prestigious universities, the University of Hong Kong, the Chinese University of Hong Kong, and the Hong Kong University of Science and Technology.

The commitment of public funds to this greatly expanded system of higher education was substantial. After the Asian economic crisis of 1997, with ongoing pressures on the economy after Hong Kong's return to China, there was a call for some rethinking of how this large public system of higher education should be sustained. One of the strategic decisions of the late 1990s was to encourage a substantial increase in the sub-degree or associate degree part of the higher education system through self-funded programs that could be managed by public higher institutions or by other social organizations. There was also a strategic decision to encourage private institutions to seek university status through review by the Hong Kong Council for Academic Accreditation, which had been established in 1990. Given that two of the most prominent private institutions, the Baptist College and the Lingnan College, had already been absorbed into the public system, there were only one or two other institutions likely to be able to meet the expected standard, one of these being Shue Yan College.

Hong Kong thus came rather late to the decision to encourage private-sector initiatives in higher education, and the way its public system had developed ensured that these were largely in the sub-degree sector of higher education. Public institutions were clearly expected to take the lead in setting standards for academic excellence and research productivity. A Research Grants Council (RGC) was established in 1991 under the aegis of the University Grants Committee (UGC). Its appropriation for research activities in the UGC-funded universities has increased from 63.8 million HK dollars in 1991/2 to 428 million in 2002/3.[20] A dynamic research base has emerged, with the majority of funds being dispersed in response to applications from individual academics in the public system and through a peer-reviewed evaluation process. A certain amount has also been set aside for the development of areas of excellence which encourage interdisciplinary and inter-institutional cooperation. Quite naturally, the profile of disbursement of these research funds reflects the academic quality of the eight public institutions, with the two oldest institutions, UHK and CUHK, as well as the HKUST, being in a position to attract much higher levels of research funding than other institutions within the system, as evident in Figure 2.

In 2001, the University Grants Committee launched a review of higher education by a committee chaired by Lord Stewart Sutherland, then principal and vice-chancellor of the University of Edinburgh. The report of this review was published in March 2002, and it shows a continuing commitment to government support for the public higher

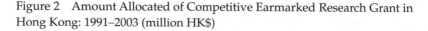

Figure 2   Amount Allocated of Competitive Earmarked Research Grant in Hong Kong: 1991–2003 (million HK$)

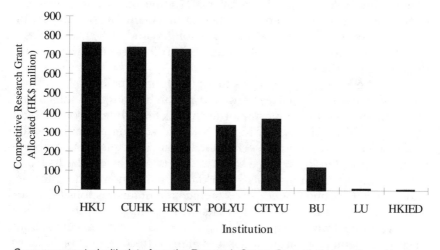

Source: computed with data from the Research Grants Council of Hong Kong, 'Appendix R: Competitive Earmarked Research Grant Exercise.' Edited by Research Grants Council Annual Report: 2002 (Hong Kong: University Grants Committee, 2003), online at www.ugc.edu.hk/English/statistics/EAppenR.pdf.

education system, combined with a decision to strategically identify a small number of institutions which should become 'capable of competing at the highest international levels.'[21] At the same time, the report makes the point that 'greater selectivity does not mean narrowing the base of higher education.'[22] Rather, a diverse set of institutions with distinctive missions will be expected to evolve, with appropriate kinds and levels of research enriching teaching in all university-level institutions. The use of a Research Assessment exercise for allocating research funds on the basis of performance, which has been developed along British lines, will be sharpened, so that 'the highest levels of research excellence can be identified and funded accordingly.'[23]

The report also recommended the establishment of a Further Education Council that should oversee the provision of programs at associate degree and parallel levels, which should expand rapidly to ensure that an even larger percentage of the age cohort receives some form of higher education.[24] All of these programs are being gradually moved to a self-funding mode, with student fees, rather than public investment, covering the major costs of expansion. While no formal target has been set, informally the government is seeking to match the levels of participation found in Shanghai, where over 70% of the age cohort gain access to higher education. Given that there is no intention to support the expansion of university-level participation beyond 18%, this means a long-term goal of over 50% of the age cohort in various forms of sub-degree higher education.

The Hong Kong government strategy is thus to maintain high standards of university-level teaching and research through a substantial commitment of public investment to this sector, while encouraging a huge expansion in short-cycle higher education through stimulating the private sector to respond to social demand and the mid-level employment needs of the knowledge society. This is seen as crucial to Hong Kong's goal of becoming 'Asia's world city,' an economically dynamic and culturally sophisticated society which maintains responsibility for its internal social and political affairs while adapting to its role as a special administrative region of China. There have been concerns about the pace of democratization and issues of press freedom, yet Beijing has largely kept its promise of non-interference into Hong Kong's internal development.

The Case of Mainland China

China's system of higher education has been fully publicly funded since the establishment of a socialist system after the revolution of 1949. Since China's strategic decision to open up to the world under Deng Xiaoping's leadership in 1978, a small number of private institutions have emerged, but these remain limited in scope and impact. Thus there were 1552 institutions in China's public higher education system in 2003, enrolling 11.1 million students, while only 173 private institutions had been accredited by the government to offer degree or sub-degree programs, with a total enrolment of 810,000 students. By far the majority of these students are in sub-degree programs.[25]

China's public higher education system was strongly influenced by the Soviet model of higher education in the 1950s, when a policy of nationalization and centralization of higher education was adopted. Under this system a small number of publicly funded universities was managed by the national ministry of education, while other state ministries and provincial governments each ran their own sectorally or regionally oriented higher education systems. Most institutions were highly specialized in curricular focus, and intended to serve a particular part of the planned socialist economy in the personnel they educated. Almost all nationally funded research was carried out in a separate set of research institutions under the Chinese Academy of Sciences or various government ministries. Research was thus separated from teaching, and teaching programs were highly specialized, with considerable overlap in provision among the different jurisdictions responsible for higher education, and a consequent waste of resources.

With the move to a socialist market economy after 1978, the Chinese government embarked on a profound set of reforms for its public higher education system, as well as making legal provision for the development of private higher institutions which could respond to burgeoning social demands. The main rationale for reform was laid out in 1985: 'to change the management system of excessive government control of the institutions of higher education ... and strengthen the connection of institutions of higher education with production organizations, scientific research organizations and other social establishments, and enable [them] ... to take the initiative ... to meet the needs of economic and social development.'[26] In 1993 a second reform document called for 'enlarging accessibility to higher education, nurturing innovative talents and carrying out cutting-edge research.'[27] In 1999 the Chinese government spelled out a specific plan for raising the participation rate of the relevant age cohort to 12.5% by the year 2000 and 15% by the year 2010, a dramatic increase from the level of about 3.4% in 1990 and 7.2% in 1995.[28]

This massive increase has taken place largely through expansion and consolidation of the public higher education system. There was a particular focus on making the system more open and efficient and breaking down the barriers among different sectors that had been put in place in the 1950s. Thus joint investment by central and local governments was encouraged, with many institutions being transferred from central to local government jurisdictions, and a large number of consortia and mergers among institutions being encouraged. This has resulted in more comprehensive institutions, with a broad range of knowledge areas, from basic arts and sciences to most fields of professional specialization. These mergers have brought about an effective reversal of the narrow patterns of specialization established in the 1950s. While expansion in the system had taken place through the creation of new institutions in the 1950s, the late 1970s, and the 1980s, in the 1990s it was achieved mainly through the expansion of institutional size, a much

Figure 3   Scale of Public Higher Education Institutions in China: 1977–2000

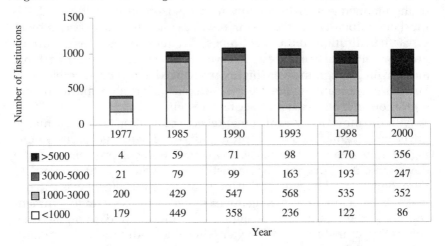

Year	1977	1985	1990	1993	1998	2000
■ >5000	4	59	71	98	170	356
■ 3000-5000	21	79	99	163	193	247
▢ 1000-3000	200	429	547	568	535	352
▢ <1000	179	449	358	236	122	86

Year

Source: computed with data from Department of Planning of Ministry of Education of China, *Achievement of Education in China 1980–1985* (in Chinese) (Beijing, China: People's Education Press, 1986); *Educational Statistics Yearbook of China 1990, 1993, 1998 and 2000* (in Chinese) (Beijing, China: People's Education Press, 1991, 1994, 1999, 2001).

more resource-efficient way of accommodating escalating student numbers. Figure 3 demonstrates this change, showing the relative stability in the number of institutions, between 1016 in 1985 and 1041 in 2000, but a dramatic rise in the number of institutions enrolling 5000 students or more, from 59 to 356.

The most dramatic increases in higher education provision occurred over the 1990s, with a more than four-fold increase in nation-wide enrolments in the public system, from 2.1 million in 1990 to 11.1 million in 2003. If the provision for students in non-formal and private institutions is factored into these statistics, the student population has been estimated at 19 million students in 2003, accommodating 17% of the age cohort in China's huge population.[29] The goals set forth for 2010 in the 1999 reform document noted above had thus already been surpassed by 2003!

In this dramatic move to mass higher education, the Chinese government has made a huge investment in the public sector, yet it has also explicitly encouraged a hierarchy of quality and talent to ensure a concentration of resources in a small number of outstanding institutions. In its 1993 reform document it announced a policy of giving enhanced financial support to 100 top institutions throughout the country, in order to enable them to attain world-class standing in teaching and research. This effort was nicknamed Project 21/1. Institutions were encouraged to garner support from local governments as well as private sources in preparing their strategic bids for acceptance into this group. In May 1998 the government made a further strategic decision to identify an even smaller number of institutions for greater concentration of public funding in the search for excellence. About 30 institutions have now qualified for the high levels of public funding that emanate from Project 98/5, which was announced at the time of the centenary celebrations for Peking University in May 1998.

Another important reform of the 1980s and 1990s has been the establishment of the National Science Foundation of China (NSFC) in 1986, which channels research funding to universities on the basis of peer-reviewed proposals. There has also been a high-technology research fund, which disburses funds for innovative technological research. The NSFC appropriation for general programs in 2001 totaled ¥797.6 million RMB,[30] and more than half of this sum went to the 30 most research-intensive universities.[31] In 2002 the top 56 research universities obtained more than ¥100 million RMB each, and their research funds totalled ¥14.2 billion RMB.[32] China's top universities are thus expected to carry out advanced and cutting-edge research activities, with an increasing amount of research funds available, as shown in Figure 4. These funds have enabled universities to compete effectively with institutes of the Chinese Academy of Sciences, which continue to play an important role in national research efforts, yet do so on the basis of competitive bids, rather than state planning, as in the system of the 1950s and 1960s. The result of these policies for the support of public higher education can be seen in Table 5, which illustrates the concentration of public resources in the 100 priority institutions which gained acceptance to Project 21/1.

While China's public higher education system is huge in comparison to that of Hong Kong, it is interesting to see how a parallel strategy has emerged. Public investment is focused on enhancing quality in the top layer of the public university system, while still ensuring basic levels of support for higher education at the regional and local levels. This is seen as crucially important to China's emerging role as a global superpower, with increasing responsibility for economic and political leadership in the Asian region and globally. China's decision to join the WTO

Figure 4   Research Funding for Public Higher Education Institutions in China: 1991–2001

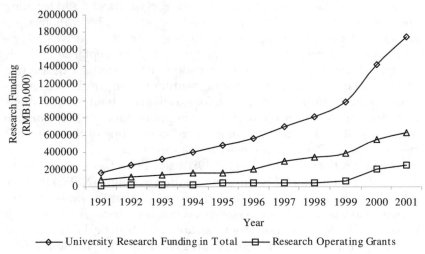

Source: Task Force on Issues of Education and Human Resources in China, *Stride from a Country of Tremendous Population to One of Profound Human Resources* (in Chinese) (Beijing, China: Higher Education Press, 2003), 638.

Table 5   Proportion of Project 21/1 Universities' Major Resources out of National Total

Resource Item	Project 21/1 Universities' Proportion (%)
Library book volume	25.65
Assets of instrument & equipment	38.70
Bachelor & sub-degree student enrolment	18.33
Master student enrolment	69.14
Doctoral student enrolment	86.01
International student enrolment	58.19
Research funds	70.10
National key laboratories	100.00
National key programs	83.61
Patent registration	72.81

Source: adapted from Guo, Xinli, 'Cong Daxue Gongneng Leiji Fenbu Guilü Kan Gaodeng Jiaoyu Zhongdian Jianshe [Key Building of Higher Education in View of the Cumulative Distribution Rule of University Function],' *Zhongguo gaodeng jiaoyu* [China Higher Education] 24:19 (2003), 16.

in December 2001, and its successful bid to host the 2008 Olympic Games, indicate the positive way it is embracing this new challenge.

Conclusion: A Strategic Role for Public Higher Education in Post-Confucian Societies

If we return to Trow's framework, it seems the three jurisdictions under examination in this paper have used public universities to maintain a balance among quality, research excellence, and accessibility. While Hong Kong and Mainland China relied heavily on the public system to cross the threshold of mass higher education, they have subsequently looked to the private sector to respond to lower levels of social demand. By contrast, Taiwan relied heavily on the private sector in reaching the threshold of mass higher education, and then increased its investment in public universities to ensure the maintenance of quality in the mass system. This was a response to concerns over quality in the private sector.

Trow also made the point that the movement of a system from elite to mass higher education wouldn't necessarily mean that the forms and patterns of the previous phase were transformed altogether. On the contrary, in a mass system elite functions might continue to be performed and even flourish, a pattern that has been evident in the United States.[33] There may be a certain necessity to this in the era of the knowledge-based economy, whose development relies not only on the overall quality of human resources but also on the capability for knowledge advancement and technological innovation. Trow further raised the question of how a system could successfully maintain diverse functions when its emphasis had shifted to forms and patterns of mass higher education.[34] The three jurisdictions we have examined in this chapter provide unique yet parallel answers to this question.

In contrast to the US situation, where many of the elite and research-intensive universities are private and have emerged out of a long process of competition and natural selection, these three jurisdictions have relied almost entirely on public universities to exercise academic and social leadership. Public resources have been marshalled to push forward research-intensive public universities at a rapid pace. This observation is particularly notable in the cases of Hong Kong and Mainland China, while Taiwan has also substantially increased investment in public higher education in the recent decade.

Within the relatively small scale of its public higher education sector, the Hong Kong government has adopted a mechanism of competition which concentrates research dollars in the three most competitive universities, while encouraging all universities to nurture a research culture in their teaching, and stimulating private-sector initiatives to respond to social demand at lower levels. Such a policy was not possible for Mainland China, given the huge size of the public higher education system. Instead, there seems to have been an increasing demarcation between the central and local governments. The central government has channelled substantial financial resources to a small group of selected elite universities to nurture their research capacity for competition at the international level. Meanwhile, the majority of public universities have turned to their local governments for extra funding, and in return take in more students from their localities and nurture the human resources suited to the needs of local and regional economic development.

This somewhat hierarchical approach does not seem to have raised much concern over the equity of higher education provision. As long as there is a perceived equal opportunity to compete for entrance to the top echelons within the system, most people are prepared to accept the differential levels of resources and differential functions given to national, regional, and local institutions. We believe the reason for this lies in China's cultural traditions. In his analysis of the miracle of Asian economic development, Vogel identified four cultural patterns that contributed to the success story: the role of a meritocratic elite, the examination ladder, the importance of the group, and an emphasis on self-cultivation or self-improvement.[35] All of these cultural patterns are consonant with highly stratified higher education systems.

Finally, theories of policy development distinguish between policies based on rational planning and policies that arise from a pragmatic reaction to internal and/or external impacts. The first is termed a 'policy blueprint' approach, and the second a matter of 'challenge and response.'[36] While Taiwan seems have taken a 'policy blueprint' approach in its move to mass higher education, the Hong Kong and Mainland China cases contain a mixture of both, with the 'challenge and response' approach predominant. The major determining factors actually producing policy changes appear to have been pragmatic responses to perceived crises: a feared brain drain in the case of Hong Kong, the urgent needs of a rapidly growing economy in the case of China.

Notes

* Ontario Institute for Studies in Education of the University of Toronto
1 Ruth Hayhoe, 'An Asian Multiversity? Comparative Reflections on the Transition to Mass Higher Education in East Asia,' *Comparative Education Review* 39:3 (1995), 301.
2 Stewart R. Sutherland, 'Higher Education in Hong Kong. Report of the University Grants Committee' (Hong Kong: University Grants Committee of Hong Kong, March 2002), 1.
3 University Grants Committee of Hong Kong 'Higher Education in Hong Kong' (Hong Kong: University Grants Committee of Hong Kong, October 1996), 16–33.
4 Ruth Hayhoe and Qiang Zha, 'Becoming World Class: Chinese Universities Facing Globalization and Internationalization,' *Harvard China Review* 5:1 (Spring 2004), 88.
5 The World Bank Group, *Hong Kong, China at a Glance* (2004 [accessed 24 Nov. 2004]); available at http://www.worldbank.org/cgi-bin/sendoff .cgi?page=%2Fdata%2Fcountrydata%2Faag%2Fhkg_aag.pdf.
6 Ruth Hayhoe, *China's Universities, 1895–1995: A Century of Cultural Conflict. Garland Reference Library of Social Science, V. 997. Garland Studies in Higher Education, V. 4* (New York: Garland Pub., 1996), 135.
7 Ruth Hayhoe, 'China's Universities since Tiananmen: A Critical Assessment,' *China Quarterly* no. 134 (June 1993), 294.
8 Martin A. Trow, *Problems in the Transition from Elite to Mass Higher Education, Reprint – Carnegie Commission on Higher Education* (n.p.: n.p., 1973), 34–9.
9 Ibid., 4.
10 Yuanjun Liu, 'Gaodeng Jiaoyu Yu Keji Fazhan: Xiankuang Yu Zhanwang [Higher Education and Advancement of Science and Technology: *Status Quo* and Prospect],' in *Ershiyi Shiji Woguo Gaodeng Jiaoyu De Fazhan Qushi [The Tendency of Higher Education Development in Our Nation in the 21st Century]*, ed. Dan jiang daxue jiaoyu yanjiu zhongxin [Education Research Centre at Danjiang University] and Ershiyi shiji jijinhui [21st-Century Foundation] (Taibei, Taiwan: Shi da shu yuan [The (Taiwan) Normal University Press], 1990), 453–4.
11 Chao-Shiuan Liu, 'Science Education and High-Tech Industry in Taiwan,' in *Proceedings of Canada-Taiwan Higher Education Conference*, ed. Philip C. Chang (Calgary: University of Calgary, 1991), 68.
12 Kirby Chaur-Shin Yung, 'Higher Education Policy of the Republic of China,' in *Proceedings of Canada-Taiwan Higher Education Conference*, 121.
13 University Grants Committee of Hong Kong, 'Higher Education in Hong Kong,' 21.
14 Wancheng Rong, *Xianggang Gao Deng Jiao Yu: Zheng Ce Yu Li Nian [Higher*

Education in Hong Kong: Policy and Conception] (Hong Kong: Joint Publishing (H.K.) Co. Ltd., 2002), 15.

15 Isidore Cyril Cannon, 'Higher Education in Hong Kong,' *Higher Education Quarterly* 51: 4 (1997), 309.

16 Government Information Service of Hong Kong, 'Hong Kong 1984: A Review of 1983' (Hong Kong: Government Information Service of Hong Kong, 1984), 3.

17 Ibid., 13.

18 Cannon, 'Higher Education in Hong Kong,' 311.

19 Rong, *Xianggang Gao Deng Jiao Yu* [*Higher Education in Hong Kong*], viii.

20 Research Grants Council of Hong Kong, 'Appendix R: Competitive Earmarked Research Grant Exercise,' in Research Grants Council Annual Report: 2002 (Hong Kong: University Grants Committee, 2003), online at www.ugc.edu.hk/English/statistics/EAppenR.pdf.

21 Sutherland, 'Higher Education in Hong Kong,' viii.

22 Ibid., vii.

23 Ibid., ix.

24 Ibid.

25 Ministry of Education of China, *2003 Nian Quanguo Jiaoyu Shiye Fazhan Tongji Gongbao* [*2003 National Education Development Statistics Bulletin*] (China Education and Research Network, 2004 [accessed 27 May 2004]); available at http://www.edu.cn/20040527/3106677.shtml.

26 Central Committee of Chinese Communist Party, 'Guanyu Jiaoyu Tizhi Gaike De Queding [Decision on the Reform of the Education System],' in *Shiyi Jie San Zhong Quanhui Yilai Zhongyao Jiaoyu Wenxian Xuanbian* [*Selection of Important Education Policy Papers since the Third Plenary Session of the 11th National Congress of Chinese Communist Party*], ed. Department of Policy & Legislature of State Education Commission (Beijing: Jiaoyu kexue chubanshe [Educational Science Publishing House], 1985), 183.

27 Central Committee of Chinese Communist Party and State Council, *Zhongguo Jiaoyu Gaige He Fazhan Gangyao* [*Outline for Educational Reform and Development in China*] (1993 [accessed 16 Sept. 2001]); available at http://www.edu.cn/special/showarticle.php?id=298.

28 State Council and Ministry of Education of China, 'Mianxiang 21 Shiji Jiaoyu Zhengxing Xingdong Jihua [Program of Educational Revitalization for the Twenty-first Century],' in *Zhongguo Jiaoyu Nianjian* [*China Education Yearbook*] 1999, ed. Ministry of Education of China (Beijing, China: Renmin jiaoyu chubanshe [People's Education Press], 1999).

29 Ministry of Education of China, *2003 Nian Quanguo Jiaoyu Shiye Fazhan Tongji Gongbao* [*2003 National Education Development Statistics Bulletin*].

30 National Science Foundation of China, *NSFC Expenditure: 1996–2001* (2001 [accessed 25 Nov. 2004]); available at http://www.nsfc.gov.cn/e_nsfc/desltop/zn/0105.htm.

31 Ministry of Education of China, *2001 Niandu Huo Guojia Ziran Kexue Jijin Mian Shang Xiangmu Zizhu De Qian 30 Suo Gaodeng Yuanxiao Mingdan* [*A List of the Top 30 Higher Education Institutions with General Program Funding from the National Science Foundation of China in 2001*] (2003 [accessed 25 Nov. 2004]); available at http://www.cer.net/article/20030612/3086683.shtml.

32 Ministry of Education of China, *2002 Niandu Keji Jingfei Chaoguo 1 Yi Yuan De Gaodeng Xuexiao Mingdan* [*A List of Higher Education Institutions with More Than ¥100 Million RMB Research Funding in 2002*] (2004); available at http://www.cer.net/article/20040618/3108368.shtml.

33 Trow, *Problems in the Transition from Elite to Mass Higher Education*, 19.

34 Ibid., 20.

35 Ezra Vogel, *The Four Little Dragons: The Spread of Industrialization in East Asia* (Cambridge, MA: Harvard University Press, 1991), 93–102.

36 A.E. Sweeting and P. Morris, 'Educational Reform in Post-War Hong Kong,' *International Journal of Educational Development* 13:3 (1993), 201.

Australian Higher Education: Crossroads or Crisis?

STEPHEN PARKER*

1. Introduction: Seventeen Years in Australia

I arrived in Australia from Mrs Thatcher's Britain 17 years ago as a senior lecturer at a good university, when my oldest daughter was just starting school. I could not believe my luck. The staff-student ratio was good. Students paid no fees, and incurred no contingent liabilities for the cost of their tuition. I had ample time for research. Internal tensions in the university and the faculty were of the deliciously trivial kind.

The honeymoon lasted all of six months. By mid-1988 fundamental changes were being injected into Australia's higher education system, the effects of which are still being felt, and the architect of whom still feels compelled to comment on them.[1]

Soon after, universities and colleges were brought together into a single, supposedly unified, mass higher education system. Many universities and colleges amalgamated with each other. The Higher Education Contribution Scheme, or HECS, of which you will hear more in this conference, was introduced. International students were admitted on a full-fee paying basis.

Since then, buffer bodies have been removed so that universities now negotiate directly with government. Performance-based funding for research has been introduced, with every sign that it will be extended to teaching performance. Competition has been progressively inculcated into the system, partly for ideological reasons, but partly possibly as a substitute for policy vision and imagination, so that market forces might take the system wherever they will.

Seventeen years later I have moved from senior lecturer to senior deputy vice-chancellor at another good university. My eldest daughter is now a law student at Monash, and active in student politics. In March this year I supported an increase in student fees. She was one of many students surrounding the administration building in protest. At one point I watched her in the distance as she pulled her phone out of her pocket and rang me up for a lift home.

There is a message here, other than about how children exploit parents. The changes in Australian higher education have been so profound and confusing that none of us is sure whether we are on the same side: staff and management; students and management; students and staff.

This paper is written from the perspective of an academic who became a dean who became a senior administrator. It has elements of warning and elements of encouragement. Which are which, is an issue for discussion.

The paper focuses on the challenges confronting Australian universities today. I suggest there are three sets: of comprehending what is happening; of responding; and of shaping or reshaping our own futures.

I will not directly describe the Australian system, because there are other comprehensive contributions at this conference from my part of the world, but I hope you will acquire a good introductory sense when I talk about the pressures to which we have been responding. [Ed: See Dawkins and Williams, and Meek and Hayden.]

I have subtitled my paper 'Crossroads or Crisis,' partly as a pun, in that the most recent review of the Australian Higher Education System commissioned by our education minister, Mr Brendon Nelson, was dubbed the Crossroads Review, and came hard on the heels of a Senate inquiry, not controlled by the minister, which asked whether Australian universities are in crisis.[2]

2. Comprehending

A significant set of challenges for all of us in Australian higher education – and, I'm sure, in other parts of the world – is to obtain a conceptual handle on just what is going on, for long enough to respond and try to influence events.

In the middle part of my research career, legal scholarship was being washed, or perhaps in hindsight only rinsed, by some critical and postmodern strands. These brought to light the simplistic ways we had been viewing social and legal phenomena, whether it was families or contracts or legal reasoning generally. I wrote a piece using the metaphor of a sound-mixing studio, which has numerous slider knobs rather than a small number of on-off switches. Even with the same musical inputs, the sound that comes out of the mixer is determined by where every knob is set on every dial. In most instances, no knob will be at the extreme end of any dial.

Many of us come from broadly similar societies with broadly similar values about higher education, but our systems have sounded somewhat different, and are diverging more, because the dials are being set in new and different places. I will continue with this metaphor for a little while because the challenge of comprehending what is going on is best met by building up a total sound from the various audio inputs.

Public-Private
From my pre-reading of other papers in this conference, a common distinction is made between public and private universities. The Australian experience suggests that it is too simple now to talk about only one public-private distinction. There are separate dials, with knobs at different points, according to whether the *funding source* is predominantly public or private, whether the *legal form* is that of a public body under statute or a private corporation, whether the *goals and value* favour public or private aspirations, and whether the *outcomes* lean towards public goods or private interests. There can be some surprising settings of the dials in relation to each other.

State-Market
So also is it too simple to distinguish clearly between the state and the market, because we now operate in state-steered competitive markets for students and research funding. The 'state,' in the form of the federal government, is the largest single purchaser of places in Australia and thereby exerts market power. From January 2005, all public universities will operate under a contractual arrangement with the government, called the Commonwealth Funding Agreement, which resembles a buyer-and-seller agreement.

Regulated-Unregulated
To distinguish simply between regulated and unregulated ignores the numerous ways in which regulatory influence is exerted through indirect means, such as the terms of the Funding Agreement mentioned above, criteria for performance-based funding, conditions attached to one-off grants for the sector, and, in relation to domestic undergraduate

students, a maximum ratio that we may maintain between government-supported places and full-fee places.[3]

National-International

In a globalizing era, it is not surprising that the distinction between national and international becomes harder to draw. For some Australian universities, however, it is becoming a core issue of identity or personality. Some have nearly 30% of their students coming from overseas. Some, like my own, have substantial operations in other countries. Monash has campuses in Australia, Malaysia, and South Africa, centres in Italy and the United Kingdom, and partnership arrangements throughout South East Asia. We recently changed the name of our Offshore Quality Assurance Committee because the very real question arose: where *is* offshore now? We are in the situation of being incorporated by statute in Victoria, under state governance requirements, whilst operating as a large, multinational organization.

Elite-Mass

Finally, the distinction between elite and mass systems is now problematic. University education in Australia certainly *was* an elite system, which then became more accessible in the 1970s through the abolition of fees, which then acquired more 'mass' through unification with the college sector, but which is arguably becoming less accessible through the introduction of tuition charging. The system is simultaneously massified and elitist.

3. Responding

As the knobs have been moving on the mixer system, Australian universities have been forced to respond to different events and in different ways.

Being reviewed

I say this with tongue partly in cheek, but almost every year now there is a major review of the whole or a large part of the Australian Higher Education system. At least some of these have drained universities of resources and management time, whilst producing little visible change. Like the bookshop customer who always gravitates to the self-help shelves in the hope that somewhere in there is the secret of contentment (or at least basic organization), our governments launch themselves into exercises in the search for palatable paths in a changing world.

Changing form

In terms of legal form, there are now 37 formally public and three private universities, whereas 17 years ago 19 were public and none private. Having said this, some public universities have their own, private, controlled entities. For example, in South Africa we established our own private higher education institution, Monash South Africa, offering Monash University degrees. In Malaysia we are partners in Monash University Malaysia, which is an accredited international university in that country. In Australia we own a private college with over 1000 students taking diploma-level and pathway courses. Two months ago we hosted a special visit from the German Rektors Conference who had singled us out as a baffling institution that they wanted to understand. Are we public and Australian? It is no longer clear.

Doing more, with less (or more)

In terms of funding mix, public contributions to university operating revenues have halved in about 20 years: from 90% of revenues in 1981 to 44%. The majority of the remainder comes from student fees; with international student fees soaring in about 15 years from very little to $1.8 billion per annum. The decline in the *public* investment per student has accordingly been very marked. The average funding per student from all sources has, however, risen slightly because of fee income.

I suspect the true situation is that some universities now have more gross revenue per student because of tuition fees, but their costs have risen because they need to market and behave in ways which attract fee-paying students. In consequence, the sector-wide student-staff ratio has gone from about 13:1 to 21:1. This is only an average, but I doubt that any university's ratio is better now than it was 20 years ago.

Reconsidering goals and values

In terms of goals and values I think it is still fair to say that all universities in Australia would espouse the modern, liberal conception of a university having to do with the discovery and transmission of knowledge as a public good as well as for private advancement.

The expressed 'missions' of Australian universities are now diverging substantially, however, with some many more avowedly vocational than others, and seeking to fashion a value proposition very much based in the private gain of the graduate. If, as is quite possible, the qualifying requirement is dropped that an Australian university must undertake research, we can expect an intensification of this trend along with the arrival of the for-profit institution.[4] One prediction is that if this occurs, we will move from 40 universities to 100 in 10 years.

Focusing on outcomes

In terms of actual outcomes, we lack the equipment to measure the balance between public good and private gain, but Australia's contingent loans scheme (which, from 2005, will cover domestic full-fee as well as subsidized places),[5] is very much premised on the belief that there *is* a balance. The voice which argues that private markets tend to under-invest in public goods is rather quiet in Australia at present.

From the universities' point of view, there is increasing emphasis on desired graduate attributes, finding out what employers seek from graduates and gathering data about 'employability' for promotional purposes. None of this is necessarily bad – quite the contrary – but the attention is shifting to the value of a university education in the first few years after graduating and away from its life-long virtues.

Moving between state and market

Australian universities have been learning how to move among state-allocation systems (in the form of government-subsidized places), quasi-markets (in the form of domestic undergraduate full-fee places up to a maximum percentage),[6] almost unregulated markets (for domestic postgraduate students), and slightly regulated markets (for international students).[7] Even in the case of government-subsidized places, from 2005 universities may charge a premium of up to 25% of the scheduled amount, thus potentially opening up competition on price. There is in any event stiff competition for students of the highest quality – for status and positioning reasons, and possibly so as to attract the best teaching staff.

If they own private educational institutions in Australia or overseas, Australian universities have to adopt a commercial mindset, and they are not always sure whether they are really 'for-profit' or 'non-profit,' because they may want to repatriate surpluses to the mother ship.

I suspect that a barometer of these changes would be how student recruitment is treated in each university. Some in the past have clearly separated their 'prospective students' function, designed to counsel applicants for government-subsidized places, from their 'marketing' function, designed to attract full-fee students from overseas or at home. The trend is to combine them because the required mindsets are now converging.

Being international

The internationalization of Australian higher education has been astonishing in my 17 years in Australia. When I arrived, international students had been coming there for three decades, largely on scholarships, as part of an 'aid' approach. In 1988 there were about 18,000 international students in Australia. In 2003 there were 210,397, almost all on full fees, and the sector is dominated by a 'trade' approach.

My own university has the largest share of 'the market,' with about 8%, which amounts to about 28% of our total student enrolments. If one adds in off-shore campuses, and distance-education students being supported at educational establishments overseas, the change has been huge. We start to face issues that multinational companies face with regulatory dissonance, in that our South Africa campus will have an accreditation visit from both the Australian and South African bodies in 2006, and we know that they have slightly conflicting requirements.

In addition, there is clearly a major need to reconsider our curriculum and general orientation to education, to take into account global changes and the new mix of our student body.

Being regulated

Australian universities are, in principle, self-accrediting, in that they do not need to seek external approval for a course or program.[8] Furthermore, the public rhetoric about university autonomy is quite strong. In practical terms, basic requirements of accountability are mutating into unprecedented levels of regulation, in the form of institutional quality audits, funding agreements, and performance criteria. I am not particularly alarmed at the current situation, but it undoubtedly requires a capacity to operate according to one's values within a more regulated environment.

Being commercial

The most significant commercial impulses for public universities come from the need to recruit full-fee students. In addition, the search is on to commercialize intellectual property and to sell other services. All universities will have a commercial arm or office of one kind or another, and all probably face internal divisions between the optimists and pessimists about how much net gain, when properly costed, commercial activities will produce. If, as I suspect, pressure increases from regulatory authorities to charge a full commercial rate, on the grounds of competitive neutrality with private providers, many consulting services may be shown to be unsustainable: that is, we attract the business because we may not always charge properly for all our overheads.

Being fair

In a strange way, the move from an elite to a mass system has not always improved equity outcomes. There are more people, and a higher proportion of people, going to institutions called universities than at any time, but the system has also become stratified in terms of prestige and opportunity. I doubt whether the major universities are any more accessible than they were two decades ago; and in some respects, for example relating to indigenous people, they may have gone backwards. The pressure is certainly mounting on universities who have done well with change to reinvest in scholarships and access programs, or operate campuses outside the main metropolitan areas.

Managing ourselves

Increasing 'managerialism' is lamented up and down faculty corridors, and with it the decline of the collegium as reflected in the dwindling influence of the senate or academic board.[9] The emergence of a cadre of career senior managers has not altogether been a *coup d'état* by failed or tired scholars, despite what is sometimes claimed. A fast-changing, semi-regulated, competitive world requires a degree of planning and coordination which a static and orderly world did not.

At some point we may turn a corner in this respect and begin to re-establish some of the collegial systems which, for all their frustrations, operated as custodians of core values and brakes against temptation. New issues will, however, keep on arising. Increasingly, universities will rely on well-trained professional administrators, often with post-graduate qualifications, who can take administrative tasks out of the hands of the academic staff and thus free them more for teaching and research. I sense we are in a transition phase in this regard.

Managing risk

Not only do we manage ourselves, we increasingly manage risks in a conspicuous way. When exposed to the market, one is exposed to its fluctuations, whether caused by an appreciating currency which increases the cost of international student places, tightened visa restrictions, or a change in academic preferences. The downturn in the IT world will have major effects on some Australian universities, many of whom have relied on full-fee students at the undergraduate and post-graduate levels. Perceptions of a whole country's attitudes or standards can change, for example because of the ranting of a racist politician or a poorly managed plagiarism scandal. We are learning from experience that the search for a place in the sun carries with it the requirement to invest in umbrellas.

Renewing ourselves
Finally, there is an emerging issue of an aging academic workforce, caused partly by widening wage differentials with the private sector, such that it is increasingly difficult to attract and retain the most talented of the young. This has been ameliorated by the recruitment from overseas of academics whose countries have weaker purchasing-power parity or worse teaching climates, but this is not a reliable source of regeneration by itself. A major challenge for the higher education sector is to show that an academic career is a rewarding one, and actually live up to the promise.

4. Reshaping

To talk about responding to pressures is to strike a negative or reactive note. On the positive side, there are opportunities for Australian universities to reshape themselves and the systems in which they operate. We are beginning to see some amazing things in our sector. We see 20-year vision statements, aspirations to diversify across several continents, and the formation of consortia which, if they succeed, will enable their members to do far more than they could do individually. We see academics surprise themselves with their boldness. My university has a centre in Florence, Italy, established by an eminent renaissance historian who, it turns out, has the same strategic acumen as the Medicis whom he studies.

I would not be surprised if a major Australian public university reaches the point where the proportion of its revenues coming from public sources becomes so small, whilst its regulatory burden across two levels of government becomes so substantial, that it will try to become a private university for the very purpose of protecting its *public* values and commitment. It may even negotiate a dowry from the government as part of its release. We shall see.

5. Crossroads or crisis?

Which takes me to my initial question: crossroads or crisis? My basic answer is that as a sector we are certainly at a crossroads in Australia, and it is one where the road we have come along is now closed off behind us. The re-election of the current federal government in October 2004 has led to the opposition abandoning its commitment to turning back the clock.

It is also a crisis for us individually, however, because those who take the wrong fork will go into decline or worse, whilst for those who take the right one there are opportunities to advance teaching and research which we have not imagined before.

For the university

Each university is at its own crossroads. If it gets it right, builds on its distinct competitive advantage, sets a tone and standards that attract good scholars and students, and makes good strategic and tactical decisions, it can thrive. In the recent Times Higher Education Supplement rankings, six Australian universities were ranked in the top 50 in the world (probably a flattering and unsustainable result, I should say), but these and some others could consolidate their position if they get it right. Equally, a university which makes wrong choices now could spiral downwards and, with regret, occupy a position in a more crowded sector.

For the scholar

Each scholar makes her or his own decisions about the university that can offer the right conditions for personal and career growth. I expect more scholars to shape their career tactically so that they increase their chances of moving to a university which offers better conditions and status. Poor decisions could lock them into a university in decline.

For the student

Each student makes decisions not only about the quality of the education they will receive but also about the future valuation of the brand behind the degree certificate. Will that university be on the list from which global employers will recruit graduates, or will a degree from it effectively lock the graduate out of certain employment markets? Will that university offer an alumni network which provides continuing opportunities in the countries where he or she is likely to live?

For local communities

Each local community and government needs to juggle the competing demands for its resources, knowing that a successful university or branch campus in its midst is an economic driver in a knowledge economy but not necessarily a vote-winner.

For governments
Each government in a developed country, faced with growing outsourcing of manufacturing and some services to developing countries, needs to think how it can sustain a knowledge economy where there is a premium on skilled graduates and a capacity to innovate. It probably does so in the context of an aging population, where it is not clear who is to pay for the health care and support of its baby-boomers, and an electorate which is opposed to immigration. The trick will be to invest sufficiently in universities whilst quietly dropping immigration controls. Universities can be a vehicle for this change, with many applications from overseas students already motivated by immigration possibilities.

6. Final thoughts

Looking ahead, it seems inevitable that some universities will make good choices, build the right relationships, have their share of luck, thrive, and move ahead. Others will go into reverse. Australia will have an increasingly stratified system, either through formal segmentation or at least functional differentiation.

I started this paper with a wistful comment about a brief period of 'good old days' in 1988. I think for some the good times will return, but the trick is not to be a university which regards the present as the good old days, because that suggests a very much worse future for them.

Notes

* Senior Deputy Vice-Chancellor, Monash University, Australia. I would like to thank my Executive Officer, Ms Michelle King, and Professor Simon Marginson of Monash University for their considerable help in preparing this paper.
1 John Dawkins in *The Australian* Higher Education Supplement, 24 November 2004.
2 One meaning of the word 'crisis' is actually a turning point, so the question evaporates, whereas other meanings point to instability, trauma, or conflict. But even this invitation to choose a meaning of crisis is a nice introduction to some of the complex and swirling ideas with which we are dealing.
3 Under the *Higher Education Support Act 2004*, Australian public universities may from 2005 admit full-fee domestic undergraduates provided they do not exceed 35% of the domestic students in that course. This system was

introduced in 1996, when the cap was set at 25%. The take-up has not been large, but it is expected to grow substantially.

4 There are no 'for-profit' universities in Australia, and to a significant extent this is because in 2000 protocols were adopted jointly by the federal and state governments about what constitutes a university. There is currently a research requirement and this has been used to block a number of private university applications. A recent review has recommended retaining this, but the federal government is nevertheless expected to try to drop it.

5 A new scheme called FEE-HELP comes into effect in 2005, as a result of which up to $50,000 of fees can be repaid through a HECS-like mechanism.

6 See above for the 35% cap.

7 The 'slightly' comes from provisions in the *Educational Services for Overseas Students Act 2000* and visa-related restrictions.

8 Unless, additionally, they want it to be recognized for particular professional purposes.

9 By which I mean the supreme academic body in a university, as distinct from the governing body or council.

Diverse Challenges, Diverse Solutions

BAHRAM BEKHRADNIA*

Ladies and gentleman, it is a pleasure to be with you this morning.

In fifteen short minutes, I can do no more than give you a brief and personal perspective on some of the challenges that the university system – certainly in the United Kingdom – has faced over the past couple of decades, and on the pressures that I think will be placed upon it in the coming years.

The higher education system has changed beyond recognition. Individual universities may look much the same – actually, most do not even look the same in England – but the system as a whole looks radically different. The most obvious difference is size. When Martin Trow describes a system with 35% of the young population participating as a mass system and one which has 50% participating as a universal system, he is exaggerating, no doubt. But there is also no doubt that in pretty well all the Western world, and beyond – in terms of its sheer size, and also the expectations of young people that they will continue their education beyond the age of 18, and increasingly well into their twenties – it is radically different. It compares, for example, with the one which we had in England until less than 15 years ago, where only a small minority of the young population – 15% or so – participated. Putting on one side the social implications of this and what it says about our society, just in terms of the nature of the university system and of individual universities, this has profound implications: not just con-

---

* Director, Higher Education Policy Institute, Oxford University. Talk delivered via teleconference.

cerning what universities teach and the way they teach it, but also regarding how the system is funded and the nature of the institutions within it.

I do not know of a single country in the world where this growth in student numbers has been matched by commensurate increase in public funding. In England, certainly, the very rapid growth of the early 1990s was matched by a 35% reduction in the funding provided per student, which poses grave threats to the quality of provision. In England, as elsewhere, these concerns about quality gave rise to the introduction of a state-run process for the quality assurance of university teaching – a curious response, you might think, to give the QA when what they needed was money, but one which actually was quite effective in my view. The other response, in England and elsewhere, has been the realization that to maintain a high-quality, and therefore a well funded, university system at the same time as meeting the aspirations of an increasing number of young people hungry for higher education necessarily implies that the state cannot be the only provider of funds. We have come to this realization rather later than you in North America, but in England, as in increasing numbers of countries, the cost of higher education is now being shared by the main beneficiaries – the state and students themselves. That is not to say, however, that this has not been a highly political and extremely difficult process. There are some countries – France and Germany, for example – where political difficulties have stood in the way of the logical, and in my view just, approach, and the introduction of student fees has been avoided. In Ireland fees were introduced, but the political party that was the opposition at the time saw political advantage in promising to abolish fees, and were obliged to do so on taking office subsequently. In New Zealand a similar dynamic led to the present government freezing the student fee when they could ill afford to increase public expenditure by the amount required. In England, the Blair government, with a parliamentary majority that is bigger than we are likely to see again, was nearly brought down by its determination to see through an approach which will lead to an increase in the student contribution.

So those are some of the implications of one of the main changes in the system: the growth that has taken place. But another equally striking consequence of the growth is that the paradigm that we, in England anyway, have taken for granted previously – of the research-led teaching university – has had to be radically modified. Funds for research have nowhere near kept pace with the increase in student numbers –

and actually there is no reason why they should. The consequence in England has been a policy decision to concentrate research funding into those universities that demonstrate the highest quality in research, which has the incidental consequence of leaving other institutions with very little funding at all for research, and in some cases no recognizable research at all. Other countries have taken a different approach and have spread funds for research, and research activity, thinly. That may be an approach that leads to a less hierarchical – and therefore more acceptable - university system, and it may in fact also be good for university teaching. I don't think, though, that it is the right approach for maximizing research impact.

The response of British governments – and in this respect the basic approach is commonly accepted by all political parties – has been pragmatic. It has been to hold up diversity as something to be cherished in its own right and encourage a diversity of institutions. Never mind that this is making a virtue of necessity, the effect has been striking. Universities differ in size from just 300 students in a specialist college of drama to 100,000 students at the Open University, which provides only for part-time students. Other universities have virtually no part-time provision at all. Some universities are entirely post-graduate, while others have very little post-graduate provision. And as I have said, some do much more research than others. Hitherto, almost all have done almost everything, though to varying extents. What is new now is the suggestion that research is not in fact a defining feature of a university. (That too I think is making a virtue of necessity, but empirically it is quite true that in some countries most research is carried out in research institutes and there is little tradition of research and university teaching being co-located.) Also new at present is the abandonment of the previous requirement for university status: that institutions must be active in a number of program areas. In England, anyway, the door has been opened to a single-discipline, private university, like a Microsoft University for example, being recognized – and perhaps even funded – by the state. That is an interesting consequence of the way things have gone.

So that is where we are now. What of the future? The fact is that universities are being asked to do an increasing range of quite different things – a great deal is asked of them and this is putting quite a strain on the system. You know well what I'm talking about, because you experience these pressures every day. Governments, for example, have become increasingly convinced of the economic role that universities will play if countries want to become modern knowledge-economies. (An interesting question for economists is whether there is some sort of a zero-sum game here, or whether all economies can become knowledge-economies – I don't know of a single country that doesn't, in its rhetoric anyway, aspire to being a knowledge-economy.) The downside of this is that governments have become increasingly interested in higher educa-tion and are increasingly interfering and making policies and doing things we could probably all do without.

What are the dimensions of this economic driver of higher educa-tion? Well, they produce new knowledge and they are seen as being those most likely to be able to apply this new knowledge, and they probably are. And that of course applies not just to science and engi-neering and so on. When we discover that we really need to know something about Islam, or about China, or even to try and explain the social breakdown on some of our housing estates, it is to academics that we look for the answers. In these cases, no less than in science and engineering, it is not possible to tell years in advance what it is that we are likely to need to know about in the future, which itself leads to interesting questions about who should decide where to concentrate our research effort.

The other economic driver is the production of highly qualified man-power – that is to say, graduates. There has been huge growth in this area recently, as I have said, and there seems little doubt in my mind that growth will continue. Those of you who have not read the book by Professor Alison Wolf, now of King's College London, entitled *Does Education Matter?* should do so. It actually takes a very sceptical stand on the question of whether education really matters in economic terms, but it shows quite clearly why there will be increasing demand for it. As more and more people become graduates, the penalties for not being a graduate increase, thereby ensuring that demand will continue to grow. The interesting question is whether, in economic terms, the state derives much benefit from this continuing increase, but that is the subject for a different conference.

Universities are expected to provide lifelong learning – not only to keep updated the skills of the workforce, but to enable people to change careers and also to enable people who perhaps missed out on education when they were younger to come back to it later in life. And in England anyway, universities are expected to be a driver for social change. Perhaps one of the liveliest – and least informed – policy discussions in recent years in England has been about the fact that the students that universities accept remain strongly biased towards what we in England rather uncharmingly call the lower social classes. It is asserted that universities have not done what they should to increase social mobility in England. That of course is only very partially a higher education issue. The main reason why there is bias in the social background of students is because of their differential achievements at school. And every country has groups that it is concerned about on precisely the same grounds. In the United States the concern is with black and Hispanic students. In Australia it is with those who do not speak English as their first language. In Bulgaria, even, such concerns exist; theirs is with Roma students. No matter that universities are only bit players in the solution to this issue, the political pressure remains.

One thing that we might *regret* is not asked of universities so much in our countries is to be the conscience of society and challengers of orthodoxy and conventional wisdom. I have been struck by the contrast in work I have done in developing countries, where universities are explicitly required to play this role. In Indonesia, for example, the preamble to the basic *Higher Education Act* speaks of 'universities as a moral force'; in Bulgaria their fundamental strategic goal for higher education is, and I quote, 'to develop a higher education system as a basis for social safety and innovation in the structural transformation of society.' Something was lost in the translation, I am sure, but the point is clear. Perhaps this role is just taken for granted in our countries, but I worry that there may be something more sinister in its omission from our discussions.

The other change that I want to mention before I finish is what I see as an ideological change that has taken place – one which affects our countries more or less equally. The market is seen as an increasingly important factor in determining the future of the higher education system and of individual universities within it. Accompanied by that is an increasingly competitive environment. The funding of universities in England is increasingly competitive. In research in particular the competition is fierce and brutal. But it is not only within our own countries that competition is increasingly important. When the World Trade Organization treats university education as a commodity whose trade is to be regulated in exactly the same way as soap powder and automobiles, that takes the notion of competition to a new dimension. And, of course, in some ways Canada, along with the United Kingdom, the United States, Australia, and other anglophone countries, has long been engaged in international competition in higher education, as we have recruited more and more overseas students, whom many universities – and the governments that fund us – regard as a cash cow. Cash cow they may be, but the presence of increasing numbers of international student raises profound questions about the nature of our universities and the courses that they provide. And the very fact that they bring in so much money means that some universities are particularly at risk to downturns in this exceptionally volatile source of funds.

In conclusion, I have no idea how the future will work out, but it is clear to me that universities will be under continuing – and increasing – pressure. And it seems to me that unless they are allowed to respond to changes in the new external environment in different ways, they are unlikely to be successful. It probably is wise, as the UK government has done, to recognize that not all universities will be successful – certainly not successful at everything – and to allow them, to require them even, to seek their own futures in different ways. That is why I have called this talk 'Diverse Challenges, Diverse Solutions.'

The Principal Challenges to Public Higher Education in the United States

ANDREW A. SORENSEN*

After reading the papers of my fellow panelists, I am convinced that there are many striking similarities in the issues we face, not only north and south of the Canada-US border, but also in Australia, Asia, and the United Kingdom. In the interest of brevity, I shall address only a few of the numerous challenges we face. Those I choose to address here could be gathered under this rubric: breaking the shackles of parochialism. We are hindered in our collective mission by pervasive parochialism, which takes several forms.

1. The first challenge is the imperative to transcend disciplinary boundaries. During the thirty-eight years I have served as a university professor and administrator, there has been a noticeable shift in the orientation of the professoriate away from fealty to their home institutions, especially as they seek and receive tenure, to loyalty to their respective disciplines. It is my conviction that this shift has increased dramatically over the past couple of decades. When I began my professorial career, faculty spoke warmly and often of devotion to their university.

Although they often complained about sub-par salaries, minimal office space, and invariably inadequate parking, even among the perennial malcontents there was grudging admiration for the traditions that the institution preserved and for the heritage the faculty felt privileged to continue – even if their enthusiasm could hardly be described as unabated.

Particularly in our research universities, as the standards for promotion and tenure have risen – exhibited by the increased emphasis on scholarly productivity (whether manifested in externally funded research and resultant publications in refereed journals or participation in juried competitions or favourable reviews of one's scholarly work) – we have perhaps unwittingly fostered allegiance to peers within the discipline, but at other institutions. As we emphasize the importance of raising the bar in search of a more prominent place in the academic landscape, in part by employing professors at peer and peer-aspirant universities to judge our own faculty, we have asserted in at least one respect that orientation to divisions within the academy supersedes allegiance to any given institution. This phenomenon receives external corroboration as our National Institutes of Health, National Science Foundation, and other prominent US funding agencies place high priority on scientific proposals that are multidisciplinary and inter-institutional.

2. This propensity to focus within disciplines provides a segue to our second challenge: to transcend institutional and political boundaries. In virtually each of the fifty states in the American Republic, support for institutions of higher education from our respective legislative bodies has declined substantially over the past few years. Nicholas Barr has observed that in some jurisdictions governments have recognized that research-intensive universities stimulate economic development and consequently have increased public funding of these institutions.[1] And Ronald Daniels and Michael Trebilcock correctly note that several states increased their funding between 1995 and 2001.[2] However, over the past three or four years, this situation has changed considerably. For the university over which I preside, the appropriations from our state legislature accounted for 38% of all university revenues in the year 2000. Four years later that had decreased by more than one-third to 24%, parallel to the situation in Australia described by Stephen Parker,[3] and the UK as described by Bahram Bekhradnia.[4]

At a meeting two weeks ago of presidents of US public universities, several commented that the support of their respective legislatures had fallen below 10%, with many noting Draconian cuts over the past several years. Daniels and Trebilcock lament the fact that in 2001 government funds accounted for 47.8% of revenues to Ontario universities, 'the lowest in Canada,'[5] but exactly twice the proportion of my university. Although a few states, including my own, are facing the prospect of modest increases in support of higher education for the next fiscal year, in most instances the magnitude of the increments will barely offset the rate of inflation and surely will not redress the substantial cuts we have experienced recently.

Here are several reasons for us to transcend our respective institutional and political boundaries in finding ways to work together:

(a) In a few instances, although I think the impact is often exaggerated, we can achieve economies of scale in integration of programs and initiatives. For example, a sister university and ours, independently of one another, were negotiating for acquisition of computer hardware and software that totalled millions of dollars annually. As a result as one, rather than two compelling parties, we saved $11 million in the first year of the contract.
(b) To my mind, a much more important consequence of transcending institutional boundaries is the synergy of scholarly endeavours that it precipitates. If the activities of faculty and staff working together across these boundaries are coordinated and territorial sensibilities are diminished, we can be enormously more effective in competing for funding and elevating scholarly productivity. This is truly a situation in which the whole can be enormously greater than the sum of its parts.
(c) A serendipitous benefit of transcending these boundaries is that faculty and staff morale is enhanced by the sincere belief that the resources of the institution are being used more effectively. If more bang for the buck is actually delivered, and the faculty have irrefutable evidence that their level of productivity has risen as a consequence, the effect on their morale is salubrious.

3. The third challenge is to transcend barriers of race and class in our search for academic excellence, which is a desired outcome of transcending disciplinary, as well as institutional and political, boundaries. There is an inevitable tension between the drive to enhance an institution's academic reputation, on the one hand, and, on the other hand, providing access to those who have not been privileged to acquire adequate preparation for university education. It is my firm belief that those two goals need not be mutually exclusive. In fact, I submit that we have a moral responsibility to provide access to our very best institutions to families who were unable to afford the economic, pedagogic, and psychological support to prepare their children for university work. In Barr's words, 'It is immoral if people with the aptitudes and desire are denied access if they cannot afford it.'[6] Over thirty years ago, Martin Trow urged us – as we made the transition from elite to mass higher education – to balance considerations of equity and

access with maintaining excellence.[7] Ruth Hayhoe offers compelling evidence from Taiwan that this balance can be achieved,[8] which I can corroborate from my own experience in Taiwan administering a graduate program sponsored by their ministry of health.

Daniels and Trebilcock appropriately recommend 'government intervention ... to ensure equality of opportunity for all students.'[9] But unless we can develop policies to dampen the effect of the regressive transfer caused by the use of general tax revenues to fund higher education, a phenomenon noted by Chapman and Greenaway – among others,[10] we shall continue to discriminate against students from low-income families. Barr offers an intriguing analysis of recent developments in the UK to overcome these disparities that merit emulation and special consideration on this side of the Atlantic.[11]

In virtually all public universities in the United States, we continue to raise tuition at a rate greater than inflation to offset cuts in legislative appropriations. This, however, merely exacerbates the regressiveness of government funding and, as Daniels and Trebilcock point out, 'reduces the opportunity of less well-off individuals to benefit from post-secondary education.'[12] In many states south of the border we have superimposed yet another layer of regressive transfer on top of the two created by government funding and student fees: we derive huge economic benefit from lottery revenues, to which the poor and near-poor contribute at a disproportionately high level.

4. The fourth challenge is to foster a truly entrepreneurial culture within the academy without compromising our institutional integrity. As we embark on this path, we must maintain our passionate commitment to open intellectual inquiry and resist what my late colleague 'Kit' Lasch characterized in *The Revolt of the Elites* as 'the university's assimilation into the corporate order.'[13] Or, in Bekhradnia's formulation, the university must be a moral conscience for our society.[14] While it is important to assert that the fiscal tail cannot be allowed to wag the academic dog, we must not be indifferent to the societal needs that funding agencies wish to address. In the United States, for example, the National Institutes of Health has provided exponential increases in funding for research into HIV infection and AIDS. It would be indefensible for a university to say: 'We refuse to do HIV research for the sole reason that we don't want the NIH telling us what to do.'

The conundrum facing us is to determine how our research universities might dip deeper into the innovation stream, and – to extend the

metaphor – simultaneously build bridges from our educational programs and technological innovations, on one shore, across that stream
to what knowledge-driven businesses need. As corporations cut back
on research and development done in-house, and are looking for external sources of innovation and breakthrough developments, we may
respond to some of their overtures without compromising the integrity
of our mission. Given our desperate need to cultivate other sources of
funding, which several of my fellow panelists have called for in their
respective papers, it is imperative that we become more aggressive in
generating revenues from the intellectual property of our faculty, and in
the process create high-quality jobs for our graduates from a variety of
sources. Given the impetus at research universities around the globe to
exploit the knowledge revolution, Bekhradnia has offered – tongue-in-
cheek – a formula for a university desirous of establishing a unique
niche in the academy: stimulate the development of an economy that is
not driven by the knowledge revolution.[15] Yet irrespective of the role
one believes is appropriate for our institutions in this increasingly global economy, there is a universal demand for upward social mobility
that our students expect their universities to facilitate.

The challenges before us are monumental, and in several respects our
near-term prospects are formidable. To borrow a theme from Jim Collins's
best-selling book, we need a 'good-to-great transformation.' But Collins
warns that such transformations 'never happened in one fell swoop.
Like pushing on a giant, heavy fly wheel, it takes a lot of effort to get the
thing moving at all, but with persistent pushing in a consistent direction
over a long period of time, the fly wheel builds momentum eventually
hitting a point of breakthrough.'[16]

I truly believe that if we find ways to transcend academic-discipline,
institutional, and political boundaries, as well as race and class barriers,
in order to elevate the quality of research and teaching in *all* North
American institutions of higher education, and at the same time invest
in the knowledge-revolution-driven industries that are capable of transforming the economies of our respective regions, we shall move from
being good to being great universities. In the process we shall accomplish far more than if we work in splendid isolation from one another,
or persist in pouring new wine into old bottles.

Quite frankly, however, success will not occur without a long-term
commitment from government, business, and education. As pointed
out by Harvard professor Michael Porter, who has served as our princi-

pal consultant on a program to foster public-private partnerships between universities and knowledge-revolution-driven industries, the race we are in is not a sprint; it's a marathon.[17] The momentum required to meet in a sustained fashion the challenges I have described will be achieved only if we are dedicated to the synergy of purpose that commitment to coherence will yield. We will be highly successful only if, in concert with our sister institutions, we are able to serve as a driving force in shaping higher education in North America for the twenty-first century.

Notes

* President, University of South Carolina

1 Barr, 'Higher Education Funding,' in this volume.

2 Daniels and Trebilcock, 'Towards a New Compact in University Education in Ontario,' in this volume.

3 Stephen Parker, 'Australian Higher Education: Crossroads or Crisis?' in this volume.

4 Bekhradnia, 'Diverse Challenges, Diverse Solutions,' in this volume.

5 Daniels and Trebilcock, ibid.

6 Barr, ibid.

7 Trow, *Problems in the Transition from Elite to Mass Higher Education* (New York: Carnegie Commission on Higher Education, 1973).

8 Hayhoe and Qiang Zha, 'The Role of Public Universities in the Move to Mass Higher Education,' in this volume.

9 Daniels and Trebilcock, ibid.

10 Bruce Chapman and David Greenaway, 'Learning to Live with Loans? Policy Transfer and the Funding of Higher Education,' paper for the Internationalism and Policy Transfer Conference, Tulane University, 2003.

11 Barr, ibid.

12 Daniels and Trebilcock, ibid.

13 Christopher Lasch, *The Revolt of the Elites* (New York: W.W. Norton, 1995).

14 Bekhradnia, ibid.

15 Ibid.

16 Collins, *Good to Great* (New York: HarperCollins Publishers, 2001).

17 Porter, in 'Governor Sanford Attends Unveiling of Monitor Report,' *The State* (Columbia, SC), 9 Dec. 2003.

What Is a 'Public' University?

DONALD N. LANGENBERG*

I must say, I feel very much at home here. I grew up just over the border from Winnipeg. I have spent most of my career on the eastern seaboard among people who sometimes detect an unusual accent but are a little vague about the geography of the American heartland. So I have taken to answering the question 'Where are you from?' by saying that I hail from the middle of the continent and am sixty miles short of being a Canadian.

We are here to discuss 'the challenges confronting public universities.' What *are* those challenges? There is a very long list, many of them worthy of an entire conference. But the fundamental and urgently important challenge that is our subject here might be characterized by answering the question with a paraphrase of a former president of mine, 'It depends on what you mean by "public"'.

I think that is the crux of the issue before us. What *do* we mean by a 'public' university? Throughout most of my life the answer to that question has been self-evident, something taken for granted by most people. But in the United States in recent years there have been clear indications of erosion and perversion of the idea of a public university. The existence of this conference suggests that that trend is North American, and my fragmentary knowledge of what has been happening in some European countries indicates that it is probably also trans-Atlantic.

I intend to confine my remarks here to the environment I know, the United States. And I would like to begin with a bit of historical context, because I believe strongly that history drives the future, especially in academe.

In my opinion, there have been just three watershed developments during the first millennium of university history. The first was the recognition in the eleventh century that there is value added in gathering different faculties together into a single institution called a 'university.' That recognition was the invention of the idea of the university and it led to the creation of Europe's oldest universities.

The second watershed event grew out of the idea that a university should not only transmit and disseminate existing knowledge by educating and training the young, but should also discover new knowledge through scholarship and research. What is commonly recognized as the world's first true research university, the University of Berlin, was founded in 1810 by Wilhelm von Humboldt in a brief but extraordinarily productive stint as a bureaucrat in Prussia's interior ministry.

The third watershed event was the inspiration of an Illinois farmer – and teacher, newspaper editor, college professor, and Yale graduate – Jonathan Baldwin Turner. In the mid-nineteenth century Turner wrote an essay entitled, 'Plan for a State University for the Industrial Classes.' Turner recognized that his country was in the midst of a transition from an agrarian society to one that depended on what we would today call knowledge-based industries. He saw that if the United States was to navigate that transition successfully, it would need well trained and educated workers and leaders in entirely new fields. And that meant educating the 'children of the industrial classes.'

Turner was both an academic and a practical man, and he realized that if his ideas were to stand any chance of practical implementation, he had to do more than publish an essay. So he found a patron, a New England congressman named Justin Morrill, whom he persuaded to introduce federal legislation mandating grants of federal lands to the states to support the development of colleges that would educate the common people in 'agriculture and the mechanic arts.'

I need not tell any of you that major higher-education issues are always ultimately political, and so it was with Morrill's bill. It was first introduced in the 1850s, but it failed to pass because the congressmen representing the southern states were not persuaded that there was any value in educating anyone other than the sons of plantation owners. When the Civil War removed them from Congress, Morrill reintroduced his bill. It passed, and the Morrill Land-Grant Act was signed into law by President Lincoln in 1862.

I would assert that that event was a major contributor to the ascendancy of the United States to social and economic leadership among the world's nations. Our first two public universities were founded in 1789, but the Morrill Act catalysed the founding of many of our nation's great public universities. It created one of the best educated and most highly skilled citizenries in the world. And it established cultural centres that have enriched the lives of individuals and communities with the fundamental values essential to a great nation.

In recent years I have become increasingly worried that my country's century-old commitment to the education of 'the industrial classes' is fading. Public universities and colleges across the US are struggling to cope with dramatic reductions in state funding. Although the immediate causes of our current woes are a shaky economy and an obsession with tax cuts, both possibly transient, I believe that they obscure clear indications of a far more troubling long-term trend in our nation's fundamental attitude toward public higher education. For decades the commonly held conviction that public higher education is a public good has been eroding into a belief that it is a merely a private benefit to individuals. For a long time now, we have been steadily privatizing American public higher education. Why?

State shares in university budgets have long been steadily declining, through both good economic times and bad. Some years ago the president of one of our greatest public universities commented that his institution had been founded as a state-supported university. It then evolved into a state-assisted university, and more recently had become a state-located university. The president of another great public university later remarked that his institution had reached the next stage and become a state-molested university. State contributions to the operating budgets of those two presidents' universities are now in the range of 10 to 20 per cent of their total annual revenues.

There are ominous indications that this trend may be just what many citizens want. A public survey conducted by the *Chronicle of Higher Education* several years ago asked, 'Who should pay the largest share of the cost of a college education?' Nearly two-thirds of the respondents said that students and/or their families should. Seventeen per cent said the federal government should. Only 11 per cent said their state government should.

I find this attitude inexplicable. When the land-grant universities were created, only a small fraction of high school graduates actually attended college. Yet, Americans and their political leaders were then convinced that these universities were sound investments of public resources that yielded important public benefits. Today, when at least 70 per cent of high school graduates enter post-secondary institutions, and when our nation depends on ever more sophisticated citizen workers, we appear to believe that higher education is not a public good but merely a private benefit to individuals.

Do we realize what we are doing? Why are we turning our backs on accessible affordable public campuses? At a time when tax cuts at both the federal and state levels are touted as the all-purpose nostrum for every societal ill, is there any hope of increased public investment in higher education? Should a public university be supported only by its current users (and perhaps its alumni), even though every citizen benefits from it, indirectly if not directly? And, if so, hasn't it become just another private university?

Then there are questions of control and regulation. State control and regulation of public universities range from moderate to excessive. If state contributions to public university budgets continue their steady slide from modest to minimal to negligible, why should universities be subject to their present levels of state control or, for that matter, any state control at all? Indeed, in many states our public universities are now seeking to shift their status from that of state agencies to that of quasi-independent non-profit organizations. And concurrently we are seeing clear indications that the federal government is preparing to move even more aggressively into university control and regulation.

Hardest of all are the questions that face students and their families. If they must bear the largest share of the cost of a college education, what about those that simply cannot afford to pay that share? Are we supposed to write them off as undeserving of a college education? What about all those striving citizens of all ages whose dream of an affordable education in a public university is withering?

The United States is currently experiencing one of the strongest tides of immigration in its history. When I look out at my physics class of 190 students, it looks like the United Nations. Is not the need to educate our 'industrial classes' stronger than ever?

It is striking how little public notice and attention these trends and the questions they raise have received. There has been a great public fuss about tuition increases and other symptoms of public higher education's current economic malaise. But these seem to be widely viewed as just a passing phase, despite strong evidence to the contrary. In my view, it is high time public academe's leaders stopped behaving like Pollyanna and started acting like Paul Revere.

Never before in my half-century of learning and leading in American universities have I been so worried about their future. Not during the riots of the sixties, nor in other troubled times. We Americans are noted for our optimism, self-confidence, ingenuity, and hard-headed practicality. Those characteristics may be in our genes, but they have certainly flowered in the intellectual sunlight of our great public universities. It is painful to watch those institutions being pushed down the path taken by the passenger pigeon.

Note

* Professor and Chancellor Emeritus, Department of Physics, University of Maryland. This presentation was adapted from D.N. Langenberg, 'Storm Warnings: Why Are We Privatizing Public Higher Education?' an opinion piece in *CURRENTS* (the journal of the Council for the Advancement and Support of Education), November–December 2003.

Challenges Facing Higher Education in America:
Lessons and Opportunities

STEVEN J. ROSENSTONE*

Higher education in America is in trouble. Deep trouble.

Over the course of the twentieth century, America created one of the world's truly great systems of higher education – a system that has generated tremendous scientific discoveries, fueled the economy, solved pressing social problems, and ensured the cultural vitality of our communities. It has educated millions of students, creating a well-trained workforce and spawning creative ideas and innovations that have improved the quality and longevity of life. Access to higher education has provided tremendous opportunities for social and economic mobility, enabling all kinds of people, including new generations of immigrants, to realize their hopes and dreams while enabling America to benefit from the creative energies of all of its people.

A well-educated citizenry is crucial to America's vitality. Well-educated citizens are more productive. They fuel economic growth.[1] They do work that leads to breakthroughs in science and industry. They create new knowledge, new products, new technologies, and new enterprises. They are more likely to have stable jobs and remain in the labour force because they have the skills needed to compete in an information economy. They are better able to manage change and complexity. They are adept at acquiring new skills and new knowledge and managing the flow of new information. They drive innovation and invention.

All told, economists estimate that increases in education account for 10 to 25% of the growth that occurs annually in the United States.[2] How well Americans are educated will determine how well America competes over the course of this new century, as human capital – creativity, knowledge, and ideas – secures its dominance as the coin of the realm.

An educated citizenry is also crucial to the social, political, and cultural vitality of our communities. Education promotes engagement and understanding of public issues as well as participation in community and political affairs.[3] Moreover, higher education helps societies chip away at socio-economic, racial, ethnic, and gender inequalities that fray the social fabric.[4] And it leads to broader social benefits, including healthier lifestyles and longer life expectancies, lower crime rates, and reduced reliance on welfare and public assistance programs.[5] Last but not least, a strong educational system nurtures the arts, whose vitality helps sustain our quality of life and the cultural and economic health of our communities.

All of the enormous contributions that education in America makes to the cultural, social, and economic vitality of our nation are at risk. This essay focuses on five challenges that threaten to undermine the system of higher education in America, with profound consequences for all Americans.

I begin by focusing on the culture shift that has occurred in America over the past two decades and has led to dramatic cuts in state support for higher education. These cuts, combined with rising costs, are jeopardizing the quality of education and have led to huge tuition increases for students. I next turn to the social impact of these mounting tuition bills: skyrocketing costs have reduced access to our universities and have increased the class, race, and ethnic disparities in college admission and attendance.

Next, I show how dramatic cuts in state support for higher education have also widened the gap between public and private universities. This widening gap is leading to a two-tiered system of higher education in which public institutions (which serve more than three-quarters of America's college students and constitute more than half of the nation's research-intensive universities) are at a distinct disadvantage.

I then turn to an analysis of risks to America's international competitiveness. Cuts in public investment in higher education, declining access, the increased barriers to international exchange, all heightened in the wake of 9/11, are weakening America's competitive position in the world.

My final point focuses on the enormous challenges American universities face to sustaining innovative research. The rising costs of research coupled with funding cuts, the looming US federal budget deficit, the lure of the marketplace, and the challenges posed by interdisciplinarity are all issues that American universities must address if they are to remain the source of important scientific breakthroughs. I conclude by offering some suggestions about strategies for the future.

From *Public* to *Private* Good: Declining State Support of Higher Education

A dramatic culture shift has occurred in America over the past two decades. It used to be more or less taken for granted that higher education was a *public good*. That consensus has vanished. A well-educated citizenry is no longer regarded universally as offering collective benefits to our community, our state, or our nation. Instead, higher education is increasingly considered a *private good* that benefits primarily the individual who receives the degree. And because the individual, not society as a whole, benefits from the education – so the argument goes – the individual, not society, should cover its cost.

This philosophical change has led to dramatic cuts in state support for public education. These cuts have had a profound impact on students, on the quality of higher education in America, and on America's capacity to compete in the global economy, not to mention on students' access to and experience of higher education. These cuts jeopardize America's entire system of higher education.

Following a period of growing commitment through the mid-1970s, state investment in higher education has been steadily declining, and the cuts over the past three years have been particularly sharp. Four decades ago, growing concerns about Soviet dominance in science and technology sent state investment in higher education soaring, from $3.59 per $1,000 of personal income (in 1961) to $10.56 in 1976. During the recessions of the early 1980s, state higher education appropriations dropped 11% to about $9.37. States took another bite out of higher education budgets during the recession of the early 1990s, when higher education appropriations dropped by another 17%, bringing levels of support down to about $7.50 per $1,000 in personal income.[6]

The most recent economic downturn brought yet another, even deeper round of cuts in state support of higher education. Nationwide, appropriations to higher education fell (in nominal dollars) a whopping $9.2 billion (13%) over the past three years, dropping the level of state support to only $6.80 per $1,000 in personal income – a third below 1976 levels. [Ed.: But see Daniels and Trebilcock p. 98 for another perspective.]

State support for higher education is back to levels last seen in the mid-1960s. State funding per $1000 of personal income has dropped

Appropriations of State Tax Funds for Operating Expenses of Higher Education per $1000 of Personal Income FY1961 to FY2004

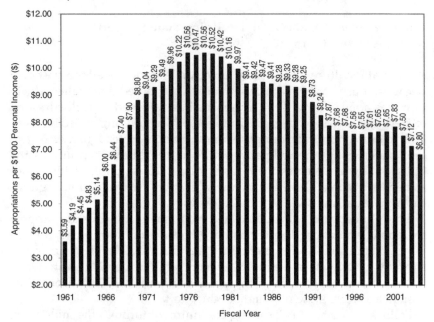

Source: Post Secondary Education OPPORTUNITY, no. 139 (January 2004), 1.

36% over the past 25 years, and the share of state budgets going to higher education has shrunk by more than one-third over the past three decades. What makes these numbers even more alarming is that the decline in support has occurred as enrollment in public higher education has soared by about 30%. These cuts translate into real appropriation losses of about $2,800 per student in a typical state. Over the same period, the real increase in public four-year in-state tuition rates averages $1,700, for a net loss to public institutions of $1,100 per student.[7]

These cuts have occurred all over America. The state of Minnesota, for example, cut appropriations for the University of Minnesota by 18% ($118 million) in 2003 and 2004, leaving its flagship public research university with a lower (inflation-adjusted) level of state support than in 1978. The state of California cut the University of California system 19% ($637 million) between 2001 and 2004, also bringing inflation-adjusted support for higher education in California back to levels last seen in the 1970s.

There are few signs that state support for higher education will turn around any time soon. State budget priorities have shifted. Some of this shift has been driven by a devolution of federal programs to the states, some by expansion of existing programs (e.g., the criminal justice system). Over a decade ago, Medicaid displaced higher education as the second largest state spending category (eclipsed only by elementary and secondary education). Medicaid expenditures and prescription drug costs continue to escalate, and baby-boomer retirements will soon place additional demands on state resources. Over the past two years, as states cut their higher education expenditures, they *increased* spending for elementary and secondary education by 3.9%; for public assistance, 6.2%; for Medicaid, 7.6%; and for corrections, 5.2%.[8]

Many states cut taxes between 1995 and 2000, only compounding the problem. These states and others are now running structural deficits and they have depleted their rainy-day funds. The upshot: state revenue is growing more slowly than in the past, and demand for those dwindling resources continues to grow. Few governors and legislators seem willing to raise taxes to provide the additional revenue needed for higher education, and there is little indication that the public is demanding that they do so.

At the same time that states have cut their support of higher education, public colleges and universities have had to face sharply rising costs due to enrollment increases, more onerous federal regulations, and increases in the cost of technology, employee health benefits, computer security, property insurance, utilities, and library acquisitions.

The combination of rising costs and reductions in state support has forced public universities to cut their investment in research, reduce faculty strength, increase class size, trim academic programs, defer maintenance and renewal of research and teaching facilities, reduce library and serial collections, freeze salaries, and reduce employee benefits. In an effort to shore up their revenue base, public universities have looked for alternatives to state funding. The result: huge tuition increases for students.

The Social Consequences of the Rising Price of Tuition

It's no secret that the price of a college education in America has skyrocketed. The cost to students has outpaced the rate of inflation, outpaced increases in family income, and outpaced increases in grants, scholarships, and other forms of student aid.

Average Published Tuition and Fee Charges, in Constant (2004) Dollars, 1976–77 to 2004–05 (Enrollment-weighted)

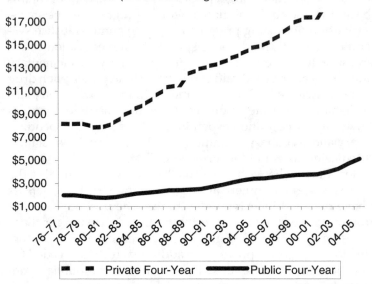

Source: College Board, 'Trends in College Pricing,' 2004, www.collegeboard.com, figure 5a.

This past fall, the average price of tuition and fees at public four-year colleges and universities in America rose to $5,132 – an increase of 158% (in *constant* dollars) since the fall of 1976. At private four-year institutions, tuition and fees averaged $20,082 – a 146% increase (in *constant* dollars) since 1976.[9] These increases have substantially outpaced cost-of-living increases and outpaced fourfold the growth in real income for families likely to have college-aged children. The rising cost of tuition hasn't just stressed families. It has priced college out of reach for most Americans.[10]

Grants-in-aid and education tax benefits (available only to some families) have helped offset some of the cost increases, but student financial aid has not kept pace with those increases.[11]

– The College Board reports that Pell Grants now cover less than 40% of the cost of tuition, fees, and room and board at an average public four-year university, compared to 69% in 1980–1.[12] The latest action by the US Congress in November 2004 froze the amount of Pell

Grants (effectively reducing the share of college costs that they will cover) and made procedural changes that will cut grant eligibility for as many as one million students.[13]

– Federal Supplemental Educational Opportunity stipends – targeted to students with significant financial need – were cut 20% over the past decade. Federal Work-Study stipends that support students who demonstrate financial need were cut 19%.[14]

– Over time, federal financial aid has shifted from grants-in-aid to loans.[15]

– A larger and larger share of student support is being targeted for merit- rather than need-based aid. Merit-based state grants-in-aid rose from 9% of the total undergraduate state grants in 1981 to 24% in 2001.[16]

– Rising costs have forced some private colleges, such as Macalester, Smith, Oberlin, and Mount Holyoke, to drop their 'need-blind' admissions policies, whereby students were admitted without regard to their ability to pay.

– Fewer than 20 private colleges and universities limit their student support to need-based (as opposed to merit-based) financial aid.[17]

The Admissions Game

In an effort to attract more students who have a 'strong academic profile,' many colleges and universities have changed their recruitment strategies, shifting their emphasis from need- to merit-based scholarships. As a result, the average amount of a scholarship awarded by public and private colleges and universities to students in the highest income quartile *exceeds* the average amount of an award provided to students in the lowest income quartile, and this gap in scholarship awards has grown over time.[18] Greater selectivity in admissions and a 'higher quality' freshman class (as measured by grades, high school class rank, and performance on standardized admissions tests) not only makes the college or university look better in *U.S. News and World Report*–type rankings, but also helps the school financially: students with 'high academic profiles' are more likely to come from more affluent families who can pay the full cost of tuition.[19]

The payoffs in income and prestige of recruiting affluent students come with a social cost. As the political winds surrounding affirmative action have changed and colleges and universities, especially the publics, are increasingly concerned about revenue and rankings, admissions directors are less compelled than in the past to make special efforts to recruit students of colour or students who are economically disadvantaged. A quarter of all admissions offices abandoned their explicit minority recruitment efforts over the course of the 1990s. Only one in three institutions in 2000 reported being engaged in special recruitment activities targeting economically disadvantaged students.[20] In the end, this recruitment gap translates into a widening enrollment and achievement gap between affluent, mostly white students on the one hand and economically disadvantaged and minority students on the other.

Because income, race, and ethnicity are so tied to the quality of a student's elementary and secondary education in America, they also affect how well a student is prepared for college, and how effectively she or he can play the admissions game.[21]

- Students of colour are much less likely to graduate from high school in four years and are far more likely to drop out without a high school diploma.
- Students of colour are less likely to take the ACT exam; less likely to take part in Advanced Placement courses; and less likely to pursue Post-Secondary Enrollment Options while they are in high school.
- The racial and ethnic disparities among those high school graduates who do take the ACT are huge. African American and Hispanic American graduates are substantially less likely than non-Hispanic whites to meet college readiness benchmarks in biology, math, and English.[22]
- This gap in college preparedness grows, in part, out of the huge disparities in funding across K–12 school districts. The funding gap for minority students nationwide is $1,099 per pupil.[23] Little improvement has been made over the past two decades in closing this gap.

And just in case the advantages of race and economic class in our K–12 systems aren't large enough, an entire industry of private admissions consultants has sprung up to coach affluent students through the college admissions process. For about $1,000, students can attend courses offered by companies such as Kaplan and Princeton Review to learn how to take the ACT and SAT exams. Parents can supplement these courses with tutors at $50 to $200 an hour to drill their children in test-taking strategies.[24] And for $5,000 to $30,000, parents can secure private consultants to help students prepare their resumes, plan and package their extracurricular activities, perform well in college interviews, and craft savvy application essays.[25]

Reduced Access to Higher Education

Skyrocketing tuition, reductions in need-based financial aid, recruitment strategies that favour students from affluent families, class and racial disparities in college preparedness and performance on standardized tests, and the ability of affluent students to game the system – taken together, these trends have led to dramatic reductions in access to higher education for students of colour and those from low-income families.

– For students from low-income families, the total charges for attending a four-year public institution accounted for about 60% of family income in 1999–2000, compared to just 5% of the family income for students from the wealthiest families.[26]
– Because low-income students are more sensitive than other students to increases in the list price, when the list price goes up, many low-income students don't even bother to apply, even though the price might be discounted by financial aid.[27] Most colleges and universities make matters worse by admitting students before aid is calculated or offered, a practice that encourages sticker shock and discourages applications from low-income students.[28]
– In 43 states, undocumented students must pay out-of-state tuition – effectively denying them access to higher education.
– According to the National Center for Education Statistics, since 1980 the college participation rate of African American high school graduates went from 4.5% behind non-Hispanic whites to 6.1% behind; the participation rate for Hispanics went from 2.2% behind non-Hispanic whites to 13.7% behind.[29]
– College participation rates for students from low income families declined by 3.5% between fall 1998 and fall 2001.[30]
– Access to higher education at the nation's 250 most selective four-year colleges and universities became increasingly skewed in favour of students from upper-income families. Students from the highest income quartile made up 54.9% of the freshman classes entering fall 2000, compared to 46.1% in 1985. Students from families in the lowest income quartile made up only 11.8% of the freshman classes,

compared to 13.0% in 1985.[31] Given the most recent trends in prices, admissions strategies, and student aid, it is likely that these class disparities have grown still larger over the past four years, just as enrollment of racial minorities in the freshman class has declined significantly this year at many top US universities.[32]

In sum, as four-year colleges and universities have grown increasingly selective, they have disproportionately turned away African Americans, Hispanics, Native Americans, and students from low-income families. This erosion of access is occurring at a time when the US population is becoming increasingly diverse and it only exacerbates the growing income and class disparities in our nation.

Growing Inequalities from Reduced Access

Growing inequalities in access to higher education have obvious consequences: growing inequalities between those who complete a baccalaureate degree and those who do not. In 1970, students from families in the top quartile of the income distribution were 6.4 times more likely than those from the bottom income quartile to have completed a baccalaureate degree. By 2002, students from the wealthiest families were 8.6 times more likely than those in the bottom income quartile to have completed a baccalaureate degree. Over the same period, the trend among high school graduates was just the reverse: the gap in graduation rates between students in the upper and lower quartiles actually narrowed significantly. Put differently, if relatively more low-income students are graduating from high school but relatively fewer are getting into and graduating from college, it is likely that erosion of access to higher education is to blame.[33]

Racial, ethnic, and class biases in admissions to America's most selective colleges have clear and lasting consequences. Students at selective colleges and universities have higher graduation rates, receive more student support, garner greater prestige, are better prepared, have better chances of being admitted to graduate and professional programs, and go on to enjoy higher lifetime earnings than students enrolled in less selective colleges and universities.[34]

Declining access to higher education has a profound and lasting impact on all of us. As the racial, ethnic, and class diversity of our universities declines, so does the quality of the education that all students receive. A diverse educational environment exposes all students to a broader range of ideas and leads to a broader and deeper under-standing of issues and perspectives. A diverse student body and a diverse faculty better prepare all students to live in a diverse society and work effectively in the global marketplace. As the US Supreme Court affirmed in *Gruttner* v. *Bollinger*, a diverse student body 'better prepares students for an increasingly diverse workforce and society ... These benefits are not theoretical but real, as major American busi-nesses have made clear that the skills needed in today's increasingly global marketplace can only be developed through exposure to widely diverse people, cultures, ideas and viewpoints.'[35] A diverse workforce, in the words of one of the corporate *amicus* briefs filed in *Gruttner*, is 'crucial to our nation's prospects.'[36] America's leadership in science, the arts, and technolgy is at risk if it continues to leave so many of its young people behind.

As James Fallows and V.V. Ganeshanathan concluded in their annual review of college admissions, 'What was once America's most powerful vehicle for social mobility is being priced out of the reach of ordinary Americans.'[37] Limited and disparate access to higher education, the great equalizer, is helping to ensure that class, race, and ethnic inequali-ties persist from one generation to the next.[38]

The Gap between Public and Private Universities is Widening

If public higher education is one of the nation's primary portals to a better life for Americans, their communities, and the nation, then the precipitous decline in state support for and access to those universities should be cause for alarm. The widening gap between the resources available to private colleges and universities and those available to the public institutions has led to a growing disparity in the respective abilities of these institutions to recruit and support outstanding stu-dents and faculty, sustain cutting-edge research, and provide high-quality education.

Access is the first casualty of this emerging two-tiered system. Grow-ing resource disparities have increasingly hampered the ability of pub-lic institutions to offer competitive financial aid packages. By and large, private institutions have deeper wells of financial resources from which to draw. As a result, they are able to support more of their students and at higher levels than can public institutions. In 1999, private four-year institutions provided financial aid to more than half of their students, including students from families in the top income quartile. The aver-

Changes in Public and Private Educational Resources over Time

	Year	Public	Private	Private Premium
Real Expenditures	1977	$8,100	$11,200	$3,100
per FTE Student	2000	$12,600	$20,000	$7,400
	growth	56.4%	79.7%	140.6%
Faculty / Student Ratio	1977	49.0	37.9	−11.1
per 1,000 FTE Students	1999	39.4	41.5	2.1
	growth	−19.6%	9.5%	−118.9%
Associate	1978	$54,300	$55,900	$ 1,600
Professor Salaries	2002	$61,500	$74,100	$12,600
	growth	13.3%	32.6%	687.5%

Source: Michael John Rizzo, 'A (Less Than) Zero Sum Game? State Funding for Public Education: How Public Higher Education Institutions Have Lost,' dissertation presented to faculty of Graduate School of Cornell University, August 2004, table 1.1.

age amount of the aid grew (in constant dollars) between 1992 and 1999, even for students from the wealthiest families. In contrast, public four-year institutions could provide financial aid to barely one-fifth of their students, with the typical grant averaging less than half the amount provided by the privates.[39] Financial aid packages at many private institutions reduce the net cost to students to a level that undercuts the lower price charged by the publics.

On a whole variety of other measures as well, the gap between public and private institutions is growing. Real expenditures per student by public institutions grew by 56.4% between 1977 and 2000; real expenditures at private institutions grew by 79.7%. Public institutions have reduced the size of their faculties to cut costs and have raised student headcounts to increase revenue. Private colleges and universities, on the other hand, have added faculty. As a result, between 1977 and 1999, the number of faculty at public institutions per 1,000 students *fell* from 49.0 to 39.4, while the number of faculty at private colleges and universities *rose* from 37.9 to 41.5 per 1,000 students. The gap in faculty salaries has also grown dramatically. In 1978, faculty salaries in public and private institutions were nearly identical; by 2002, faculty salaries at private institutions had zoomed ahead of those of public institutions.

The public-private gap in resources for faculty has grown even larger over the past two years as public universities have had to absorb deep cuts in state support. Between fall 2002 and fall 2003, salaries of con-

Average Faculty Salary at Doctoral Universities, 2003–04

Academic Rank	Public	Private	Private Premium	% Public-Private Gap
Professor	$94,606	$122,158	$27,552	29.1%
Associate	$66,275	$ 78,863	$12,588	19.0%
Assistant	$56,277	$ 68,218	$11,941	21.2%
Instructor	$37,972	$ 45,200	$ 7,228	19.0%

Source: American Association of University Professors, 'Don't Blame Faculty for High Tuition: The Annual Report on the Economic Status of the Profession 2003–04,' www.aaup.org/surveys/04z/04z.pdf, table 4.

tinuing faculty at public doctoral institutions rose 2.7%, compared to 3.9% at private doctoral institutions. Average salary increases exceeded 4% at only *one in four* public institutions; increases exceeded 4% at *more than half* of the private colleges and universities. Salaries of full professors at public doctoral institutions now stand, on average, $27,552 behind those of their counterparts at private institutions.[40] Twenty-five years ago, the salary gap was negligible.

In their effort to recruit outstanding faculty, private institutions can offer much more than higher salaries. The array of other benefits includes prestigious endowed chairs, lighter teaching loads, smaller classes, research support, better equipment and facilities, fellowships to recruit and support top graduate students, mortgage assistance, tuition benefits for one's children, and more. Publics are often outflanked and outspent in competing against this vast array of resources to recruit and retain outstanding faculty.

As state support for public higher education has tumbled, public universities have beefed up their efforts to secure private support. It's been an uphill climb: the tradition of private giving to public institutions is less well established than it is at private colleges and universities; and despite their large numbers, public school graduates' institutional ties are weaker and their average earnings and net worth are lower. Aggressive fundraising drives at public institutions over the past decade have made up some of the lost ground, typically raising $1 billion to $2 billion over five or more years. And yet, despite these aggressive and very successful fundraising efforts, the endowments of private institutions continue to grow faster than those of the publics. Moreover, the yield from those growing public endowments usually does not keep pace with the loss of state support.

Growing Endowments of United States AAU Member Institutions

AAU Institution	Average Market Value of Endowment* 6/30/02	6/30/03	Average Growth in Endowment Amount*	%	Average New Endowment Revenue*	Average Change in State Support* in FY03	Average Net Position*
Publics	$1,186	$1,216	$ 29.7	4.7%	$1.3	–$24.6	–$23.3
Privates	$3,618	$3,742	$123.8	1.5%	$5.6	0	+$ 5.6

*In $ millions
Source: The Chronicle of Higher Education Almanac Issue, 2003–04 and 2004–05; Center for the Study of Education Policy at Illinois State University, www.coe.ilstu.edu/grapevine/.

The 33 US public universities that are members of the American Association of Universities (AAU)[41] increased their endowments by an average of 4.7%, or $29.7 million between 30 June 2002 and 30 June 2003. The private AAU universities increased their endowments by 1.5%, on average, but this translated to a boost in the average endowment value of $123.8 million because they had substantially larger endowments to begin with. An average AAU public university earned $1.3 million off its incremental endowment; an average AAU private university earned an incremental 5.6 million.[42] But enter the state cuts into the calculations and it quickly becomes apparent that public university endowments are not growing fast enough to keep up with the cuts in state support. The AAU publics lost an average of $24.6 million in state support, not only eating up all of the new endowment revenue, but leaving the publics even farther behind the privates. Also keep in mind that any gain in endowment income at a private university is likely to stretch further than a comparable gain in a public university because private universities serve substantially fewer students.

To illustrate the challenge facing the publics, consider Harvard University's endowment, which rose 17.5% between 2003 to 2004, reaching an astronomical $22.1 billion, or about $1.1 million of endowment per student. At the same time, the University of Texas System endowment, the largest endowment of any public university in the country, rose 18.7% to $10.3 billion – about $58,000 per student.[43] The incremental revenue available to Harvard from its growth in endowment is about $148 million, or about $7,500 per student. The incremental revenue available to the University of Texas System is $73 million, or about $621 per student. If you deduct from the University of Texas System's $73 million in new endowment income the $40.2 million it lost in state support, the net gain in revenue drops to $32.8 million, or about $280 per student.

Even fundraising on a grand scale by public institutions is going to have a difficult time closing the gap between the publics and the privates. A public university would need to raise $2.2 billion in (unrestricted) gifts to create an endowment sufficient to replace a $100 million cut in state support (assuming an annual endowment payout of 4.5%). To secure an incremental $2.2 billion in endowment funds, all but five public universities in the nation would have to more than double the size of their current endowments, and this would merely leave them even with where they were prior to the state cut. Very few public universities are in a position to make this happen.

Making matters worse, at the same time that public universities have embarked on capital fundraising drives to mitigate the consequences of cuts in state funding, private universities are also off securing new resources. Several private universities have embarked on massive fundraising drives to dramatically increase the size of their faculty. In September 2002, the University of Southern California's College of Letters, Arts and Sciences, for example, announced a three-year initiative designed to add 100 professors – increasing the size of their faculty by 25%. Two years later, New York University announced a $2.5 billion campaign to raise money for 125 new faculty hires and build by 20% its arts and sciences programs.

These well-financed hiring sprees by the privates come at a time when public universities are cutting faculty positions, closing programs, and trimming support for research, students, and compensation. Competition will further intensify as baby-boomers begin to retire over the next decade, increasing the number of open faculty positions beyond the number of outstanding scholars and teachers in the hiring pool. Unless the gap in resources between public and private institutions is significantly narrowed, only a very few of the nation's public universities will be competitively positioned to recruit and retain distinguished faculty and talented graduate, professional, and undergraduate students.

As public universities struggle with these new financial realities, they do so under an additional set of constraints. The best private research universities – even the large ones – are more agile organizations than are the best public research universities in America. This is so in part because private research universities have a more focused academic mission. They support fewer degree programs, and are partitioned into fewer administrative units. This more streamlined structure facilitates decision making and lowers transaction costs.

Private universities also are subject to fewer external pressures. Privates and publics alike must negotiate with and respond to external forces such as boards of overseers, donors, corporate sponsors and partners, the communities in which they live, and the vagaries of the economy. But the privates are substantially more insulated from the ebbs and flows of state budgets and from the political pressures that legislatures and taxpayers can and do apply. When public money is involved, even if it's pennies per capita, public scrutiny is high. And taxpayers are not shy about leveraging their financial stake in their state's university. They weigh in on, and their elected representatives make decisions about, everything from what lines of research to support to how much professors will be paid, how much tuition will be charged, and which special programs or campuses will be protected.

All of these factors combined – their breadth, size, and complexity, and the broader and more intractable set of external demands and constraints that they must negotiate – make public universities far less nimble than the privates. The public universities are less able to make timely, effective decisions, are less able to respond deftly to change, and are less able to reconfigure themselves to pursue new initiatives. That they are answerable to so many and such diverse external constituencies and are situated directly in the path of political and cultural winds puts public institutions at a disadvantage.

In conclusion, over the past several years, a perfect storm has been brewing, and public universities are losing their mooring at the centre of that storm. If states do not boost their support for public colleges and universities, American higher education will drift toward a two-tiered system, with the *haves* (the privates) riding the waves, able to recruit the best students and faculty and sustain the most innovative programs of teaching and research, and the *have-nots* (the publics) left in the wake. With more than three-quarters of the nation's college students enrolled in public institutions, the widening gap in resources threatens to swamp the entire system of higher education in America.

America's Declining International Competitiveness

As the US economy struggles, the United States is trying to maintain its competitive edge in global markets. The strength of a nation's system of higher education is a powerful measure of a nation's ability to sustain

4-Year College Continuation Rates in OECD Countries in 2001

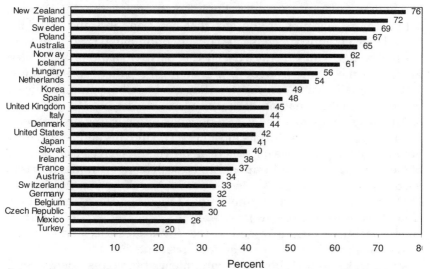

New Zealand 76
Finland 72
Sweden 69
Poland 67
Australia 65
Norway 62
Iceland 61
Hungary 56
Netherlands 54
Korea 49
Spain 48
United Kingdom 45
Italy 44
Denmark 44
United States 42
Japan 41
Slovak 40
Ireland 38
France 37
Austria 34
Switzerland 33
Germany 32
Belgium 32
Czech Republic 30
Mexico 26
Turkey 20

Percent

Source: Organization for Economic Cooperation and Development (OECD), published by National Center for Education Statistics in *The Condition of Education*, at www.nces.ed.gov/programs/coe/2004/section3/table.asp?tableID=58. [Ed: Data for Canada were not available for this OECD survey.]

its position in a global knowledge economy. By this measure, the United States is not faring well.

The United States is in a weaker position to compete for the world's best and brightest students, faculty, and researchers than it was a decade ago. Cuts to public investment in higher education; declining access to college; the growing political isolation of the United States; increased barriers to international exchange and to the ability to recruit faculty and students from other countries – all of these factors, heightened in the wake of 9/11 – have weakened America's competitive position.

The proportion of the population that goes on to a four-year college or university is a leading indicator of how well a nation is prepared to compete in a global knowledge economy. Declining access to higher education in the United States bucks the international trend of growing state commitments to ensuring an educated workforce. Americans are less likely than citizens in other OECD countries to go on to four-year colleges or universities. Fourteen nations – including the Scandinavian countries, New Zealand, Australia, Hungary, Poland, Korea, Spain, the

United Kingdom, and Italy – have college continuation rates that are higher than America's. America stands 5 points below the OECD mean.

Even more alarming is the fact that between 1998 and 2001, the typical OECD country *increased* its college continuation rate by an average of 7 points, while the rates declined in only two nations (the United States and the United Kingdom). In short, the pattern in the United States stands in stark contrast to what has been happening in many other industrialized nations of the world.[44]

America's competitive edge also depends upon its universities serving as magnets for the world's most talented students and researchers. For most of the past 60 years, American universities have been the envy of the world, affording educational and research opportunities unparalleled at any but a few other institutions. Over 30 years, the share of PhDs granted by American universities to temporary residents of the United States rose from 10 to 26%. In 2002, nearly 40% of all PhDs American universities awarded in the physical sciences and 55% of those in engineering were to temporary residents.[45]

In the wake of 9/11, however, enrollment of foreign students in US colleges and universities has declined dramatically. The number of foreign students on American campuses dropped in the 2003–4 academic year by 2.4% – the first drop in enrollment of students from abroad in more than 30 years. The decline came after a year of almost no growth. A recent study of major graduate institutions conducted by the Council of Graduate Schools found a 28% decline in applications and a 6% decline in new foreign enrollments in fall 2004, the third year in a row with a substantial drop.[46] Declines were particularly steep in the number of applications to science and engineering programs.[47]

The steep decline in applications suggests than many students have become discouraged by the new visa restrictions and the increasingly onerous and sometimes offensive security checks associated with visa applications. Stories abound: Foreign graduate students travel home for the holidays and are unable to return to resume their studies. Foreign students and faculty at US institutions travel abroad to attend scholarly conferences, but are unable to get back in the country. Prominent scholars and scientists are unable to secure visas to attend scholarly meetings or lecture in the United States. Students and scholars endure long waits at consular offices for visas to be processed and interviews to be scheduled. Scientific meetings are moved outside the United States because foreign scientists cannot gain entry.

There is no way to quantify these occurrences, but the prevailing

Percentage Change from 2002–03 to 2003–04 in
Foreign Graduate Students in the United States

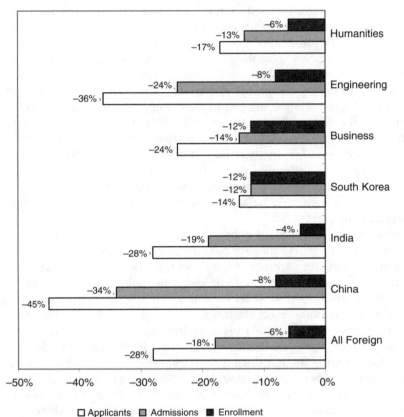

□ Applicants ■ Admissions ■ Enrollment

Source: Council of Graduate Study

anecdotal evidence, coupled with the tremendous drop in foreign students applying to American graduate programs, suggests that America's image as the centre of the universe for graduate education, scientific exchange, and discovery has been tarnished. As James Langer, vice-president of the National Academy of Sciences, told the United States Senate Science and Technology Caucus in May 2004, 'American science is being isolated from the rest of the world.'[48]

And the rest of the world is moving into the breach. While the United States has erected new barriers to foreign students and scientists, other countries – most notably Australia, Britain, and Canada, but also New Zealand, South Korea, Malaysia, and Singapore – have seen a boom in the number of international students.[49] These nations are growing hubs for international students and scholars.

The long-term implications of the continued drop in the number of graduate students and scientists coming to the Unites Statea are dire. Amid fierce international competition for human capital, America is closing its doors to people of enormous talent and creativity. And because of their declining interest in pursuing advanced training in the sciences and engineering, American students are unlikely to fill the gap. In the end, there will be too few US scientists and engineers to sustain research and teaching in these key disciplines. As Albert H. Teich, director of science and public policy at the American Association for the Advancement of Science, concludes, failure to improve the visa situation 'will do irreparable harm to scientific progress as well as U.S. competitiveness.'[50]

These trends are part of a broader set of concerns that have led Richard Florida, Heinz Professor of Economic Development at Carnegie Mellon and a visiting scholar at the Brookings Institution, to warn that the United States is on the verge of losing its ability to attract creative talent from around the world. Paralleling the drop in graduate school applications, he notes, is an alarming 55% drop since 2002 in the number of US government–issued visas for immigrants to work in science and technology, with parallel, though smaller, declines in other fields.[51]

Florida reminds us that during the 1980s and 1990s, 'talented, educated immigrants and smart, ambitious young Americans congregated in and around a dozen U.S. urban regions ... Now the rest of the world has taken notice of our success and is working hard to reproduce it.'[52] He notes that in countries such as Belgium, Canada, Finland, India, Ireland, the Netherlands, and Sweden, government-subsidized laboratories, partnerships between universities and industry, and investments in higher education have begun to lure creative talent – scientists, students, researchers, entrepreneurs, artists, and the like – from around the globe (including from the United States), building creative industries that used to be America's province.[53] Florida concludes ominously, 'For the first time in modern memory, top scientists and intellectuals from elsewhere are choosing not to come here.'[54]

Florida suggests several remedies for rebuilding America's creative infrastructure, but singles out higher education as the generator and wellspring of talent and creativity. We must, he concludes, 'spend radically more on research and development and higher education, opening up universities and colleges to more Americans and to more of the world's best and brightest.'[55]

Sustaining Innovative Basic Research

The quest for knowledge about the underlying principles and laws that govern our social, cultural, political, physical, and natural worlds is a primary mission of a university. Pathbreaking discoveries – discoveries that reshape the way people think about and understand the world; that advance theoretical understanding; that reframe the fundamental questions we ask; and that have broad impact and enduring value – distinguish great universities from all other kinds of institutions.

The scientific advances from basic research create and feed the wellspring of scientific capital from which practical applications and new products are developed. Basic research does not necessarily yield immediate practical benefits. It is a painstaking, long-term process whose applications might be many years down the road. But the results are worth the investment and worth the wait. Theodore Maiman built the first laser in 1960, but his discovery depended upon four decades of basic research by mathematicians and physicists, including Albert Einstein, who first recognized in 1917 the theory of 'stimulated emissions,' and Columbia University professor Charles Townes, who discovered how to create a focused microwave beam. Computerized Axial Tomography (the CAT scan), which revolutionized medical imaging and diagnosis in the early 1970s, owes a debt to the basic mathematical research that physicist A.M. Cormack conducted a decade earlier.

Some of the long-term applications of basic research are neither intended nor forseen. However consequential his findings, Einstein could not, for example, have anticipated Maiman's breakthrough. Indeed, more than half of the discoveries in biomedical science in the late twentieth century resulted from basic research never intended for the specific application that emerged.[56] Nonetheless, although decades may pass before new scientific knowledge helps solve a practical problem, without the knowledge gained from basic research, the practical application would not be possible.

Basic research is crucial to the advancement of human knowledge, understanding, and problem solving. However, because its practical benefits are neither immediate nor transparent, its value is not always appreciated. Universities across America are struggling to meet the rising costs of basic research, balance scientific priorities with the financial enticements of the market, and sustain creative environments on their campuses – all essential battles that must be won if cutting-edge basic research is to advance.

Financial Challenges to Sustaining Research

The changing nature of research has sent the costs of scientific research soaring. Supercomputers have replaced slide rules; buildings that house multimillion-dollar instrumentation facilities have replaced labs with bunsen burners; electronic air-filtration systems have replaced fume hoods; teams of researchers have replaced individual scholars; grant administrators conversant with complex federal regulations have replaced accountants. And multimillion-dollar start-up packages, not a train ticket and a typewriter, are needed to recruit the world's top researchers.

Big science requires big financial investments, and for the most part, the federal government has been the chief funder of basic research in America – to the tune of about $50 billion a year. But at the same time states were cutting their support of public universities, the federal government was also cutting the funds it provides universities to sustain their research infrastructure (e.g., libraries, buildings, computer networks, and grants administration). As the federal government reduced its indirect-cost recovery rate, US universities needed to dramatically increase their own contribution to research and development to meet the rising costs. Between 1972 and 2000, the proportion of their total research and development expenditures that universities have paid out of their own pockets nearly doubled, from 11 to 21%.[57] Public and private universities alike have drawn resources from their teaching and the educational mission to subsidize the rising costs of the research side of the house.[58]

An even larger financial threat to university-based research is looming on the horizon. Over the next few years, and beyond, the US federal budget deficit and the mounting national debt will profoundly diminish the capacity of the federal government to fund research and development. With a budget deficit of $422 billion in 2004 (about 18% of the total budget) and a national debt that now tops $4 trillion, the federal government is unlikely to increase its investments in research. It may even need to reduce spending from current levels. Demographics will continue to drive the need for more spending on Medicare, Medicaid,

and Social Security. The costs of homeland security and national defence will likely continue to rise as well. These demands on federal
resources, in conjunction with the revenue losses from the 2001 and
2003 tax cuts, suggest that the federal deficit is not likely to go away
anytime soon. In fact, the Congressional Budget Office estimates that
the national debt will climb to $6.3 trillion by the end of the decade,
necessitating annual interest payments of close to $600 billion a year. As
Brookings fellows William G. Gale and Peter R. Orszag conclude, 'The
United States has never before experienced such large long-term fiscal
imbalances.'[59]

The federal budget deficit and growing national debt are already
slowing the pace of federal research support. Between FY01 and FY04,
non-defence federal research and development (R&D) grew an average
of 7.8% a year (in constant dollars). Non-defence R&D is projected to
grow a mere 0.2% in FY05. The National Science Foundation's budget
will be cut by 2.0%. With little or no new incremental federal investment in research, universities will need to find new ways to sustain
their current research infrastructure and fund major new initiatives.

Perhaps in anticipation of the reduction in federal research dollars,
some states have decided to invest heavily in high-profile, high-priority
projects. To help ensure California's leadership in biotechnology, for
example, Californians recently voted to provide $3 billion in state funds
($300 million a year for ten years) to support research involving embry-
onic stem cells. Other states have been advancing similar mega-initia-
tives. Wisconsin Governor Jim Doyle recently announced a plan to
spend $750 million on biotechnology and stem-cell research at the
University of Wisconsin and several hospitals in the state.

Threats to Basic Research

As the cost of research has soared and the demands placed on universities' own resources have grown, corporate America has stepped in to
help by providing funds for buildings and equipment, support for
distinguished researchers and stellar students, contracts to support
research, and partnerships to take university-based discoveries out to
the marketplace. Universities, in their search for new revenue, have also
intensified their focus on the marketability of their discoveries through
licensing agreements, technology transfer, and spinoff companies.[60]

As lucrative as these arrangements can be, they can have a subtle
(and sometimes not so subtle) impact on academic priorities, steering

research to revenue-producing projects that might be attractive to corporate partners.[61] Some observers have voiced concern that universities are slipping as places where independent, basic research is nurtured and protected,[62] warning that if the reward structure – including the granting of tenure, the awarding of endowed professorships, the allocation of laboratory space, salary increases, and the granting of new faculty lines – is tied to profitability rather than intellectual merit, then a core mission of the university will be undermined.[63]

Universities must remain places where faculties can set research agendas based on the theoretical importance of the inquiry, not on its commercial profitability. Universities must remain places that value and nurture the free exchange of ideas, not proprietary arrangements that embargo results from publication.[64] In short, for universities to serve society effectively through the advancement of knowledge, basic research and the free flow of information must be sustained. By advancing basic research, universities provide an important public good for which there are inadequate private incentives for industry to provide support. If basic research is neglected, applied and translational research will founder.

Sustaining a Creative Environment for Innovation

Universities also need to cultivate a culture of excellence that continually sparks and nurtures innovation by encouraging faculty and students to work on important, pathbreaking projects, take intellectual risks, challenge theoretical assumptions, undertake bold experiments, and integrate different forms of knowledge in novel and creative ways. Universities need to provide the opportunities and incentives, the time and the resources, the facilities and the space to enable the breakthrough discoveries that will reshape our understanding of the human condition.

Although universities need to protect the strength of their academic programs, they must also overcome the hurdles that disciplinary boundaries often create, preventing faculty across the university from working together, in new combinations, to provide the multiple perspectives needed to solve some of the most challenging scientific questions. We need to find ways for faculty to overcome their clan mentality and interact more with colleagues who bring different epistemological and disciplinary perspectives to a question. We need to find ways to overcome the sheer size of our campuses, which has spread faculty over scores of buildings, making such encounters unlikely.

If universities are to remain creative centres for research, innovation, and knowledge creation, then they must create incentives and opportunities for these kinds of creative enterprises to thrive – opportunities and support to bring researchers from diverse disciplines together for creative discussion. Universities need to be incubators for breakthrough research and creative work that will solve the world's most vexing problems.

Conclusions

Higher education in America is in trouble.

- State funding cuts have put at risk the ability of public colleges and universities to serve the people of their state.
- Declining access to higher education has diminished the ability of our nation to harness the creative energies of all of its people and ensure opportunities for social and economic mobility.
- The growing gap in resources between public and private institutions has put at risk the ability of public colleges and universities to recruit outstanding students and faculty and provide the three-quarters of America's college students that they serve with an education equal to that provided by private institutions.
- Declining access to higher education as well as new barriers to international exchange have put at risk America's international competitiveness.
- Rising costs coupled with declining federal investment in R&D have put at risk the ability of universities to generate the scientific breakthroughs needed to advance knowledge and address our nation's most profound needs.

While the political debate over whether higher education is a public good rages on in America, all of the enormous contributions that our colleges and universities have made to educating the people and advancing the knowledge needed to ensure the economic, social, cultural, and political vitality of our communities, states, and nation are at risk. How do we get ourselves out of this predicament?

Part of the solution lies in politicians moving beyond the short-term time horizon that drives many of their decisions. Elected officials need to provide long-term solutions rather than politically expedient fixes that leave our system of higher education at risk. Governors, legislators, civic leaders, colleges, and universities must lead public discussion of what it is going to take to save public higher education in America. And elected officials must make the tough political decisions necessary to save it.

Colleges and universities also must avoid expedient choices that fix this year's budget, but do not ensure the long-term vitality of their institutions.

Colleges and universities must find a better way to balance the incentives of the marketplace with their core values. We compete in global markets for the best students and faculty, for research dollars, for donor support, and for corporate partners. Markets influence how much students will pay, the institutions at which faculty will work, their level of compensation, and the research projects they will get to pursue. Markets create incentives for universities to build centres of excellence and they create incentives for universities to offer great academic programs and research capacities that attract outstanding student and faculty. But markets can also lead institutions to make choices that maximize the financial bottom line at the cost of such core objectives as high-quality education, service to the community, and path-breaking research that advances the frontiers of knowledge (even if the research is not financially rewarding). While market forces will inevitably influence the decisions that colleges and universities make, financial rewards need to be balanced against the core values that are at the heart of any great institution of higher learning.[65]

America's decentralized system of higher education is both a strength and a weakness. Decisions about everything – which courses and degree programs to offer; how many and which students to admit and how much they will be charged; who will be on the faculty and how much they will be paid; what lines of research should be pursued; and what facilities to build – can be made by individual institutions, and in some cases by individual members of their faculty. Over the years, those many decisions have created a truly great system of higher education. But, as we well know, even if the micro-level choices are perfectly rational, they don't always aggregate into rational macro-outcomes.[66] We need to do a better job of connecting the dots, both within our own institutions and across the colleges and universities that constitute America's system of higher education.

In the aggregate, we need to ensure a system of higher education that
- provides excellent academic programs for our students;
- supports path-breaking research and scientific achievement that advances the frontiers of knowledge and provides the empirical and theoretical breakthroughs needed to fuel basic and applied research;
- provides access to all qualified students regardless of their race, national citizenship, or personal financial circumstances;
- meets the state's workforce needs by producing graduates able to contribute to every sector of society;
- works in an efficient and cost-effective manner;
- links colleges and universities to business, government, and cultural institutions to effectively leverage university resources and research;
- allocates resources based on a competition of ideas, not history, politics, or privilege; and
- evolves, changes, and adjusts in response to new opportunities, conditions and needs.

The future of higher education in America will ultimately boil down to priorities. America is the richest country in the world, and the leaders of our nation, states, colleges, and universities can decide to reverse the trend and shift college education costs away from those least able to afford it. States can decide to boost their investment in public education to develop the human capital needed for all of its people to contribute to the community or they can continue to build prisons to incarcerate those who turn to crime rather than education as a road to a better life.

Colleges and universities need to stop chasing rankings that measure only the selectivity of their freshman class, not the quality of the education they are providing their students. We need to start focusing attention on the more difficult tasks of building a diverse pipeline of talented students, uncovering and recruiting the most creative, inventive, and promising students, and providing scholarship support to those most in need. We must focus our attention on the quality of the education we are actually providing to those we serve.

Over the past two centuries, an extraordinary system of higher education has evolved in America. The system has led to tremendous scientific discoveries, the education of millions of students, the creation of a well-trained workforce, and ideas and innovations that have improved the quality and longevity of human life. It has fueled the economy, solved pressing social issues, and ensured the cultural vitality of our communities. The American higher education system has also provided opportunities for tremendous social and economic mobility, enabling new generations of immigrants to realize their hopes and dreams.

As we grapple with the challenges facing higher education in America, we have an opportunity to make choices that will ensure not only the excellence of that system, but also ensure that our colleges and universities will continue to serve our communities and our nation.

Notes

* Dean, College of Liberal Arts, University of Minnesota. I first presented the key points in this essay at a roundtable discussion on 'Higher Education in America: A Model for Europe,' sponsored by the University of Minnesota's Center for German and European Studies on August 23, 2004. I am grateful to University of Toronto Interim President Frank Iacobucci and University of Toronto Vice-President Carolyn Touhy for their generous invitation to codify those ideas into the current essay. I also want to express my gratitude to my University of Minnesota colleagues who assisted in this project. Peter Radcliffe skillfully helped with the some of the data analysis. Eugenia Smith helped sharpen the prose over the course of several drafts. Jennifer Cieslak, Mary Hicks, and Susan Banovetz provided thoughtful feedback at various junctures of the project. Sarah Knoblauch and Peggy Berkowitz helped whip the manuscript into final form. I am also indebted to the McKnight Foundation and the University of Minnesota for the resources provided by the McKnight Presidential Leadership Chair. Without the generosity, support, and understanding of my family – Maria Antonia, Sara, Anna and Samuel – I would not have had the time that I devoted to this essay.

1 Emily Hannun and Claudia Buchmann, 'The Consequences of Global Educational Expansion: Social Science Perspectives,' American Academy of Arts and Sciences, 2003; Edward L. Glaeser and Albert Saiz, 'The Rise of the Skilled City,' NBER Working Paper #10191 (December 2003).

2 Joint Economic Committee, United States Congress, Investment in Education: Private and Public Returns, January 2000. www.house.gov/jec/.

3 Steven J. Rosenstone and John Mark Hansen, Mobilization, Participation, and Democracy in America (New York: Longman, 2003).

4 Emily Hannun and Claudia Buchmann, 'The Consequences of Global Educational Expansion: Social Science Perspectives,' American Academy of Arts and Sciences, 2003.

5 College Board, 'Education Pays: The Benefits of Higher Education for Individuals and Society,' 2004. www.collegeboard.com; Emily Hannun and Claudia Buchmann, 'The Consequences of Global Educational Expan-

sion: Social Science Perspectives,' American Academy of Arts and Sciences, 2003.

6 'State Tax Fund Appropriations for Higher Education FY1961 to FY2004,' *Postsecondary Education OPPORTUNITY*, no. 139 (January 2004).

7 Michael John Rizzo, 'A (Less Than) Zero Sum Game? State Funding for Public Education: How Public Higher Education Institutions Have Lost,' dissertation presented to the faculty of the Graduate School of Cornell University, August 2004.

8 National Association of State Budget Officers, State Expenditure Report 2003, www.sasbo.org, 5.

9 College Board, 'Trends in College Pricing,' 2004, www.collegeboard.com. The full cost of attending college, including room and board, books and supplies, transportation, and other expenses is $14,640 at public four-year institutions and $30,295 at private four-year colleges and universities.

10 College Board, 'Trends in Student Aid,' 2003, www.collegeboard.com, fig. 4.

11 Over the past decade, the *net* price (after the impact of student aid has been taken into account) of public four-year colleges and universities (in constant dollars) rose 16%; the *net* price of private four-year colleges and universities (in constant dollars) rose 14%. College Board, 'Trends in College Pricing,' 2004, www.collegeboard.com, table 8.

12 Edward P. St. John, 'The Access Challenge: Rethinking the Causes of the New Inequality,' Policy Issue Report #2002-01, Indiana Education Policy Center, Indiana University, 3.

13 Associated Press, 'Pell Grant Change May Affect Students,' *New York Times*, 23 November 2004.

14 College Board, 'Trends in Student Aid,' 2003, www.collegeboard.com, table 3.

15 In 1982–3, 50% of the total aid was in the form of grants and 46% in the form of loans (the rest was work study or tax credits). Two decades later, grants had fallen to 40% of the total and loans had risen to 54% of all aid. College Board, 'Trends in Student Aid,' 2003, www.collegeboard.com, fig. 6.

16 College Board, 'Trends in Student Aid,' 2003, www.collegeboard.com, fig. 10.

17 Ronald G. Ehrenberg, 'Key Issues Facing American Higher Education,' 3; paper presented at the NACUBO annual meeting, Milwaukee, Wis., July 2004.

18 College Board, 'Trends in Student Aid,' 2003, www.collegeboard.com, fig. 12.

19 College-bound high school seniors whose parents have incomes over $100,000 are 62% more likely to have high school grade point averages of A– or better than are students from families with incomes below $10,000. The average ACT composite score for college-bound high school seniors with family incomes over $100,000 is 23.4 compared to 17.9 for students

from families with incomes below $18,000. ACT scores for African Americans lag 4.7 points behind non-Hispanic whites; the scores of Hispanics are 3.3 points behind and the scores of Native Americans are 3.0 points behind. College-bound high school seniors with family incomes over $100,000 score an average of 135 points higher (555 versus 420) on the SAT I Verbal test and 124 points higher (568 versus 444) on the SAT Math test than students from families with incomes below $10,000. College Board, 2003.

20 Anthony P. Carnevale and Stephen J. Rose, 'Socioeconomic Status, Race/ Ethnicity, and Selective College Admissions' (New York: Century Foundation), March 2003, 25.

21 Jonathan Kozol, *Savage Inequalities: Children in America's Schools* (New York: Crown, 1991).

22 ACT, 'Crisis at the Core: Preparing All Students for College and Work, www.act.org, figs. 1 and 5.

23 Kevin Carey, 'The Funding Gap 2004,' The Education Trust, www.edtrust .org.

24 See, for example, Coeli Carr, 'The Multiple Choices of Prepping for the SAT,' *New York Times*, B1–8.

25 See, for example, Nicholas Confessore, 'Independent Counsel,' *Atlantic Monthly*, October 2004, 135–40.

26 College Board, 'Trends in College Pricing,' 2003, www.collegeboard.com.

27 Donald E. Heller, 'Student Price Response in Higher Education: An Update to Leslie and Brickman,' *Journal of Higher Education* 68: 6, 624–59.

28 Anthony P. Carneval and Stephen J. Rose, 'Socioeconomic Status, Race/ Ethnicity and Selective College Admissions,' Century Foundation, March 2003, www.tcf.org, 26.

29 Edward P. St. John, 'The Access Challenge: Rethinking the Causes of the New Inequality,' Policy Issue Report #2002-01, Indiana Education Policy Center, Indiana University, 4.

30 *Postsecondary Education OPPORTUNITY*, no. 133 (July 2003), 7.

31 Alexander W. Astin and Leticia Oseguera, 'The Declining "Equity" of American Higher Education, *Review of Higher Education* 27:3 (Spring 2004), 321–41.

32 Significant drops in the number of African American freshmen occurred, for example, at the University of Michigan, Penn State University, University of Minnesota, University of Georgia, Ohio State University, University of Illinois at Urbana-Champaign, the University of Pennsylvania, University of North Carolina, Chapel Hill, and many campuses of the University of California system. Michael Dobbs, 'Universities Record Drop in Black Admissions,' *Washington Post*, 22 November 2004, A1.

33 *Postsecondary Education OPPORTUNITY*, no. 143 (May 2004), 1.

34 Ibid., 11–20.

35 *Gruttner* v. *Bollinger*, 539 U.S. (2003), 18.

36 'Brief of General Motors Corporation as *Amicus Curiae* in Support of Appellants in *Grutter* v. *Bollinger*,' 30 May 2001, 29.

37 James Fallows and V.V. Ganeshanathan, 'The Big Picture,' *Atlantic Monthly*, October 2004, 122.

38 See William G. Bowen and Derek Bok, *The Shape of the River: Long-Term Consequences of Considering Race in College and University Admissions* (Princeton, NJ: Princeton University Press, 1998).

39 College Board, 'Trends in Student Aid,' 2003, www.college.board.com, figs. 11 and 12.

40 Many private universities provide additional benefits not available at public institutions, such as free tuition for children of faculty, which increases the public-private gap in total compensation to $34,493 for full professors at doctoral institutions. American Association of University Professors, 'Don't Blame Faculty for High Tuition: The Annual Report on the Economic Status of the Profession 2003–04,' www.aaup.org/surveys/04z/04z.pdf, tables 1–4.

41 The AAU comprises America's research-intensive universities.

42 This assumes that everyone has the same draw of spendable income off their endowment of 4.5%.

43 'Total Endowment Assets' from the National Association of College and Business Officers. The incremental revenue assumes an annual endowment payout of 4.5%.

44 'International Comparisons of 4–year College Continuation Rates, 1998 and 2001,' *Postsecondary Education OPPORTUNITY*, no. 144 (June 2004), 11–16.

45 Thomas B. Hoffer et al., Doctorate Recipients from United States Universities: Summary Report 2002' (Chicago: NORC at the University of Chicago, 2003), table 11. At http://www.norc.uchicago.edu/issues/sed-2002.pdf.

46 Burton Bollag, 'Enrollment of Foreign Students Drops in U.S.,' *Chronicle of Higher Education*, 19 November 2004, A1.

47 Heath A. Brown and Peter D. Syverson, 'Findings from U.S. Graduate Schools on International Graduate Student Admissions Trends,' Council of Graduate Schools, Summer 2004.

48 Richard Florida, 'America's Looming Creativity Crisis,' *Harvard Business Review*, October 2004, 130.

49 Paul Mooney and Shailaja Neelakantan, 'No Longer Dreaming of America,' *Chronicle of Higher Education*, 8 October 2004, A41. Foreign student enrollment is up 75% in Australia between 2000 and 2004; up 18% in Great Britain between 2000 and 2002; and up 60% in Canada between 2000 and 2003.

50 Burton Bollag, 'Wanted: Foreign Students,' *Chronicle of Higher Education*, 8 October 2004, A40.

51 Richard Florida, 'America's Best and Brightest Are Leaving ... and Taking the Creative Economy with Them,' *Across the Board* 41:5 (2004), 34–40.
52 Ibid.
53 Ibid. and Florida, 'America's Looming Creativity Crisis.'
54 Florida, 'America's Best and Brightest Are Leaving.'
55 Florida, 'America's Looming Creativity Crisis,' 134.
56 Martin Kenney, *Biotechnology: The University-Industrial Complex* (New Haven, Yale University Press, 1987); quoted in James S. Fairweather, 'The University's Role in Economic Development: Lessons for Academic Leaders,' *SRA Journal/Features*, Winter 1990, 7.
57 Ronald G. Ehrneberg, Michael J. Rizzo, and George H. Jakubson, 'Who Bears the Growing Cost of Science at Universities,' Cornell Higher Education Research Institute Working Paper WP35 (April 2003); www.ilr.cornell .edu/cheri.
58 Ronald G. Ehrenberg, 'Key Issues Currently Facing American Higher Education,' paper presented at the NACUBO annual meetings, Milwaukee, July 2004.
59 William G. Gale and Peter R. Orszag, 'The Budget Outlook: Projections and Implications,' *The Economists' Voice* 1:2 (2004), 1:6; www.brook.edu/ views/papers/20040910orszaggale.htm.
60 See, for example, Scott Shane, *Academic Engrepreneurship; University Spinoffs and Wealth Creation* (Northampton, Mass. Edward Elgar, 2004).
61 For an example of the clash between the scientific and ethical concerns and economic incentives to create commercializable products see 'Defending Medicine: Clinical Faculty and Academic Freedom,' November 2004, at http://www.caut.ca/en/issues/academicfreedom/DefendingMedicine .pdf.
62 See Sheila Slaughter and Larry L. Leslie, *Academic Capitalism: Politics, Policies, and the Entrepreneurial University* (Baltimore: Johns Hopkins University Press, 1997); Eyal Press and Jennifer Washburn, 'The Kept University,' *Atlantic Monthly*, 2000, 50; and Derek Bok, *Universities in the Marketplace: The Commercialization of Higher Education* (Princeton, NJ: Princeton University Press, 2003), chap. 11.
63 See Peter D. Blumberg, 'From "Publish or Perish" to "Profit or Perish": Revenue from University Technology Transfer and the 501(c)(3) Tax Exemption'; and Rebecca S. Lowen, *Creating the Cold War University: The Transformation of Stanford* (Berkeley: University of California Press, 1997).
64 See Derek Bok, *Universities in the Marketplace: The Commercialization of Higher Education* (Princeton, NJ: Princeton University Press, 2003), chaps. 4 and 8; and David L. Kirp, *Shakespeare, Einstein, and the Bottom Line: The Marketing of Higher Education* (Cambridge, Mass.: Harvard University Press, 2003), chap. 11.
65 See Bok, *Universities in the Marketplace*, chap. 11.
66 See Thomas C. Schelling, *Micromotives and Macrobehavior* (New York: W.W. Norton, 1978).

Towards a New Compact in University Education in Ontario

RONALD J. DANIELS AND MICHAEL J. TREBILCOCK*

Over the past decade, a number of different industrialized democracies have critically examined the structure and performance of their post-secondary education systems. By and large, the focus of this attention has been on the capacity of the state to support the needs and aspirations of the traditional publicly funded research-intensive university. In the received model, the public research university receives significant levels of funding from the state to support its research and teaching activities, but is subject to some level of state oversight and control so as to render the activities of the institution congruent with the public interest. The level of state intervention in the affairs of the public research university (and its precise form) varies of course from jurisdiction to jurisdiction, but typically involves some regulation of programs (priority may be placed on education and research programs that are geared to the local economy), tuition fees (typically set at below market rates), student financial assistance, and admissions (preferential treatment for in-state versus out-of-state or out-of-country students). In contrast, privately funded research universities (to the extent that they are permitted to operate in jurisdictions supporting public university education) are not subject to the same degree of oversight, but also do not receive the same degree of public funding.[1]

Concerns over the capacity of the publicly funded research university to respond to social needs emanates from a number of different sources. First, given the significant private benefits that are conferred on university graduates (in terms of both their increased social status and enhanced earning power), there is concern over the ability of the publicly funded university system to accommodate the burgeoning interest of students (and their families) in obtaining higher education. In a setting where publicly funded universities enjoy a statutory monopoly on the provision of university education, and assuming that the quality of existing programs is to be held constant, any expansion in university enrollment necessarily requires either an increase in the level of state support for the system and/or relaxation of some of the tuition constraints set by government so that students end up bearing more of the costs of their education relative to the benefits received. Second, concern over capacity constraints in the public university system may also lead the state to consider the scope for entry by private institutions, which in turn raises questions of the appropriate scope for governmental financial support and regulation. Third, another concern is the growing competitive threat posed by elite private universities (particularly in the United States) for the very best students and faculty. To the extent that publicly funded research universities lack the resources or flexibility to attract and retain outstanding faculty and students, the quality of their institutional performance will suffer accordingly. Not surprisingly, the intensity of the threat posed by well-funded private universities to the publicly funded university has spawned a debate over the suitability of relaxing certain constraints that govern the affairs of the public university system.

In much of our scholarly or government advisory work on public policy issues in the past, we have emphasized the importance of the appropriate choice of instrument in vindicating widely-shared public policy goals. In the context of post-secondary education, it is at least as important to be clear on the goals or ends of post-secondary education and then to evaluate whether a superior choice of instrument or means is available than policies presently exhibit to more fully vindicate these goals or ends. Thus, we first examine the desired ends of higher education. We then discuss the various rationales for government intervention. Next we proceed to explore in greater depth the various criticisms and problems of the present instruments governing publicly funded research-intensive universities throughout the industrialized democracies. We then focus specifically on problems facing the Ontario post-secondary sector. Finally, we propose modifications to the current Ontario model designed to increase the level of public and private revenue for public universities which in our view would enhance international standards of excellence in teaching and research while enhancing student equality of opportunity – modifications that in our view will provide a better fit of goals and instruments (ends and means).

1. The Ends of Post-Secondary Education and the Rationales for Government Intervention

There are two quite different but complementary enterprises that motivate the existence of post-secondary institutions.[2] The first is a teaching or educational mandate. As with primary and secondary education, this educational mandate can be understood as having two motivations. The first motivation is that of instilling in students the skills and knowledge that are required to engage in a specific profession or vocation. University professional programs – medicine, dentistry, pharmacy, nursing, law, management, and engineering – fall squarely into this 'skills' portion of the educational mandate. These programs confer substantial private benefits on students in the form of increased human capital. Riddell, for instance, has found most estimates place 'average real rates of return to post-secondary education at 6–9% for men and 8–10% for women, although there are substantial differences across fields of study.'[3] The second aim of the teaching mandate is to enable students to mature into effective citizens – fully capable participants in a culturally rich, diverse, democratic society. The fulfillment of this aim is largely the domain of undergraduate arts programmes and advanced liberal arts graduate programmes, although to some extent all programs contribute to this end. The second enterprise that motivates the existence of post-secondary institutions is the pursuit and amplification of knowledge through rigorous scholarly research. Such research can be conducted at either a basic or applied level (or, typically, at both levels), and confers significant benefits on humankind in the form of new understandings of the human condition and the physical environment.[4] In the research-intensive university, neither of these activities can be said to take precedence over the other. Its teaching and research missions fortify and complement one another, and account for its distinctive strengths and longevity.

Given this time-honoured role of the research-intensive university, what is the rationale for government intervention in this area? There are three main rationales that to varying degrees support public involvement in post-secondary education. First, the positive externalities associated with post-secondary education, emanating from the civic virtue and citizenship values that are nurtured in students, ground a case for public subsidization. So, too, do the positive externalities associated with various types of research activities. Second, there may be a weak paternalism role for government insofar as students may suffer from informational deficiencies when determining which program of study to pursue at which institution. Third, given the human-capital market limitations that constrain private capital available to students, there is a strong case for government intervention based on equality of opportunity goals.

Positive Externalities

Markets fail to reach efficient outcomes when decision-makers do not experience the full consequences – that is, bear all the costs and reap all the benefits – of their actions. Therefore, a case for government subsidization in the market for post-secondary education is made out to the extent that a significant portion of the benefits of post-secondary education – an enhanced civic culture, valuable research breakthroughs, and increased community cohesion – accrue to the public good and not to individual decision-makers alone (i.e. potential students). It makes intuitive economic sense to argue that the government should subsidize the cost of post-secondary education to the extent that society at large reaps the benefits, and because they are likely to be sub-optimally supplied. Concomitantly, individual students should pay the costs of post-secondary education to the extent that they individually reap the private benefits of their post-secondary education. If such a system operated in a world of perfect information and rationality, a socially optimal level of post-secondary education would be 'produced' and 'consumed' in the marketplace.[6]

Although drawing this dichotomy in the benefits of post-secondary education is overly simplistic and fraught with measurement difficulties, it has utility as a framing idea. Consider the fact that typically post-secondary education that increases a student's future income[7] will increase societal wealth and, derivatively, government tax revenue, thereby providing concrete benefits to society.[8] In this way, even the most skills-oriented program is likely to generate social benefits. However, the intangible positive externalities – the creation of a robust civic culture and increased community cohesion – associated with post-secondary education in the arts and professions are probably at least as valuable in the long run as these indirect fiscal dividends.[9] In any event, using the public/private benefit dichotomy we have a *prima facie* case for government intervention in post-secondary education to the extent that mixed private and public funding is required to match the costs of post-secondary education with those garnering the benefits flowing there from.

Another related rationale for public intervention in relation to post-secondary education concerns the university's research activities. Because basic (and even applied) research has the character of a public good (its benefits are appropriable by all), it will be under-supplied by the market; as a consequence, there is a role for government in subsidizing the production of research. Absent this supplementary funding, it is highly unlikely that private parties will dedicate a socially optimal amount of their own resources to research if they will not be able to reap the full range of benefits.[10] In the last decade or so, considerable attention has been devoted to the role played by research-intensive universities in spawning industrial innovation. In light of this recognition, governments in a number of jurisdictions have increased the level of public funding keyed to both basic and applied research.[11] Riddell contends that the social benefits of post-secondary education are substantial and may, in fact, approximate the private returns (7–10%).[12]

Paternalism

Participation in post-secondary education, unlike participation in primary and secondary education, is not mandatory but optional. Accordingly, one can assume that each individual is making a rational choice to acquire a set of skills or form of learning that will be of significant personal value to them upon graduation. In these terms, government should be understandably wary of exercising a paternalistic role in shaping choices in relation to post-secondary education, because the choice of one's vocation is central to one's mode of life and thus to one's very sense of self-fulfillment. Moreover, given that nearly all potential post-secondary students will have already completed twelve years of formal education before making these choices, they should be regarded as being capable of making rational and informed decisions regarding the appropriate future course of their education.

There may be some modest scope for government intervention grounded on paternalism rationales in the form of a government-mandated disclosure system that would seek to attenuate information asymmetries existing between students and post-secondary institutions, although it is not clear that students themselves are incapable of recognizing the existence of these asymmetries and securing privately produced information (in the form of rankings, university evaluations) that would assist them in making informed choices. Government-mandated disclosure would require institutions receiving public funds to publish information respecting the quality of the entering class, the quality and character of the academic program (course offerings, class sizes, faculty/student ratios), student completion rates, faculty research activity, and career placement patterns for graduates.

Equality of Opportunity

Although post-secondary education should not be considered a right available to all citizens irrespective of individual merit, true equality of opportunity among equally meritorious citizens (however one defines meritorious in this context) is a benefit of considerable importance. Professional schools play a pivotal 'gatekeeper' role in determining access to the corridors of power within a democratic system.[13] The representation of various communities in positions of power and in the professions must be of concern. Thus, we should take seriously the broader social consequences of admissions policies in such institutions. However, given the current competitive landscape, and the role of various legal restrictions on discriminatory admissions practices, most universities are committed to recruiting the strongest possible student body, and thus the admissions decision is typically merit driven. The difficulty, however, arises in relation to the capacity of the admitted student to afford the prescribed tuition levels, particularly when limitations in human capital markets constrain the capacity of meritorious students to borrow to finance their education against the collateral of their human capital. Consequently, there is a need for government intervention to compensate for these failures and to ensure equality of opportunity for all students.

2. Modes of Government Intervention: Problems in the Present System

As indicated earlier, there is a significant distinction between the private and public university models in terms of the level of institutional flexibility and overall resource support enjoyed by each. However, even within the public university model, there is considerable variation across jurisdictions in the precise way in which funding is transferred to institutions by the state (number of levels of government involved, performance- or non-performance-based funding, tied or untied program funding, degree of tuition pricing flexibility). Of course, there is also considerable variance across jurisdictions in the actual magnitude of state support that is provided to public universities. Yet despite this variance in the character and level of state support, the demands that have been placed on the public university have forced re-examination of the central tenets of government intervention in this area. In the following discussion, we briefly highlight some of the defects in state support in order to consider the desirability and design challenges of an alternative model.

Increased Demand for Higher Education

One of the most significant challenges facing the received system of publicly delivered university education emanates from the growing level of student interest in obtaining a university education. Over the last two decades, there has been a steady increase in the demand for university education, at both the undergraduate and graduate levels. This trend reflects, of course, underlying population trends (i.e., the rise in the number of children in the 'echo-boom' cohort), but also a secular increase in the demand for higher education programs among the cohort. Further fuelling the demand for higher education in developed countries is the rapidly surging population of students from developing countries who are interested in securing a university education abroad (particularly in OECD countries). In tandem, these demands have placed excessive strain on existing public systems, particularly where enrolment increases require enhanced funding support from sponsoring governments in order for universities to expand programs and facilities.

   To the extent that governments have not been able to support program expansion through enhanced public funding, universities have reacted in a number of different ways. Some have simply refused to increase their enrolment base, which means that otherwise qualified students may be deprived of the benefits of higher education. Alternatively, public universities may agree to enroll additional students (as a result of pressure from sponsoring governments), but their decision to do so has come at the cost of reduced program quality, as universities have increased student-faculty ratios or reduced program offerings. Other universities have sought to accommodate enrollment increases by enlisting additional external financial support for the university from private benefaction, industry, or private foundations. In some

cases, public institutions have sought and obtained increased governmental support for tuition increases, but typically these are still severely constrained, and often seek to differentiate funding support on
the basis of student residency (in or out of state) or the character of
program study. In the former case, the striking disparities in the level of
fees charged by institutions depending on the jurisdiction of the participating student may raise vexing distributional questions when, for
instance, the least advantaged students from developing countries are
required to pay a substantial tuition premium relative to much more
privileged domestic students in developed countries. A further problem with differential student fees relates to the discriminatory impact
that this fee structure has on freedom of movement within nations
when deployed by lower-level governments.

Regressive Subsidization

Another challenge facing the current system of publicly funded universities relates to the highly regressive character of the funding formulas
typically used to allocate funds to recipient universities. Because public
universities are typically funded out of consolidated revenues (on a per
student basis), and because children of higher socio-economic groups
participate disproportionately in higher education, the system of flat
based funding constitutes a regressive transfer from poorer to more
affluent families.[14] This pattern of public support that perpetuates,
rather than attenuates, intergenerational advantages has long been the
subject of criticism by commentators from several different political
perspectives. Because of this regressive transfer, Nicholas Barr, among
others, is highly critical of using general tax revenues to finance higher
education. 'The taxes of poor families contribute to the consumption by
the rich of a university education which helps to keep them rich.'[15]
Chapman and Greenaway argue that 'not only is it the case that graduates receive high returns on average to investment in university there is
also no doubt that university students are more likely to come from
more privileged backgrounds.'[16] The authors argue that the combination of these factors makes a system that does not charge (or minimally
charges) students for their post-secondary educations 'unquestionably
regressive.'[17] That is, taxpayers, who do not receive as many benefits
from post-secondary education as graduates, are required to finance the
majority of others' educations.

Quality

Quite apart from the distributional concerns that are associated with existing systems of public delivery of university education, another set of challenges relates to the quality of programs that public universities can offer, particularly in relation to elite private institutions. At one level, the problem is one of the overall level of resources. Overall expenditure levels at elite private institutions are significantly higher than comparable levels at public universities, particularly when expressed on a per student basis. This funding advantage reflects the much greater regulatory latitude enjoyed by private institutions in securing tuition fees from students, which are typically only constrained by the market. This tuition revenue advantage is further buttressed by the large accumulated endowments (which generate significant income) and discretionary public research subsidies received by many elite private institutions. In conjunction, the higher levels of revenue enjoyed by elite private institutions confer a significant advantage on these institutions in recruiting and retaining outstanding faculty in an increasingly competitive international labour market, in mounting innovative teaching programs, and in supporting complex and novel research activities.[18] The failure to allow public institutions to secure the funds necessary to create outstanding programs is especially regrettable in light of the large capital investments that states have previously made in these institutions.

Inflexibility

At another level, however, the principal challenge for publicly funded universities increasingly relates to the foregone efficiencies that could be realized from less-stringent regulation of their conduct. Tuition price caps and uniform public subsidies that do not differentiate on the basis of institutional or program performance (or only crudely track it) limit the incentive and the capacity of institutions to invest in the development of innovative programs that are responsive to student preferences.[19] This lack of differentiation means that students are deprived of the fullest possible range of programs in their home jurisdictions. It also means that even if there is some realm for meaningful choice in selecting among different publicly funded programs, students will not have access to important price information that, in conjunction with other forms of data, serves as a useful guide to institutional quality. In conjunction, the demand and supply side distortions introduced by tuition restrictions and non-differentiated state funding formulas are likely to result in significant efficiency losses.

Attrition

A final challenge confronting publicly funded universities relates to the lower levels of student program completion relative to private institutions. The seminal study is by Friedman and Friedman, which compared student attrition rates at representative public and private institutions in the United States, and found that whereas the attrition rate at UCLA (publicly funded) was 50%, it was only 5% at Dartmouth (privately funded).[20] Canadian evidence supports the linkage of lower tuition fees with higher dropout rates.[21] The Smith Commission found that 42% of students entering Canadian universities in 1985 failed to obtain a degree within five years, and that the attrition rate in graduate programs was lower, but still highly significant, at about one-third.[22] The Smith Commission concluded that such statistics are 'a symptom of inadequate quality in the organization and delivery of [post-secondary] education.'[23] Another explanation may be that tuition fees at publicly subsidized institutions historically have been so low that they do not impress adequately on students the seriousness of the forgone benefits associated with the non-completion of their post-secondary education and the magnitude of the opportunity costs of forgoing workforce participation for several years.

3. Post-secondary Education in Ontario

All provincial governments in Canada, including Ontario's, are extensively involved in the provision and financing of post-secondary education. Post-secondary education provides a variety of social benefits such as equality of opportunity for economic success, increased information and analysis of political decisions, and increased economic growth through innovation and research. It also provides significant private benefits to individuals, not the least of which is higher incomes, particularly in the case of professional degrees. The mix of public and private benefits points to a mixed role for governments and markets.

Post-secondary education (in universities and colleges) in Ontario is primarily publicly funded. Canadian investment in post-secondary education presents a mixed picture. Canadian expenditure per student is the second highest, after the United States, among the G-7 countries, and is substantially above the Australian and OECD average. As a proportion of Gross Domestic Product, Canada places second behind the US in the OECD, at 2.5% as compared to 2.7%.[24] However, the composition of the expenditure in the US and Canada differs markedly, with Canada spending a much lower fraction of GDP on *university* education and a much larger proportion on non-university post-secondary education.[24] At the community-college level, Canada's expenditure per student exceeds that of the US and all other G-7 countries.

Within Canada, the fraction of provincial GDP devoted to post-secondary education in Ontario is lower than in all other provinces, and substantially below the national average.[26] Further, spending by the Ontario government on university operating grants fell dramatically between 1988 and 2001, as a percentage of the provincial budget (a 33% decrease).[27] This decline is in sharp contrast to spending on health, which has risen over the period from approximately 32% of the provincial budget in 1986/7 to 39% by 2001/2.[28] Spending priorities have obviously shifted from education to health care over this period. This shift in spending has obvious implications for inter-generational equity (the lion's share of health care funding is received by older citizens), as well as long-term productive capacity of society.

Strikingly, Ontario has been at the bottom of all provinces in terms of spending on universities per capita for the last eight years – per capita spending on post-secondary education in 2003, adjusted for inflation, was 20 per cent below its 1989 level.[29] In spending on universities per student, Ontario has been tenth and last of all provinces for the past three years and ninth for the five years before that.[30] By 2003, Ontario was last among all provinces in university spending per student, per capita, or by any other measure.[31] Tuition, on the other hand, rose over the period from $2,200 to $4,700, an increase of 117%, before being capped by the provincial government.[32] Ontario student fees account for an increasingly high percentage of university operating revenues, and are the second highest in the country behind Nova Scotia's, and are reflected in sharply rising student debt loads.[33] However, Ontario university tuition is comparable to Australian fees and significantly lower than those of public universities in the United States.[34] Interestingly, Ontario college fees are among the lowest in Canada.[35]

While Ontario's funding of post-secondary education has declined relative to other provinces, its position in relation to public universities in many American states is even more unsettling. Provincial funding per full-time student in Ontario is now only half of per-student funding of public institutions in California and North Carolina, and 60% of that in Florida and Michigan. Compared to 12 American peer states, including eight in the Great Lakes Region, the provincial government provides only two-thirds of the funding that state governments provide to their public institutions. Between 1995/6 and 2000/1, Illinois, Michigan, Indiana, Minnesota, New York, Ohio, Pennsylvania, and Wisconsin increased their state funding by between 20% and 35% while Ontario's spending actually diminished by about 3%. [Ed: But see Rosenstone, pp. 57–59, for another perspective.] As well, the federal government provides grant funding that amounts, on a per-student basis, to less than half of the funding provided by the US government to its public institutions. This gap was not closed by increased Canadian tuition revenues. In 2001, on average, Ontario's universities charged only 82% of what their public American peer group charged, further exacerbating the revenue differential. The gap in funding raises the danger of an excellence and accessibility gap.

Has the funding in Ontario translated into accessible, high-quality education and innovative research? For the country as a whole, 54% of the Canadian adult population has completed some form of post-secondary education. This proportion is double the OECD average of 26% and higher than that in the US, where 37% of the population has completed post-secondary education.[36] Canada has a much higher percentage of students who complete college, as opposed to university, programs than either the US or other OECD countries. In terms of students who complete university, Canada is above the OECD average (20% versus the OECD average of 15%) and similar to Japan and Britain, though substantially below the US, where 28% have graduated from university, and further below the US in terms of percentage of students who complete post-graduate degrees. However, 34% of Canadians have non-university post-secondary education, triple the OECD average and more than twice that of any G-7 country.[37] In 2001, Ontario had the highest proportion of its population with a university degree of all provinces (24% versus the national average of 21%) and was slightly below the national average of 34% in terms of individuals with a non-university post-secondary education.[38]

However, the reduced public funding and rising tuition levels in Ontario are raising concerns about accessibility to post-secondary education in the province and, in particular, to university education. Even

before the decline in funding in the 1990s, there was a growing disparity in university education between rich and poor. Between 1986 and
1994, participation in university education increased for 18–to-24-year-
olds of all socio-economic backgrounds. However, participation was
lowest and increased least for those from the lowest socio-economic
families. Individuals from middle socio-economic families participated
at a higher rate than those from lower socio-economic families, and
their rate increased the most prior to 1994. Individuals from the highest
socio-economic status had the highest level of participation in university education over the period. These relative rates of participation
continued in the latter part of the 1990s, yet the pattern of change was
different. Individuals from middle- and high-income families were still
more likely to go to university than individuals from low-income families, but their participation rates declined between 1994 and 1997. The
participation rate for individuals from low-income families, on the
other hand, increased over this period.[39] Looking at post-secondary
education as a whole, students from lower-income families had about
the same rate of college participation as students from higher socio-
economic families. College, therefore, plays a greater role than universities in aiding these individuals.[40]

The restraints on increased funding also raise concerns that the quality of Ontario's post-secondary education is not being maintained. The
student-faculty ratio provides one measure of the quality of post-secondary education in terms of teaching. This ratio in Ontario universities
is dramatically above the average for the other nine provinces, and
international comparisons are equally dismal.[41] Further, in the coming
decade, Ontario will need to hire 11,700 faculty to deal with predicted
retirements and enrolment increases and to keep student-faculty ratios
from deteriorating further.[42]

However, there is intense competition internationally for the best
academics. While there may not be an overall brain drain from Canada
to the US, certain groups are leaving the country at a disproportionate
rate, including university professors, engineers, and scientists. Ontario
universities require the funding to attract and retain outstanding researchers and teachers.[43]

The reduced funding raises concern not only about the loss of faculty
but also about the deterioration of facilities. Ontario universities are
facing a very high level of deferred maintenance costs over the coming
years. While Ontario has invested in some capital funding in recent
years, the existing university facilities are aging, in need of repair, and

badly lacking in space for faculty and students. The Council of Ontario Universities estimated that in 2002 deferred maintenance amounted to $1.3 billion or $1.56 billion when adaptation and renewal renovations are included. Over $100 million per year is required merely to maintain the status quo.[44]

One question that arises is whether Ontario (and Canada as a whole) is misallocating resources by spending so much on non-university post-secondary programs and having such a large number of graduates from those institutions. Some commentators argue that this reflects a lack of ambition on the part of Ontarians that needs to be remedied in order for the province to prosper.[45] An alternative explanation is that the funding of non-university programs reflects demand in the labour market and allows diversity of learning.

The economic effect in terms of private returns to the individual is substantial for all types of education. University programs, and in particular post-graduate degrees such as those in medicine and veterinary medicine and PhDs, have the largest impact on individual earnings. College programs and trade schools have a lower impact than universities on the earnings of those who complete high school, although they substantially increase the incomes of those who did not finish high school. In both cases, the impact of post-secondary education on earnings is greater for women than for men. As well, the increased returns have been found to arise because education makes individuals more productive (not because they merely signal existing differences in people). These results suggest that universities do play a central role in economic returns for Ontarians and provide a larger return to the individual than a non-university post-secondary program. However, colleges and trade schools also play a pivotal role in increasing the economic opportunities of and returns to Ontarians, including those who dropped out of high school.[46]

Top Canadian universities perform reasonably well with respect to the volume of scholarly publications they produce, but lag substantially behind the top US universities in terms of the recognition that their research garners from scholars. It is fair to say that the quantity of research emerging from Canadian universities is comparable, proportionately, to the quantity produced by US universities, but that the quality of research in Canada, which is what really matters, falls substantially behind the output found in top US institutions.[47] This gap can be attributed to proportionately lower levels of provincial financial support for Canadian universities than is provided by US states to their public institutions, to proportionately lower levels of federal research funding in Canada, to poor allocation of research funding, and to systematically lower salary levels in Canada that hinder the ability of Canadian universities to hire and retain the best and the brightest.

The policy environment for post-secondary education in Ontario over the past two decades has been highly unstable. Apart from declining levels of public funding, the system has endured the salary rollbacks associated with the Rae government's Social Contract, the draconian budget cuts associated with the Harris government's Common Sense Revolution, the subsequent partial liberalization of tuition pricing policy, and then recently the McGuinty government's complete freeze on tuition increases. These policy discontinuities have severely compromised the ability of universities to engage in serious forward-planning, including the ability to make salary commitments to hire and retain faculty and invest in infrastructure. A new and more stable compact between government and the post-secondary sector is sorely needed.

4. Towards a New Compact for University Education in Ontario

The economic, social, and political benefits of post-secondary education point to the need to foster a strong, broad-based educational system. There are a number of reforms that should be made to improve the post-secondary education system in Ontario. For example, the government should improve the information available to students on employment and earnings associated with different programs so that students can make better decisions about which programs to pursue. It should also require post-secondary institutions to provide more informative grading to aid both employers and students in making employment and other decisions. Further, the government should improve accessibility and opportunities for students by expanding co-op programs and improving the integration of colleges and universities.[48]

However, the greatest challenges facing post-secondary education in Ontario relate to the funding of institutions, the quality of teaching and research, and the accessibility of post-secondary education. The government can have the greatest impact on the financing, quality, and accessibility of post-secondary education by reforming its funding and tuition policies to promote excellence and diversity among programs. Not all institutions or programs should be exactly the same and, as Cameron notes, 'there is much to be said for increased diversity [in research intensity].'[49] The current system aiming for similar programs at all universities hobbles our universities' health as engines of innovation, creativity and enlightenment. Promoting institutions and programs with a variety of goals can aid in tailoring the post-secondary education system to the needs of Ontarians. Some institutions should focus on teaching, some on research, some on a combination of the two, and some on vocational training. Moreover, there should be incentives to promote excellence in particular programs rather than forcing or encouraging all institutions to deliver similar programs. Finally, because education holds the key to equal economic and social opportunities, any reforms must ensure that individuals are not hindered from obtaining post-secondary education because of their socio-economic background.

Specifically, the province should undertake a four-part plan to promote diversity, quality, and accessibility in post-secondary education. First, the amount of public money that is spent on post-secondary education should be substantially increased so that on a public expenditure per student basis Ontario is the leading province not the last province. Second, the amount of increased public funding for each program should be tied to performance – that is, programs that provide better quality should receive additional money. Third, tuition policy should be deregulated to permit different fees for programs of different quality, subject to the maintenance of effective financial aid programs and policies administered by universities. Fourth, in order to ensure that the cornerstone of a society in which each citizen is able to realize his or her full potential – accessibility – is maintained, the province should institute an income-contingent loan program and target an enhanced grant and loan program at increasing participation of individuals from lower income backgrounds in post-secondary learning, particularly university education.

Public Money and Performance Funding

Ontario invests substantial funds in post-secondary education. This money should be leveraged to ensure it is used to promote excellence in teaching and research and a diversity of programs that will benefit Ontarians. This leveraging can occur through performance funding.[50]

In Ontario, performance-based funding currently plays a very limited role. For 2000–1, the Ministry of Training, Colleges and Universities distributed $16.5 million (relative to grants to universities of approximately $1.7 billion)[51] on the basis of three performance-based mea-sures: graduation rates, graduate employment after six months, and graduate employment after two years. Alberta and other U.S. states have also used crude indicators, such as graduation rates and employ-ment rates, in implementing similar performance-based funding schemes.[52] These indicators do not assess the quality of the research taking place at an institution, nor do they adequately reflect the quality of its graduates or the jobs they take. This performance funding repre-sents only a modest beginning, comprising less than 1% of the $1.7 billion distributed to Ontario universities in the form of operating grants.

The majority of the Ontario government's funding for the university system has been based on a flawed funding mechanism. Since the 1960s, funding has been based on a weighted average of the number of students in various programs. The weights are determined by the rela-tive cost of educating students in various programs.[53] Provincial fund-ing for the post-secondary sector is distributed essentially on the basis of student enrolment, or full-time equivalent (FTE) enrolment, with program weights then applied to enrolment numbers to yield Basic Income Units (BIUs).[54] Enrolment numbers therefore drive university funding in Ontario without reference to quality – the strongest and the weakest programs get largely the same financing. A key concern with this funding mechanism is that it does not adequately take into account both teaching and research. The government does increase the BIU weight for students in more research-intensive graduate programs. However, within each type of program, the funding mechanism does not account for differences in the quantity or quality of research and therefore for the costs of a greater volume of research or higher-quality research.[55] To be sure, in recent years both the federal and provincial governments have launched a number of initiatives to enhance research-based funding for Ontario universities.[56] The federal govern-ment, in particular, has taken significant steps to bolster leading research, such as establishing Canada Research Chairs to fund outstanding scholars.[57]

Still, the provincial funding mechanism does not distinguish between high- and low-quality educational programs. Ontario universities are relatively homogeneous in large part because the formula provides the same funding for all programs and does not allow differences in tuition fees to reflect variances in quality – with the recent exception of profes-sional programs. Ontario institutions and programs vary less in terms of quality and specialization than do institutions and programs in many

US states or in Britain. At the present time, Ontario lacks research-intensive universities with the reputation of top US state-funded universities, such as the University of California, Berkeley, or the University of Michigan.[58]

We recognize the challenges in designing appropriate performance-based funding systems as pointed out in several papers in this volume – performance criteria that key on academic inputs, not outputs, or preferably outcomes (which are admittedly difficult to measure or evaluate directly), and perverse incentives or gaming behaviour that inappropriate performance proxies can engender. However, asking governments simply to write larger blank cheques on an across-the-board basis to the post-secondary sector is politically untenable. In a setting of intense fiscal pressure, governments must, by necessity, demonstrate that any new public investment, is strategic, and can yield demonstrable improvements to the quality of publicly supported services. Therefore, to respond to the need for differentiated performance-based investment, but without an administratively cumbersome bureaucratic structure that will subvert sound academic planning and performance, we recommend, in skeletal form, a four-tiered performance-based system that would be structured as follows.

At the undergraduate level, additional public funding should be made available for programs and institutions prepared to commit over time to restoring tenure-stream faculty-student ratios to their 1990 level (e.g., 17 to 1, not 27 to 1), given evidence that class size seems to be highly correlated with the student undergraduate academic experience. This funding should be significantly weighted by quality of the student entering cohort to provide incentives for independent program improvement. At the post-graduate level, additional multi-year public funding should be made available to create and reinforce a very small number of internationally competitive post-graduate programs in most of the major disciplines to enable the hiring and retention of internationally recognized faculty, to attract and support top graduate students domestically and internationally, and to finance necessary enhancements in physical infrastructure. This funding would be allocated by a specialized provincial granting agency (like the federal granting agencies) in peer-reviewed competitions with well-defined evaluating criteria and subject to periodic *ex post* peer review. Third, project-specific research support would continue to be allocated by the federal granting agencies in peer-reviewed periodic competitions. Fourth, public support for infrastructure enhancements might primarily take the form of matching grants for donor-supported projects to enhance incentives for universities to place a high premium on alumni satisfaction and to cultivate and exploit their alumni and donor networks.

If performance-based funding were awarded to individual programs instead of to entire institutions, top programs could be produced across the province, although some institutions may always have a concentration of excellent programs. Universities that cannot compete against a large institution like the University of Toronto would not be left out because they could focus their resources on those areas in which they have a comparative advantage. Indeed, Ontario's universities would be encouraged to identify their strengths and improve programs that they know are competitive provincially, nationally, or internationally.

In other words, most universities, rather than pursuing many mediocre programs, would have incentives to create a few internationally recognized, excellent ones (somewhat analogous to, but more ambitious than, the 'Centres of Excellence' that the province has promoted in the recent past). This specialization introduces competition among universities for enhanced funding and, perhaps most importantly, improves the overall efficacy of Ontario's university system by eliminating wasteful duplication and making strong programs even stronger. As a province, Ontario will have better programs and scholarship. Talent can be attracted from other provinces and countries, and the education of top graduate and professional students can be enriched. However, an important feature of this funding regime is that no institution actually loses financing that it is currently receiving – that is, no university is punished or deprived of funding for failing to meet certain standards. Enhanced funding is used to reward excellence and to create incentives to excel in the future.

It is important to recognize that colleges are also a key component of the post-secondary education system in the province. They provide a wide range of students with the skills to compete for rewarding work. They also play a particularly important role in providing education to students from lower socio-economic backgrounds, as well as to those who have dropped out of high school. The importance of colleges raises the need for Ontario to provide sufficient public funding, yet there is insufficient evidence to determine whether the financing of colleges versus universities is out of balance. There are steps the province can take to improve access to and choice in college education. First, Ontario should enter into a Labour Market Development Agreement with the federal government, enabling the province to better aid in tailoring college programs to the needs of Ontarians.[59] Second, as with universities, additional funding for colleges should be performance-based to develop and reward excellence in college programs. Third, the province should take an active role in ensuring the provision of information to students, such as the employment and income profiles of graduates from each university and college program, to enable them to make informed choices. Finally, the province should take steps to promote the integration of colleges and universities to provide greater access to post-secondary education, especially in areas where there are no universities, and greater movement between post-secondary programs as students assess their abilities and interests.[60] To date, there has been only limited collaboration between universities and colleges.

Tuition, Choice, and Accessibility

Government funding of post-secondary education reflects the social benefits derived from a strong post-secondary system, as well as the information and funding problems facing students. The reality is that under any scenario there are insufficient public funds to close the excellence gap between Ontario universities and top international public institutions. As noted, post-secondary education produces substantial private returns. Full government funding of post-secondary education results in all Ontarians bearing the costs of educating individuals who stand to obtain very large personal returns. Because such subsidies are financed through taxes, they either reduce the amount of public money available to finance other programs, or they necessitate higher taxes. As a result of this mix of the private and social effects of education, both the provincial government and the individuals who stand to gain should invest in post-secondary education. In 2001, student fees accounted for 26.3% of Ontario universities' revenue, among the highest in Canada. Government funds accounted for 47.8% of revenues, the lowest share in Canada.[61]

When individuals must pay part of the cost of their education, they will be more selective about their programs, and thus institutions would have greater incentives to pay attention to students' interests. These incentives would be even sharper if programs were able to set different fees. Programs of higher quality could charge higher tuition, although they would have to demonstrate the justification for the higher cost to students.

However, tuition payments by individuals raise concern about a key tenet of the education system in Ontario – accessibility. Education should be equally available to all qualified individuals, regardless of their family or personal background – that is, their socio-economic status. While individuals tend to obtain higher incomes as a result of post-secondary education, financial institutions are in general reticent to lend money for this type of investment in human capital because human capital cannot be collateralized like other assets. As a result, without specific arrangements to promote accessibility, raising tuition fees will reduce the opportunity of less well-off individuals to benefit from a post-secondary education. Further, even where funds are available to aid such students, they may hesitate to apply to universities because of the 'sticker shock' from the high tuition levels.

Rising tuition fees in Canada have increased the debt level of students. For example, by 1995, 46% of bachelor's graduates borrowed for their education, with the mean amounts of the loans rising sharply from around $6,000 in 1982 to $13,600 in 1995.[62] The average government-student-loan debt of students who went to university for four years and finished their program in 2002 was $21,500.[63] The federal and provincial governments help with loans through the Canada Student Loan Program and the Ontario Student Assistance Program. These loans are similar to mortgages in that they must be repaid following graduation, with interest. As well, students' access to loans is limited because not everyone qualifies for them, as they are means-tested on the basis of family income. Such means testing presumes unencumbered access of individuals to family resources. However, those in charge of the distribution of household finances to household members may not have the prospective student's view of the value of education.[64] In addition, a large number of students default on their loans,[65] partly because there are no serious disincentives to prevent them from doing so.[66] The high costs of these defaults are absorbed by the government. For example, the cost to the federal government of collecting at-risk student loans is estimated at between 19 and 28 cents per dollar.[67] Furthermore, since the government guarantees the loan to the university or college by paying the student's fees up front, universities and colleges put too little effort into debt recovery or into screening students adequately to determine their prospects for successful completion of programs. There is a wide variation of institutional performance on repayment.

More importantly, under the current system, some students may be reluctant to borrow out of fear of not meeting future repayment obligations. This concern arises because these loans for education are insensitive to the borrower's changing financial circumstances. These prospective students will not borrow and therefore will not attend university or college.[68] The fear of not being able to pay back the loan will likely have a disproportionate effect on the disadvantaged. This impact of the current loan programs therefore has important consequences for the accessibility of post-secondary education.

A better approach to student financing involves income-contingent loans (ICLs). An ICL involves students contracting with the government to repay deferred fees in proportion to their future income. Students pay up front only as much as they can, with the rest deferred until they graduate and are working. The government supplies the university or college with the fees that students have deferred. Students eventually repay their deferred fees through the income-tax system, in proportion to their earnings. The introduction of such regimes in other countries is often accompanied by deregulated tuition fees and direct subsidies for low-income students.

The main attraction of ICLs is that they can be designed to avoid the problems associated with Ontario's current system of traditional loans. First, there is no concern with intra-family sharing so long as the scheme is universal. No students would be denied access through the imposition of means-testing arrangements that could exclude some whose parents or partners are unwilling to help.[69] Second, the default issue for the government is largely addressed by deploying the tax system to collect the debt, since it is extremely difficult for the vast majority of graduates to avoid repayment.[70]

Some students will not pay back their deferred fees in full because ICLs are designed to forgive the fees of students whose lifetime incomes are below a certain threshold. Those students may be able to pay back a portion of their fees, which is an improvement over the complete defaults occurring under the current system. Students who earn incomes below a certain threshold will not have to make any contribution through the tax system in that year, though they will when their career prospects improve. In other words, ICLs mitigate the risks that students face when they invest in higher education.

Since 1989, Australia, New Zealand, and Britain have introduced ICLs for post-secondary education. These countries had in the past offered essentially free post-secondary education. The Australia and New Zealand systems have loan repayments dependent on an individual's income and reduce the costs of the program by having the payments collected through the tax system. In each case, there is a minimum threshold below which the loan does not have to be repaid, with a progressive rate of collection, depending on the individual's income. In both cases, institutions are now permitted to set their own fees.

In Australia, accessibility appears to have been maintained. The socio-economic make-up of the higher education student body was about the same in the late 1990s as it was before these loans were introduced.[71] This can be explained by a number of factors. First, ICLs will not deter students in the same way that up-front loans can – by shocking lower-income students with immediate, large debt. As well, post-secondary enrolments in Australia have increased by some 50% as a result of the increases in tuition and increased post-secondary spending by the Australian government. Finally, the recent reforms of 2003 emphasize the importance of improving the performance of indigenous peoples and disadvantaged minorities through scholarships and other equity-based measures.

Overall, income-contingent loans appear to have been a successful innovation in post-secondary funding in Australia and New Zealand. Their use of the national income-taxation infrastructure stands out as a crucial feature of a well-designed ICL program.[72] Britain is moving in a similar direction after introducing a limited form of ICL in 1997. A review of higher education in 2003 is pointing towards an expanded ICL program with universities setting their own tuition levels, subject to a cap, and students making ICL repayments after graduation through the income tax system.

The Australian, New Zealand and U.K. reforms provide a clear direction for Ontario.[73] No students, regardless of family income, should be required to pay tuition up front, although they may if they choose. Loans for post-secondary education should be repayable after graduation on an income-contingent basis, that is, they should depend on a student's future income, and the most efficient mechanism by which they can be collected is through the income tax system. With such arrangements in place, the regulation of tuition fees can be substantially loosened, permitting universities and colleges to more effectively supplement their public subsidy with contributions from students. Since these contributions are income-contingent, they will be made in proportion to the earnings advantage that individual students enjoy as a result of their education.

An ICL program would address the risk inherent in human capital investments, because those whose post-graduation earnings are below average are not faced with high debt loads, as would be the case under a conventional student loan program. Those whose earnings are below average may repay less under ICLs, but those who achieve above-average earnings will likely repay more than under the current system.[74] Other advantages of ICLs include a scheduling of payments that is more closely aligned with the evolution of the individual's ability to pay, reduced administrative costs, and lower default rates.

Further, when a student defers his or her tuition fees, the province should supply the university or college with the deferred amount. These payments will enable post-secondary institutions to operate free of uncertainty with respect to yearly tuition revenues. Once the student has graduated and is working to pay off the ICL, the provincial government will assess contributions to be paid through the income tax system, thereby recouping its original loan. In order to enhance institutional incentives to screen students for prospects of successful program completion, the college or university should bear some part of the risk of default, such as through reduced public funding based on default rates.

In order to maximize the benefits of diversity of institutions and increase choice in post-secondary education in Ontario, when the province has introduced an ICL program it should deregulate tuition fees. Deregulating tuition fees would encourage universities and colleges to expand enrolment to meet the demand for their programs and enable outstanding programs to differentiate themselves and aspire to even higher levels of international excellence. It would also provide colleges and universities with funding they need because of the recent reductions in public funding. This added funding would aid in improving the quality of higher education in Ontario.

Deregulating tuition, even with ICLs, raises concerns about participation by individuals from poorer socio-economic backgrounds. If education is to have the benefits it potentially could have in terms of reducing inequality and opening up opportunities for the less well-off, higher education needs to be a viable option for all Ontarians. The province, therefore, should supplement an ICL program with a grant program to increase the participation in post-secondary education and, in particular, university education by individuals from less-privileged socio-economic groups. The federal government has taken some steps in this regard through the Millennium Scholarships Program, as has Ontario through the Ontario Student Opportunities Trust Fund.[75] These programs have led to an increase in participation by lower-income individuals in the latter part of the 1990s.[76] However, more needs to be done to increase the participation rate of these individuals. The province should increase the funding of grants and monitor this participation rate with a view to increasing it significantly over time, perhaps towards a specific targeted level.

Deregulating tuition, combined with ICLs and increased grants, would allow institutions to differentiate themselves and to foster outstanding programs. However, the province should not attempt to micromanage post-secondary admissions and program offerings.[77] Evidence from Britain indicates that micromanagement by the state decreases university independence and results in lower standards.[78] Institutions should make the decisions about which programs to develop and how to meet the needs of students. Unlike the province, these institutions have the information to make the creative and innovative decisions necessary to foster excellence. The public interest in post-secondary education in a system centred around institutional diversity can be protected in two ways. First, as noted above, there will continue to be public funding of universities, which will allow the province to maintain incentives for institutions to pursue the public interest. Second, a diverse, and vocal, set of stakeholders, including the public, have input into the decisions of post-secondary institutions through the governance regimes of individual universities and colleges. There has been no scarcity of scrutiny and debate in these fora in the past over the ways in which excellence and accessibility can be promoted and it is unlikely that there will be a shortage in the future. This form of civic engagement in the decisions of institutions helps allay concerns that they will use public funding or increased tuition revenue in ways that do not promote the public interest. To aid both these avenues of monitoring, the province should require every university and college governing council to demonstrate that they have a credible access program in place. Each governing council should be required to make a public report to the government every three years on the effectiveness of its access program. Such reporting would ensure that the province and the public have the information necessary to assess progress on accessibility.

5. Conclusion

Ontario needs a new relationship between government and students to ensure high-quality, accessible post-secondary education. To this end, spending on post-secondary education in Ontario should be, on average, the highest in Canada on a per student basis. In order for Ontario to achieve the highest levels of public support per student in Canada (not the lowest), the recent report of the Panel on the Role of Government in Ontario[79] roughly estimated, this would entail additional public expenditures of $1.3 billon per year, phased in over several years. This number needs to be put in perspective. The total provincial expenditure budget as of 2004 is about $80 billion. Of this, about $30 billion is spent on health care and only $4 billion on post-secondary education. An additional infusion of public funding of $1.3 billion, if appropriately structured, along with a further infusion of revenues from deregulated tuition fees, have the potential for a transformatory impact on the post-secondary sector, promoting institutional specialization in internationally competitive programs, enhancing the student learning experience at both undergraduate and post-graduate levels, and enhancing student accessibility to higher-quality programs through income-contingent loans and grants to meritorious students from disadvantaged backgrounds.

These reforms represent a new partnership between government and students and will promote both excellence and accessibility in post-secondary education in Ontario.

Notes

* Faculty of Law, University of Toronto. This paper draws on work undertaken for the Ontario Role of Government Panel, with which both authors were associated, and on our forthcoming book, *Rethinking the Welfare State: Government by Voucher* (London: Routledge, 2005). Andrew Green and Roy Hrab made important contributions to the development of the analysis of the Panel on the Role of Government. We also wish to acknowledge the useful comments of Ian Clark and Frank Milne on an earlier version of this chapter delivered at the conference.

1 The boundary between public and private universities should not, however, be drawn too starkly. Many elite private institutions receive significant levels of state support in the form of competitively allocated research grants and student-based financial aid assistance, which mutes the difference between these two modes of provision.

2 For a general discussion, see Douglas Auld, *Expanding Horizons: Privatizing Universities* (Toronto: University of Toronto Press, 1996), chap. 1.

3 W. Craig Riddell, 'The Role of Government in Post-Secondary Education in Ontario,' Report to the Panel on the Role of Government in Ontario (2003), 49. Available online at http://www.law-lib.utoronto.ca/investing/reports/rp29.pdf. Riddell notes that these private returns have remained

high despite considerable increases in the number of educated workers over the last several decades. Riddell further notes that the impact of education on earnings is causal, that is, workers are more productive as a result of education rather than education being simply a means of signaling worker quality.

4 Somewhat more broadly, there is a literature showing that, particularly in a human capital economy, university research contributes significantly to societal wealth. See Anna-Lee Saxenian, *Regional Advantage: Culture and Competition in Silicon Valley and Route 128* (Cambridge, MA: Harvard University Press, 1994). See also the very thoughtful contributions made by David Dyzenhaus and Andrew Green in this volume.

5 By the term 'extent' it is suggested that the state, which is the ultimate beneficiary of the public benefits, should be a proportion of the costs of higher education relative the overall benefits of higher education. In this way, the rates of return for both the private and the public expenditures on post-secondary education would be equalized, without privileging either.

6 The fact that the benefits to society and to the individual are largely intangible and probably impossible to measure accurately does not undermine the theoretical cogency of this argument. A system that at least *attempted* to do this would probably reach a more efficient outcome than our system does at present.

7 Some have argued that university education does not actually cause one's income to be higher. The screening hypothesis argues that post-secondary education may just be a signal of some other attributes to which employers assign value. See Nicholas Barr, *The Economics of the Welfare State*, 3rd ed. (Stanford, CA: Stanford University Press, 1998), 324.

8 For a further discussion of this idea, see Barr, ibid., 325.

9 Even more than at the primary and secondary levels, the positions of Martha Nussbaum, *Cultivating Humanity: A Classical Defence of Reform in Liberal Education* (Cambridge University Press, 1998), Amy Gutmann, *Democratic Education* (Princeton, NJ: Princeton University Press, 1987), and Allan Bloom, *The Closing of the American Mind* (New York: Touchstone Books, 1988) are important. That is, it is at the university level that they are most concerned with promoting a vision of liberal education as formative of a certain character and way of experiencing the world, not merely as imparting marketable skills.

10 In actual fact, even with government subsidization investment in research will probably be deficient because research does not have guaranteed payoffs and most investors are risk averse. That is, a guaranteed return is to some extent preferred to a higher expected, but more variable return. Note that investment in applied research will probably be less deficient than investment in pure research because of the greater prospect of appropriating the benefits therefrom via patents.

11   See, for instance, Robert J. Barro, 'Human Capital and Growth,' *American Economic Review* 91:2 (2001), 12–17 and Robert J. Barro and Eaverier sala-i-Martin, *Economic Growth* (New York: McGraw-Hill, 1995).

12   Riddell (see note 3), 24.

13   Ronald Dworkin, 'DeFunis v. Sweatt,' in Marshall Cohen, Thomas Nagel, and Thomas Scanlon, eds, *Equality and Preferential Treatment* (Princeton, NJ: Princeton University Press, 1977), 63.

14   In the US, private universities often pursue 'need-blind' admissions policies and then provide varying degrees of student assistance to those who are in financial need. The net result is that education is means-tested at private American universities. Another way to describe this policy, however, is to say that private American schools engage in a system of price discrimination that is designed to extract the maximum amount of money from each student. Given that private universities in the US are non-profit institutions interested in educating the strongest students possible, from an equity standpoint this regime of price discrimination is not necessarily repugnant, but at worst benign and perhaps even desirable. It serves as a way for students from wealthier families to cross-subsidize students with a lower ability to pay, while ensuring that only the most able applicants are granted admission. Many private universities supplement the federally sponsored loan program with internal income-contingent repayment plans (ICRPs) for loans that they grant to students in need of financial aid. The price discrimination regimes combined with ICRPs make access to education relatively equitable at private universities – despite the high tuition fees – for students confronting affordability problems. In terms of accessibility, then, private universities are arguably well ahead of their public counterparts.

15   Barr (see note 7), 347.

16   Bruce Chapman and David Greenaway, 'Learning to Live With Loans? Policy Transfer and the Funding of Higher Education,' Paper for the Internationalism and Policy Transfer Conference, Tulane University (2003), 8. See also O. Mehmet, *Who Benefits from the Ontario University System: A Benefit-Cost Analysis by Income Groups* (Toronto: Ontario Economic Council, 1978), 45: 'The principal net gainers from the university system are the middle and upper-income groups at the expense of lower-income groups. In this sense, the university system is a large public expenditure program in which the relatively poor groups tend to subsidize the relatively rich.'

17   Chapman and Greenaway, ibid., 8.

18   In extreme, some public institutions confront a combination of caps on faculty salaries, mandatory salary disclosure, and tuition-fee restrictions, making it increasingly difficult for these institutions to attract and retain the most sought-after professors. For instance, in 1980 in the US the average gap in salary between full professors at public and private univer-

sities was $1,300. By 1998, this gap had widened to $21,700. 'United States: The Gap Widens,' *The Economist*, 22 April 2000.

19 This lack of flexibility is perhaps most evident in relation to the relatively poor response of public universities to the growing needs of mature and part-time students. Whereas only 27% of US college students were twenty-five or older in 1970, by 1991 this segment of the student body had risen to constitute 45% of students. Entrepreneurial private institutions in the United States that cater to mature and part-time students through an array of online correspondence and other materials have begun to fill the void left by slowly moving public and well-established private institutions. New opportunities will arise as technology becomes more reliable, more interactive, and more ubiquitous. However, it is not clear that public institutions have been nearly as responsive to these needs.

20 Milton Friedman and Rose Friedman, *Free to Choose* (New York: Harcourt Brace Jovanovich, 1980), 176–7.

21 An alternate explanation may be that high tuition rates dissuade high-risk students from attending universities with high tuition. Instead high-risk students prefer to attend where they can make a lower-valued investment in their post-secondary education (and therefore have less to lose in the case of abandonment).

22 Commission of Inquiry on Canadian University Education, *Report* (Ottawa: AUCC, 1991), 105.

23 Ibid., 106.

24 Government of Ontario Post-Secondary Review (Rae Review), 'Discussion Paper' (2004), 25.

25 Canadian post-secondary education expenditure per student is only 70–80% of the US level. Furthermore, if post-secondary education expenditure is divided into university and non-university components, Canada's university expenditure per student is only 60% of the US level. Riddell (note 3), 27.

26 Ontario's spending is about 84% of the Canadian average, although this comparison is biased downward somewhat due to transfer/equalization payments from the federal government that allow for increases in educational funding in poorer provinces by taking some GDP away from richer provinces. Riddell, 88.

27 Council of Ontario Universities, *Ontario Universities: 2000 Resource Document* (2000), table 1.5, online at http://www.cou.on.ca/_bin/briefsReports/onLine/2000resourceDocument.cfm.

28 G. White, 'Change in the Ontario State 1952 – 2002,' Report to the Panel on the Role of Government in Ontario (2003).

29 University of Toronto, 'The Choice for a Generation: Investing in Higher Education and Ontario's Future,' *University of Toronto Submission to the Rae Review* (November 2004), 4.

30 Council of Ontario Universities, *2002 Resource Document* (2002), at http://www.cou.on.ca/_bin/briefsReports/onLine/resource2002.cfm.
31 R. Birgeneau, President, University of Toronto, 'Open Letter to All Ontarians,' 19 Sept. 2003, at www.utoronto.ca/president/190903.htm.
32 Council of Ontario Universities (note 27).
33 Council of Ontario Universities (note 27); Government of Ontario (note 24), 24.
34 Government of Ontario, 24.
35 Ibid.
36 Riddell, 33.
37 Ibid. However, Canada's definition of post-secondary education is more generous than the American definition because it includes those with trade certificates. However, Canada has a higher percentage of individuals with post-secondary education even when this definitional issue is taken into account.
38 Ibid., 36.
39 M. Corak, G. Lipps, and J. Zhao, 'Family Income and Participation in Post-Secondary Education,' *Statistics Canada Research Paper, Cat. no. 11F0019MIE – 210* (October 2003).
40 Keith Banting, 'Responding to Social Risk in Ontario: Are We There Yet?' Report to the Panel on the Role of Government in Ontario (2003). Between 1986 and 1994, the percentage of 18–21 year olds attending university increased for individuals from low socio-economic status (SES) backgrounds from 13.7% to 18.3%, for individuals from middle SES backgrounds from 14.5% to 25.3%, and for individuals from high SES backgrounds from 32.9% to 40.3%.
41 University of Toronto (note 29), 12. This state of affairs is the result of a long term deterioration in Ontario.
42 Council of Ontario Universities, *Biennial Report 2000–2002* (May 2003), at http://www.cou.on.ca/content/objects/Biennial20002002Report.pdf.
43 D. Cameron, 'The Challenge of Change: Canadian Universities in the 21st Century,' *Canadian Public Administration* 45:2 (2002), 145.
44 Council of Ontario Universities, *University Education in Ontario: Shared Goals and Building Blocks* (September 2003), at http://www.cou.on.ca/content/objects/Shared Goals 7 w1.pdf.
45 R. Martin and J. Milway, 'Unleashing Higher Learning,' *Globe and Mail*, 30 Aug. 2003, A15.
46 Riddell, 47.
47 J. Chant and W. Gibson, 'Quantity or Quality? Research at Canadian Universities,' in D. Laidler, ed., *Renovating the Ivory Tower: Canadian Universities and the Knowledge Economy* (Toronto: C.D. Howe Institute, 2002).
48 See Riddell, 50, for a description of these potential reforms.
49 Cameron (note 43), 171.

50 For a recent comparative review of the role of performance-based funding in higher education in eleven OECD countries, see Ben Jongbloed and Hans Vossensteyn, 'Keeping Up Performances: An International Survey of Performance-Based Funding in Higher Education' (2001) *J. of Higher Education Policy Management* 127.

51 Council of Ontario Universities (note 27).

52 Council of Ontario Universities, *A Background Report Prepared for the Working Group on Performance Funding: Lessons from Other Jurisdictions* (March 2001), at http://www.cou.on.ca/content/objects/Performance Funding_Lessons.pdf.

53 This 'Basic Income Unit' system was introduced in 1967–8. A major modification in 1987–8 severed the direct link between funding and student enrolment by introducing a 'corridor' within which changes in student numbers do not result in changes in funding. Panel on the Role of Government, *Staff Report: Creating a Human Capital Society for Ontario* (March 2004), 64.

54 Every year, the Ministry of Training, Colleges and Universities produces 'The Ontario Operating Funds Distribution Manual,' which fully details the funding formula and regulatory policy. Panel on the Role of Government, *Staff Report*, 64.

55 Riddell 62.

56 'At the federal level these include the Canada Foundation for Innovation and indirect funding for research. At the provincial level these include the Ontario Research and Development Challenge Fund, the Ontario Investment Trust, and the Premier's Research Excellence Awards.' Riddell, 62.

57 Cameron (note 43).

58 Riddell, 62.

59 For a more extensive discussion of Labour Market Development Agreements, see Panel on the Role of Government, *Staff Report: Creating a Human Capital Society for Ontario* (March 2004), 77; alternatively, H. Lazar, *Shifting Roles: Active Labour Market Policy in Canada under the Labour Market Development Agreement* (2002), online at www.cprn.org.

60 Riddell, 77.

61 Statistics Canada, 'University Finance,' *The Daily*, 11 June 2003.

62 R. Finnie, 'Student Loans: Is It Getting Harder? Borrowing, Burdens and Repayment' (Kingston, ON: School of Policy Studies, Queen's University, 2000), 4.

63 Government of Ontario (note 24), 8. Government student debt has increased by 25% over the past five years for four-year university students, as compared to only 6% for two-year college students.

64 Chapman and Greenaway (note 16), 9.

65 Finnie finds that 40–50% of Fine Arts and Humanities graduates in 1995 reported repayment problems. Finnie (note 62), 11. In the US, Harrison

notes that in some US colleges the default rate is as high as 50%. M. Harrison, 'Default in Guaranteed Student Loan Programs,' *Journal of Student Financial Aid* 25 (1995).

66 Edwin G. West, *Ending the Squeeze on Universities: Canada in a World Perspective* (Ottawa: Carlton University, 1993), at www.ncl.ac.uk/egwest/pdfs/ending%20the%20squeeze.pdf. According to the Rae Review Discussion Paper there has been a decline in the likelihood of student default, although no explanation is provided for this improvement. Currently, 'National data shows 30% of college and 24% of university graduates report difficulty in repaying their loans.' See Government of Ontario (note 24), 24, 26.

67 West, ibid.

68 For analysis of this issue, see B. Chapman, 'Conceptual Issues and the Australian Experience with Income Contingent Charging for Higher Education,' *Economic Journal* 107 (1997), 1178.

69 Chapman and Greenaway, 9.

70 A significant concern relates to former students emigrating, thereby detaching themselves from their home country's taxation system. This relatively minor loss is to be weighed against the larger benefits of ICLs and the greater tuition revenue that they facilitate.

71 B. Chapman and C. Ryan, 'Income Contingent Financing of Student Higher Education Charges: Assessing the Australian Innovation,' *Welsh Journal of Education* 11 (2002), 64.

72 New Zealand has higher administrative costs than Australia as it has a more complicated system relating to interest on the debt.

73 The federal government attempted to put in place an income-contingent loan program in 1994. However, the program was not well conceived and was abandoned when it ran up against significant opposition from the provinces, students, and universities. Cameron (note 43).

74 Riddell, 70.

75 Banting, *supra* note 40.

76 Corak et al. (note 39), note that the lower increase in participation in the early 1990s by individuals from low income families was likely the result of increases in tuition without corresponding increases in loans and grants, which did not increase until the latter part of the 1990s.

77 See 'Pay or Decay,' *Economist*, 24 Jan. 2004, 11; 'Who Pays to Study?' *Economist*, 24 Jan. 2004, 23.

78 Ibid.

79 See Report of the Panel on the Role of Government in Ontario, *Investing in People: Creating a Human Capital Society for Ontario* (February 2004), 70.

PART II

The Case for the Public University:
Rationales for and Modes of Public Intervention

Public Funding of Teaching and Research in Universities: A View from the South

PETER DAWKINS AND ROSS WILLIAMS*

Debate over the structure and funding of higher education revolves around three main groups of issues. The first and overriding issue is the nature of the higher education system. Should there be a range of institutions with different missions or should each institution attempt to meet the full range of society's needs? Put more specifically, should all institutions offer doctoral programs (the Australian model) or should there be a hierarchy of institutions ranging from technical colleges to liberal-arts colleges to PhD-granting institutions. The broad structure of higher education is a regulatory rather than a funding issue; it is a matter for society to decide through government.

The second contentious issue is who should contribute to the resourcing of higher education and the related question of what is the appropriate level of overall funding? What should be the relative roles of government and private contributions? A third issue is the nature and extent of research funding and the relationship between research activity and teaching/scholarship. This relates back to the nature and aims of the system as a whole.

Ultimately, decisions about the structure of the higher education system are made by government. A number of major reviews of Australian higher education have been undertaken by federal governments over the last 15 years.[1] These have involved soliciting the views of interested parties such as educationalists, academics, employers, professional bodies, alumni, and students. Different federal ministers have placed quite different weights on the views of groups and individuals. Government education policy has also interacted with policy in other areas, such as regional policy.

Internationally, there is considerable diversity in the structures of higher education. The structure in the United States is the most diverse, encompassing both private and public institutions of disparate size and mission. At the other extreme lie the centralized systems of a number of European countries. In the past decade there has been a movement away from very centralized models. The trend away from centralization is being driven by the growing complexity of the demand for higher education. As Nicholas Barr (1998, 180) has written: 'In the past, universities offered a limited range of fairly standard packages to a limited group of full-time, usually young students. Today, in contrast, the educational package is more complex, is changing, and will continue to change; and there are many more students, their needs are more diverse, and education will increasingly be a repeated exercise. As a practical mater, the task has become too complex for central planning any longer to be possible.'

Decentralization of decision making does not of itself imply a change in who pays for the sector. Voucher schemes, for example, merely transfer direct government funding from institutions to individuals. In practice, however, governments are reluctant to devolve decision making for funds they provide.

The plan of the paper is as follows. In section 1 we discuss the regulatory framework, which logically comes before funding. In section 2 we explore funding issues for coursework programs, and in section 3 funding for research and research training. Performance measures are discussed in section 4 and we end, in section 5, with some concluding remarks. In an appendix we provide an overview of current regulatory and funding mechanisms in Australia.

1. The Regulatory Framework

We start from the assumption that some government intervention is required to at least monitor the university sector. We go further and believe that some form of formal accreditation of institutions is required in order to provide information to clients in an efficient manner. The central issue then is how much regulation is needed? Should there, for example, be an official certification of the name 'university' in the title of a higher education institution? Should all institutions be able to offer the full range of courses from certificates, through bachelor degrees and the PhD? The Californian model, for example, consists of tiers of institutions, with only designated public-funded institutions able to offer PhD programs.

It is inevitable and proper that governments regulate public universities which they are funding. Ideally, regulation should include the following in its aims:

- Efficient provision of society's demands for higher education, taking account of the diversity of talents, interests, and desires
- Minimum standards for award courses
- Transferability of credits and awards across institutions in the government's jurisdiction

The first aim might best be achieved by regulation which encourages or compels the existence of a range of higher education institutions and avoids excessive duplication. This can involve vertical or horizontal specialization or a combination of both. In vertical specialization with a hierarchy of institutions it is essential to encourage and facilitate the movement of students and academic staff between the tiers.

In federations (and unions) it is important to harmonize the regulations imposed by the federal government and the state/provincial governments. Particularly in federal/state matters, it is not only what might be termed 'academic regulation' that needs to be harmonized, but regulations in areas such as employment conditions, occupational health and safety, and finances and financial reporting.

Under the regulation framework it is necessary to include all aspects of university activity: coursework teaching, research training, and research. What place should universities have in the research effort of the nation or state/province? What should be the relationship between research institutions funded by government outside universities (e.g., in Australia, CSIRO and specialized medical research institutes)? Is the dual research model inefficient or does it promote vigorous competition?

A question frequently addressed by universities, government, and the private sector is, what type of research should be undertaken in universities? Academics put greatest weight on pursuing research into what they as individuals consider to be important and intellectually interesting. Governments tend to favour research which will have a payoff to the nation in the medium term. Business groups emphasize the importance of immediate relevance. These demands need not be conflicting if the regulatory framework encourages cooperation.

2. The Case for Public Funding of Coursework Programs

2.1 Direct Funding of Universities for Coursework Programs

Evidence suggests that students gain considerable *private* benefit from a university education in the form of higher earnings. Borland (2002) estimates for Australia that the average private return to a person with a bachelor's degree lies between 9 and 15%. The private returns vary across disciplines: Borland's results range from 11% for science graduates to 19% for engineering graduates. Further similar estimates of private rates of return are given in Borland, Dawkins, Johnson, and Williams (2001).

Why then should the government subsidize higher education? The rationale for subsidizing higher education is essentially that it leads to 'external benefits' to society that go beyond the private benefits that accrue to the individual who receives the education.

The lower bound on the social rate of return for bachelors graduates is estimated by Borland, Dawkins, Johnson, and Williams (2001), using Australian data, to be 16.5% for a three-year degree and 14.5% for a four-year degree. On the benefit side these estimates use only the extra gross income earned by a graduate compared with a non-graduate. If it is assumed, for example, that aggregate employment expands by one for every extra ten persons who acquire a university degree, the social rate of return increases to 20.5% for a three-year degree and 17.5% for a four-year degree.

Borland et al. also use a balance-sheet approach to government expenditure on and income from higher education. The findings are that, in Australia, the value of extra tax earnings from higher graduate income exceeds the cost of the teaching component to government in all of the last twenty years. Because of the lags in the repayment schedules of students the net gain of the government in likely to increase in future years. Again, this estimate excludes the more general external benefits that might accrue from having a more educated workforce.

These external benefits can be of various kinds. There is some evidence that an educated workforce is more adaptive to new technology and thereby stimulates economic growth in a way that goes beyond the private benefits to those with high levels of formal education. More educated people may make a greater contribution to voluntary work; a more educated society might be a more cultured society, with resulting societal benefits that are not adequately reflected in wages paid to the more highly educated.

If the externalities are similar for each discipline, then government funding should take the form of a block grant for teaching. However, a priori one might expect differences across disciplines. In an Australian survey by Round and Siegfried (1998) of a sample of people who could perhaps be described as 'experts' (attendees at a higher education conference), the respondents were asked what kind of disciplines they believed generated the greatest external benefits (benefits that exceed those returned to the individual). Subjects like Nursing, Music, Education, Performing Arts, English, and History came near the top of the poll. Subjects like Accounting, Commerce, Management, Law, and Veterinary Science came near the bottom. It should be stressed that these were opinions and should not be regarded as a scientific ranking of the actual externalities.

Larkins (2001) estimates rates of return using data on Australian graduates classified into two groups (Science & Technology and Humanities & Social Sciences) and two levels (three- and four-year degrees). He concludes that the 'social rate of return is very similar for all the bachelor degrees' and is 'in the range 8.7 to 12.1 per cent' (410). Again, this does not include all the possible spillover effects.

There are three conditions under which direct public funding might be differentiated by type of program or university. First, there may be particular types of programs that the government concludes would be under-provided in a consumer-led system. High-cost programs with low private rates of return (e.g., nursing) might be under-subscribed from a public-interest point of view. In other words, this is a situation where the external benefits of a program require larger than average subsidies. Second, government may wish to subsidize universities in regional areas to foster decentralization or for labour market reasons. Third, contingent funding could be given for the provision of equity scholarships for students from disadvantaged backgrounds or to provide additional teaching and pastoral support.

Should that part of the funding for coursework programs which effectively funds research rather than teaching be separated out and allocated differently from the teaching component? This is an important question to address and deserves serious consideration. It is clear that the quantity and quality of research varies considerably between different academic staff and different fields of study in different universities. This presents an a priori reason for varying that part of the operating grant that supports research in the form of the time of 'teaching and research' staff devoted to research.

2.2 Direct Government Funding of Students for Coursework Programs

Government funding does not necessarily imply direct funding to universities. Public funds to universities can be directed to the institutions, students, or a combination thereof. The argument for directly funding students is one of consumer sovereignty. In its most general expression it takes the form of 'learning entitlements' over a period of time, possibly a lifetime. These entitlements are exchanged for educational services, and can vary in amount from the full cost of a course to a much lower percentage. This idea of portable tuition subsidies has considerable merit. It has also received endorsement from a number of authoritative sources in Australia, such as the West report (1998) and the writings of Karmel (2001, 2002), and internationally from Barr (1998).

Alongside the idea of paying portable subsidies to students, there is a case for greater flexibility in the price of programs, to allow a greater variety of offerings to come forward and allow those courses that consumers are willing to pay more for to receive a higher price. This was also supported by West (1998), Karmel (2001, 2002), and Barr (1998).

In addition to deciding whether to direct subsides to students or to universities, a number of issues have to be addressed. They relate to the following questions:

- Should there be funded 'learning entitlements' for all students eligible for entry into higher education, or should there be a restricted number of rationed vouchers?
- How portable should these 'vouchers' or 'learning entitlements' be?
- Should the teaching and research components of universities' operating grants be separated?
- How should the level of the subsidy vary across students, fields of study, and universities?
- How much flexibility should universities be allowed in setting the prices of courses?

If subsidies are provided directly to students, arguably the simplest way to proceed with such student subsidies would be to grant an equal amount to all students as they enter the higher education system. This has a strong equity basis. It can also be defended on efficiency grounds, on the basis that it is difficult to identify the variations in the size of the externalities associated with higher education. It may, however, lead at times to a mismatch between demand and supply in some occupations.

Can any arguments be advanced for adopting a different basis than equal-value subsidies paid directly to students? The idea of providing higher subsidies to courses in areas that have historically been more costly can be criticized on two grounds. First, historical costs are really historical expenditures, which in turn have depended largely on the public subsidies.[2] There is a certain circularity in this which tends to make the historical costs adopted in such a funding approach self-fulfilling. Under this arrangement, cost effectiveness is not really tested. The second criticism is that there is no obvious reason why the externalities associated with a student's education (the theoretical basis for subsidies) is correlated with the costs of providing that education.

It is interesting to look back at the ranking of fields of study by the perceived level of externality in the survey by Round and Siegfried (1998) referred to in section 2.1 above. While that was not a scientific ranking of actual external benefits, it does throw some doubt on the idea that the highest priced or highest costs courses would have the highest external benefits. Some of those courses that were thought to have the highest external benefits would probably be amongst the lower priced courses and lower cost courses, e.g. History, while some with lower perceived externalities, such Veterinary Science, would be amongst the higher priced and higher cost course.

2.3 A Hybrid Model of Funding Coursework Programs

A hybrid model is one where student entitlements exist to promote flexibility in the system, but there is also direct public funding to universities. The funding might be directed heavily to areas where serious shortages of supply might exist, such as science or nursing, or be earmarked for disadvantaged students so that they paid little or nothing in the way of top-up fees. These shortages of supply might show up in unfilled vacancies for nurses. In the case of scientists this shortage may be less evident. But if there are substantial social benefits from scientific research, there is a danger that there would be an under-investment in science training without such direct funding.

Each university would then charge a fee for each of its programs (possibly with some constraints). Students could combine their learning entitlement with any university-specific scholarship obtained to help them pay the price for the course. For the residual amount they would have access to an income-contingent loan. If they did not obtain a scholarship in the university of their choice, their subsidy would be entirely in the form of the learning account, and the remainder could be covered by an income-contingent loan.

In this system universities would be free to determine the courses that they offer, the number of places on those courses, and the prices charged. There may be some limits imposed on the prices. One feature of a model of this kind is that it makes the full price of each program much more transparent.

The cost differential between laboratory-based programs and non-laboratory programs, especially in advanced undergraduate years, is heavily influenced by the infrastructure costs of the former: both buildings and equipment. If public funds were used to cover these overhead costs and the 'price' that students faced was based on the remaining costs (labour and consumables), then the case for learning entitlements of equal value would be very strong. For efficient national delivery of programs, capital should be utilized in all of undergraduate programs, research training, and research. The quid pro quo for government provision of infrastructure would be the need for universities to specialize.

2.4 The Australian Model

Qualified students commencing undergraduate programs in Australia from 2005 will have seven years of learning entitlements. This is a guarantee of government subsidy for up to seven years of equivalent full-time study. The entitlement is to any program of study that a student is admitted to as a Commonwealth Supported Student. The amount of the subsidy is program-specific and is fixed by the federal government. The subsidy in 2005 varies from A$1472 p.a. for law to A$15,047 for medicine. The difference between the price for each course and the course subsidy is paid for by the student, either up front or through the system of income-contingent loans repaid through the tax scheme. The annual price of each course is set in each institution subject to a maximum level for each course. (In 2005 the top-up fee imposed by universities must not exceed 25% of the government-determined basic fee.) If an institution sets prices at the maximum allowable, the direct government subsidy varies from 16% for law to 65% for medicine.

Public universities can also offer full-fee-paying places up to a maximum of 35% of government subsidized places in each degree program. In practice these places are taken by students who would prefer a full-fee place at one university to a government-subsidized place in another university. This results in a net increase in the number of university places. There is no cap on the price charged for full-fee-paying students, and the fees are also repayable through an income-contingent loan of a maximum value of A$50,000.

The Australian model has the virtue of making explicit the price of a program and the extent of government subsidy. The program-specific subsidies are, however, largely a carry-over from the previous funding model and are a mixture of cost and demand factors. The subsidies are not related to externalities. The model of itself does not change public funds allocated to universities for each student in a given program, but it permits universities to obtain more revenue through the top-up fees.

The model has the potential advantage of encouraging diversity in teaching relative to the previous arrangements, where prices did not vary much between universities: now an institution can choose between offering a resource-rich program at a premium price or a more modest program at a lower price. This should also encourage efficient methods of delivery, although the price caps restrict the price variations.

3. Public Funding of Research and Research Training

Precise quantification of the returns to research and development funding is difficult. The benefits are spread widely across society and nations, and the time lags can be very long. In his survey of studies of returns to R&D expenditure by firms in the US and OECD, Dowrick (2002) quotes social rates of return of between 50 and 60% and private rates of return of 20 to 30%. Even within the private sector the social rate of return is much higher than the private rate.

The social rate of return to R&D conducted within universities might be expected to be similar to those for the private sector, at least for research in the areas of engineering, science, and medicine. The private rate of return to university researchers will vary depending on intellectual property arrangements but can be expected to be less than in the private sector, where R&D returns feed directly into profit.

In short, the gap between social and private returns to R&D activity undertaken within universities is large. The case for government funding is overwhelming. The more difficult issue is what the level of funding should be and how it should be allocated.

In the absence of government funding, the greatest under-funding will occur with fundamental research, as this is less likely to be undertaken in the private sector. This leads to the conclusion that fundamental research should be funded almost entirely by governments, but that development and applied research should involve industry or industry associations (see Romer 1993). Block public funding should be primarily for pure research which meets international standards of excellence, and it should not attempt to pick winners.

Governments also provide funds for research through project grants which are awarded on a competitive basis. Project funding has two objectives: (i) it funds the best researchers and encourages specialization, and (ii) it funds research in areas of national importance. In Australia, project funding often does not cover full costs, and some project overheads must be covered from other sources. Such a model has the undesirable effect of using block funding to top up project funding.

Turning to research training, this fulfils a dual purpose: to train the next generation of researchers and to train the next generation of teachers and scholars. Any estimates of the social rate of return must therefore be treated with caution. Many estimates of the *private* rate of return are low. Using British data, Blundell et al. (2000) look at the effect of higher education on hourly wages. After controlling for age, ability, family and demographic effects, and employment characteristics, they found that males with a higher degree (including coursework) earn 8% cent more than males who qualified for university but did not go. This is less than the 12% differential for males with only a first degree. The returns to degrees are estimated to be much higher for females, but they are estimated to be the same for both a first degree and a higher degree – at around 30% compared with someone with only GCE 'A' levels. Using Australian data, Larkins (2001) estimates that the private rate of return to research higher degrees is lower than the private rate of return for bachelor degrees.

Turning to social rates of return, Larkins (2001) finds that the direct social rates of return for research higher degrees are in the range 5 to 7%, increasing to 9 to 11% if some allowance is made for the effect on growth in gross domestic product. These are conservative figures.

It seems clear that because of the high social rates of return to research the training of researchers should be heavily subsidized by government. The difficult question is how many places should be provided and at what funding levels per student? A funding model which provides good infrastructure funding for quality specialist groups would allow research-degree students to be taken on at lower direct cost. The Higher Education Funding Council for England (HEFCE) uses a model which integrates research and research training and acts to promote greater specialization.[3] The HECFE allocates a block research grant to universities based on the quality and volume of research activity in each subject area. The quality of departments is determined by detailed peer evaluation of the quality of output. Research students in their second or third full-time year are funded from the research budget. Only first-year post-graduate research students are funded from the teaching budget of the HEFCE. This recognizes the fact that the learning component for students in their first year dominates the research-output component.

The English model, by allocating no infrastructure funds to some institutions, will inevitably cause very differentiated research agendas across English universities, with the highly ranked institutions undertaking most of the pure curiosity-driven research and the lower ranked institutions either concentrating on applied research or becoming more like the US liberal arts colleges, with an emphasis on scholarship and teaching. Movement of academic staff, in both directions, will reinforce the differentials. The movement towards a tiered system can therefore be achieved over time by a funding formula rather than regulation.

Any system of higher education that differentiates between research-intensive institutions and others in its funding mechanisms should facilitate the transfer of able students in the lower tiers to research-intensive universities for research higher degrees.

To summarize this section, there is an overwhelming argument for government to fund both basic research in universities and research training. There is an argument for applied research to be jointly funded by government and the private sector. In order to provide a balance between long-term research and current perceived needs, there is a case for both block funding and project funding.

4. Performance Measures

Sir Gareth Roberts (2003) asserted in the preface to the review of research assessment in the UK that 'all evaluation mechanisms distort the process they purport to evaluate.' He nevertheless went on to support the use of performance measures for research funding. The point being made is, of course, that performance measures need to be well chosen so that they cannot be easily manipulated. Performance measures have their role in encouraging and rewarding good practice. They need, however, to be an adjunct to core funding in order provide some certainty for medium-term planning.

The most difficult area for performance evaluation is coursework programs. Allocating funds on the basis of pass rates and honours grades can lead to grade inflation. Student evaluations have a role, but raise issues of comparability across discipline areas and institutions. Dealing with differences in the level and mix of student intake poses particular difficulties.[4] Evaluation by peers would seem the preferred method, albeit an expensive one.

Research performance is more readily measured. The selection of funding for projects or individuals is based on past research performance, the quality of which is readily measured though refereeing and through publication and citation lists such as ISI. Aggregation up to discipline or institutional level is more complex. The Roberts (2003) review of the funding of research in the UK had as its core recommendation that '[a]ny system of research assessment designed to identify the best research must be based upon the judgement of experts, who may, if they choose, employ performance indicators to inform their judgement.' In order to reduce complexity, the peer review needs to be a streamlined one. There seems little point, for example, in reworking the activity of editors and referees of leading journals to judge the value of an article.

Performance in research training can be measured by variables such as the placement of graduates, publications by graduates, and student surveys. But research training should also be evaluated in the full context of the research performance of a discipline or institution.

5. Concluding Remarks

The case for public subsidy of universities is highest for research and research training. The high infrastructure costs of research in the sciences means that specialization across universities is required. It may well be that the optimal amount of research infrastructure in a province or nation, when combined with the desirability of specialization, means that not all institutions of higher education should offer PhD programs in the sciences, broadly defined to include natural and physical sciences, health sciences, and engineering. This can be brought about either by regulation or by default through funding formulae.

Spreading the cost of infrastructure also has implications for funding undergraduate programs. In many ways it would be desirable to husband resources by encouraging specialization at the advanced undergraduate level. This approach might, however, lock some able students out of PhD programs because of their inappropriate undergraduate programs unless provision was made for conversion programs, even of relatively short duration.

If infrastructure costs are covered through public funding, then the financing of undergraduate programs is much simpler. The net costs per student are then much more similar across disciplines, which makes either learning entitlements, further government funding, or student contributions much easier to implement, as there is little need to differentiate by discipline. In this model, government would effectively be limiting the funds available for subsidized places in the sciences and, in effect, the number of student subsidized places, although student and institutional choices would still determine the mix within the sciences. Thus, for example, a shift in demand from the physical to the biological sciences could easily be accommodated under this model.

Appendix: The Current Australian Model[5]

The Australian higher education system comprises 38 public universities, 42 institutions that have federally funded student places, and approximately 86 higher education private institutions. In addition, there is a state-based system of colleges of technical and further education.

Under the Australian constitution, education is a matter for state governments. The public universities in each state were established by acts of state parliament. Prior to 1973 state governments were the main source of public funds for the public universities. In 1973 the commonwealth government took over the responsibility of funding public universities under its powers that it can grant funds to the states for any purpose. The anomaly remains that the governing bodies of state universities are responsible to state governments who now provide only about 2% of funds. The two universities located in the Australian Capital Territory come under federal-government legislation.

Approval to use the name 'university' is given by the relevant state government. The state and federal governments have agreed on a series of conditions that must be met before an institution is accredited. These conditions include the requirement of an active research program.

Enrolments in private universities are small – the largest, Bond University, has fewer than three thousand students. Students at private universities are now able to take advantage of income-contingent loans. Foreign institutions have on occasion set up small campuses in Australia. In November 2004 the state government of South Australia gave permission for Carnegie Mellon to establish a private university campus in that state.

Australia has the largest percentage of foreign students of any OECD country; in absolute terms it is the fourth-largest provider of tertiary education to foreign students after the USA, UK, and Germany.[6] The majority of students are from Southeast Asia. Fees paid by foreign students now account for 14% of the sector's revenue

Over the last decade public funding of universities (federal and state) has been relatively static in real terms. As a share of the revenue of public universities it has fallen from over 60% in 1994 to 44% in 2003. Of the funds available for the provision of coursework programs (teaching and learning) in 2003, 43% were provided by the federal government, 33% by Australian students (either up front or through income-contingent loans), and 24% by foreign students. These percentages vary greatly across universities and disciplines – foreign students are heavily concentrated in the areas of business and IT.

OECD figures suggest that as a percentage of GDP *total* expenditure on higher education in Australia is above the OECD mean (1.4% in 2001 compared to an OECD mean of 1.0), but public expenditure for all tertiary education is below the OECD mean (51% of the total in 2001 compared with an OECD average of 78%).[7] Australia has been an outlier, in that private expenditure has tended to substitute for public expenditure. As the OECD (2004, 240) notes: '[P]ublic investment in education has increased in most OECD countries for which 1995 to 2001 data are available, regardless of changes in private spending. In fact, some of the OECD countries with the highest growth in private spending have also shown the highest increase in public funding of education. This indicates that increasing private spending on tertiary education tends to complement, rather than replace, public investment. A notable exception to this is in Australia where the shift towards private expenditure at tertiary level has been accompanied by a fall in the level of public expenditure in real terms.'

Block funding for research is provided by the federal government through two channels: the Infrastructure Grant Scheme (IGS) and the Research Infrastructure Block Grant (RIBG). These block grants amount to only 3.4% of total university revenue. The RIBG is designed to provide infrastructure for project funds obtained from government and private sources and is allocated to universities on the basis of their external research revenue. The IGS is allocated on the basis of external research income, research publications, and research student load.

In recent years government policy has moved in the direction of linking research and research training. This trend recognizes the joint nature of much of these activities and the need to efficiently use expensive capital equipment in the scientific disciplines. The most obvious nexus is the inclusion of the research training load as a determinant of the IGS, with a weight of 30%.

Funding to institutions for research training is provided through the Research Training Scheme (RTS). It is allocated on the basis of research student completions, research income, and research publications, with a guarantee that no university will be awarded less than 95% of the previous year's funding.

Funding to individuals for research training is provided through the Australian Postgraduate Awards (APA) Scheme; a similar scheme operates for foreign students. These funds are allocated to institutions according to the RTS formula. Nearly all Australian research students are exempt from making any contribution to the cost of their training. Research students from overseas pay full fees if they do not receive a scholarship.

Public project funding is through the Australian Research Council (ARC) and the National Health and Medical Research Council (NH&MRC), whose funds are allocated on a competitive basis using peer review.

Notes

* Peter Dawkings is the Ronald F. Henderson Professor and Director, and Ross Wiliams a Professorial Fellow, at the Melbourne Institute, University of Melbourne.

1 Major reviews were conducted by Dawkins (1987, 1988), West (1998), Kemp (1999a, 1999b), and Nelson (2002, 2003).

2 In a higher education system with a well-developed private sector, such as that in the US, the 'cost of a course' *in a given discipline* varies greatly across institutions. The resources devoted to, say, an undergraduate arts course at Harvard exceeds the resources devoted to science courses at many public universities. In other words, each discipline can be taught at various levels of resourcing, and the 'cost of a course' is not a well-defined concept.

3 See 'Funding Higher Education in England: How the HEFCE Allocates Its Funds,' May 2004, at www.hefce.ac.uk/Pubs/hefce/2004/04_23/.

4 In a recent study looking at the international standing of Australian universities, Williams and Van Dyke (2004) use four criteria for the quality of
   undergraduate programs: staff-student ratios, attrition rates, surveys of
   how recent graduates perceived their program, and progression to further
   study.
5 A convenient description of the system is to be found in DEST (2004).
6 See OECD 2004, 293–7.
7 See OECD 2004, table B2.1c (p. 231) and table B3.2b (243).

References

Barr, N. 1998. 'Higher Education in Australia and Britain: What Lessons?'
   Australian Economic Review 31:2, 179–88.
Blundell, R., L. Deardon, A. Goodman, and H. Reed. 2000. 'The Returns to
   Higher Education in Britain: Evidence from a British Cohort' *Economic
   Journal* 110:461, F82–99.
Borland, J. 2002. 'New Estimates of the Private Rate of Return to University
   Education in Australia.' *Melbourne Institute Working Paper* 14/02.
Borland, J., P. Dawkins, D. Johnson, and R.Williams. 2001. 'Rates of Return to
   Investment in Higher Education.' *Australian Social Monitor* 4:2, 33–40.
Dawkins, J. 1987. 'Higher Education: A Policy Discussion Paper.' AGPS,
   Canberra.
– 1988. 'Higher Education: A Policy Statement.' AGPS, Canberra.
Department of Education, Science and Training (DEST). 2004. *Higher Educa-
   tion, Report for the 2004–2006 Triennium.* Available at www.dest.gov.au/
   highered.
Dowrick, S., 2002. 'The Contribution of Innovation and Education to Eco-
   nomic Growth.' Paper presented to 2002 Economic and Social Outlook
   Conference, University of Melbourne, April.
Karmel, P. 2001. 'Public Policy and Higher Education.' Joseph Fisher Lecture,
   University of Adelaide.
– Karmel, P. 2002. 'Priorities in Higher Education Reform.' Paper presented to
   Towards Opportunity and Prosperity Conference, University of Melbourne,
   April.
Kemp, D. 1999a. *New Knowledge, New Opportunities.* Commonwealth Depart-
   ment of Education, Training and Youth Affairs (DETYA), June.
– 1999b. *Knowledge and Innovation: A Policy Statement on Research and Research
   Training.* DETYA, November.
Larkins, F. 2001. 'The Economic Benefits of Australian University Degrees:
   Bachelor and Research Higher Degrees.' *Australian Economic Review* 4:4,
   403–14.
Nelson, B. 2002. *Higher Education at the Crossroads.* Ministerial discussion
   paper, Commonwealth Department of Education, Science and Training.

Nelson, B. 2003. 'Our Universities: Backing Australia's Future.' Commonwealth of Australia, May.

OECD. 2004. 'Education at a Glance, OECD Indicators 2004.' OECD.

Roberts, Gareth. 2003. 'Review of Research Assessment, Report to the UK Funding Bodies, May.' At www.raveview.ac.uk/reports/roberts.asp.

Romer, Paul M. 1993. *Implementing a National Technology Strategy with Self-organizing Industry Investment Boards*, 345–90. Brookings Papers on Economic Activity, Microeconomics.

Round, D.K., and J.J. Siegfried. 1998. 'Discounts for Degrees: External Benefits and University Fees.' *Australian Economic Review* 31:2, 167–78.

West, R. 1998. *Learning for Life*. Review of Higher Education Financing and Policy, DETYA.

Williams, Ross, and Nina Van Dyke. 2004. *The International Standing of Australian Universities*. Melbourne Institute, University of Melbourne; available at www.melbourneinstitute.com.

The Social Benefits of Education: New Evidence on an Old Question

W. CRAIG RIDDELL*

Education has numerous consequences for individuals and society. For many people, there is some 'consumption value' from the educational process. Human beings are curious creatures, and they enjoy learning and acquiring new knowledge. Education also has considerable 'investment value.' Those who acquire additional schooling generally earn more over their lifetimes, achieve higher levels of employment, and enjoy more satisfying careers. Education may also enable people to more fully enjoy life, appreciate literature and culture, and be more informed and socially involved citizens.

An important distinction is that between the private and the social returns to education. Private returns refer to benefits received by the individual who acquires the additional schooling.[1] These include economic benefits such as higher lifetime earnings, lower levels of unemployment, and greater job satisfaction. They may also include consequences such as improved health and longevity. Social returns refer to positive (or possibly negative) consequences that accrue to individuals other than the individual or family making the decision about how much schooling to acquire. They are therefore benefits (possibly also costs) that are not taken into account by the decision-maker. If such 'external benefits' are substantial, they could result in significant underinvestment in education in the absence of government intervention.

Many observers have suggested that schooling has substantial social benefits, and on this basis have advocated government involvement in the financing and provision of education. Indeed, when discussing education policy, many classical economists departed from their usual *laissez-faire* position on the appropriate role of government. For example, in *The Wealth of Nations*, Adam Smith states: 'The state derives no inconsiderable advantage from the education of the common people. If instructed they ... are less liable to the delusions of enthusiasm and superstition, which among ignorant nations, frequently occasion the most dreadful disorders' (Book V, part III, article 2). A more contemporary illustration of this point is Milton Friedman's position on the role of government in schooling: 'A stable and democratic society is impossible without widespread acceptance of some common set of values and without a minimum degree of literacy and knowledge on the part of most citizens. Education contributes to both. In consequence, the gain from the education of a child accrues not only to the child or to his parents but to other members of the society; the education of my child contributes to other people's welfare by promoting a stable and democratic society' (Friedman 1955).

This paper summarizes recent evidence on the social benefits of education. In the past, many observers and policy-makers have suggested that investing resources in education is likely to yield substantial benefits to society at large. Indeed, the extensive government involvement in the financing and provision of education is to an important extent based on this belief. However, until recently empirical evidence on the magnitudes of such benefits has been lacking. Recent advances have allowed the consequences of education to be estimated in a credible fashion. As a result, we know much more about the private and social benefits of additional schooling than we did even a decade ago. The purpose of this paper is to provide an overview of these recent advances, and to examine the implications of this new evidence for education policy.

The paper is organized as follows. The first section briefly discusses the role of government in education. The rationales for government intervention in the provision and/or financing of education have been described elsewhere (see, for example, Haveman and Wolfe 1984; Poterba 1995; Behrman and Stacey 1997; Wolfe and Haveman 2001; and Laidler 2002), so it is not necessary to provide a detailed discussion here. However, because this issue is central to the main objective of the paper, some discussion is warranted. In addition, a clear statement of the reasons why government involvement may improve matters is often helpful in assessing the form that such involvement should take. The second section discusses the challenges that one faces in obtaining credible estimates of the private and social consequences of education. Recent Canadian evidence on the private benefits to schooling is also briefly summarized. The magnitudes of the private returns provide a useful benchmark against which to compare estimates of the social benefits. The paper then reviews the current state of knowledge regarding the social benefits of education – ranging from impacts on crime, health, volunteer activity, and democratic participation to benefits associated with economic growth via the creation of new knowledge. Section 3 constitutes the main body of the paper. The last section summarizes its conclusions.

1. Rationales for Government Involvement in Post-Secondary Education

All Canadian jurisdictions are characterized by extensive government involvement in the provision and financing of education. This involvement may be justified on both efficiency and equity grounds. Efficiency gains result in an increase in society's total output of goods and services, and thus allow achievement of higher average living standards. Equity considerations relate not to the average standard of living, but to how society's total output is distributed among citizens.

One efficiency rationale – arguably the principal such rationale – was discussed in the introduction. This is based on the presence of benefits from education that accrue to society as a whole in addition to the private benefits that accrue to those receiving the education. A second argument for intervention is the observation that – in the absence of interventions such as student loan programs – individuals who might benefit from higher education but who do not have the financial resources to finance the investment are typically unable to use their potential human capital as collateral for a loan. As a consequence, the talents of the population may not be fully utilized and the total output of goods and services may fall short of its potential. In this respect there may be a case for governments to be involved in the financing of post-secondary education, especially for those from less advantaged backgrounds.

Both of these efficiency rationales involve a potential 'market failure.' The first arises because of positive 'external benefits' associated with education – social benefits that exceed private benefits. The second arises because of a failure in credit markets that results in some individuals being unable to finance productive investments. This feature of credit markets makes investments in human capital fundamentally different from those in physical capital. Institutions such as limited liability, financial markets such as equity, bond, and venture capital markets, and financial institutions such as banks generally ensure that investments in physical capital with a high potential payoff (after adjusting for risk) can be financed. Similar institutional arrangements do not exist for financing human capital investments – in part because of the abolition of slavery and other forms of indenture.[2]

In addition to human capital investments not being easily collateralized, the risks associated with these investments are inherently non-diversifiable. An individual choosing to become, say, a pilot cannot diversify the risk associated with this occupation by selling claims on future income and purchasing claims on the future income steams of alternative occupations such as pharmacists, electricians, and geologists. Inability to diversify risks is another way in which human capital investments differ from investments in physical capital.

Government intervention is also often justified on equity grounds – that is, promotion of equal opportunity, social mobility, and a more equal distribution of economic rewards. Although important, these issues are not examined in this paper. However, some of the intergenerational effects of education – which are discussed here – are closely related to issues of equal opportunity and social mobility.

Even if there were no 'market failures' relating to human capital acquisition – that is, no social returns in excess of private returns and no credit-market failures prohibiting individuals from financing productive human capital investments – there may nonetheless be a role for some government intervention. This is the case because the market for higher education suffers from pervasive problems of incomplete information – a different type of market failure (Romer 2000). Government intervention has the potential to improve the quantity and quality of information and thereby enable individuals to make more informed decisions.[3]

Before examining the evidence on social returns, I briefly discuss the challenges that one faces in estimating the private and social returns to education.

2. Estimating Private and Social Returns to Education

As many studies have documented, education is one of the best predictors of success in the labour market. More educated workers earn higher wages, have greater earnings growth over their lifetimes, experience less unemployment, and work longer. Higher education is also associated with longer life expectancy, better health, and reduced participation in crime.

The strong positive relationship between education and earnings is one of the most well established relationships in social science. Many social scientists have, however, been reluctant to interpret this correlation as evidence that education exerts a causal effect on earnings. According to human capital theory, schooling raises earnings because it enhances workers' skills, thus making employees more productive and more valuable to employers. However, the positive relationship between earnings and schooling may arise because both education and earnings are correlated with unobserved factors such as ability, perseverance, and ambition (hereafter simply referred to as 'ability'). If there are systematic differences between the less- and well-educated that affect both schooling decisions and labour market success, then the correlation between education and earnings may reflect these other factors as well. According to signaling/screening theory, such differences could arise if employers use education as a signal of unobserved productivity-related factors such as ability or perseverance (Spence 1974). In these circumstances, standard estimates of the return to schooling are likely to be biased upwards because they do not take into account unobserved 'ability.'

This 'omitted ability bias' issue is of fundamental importance for the correct interpretation of the positive relationship between earnings and schooling. To the extent that estimates of the return to schooling are biased upwards because of unobserved factors, estimated average rates of return to education may substantially over-predict the economic benefits that a less-educated person would receive if he/she acquired additional schooling. The estimated average rates of return in the population reflect both the causal effect of schooling on productivity and earnings and the average return to the unobserved ability of the well-educated. However, if those with low levels of education are also, on average, those with low ability or ambition, they can only expect to receive from any additional schooling the return associated with the causal effect of schooling on earnings. That is, average rates of return in the population reflect the causal effect of schooling on earnings and the return to unobserved factors. The marginal return – the impact of additional schooling for someone with low levels of education – may be substantially below the average return. In these circumstances, education may not be very effective in improving the employment or earnings prospects of relatively disadvantaged groups.

Credible estimates of the causal effect of education on earnings are thus important. How can such estimates be obtained? The most reliable method would be to conduct an experiment. Individuals randomly assigned to the treatment group would receive a larger 'dose' of education than those assigned to the control group. By following the two groups through time we could observe their subsequent earnings and obtain an unbiased estimate of the impact of schooling on labour market success. Random assignment would ensure that, on average, treatment and control groups would be equally represented by 'high ability' and 'low ability' individuals.

In the absence of such experimental evidence, economists have tried to find quasi-experiments or 'natural' experiments that isolate the influence of education from the possible effects of unobserved ability. A large number of such studies have recently been carried out, using data on identical twins or on sources of variation in education such as those implied by compulsory schooling laws or proximity to a college or university. Card (1999, 2000) provides a discussion of the issues in this literature as well as a review of empirical findings. A consistent result is that conventional estimates of the return to schooling tend, if anything, to *underestimate* rather than overestimate the causal impact of education on earnings. Thus conventional estimates appear to provide a lower bound for the causal impact of education on earnings.[4] Subsequent research by Oreopoulos (2003) provides additional evidence on the effects of increases in education brought about by compulsory schooling laws. He finds that an additional year of schooling raises annual earnings among those affected by these laws by 10–14% in the US, Canada, and the UK.

Many studies have used conventional multivariate regression methods to analyse the relationship between education and labour market outcomes such as earnings.[5] Canadian studies obtain estimates of the 'return to schooling' that are similar to those obtained in studies carried out in other developed countries: rates of return (in real terms, i.e., after adjusting for inflation) of approximately 8–10% for the labour force as a whole.[6] Such estimates compare favourably with rates of return on physical capital investments. In Canada, women tend to benefit more from education than men. For example, a recent study found real rates of return to investments in education of approximately 9% for females and 6% for males (Ferrer and Riddell 2002). In addition to the effects of employment and earnings, a number of benefits discussed subsequently – such as improved health and longevity – are at least partly private in nature. As a consequence, there are strong incentives for individuals and families to invest in education.

The challenges one faces in estimating the social impacts of education are similar to those associated with determining the causal impacts on employment and earnings. For example, it has been known for some time that there is a strong positive correlation between education and health outcomes. Does this association arise because acquiring additional schooling causes individuals to adopt healthier lifestyles? Or does the association arise because both education and health are related to some unobserved factors? For example, it is possible that people who are more 'forward looking' choose to acquire more schooling and to pursue better health practices than do their more myopic counterparts who seek immediate gratification. In this case, the correlation between education and health may not reflect a causal influence.

Recent research on the social impacts of education has adopted a similar research strategy to that described above for analysing the private returns to schooling. That is, researchers have used quasi-experimental methods (or natural experiments) to isolate the causal impact of education from other influences on social outcomes. Many of these natural experiments reflect policy changes that took place many years ago, so the subsequent impacts on outcomes such as health, civic participation, and even the well-being of children can be traced over time. An important source of variation in educational attainment in several countries is that due to changes in school-leaving laws. The way in which these types of variations in education are utilized is described more fully in the next section.

3. Social returns to education

Social returns to education refer to positive or negative outcomes that accrue to individuals other than the person or family making the decision about how much schooling to acquire. They are therefore benefits (potentially also costs) that are not taken into account by the decision-maker. If such 'external benefits' are quantitatively important they could result in significant under-investment in education in the absence of government intervention. A substantial amount of empirical evidence is now available on at least some of these outcomes. Several useful surveys of this literature have recently appeared, and I refer to these and some of the individual studies in this paper. Most of the empirical evidence comes from the United States. Much of the earlier literature focused on the correlation between educational attainment and various outcomes. Recent contributions have paid much more attention to distinguishing between correlations and causal impacts.

The content of education clearly matters. In totalitarian societies schooling is often used as a form of indoctrination. The discussion here presumes that the nature of education is similar to that in Canada and other Western democracies.

I first discuss social benefits that take the form of market outcomes such as productivity, earnings, and output of goods and services. This is followed by an examination of non-market outcomes such as health, civic participation, and criminal activity.

3.1 Innovation, Knowledge Creation and Economic Growth

The factors that determine long-term growth in living standards have received substantial attention in the past two decades. Much of this research has been dominated by 'new growth theory' that emphasizes the contribution of knowledge creation and innovation in fostering advances in living standards over time.[7] The influence of these new perspectives has been reinforced by empirical evidence that supports the view that education plays an important role in economic growth (see, for example, Barro 2001).

The importance of economic growth (growth in average living standards) deserves emphasis. Even apparently small differences in growth rates will, if they persist over extended periods of time, make huge differences to the living standards of the average citizen. For this reason many economists have noted that understanding the determinants of long-term growth is one of the most significant economic problems. As stated for example by Lipsey (1996, 4): 'All the other concerns of economic policy – full employment, efficiency in resource use, and income redistribution – pale into significance when set against growth ... All citizens, both rich and poor, are massively better off materially than were their ancestors of a hundred years ago who were in the same relative position in the income scale. That improvement has come to pass not because unemployment or economic efficiency or income distribution is massively different from what it was a century ago but because economic growth has increased the average national incomes of the industrialized countries about tenfold over the period.'

A central tenet of the new growth theories is that knowledge creation and innovation respond to economic incentives, and can thus be influenced by public policy. The education and skill-formation systems play an important role in fostering innovation and advancing knowledge. There are three main dimensions to this role. One is related to the research function of educational institutions, particularly universities.

Such research can be an important source of new ideas and advances in knowledge. The other dimensions are related to the teaching function of universities and colleges. These educational institutions train many of the individuals who will make future discoveries. They also play a central role in the transfer of accumulated knowledge to new generations. According to this perspective, the human capital of the workforce is a crucial factor facilitating the adoption of new and more productive technologies.

The transfer-of-knowledge function should be reflected in the private returns to education. Those receiving education will become more productive and thus more valuable to employers. The 'return' to this investment takes the form of higher earnings than would have been possible without additional education.

In contrast, there will generally be social benefits associated with encouraging innovation and scientific advances that arise from the 'public good' nature of knowledge. The potential market failure associated with the public-good nature of knowledge is recognized by adoption of patent laws and other institutional arrangements to encourage invention and innovation. In addition to these 'dynamic externalities' that may contribute to greater growth in living standards over time, there may also be 'knowledge spillovers' of a more static form if more educated individuals raise the productivity and earnings of those they work with or interact with in the community.

The magnitudes of these 'knowledge spillovers' – both the dynamic and static types – has been the subject of substantial recent research. Davies (2002) provides a careful review of this literature. He concludes that there is substantial evidence of dynamic externalities associated with education, although he cautions that there remains considerable uncertainty about their magnitudes. These dynamic externalities appear to operate primarily via technology adoption and innovation. His estimate of the magnitudes of these growth-enhancing social returns in excess of private returns is one to two percentage points. This estimate is consistent with the results of a number of studies of the relationship between education and growth. For example, the ambitious study of both static and dynamic impacts of education on economic growth by McMahon (1999) covering 78 countries over the 1965–90 period obtains estimates of total returns to education for the US of 14%, of which private returns constitute 11–13%. Comparable estimates for the UK are total returns of 15% and private returns of 11–13%.

Another noteworthy finding in this literature is that post-secondary education is relatively more important for explaining growth in OECD countries, while primary and secondary schooling is more important in developing countries (Gemmell 1995; Barro and Sala-i-Martin 1995). This result is consistent with the view that tertiary education has a special role to play in preparing workers for technological adoption and innovation in the more advanced countries.

3.2 Knowledge Spillovers

Static knowledge spillovers arise if more education raises not only the productivity of those receiving the education but also the productivity of those they work and interact with. For example, in *The Economy of Cities*, Jane Jacobs (1969) argues that cities are an 'engine of growth' because they facilitate the exchange of ideas, especially between entrepreneurs and managers. Such knowledge spillovers can take place through the exchange of ideas, imitation, and learning-by-doing. Evidence of the role of knowledge spillovers in technological change has resulted in substantial attention being focused on the clustering of the agents of innovation – firms, end users, universities, and government research facilities (Bekar and Lipsey 2002).

Rauch (1993) did the first study of human capital spillovers employing cross-sectional evidence on US cities. He found evidence that higher average education levels in cities is correlated with both higher wages of workers (even after controlling for the individual's own education) and higher housing prices. Similarly, Glaeser, Scheinkman, and Shleifer (1995) found that income per capita grew faster in US cities with high initial human capital in the post-war period. In one of several studies of specific industries, Zucker, Darby, and Brewer (1998) note an impact of the concentration of outstanding scientists in particular cities on the location decisions of new biotech firms. These studies provide some indirect evidence of human capital externalities. However, they are not conclusive because cities with higher average schooling levels could also have higher wages for a variety of reasons other than knowledge spillovers. In addition, the direction of causation could be the reverse – higher incomes could lead to more schooling. Recent contributions have used 'natural experiments' and other techniques to assess whether there is evidence of knowledge spillovers that is causal in nature.

Acemoglu and Angrist (2001) use variation in educational attainment associated with compulsory-schooling laws and child labour laws in the US to examine whether there is evidence of external returns to higher average schooling at the state level.[8] They find small (about 1%) social returns in excess of private returns, but these are imprecisely estimated and not significantly different from zero. Because compulsory-schooling laws principally influence the amount of secondary schooling received, these results suggest that there are not significant knowledge spillovers associated with additional high school education. However, subsequent studies by Moretti ([1998], 2003[a], 2004) and Ciccone and Peri (2002) find stronger evidence of externalities associated with post-secondary education (graduates of four-year colleges in US). These studies use a variety of data sources and focus on spillovers at the city level. Moretti (2003[b]) provides a useful survey of evidence on these city-level spillovers. Although this literature is still in its infancy, the most recent research indicates moderately large social returns due to knowledge spillovers from post-secondary (college in US or university in Canada) education. For example, Ciccone and Peri (2002) estimate social returns of 2–8% in excess of private returns. A cautious assessment of this recent literature would be that there are social returns of 1–2% associated with static knowledge spillovers from post-secondary education in advanced economies. Together with the growth-enhancing dynamic effects, this evidence suggests that social benefits associated with technological adoption, innovation, and productivity enhancement from knowledge spillovers may yield social returns in the range of 2–4%.

3.3 Non-Market Effects of Education

The non-market benefits of education considered are consequences other than those received in the form of higher wages or non-wage benefits from working. Some of these non-market effects – such as improved own health or child development – may be considered private in nature, or at least private to the family, and thus may be taken into account by individuals in choosing the amount of education to acquire. If so, they should not be treated as social benefits. Nonetheless, they are benefits that accrue to the individual or family, and thus should be added to the private benefits associated with higher lifetime earnings. In addition, even effects such as improved health outcomes may be of some public value if they reduce reliance on publicly funded programs.

Berhman and Stacey (1997), McMahon (1997), Wolfe and Zuvekis (1997) and Wolfe and Haveman (2001) provide recent surveys of the literature that attempt to quantify the social and non-market effects of education. This research analyses data from both developed and developing countries. The empirical studies that these authors survey generally find considerable impacts of education on a wide variety of non-market and social benefits, even after controlling for such factors as income, age, and race. These include

- Effect of wife's schooling on husband's earnings.
- Effect of parents' education on child outcomes (intergenerational effects): education, cognitive ability, health, and fertility choices.
- Effect of education on own health and spouse's health.
- Effect of education on consumer-choice efficiency, labour-market search efficiency, adaptability to new jobs, marital choice, savings, and attainment of desired family size.
- Effect of education on charitable giving and volunteer activity.
- Effect of schooling on social cohesion: voting behaviour, reduced alienation, and smaller social inequalities.
- Effect of education on reducing reliance on welfare and other social programs.
- Effect of schooling on reduced criminal activity.

Many of the studies also find relationships between the average education levels in the community and positive non-market benefits. For example, higher average education levels in the community (particularly among young adults) lower the school dropout rates of children. However, not all of this research is able to control appropriately for unobserved factors that may impact both education and these non-market outcomes. Thus considerable care needs to be exercised in treating correlations between education and various outcomes as being causal in nature.

Brief summaries of the state of knowledge relating to these non-market social benefits of education are provided below. Special attention is devoted to recent research, which has generally devoted considerable attention to trying to estimate the causal impacts of education on various outcomes.

3.4 Intergenerational Effects

Parents' education has strong effects on children, resulting in large intergenerational effects. As a consequence, the benefits of higher education accrue over extended periods. Surveys by Greenwood (1997) and Maynard and McGrath (1997) summarize the literature on these effects. Additional evidence is reported in recent studies by Currie and Moretti (2003) and Oreopoulos, Page, and Stevens (2003). The research shows an impact of parental education on a number of child outcomes, including

- Higher parental education is associated with lower fertility, via increased efficiency of contraception, as well as via raising the age of both marriage and first pregnancy. The resulting lower population growth is positive for economic growth in developing countries.
- The incidence of teenage childbearing is much higher for children of less educated parents. Teenage parents have elevated probabilities of dropping out of high school, demonstrated lower parenting skills, and experience higher rates of poverty. This has subsequent negative impacts on the children of teenage parents, as outcomes for these children are generally worse than for other children.
- Child abuse and neglect are also associated with parental education levels.
- Higher parental education is associated with more substantial family investments in children, and these investments have an effect far greater than the societal educational investments made when the child enters school. Children of more educated parents generally perform better in school and in the labour market, and have better health. These impacts are significant even after controlling for parental income. The higher family investments typically take the form of parental time and expenditures on children. Using US data, Oreopoulos, Page, and Stevens (2003) find that increases in the education of either parent reduces the probability that a child repeats a grade and significantly lowers the likelihood of dropping out of school.
- Children of less educated parents generally cost more to educate, needing special compensatory programs, as well as being more likely to require expensive programs like foster care and juvenile diversion.
- Higher parental education is associated with lower criminal propensities in children. It is also associated with lower probabilities of parental abuse and neglect, which also may reduce criminal behaviour and the need for the removal of children from the home.
- Higher parental education is associated with improved child health. Currie and Moretti (2003) provide recent US evidence on the effect of maternal education on infant health, as measured by birth weight and gestational age. They also find that higher maternal education

increases the probability that a new mother is married, reduces parity, increases the use of parental care, and reduces smoking, suggesting that these may be important pathways for the ultimate effect on child health.

Although many of these consequences are internal to the family, and thus should be treated as private benefits, a number of these intergenerational effects of education also have benefits for society. These include lower education costs, less use of foster care and juvenile diversion, lower crime, lower health costs, and lower dependence on welfare transfers.

3.5 Health and Longevity

Grossman and Kaestner (1997) and Wolfe and Haveman (2001) survey a huge amount of empirical research on the causal effects of education on health. The overriding conclusion of these authors is that the empirical evidence supports the belief that education has a causal impact on health outcomes in the US, other developed countries, and developing countries. Many studies are careful in uncovering causal impacts rather than simply correlations between education and health outcomes (which are known to be strong). In addition, as noted previously, there is also considerable evidence that child health is positively related to parents' education (Wolfe and Haveman 2001).

There is less evidence on the actual pathways by which education impacts health. Education may impact how individuals assess information on how to improve health, and it may increase the efficiency by which individuals use that information in lifestyle choices. It may also impact individuals' rate of time preference, with more educated individuals discounting the future less, and thus undertaking actions that improve health (e.g., smoking less). In a widely cited study, Kenkel (1991) found that education is associated not only with better health outcomes but also with superior health behaviours such as reduced smoking, more exercise, and lower incidence of heavy drinking. Interestingly, however, the influence of schooling does not mainly operate through its impact on health knowledge – the estimated impact of additional education did not decline substantially when controls were included for health knowledge. This suggests that the effect of education on health occurs mainly through the utilization of health knowledge rather than the acquisition of such knowledge.[9]

Recent research by Lleras-Muney (forthcoming) reinforces the conclusion that there is a strong causal effect of education on mortality in the US. She finds that an extra year of schooling results in a decline in mortality of at least 3.6% over a ten-year period, an impact that is larger than prior estimates of the effect of education on mortality. To deal with unobserved characteristics that impact both education and health she uses variation in educational attainment due to compulsory-schooling laws as employed by Acemoglu and Angrist (2001) and others. This methodology results in estimates that focus on the impact of additional high school on mortality, rather than on higher levels of post-secondary education.

Lleras-Muney and Lichtenberg (2002) examine one of the mechanisms by which education may impact health outcomes. They investigate whether education is correlated with adoption of newer prescription drugs. If more educated people are more likely to adopt newer drugs, due to more information or a better ability to learn, and those newer drugs improve health, then this may be one mechanism by which education leads to better health. They find that education is correlated with the purchase of drugs that are more recently approved, after controlling for the medical condition, individual income, and health insurance status. The impact of education is generally felt only for chronic conditions, where prescriptions are bought regularly for the same condition. This suggests that the more educated are better able to learn from experience.

Although better health is principally a private return, it may also be a social benefit if it means less reliance by people on publicly provided health care or welfare payments. In this respect, there is an important difference between morbidity and mortality. From the perspective of the public finances, reduced morbidity has a positive effect, whereas increased longevity is more likely to negatively affect publicly funded programs such as pensions and medical care.

3.6 Criminal Activity

Until recently the evidence from empirical studies of the impact of education on crime was mixed. For example, in their reviews of the literature Witte (1997) and McMahon (1999) concluded that the available evidence does not find that education impacts crime once other factors are controlled for.[10] However, recent work by Grogger (1998), Lochner (2004), and Lochner and Moretti (2004), focuses specifically on the role of education and does find an impact of schooling on crime. Higher education levels may lower crime by raising wage rates, which increase the opportunity cost of crime. Education may also raise an individual's rate of time preference (the extent to which future consequences are discounted), thus increasing the cost of any future punishment as a result of crime. Lochner (2004) estimates the social value of high school graduation through reductions in crime, taking into account the costs of incarceration and costs to victims. The extra social benefits amount to almost 20% of the private returns to increases in high school completion. This may even be a conservative estimate, as a number of crimes are not included in the analysis, nor are the potential benefits to citizens associated with feeling safe. In addition, some of the costs (such as criminal justice and law enforcement costs) are also not taken into account.

In subsequent research, Lochner and Moretti (2004) utilize a variety of data sets to examine whether increasing education levels cause reductions in crime among adult males in the US. They employ three sources of information: incarceration, arrests, and self-reports of criminal activity. The authors find that higher education levels, particularly graduation from high school, consistently lower the probabilities of incarceration, of criminal arrests, and of self-reports of undertaking criminal activity. In US census data the probability of incarceration is negatively correlated with education levels, and is much higher for blacks than whites. This correlation may not be causal, however, if there are unobserved individual characteristics which both raise education and lower criminal activity. Following the methods used by Acemoglu and Angrist (2001) discussed previously, the authors employ compulsory school attendance laws as an independent source of variation in educational attainment. Their casual estimates of the impact of education on incarceration indicate that high school graduation lowers incarceration probabilities by 0.8 percentage points for white males and 3.4 percentage points for black males. Differences in educational attainment can explain as much as 23% of the black-white gap in male incarceration rates.

Data from the FBI's crime reports allows the impact of education on different types of crime to be estimated. Education was most effective in lowering violent crime rates like murder and assault, as well as motor vehicle theft. The third data set employed was a longitudinal survey that asked respondents about crimes they have committed. This source of information usefully supplements the data on arrests and incarceration because it is possible that more educated people commit as much crime as less educated people, but are better at avoiding arrest or obtaining lighter sentences. The evidence, however, is that education has very similar impacts on self-reported criminal activity to that which it had on arrests and incarceration.

On the basis of this evidence, Lochner and Moretti (2004) calculate that raising the high school graduation rate by 1% will reduce the costs of crime by approximately $1.4 billion per year in the US.

3.7 Civic Participation

The impact of education on civic participation has been analysed by political scientists for a long time. The correlation between education and voting is strong. Higher education is also associated with greater charitable giving and more volunteerism. Helliwell and Putnam (1999) also find that education is correlated with typical measures of social capital: trust and social participation (club memberships, community work, hosting dinner parties). However, only recently have studies attempted to determine whether education exerts a causal influence on civic participation, or whether the correlation arises because both education and civic participation are jointly influenced by unobserved factors. Two recent papers that attempt to do so are Milligan, Moretti, and Oreopoulos (2004) and Dee (2004).

Milligan, Moretti, and Oreopoulos (2004) analyse the question of whether education improves citizenship. The authors focus on the US and the UK, but provide some results for Canada also. The main question is whether people who have more education are more likely to vote in elections. Analysis is also conducted on whether education raises the 'quality' of people's involvement in society. Here 'quality' is measured by such things as whether people

1. follow the news and political campaigns,
2. attend political meetings,
3. work on community issues,
4. try to persuade others to share their views,
5. discuss political matters with friends,
6. consider themselves politically active,
7. consider themselves close to a political party, and/or
8. trust the federal government.

As in previously discussed studies by Acemoglu and Angrist (2001) and Lochner and Moretti (2004), Milligan, Moretti and Oreopoulos

(2004) use variation in educational attainment generated by compulsory-school-attendance laws and child-labour laws. The estimates thus relate to the impact of additional secondary schooling on civic participation.

Generally the authors find that having a higher level of education does raise the probability of voting in the US, but not in the UK. They suggest that this may be due to different voter registration methods in the two countries. In the US, registration is the responsibility of the individual, and thus many people are not registered. In the UK, registration is undertaken by local authorities, and is required. Thus the vast majority of citizens are registered. If estimates of the impact of education on voting are made conditional on registration, the effect of education becomes much less in the US. There is little change in the UK, as we would expect given the high level of registration. Canada has registration laws more closely resembling the UK's, and the impact of education on voting behaviour is much more muted than in the US. Graduation from high school raises the probability of voting by close to 30% in the US (not conditional on registration), while the estimated impact is around 9% in Canada. The authors also find strong impacts of education on the measures of the 'quality' of citizenship listed above.

Dee (2004) analyses the impact of education on voting and civic behaviour in the US, using comparable methods to Milligan et al. (2004) but with different data sources. He also finds a strong causal impact of education on voting behaviour, the probability of reading newspapers, and support for free speech by various groups. Some of his results also provide evidence on the impact of post-secondary education on voting behaviour. For example, he finds that college entrance raises the probability of voter participation by approximately 20 to 30 percentage points. He also concludes that an additional year of high school increases the probability of voting in presidential elections by around 7 percentage points. Education also increases certain measures of civic engagement and knowledge: the frequency of newspaper readership, and support for free speech by anti-religionists, communists, and homosexuals. He also finds that additional education does not increase support for free speech by militarists (someone who advocates outlawing elections and letting the military run the country) or racists.

In addition to these studies based on individual data, cross-country studies find that higher education has a positive effect on democratization and political stability – the type of relationship suggested by the quotes from Adam Smith and Milton Friedman in the introduction to this paper. For example, McMahon (1999, 2001) finds significant effects of secondary schooling on measures of democratization, human rights, and political stability, after controlling for income per capita and military spending as a proportion of total public expenditure. McMahon also finds strong feedback effects on economic growth that operate through democratization and political stability.

3.8 Tax and Transfer Effects

Several studies discussed by Wolfe and Haveman (2001) find that those with more education are less likely to rely on public transfers, even when eligible for benefits. Indeed, evidence indicates that the mother's education even lowers take-up of welfare by eligible children. Although these consequences of education should not be ignored, the quantitatively most important effect is the impact of higher lifetime earnings on government tax receipts (Davies 2002). For example, in Canada the modal marginal tax rate on university graduates – taking into account sales, excise, and income taxes – is in excess of 50%. Thus each additional $1000 in labour market earnings generates an additional $500 in tax revenue. Collins and Davies (2003) recently estimated the gap between before-tax and after-tax rates of return to a university bachelor's degree in Canada and the US. In Canada, for men and women together, the median reduction in the rate of return due to taxes was 1.9 percentage points. In the US the corresponding reduction was 1.1 percentage points. On the basis of these calculations, Davies (2002) notes that the tax revenue associated with higher earnings adds approximately 2 percentage points to the social benefits of higher education.

Because of the progressive nature of income tax, the reductions in the rate of return due to taxation are larger at higher income levels. For example, Collins and Davies (2003) estimate reductions of 2.8 percentage points for Canadian men at the 90th percentile of the earnings distribution and 1.9 percentage points for corresponding US men.

4 Summary and Conclusions

A central reason for public funding – and in many cases also provision – of education has been the belief that there are major social benefits from schooling, in addition to the private benefits. However, until recently evidence on the magnitudes of these external benefits has been lacking. Beginning in the 1960s and 1970s, with the availability of large micro data files on individuals, social scientists have confirmed that educational attainment is correlated with numerous individual and social outcomes such as lifetime earnings, health, and civic participation. However, it remained unclear to what extent the positive correlation between schooling and outcomes such as earnings and health reflected a causal impact of education or was due to both schooling and individual outcomes being related to some unobserved factor. Resolution of this issue is crucial, as the case for public subsidization rests on education causing social benefits to occur. Recent research using natural experiments and related statistical methods has strengthened the case for believing that the social benefits of education are substantial.

Summarizing the evidence surveyed in this paper yields the following approximate estimates of the social returns to schooling:

1. Dynamic externalities associated with
   economic growth   1–2 percentage points
2. Static knowledge spillovers   1–2 percentage points
3. Non-market external benefits   3–4 percentage points
4. Social benefits associated with taxation   2 percentage points
   Total   7–10 percentage points

The quantitative estimate for non-market benefits is based on calculations by Wolfe and Haveman (2001) after removing benefits associated with intergenerational effects and health, both of which are arguably principally private to the individual or family. The other estimates were discussed previously.

These estimates suggest that the social benefits of education may be similar in magnitude to the private benefits associated with higher lifetime earnings, which are also in the range of 7–10%. If so, the social returns to education are substantial and justify significant public subsidization of this activity.

The estimated (real) social return of 7–10% is arguably a conservative estimate. After a detailed survey of the available evidence, Wolfe and Haveman (2001) conclude that the social return from non-market effects of schooling are of the same order of magnitude as the private returns to education from higher earnings. They do not, however, include the social benefits from higher tax revenue or the growth-enhancing effects of knowledge creation and innovation. Still, they do include in their calculations the intergenerational effects and the impacts of education on health, both of which are excluded from the above estimates on the basis that they are principally private in nature. Similarly, Davies (2002) also concludes that the social returns are similar in size to the private returns. His estimates are similar to those above except that he estimates a value of zero for static knowledge spillovers. The main reason for this different conclusion is that Davies (2002) did not have access to the very recent research by Moretti (2003[a], 2004) and Ciccone and Peri (2002) that finds evidence of knowledge spillovers associated with post-secondary education in US cities. Davies's conclusion was principally based on earlier research by Acemoglu and Angrist (2001), who concluded that additional secondary schooling did not have positive external effects on the earnings of other workers in the same state.

Several additional observations are warranted. First, there remains considerable uncertainty about the magnitudes of the social benefits of schooling. In contrast to the substantial amount of research that has been carried out on the relationship between schooling and earnings, much less is known about the causal impact of education on other outcomes. This is particularly the case with respect to Canadian evidence. As indicated in the previous section, most of the evidence on causal impacts comes from US studies. Some of the impacts of schooling may be universal in nature, but others are likely to depend on the social and institutional setting. This situation was evident in the case of civic participation, where education appears to have a much larger effect on voting behaviour in the US than it does in Canada and the UK, for reasons that seem to be related to systems of voter registration in the respective countries. It is quite possible that the magnitudes of the impacts of education on Canadian criminal activity and health outcomes are different from those in the US, even if the direction of the influence is the same in the two countries.

Second, there is substantial uncertainty about the size of the social benefits associated with post-secondary education. Much of the US evidence on causal impacts of schooling uses as a source of independent variation in educational attainment the changes in compulsory-school-attendance laws and child-labour laws. As discussed, these studies provide evidence on the causal impact of additional schooling at the secondary level. The clearest evidence of positive social benefits from post-secondary education is that associated with growth-enhancing effects from technological change and innovation and knowledge spillovers from more educated workers. There is also some evidence that post-secondary education enhances civic participation. Many of the studies of intergenerational effects also report evidence of significant impacts associated with post-secondary education.

A third observation is that I have not included in the above calculation of social benefits the evidence of intergenerational effects such as those on child development, health, and education associated with the educational attainment of the parents. Nor have the effects on the individual's health behaviours and health outcomes (as well as those on the spouse) been included. Whether these are appropriately viewed as private or social benefits depends to an important extent on whether individuals take these consequences into account at the time they choose how much education to acquire. The case for regarding these consequences of additional schooling as private benefits is based on the argument that a rational individual should take these effects into account in making their educational choices (even if they do not yet have a spouse or children). Although many individuals appear to be motivated in part by career prospects in making their educational decisions, it is less clear that they take into account these other benefits. If they generally do not do so, there is a case for including these consequences as social benefits, as is done by scholars such as Wolfe and Haveman (2001). In these circumstances, the above estimates understate the social benefits from education. On the other hand, if we treat the inter-generational effects and health-and-longevity consequences as being strictly private benefits, then the total private benefits are much larger than is commonly believed. This conclusion may enhance the case for government involvement in the financing of post-secondary education, in order to help ensure that individuals from disadvantaged backgrounds can take advantage of investments with potentially high returns. In addition, there may also be a case for governments providing more information than is currently available on the non-market consequences of additional schooling, rather than focusing principally on the consequences for future employment and earnings.

In summary, although more research on these issues is needed (especially more Canadian research), the value of the social benefits of education appears to be similar in size to the private market returns to education from higher lifetime earnings. Thus the benefits of education are considerable, and any decisions regarding public support for education should take these social and non-market benefits into account.

Notes

* Department of Economics, University of British Columbia. I thank Mick Coelli for research assistance.
1 Because decisions relating to investments in education are often taken at

the family rather than individual level, the private benefits may refer to those received by the family. This point is discussed more fully later.

2 There are a few exceptions. For example, the Canadian Armed Forces' Regular Officer Training Program (ROTP) provides heavily subsidized university education in return for a commitment to serve in the Armed Forces for a minimum amount of time (currently 5 years) following graduation.

3 See Riddell 2003 for a discussion of these issues in the Canadian context.

4 See Card (1999, 2000) for further discussion of this evidence, and Riddell (2002, 2004) for a review of Canadian evidence on causal impacts.

5 Earnings is the most commonly used measure of labour market success because it captures both the wage rate or 'price' of labour services and employment (hours, weeks, and years of work).

6 These are before-tax rates of return. I discuss the impact of taxation below.

7 Previous theories of economic growth placed greater emphasis on 'inputs' into production – i.e., on the accumulation of physical and human capital.

8 Such laws result in variation in educational attainment (in this case, additional secondary schooling) that is independent of individuals' educational choices.

9 An important exception is the case of smoking, where Kenkel (1991) found evidence of an important interaction between health knowledge and education. Those with more schooling reduced their smoking more for a given increase in knowledge of the consequences of smoking. He also points out that prior to the report of the US Surgeon General in the 1960s (which had a major impact on knowledge about the health consequences of smoking) higher education was not related to lower incidence of smoking.

10 There is however strong evidence of a link between time spent productively occupied – either employed or in school – and crime.

References

Acemoglu, Daron, and Joshua Angrist. 'How Large Are Human Capital Externalities? Evidence from Compulsory Schooling Laws.' *NBER Macroeconomics Annual 2000* (2001), 9–59.

Barro, Robert J. 'Human Capital and Growth.' *American Economic Review* 91:2 (May 2001), 12–17.

Barro, Robert J., and Xavier Sala-i-Martin. *Economic Growth*. New York: McGraw-Hill, 1995.

Behrman, Jere R., and Nevzer Stacey. *The Social Benefits of Education*. Ann Arbor: University of Michigan Press, 1997.

Bekar, Clifford, and Richard G. Lipsey. 'Clusters and Economic Policy.' *ISUMA: Canadian Journal of Policy Research* 3:1 (Spring 2002), 62–70.

Card, David. 'The Causal Effect of Education on Earnings.' In *Handbook of*

Labor Economics, volume 3A, ed. Orley Ashenfelter and David Card, 1801–63. Amsterdam: North Holland, 1999.

– 'Estimating the Return to Schooling: Progress on Some Persistent Econometric Problems.' National Bureau of Economic Research Working Paper 7769, June 2000.

Ciccone, Antonio, and Giovanni Peri. 'Identifying Human Capital Externalities: Theory with an Application to U.S. Cities.' IZA Working Paper 488, April 2002.

Collins, Kirk, and James B. Davies. 'Tax Treatment of Human Capital in Canada and the United States: An Overview and an Examination of the Case of University Graduates.' In *North American Linkages: Opportunities and Challenges for Canada*, ed. R.G. Harris, 449–84. Calgary: University of Calgary Press, 2003.

Currie, Janet, and Enrico Moretti. 'Mother's Education and the Intergenerational Transmission of Human Capital: Evidence from College Openings.' *Quarterly Journal of Economics* 118 (November 2003), 1495–1532.

Davenport, Paul. 'Universities and the Knowledge Economy.' In David Laidler, ed, *Renovating the Ivory Tower: Canadian Universities and the Knowledge Economy*, 39–59. Toronto: C.D. Howe Institute, 2002.

Davies, Jim. 'Empirical Evidence on Human Capital Externalities.' Paper prepared for Tax Policy Branch, Department of Finance, Government of Canada. Mimeo, Department of Economics, University of Western Ontario, February 2002.

Dee, Thomas S. 'Are There Civic Returns to Education?' *Journal of Public Economics* 88 (August 2004), 1696–1712.

Ferrer, Ana, and W. Craig Riddell. 'The Role of Credentials in the Canadian Labour Market.' *Canadian Journal of Economics* 35 (November 2002), 879–905.

Friedman, Milton. 'The Role of Government in Education.' In *Economics and the Public Interest*, ed. R.A. Solo. Rutgers University Press, 1955.

Gemmell, Norman. 'Endogenous Growth, the Solow Model and Human Capital.' *Economics of Planning* 28:2–3 (1995), 169–83.

Glaeser, Edward. L., Jose A. Scheinkman, and Andrei Shleifer. 'Economic Growth in a Cross-section of Cities.' *Journal of Monetary Economics* 36:1 (August 1995), 117–43.

Greenwood, Daphne T. 'New Developments in the Intergenerational Impacts of Education.' *International Journal of Education Research* 27:6 (1997), 503–12.

Grogger, Jeff. 'Market Wages and Youth Crime.' *Journal of Labor Economics* 16:4 (October 1998), 756–91.

Grossman, Michael, and Robert Kaestner. 'Effects of Education on Health.' In *The Social Benefits of Education*, ed. Jere Behrman and Nevzer Stacey. Ann Arbor: University of Michigan Press, 1997.

Haveman, Robert, and Barbara Wolfe. 'Schooling and Economic Well-Being: The Role of Non-Market Effects.' *Journal of Human Resources* 19 (Summer 1984), 377–407.

Helliwell, John F., and Robert D. Putnam. 'Education and Social Capital.' NBER Working Paper 7121, May 1999.

Jacobs, Jane. *The Economy of Cities*. New York: Random House, 1969.

Kenkel, Donald S. 'Health Behavior, Health Knowledge, and Schooling.' *Journal of Political Economy* 99:2 (April 1991), 287–305.

Laidler, David, ed. *Renovating the Ivory Tower: Canadian Universities and the Knowledge Economy*. Toronto: C.D. Howe Institute, 2002.

Lipsey, Richard G. *Economic Growth, Technological Change, and Canadian Economic Policy*. C.D. Howe Benefactors Lecture. Toronto: C.D. Howe Institute, 1996.

Lleras-Muney, Adriana. 'The Relationship between Education and Adult Mortality in the United States.' *Review of Economic Studies*, forthcoming, 2004.

Lleras-Muney, Adriana, and Frank R. Lichtenberg. 'The Effect of Education on Medical Technology Adoption: Are the More Educated More Likely to Use New Drugs?' National Bureau of Economic Research Working Paper 9185, September 2002.

Lochner, Lance. 'Education, Work and Crime: Theory and Evidence.' *International Economic Review*, forthcoming, August 2004.

Lochner, Lance, and Enrico Moretti. 'The Effect of Education on Crime: Evidence from Prison Inmates, Arrests and Self-Reports.' *American Economic Review* 94 (March 2004), 155–89.

Maynard, Rebecca A., and Daniel J. McGrath. 'Family Structure, Fertility and Child Welfare.' In *The Social Benefits of Education*, ed. Jere Behrman and Nevzer Stacey. Ann Arbor: University of Michigan Press, 1997.

McMahon, Walter W. *Education and Development: Measuring the Social Benefits*. Oxford: Oxford University Press, 1999.

– 'The Impact of Human Capital on Non-Market Outcomes and Feedbacks on Economic Development.' In *The Contribution of Human and Social Capital to Sustained Economic Growth and Well-being*, ed. John Helliwell. Vancouver: UBC Press, 2001.

McMahon, Walter W., guest ed. 'Recent Advances in Measuring the Social and Individual Benefits of Education.' Special issue of *International Journal of Education Research* 27:6 (1997), 447–532.

Milligan, Kevin, Enrico Moretti, and Philip Oreopoulos. 'Does Education Improve Citizenship? Evidence from the U.S. and the U.K.' *Journal of Public Economics* 88 (August 2004), 1667–95.

Moretti, Enrico. 'Social Returns to Education and Human Capital Externalities: Evidence from Cities.' Center for Labor Economics, University of California, Berkeley, Working Paper 9, November 1998.

– 'Estimating the Social Return to Higher Education: Evidence from Longitudinal and Repeated Cross-Sectional Data.' National Bureau of Economic Research Working Paper 9108, August 2002. *Journal of Econometrics*.

- 'Workers' Education, Spillovers and Productivity: Evidence from Plant-Level Production Functions.' University of California at Los Angeles, Working Paper, January 2003[a].
- 'Human Capital Externalities in Cities.' Forthcoming in *Handbook of Regional and Urban Economics*. North Holland-Elsevier, March 2003[b].
- Oreopoulos, Philip. 'Do Dropouts Drop Out Too Soon? International Evidence from Changes in School-Leaving Laws.' NBER Working Paper 10155, December 2003.
- Oreopoulos, Philip, Marianne Page, and Ann Stevens. 'Does Human Capital Transfer from Parent to Child? The Intergenerational Effects of Compulsory Schooling.' Working Paper, University of Toronto and University of California, Davis, November 2003.
- Poterba, James M. 'Government Intervention in the Markets for Education and Health Care: How and Why?' NBER Working Paper 4916, December 1995.
- Rauch, James E. 'Productivity Gains from Geographic Concentration of Human Capital: Evidence from the Cities.' *Journal of Urban Economics* 34:3, (November 1993), 380–400.
- Riddell, W. Craig. 'Is There Under- or Over-Investment in Education?' In *Towards Evidence-Based Policy for Canadian Education*, ed. Patrice de Broucker and Arthur Sweetman, 473–96. Montreal and Kingston: McGill-Queen's University Press and John Deutsch Institute for Economic Policy, 2002.
- 'The Role of Government in Post-Secondary Education in Ontario.' Background Paper for the Panel on the Role of Government in Ontario. August 2003.
- 'Education, Skills and Labour Market Outcomes: Exploring the Linkages in Canada.' In *Educational Outcomes for the Canadian Workplace*, ed. Jane Gaskell and Kjell Rubenson. Toronto: University of Toronto Press, 2004.
- Romer, Paul M. 'Should the Government Subsidize Supply or Demand in the Market for Scientists and Engineers? NBER Working Paper 7723, June 2000.
- Spence, A. Michael. *Market Signaling: Informational Transfer in Hiring and Related Screening Processes*. Cambridge, MA: Harvard University Press, 1974.
- Witte, Ann D. 'Crime.' In *The Social Benefits of Education*, ed. Jere Behrman and Nevzer Stacey. Ann Arbor: University of Michigan Press, 1997.
- Wolfe, Barbara, and Robert Haveman. 'Accounting for the Social and Non-Market Benefits of Education.' In *The Contribution of Human and Social Capital to Sustained Economic Growth and Well-being*, ed. John Helliwell, 221–50. Vancouver: UBC Press, 2001.
- Wolfe, Barbara, and Samuel Zuvekis. 'Nonmarket Outcomes of Schooling.' *International Journal of Educational Research* 27:6 (1997), 491–502.
- Zucker, Lynne G., Michael R. Darby, and Marylinn B. Brewer. 'Intellectual Human Capital and the Birth of U.S. Biotechnology Enterprises.' *American Economic Review* 88:1 (March 1998), 290–306.

The Case for Public Investment in the Humanities

DAVID DYZENHAUS*

I dare hope why it might now begin to be clearer why I am arguing that an education which includes the 'humanities' is essential to political wisdom. By 'humanities' I especially mean history; but close behind history and of almost, if not quite equal importance are letters, poetry, philosophy, the plastic arts, and music. Most of the issues that mankind sets out to settle, it never does settle. They are not solved because ... they are incapable of solution properly speaking, being concerned with incommensurables. At any rate, even if that be not always true, the opposing parties seldom do agree upon a solution; and the dispute fades into the past unsolved, though perhaps it may be renewed as history, and fought over again. It disappears because it is replaced by some compromise that, although not wholly acceptable to either side, offers a tolerable substitute for victory; and he who would find the substitute needs an endowment as rich as possible in experience, an experience which makes the heart generous and provides the mind with an understanding of the hearts of others.

Learned Hand[1]

I will make the case today for public investment in the Humanities and I will do so by reflecting on Learned Hand's celebration of the Humanities. The question for this conference is not whether there should be public investment in Ontario's universities but rather how extensive an investment. Framing the question that way might seem to do away with the need to make a case for public investment. But in a world of scarce resources, the two questions – 'Should there be investment?' and 'How much should there be?' – are linked. And we all know that it is fairly easy to argue that engineering, or medicine, or even the pure sciences should be publicly funded because these disciplines seem to have either immediate or indirect cash value in the real world. Graduates in these disciplines have a clear route to jobs and the economy is a clear beneficiary. There is a direct return or, at worst, an indirect return on public investment.

But we also all know that it is not so straightforward to make the case for public investment in the Humanities. In South Africa, where I did my first five years of university, the BA degree was commonly and not kindly said to stand for Bugger All, since bugger all 'useful' was learned. And this kind of attitude towards the Humanities is hardly confined to South Africa.

One response to this kind of attitude is John Henry Newman's, who in 1852 in his famous lectures on the topic, *The Idea of a University*, argued that '[k]nowledge is, not merely a means to something beyond it, or the preliminary of certain arts into which it naturally resolves, but an end sufficient to rest in and to pursue for its own sake.'[2] As Jaroslav Pelikan has pointed out in his re-examination of the same topic, Newman felt compelled to engage in a polemic against utilitarianism because he had to deal with a campaign to eliminate from the curriculum 'traditional fields of inquiry that could not be justified on the grounds of their usefulness.'[3] And Newman's task was made even harder by the fact that his lectures were delivered as part of a campaign of his own – to procure support for the foundation of the Catholic University of Ireland. As a result, he argued in his lectures that theology had not only a place, but the central place, in the curriculum.

But knowledge for knowledge's sake is not only an inadequate slogan to combat an even more unrelenting utilitarian campaign than Newman faced; it is also inadequate for reasons that go beyond the expedience of the moment. For it might be right that if the Humanities are not useful, there is no reason for the public to invest in them. At most, they should be preserved in the great private universities of the United States of America – a luxury for those institutions which can fund useless inquiry from private pockets. Indeed, Newman found himself in some tension here, as those who wanted him to direct the Catholic University had in mind an institution which would equip young Catholic men to enter the establishment on equal terms with those who were educated at Oxbridge.

The problem, in my view, lies not in utilitarianism's focus on consequences or on usefulness, nor in the general instrumental character of its arguments. Rather, the problem lies in the kinds of consequences utilitarianism deems relevant and thus the goals which figure in its instrumental arguments. The problem arises when we deem the category of the useful to be confined to that which is capable of contributing directly or indirectly to the gross domestic product.

There is, however, another more expansive sense of usefulness even in the utilitarian tradition; as John Stuart Mill put it, utility is best understood as 'grounded on the permanent interest of man as a progressive being.'[4] And it is just that sense of usefulness, one to be found in a tradition of thought I will call pragmatic liberalism, on which Learned Hand relies.

The Experience of Being Human

The lengthy passage from Learned Hand comes not from a discussion of the Humanities but from a discussion of the skills he thought required of a jurist and, more generally, of those who participate in whatever way in legal order. I emphasize this point because lawyers, like medical doctors, can claim a place as indirect contributors to the economy; just as medical doctors keep us fit for work, lawyers provide both the framework of rules that make it possible for individual interaction to be productive as well as solutions to the problems that arise when the rules are not sufficient to maintain interaction. It is significant that Hand, who was not only one of the great practitioners of the law in the United States, but also one of the pioneers of the Law and Economics approach to law, thought a training in the Humanities to be indispensable for a lawyer. I am, though, less interested in that bare fact than in his argument for the fact, which argument can be broken down into the following propositions:

1 There are no permanent solutions to most of humankind's problems, and even where there do appear to be such solutions, not all parties will agree that this is the case.
2 However, we do move ahead and that is because we are capable of reaching compromises, which, while not wholly satisfactory to either side, are a 'tolerable substitute for victory.'
3 In order to be capable of finding such a compromise one must have certain attributes: 'an endowment as rich as possible in experience' and an experience of a particular kind – one which 'makes the heart generous and provides the mind with an understanding of the hearts of others.'

The third proposition is one about the kinds of persons who might contribute to solving the problems of humankind because of their ability to reach productive compromises. That kind of person has to be capable of being open to others, a capacity which Hand seems to suggest can be cultivated by one's educational experience. But the importance of experience goes beyond the educational experience in which this personality is cultivated. The kind of person Hand depicts is one who is willing to let her ideas be tested against experience. And since one of her attributes is the ability to reach compromises with other people, openness is not only to experience but to the understandings of experience of the others with whom one has to find compromise.

The experience Hand has in mind is not the experience of the natural world, which forms the testing ground for scientific hypotheses, nor is it the hard data of people's lives, which are the subject of the social sciences. Rather, it is people's *lived* experience – the way they understand their economic, social, political, and quite personal moral experience. It is in the Humanities that questions about this kind of experience are studied. But if one values education in the Humanities for these reasons, one will also not think that that education stops as one exits the university for the 'real' world. For an education in the Humanities is supposed to issue in a kind of person who is prepared for a lifelong process of education, through the capacity to be open to learning from others.

What we have here is an understanding of the excellent citizen – of someone who will benefit the public even if his activity is confined to the private realm. This understanding is liberal and pragmatic. It is liberal in its optimistic view of the individual as capable of continual, self-directed improvement of both him- or herself and the world. It is pragmatic because of its emphasis on experience as the testing ground for our ideas.

Let us contrast this liberal, pragmatic kind of person with the kind of person encouraged by what I will call crude utilitarianism: the relentless maximizer of personal satisfaction. Crude utilitarianism holds that there is no measure of goodness outside of this person's own set of preferences and judgments about the means to satisfy preferences. Other people are there to be used as resources in the maximization project, and constraints on such use are only those constraints that are necessary to make it possible for all people to be relentless maximizers. Similarly, the only public resources crude utilitarianism needs are those that create a framework which makes it possible for people to interact without harming each other.

Now crude utilitarianism makes a claim with a public aspect. It claims that we will all be better off if its understanding of the person is adopted. But it has no place in its design of public space for institutions other than those that will facilitate the pursuit of individual satisfaction. Moreover, educational institutions should benefit from public investment to the extent necessary to compensate for market failure – for those gaps that private initiative will not by itself fill, but which must be filled if the framework for individual interaction is to be maintained. Finally, such public investment as there is in education should be confined to the skills that are necessary to sustain, either directly or indirectly, the framework. Other kinds of inquiry including the Humanities are not ruled out. Rather, they are luxuries in which people may indulge only if they as individuals are willing to bear or to subsidize the costs.

There is at least one severe tension in this crude utilitarian view of education. The view is itself a product of the interaction of social, economic, and political currents; but like any idea it is much more than that. Its force as an idea, an idea which plays its own role in promoting certain currents rather than others, comes from its articulation. And that articulation is most elaborate and sophisticated in university departments: for instance, in philosophy, political science, and economics departments. Indeed, economics departments and even many political science departments now sometimes seem to be for the most part decidedly anti-humanistic in their orientation, focused on mathematical or quasi-mathematical inquiries in which human beings figure only as stripped-down maximizers.

But one should recall both that this idea of the person had to be forged before it could drive inquiry and that it was forged by economists who pursued their inquiries in a distinctly humanistic mode – a group which in my view includes Adam Smith, but also Friedrich von Hayek and Milton Friedman.[5] In sum, the idea of the person promoted by crude utilitarianism leads to a view of education which is at odds with the education it took to produce that idea. It is as though crude utilitarianism supposes that one can climb the ladder of the Humanities and that at the top, having reached the truth about the nature of the rational person, one can kick the ladder away.

But the ladder cannot be kicked away so easily. The very utility of this idea of the person is subject to challenge from within the discipline of economics, most notably by Amartya Sen. Sen, I think it is fair to say, wishes to make the 'science' of economics more humanistic in order that it might better promote the welfare of the individuals whose interests it aims to serve.

It is thus important to see that the conception of the individual as a relentless maximizer arose from the Humanities. But it is even more important to see that challenges to it are inevitable and vital. We continue to challenge our conceptions and we continue to inquire into how we are or ought to be as human beings. This inquiry is the stuff of the Humanities. And it is what enables us to fully live up to our potential.

We are not yet at the point of establishing the case for public investment in the Humanities. But the contrast between the liberal pragmatic view of the person and the crude utilitarian view is instructive. First, the liberal pragmatic view does not exclude the crude utilitarian view from having any role in inquiry. As my colleagues in the law faculty who work within the discipline of Law and Economics argue, the crude utilitarian view can be extremely helpful when it comes to exploring the incentive structure created by different regulatory schemes. But that is because they are all, as far as I can tell, liberal pragmatists, who conceive of the discipline of law as humanistically as any philosopher. In contrast, those who think that the crude utilitarian view is not just a useful tool for some inquiries, but a normative base for public policy in general, exclude other conceptions of the person from debate about appropriate public policy. Second, the liberal pragmatist is at the least agnostic about whether the educational space within which ideas about personality are to be cultivated should be publicly or privately funded. In contrast, as we have seen, for crude utilitarians, public policy and public institutions are instrumental only to very particular goals. A society should take collective action and establish institutions which make such action possible only when successful individual interaction, aimed as maximizing satisfaction of preferences, is not possible without such interventions. In short, the public realm is there only in so far as it is necessary to compensate for market failure. Together, these two differences are from the crude utilitarian perspective lethal to a case for public investment in the Humanities.

I said that the liberal pragmatist is at the least agnostic about whether the educational space within which the individual is to be cultivated should be publicly or privately funded. But it is important to emphasize the phrase 'at the least.' For liberal pragmatists, as I will now argue, must be committed to much more than the proposition that public investment in the Humanities is merely legitimate, in that it cannot be excluded a priori, as crude utilitarians would prefer. They must, that is, be committed to the view that public investment in the Humanities is required.

The Public Nature of the Humanities

The liberal pragmatic conception of the person has a much more robust public aspect to it than does crude utilitarianism. The beneficial consequences that flow from it are not limited to the wealth of a society measured in monetary terms. They are consequences for, or are instrumental to securing, a stock of public goods – human capital, as it is sometimes put. And here 'human capital' is not understood in terms of what is capable of generating economic returns on investment: the average student trained in philosophy will contribute $X to GDP over her life. Rather, it is understood in close proximity to the idea of the Humanities – of the cultivation of people who are humane in the way Hand describes, or as the *Oxford English Dictionary* does: 'Characterized by such behaviour or disposition towards others as befits a man: civil; courteous, obliging ...; kind, benevolent.' Such people constitute a stock of public goods because they carry in themselves the resources of a civilized society.

It is, in my view, difficult to overestimate how valuable a resource this conception is. Each generation of students needs to ask questions about what it is to be a citizen, to be benevolent, to be human. The Humanities are the location of this engagement. To the extent that professional faculties and the applied sciences have become more, or even considerably, occupied by the need to answer such questions within their own curricula, they have, to use a word I only just learned from the *Oxford English Dictionary*, been humanized.

In asking such questions, each generation of students will be led to further questions; for example, the question whether genes, sociological circumstances, and the contingencies of history determine behaviour, so that there is no making sense of praise or blame for worthy or odious acts, or even the question whether it makes sense to use the labels 'worthy' and 'odious.' The issue is not whether questions about free will and determinism can ever be settled, but to see, with Learned Hand, that it is in the asking of such questions, in our engagement with them, that we learn something crucial about what it is to be human.

It is worth noting that the Humanities attract a disproportionate share of students. This is because it is in the Humanities that deep, subtle, and pressing questions are advanced: What is of value in life? How did we get to where we are, socially, politically, and morally. Students sense that these questions are essential. But my question is: should government also adopt that sense?

The problem with crude utilitarianism is not only that is does not think such questions worth asking, since it believes that they have been settled, but that it supposes that the funds for those who wish to engage in such questions should be entirely private. But civil society is a not a private matter. It is profoundly public, something which, as Thomas Hobbes argued, has to be put in place in order to make successful private interaction at all possible. I mention Hobbes because he is often thought of as the arch individualist, even as the founder of the crude utilitarian conception of the person. But there is no more powerful expositor than Hobbes of the argument that the public is prior to the private, such that the public establishment of a civil society is necessary for successful private interaction. And for him an education in which universities have a central role is a crucial component in the structure of such a society.[6]

Now it is perhaps possible to imagine a society in which education in the Humanities is provided by private investment only. But one would have good reason to doubt that society's commitment to being a civil society. A society that wants to be a civil society, to be humane or decent, is also a society that understands that a public realm has to be maintained as a priority over the realm of private interaction. And such a society would be hypocritical if it did not invest resources in maintaining the public realm.

This idea is well understood by Canadians, who regard universal health care as an achievement, as a public good whose value cannot be reduced to economics, since it is an expression of a commitment to living in a decent society. As far as health care is concerned, it is important not only that every individual in a decent society has access to it, but that the resource of health care is regarded primarily as a public one. We as a public are required to invest in universal health care, because if we did not do so our understanding of our society as one in which individuals are committed to treating each other with equal concern and respect would be in doubt. And the argument is consequentialist or instrumental to its core – it is about the consequences to us as human beings should we move too far away from that commitment. It is not, then, just our understanding of society that is at stake but our understanding of ourselves as fully human.

Of course, in a world of scarce resources we cannot have all we want, even when it comes to health care. But the default position for liberal pragmatists is that when it comes to what we can call public goods, goods that are constitutive of the public realm, the public must be committed to maintaining the resources necessary to them. Only if it is clear that the society cannot muster the resources to do this should private markets be considered as having a place in compensating for public failure. It is a serious mistake, then, to let one's outlook be framed by an idea that the state is there solely to compensate for market failure. On the most important issues, when it comes to public goods, the public realm comes first. And if that deeply humanistic argument is right, then the case is now complete for public investment in the Humanities, at the highest possible level a society can maintain. The case is complete if what we want to be is a humane, decent, or civil society.

Notes

* Professor of Law and Philosophy, Associate Dean of Law (Graduate), University of Toronto. I thank Donald Ainslie, Andrew Green, Cheryl Misak, and Michael Trebilcock for helpful comments on drafts of this paper.

1 As quoted in Frank M. Turner, 'Newman's University and Ours,' in F.M. Turner, ed., John Henry Newman, *The Idea of a University* (New Haven: Yale University Press, 1996) 300.

2 Newman, ibid., 78. Newman went on to say of knowledge: 'That further advantages accrue to us and redound to others by its possession, over and above what it is in itself, I am very far indeed from denying; but, independent of these, we are satisfying a direct need of our nature in its very acquisition; and whereas our nature, unlike that of the inferior creation, does not at once reach its perfection, but depends, in order to it, on a number of external aids and appliances. Knowledge, as one of the principal of these, is valuable for what its very presence does for us after the manner of a habit, even though it be turned to no further account, nor subserve any direct end' (79). A careful reading of this passage does make is susceptible to a much more instrumental understanding of knowledge than Newman seems to want – knowledge is important for us to be fully human and, by implication, the world is better off if it is populated by fully human beings.

3 Jaroslav Pelikan, *The Idea of the University: A Reexamination* (New Haven: Yale University Press, 1992), 33.

4 John Stuart Mill, *On Liberty* in *Collected Works*, vol. 18, ed. J.M. Robson (Toronto: University of Toronto Press, 1984), 275.

5 Of course, some of the people who work in this mode might have thought of their work as more scientific than humanistic and might even have seen it as a reaction to what they regarded as the bad modes of thought promoted in the Humanities of their day. I am thus using 'Humanities' anachronistically to describe work of the sort that would today be done within the Humanities, including the more Humanities-oriented parts of the social sciences, for example, political theory or political economy.
6 Thomas Hobbes, *Leviathan*, ed. Richard Tuck (Cambridge: Cambridge University Press, 1996).

On Complex Intersections: Ontario Universities and Governments

GLEN A. JONES*

Universities and governments share many common interests and characteristics, but the one common characteristic that receives surprisingly little attention in discussions of their relationship is that both are enormously complex organizational forms. For those who study the relationship between universities and the state, there has been a quite natural tendency to categorize and simplify, these organizational complexities. In order to study we define, and in doing so delimit the scope of our analysis; in order to measure we count, and in doing so make decisions about the 'what' we are measuring.

Discussions of the public role and importance of universities are interesting examples of this tendency to categorize, simplify, and define. We have learned a great deal from the economic analysis of the relationship between educational attainment and lifetime earnings and the macro-analysis of the role of the university in economic development. We know a great deal about aggregate demand for access to post-secondary education, participation rates, and certain types of accessibility. In short, we know much more about the public impact and nature of universities, especially in economic and social terms, than we did when the Government of Canada decided to invest in the mammoth expansion of our higher education system in the middle of the last century by providing direct grants to universities, a decision that initiated what J.A. Corry referred to as the Canadian university's transition 'from private domain to public utility' (1970, 101).

My objective in this paper is to contribute to this discussion by taking a step back into the organizational complexity of both universities and governments in order to demonstrate that there are important components of the public role of universities, and important components of the relationship between governments and universities, that are frequently missing from the debate. My goal is to illuminate a few important examples, rather than provide a comprehensive overview, of these missing components. The paper is organized into three major sections. The first focuses on the organizational complexity of the university in order to shed light on contributions to our society, while the second focuses on the organizational complexity of government. The third deals with issues of intersection between these complex organizational forms, and offers some observations on the provincial coordination of higher education in Ontario.

The Organizational Complexity of the University

Universities are highly complex institutional forms. The complexity of their organizational arrangements is largely a function of two complementary characteristics. The first is that universities are knowledge-driven organizations. The expansion of knowledge has led to increased specialization, and increased specialization has led to the emergence of new academic programs and organizational units such as research centres and institutes (Clark 1995). In 1963 Clark Kerr (1982) used the term 'multiversity' to describe what he perceived to be a new, complex organizational form of the university comprising semi-autonomous academic units defined by the disciplines or professions and held together by a central administration. Forty years later, the picture of the multiversity painted by Kerr appears to capture the relative simplicity of an academic world before the rise of virtual research networks, research clusters, and a plethora of new and emerging external partnership arrangements.

The second characteristic that obviously contributes to universities' organizational complexity relates to the tremendous diversity of activities, operations, and services that they administer. Universities maintain classrooms, laboratories, and libraries, but they also run restaurants, residences, counselling services, publishing companies, art galleries, animal care facilities, daycares, schools, medical centres, and bookstores. This list of activities can be impressively long even for small institutions, and for large universities it may be a challenge to even compile a complete list of operations, services, and specialized facilities.

Given this organizational complexity, it is not particularly surprising that when asked what universities do, university leaders tend to return to the three words that capture what are commonly accepted to be the core activities of Canadian universities: teaching, research, and service. The case for public funding is based on the public dimension of these concepts. The evidence used to support the argument for public investment in higher education is based on the analysis of institutional and system-level data.

The problem, of course, is that there are types of activities that we know universities are engaged in but where there is relatively little data, even at the institutional level. There are ways in which our universities contribute to Canadian society that can only be discussed in the broadest terms, in large part because these are activities that take place at what Clark (1983) refers to as the understructure or basic-unit level of the university but are largely invisible in system-level policy discussions.

For example, we know relatively little about the teaching activities of Canadian universities that are not associated with formal degree programs. Public discussions of universities in Ontario focus almost entirely on participation in undergraduate and graduate degree programs, and our institutional and system-level data systems obviously focus on the registration of students in programs that 'count' under provincial funding mechanisms. At the same time, we know that universities are increasingly engaged in continuing-education programming, especially in the professions, and that these activities play an important role in the complex intersections between universities, governments, and the broader society (see Brooke and Waldron 1994; Jones 2001).

Continuing education and extension programming takes place at the basic-unit level of the university, and while most universities have a unit with a specific mandate to offer and coordinate continuing education, in reality these activities, broadly defined, are dispersed throughout the understructure and represent attempts on the part of these local units to respond to the needs of the broader society as well as the particular professional or knowledge communities to which they are directly affiliated. The form of these activities range from informal public workshops to extremely formal programs of study leading to a non-degree credential such as a specialized certificate or diploma. For professional program units, these activities may include highly structured continuing professional-development activities designed to teach professionals about new research findings related to practice, or to upgrade practising professionals in light of new professional standards. On the other hand, these activities can promote informal interaction between knowledge creators and knowledge users by creating sustained relationships through workshops, alumni activities, and partnership arrangements between the university, employers, and/or professional organizations.

There are undoubtedly social benefits associated with these continuing-education activities, whether they involve introducing citizens to new ideas and new understandings, or whether they focus on ensuring that licensed professionals are aware of the newest research findings related to practice. There is also both a public and private dimension to these activities; there are continuing-education markets in some sectors where students pay high tuition, while there are also examples of heavily subsidized activities based on the need to serve particular populations. There is a body of scholarship on continuing education, but for the most part the literature focuses on the relationship between the relevant component of the university and the populations that they serve (for example, continuing medical education and the health professions).[1] In other words, we know something about what is taking place at the understructure of the university, but relatively little about the scope and nature of these activities across the university and how the sum of these locally initiated activities relate to the more 'traditional' teaching and research activities of the institution. When public resources for formal degree programs are scarce, do local units shift their energies towards the development of revenue-generating continuing-education programs? Are subsidized extension programs retained despite decreases in government operating support because of the importance placed on the real or perceived social benefits that these activities produce?[2]

A second example of activities that receive little attention in system-level discussions of higher education is the work and role of faculty in terms of contributing to informed public debate of social issues and public policy. At the system level we know relatively little about university faculty other than the most basic information such as age, gender, salary, and area of study. At the same time, we know that the nature of faculty work differs enormously by discipline. As Braxton and Hargens have noted, the 'differences among academic disciplines are profound and extensive. Their manifestations range from global characteristics, such as disciplinary structural patterns, to individual scholars' everyday teaching and research experience' (1996 35).

We also know something about the role that faculty play in terms of contributing new knowledge and critical analysis to social and political debates that take place outside the academy. Faculty obviously disseminate their research through the traditional venues of the scholarly disciplines, but many are also not infrequent contributors to popular media discussions of social issues.

Faculty expertise is also used as a resource by government. Almost fifteen years ago I conducted a small study of selected political activities of University of Toronto faculty (Jones 1993). Of the 450 professors responding to the survey, 17% indicated that they had been asked for advice by representatives of the Ontario government in the previous year. In addition, more than one-in-four respondents indicated that they had attempted to influence provincial government policy in some way during the previous year. While larger numbers of faculty in the social sciences and health professions reported involvement in these types of activities than other fields of study, over one-quarter of all faculty in all of the eight broad disciplinary categories reported some level of public or political engagement. The list of activities included everything from sitting on government committees to simply writing a letter. Of course some of these activities were more directly related to the role of faculty as 'citizens,' but many involved activities where faculty members believed that they had a professional responsibility to apply their scholarly expertise to important policy issues.

One might well assume that there are social benefits associated with the contributions that faculty make to public debate and public policy, but these are not contributions that have been systematically studied or discussed at the system level. Given the role of faculty in Ontario universities, it is rather shocking to note that there have been few systematic studies of what they do, what their ambitions are, or how they understand their public role. We know little about the relative emphasis that Ontario university faculty members place on their teaching, research, and service activities, and how this emphasis varies by discipline and by university. We know little about how changes in government funding or system policy affect the day-to-day experience of our faculty.

The Organizational Complexity of Government

The discussion and analysis of the relationship between universities and governments almost always focuses on the direct relationship between universities, represented by their institutional leadership, and governments, represented by a ministry or agency assigned responsibility for higher education policy. These discussions frequently ignore the complex organizational arrangements of government, just as they tend to ignore the complexity of the university in terms of the wide range of public activities associated with the institutional understructure.

As I have already noted, universities engage in a broad range of activities, and discussions of university–government relations frequently ignore the fact that many of these activities are regulated by other component parts of government, largely because the activities are outside the boundaries of what is normally thought of as higher education policy. University-operated daycares must fulfil the same licensing standards and regulatory requirements of other child care facilities. Restaurants and food service facilities must meet government guidelines related to the preparation and serving of food. Specialized research facilities are regulated by health and safety codes, environmental regulations concerning the use, storage, and disposal of certain chemicals, and a myriad other government standards designed to protect the health and safety of workers, establish appropriate guidelines for the treatment of animals, and protect the broader public interest. In other words, the fact that universities are engaged in a range of activities means that they are regulated by multiple levels of government under legislation that has little if anything to do with higher education policy. The enormous complexity and diversity of university activities implies that they operate under a wider range of government oversight and regulatory agencies than most other organizations or corporations. Government regulation in all of these areas has a direct impact on how universities do what they do, but it is generally assumed that, with some important exceptions, universities should be treated like other firms.

There are also a wide range of relationships between component parts of government and component parts of the university that emerge as a function of the university's role in teaching, research, and service. Perhaps the most obvious examples of these direct relationships involve the complex interactions between professional schools, professional organizations, and government units assigned responsibility for issues of professional practice within a particular sector. These are areas of activity where government has determined that it is in the broader public interest to intervene and regulate professional practice.

The certification of school teachers has long been the responsibility of the Ministry of Education in the province of Ontario, and at one point the education of teachers was the direct responsibility of government through ministry-funded colleges and normal schools. In the 1960s Ontario, like many other jurisdictions, reorganized teacher education and assigned universities with the public responsibility for educating

teachers for practice. More recently, the provincial government established the Ontario College of Teachers, an agency that has assumed
responsibility for the review and accreditation of teacher education
programs, for the establishment of standards for teacher certification,
and for regulating the continuing professional education of teachers.
Faculties of education have a direct relationship to the Ministry of
Education. The ministry influences the number of students enrolled in
teacher education programs, in some cases quite directly through targeted funding programs facilitated through the Ministry of Training,
Colleges and Universities. Programs designed to prepare teachers for
practice and professional certification are accredited in accordance with
standards determined by agencies outside the university operating
under government regulation.

There is considerable variation in how professions are regulated and
the relative authority assigned to professional bodies, government agencies, and the university in professional education, but the key point here
is that these arrangements are almost always worked out within policy
communities that involve both governments and universities, but which
are beyond the boundaries of what one would normally consider higher
education policy. Ernest Sirluck (1977) once described these types of
relationships as 'secondary' to the principal relationship involving the
central administration of the university and the government agency
assigned responsibility for higher education policy, but Sirluck was
writing as a university president with an institution-level perspective
on university-government arrangements. From the perspective of the
university understructure, these relationships may be central and extraordinarily important in their day-to-day activities. Health-care sector reforms may have a much greater impact on decisions within a
faculty of medicine than almost any regulatory change more directly
associated with higher education policy. Nursing is perhaps the most
dramatic recent example of the importance and influence of these relationships. The shift towards the baccalaureate degree as the minimum
requirement for entry-to-practice in the nursing profession has led to
significant changes in the demand for degree programs, and the development of new partnerships between university and college nursing
programs.

These are not, of course, simply one-way hierarchical relationships
involving authoritarian governments and subservient university units,
but rather are extraordinarily complex policy communities. Governments ask universities for advice on professional standards, they em-

ploy faculty as consultants, and they appoint faculty to advisory boards. In other words, universities frequently play a special role in these discussions that revolves around the specialized expertise of faculty and the university's teaching and research function. University faculty also play an extremely important role as expert critics of professional standards and practices, and as research-informed advocates for reform.

This is, of course, the other side of the same set of activities that I discussed in relation to the work of faculty. Governments draw on the university as a public resource. They seek the technical advice and expertise of faculty in a wide range of policy areas. In some cases these 'other' parts of government provide financial support to fund specific university initiatives and projects. They may fund university research initiatives in strategic areas related to the ministry's mandate (think, for example, of the research needs of agriculture, transportation, and natural resources).

However we understand and define higher education policy, it is important to recognize that there are a plethora of other interactions between universities and governments that involve other component parts of government in intersection with specific programs and expertise operating at the understructure level of the institution.

Complex Intersections, Public Purpose, and Government Coordination

In the early years of the twentieth century, the question of whether Canadian universities should be supported by the public purse was open to debate. The majority of Canadian universities were private, denominational institutions, and few of these institutions received provincial operating grants. A year after Confederation the Government of Ontario decided that it would only provide provincial support to secular universities.

The question of whether the universities that received public operating support were 'public universities' was, and continues to be, open to debate. Unlike the university arrangements that emerged as a function of the national reforms in continental Europe in the nineteenth century, Canadian universities were never viewed as public institutions in terms of state ownership or control (Amaral, Jones, and Karseth 2002). In legal terms they were established as independent, not-for-profit, private corporations. They were never owned by provincial governments, and were subjected to relatively little government regulation until provincial governments began to coordinate expansion in the 1960s (Jones 1996).

By the early 1970s the higher education landscape had changed dramatically. The lure of provincial government investment had led many denominational institutions to secularize and become eligible for operating support, while many others entered into federation or affiliation arrangements with publicly supported institutions. Every university in Canada received government funding, and while the arrangements varied by province, these publicly supported institutions were assigned a public monopoly over the ability to grant secular degrees (Jones 1996; Skolnik, 1987). Even with an assigned monopoly over degree-granting and government operating grants, the universities of Ontario tended to refer to themselves as 'provincially assisted' rather than 'public' institutions (Monahan 2004, 41). This phrase reflected the other reality of Canadian universities, that universities continued to be funded through a combination of both public and private (tuition fees, gifts, sale of goods, contracts, etc.) sources.

It is government, rather than the universities, which has historically played the central role in determining the balance between private and public funding. Given that the two largest components of university operating revenues are government grants and tuition fees for degree programs, it is important to note that provincial governments across the country have had considerable experience in influencing, if not directly controlling, both the level of grants and the level of fees (Jones 1996).

The question of whether Canadian universities should be supported by the public purse is no longer a matter of debate. Canada's provincial governments, like every other government on earth, have come to recognize the public importance of higher education. There is also no question as to whether universities contribute to the broader society. We know that there are both private and social benefits associated with a university education. We know that universities contribute to the economic development of our nation.

The problem, as I have attempted to illustrate, is that there are also a range of university activities that contribute to our society that we know surprisingly little about. We know something about the social benefits associated with our formal degree programs, but we know relatively little about the social benefits associated with the wide range of other teaching and educational activities that take place within our universities. We know that university faculty contribute their expertise to public debates. They offer expert analysis and opinions through publications and media coverage. Governments ask them for advice, and engage them as consultants. In short, universities may play a very special role within our democratic society as a source of technical expertise, scholarly criticism, and policy alternatives. We know something about the economic benefits of higher education for our students, but surprisingly little about the impact of university education on other dimensions of their lives. This is far from an exhaustive list of activities that receive relatively little attention in the discussion of the contributions of the university to our society. This list does, however, provide support for the conclusion that our current attempts to measure the social and economic benefits of higher education barely scratch the surface. There are a wide range of university activities that involve social benefits and the broader public interest that we know surprisingly little about.

Given these already complex intersections between universities and governments, how should the Government of Ontario coordinate universities? Perhaps the most obvious observation is that a highly centralized approach is problematic if not impossible. It is problematic because a centrally controlled approach to coordination would have an impact on the capacity of local units to respond to their knowledge communities, industries, professions, and students. Given the complexities of government, it would be impossible because of the level of collaboration between the various government departments with a direct interest in universities that would be necessary in order to develop a coordinated approach.

This observation is also supported by policy trends in many other jurisdictions. Many of the countries that previously employed highly centralized approaches to coordinating and regulating higher education have taken a step back in the last few decades in order to provide universities with greater autonomy. This includes Japan, Sweden, and many of the countries of continental Europe (see Amaral, Jones, and Karseth 2002; Meek 2002, 2003). The Canadian approach to university coordination, in contrast, has been highly decentralized, and Canadian universities have historically had very high levels of institutional autonomy (Anderson and Johnson 1998; Jones 1996).

A second observation is that given the complex intersections between governments and universities, the notion of a 'buffer body,' an agency designed to separate universities from the political interference of government, may no longer be a viable structural mechanism for coordination. With the University Grants Commission of the United Kingdom as perhaps the most frequent example, it was once argued that 'buffer bodies' provided a mechanism for coordinating higher education at arm's-length from the dangerous interventions of partisan politics (Meek 2002). The problem, however, is that the interactions between universities and governments now involve such a wide range of government sectors and university units that a 'buffer' may do more harm than good. In other words, among the possible roles that might be assigned to some sort of advisory body for higher education in Ontario, I do not believe that it is reasonable to assume that this agency can and should protect the universities from government, any more that we should assume that the agency can and should protect the government from universities. The intersections between government and university activities are simply too complex and multifaceted to be structurally routed through some form of buffer agency.

In my opinion, the problems with our current coordinating arrangements in Ontario stem from two basic issues. The first is that these arrangements need to consider the enormous complexity of higher education as a policy sector. In this paper I have tried to provide some indication of the organizational complexities of both the university and government, but the moment that we begin to discuss the coordination of higher education in Ontario we need to consider the complexities associated with coordinating a system composed of many universities and colleges of applied arts and technology. It is also a system that is increasingly influenced by two levels of government, rather than one. We now have a range of federal government initiatives designed to increase the research capacity of our universities. We now have a community college sector that grants applied degrees, and a university sector that is increasingly involved in certificate and diploma programs. We now have a small number of new private universities, and a growing private/vocational proprietary sector.

What has been the impact of these shifts in policy direction? The first problem with our current coordinating arrangements in Ontario is that we really do not know the answer. The Ministry of Training, Colleges and Universities spends over $4 billion a year, but it has almost no research capacity in terms of studying and monitoring higher education. As these major changes suggest, the problem is not whether the government has the capacity to make decisions, but rather whether it has the capacity to make informed decisions. We need more systematic research about higher education in Ontario. We need to know more about the work of our faculty and the role of higher education in the lives of our students.

The second problem is that the Government of Ontario has never really adopted a system-wide perspective to the coordination of higher education in this province. Ontario has a long tradition of binary, sectoral policy development, despite the evidence that one of the most important policy issues is associated with the relationships between the Ontario college and university sectors (Jones 1997). We need an approach to coordination that recognizes that there is a public interest in higher education that may, at times, transcend sectoral and institutional interests. I am not arguing for greater government interference in higher education policy, I am suggesting the development of system-level higher education coordination that is mindful of the organizational complexities of our system. My sense is that both universities and colleges are best served by high levels of institutional autonomy, but that the government has a responsibility to steer.

These two problems are obviously closely related. You can't steer without some sense of where you are and where you want to go. Higher education in Ontario is clearly moving, but without a clear sense of who is going in what direction it has been difficult to decide who should pay for the gas, let alone understand the benefits of taking the ride. Given the complex intersections between universities, governments, and the broader society, it is also important to know what is happening on the ground.

Notes

* Professor of Higher Education, Department of Theory and Policy Studies in Education, Ontario Institute for Studies in Education of the University of Toronto.
1 Houle (1980) is perhaps the most cited work on the role of continuing education in the professions, though most of the empirical work in this area can be found in the specialized educational journals of the various professions. The *Canadian Journal of University Continuing Education* provides a forum for research findings on the role and work of central continuing education and extension units within the university.
2 One might logically presume that the answer to the first question is yes and

the answer to the second no, but in the analysis of markets and influence in higher education there are often unanticipated findings (see Teixeira, Jongbloed, Dill, and Amaral 2004).

References

Amaral, A., G.A. Jones, and B. Karseth. 2002. *Governing Higher Education: Comparing National Perspectives.* In Amaral, Jones, and Karseth, eds, *Governing Higher Education: National Perspectives on Institutional Governance*, 279–98. Duderstadt, The Netherlands: Kluwer Academic Publishing.

Anderson, D., and R. Johnson. 1998. *University Autonomy in Twenty Countries.* Technical report. Canberra, Australia: Department of Employment, Education, Training and Youth Affairs.

Braxton, J.M., and L.L. Hargens. 1996. 'Variation Among Academic Disciplines: Analytical Frameworks and Research.' In J. Smart, ed., *Higher Education: Handbook of Theory and Research*, vol. 11, 1–46. New York: Agathon.

Brooke, M., and M. Waldron. 1994. *University Continuing Education in Canada: Current Challenges and Future Opportunities.* Toronto: Thompson Educational Publishing.

Clark, B.R. 1995. *Places of Inquiry: Research and Advanced Education in Modern Societies.* Berkeley: University of California Press.

– 1983. *The Higher Education System.* Berkeley: University of California Press.

– 1970. *Farewell the Ivory Tower.* Montreal: McGill-Queen's University Press.

Houle, C.O. 1980. *Continuing Learning in the Professions.* San Francisco: Jossey-Bass.

Jones, G.A. 2001. 'Islands and Bridges: Lifelong Learning and Complex Systems of Higher Education in Canada.' In D. Aspin, J. Chapman, M. Hatton, and Y. Sawano, eds, *International Handbook of Lifelong Learning*, vol. 2, 545–60. Dordrecht, The Netherlands: Kluwer Academic Publishers.

– 1997. 'Higher Education in Ontario.' In G.A. Jones, ed., *Higher Education in Ontario: Different Systems, Different Perspectives*, 137–60. New York: Garland Publishing.

– 1996. 'Governments, Governance, and Canadian Universities.' In J.C. Smart, ed., *Higher Education: Handbook of Theory and Research*, vol. 11, 337–71. New York: Agathon Press.

– 1993. 'Professorial Pressure on Government Policy: University of Toronto Faculty.' *Review of Higher Education* 16:4, 461–82.

Kerr, C. 1982. *The Uses of the University.* 3rd ed. Cambridge: Harvard University Press.

Meek, V.L. 2003. 'Introduction.' In A. Amaral, V.L. Meek, and I.M. Larsen, eds, *The Higher Education Managerial Revolution?* 1–30. Dordrecht, The Netherlands: Kluwer Academic Publishing.

– 2002. 'Changing Patterns in Modes of Co-ordination of Higher Education.'
In J. Enders and O. Fulton, eds, *Higher Education in a Globalising World:
International Trends and Mutual Observations*, 53–71. Dordrecht, The Nether-
lands: Kluwer Academic Publishers.

Monahan, E.J. 2004. *Collective Autonomy: A History of the Council of Ontario
Universities, 1962–2000*. Waterloo: Wilfrid Laurier Press.

Sirluck, E. 1977. 'University Presidents and the Politicians.' *Canadian Journal of
Higher Education* 7:1, 1–12.

Skolnik, M.L. 1987. 'State Control of Degree Granting: The Establishment of a
Public Monopoly in Canada.' In C. Watson, ed., *Governments and Higher
Education: The Legitimacy of Intervention*, 56–83. Toronto: Higher Education
Group, Ontario Institute for Studies in Education.

Teixeira, P., B. Jongbloed, D. Dill, and A. Amaral, eds. 2004. 'Markets in
Higher Education: Rhetoric or Reality?' Dordrecht, The Netherlands:
Kluwer Academic Publishers.

Equality of Opportunity
and University Education

ANDREW GREEN*

In beginning any discussion of university education, it seems obligatory to mention its importance in providing opportunities to individuals. Sometimes such opportunities seem to be viewed as one of the purposes of the university system; other times they are discussed as one of the broader social benefits of university education. The discussion will often then veer off to focus on the economic opportunities from university education and their implications for economic growth. The trend over the past decade has been to argue that investing in 'human capital' is the answer to all problems – it is seen as increasing the ability of individuals to obtain high-paying work, growing the economy, reducing inequality, addressing problems in the health-care sector, and generally overcoming just about any other current social and economic problem.[1] It is often tied to concern about preparing for or taking advantage of the 'new economy.'[2] Higher education is seen as central to this approach.

While economic opportunities are a key function of higher education, they are not all that a university education provides or promises, nor are they the solution to all problems. In fact, the primary focus on the economic nature of human capital from university education may be detrimental to finding solutions to many of the social issues it is purported to address. Part of the reason is that this view fails to take into account broader notions of equality of opportunity and their importance in a pluralistic society. These broader notions of opportunity are not an interesting by-product of university education, but are central to understanding the role of universities and the impact of different institutional structures for higher education.

This article discusses these broader notions of equality of opporttunity and their connection to the role and institutional structure of universities. It begins by setting out why equal opportunity is important. It takes the general concept of equal opportunity from Nobel prize–winning economist Amartya Sen's notions of freedom and capability – every individual of a society should have an equal opportunity (freedom) to do the things, and lead the life, he or she has reason to value.[3] Individuals should have the ability to make choices about, and take responsibility for, their goals. This paper briefly sets out the two aspects of equal opportunity – the process aspect (freedom from constraints or barriers) and the capability aspect (the capacity to take advantage of those freedoms). Education is fundamental to the capability aspect of equal opportunity.

However, while there is a threshold of education that we may want everyone to have, not everyone needs, wants, or should have a university degree, let alone a graduate degree. This paper therefore next draws out connections between equal opportunity and university education. In particular, it focuses on the connection between university education, deliberative democracy, and self-fulfilment. It then discusses some of the implications of this notion of equal opportunity for the design of the institutions surrounding university education. These institutional design issues are central to universities' role in promoting fairness, not only in providing opportunities to individuals but also in defining what those opportunities are and should be.

1. Why Equal Opportunity?

The first step in discussing the connection between equality of opportunity and the university sector is to define what is meant by equality of opportunity. At its core, equality of opportunity focuses on enabling each individual to pursue the goals and make the choices he or she has reason to value. A diverse society can never decide on one view of life that is best and to be valued.[4] Canadian society has always been diverse (whether it has been acknowledged to be so or not) and has become increasingly so over time. Canada has had a number of large influxes of immigrants in the past century and continues to expand through immigration, particularly in cities such as Toronto.[5] It is increasingly diverse in many other ways, as seen for example in its changing family structures (with greater numbers of lone-parent and dual-income families)[6] and its increasing income inequality (both market income and income after taxes and transfers).[7]

Such diversity is a source of strength and vibrancy in Canada, but it also means that it is difficult (if not impossible) to imagine complete agreement on what type of life people should live or should value. Different religious, cultural, and linguistic backgrounds and social situations mean that Canadians develop their own views of life and how to live it – some people value individual happiness, but others value religious purity or self-sacrifice or community service or other aspects of life regardless of their impact on happiness. It is hard to treat individuals equally when the concept of what should be equalized is valued differently by different people.[8] Moreover, even if a society could develop some definition of what all individuals should value (such as pleasure or satisfaction) and attempt to make everyone equal in that respect, it would be difficult, if not impossible, to measure each person's status (for example, their level of happiness).[9]

Because of these difficulties in defining and measuring the type of life everyone should value, it is important to focus on the ability of individuals to pursue the types of lives they each have reason to value. The aim then would not be to achieve some agreement by all citizens on what type of life should be most valued and try to measure how each person is faring towards that goal. Instead, each individual has the responsibility, and should be provided with the opportunity, to make the decisions about the type of life he or she wishes to lead. It is an attempt to find common ground in a diverse society that does not speak to any overall concept of the good life, but instead looks to finding the conditions necessary for individuals to pursue their own visions of the good life in a diverse society.[10] Such equal opportunity is concerned with expanding the options for people to choose and pursue the life plans they have reason to value.

It is important, however, to consider not just opportunity but equality of opportunity. This requires consideration of two interconnected aspects of opportunities: a *process* aspect relating to how decisions are made and a *capability* aspect relating to individuals' ability to make decisions.[11]

The Process Aspect of Opportunity

The process aspect of the term 'opportunity' encompasses freedom from barriers to taking actions such as participating in the market or in political discussions. It focuses on the removal of constraints on individuals' choice – including restrictions on the use of property (for example, acquiring and transferring property), on speech, on association, and on religion.[12] Individuals should be free to the extent possible to make their own decisions – each individual should have as much freedom as is consistent with the freedom of all others.[13] This freedom expands individuals' opportunities to choose the type of life they have reason to pursue. The process aspect of opportunity also encompasses the ability of individuals to become involved in decisions. For example, individuals need a right to vote or to challenge government choices (such as in court) in order to become meaningfully involved in political decision-making.

The Capability Aspect of Opportunities

The process aspect of opportunities, standing alone, ignores the contingent nature of the exercise of rights. Freedom to take action is meaningless for people who, given their talents, disadvantages, or background, are unable to actually take the action.[14] Therefore for opportunities to be meaningful, it is necessary to foster 'the actual ability of a person to achieve those things she has reason to value,'[15] thereby expanding her actual, effective choices. For example, an individual who cannot read will not be able to take advantage of a wide range of opportunities for employment.

Education is central to providing equality of opportunity. The structure of its institutions determines whether there are barriers to individuals obtaining the capacities, training, and knowledge that they want in life. Its form therefore impacts the process aspect of opportunity. Moreover, it is particularly important in terms of the capability aspect of opportunity. For example, an individual who lacks an education has fewer choices of jobs and greater probability of unemployment.[16] Education levels, at the same time, influence other aspects of individuals' lives such as political participation and even health.[17] The next section discusses some of the manners in which university education impacts important capabilities of individuals.

2. Education, Universities, and Expanding Opportunities

Education both at lower levels and at universities plays an essential role in expanding opportunities for individuals by enhancing capabilities. As mentioned above, in general, discussions about universities make a brief reference to broader social opportunities and then focus on economic opportunities.[18] In this section I intend to do the opposite. I want to make a brief reference to the important role universities play in expanding economic opportunities directly. I then move on to provide some examples of other ways in which universities expand opportunities.

Technical Skills, Knowledge, and Economic Opportunities

All levels of education can expand individuals' ability to obtain meaningful work. Basic education aids individuals in obtaining minimal levels of skills (such as reading, writing, mathematics, and general skills) to hold jobs and function in an advanced market economy. In fact, some argue that by far the greatest impact from education on economic returns comes from the lower levels – early childhood education and primary and secondary school.[19] University education adds considerable benefits, but its relative role in the education system must be borne in mind.

Higher education can add skills and knowledge related to economic opportunities, either through general study or study tied more specifically to an area of specialty. Such skills and knowledge vary across disciplines and types of education, from the more abstract skills and knowledge of a general arts and science degree to the more tailored focus of graduate degrees and professional schools. The private economic returns from higher education are significant.[20] Opening up these economic opportunities to all members of society, rich and poor, established and immigrant, is one of the most important functions of a university system.

Education therefore aids in increasing economic opportunities in part by providing skills and disseminating information that help individuals either obtain work or succeed in the workplace. In addition to these private economic returns, education may expand economic opportunities for all individuals in a society through its impact on economic growth. For example, it can increase the returns to, and productivity of, not only the individuals themselves but also of others. More educated workers appear to make those around them more productive.[21] Further, universities can aid in the creation and application of ideas. Both primary and applied research at universities in a wide variety of areas can lead to increases in productivity and economic growth. This connection has led to the focus of federal funding on science, technology, and the 'new economy,' although such tailoring of research funding has come under attack.[22] The creation of new ideas and the dissemination of current knowledge, therefore, can spur economic growth, expanding opportunities for everyone in society.

Empathy and Inequality

Universities can also play a role in developing and expanding other capabilities of individuals that are different from, though connected to, those that expand economic opportunities. One example is empathy, or what Adam Smith calls 'sympathy' and Martha Nussbaum terms 'narrative imagination.'[23] I want to illustrate the role of empathy by discussing the potential role of human capital in addressing income inequality.

The arguments for the role of education, and in particular university education, in expanding economic opportunities have led to calls for focusing public policy on human capital formation.[24] Human capital has at its core generally been meant in the economic sense of skills and knowledge related to economic opportunities.[25] These calls for investing in human capital changed public policy in Canada in the 1990s. The emphasis of policy shifted, at least in rhetoric, from supporting individuals who were not succeeding (safety nets) to providing them with the skills and training that was felt necessary for them to succeed (trampolines).[26] On this theory, education and training can help everyone succeed. Those with the education and training (the human capital) have the opportunity to increase their income (that is, obtain higher-paying jobs). Those who have not invested in human capital will also be helped because their numbers will go down and they therefore will be able to command higher wages. As a result, on this view everyone will be better off and inequality will be reduced.[27]

However, there are a number of concerns with this view. First, even if the underlying theory is correct, policy has only partially adapted to this approach. In the 1990s, governments cut back on funding for safety nets in the form of welfare payments, health care, and unemployment insurance. They did not, however, undertake the second half of the policy – investing in training and education. There has been an increase in funding in recent years, but it is not clear it is sufficient to meet the demands of the new 'human capital' agenda or to permit a fair transition to the new approach.[28]

Second, even if the funding was sufficient, there have been concerns raised about whether the focus on 'human capital' can have as significant an impact as has been claimed. For example, there is some evidence that the focus on human capital may actually increase income inequality. Instead of the decrease in supply of those who have not invested in education leading to an increase in their wages, the increase in supply of those who *have* invested may draw capital away from low-skilled work towards high-skilled work. The result may then be that instead of catching up, the low-skill workers fall further and further behind.[29]

The impact of such concerns may be evident in the increase in income inequality throughout the 1990s. While I do not want to enter into the substance of these debates, if they are correct, the answer – invest more in human capital – is not a sufficient answer to either concern. It is obviously not sufficient if the impact of such investment is the opposite of that claimed – that is, it does not expand and in fact contracts economic opportunities for some elements of society. Further, it is not sufficient if the political system does not recognize or address the equality-of-opportunity issue at the core of the human-capital agenda.

Underlying these issues is society's notion of individual responsibility. Society must define the basic capabilities an individual requires to pursue the life he or she has reason to value. However, it must also decide what is to be done if an individual does not succeed, either because of bad luck or because they have failed to take advantage of the capabilities or opportunities provided. The social welfare system that developed in Canada and other developed nations in the 1950s and 1960s may in part have stemmed from the Great Depression. The Depression made salient to almost everyone in society that they were vulnerable to misfortune. Poverty became seen not solely as due to the moral fault or laziness of the individual but as something that was in part beyond everyone's control. This 'There but for the Grace of God' view, combined with an expanding economy, led to increasingly generous social programs based on safety nets.[30]

The human-capital approach, and in one way an equal-opportunity approach, can be seen as changing the nature of this view. This change has both a beneficial and a troublesome aspect. The focus of equal opportunity is on fostering the ability of each individual to pursue the life he or she has reason to value. Each individual has the responsibility to determine his or her own life plans. Such a responsibility avoids the loss of 'motivation, involvement and self-knowledge' that results from placing the responsibility for determining the life plan of one person in another's hands (such as the government).[31] Society must therefore reach some agreement about what are the necessary capabilities – for example, the required opportunities for investing in education. However, there is also the further issue of what society's role is once it has offered the opportunities to invest in human capital and some have not invested. Do we as a society offer anything to those who choose not to invest for whatever reason? To what extent do we worry about the incentive effects from policies supporting these individuals?

This issue is too large for this paper, but it is important to recognize that education has a role to play. Education, including university education, at its best fosters empathy for others. Adam Smith in *The Theory of Moral Sentiments* discusses this capacity, which he calls sympathy:

> As we have no immediate experience of what other men feel, we can form no idea of the manner in which they are affected, but by conceiving what we ourselves should feel in the like situation. Though our brother is upon the rack, as long as we ourselves are at our ease, our senses will never inform us of what he suffers. They never did, and never can, carry us beyond our own person, and it is by the imagination only that we can form any conception of what are his sensations. Neither can that faculty help us to this any other way, than by representing to us what would be our own, if we were in his case. It is the impressions of our own senses only, not those of his, which our imaginations copy. By the imagination we place ourselves in his situation, we conceive ourselves enduring all the same torments, we enter as it were into his body, and become in some measure the same person with him, and thence form some idea of his sensations, and even feel something which, though weaker in degree, is not altogether unlike them. His agonies, when they are thus brought home to ourselves, when we have thus adopted and made them our own, begin at last to affect us, and we then tremble and shudder at the thought of what he feels. For as to be in pain or distress of any kind excites the most excessive sorrow, so to conceive or to imagine that we are in it, excites some degree of the same emotion, in proportion to the vivacity or dulness of the conception.[32]

Adam Smith argued that public education aids in developing broader capabilities and connects these capabilities to the ability to participate in public decisions.[33] Similarly, Martha Nussbaum calls this capacity 'narrative imagination,' which she defines as 'the ability to think what it might be like to be in the shoes of a person different from oneself.'[34] She argues that 'narrative imagination' can be developed through courses in literature and the arts. However, it is also developed not only through students taking these courses but by having researchers thinking and

writing about these areas and bringing ideas about them to the class-
room and to the public more generally.

Such empathy or imagination is a necessary part of any democracy. It
allows decisions to be made which impact the lives of others; it improves the deliberation necessary to undertake decision-making in a
diverse society. A shift to policies based on investment in human capital
is going to require significant public funding. Empathy will be an
important capacity for Canadians in deciding to what extent equality of
opportunity demands greater investment in higher education and how
to aid individuals in the transition to policies based on human capital. It
will also aid society in making fairer decisions about society's responsibilities for those who are not helped by this approach, either because
human capital does not aid everyone or because some choose not to
invest. Each society must make its own determination concerning what
is fair. Empathy or narrative imagination developed in part through
universities will aid in making these determinations in a manner that
takes account of everyone in society.

Political Opportunities and Openness

University education also feeds into political decision-making in another manner. Equal opportunity to pursue the life one has reason to
value means it is important for individuals to be able to make decisions
about their own lives. However, this responsibility of each individual
does not preclude individuals from making aspects of this decision with
the other members of their community. In fact, fostering political and
community action – the existence of and capability of participating in
political opportunities – is an essential component of equal opportunity.

As noted above, political opportunities enable societies to determine
what each individual needs to pursue his or her own life plans and for
which decisions or choices he or she will be held responsible. They also
allow individuals to work together towards common goals that they
would not be able to pursue on their own. For example, Joseph Heath
argues that Canadian society is very efficient at meeting the needs and
desires of Canadians because Canadians permit a variety of institutions, including government, to make decisions and provide goods and
services that other countries, such as the United States, leave to the
market.[35] Further, political opportunities provide individuals with the
ability to develop collective aspirations about their society, such as
what level of environmental protection they want.[36]

These political opportunities encompass, for example, the ability to participate in decisions such as through providing information or voting, to debate issues with fellow citizens, to challenge decisions of government, and to run for office. Fairness requires providing all citizens with the ability to participate in political decisions relating to their community. Education provides a means of providing these abilities and improving collective decisions. It permits individuals to gain a greater appreciation of the issues that society faces and therefore to engage in better deliberation and decisions. While all levels of education are helpful and necessary in this regard, higher education has an important role to play in both developing and disseminating ideas that are central to these debates. Individuals with a range of different educational backgrounds can bring different concerns into democratic deliberation. Such deliberation, for example, is improved by the same skills and knowledge that lead to economic opportunities. However, it also requires other capacities that are not valued in or directly tied to economic opportunities.

One example, related to but different from empathy, is an openness to and understanding of other cultures and societies. University education should aid in developing the ability in individuals 'to see themselves as not simply citizens of some local region or group but also, and above all, as human beings bound to all other human beings by ties of recognition and concern.'[37] Such ability is important in making decisions in a society that is increasingly diverse – that is taking in a wide range of immigrants from different areas of the world. Decisions in such a society may require partial agreements which allow those with different viewpoints to attain a minimal level of political agreement and work together as a society, reaching what Rawls terms an 'overlapping consensus.'[38] The ability to reach such an agreement allows individuals to hold different views, but is aided by a greater understanding of other people and their cultures. Universities can foster such understanding through, for instance, general liberal arts courses and courses related to different world views.[39]

However, such understanding also has another impact in a world that is increasingly integrated in economic and other ways. The rise of issues that transcend national borders requires some form of international action. Different nations will need to come together to resolve a range of issues such as transboundary environmental matters like climate change, international trade disputes, and duties to address civil strife in other countries. It is difficult enough to make decisions within a relatively defined national community. International decisions will require even greater openness to and understanding of other cultures and peoples. Again, such education for 'world citizenship' occurs in part through general liberal arts education and courses which include different world views.[40] Without this broader education and ability to understand their place in the world, Canadians will be ill equipped to effectively participate in increasingly important international debates and decisions.

Social Opportunities and Self-Critical Thought

Universities also aid in expanding social opportunities. The area of social opportunities is broader than economic or political opportunities and harder to delineate. Social opportunities relate to the basic capabilities of individuals to form and actively pursue the lives they have reason to value. They encompass such issues as health care, education, basic income needs, and the environment. There is evidence, for example, that higher education provides individuals with a range of non-economic private benefits such as better health, lower probability of engaging in crime, and better outcomes for their children. As with economic opportunities, there are also corresponding non-economic public benefits such as enhanced 'social cohesion' and reduced criminal activity.[41]

One source of such private and public non-economic benefits is the self-critical abilities formed in universities. As noted above, equal opportunity is centred on the notion that individuals should have the ability to pursue lives 'they have reason to value.' The focus is on lives individuals have 'reason to value' because individuals need to be in a position to make reasoned decisions about their lives. Individuals' preferences or desires adapt to circumstances. The emphasis is not on 'rational' or 'reasonable' decisions but on the individual being in a position to make a decision between life choices based on reasons, not because of constraints.

In her defence of the 'liberal arts' higher education, Nussbaum places this self-critical capacity at the top of the list of reasons such education is valuable in society. It is the 'capacity for critical examination of oneself and one's traditions – for living what, following Socrates, we may call "the examined life."'[42] She argues that philosophy is central to this capacity. However, while philosophy can provide formal instruction related to this capacity, it also arises in study and research in other disciplines which critically examine existing norms and institutions, including some more directly related to economic opportunities. Universities must provide an opening for both teaching that fosters this capacity and research that sets the basis for development of this capacity in a wide range of areas. Such openings are central to the power of higher education to better enable individuals to make reasoned decisions about their lives. They also, not surprisingly, may aid individuals in taking advantage of economic and political opportunities.

3. Equal Opportunity, Goals, and Institutions

University education therefore may expand a wide range of economic, political, and social opportunities.[43] Further, such opportunities are interconnected. Increased health improves individuals' lives directly, but also can increase economic growth by increasing individuals' willingness to save over the course of their longer lives. Increased economic growth can provide individuals with private funds to meet their needs, but also enhances government's ability to finance social spending by increasing tax revenue.[44] More importantly for the purposes of this paper, capacities related to political and social opportunities help shape the content and implications of economic and other opportunities. Universities play a central role in both the provision and definition of these various opportunities.

The structure of the institutions surrounding universities therefore must take account of all these impacts on opportunities for citizens. Expanding economic opportunities is an important function of university education, but designing the institutions around it to focus only on these opportunities does not allow universities to fulfil their promise for expanding the relevant opportunities of all individuals and improving the functioning of democracy. Of course, the difficult part is designing institutions to capture these benefits.

As the many connections between this broader equality-of-opportunity approach and the institutions surrounding universities are too numerous for this paper, I will focus on two points. First, while the case for public funding of university education is clear, the form of that funding is crucial to the type and quality of capabilities that universities foster. Second, measuring the value and impact of higher education must take into account these broader capabilities more explicitly.

Public Funding, Markets, and Opportunities

The connection between universities and economic, social, and political opportunities provides an argument for public funding of universities. It does so for two reasons.[45] First, as noted above, higher education has private benefits for individuals, but also has benefits to society as a whole that the individual only partially enjoys. Individuals will not fully take into account these broader social benefits, which include greater productivity growth, reduced crime, lower health care costs, and enhanced democratic decision-making. They point to the need for at least a partial public subsidy of higher education, as without public funding, education will be under-provided.[46] Individuals do not base their demand on the entire benefit from higher education. Further, Arthur Ripstein argues that these broader public benefits require partial public funding of education on fairness grounds – on a fair apportionment of responsibility for the cost of providing the private and public benefits.[47]

Second, from a position of fairness, all citizens of a society should have the opportunity to take full advantage of the opportunities for private benefits to the extent of their abilities and willingness. They should not be denied these opportunities for reasons such as family background or lack of wealth. Government therefore has a role in ensuring that the institutions and funding in place do not hinder an individual from obtaining a higher education because of such reasons, although the private benefits of education imply some individual responsibility for the cost of education.[48]

While the case for some public funding is clear, there is a connection between the form of public funding and equality of opportunity that points to the need for care in designing the institutions around such funding. The form of public funding will have an impact on the course offerings at universities and therefore on the possibilities that are open to students. Further, it may affect the research that is conducted at universities in terms of both type (such as basic versus applied research) and subject matter (science and technology versus humanities).[49]

Public funding does not necessarily mean that the funds must be paid directly to universities. There has been and continues to be considerable interest in deregulating tuition and shifting funding from universities to students, as through income-contingent loan and grant programs.[50] Such an approach promotes individual choice. To the extent they are well informed, individuals can make decisions between universities and programs that reflect their information and preferences. Individuals in many cases may have the best information about important skills or knowledge that they need to succeed or live the lives they wish to lead.[51] For such choices to be effective, universities must have the capacity to adapt to differing demands. Ensuring that individuals have appropriate funding to make choices and allowing institutions to adapt to these choices promotes individual responsibility and the flexibility and diversity the system needs to adapt to changing preferences.

However, a market-based approach consisting of individual funding and choice cannot be the whole answer. First, as noted above, individuals will not take into account the broader societal benefits from their choices. The issue is easier to see in the case of harms (negative externalities) such as pollution. Suppose a company emits pollutants that harm its neighbours. If that company does not have to pay the costs of the harm (assuming they can be measured), it will face too low a cost of production and emit too much pollution. Conversely, the broader social benefits of education are positive externalities – an individual's education creates benefits for others in society that the individual does not fully take into account. To the extent that there are benefits for democracy from individuals developing an openness to other cultures or a sense of empathy, programs which develop these capacities will be under-provided in a system in which individual choices determine the exact content of university curricula.

Second, individuals may not even take full account of the private benefits of capacities related to non-economic opportunities. They may not understand these less tangible benefits or may not appreciate their value until much later in life. To the extent that students lack information or are essentially short-sighted in choosing courses and programs, they will not demand the courses that foster these broader capabilities. This point relates to more than the need for public funding. It goes to how decisions are made about what universities deliver. Even with public funding of universities to account for the public benefits from individuals undertaking higher education, individuals cannot (on their own) choose courses which provide them with benefits they do not yet understand or appreciate. University education, and in particular some programs such as the humanities, provide these broader non-economic capacities such as empathy or openness. It would be odd, and counterproductive, to base a system wholly on individual choices where the individuals do not yet have the ability to appreciate the choices. It is different for most capabilities tied to economic opportunities. We can have more confidence that individuals can appreciate the value of attaining the more tangible benefits of these capabilities than the less tangible and less easily understood capabilities related to political and social opportunities. This is not to argue students should be forced to take particular courses, but that the offering of courses, should not be tied to student choices where such choices require capabilities that are not yet developed.[52]

Markets, based on student choice, therefore may lead to under-provision of programs that foster these broader capabilities. As discussed in section 5, the public nature and benefit of these capabilities may point to different forms of government intervention such as funding made directly to universities, subsidized information programs aimed at program choice by students, or even an overall higher education policy set by government. The point here is narrower. The different nature of these capabilities means that the same institutions which foster capabilities that promote economic opportunities may not work for capabilities that promote political and social opportunities.[53] These implications must be borne in mind in designing institutions in the university sector.

Measuring the Value of Universities

A second issue connecting equality of opportunity and universities relates to measuring the value of university education. How we measure opportunity and its impacts will influence our approach to the university sector. Because of the richness and complexity of opportunities, it is impossible to reduce their examination to a single metric. For example, such measurement cannot be based solely on the impact of educational policies on GDP per capita. GDP per capita is a common economic indicator of 'standard of living.' It tends to be used because it measures the output of an economy and because it allows for 'easy benchmarking' across and within jurisdictions.[54] Further, proponents of GDP per capita argue that if a jurisdiction can increase its GDP per capita, it can increase the social, political, and economic opportunities for its citizens by increasing both the private and public resources available to open up these opportunities. However, while economic growth is clearly important in this regard, it will not necessarily have these benefits. The opportunities may not be equally distributed across society, for example, because the system does not increase private resources for some parties and public resources are not provided to these parties, such as through better health care or public education systems.

Any single metric (such as GDP per capita or even the UN Human Development Index) hides important information.[55] The key is, to the extent possible, to examine the impact of institutions on the breadth of opportunities for individuals.[56] Full analysis will require breaking down impacts across subgroups of society such as by age, gender, social and ethnic groups, and income. More work must be done on developing indicators which aid in assessing the impact of the institutional structure of the university sector on opportunities broadly conceived. The current attempts at measuring the broader social impacts of education mainly focus on the impact of secondary education and not higher education. Further, they tend to focus on correlations rather than causation between education and some indicators of broader benefits, such as voting rates or voluntarism. Finally, some attempts have been made to determine a 'social rate of return' from education, even though the impact of these broader opportunities is primarily non-economic.[57]

It will be difficult to determine appropriate measures of the impact of university education on broader, largely non-economic capabilities, although at the very least the studies of the social benefits of education could be extended to university education. They could also potentially be focused on the institutional features of the university sector, such as breadth of course offerings or types of funding. The difficulties in designing measures do not point to abandoning broad examinations and returning to narrower measures such as GDP per capita. The description or measurement of value may preference certain aspects of universities in any debate over their structure. The expansion of opportunities for all Canadians is too important to neglect important distributional and other impacts from these institutional choices.

4. Opportunities and the Design of the University Sector

Universities therefore play an important role in both providing and defining the capacities required for equality of opportunity, broadly conceived. This role raises two central points about the debate over the direction of university education. First, the language of the debate is important. The focus of debate around universities is often on 'human capital' in its more narrow economic meaning or, where public benefits are taken into account, on their impact on economic measures such as GDP per capita. Such a focus neglects important aspects of universities and university education including those relating to deliberative democracy. It frames and narrows the debate in a manner which under-mines the purpose and promise of universities.

Second, the debate over the institutional structure of the university sector must not lose sight of the impacts of the structure on the broader, less tangible political and social benefits. There is clearly a need for government funding related to these benefits, but the issue of how this funding is provided will also be important. Permitting student choices (even with public subsidies) to drive education policy is problematic if these students are essentially myopic about the value of different types of programs. Such myopia could potentially be mitigated through gov-ernment subsidizing or providing information to students on the value of different programs. However, even with information provision, there remains a concern that the greater tangibility of the benefits of pro-grams aimed at economic opportunities will lead to lower than optimal demand for programs fostering political and social opportunities.

If student choices are not the whole answer, that raises the question of who should decide on whether and to what extent programs such as the humanities exist. Governments may be able to take account of broader societal benefits in a deliberative fashion, but they face serious informa-tion problems. Moreover, they themselves have been criticized for dis-torting university teaching and research through favouring the 'new economy' agenda.[58] University governance bodies, where broadly based, may have greater ability than governments to respond to student de-mands. Further, permitting universities to make such decisions allows space for diversity across the sector.[59] However, university governance bodies face their own set of incentives and may not fully take account of the benefits to society generally of the programs they offer. Such con-cerns about both government and universities may or may not be solved by an independent intermediary body providing advice or other functions related to university programs. The point is not to decide this issue of the appropriate structure, but merely to point out that whatever institutional structure is chosen will have implications for how and to what extent different programs are offered. Any discussion over the structure therefore cannot lose sight of its impact on the less tangible but nonetheless essential broader benefits of universities.

It is particularly vital in an increasingly diverse and globally inte-grated country like Canada to use the university sector to promote opportunity for all citizens. By providing a broader range of capacities, universities can improve deliberative democracy. Enhanced delibera-tion will be essential as Canadians attempt to address a range of contentious issues nationally, such as what to do about individuals who are left behind by the drive for a 'human capital' society. It will also be essential for Canadians as they attempt to participate in an increasingly wide range of international decision-making institutions. Further, these broader capacities will aid individuals in leading fuller lives and taking advantage of the social opportunities available in Canadian society. Incidentally, they will also aid in enhancing both private and public economic opportunities.

Notes

* Assistant Professor, Faculty of Law, University of Toronto. I would like to thank Michael Trebilcock, David Dyzenhaus, David Green, Arthur Ripstein, Ed Iacobucci, and Lorne Sossin for discussions about issues and comments on earlier drafts of this paper.

1 See T. Courchene, *A State of Minds* (Montreal: Institute for Research in Public Policy, 2001) and C. Riddell, 'The Role of Government in Post-Secondary Education in Ontario' (Research paper no. 29, Ontario Panel on the Role of Government, 2003), discussing the many potential benefits of a focus on human capital.

2 J. Chant, Comments on *Higher Education in Canada* (John Deutsch Institute conference, Queen's University, 2004) and D. Laidler, 'Incentives Facing Canadian Universities: Some Possible Consequences' (ibid.).

3 A. Sen, *Development as Freedom* (New York: Anchor Books, 1999).

4 This section is based on R. Dworkin, *Sovereign Virtue: The Theory and Practice of Equality* (Cambridge, MA: Harvard University Press, 2000).

5 In Ontario, for example, 26.8% of the population was foreign born in 2001 with 17.8% immigrating before 1991 and 9.1% between 1991 and 2001. In Toronto, the percentages of recent immigrants were even higher, with 43.7% of the population being foreign born (26.6% immigrating before 1991 and 17% between 1991 and 2001) (Statistics Canada, *2001 Census*, available at www.statscan.ca). D. Foote, 'Demographic Change and Public Policy in Ontario' (Research paper no. 3, Ontario Panel on the Role of Government, 2002) notes that post-war annual immigration was at a high in 1957 at 282,000 and dropped to a low of 72,000 four years later, but has exceeded 200,000 for most of the 1990s.

6 J. Maxwell, 'The Great Social Transformation: Implications for the Role of Government in Ontario' (Research paper no. 5, Ontario Panel on the Role of Government, 2002) notes about 15% of families are led by a lone parent (generally a woman), up from 9% in 1971. Further, in 1951 32% of families had two income earners; in 1999 it was 64%.

7 According to the census (2001), the average income of individuals in

Ontario employed full-year and full-time increased by 7.8% between 1990 and 2000. However, see E. Saez and M. Veall, 'The Evolution of High Incomes in Canada: 1920 to 2000' (Manuscript, December 2002) (finding that, as in the US, the income shares of the top 5% of income earners in Canada, and particularly the top 1%, fell in the immediate post-war period, but have increased dramatically since the 1970s to return to pre-war levels, to an income share of almost 30%) and M. Frenette, D. Green, and G. Picot, 'Rising Income Inequality in the 1990s: An Exploration of Three Data Sources,' in D. Green and J. Kesselman, eds, *Dimensions of Inequality in Canada* (Vancouver: UBC Press, forthcoming).

8 Dworkin (2000).

9 Hayek argued that a key problem in determining social rules is that knowledge of circumstances is not and cannot be known to one person or planner but instead is dispersed across all individuals. Hayek concludes that the market (and the price system) is much better than government in utilizing such information. (F. Hayek, 'The Use of Knowledge in Society,' *American Economic Review* 35 [1945], 519). Such dispersed knowledge and information on individuals' preferences is key to understanding the difficulty in equalizing happiness or some other version of individual welfare. However, as will be discussed below, determining the role of government in promoting equal opportunity will require examining the relative advantages and disadvantages of a range of institutions including markets, governments, courts, and communities. In certain circumstances, markets have failures or limitations that may make government action preferable.

10 John Rawls, 'Commonweal Interview with John Rawls,' in S. Freeman, ed., *John Rawls: Collected Papers* (Cambridge, MA: Harvard University Press, 1999).

11 Sen (1999) (arguing that freedom should be the goal of society and that freedom also has both a process and an opportunity aspect). See also Arthur Ripstien, 'Public and Private Benefit in Higher Education' in this volume for a discussion of distributive justice.

12 This view of the process aspect of opportunity stems from Isaiah Berlin's famous *Two Concepts of Liberty* (Clarendon Press, 1962) in which Berlin distinguishes between two types of freedom: positive and negative. It also accords with the libertarian view put forward by Robert Nozick in *Anarchy, State and Utopia* (New York: Basic Books, 1974).

13 J. Rawls, 'The Idea of Overlapping Consensus,' in S. Freeman, ed., *John Rawls: Collected Papers* (Cambridge, MA: Harvard University Press, 1999 [henceforth 1999a]).

14 Sen (1999).

15 A. Sen, *Rationality and Freedom* (Cambridge, MA: Harvard University Press, 2002), 10.

16 A. Sweetman, 'Working Smarter: Education and Productivity,' in A. Sharpe, F. St-Hilaire, and K. Banting, eds, *The Review of Economic Performance and Social Progress (2002): Towards a Social Understanding of Productivity* (Montreal: Institute for Research on Public Policy, 2002).

17 Riddell (2003).

18 M. Skolnik, 'Does Structure Matter? (Where) Do Questions about Structure Fit on the Higher Education Policy Agenda' (Higher Education in Canada conference, 2004) (discussing an increased emphasis on the economic contribution of universities).

19 J. Heckman, 'Policies to Foster Human Capital' (Paper for the Aaron Wildavsky Forum, Richard and Rhonda Goldman School of Public Policy, University of California at Berkley, 2000).

20 For example, see Riddell (2003) (noting that the returns vary, but on average the real rate of return from the impact of higher education on earnings has been about 7 to 10% over the past decade).

21 Riddell (2003).

22 Chant (2004) and Laidler (2004).

23 Adam Smith, *The Theory of Moral Sentiments* (New Rochelle, NY: Arlington House, 1969) and Martha Nussbaum, 'Education for Citizenship in an Era of Global Connection,' *Studies in Philosophy and Education* 21 (2002) 289.

24 See, for example, Courchene (2001).

25 See M. Trebilcock, R. Daniels, A. Green, and R. Hrab, *Creating a Human Capital Society for Ontario* (Staff report, Ontario Panel on the Role of Government, 2004) (arguing for a broad definition of human capital, including both economic and social aspects).

26 K. Banting, 'Responding to Social Risk in Ontario: Are We There Yet?' (Research paper no. 31, Ontario Panel on the Role of Government, 2003).

27 Riddell (2003).

28 Banting (2003).

29 P. Beaudry and D. Green, 'Wages and Employment in the U.S. and Germany: What Explains the Difference?' *American Economic Review* 93:3 (2003), 573.

30 A. Green, 'The Evolution of the State as Risk Manager in Canada' (Research paper no. 4, Ontario Panel on the Role of Government, 2002).

31 Sen (1999), 283 and Dworkin (2000).

32 Smith (1969), 3–4.

33 In *The Wealth of Nations* (New York: The Modern Library, 1937), Smith stated: 'The man whose life is spent in performing a few simple operations ... has no occasion to exert his understanding, or to exercise his invention in finding out expedients for removing difficulties which never occur. He naturally loses, therefore, the habit of such exertion, and generally becomes as stupid and ignorant as it is possible for a human creature to become. The torpor of his mind renders him, not only incapable of relish-

ing or bearing a part in any rational conversation, but of conceiving any generous, noble, or tender sentiment, and consequently of forming any just judgement concerning many even of the ordinary duties of private life. Of the great and extensive interests of his country he is altogether incapable of judging.' (734–5). He then connects the development of these broader capacities to general education. D. Green and J. Kesselman, 'Overview and Summary of the Volume,' in Green and Kesselman, *Dimensions of Inequality in Canada*.

34 Nussbaum (2002).
35 J. Heath, *The Efficient Society: Why Canada Is as Close to Utopia as It Gets* (Penguin: Toronto, 2001).
36 Dworkin (2000); C. Sunstein, *After the Rights Revolution* (Cambridge: Harvard University Press, 1990).
37 Nussbaum (2002), 295.
38 Rawls (1999a) and Sen (1999).
39 Nussbaum (2002).
40 Nussbaum (2002), 299.
41 Riddell (2003).
42 Nussbaum (2002), 293.
43 Sen (1999) (arguing for five types of opportunities or freedoms, although the three discussed in this paper – economic, political, and social opportunities – are taken to include all five of Sen's areas).
44 See, generally, K. Banting, A. Sharpe, and F. St-Hilaire, 'Towards a Social Understanding of Productivity: An Introduction and Overview,' in Sharpe, St-Hilaire and Banting, eds, *The Review of Economic Performance and Social Progress (2002): Towards a Social Understanding of Productivity* (Montreal: Institute for Research on Public Policy, 2002).
45 However, the scope of the opportunities from education in all its forms should give rise to caution about claims about the relative importance of public investment in the university sector. As noted above, the benefits from universal early childhood education and primary and secondary school may be greater than that from university education. Heckman (2000).
46 Trebilcock, Daniels, Green, and Hrab (2004) and Riddell (2003).
47 Ripstein (2004) (discussing how distributive justice points to both public and private funding of higher education).
48 Ripstein (2004) and Trebilcock, Daniels, Green, and Hrab (2004).
49 Laidler (2004).
50 R. Daniels and M. Trebilcock, 'Towards a New Compact in University Education in Ontario' in this volume and Trebilcock, Daniels, Green, and Hrab (2004).
51 N. Barr, *The Economics of the Welfare State*, 4th ed. (Oxford: Oxford University Press, 2004) and N. Barr, 'Higher Education Funding,' *Oxford Review of*

Economic Policy 20:2 (2004 [henceforth 2004a]), 264 (discussing the importance of well-informed choice to the efficiency case for variable fees and
student choice).

52 Martha Nussbaum, 'Capabilities as Fundamental Entitlements: Sen and
Social Justice' (forthcoming, *Feminist Economics*) argues that in order to
respect pluralism, the focus of society should be on capabilities (what
individuals are actually able to be or do) not functionings (that is, ensuring everyone takes up a specific capability), since requiring individuals to
have a specific functioning (rather than the opportunity to achieve that
functioning) neglects or overrides personal choice.

53 Note that this is a different point than saying that student markets are
completely irrelevant to these programs. It may still be the case that
student choice and demand for particular programs provide some in
formation about the quality of the program – the number and quality of
students attempting to get into a particular philosophy department provides information about the quality of that program relative to philosophy
departments in other universities. A. Green and E. Iacobucci, 'Public
Funding, Markets, and Quality: Assessing the Role of Market-Based
Performance Funding for Universities' in this volume. See also Barr
(2004a) (arguing that while some subjects, such as accounting, law, and
economics, may not need added help, others such as classics may need
specifically targeted resources).

54 Institute for Competitiveness and Prosperity, 'Measuring Ontario's Prosperity: Developing an Economic Indicator System' (Working paper no. 2,
Ontario Institute for Competitiveness and Prosperity, 2002), 13.

55 The UN Human Development Index ranks performance of countries
based on three goals or ends: longevity (measured by life expectancy at
birth), knowledge (measured by adult literacy and educational achievement), and standard of living (measured by real per-capita income).
Although better than merely examining GDP per capita, it has been
criticized because of its narrow focus and complex weighting system.
See, for example, L. Osberg, 'Needs and Wants: What Is Social Progress
and How Should It Be Measured?' in K. Banting, A. Sharpe, and F. Hilaire,
eds, *The Review of Economic Performance and Social Progress: The Longest
Decade: Canada in the 1990s* (Montreal: Institute for Research on Public
Policy, 2001).

56 Sen (1999).

57 Riddell (2003) (discussing attempts to measure the social benefits of
university education).

58 Chant (2004) and Laidler (2004). See also Daniels and Trebilcock in this
volume discussing the issue of micromanagement.

59 Daniels and Trebilcock in this volume.

PART III

Responding to the Challenges: Performance-Based Government Operating and Capital Support

The Unbearable Lightness of Being: Universities as Performers

JANICE GROSS STEIN*

It is no accident that as soon as we begin to talk about public reinvestment in higher education, we move quickly to a parallel discussion of accountability and performance measures. The political bargain is clear: in return for the investment of public funds, governments acting on behalf of the public demand 'results' from their partner institutions. The conversation has moved beyond 'transparency' about the *way* public money is spent to a discussion of *what* public money is buying. We are now in the Auditor General's world of 'value for money.' Is the public getting 'value' for the 'money' it is spending on higher education?

In this paper, I make the following assumptions and arguments:

- Neither governments nor auditors can determine whether universities are providing 'value for money.' It is a serious mistake to try, and universities will come to grief as have other public institutions if we try seriously. We should resist this particular conversation strenuously.
- Public evaluation of performance is here to stay. It is embedded in the political vocabulary.
- Evaluation of our performance is important to the academic community. If it is done well, it can stimulate self-reflection, learning, and improvement.
- Which measures we choose matters. We need to understand the limits of performance measures as measures and their power as incentives to drive strategic behaviour.

This line of reasoning leads to three broad guidelines to the construction of performance measures for higher education. We need to choose the 'lightest' possible basket of measures which

- minimizes the incentives to reduce the quality of educational programs;
- increases the opportunities for universities to gather valuable information about their performance at reasonable cost and to learn so they can improve their performance; and
- rewards experimentation and innovation.

1. Procedural and Substantive Accountability

Performance measures are the tangible manifestation of the far more complex concept of accountability. Indeed, we cannot understand performance measures without embedding them in the larger context of accountability. At the core of accountability is the demand by one who is entitled to do so for an 'account' from another. Accountability presumes a relationship of entitlement, information, and the power to sanction those who provide the information. The essence of accountability is that the initiative is held by the questioners, who have the power to punish if they are dissatisfied with the answers.

We can think about accountability in public institutions in two ways. There is accountability about rules and procedures – the way I do things – and accountability about substance – what I do. Procedural accountability is fairly easy. Over time we have agreed more or less on a set of procedures in public life, on fair rules, which constitute reasonable due process. When leaders break these rules, when they violate conflict-of-interest guidelines, when they give contracts to their friends outside of normal channels, when they fail to follow appropriate procedures, when they profit privately from public money, they can be held accountable and sanctioned.

It is entirely legitimate that governments demand that universities be accountable for their procedures. It is also legitimate for the auditor to audit the procedures that universities use to disburse public funds. Undoubtedly, the auditor will find some procedural violations and the universities will quickly fix these violations. Procedural accountability is a 'no-brainer.'

Substantive accountability is far more challenging. The issue is not 'How have I done it?' but 'What have I accomplished?' What 'results' have I delivered? It is here that we begin the slide down the treacherous slope of 'value for money.' The pitfalls along the way are many. The fundamental trap is, I think, obvious: we are asked to quantify and monetize the value of a university education that students receive, of the research that we do, and of the public education that we provide. In anything but a trivial sense, this is not only a technically impossible series of tasks, it is seriously wrong-headed.

How does substantive accountability work now, at least in theory? In public institutions, we report, or give an account of what we have done, to a superior. In hierarchical organizations, with clearly drawn reporting lines neatly represented in an organizational chart, and clear command and control structures, accountability seems fairly obvious. These neat diagrams, however, often hide very large contradictions that usually escape our notice. At the core of accountability are five questions.

The first, often surprisingly difficult question is – who is accountable and to whom? In my university, the lines of accountability seem to be quite clear. I report annually to the chair of my department, who in turn reports to the dean, who reports to the chief academic officer, who reports to the president, who reports to the Board of Governors. Accountability seems to flow neatly upward on the organizational chart. If we looked only at the formal procedures, however, we would miss most of what is happening.

The chart tells me that I am accountable to my chair, but I feel that I am – and indeed I am – also accountable to the students that I teach and work with every year. Two problems immediately become obvious. First, I am simultaneously accountable to at least two groups – my students and the university administration through my chair – that at times may have compatible expectations but, at times, may differ in what they expect. And second, although my students evaluate my teaching and forward the information annually to the chair of my department, they have at best only very limited capacity to punish me for what they may consider my poor performance. When a student once told me that he deserved a medal for staying awake through my course, I could only commend him for his perseverance.

It gets worse. I also feel accountable to my colleagues for the work that I do in my department, and to a wide network of scholars in other universities and research institutes who work in the same field for the quality of the research that I do. Finally, I work in a university which receives significant public funding, so I feel that I am accountable to the public for what I do. I have multiple accountabilities – to institutions, to networks, to peers, and to my students – with very different expectations and standards. These do not always sit comfortably together. When they do not, to whom do I give priority? The language of accountability, the rendering of accounts, will not help me very much here. Nor does a discussion about 'value for money' that reduces a complex problem to a single dimension of measurement.

I have to look outside the formal structure for help in solving that problem of competing obligations. The danger here is obvious: to resolve the problem of multiple and at times competing accountabilities, I will look to measures of performance to provide guidance about what really matters. In short, in a context of multiple accountabilities, performance measures act as silent incentives for some kinds of behaviour rather than others.

The next two questions – for what am I accountable and by what standards? – are even more difficult. The 'what' of accountability focuses on results. Am I succeeding in what I hope to accomplish? Am I meeting the standards? Another way of putting these questions is to ask what 'numbers' do I provide to 'measure' my 'success'? Do I report on the number of published articles, or on their quality? Who judges quality and how? Do I report on whether I encouraged someone to think more deeply about some piece of conventional wisdom? If I spend two years writing a book, and publish nothing else while I am doing so, am I 'unproductive?' Would one 'good' book be the equivalent of two, three, five shorter publications? How do I know whether what I write 'matters'? Peer review by my colleagues helps to answer these questions, but not completely. The opinions of my peers often range quite widely and review processes push to compromise, often leaching out the sharp edges of arguments. Often, after an elaborate process of peer review and revision, no one is satisfied.

The problem becomes even more complicated when we turn to my students. They evaluate my teaching every year, but are their opinions decisive? Is it my 'job' to please my students, or to push them, to make them so uncomfortable that they begin to challenge, to create uncertainty so that they begin to wrestle with difficult questions? Do I spend more time teaching my students what we do know, or what we don't know? And how do I report on whether my students are more uncertain, more open, more critical, more independent-minded, and more troubled and troublesome at the end of the year than they were at the beginning? Is the opinion of every student of equal weight? What I am accountable for is often a subject of deep controversy, a controversy that engages important values, different visions, and quite a broad spectrum of possible 'results.'

Finally, how am I sanctioned for poor performance? My students can do so only very indirectly, by reporting my failures to my chair. My colleagues can comment on the poor quality of my research and my failure to advance knowledge. My performance is reviewed annually and I can be deprived of promotion or of a modest increase in salary as a signal of displeasure. But the university, like other institutions in public life, has quite deliberately built in protection against summary dismissal, to protect members of faculty who have passed the tests of tenure against those who would sanction them for what they say. Universities did so to provide safe space for dissent and criticism, for unpopular challenges to conventional wisdom. They long ago made a choice to give highest priority to the free and safe exchange of ideas, even at the sacrifice of some accountability. That choice invokes larger public values and a commitment to a public good.

This kind of choice is not unique to universities. Constitutional systems often create institutions that are deliberately not held accountable.[1] The Supreme Courts in the United States and in Canada, when they interpret the constitution and rule legislation unconstitutional, are not acting as agents of the public. The public cannot hold judges accountable in the usual ways by measuring their performance. How, in any event, would they conceivably do so? These two courts are acting as trustees of the public good, free to make decisions which may be widely unpopular, at least for a time.

Much of the discussion of accountability uses the convenient fiction of the individual in order to grapple with these issues. It is far easier to think about procedural and substantive accountability when we think about individuals. Who gave the order? Who broke the rule? Who got poor results? In my office at the university, when I ask 'How could this have happened?' I intuitively think someone who must have been the weak link in a high-performing chain. But most decisions in public institutions and their results are the result of chains of collective action. When we look at substance – whether it is the improvement of security or the creation of new knowledge – it is collaborative and collective action, flowing through complex causal chains, that produces or fails to produce results. Individual accountability, conclude two seasoned observers of public institutions, is nothing more than a useful myth to affirm control and to motivate people to do their best.[2]

2. The Costs of Accountability and Performance Measures

The language of accountability, so pervasive now in our societies, does not take us far enough. It does not because of the difficulties in holding collectivities rather than individuals to account. It does not because so much of what matters to us is difficult to measure, to translate into the numbers that a culture of accountants, comptrollers, regulators, and auditors require. I had an astonishing conversation recently with a public auditor who was preparing to audit the Department of Foreign Affairs in Canada. He wanted to know whether the fact that the government had appeared to change its policy about the war in Iraq bespoke a lack of accountability. Were we, he asked me, getting 'value for money' from the Department of Foreign Affairs? He could not understand why I was utterly confounded by the question. This is the kind of risk we run when we monetize our public culture.

Accountability favours measurable and comparable accounts – numbers that we can add and subtract. We only see what we measure and miss what we don't, and much of what is important in public institutions cannot be measured and compared. A focus on accounting, on the ledger, channels our public conversation into the concrete, the tangible, and leaves little room for the intangible, for what we cannot measure. Taken to extremes, a culture of accountability transforms the conversation about the public good into a discussion of the public's business. It impoverishes our conversation, not only about our universities but about all our public institutions.

That is not the only cost of accountability. Accountability has been most successful when it focuses on procedure, on the rules, and on those who break them. The scandals that have riveted public attention in the last few years have all focused on those who break the law – in corporations, in government, in the civil service, in the voluntary sector. With each wave of scandals, governments and regulators enact a new set of rules, designed to close the loopholes that allowed the violations to happen. Some of these rules are wise and necessary – the restrictions on conflict of interest, peer review of candidates for senior appointments, legislation to protect whistle-blowers. Many of the rules, however, only add to the cumbersome burden of regulation, and stifle initiative and creativity.

The same kind of problem exists in universities. Universities in Britain spent vast amounts of time, energy, and money collecting the data that were needed for agreed-upon performance measures. Measuring and reporting consumed an ever-increasing amount of resources. Universities raided each other's faculty before every review to increase their own research profile with 'productive' faculty members. An examination of the report by the British Auditor General and Comptroller as early as 1994 tells the tale of what was to unfold. 'On the basis of financial criteria alone,' the Auditor General wrote, 'an institution can be judged as healthy but may be engaged in activities which are not viable and which can eventually impact on overall health, for example, *courses which do not attract sufficient students, research work which fails to attract financial support,* and an infrastructure which is inefficient or under invested.'[3] The language, I think, speaks for itself. To compensate for the monetization of measures, the Funding Council reviews the quality of higher education, but virtually all the subjects reviewed were rated as satisfactory or better. Despite the obligatory rhetoric about quality, the yardstick for measurement was clear.

One unexpected result was the creation of a market for highly visible faculty within the British university system and a sharp increase in salaries for the select few. The other – expected – consequence was that university leaders became even less willing to take risks, to innovate, to create, and to experiment. They focused their attention on improving their relative standing on agreed-upon measures and diverted resources from other sectors of the university so they would 'rank' higher. Their behaviour is not unlike that of our own universities when it comes to the annual rankings in *Maclean's* magazine. Teachers almost always teach the test when the test results of their students are made public. In other words, we 'game' the system and performance measures become the game.

The encouragement of innovation and creativity in research is one of the most important – and neglected – challenges in public universities. Leaders of the Howard Hughes Medical Institute recently built a new laboratory, the Janelia Farm Research Campus, explicitly designed to enable scientific creativity. Its operations are modelled on two research centres with outstanding records of scientific discovery – Bell Labs and the Laboratory of Molecular Biology, funded by the Medical Research Council of Britain. The formula at the new lab, explained Dr Gerald M. Rubin, vice-president of the Hughes Institute, is designed to free the scientists to do their work without constant accounting for results. Scientists work in small groups, led by people who do hands-on research. They receive ample financial and technical support, so that they are freed from the constant distraction of grant-writing and grant-management. The only directive is that people work on an interesting problem, however long it might take. This model is completely *inconsis-*

tent with any set of measures used to measure performance in universities on an annual basis. Why would Hughes create and support this kind of laboratory?

Funding agencies, leaders at Hughes explained, demand safe research and predictable results. A demanding system of peer review screens out high levels of risk and 'mainstreams' most research projects. The Hughes Institute encourages young scientists to commit to long-term research projects, to projects that may be high-risk, or to projects that are unlikely to be supported by granting agencies. The vision at Janelia Farm – long-term goals, research that makes a critical difference, no pressure to generate practical results, no annual performance review, no grant-writing, no administration, and genuine multidisciplinary work – is very different from established university practice. More to the point, it self-consciously acknowledges that some of its bets on young scholars will fail, but accepts these carefully thought through failures as the cost of innovation. It frees scientists to do their work, recognizing the serious costs of constant reviewing and measuring to innovation, experimentation, and risk-taking.[4]

This kind of model is not a substitute for established structures of research and teaching in public universities. Indeed, Gerald Rubin explicitly insists on the complementarity between the two kinds of structures. Nevertheless, universities need to make much greater space for long-term experimentation, and to think seriously about performance measures which encourage and reward risk-taking in research and teaching. This may mean moving beyond established standards of peer review and citations in 'high-impact' journals, which often serve as gatekeepers of conventional wisdom.

This overview of performance measures focuses explicitly on their costs and identifies several that merit serious consideration. Perverse strategic behaviour and the expenditure of large amounts of scarce resources – time, energy and money – on data collection and manipulation are two of the most obvious. Performance measures tend to stifle innovation and risk-taking, as they channel activity into improving performance on agreed-upon standards.

Performance measures also tend to focus on the tangible and the quantifiable, in part because quality is so difficult to measure in so many areas. The University of Toronto, for example, publishes an annual report on its performance.[5] It uses measures such as student retention and degree completion, class size, research council funding, research yields, and research revenue, all quantitative measures of performance.

Only faculty honours and citation counts try to get at the quality of research, and citation counts raise some special issues, principally in the social sciences and humanities, but even in the sciences. This reliance on quantitative measures drives the university system in perverse ways. 'Once a phenomenon has been converted into a quantitative measure,' argues Deborah Stone, 'it can be added, multiplied, divided, or subtracted, even though these operations have no meaning in reality. Numbers provide the comforting illusion that incommensurables can be weighed against each other, because arithmetic always "works" ... Numbers force a common denominator where there is none.'[6] Stone is right.

Any analysis of performance measures needs to concentrate not only on what is measured and how it is measured, but also on the incentives these measures create within the university system and on the opportunities they provide for institutions to learn about quality.

3. Measuring Performance: The OECD Experience

How do other societies fund their universities as performers? The closest comparators are likely within the OECD countries. Most fund universities through a combination of input factors – or resources universities use – and outputs – teaching and research. Typically these outputs are measured quantitatively: the number of credits that students accumulate, the number of students that receive degrees, the number of research publications, and the number of patents and licences researchers receive. In addition, some governments include measures of the relative success of graduates on the labour market, the number of graduates working in jobs related to their training, and the success of universities in attracting outside funding.[7]

Three problems are immediately obvious. The first is the relative inattention to quality, largely because of the inherent difficulties in measuring quality across different domains. Consequently, as Jongbloed and Vossensteyn observe, 'Every output indicator ... will have its shortcomings. The main reason for this is that the services of a university are not sold in a kind of market where supply is meeting demand and prices reflect costs, quality, and scarcity.'[8]

Second, some of the performance measures clearly reflect the political agendas of funding governments. This should come as no surprise. Measures of effectiveness – the political terrain on which the battles of accountability are fought – are constructed in society. Although the polemics revolve around measures, that is often not what the debates are about. Hidden beneath the polemics are arguments about goals and values, where measures serve as surrogates. The fundamental issues of any conflict over policy come alive in how we choose to count the dimensions of the problem. The choice of measures becomes deeply political, reflecting these often hidden differences.

Finally, it is obvious how universities can treat these measures as incentives when their funding is conditional on their performance. Universities may accelerate their students' progress by lowering standards, they may encourage their faculty to publish quantities of research rather than focus on quality, and they may skew their teaching programs to align closely with current employment opportunities. Any of these would be a serious mistake which could undermine the capacity of the university to deliver a 'high quality performance' over the longer term.

How significant is performance-based funding as a component of general funding of universities within the OECD? Less than one might think. In eleven of the OECD countries, teaching and research budgets are 'lumped' together and universities are free to use the funding in any way they see fit. In Germany, for example, the total funds allocated are based principally on last year's budget, with appropriate adjustments for price changes and policy adjustments.[9] Only in Belgium, New Zealand, and the United Kingdom is research funded on the basis of a formula which incorporates some performance measures.

In Belgium and New Zealand, funding is driven largely by student numbers or the number of graduates. Only in the UK does research funding depend significantly on measures that tries to build in some qualitative amidst the largely quantitative indicators. The funding councils rate departments on their quality once every four to five years, using peer reviews. Those who are ranked highest receive approximately four times as much funding for research infrastructure as do those in the middle, while those at the bottom receive no funding at all. Surprisingly, once universities receive the funds, they are free to allocate the funds across departments in any way they wish. Recently, the UK has begun to try to reduce the burden of data collection and analysis that the Research Assessment Exercise requires.

A review of the funding of higher education among OECD countries finds that the role of output measures in funding decisions is relatively small. 'With a few exceptions,' Jongbloed and Vossensteyn observe, 'one cannot speak of a high degree of performance orientation' in the OECD countries.[10] Performance measures are more important as learning tools for universities and for students than they are as mechanisms of accountability. That is probably as it should be.

4. Constructing Performance Measures

We need to be measured in our use of performance measures, mindful of their capacity to drive behaviour as well as their capacity to assess achievement. We need to understand as well that performance measures tend to focus on quantity, at the expense of the much more difficult challenge of quality.

First, we must minimize the incentives of a set of performance measures to reduce the quality of research and teaching in order to increase quantity. When we count the number of students that we graduate, for example, we must also examine student-staff ratios and the size of classes, and ask students to evaluate the quality of their experience. Are students able to meet with faculty during a semester, are they given opportunities to participate in research? Taken together, a composite of these measures is more likely to reflect how well a university is meeting its obligations to its students.

Graduate students cross the boundary between teaching and research and blur the two in helpful ways. When we recruit graduate students, are we getting our first choices? Where do our graduates go when they leave us? Do they go to other excellent universities, to leadership positions in the private or voluntary sector, or into the public sector? Do they work mainly in Canada or internationally? What have our graduates accomplished ten years after they leave us? We need to ask them whether they feel they were given the highest-quality education to prepare them for the careers they have followed.

When we count the research dollars a university receives, and add up the number of faculty publications and honours, we also need to ask faculty whether they feel they have adequate time to do research. Are younger faculty members mentored by more senior faculty? Do they get helpful advice and support? Is the research infrastructure adequate? Citation counts are helpful in assessing quality, but they can be misleading as well. Studies often cite other studies that support their research findings, or attack a line of investigation that is critical. We need to explore reputational effects: where do other excellent universities send their students to do graduate work? Who is doing innovative and exciting work in this field and where are they? When we are recruiting faculty, are we getting our first choice most of the time, some of the time, or rarely? Why? How are we different from other departments working in the same field? These kinds of questions are likely to turn up answers that can be helpful to departments as they evaluate their record and seek to improve their performance. They are, in other words, useful learning tools.

Performance measures, if they are to be useful in encouraging change, need to be dynamic rather than static. They need to help us understand processes rather than take snapshots at a given moment in time. We need to ask faculty members who is doing innovative and experimental work in their field. Where are new approaches and discoveries likely to come from? What have we tried in the last five years that has succeeded? What have we tried that has failed? Answering that second question is just as important as answering the first. *If we cannot identify any failures, it is very unlikely that we have a culture of risk-taking at all.* What programs have we closed to make room for innovative, high-risk, ambitious research?

For performance measures to be valuable to universities and to those they serve, they must sit lightly. Collection and analysis of data can consume millions of scarce dollars and even scarcer faculty time and energy. The Research Assessment Exercise in Britain, which is widely regarded as onerous, takes place once every five years for research units and departments. Therein, I suspect, lay an important message. Annual performance measures do not tell us much; the variation can be the product of small shifts that are not terribly meaningful. We need to lengthen the time horizon of evaluation, and look for improvement that is built over several years. Short time horizons work against innovation and risk-taking, and in favour of continuing to do what we are already doing.

Designing performance measures that focus on quality requires careful and deliberate staging over time, so that the building blocks are put in place one after another without skewing the system of higher education. The measures must include subjective as well as objective indicators if we are to capture quality. They must explicitly build in indicators that help universities to learn and to improve. They must have long enough time lines so that risk-taking and intelligent failures can be recognized.

Above all, we must avoid the trap of monetizing the value of a university education. No auditor-general can reach a judgment about whether universities are providing 'value for money.' In the choice of a light basket of measures, phased in over time, we can help to inform the judgment of whether we are doing the very best that we are capable of doing. Which measures we put into the basket of accountability will shape the system of higher education over the next several decades. Measures and numbers are contested because they are surrogates for political conflict over values. Our world, G.K. Chesteron wrote a century ago, 'looks a little more mathematical and regular than it is; its exactitude is obvious, but its inexactitude is hidden; its wildness lies in wait.'[11] As we construct a more demanding architecture of accountability, we need to understand clearly why we are counting what we are counting, who chooses the measures and how they are chosen, how the measurers and the measures are politically connected, and what incentives these measures will create.

Notes

* Belzberg Professor of Conflict Management and Director, Munk Centre for International Studies, University of Toronto.
1 Robert Keohane, 'Political Accountability,' paper prepared for Conference on Delegation to International Organizations, 8.
2 James G. March and Johan Olsen, *Democratic Governance* (New York: Free Press, 1995), 157–8, 161.
3 Report by the Comptroller and Auditor General, *The Financial Health of Higher Education Institutions in England* (London: House of Commons, 1994).
4 See Nicholas Wade, 'New Hughes Haven for Science Reaches for the Stars,' *New York Times*, 19 October 2004, D2.
5 University of Toronto, Office of the Vice-President and Provost, *Performance Indicators for Governance*, Annual Report, September 2004.
6 Deborah Stone, *Policy Paradox and Political Reason* (New York: Harper-Collins, 1988), 136.
7 Ben Jongbloed and Hans Vossensteyn, 'Keeping Up Performances: An International Survey of Performance-Based Funding in Higher Education.' *Journal of Higher Education Policy and Management* 23:2 (2001), 127–45.
8 Ibid., 129.
9 Ibid., 132.
10 Ibid., 135.
11 G.K. Chesterton, *Orthodoxy* (New York: Dodd, Mead, 1908; repub. Image Books, Doubleday, 1990), 81.

The Political Economy of Performance Funding

DANIEL W. LANG*

It has now been more than a decade and a half since Guy Neave introduced the phrase 'the Evaluative State' (Neave 1988). At that time Neave was reflecting on a variety of practices and policies that had been installed to assist universities and, more often, the states that supported them, to cut the higher educational suit to fit the public-purse cloth by quantitative measurement. Also, at that time most of the measures, although flawed, were accepted as temporary but necessary rough justice.

A decade later Einhard Rau presented a small but important paper that asked, 'Performance Funding in Higher Education: Everybody seems to love it but does anybody really know what it is?' (Rau 1999). The title of Rau's paper was telling. By the turn of the century, practices that previously had been tolerated on an assumption that they were ephemeral and would go away, were not only still in use but were also more popular, at least among governments and other agencies that provided financial subsidies to higher education. Moreover, and perhaps more importantly, Rau's research indicated that despite a decade of experience, mainly of the trial-and-error variety, performance funding was poorly understood and, in the views of many, still seriously flawed.

Even the language of performance funding is problematic. Performance funding, performance indicators, accountability, Total Quality Management, benchmarking, best practice, incentive funding, performance budgeting, performance reporting, performance agreements – they all seem at once to be different and the same. In addition to not knowing exactly what performance funding is, we are not certain that it works or, if it does, why.

An Illustrative Anecdote

The purpose of these introductory comments is to locate performance funding in a larger context of the structure and purpose of public higher education. Performance funding is not a new idea, except perhaps in terminology. One could argue that it is typical of any principal–agent relationship that surrounds a production function for which there is a public subsidy. One could further observe that what is labelled 'performance funding' at the beginning of the twenty-first century is not substantially different from enrolment-sensitive funding formulas that were first devised at the beginning of the twentieth century, or the PPBS and zero-based budgeting schemes that were introduced in the 1950s (Serban 1998).

Let us take recent events in the Province of Ontario as an introductory example. The province has a system of 'key performance indicators' that are used to allocate less than 2% of the operating funding available to the province's colleges and universities. What now is in place in Ontario may not really be either performance indicators or performance funding. The emphasis here is on the word *performance*. To understand this we have to return to some of the broad economic ideology that a *conservative* government brought to the public sector when it took office in 1995, much of which a *liberal* government that followed has left in place.

The fundamental spending question for any government, indeed for any public institutions like universities, is 'How much is enough?' This question becomes more essential and more difficult as the availability of public funding becomes more constrained. Although there are many opinions about why funding is constrained and whether or not it ought to be, the reasons are unimportant here. The point is that as long as funding is limited, decisions have to be made about when, in the case of post-secondary education, enough capacity, or enough quality, or enough breadth, or enough distribution has been funded. Scale, breadth, quality, and distribution, when added to efficiency, constitute the basic factors in the political economy of a system of higher education. When resources are limited, how can an efficient balance be struck among those factors?

In the private, for-profit sector, this question usually is answered by signals from a market. As Simon Marginson has demonstrated, there can be markets within a public sector too (Marginson 1997). But for most public universities, there is, at most, a quasi-market, and usually less than that. For universities, like most public institutions, the majority of funding usually comes from sources other than those persons who actually receive the goods or services that the institutions provide. As high as university tuition fees have become in the eyes of some, they still are not true prices in the sense that they do not indicate the real cost of the education that they nominally purchase. The same is true of heavily endowed private universities. If students (or, for that matter, employers and politicians) do not know the real cost of education, they cannot know its net economic worth and relative social benefit; and they usually don't.

What does this little exposition of market behaviour have to do with performance indicators and performance funding, and a particular event in one Canadian province? It explains why the province's conservative government began its first mandate with a particular interest in deregulation and higher user fees, which in the end is what a tuition fee is. The idea was to bring as much market behaviour as possible to the public sector, and then to let the respective markets thus created answer the 'How much is enough?' question.

For universities, however, the markets were still imperfect. Even as tuition fees rose, the real cost and, in turn, the real net worth of various programs remained disguised. *De*-regulation, was really *re*-regulation as programs were placed into new categories to which different fees and fee regulations then were applied. But fee differentiation, unlike the provincial funding formula of the day, was based more on prospective earnings of graduates than on the costs of production. Students as consumers still could not apply a reliable market test. Moreover, and much to the consternation of a government ostensibly committed to free markets, students as consumers seemed to be making their very worst market choices about educational programs that were being offered by private post-secondary vocational schools. For the PVS sector, rates of employment were dropping while their rates of loan default were rising.

What was to be done? The government's answer was to supplement the information about market choices, and here is the key point, to introduce performance indicators, which were formally termed 'Key Performance Indicators' or KPIs. The basic idea behind the key performance indicators was that students as consumers needed to know more about the province's colleges and universities. When Michael Spence received the Nobel Prize in 2001, he was asked by a journalist 'whether it was true that you could be awarded the Nobel Prize in Economics for simply noticing that there are markets in which certain participants don't know certain things that others in the market do know?' (Spence 2001). The answer, of course, was yes: the degree of asymmetry, if not simple, was surprising. In economic terms, the market for higher education is highly asymmetrical. This is exemplified by research on college choice that reveals erroneous but forceful perceptions that applicants have about the selection process (McDonogh 1997, Lang and Lang 2002).

Thus the original idea behind the Key Performance Indicators was to strike a balance of information between buyers and sellers in a market for higher education. That being the objective, the first deployment of performance indicators in Ontario was for the purpose of public information. The reasoning was that if the information provided by performance indicators was added to the information already available in the market from universities and colleges, students would then make better choices and, in theory anyway, select programs and institutions with higher employment rates, lower default rates, and so on. Thus at the time that the Key Performance Indicators were designed and introduced, they had nothing directly to do with accountability, with funding, or with modifying institutional behaviour – all of which were normally associated with performance indicators elsewhere, and with which they would later be associated in Ontario.

The next step in the evolution of Key Performance Indictors in Ontario was to cast the indicators as standards. As public information, the performance indicators displayed results in ranked order, but there was no indication of what amounted to satisfactory or unsatisfactory performance. They were something like the lists on the David Letterman show: each quip is funny but the audience is left to decide which is the funniest. So complicated break points were introduced at which some funding liabilities – but not rewards – would come into play. This use of performance indicators as standards did not really add much to public information. In fact, they never were really explained to the public. Moreover, functionally, they were aimed mainly at the private vocational school sector.

At about this time the government introduced a program called ATOP (Advanced Technology Opportunity Program) that was designed to induce colleges and universities to expand their capacities in certain areas like computer engineering, and to induce students to select those programs over others. What does this have to do with our discussion of the evolution of performance indicators and performance funding? The answer is 'a lot,' because ATOP was an implicit repudiation of the government's market *cum* key performance indicators experiment in higher education. The government in practical effect, if not conscious admission, decided that it could not trust the market to balance supply and demand in areas that it believed were critical to economic growth. The market had to be 'fixed' and the means that the government chose were those that one normally associates with a centralized command economy. The Key Performance Indicators ceased to be instruments for informing students as consumers. Without modification the indicators were redeployed as 'carrot and stick' financial incentives in a centrally planned regulatory system.

The ATOP program thus coincided with the next step in the evolution of performance indicators and performance funding in the province. The primary purpose of Ontario's Key Performance Indicators would no longer be to inform students as consumers or to set standards. The purpose was to provide a basis for allocating a portion of annual operating funding. Two per cent of the provincial operating grant to universities was set aside for allocation on the basis of annual performance as measured by the Key Performance Indicators. Although their purpose again changed, the indicators themselves did not.

Perhaps this evolution of ends but not means should not be surprising. Governments also are buyers in the higher education market (or perhaps in two higher education markets, because research follows a different production function). To the extent that governments provide subsidies to colleges and universities in order to increase productivity and stimulate economic growth, they are making investments from which they expect certain returns. In these cases the purchase is of education or, in economic terms, of increased human capital. In the case of the ATOP program the government decided, market signals notwithstanding, that the provincial economy required more graduates in certain science and technology disciplines, and deployed a regime of performance funding to ensure that institutions and students would behave accordingly.

Compared to other jurisdictions, Ontario's use of performance indicators could be construed in different ways. Their purpose could be to influence institutional behaviour without direct government intervention, and thus with a healthy respect for institutional autonomy. Or their purpose could be to allocate funding more reliably than funding formulas do. The proof of the pudding is in the eating. Just as public subsidies and private endowments discount and disguise tuition fees as prices, the amount of funding attached to the Key Performance Indicators in Ontario bore no particular relation to the costs that colleges and universities had to incur in order to alter their performance according to the indicators. This fact suggests that the real point of indicator-regulated performance funding sometimes is to influence institutional behaviour instead of to measure institutional behaviour.

The same fact reveals a conundrum that is often typical of performance funding that is allocated on the basis of performance indicators. If the funding allocated under the Key Performance Indicators does not relate to the performances that the indicators are putatively meant to change, how can colleges and universities afford to modify their behaviours to align with the indicators? The fact that this conundrum exists at all is a reason for suggesting that the example of Ontario reveals something different from performance indicators and performance funding per se. The most apt description would appear to be that, at least sometimes, 'performance' means 'compliance' with government policies aimed at cost efficiencies in units of output, the cost of student loan defaults, and satisfying labour market demand. Even if this description is less than perfect, it suggests that the language of performance funding requires more precision.

The Lexicon of Performance Funding

Performance indicators, as the example of the Province of Ontario demonstrates, are not necessarily associated with *performance funding,* at least not directly. A jurisdiction may deploy performance indicators without deploying either performance funding or performance budgeting. This use of performance indicators alone is often called *performance reporting.* Performance indicators unconnected to performance funding may be installed for several different reasons.

Market symmetry. As in the case of the Province of Ontario's initial installation of performance indicators, their purpose may be to 'level the playing field' of a higher education market by injecting information that otherwise might not be available to students as consumers, or might not be available at all. This use of performance indicators depends on several presumptions.

The first is that universities modify their performance as organizations in response to competition (Ben-David 1972, Dill 1997). The second assumption is that competition is greatest when colleges and universities are relatively independent. Ben-David (1972), Clark (1998), MacTaggart (1998), and Altbach (2004) have all advanced similar cases for institutional autonomy *cum* competition. This implies a performance paradigm rooted in organizational behaviour and system structure. From this follows an intriguing paradox: as governments pursue improved institutional performance through the construction of more highly regulated and planned systems of higher education they may in practical fact be discouraging the competitive market behaviour that stimulates innovation and responsiveness.

The third assumption is that tuition fees, even when discounted, must be high enough to simulate prices and, in turn, market choices on the part of students as consumers. It is theoretically true that, in the absence of tuition fees, students will still incur major opportunity costs and realize large returns on their private investments, but this requires a level of economic literacy that most students do not have (McDonogh 1997, Sedaie 1998).

Comparison. Colleges and universities throughout much of the world are regularly compared to one another. Sometimes they do this by their own choice, usually either to benchmark their costs and performance or to determine their competitive market positions. At other times they are compared and ranked by the press, a practice that most colleges and universities on the one hand decry, and, on the other hand, cannot resist (Just 2002).

At yet other times, usually in the name of accountability, governments whose systems of higher education are centralized compare colleges and universities, at least those within their own systems. Sometimes the systems themselves are compared, in which case quality often is not the primary index. Often the degree of diversity within each system becomes a point of comparison, usually with respect to questions about how differentiation among institutions might be measured and promoted, and how distinctive institutional missions and roles might be recognized within each system.

Measuring performance in terms of quality and diversity is not easy. This is not only a matter of objective quantification and comparison. It also has a lot to do with how universities change in order to improve performance. What events and conditions might cause a university to change its organizational behaviour? This is not a matter of simple instrumentalism. For example, as Pike's research (2004) demonstrates, infusions of resources do not necessarily improve or signify quality in higher education. Frederiks and Westerheijden (1994) came to a similar conclusion after studying the results of performance funding in the Netherlands.

Robert Birnbaum, who has written extensively about diversity in higher education identified two different paradigms – 'natural selection' and 'resource dependence' – that may explain institutional behaviour (Birnbaum 1983). In both cases, the forces that lead to change are essentially external. Because they are external, they inherently involve comparison.

Best practice and benchmarking. Benchmarking in higher education is an import from business in the for-profit sector. In the view of some, although benchmarking did not originate in higher education, it has become a virtually mandatory practice for colleges and universities (Alstete 1995). Benchmarking sometimes looks very similar to comparison. On close examination, however, we see that they are different. Comparisons are almost always organizational, that is, the indicators measure in various ways the performance of institutions or, in some cases, faculties and schools within institutions. However, the best 'practices' that benchmarks measure are processes (Birnbaum 2000).

Benchmarking for best practice, because it focuses on processes, is the most laborious utilization of performance indicators. It can also be the most risky. It is laborious (and, in turn, expensive) because of the large amounts of data that must be collected and statistically analysed (Gaither, Nedwek, and Neal 1994; Lang 2002). It is risky, because, in the absence of a corollary effort to insure that best practices are drawn from institutions that are peers, there can be no assurance that what is a best practice in one institution can be a best practice in another (Lang 2000). As Robert Birnbaum observed, when that happens, a benchmark that is converted into a performance indicator is for practical purposes arbitrary (Birnbaum 2000).

Performance funding does not have to be based in performance indictors. Indeed, one can argue reasonably that performance funding is, when stripped of management jargon, formula funding based on outputs instead of inputs (Layzell and Caruthers 1999, Lang 2005). For example, an enrolment-sensitive funding formula can be based either on enrolments of students as degree candidates – that is, as inputs – or of students as degree recipients – that is, as outputs.

Output-based incentive or performance formulas are usually combined with other types of formulas that are used to allocate most of the funding available for distribution; a portion is withheld and allocated on the basis of performance. In these cases performance is measured in a number of ways, for instance, by programs accredited, the performance of graduates on standardized tests, the evaluation of programs and services, peer evaluation, and success in attracting competitive research grants and contracts. Separate funding – often called an 'envelope' – is set aside for each category of performance or policy incentive. For each envelope or incentive there is then a formula.

Incentive-funding, or performance-funding, formulas are the most policy-oriented of funding formulas. They are not neutral. On the one hand, this type of formula respects institutional autonomy in the sense that a college or university may choose to ignore the incentive and forgo whatever funding it might have provided. Still, on the other hand, the express purpose on an incentive or performance formula is to modify institutional behaviour.

Although technical, there are two fundamental aspects of incentive and performance formulas that influence their effectiveness in terms of the institutional behaviours that they engender. The first aspect is not so much about the formula's funding algorithm as it is about the source of the funds that the formula allocates. If the funds available for allocation are new or additive, the incentive is truly a carrot that institutions may, literally, take or leave according to their autonomous judgment. If, however, the funds available for allocation come from existing public grants to colleges and universities, the incentive may be as much a stick as a carrot, and as such will be harder for institutions to ignore, regardless of their autonomy.

The other fundamental factor that influences the effectiveness of incentive and performance formulas has to do with cost. To a casual observer an incentive or performance formula will look a lot like a composite formula: a series of separate funds and a separate algorithm for each fund. They are, however, basically different. The first is that incentive and performance formulas virtually never operate alone to allocate all of the public funds available to colleges and universities in a given post-secondary system. Incentive and performance formulas account for only a small fraction – usually less than 10%, and often as low as only 1 or 2% – of public funding for colleges and universities. The second difference follows from the first: many incentive and performance formulas are distinct only in the sense that they allocate funds earmarked for a particular purpose. Their allocative arithmetic may be the same as that of the larger formula with which they are associated. For example, an incentive or performance formula aimed at increasing rates of graduation will use the number of graduates instead of total enrolment as its coefficient. But the program weight that it assigns to each graduate to reflect differences in costs will be the same as the weight in the enrolment-based formula with which it is associated. In other words, the measure of volume is different but the cost is not. Even when the measure of cost is different, incentive and performance formulas almost always use one or more of the major forms of formula funding (Burke 1997).

The third difference is the most basic. Composite funding formulas that include incentive and performance components are used when high degrees of accuracy in costing and funding are desired. In terms of costs, incentive and performance formulas are more inaccurate than any other type of funding formula. The amounts of funding set aside for the outcomes or other behaviours that any given incentive or performance formula is put in place to engender often bear no realistic connection to the costs of any given outcome. Let's again use rates of graduation. To improve rates of graduation a college or university might take several steps that involve additional expense, for example, more academic counselling, writing labs, math labs, teaching assistants, and financial aid. The list could be longer, but the length of the list of measures that might be taken to improve rates of graduation is not the point. The point is the cost of the list. If the amount of funding set aside does not reflect, at least approximately, the cost of the institutional performance for which the formula calls, the incentive will be ignored. Indeed, performance and incentive funding often is ignored (El-Khawas 1998, Rau 1999, Schmidtlein 1999, Schmidt 2002, McColm 2002).

Performance budgeting is often identified with performance funding, but in fact is quite different. The two are linked by their use of performance indicators. Performance budgeting, which is much more frequently deployed than performance funding, allows the discretionary use of performance indicators by government funding agencies to supplement allocations to institutions. The key word in this definition is 'discretionary': there is no arithmetic or formulaic connection between an institution's performance as measured by the indicators and the supplementary allocation that it receives. Performance budgeting thus is much more destabilizing and unpredictable than performance funding, even though they use virtually the same arrays of performance indicators.

Inputs, Throughputs, Outputs, and Outcomes: The Anatomy of Performance Funding

Critics of performance funding often claim that it is only about outputs, and in turn that it is only about those outputs that can be conveniently measured (Gaither, Nedwek, and Neal 1994, Ewell 1998). There are

Input indicators	Process indicators	Output indicators	Outcome indicators
market share of of applicants	student workload	graduation rate	employer satisfaction with graduates
student:faculty ratio	persistence and retention	number of graduates passing licensing	job placement of graduates
funding per student	class size	cost per student	reputation measured externally
faculty workload	student evaluation of teaching	rate of PhD completion	graduate satisfaction
amount of space	peer review of curricula	research publication	patents and royalties from research
quality of space	peer review of teaching		research citations
percentage of faculty with doctorates	peer review of research		

instances in which those assertions are borne out. In fact, however, performance funding is more complex, involving a variety of inputs, throughputs, and outcomes, as well as outputs. The accompanying table is an expanded version from a study that was conducted by Bottrill and Borden (1994), and developed further by McColm (2002). This table is not inclusive. It is not meant to be. There are literally hundreds of performance indicators for higher education (Taylor, Meyerson, and Massy 1993; Taylor and Massy 1996). The purpose of the table is to describe the texture and variety of performance indicators. It is possible to over-generalize about performance indicators, which are different because they measure different performances, only some of which are outputs. The table is also important because, in terms of causality, it demonstrates that the connections between performance funding and the institutional behaviours that they are supposed to engender are more often than not indirect. Let us take the table's several research indicators as examples. The number of faculty who hold earned doctorates is an *input* to the research-production function, just as research grants would be. Their *input* was the expense of the research. Performance funding can be attached to input for two purposes. The first would be to act as an incentive to engage in more research. But because so little funding is allocated on the basis of performance, we see another less obvious but more forceful purpose: to leverage other funding to underwrite an otherwise unaffordable public-policy objective. In this context the deployment of performance funding amounts to an implicit recognition on the part of government that they either already are or are becoming minority partners in the nominally public enterprise of higher education.

Next, the *process* of research can be measured by peer review. The research process – in terms of either quality or efficiency – can be the same regardless of the significance of the results of the research. The *throughput* was the process by which the paper was produced. When performance funding is attached to throughput or process we see a quite different purpose, which is essentially to modify institutional behaviour and encourage putative best practice. It is when performance funding is deployed in this way that it becomes most intrusive on institutional autonomy and tends to promote monocultures and undermine diversity. The mismatch of funding to purpose is most troublesome in terms of process and throughput; it is these performances that actually incur costs.

The most common measure of research *output* is the rate of peer-reviewed publication. Applying performance funding to outputs is a relatively simple concept: you get what you pay for. This is the application of performance funding that is most often associated with accountability, compliance with regulation, and value for money measured in terms of cost-benefit.

One might expect the performance-indicator continuum to stop there. But there is another step: *outcomes*, which can be thought of as measures of the significance or added value of research. Ideally, we should most want to link performance funding with outcomes, which in turn amounts to value for money measured in terms of quality, significance, and influence – in other words, with the difference that performance makes. This, however, is the purpose that performance funding is least capable of fulfilling. Here is why. First, this is the area of performance funding that is most damaged by the 'one size fits all' homogenizing effect of performance indicators. Performance indicators, at their very best, rarely measure quality reliably. This why commercial surveys and rankings of universities – like those of *U.S. News & World Report* and *Maclean's* – in actual effect substitute reputation for quality.

Second, it is this use of performance indicators that most assumes the marketization of university education. In the public higher educational market the results of performance measurement is assumed to influence student choice, private philanthropy, and funding for research – all of which as sources of funding for universities are far more significant than even the most generous performance funding schemes. Again we see performance funding as a financial matching device by which governments, as minority partners in the enterprise of higher education, seek to leverage and influence the behaviour of the majority partners.

This example of research is another illustration of the problem that market asymmetry poses for performance indicators and performance funding. Superficially, research might seem to be the area of university performance that is most amenable to performance funding. It isn't.

Much of the complexity of developing measures of research performance or productivity in universities can be understood by reference to the economic concepts of *principal* and *agent*. This is usually called the *agency problem*. With a few exceptions principals fund research, but do not conduct it themselves. Instead, they purchase research from agents, who may be seen as either individual researchers in universities or as the universities themselves. Funding agencies as principals may have different motives and expectations from those of researchers as agents. It is difficult, if not impossible, for the sponsors of research to know and, more to the point, to evaluate the actual processes of research. As Michael Spence might have said in this context, the market for university research is ineluctably and inherently asymmetrical. But to a considerable degree, as our table illustrates, it is those processes that productivity is about.

Experts who think a lot about agency relationships recommend contractual arrangements that are based on outcomes (instead of process) as a means of limiting opportunistic behaviour on the part of agents. Opportunistic behaviour, whether implicit or explicit, diminishes productivity; at least, that is what the sponsors of research fear. The objective, therefore, becomes an alignment of the funding agency's interests with the agent's interests.

That sounds a lot like performance funding based on performance indicators. It also seems simple and straightforward until one considers that the process of conducting research is poorly suited to the normal understanding of the *principal–agent* relationship. Principals, as the financiers of research, normally think in terms of outputs. The processes by which the outputs are created are essentially unimportant to the principals. Ends count, means do not. The logic of this suggests that performance funding that focuses on process amounts to unproductive micromanagement.

Nevertheless, of the four elements of performance funding *cum* performance indicators, it is most important to understand process. The subtitle of James Scott's *Seeing Like a State* (1998) explains the special significance of process in understanding performance funding: *How Certain Schemes to Improve the Human Condition Have Failed*. Scott did not discuss performance indicators and performance funding explicitly, but if he had, he might have described them as 'social simplifications' under his heading 'limits of measurement.' Scott presents a series of plans that not only failed to improve the human condition but also made it worse, for example, the Soviet collectivization of agriculture. Performance funding is not on that scale, but it may nevertheless be a social simplification subject to the limits of measurement. The key to each of the fiascoes that Scott dissects was a failure to understand process. For example, Soviet central planners did not have enough knowledge of how certain crops were grown to know which ones would be successful under large-scale collectivized agriculture and which ones, regardless of political or economic ideology, could be grown only on small-scale family farms. In terms of Scott's metaphor, what the state 'saw' and what the farmers 'saw' were different. The state saw a political control and compliance problem while the farmers saw an agricultural process.

This lesson about process and the sight of the state can help us better understand performance funding. The rate of graduation provides a good example. It is a performance indicator in most performance funding schemes, and it is a lot more complicated than it at first seems to be. The process dimension of the rate of graduation does not begin with what otherwise might seem obvious: quality of teaching, class size, academic services, and so on. It begins with the selection of students for admission. The most straightforward and least costly means of improving rates of graduation are to raise standards for admission and introduce more selective and more predictive selection processes. After that, improvements in instruction, academic services, financial aid, and other interventions come into play. The simple measure of rate of graduation does not necessarily 'see' these processes. Moreover, the measurement may misconstrue the process. For example, an increase in the rate of graduation that was induced by raising standards for admission would not be the result of any actual change in an institution's educational performance, but it would nevertheless be rewarded with performance funding.

Another example of the state's inability to 'see' process can be found in the Province of Ontario's initial attempt to deploy performance indicators without performance funding. As previously discussed, in that case the government through the lens of market capitalism assumed that students would choose colleges and universities differently if they had more and better information about institutional performance as measured by three indicators: rate of graduation, rate of graduate employment, and rate of default on student loans. The scheme didn't work; students did not use the information and did not change their patterns of choice. The fact that the government did not 'see' the process by which students choose colleges and universities was not due to a lack of information about the process. There is plenty (McDonogh 1997, Hossler, Schmit, and Vesper 1999, Lang and Lang 2002). Instead, the lack of sight was due to the lens, or what Scott called the 'hieroglyphics of measurement' that can cause governments to oversimplify and over-unify processes that are neither simple nor uniform. One need only look through an issue of either the annual survey and ranking of colleges and universities *U.S. News & World Report* or *Maclean's* to see how complex and disparate the process of choice really is.

The Track Record of Performance Funding

Performance funding of various stripes has been in place in North America since the mid-1970s. Before then some funding formulas had performance components that could have powerful steering effects, mainly to encourage or discourage the expansion of enrolment (Darling et al. 1989). Beginning in the mid-1990s the Nelson A. Rockefeller Institute of Government conducted a series of surveys of the use of performance funding in the United States. The deployment of performance funding grew rapidly from 1979 to 2001, at which time it was in place in some form in 19 states. However, between 2001 and 2003, four states discontinued the practice, and none has been taken it up since. Also, of the remaining 15 states where performance funding is still in place, two use it for two-year colleges only. Thus, as of 2003, performance funding for universities was in use in only 13 American states, or in about two-thirds of the historical high.

In approximately the same period in Canada, two provinces – Alberta and Ontario – introduced performance funding. In both of the Canadian cases, although performance funding remained in place, the amounts of funding allocated on the basis of performance were reduced to nearly negligible levels.

The Rockefeller Institute, in speculating about the levelling off or actual decline in the use of performance funding in the United States, said that '[t]he volatility of performance funding confirms the previous conclusion that its desirability in theory is matched by its difficulty in practice. It is easier to adopt than implement and easier to start than to sustain' (Burke, Rosen, et al., 2000).

What makes performance funding volatile? One explanation has already been mentioned: the amounts of funding associated either with performance funding generally or with specific performance indicators usually do not correspond with the cost structures of the performances that are being measured and putatively rewarded. For example, given the efforts that a university would have to exert in order to raise rates of graduation – smaller classes, enhanced academic services, supplementary financial aid – the costs that the university would have to incur might be greater than the additional income that those efforts would generate. This is a greater problem if the purpose of performance funding is to modify institutional behaviour by means of incentives. If the purpose is compliance or accountability, the problem is less serious.

Also in terms of cost structures, performance funding often fails to take into account the fact that universities have long production cycles. For example, the typical undergraduate program takes four years to complete; many programs take longer. For that reason universities are something like super-tankers: it takes a long time to change their direction, even when they are willing to change in response to financial incentives. Let us again take the rate of graduation as an example. First, the rate of graduation is not a simple sum of annual retention rates. Most graduation rate performance indicators are not calculated until one or two years after the normal program length, for example, after the sixth year for a four-year program. This allows for the inclusion of students who 'stop out' or temporarily switch from full-time to part-time status, but who nevertheless eventually graduate. Thus, even if a university makes every possible authentic effort to increase its rate of graduation, the results of those efforts will not be seen until several years later. But performance funding universally operates annually. This means that a university must incur costs long before it receives supplementary 'performance' revenue to cover those costs, and even then usually partially instead of fully.

Even the delayed recovery of costs is problematic. One of the reasons most often cited for the disinclination of some universities to take performance funding seriously is uncertainty about the future (Burke and Modarresi 2000). Will the definition and calculation of performance indicators change over time? Will the amount of funding attached to performance change? Will new indicators be introduced that offset older indicators? These concerns about stability are not unfounded. In Ontario, for example, the performance funding *cum* performance indicators program changed four times in eight years.

Some jurisdictions deal with the problem of costing by limiting the number of indicators so that the performance funding available to each indicator will be higher and therefore closer to a reflection of the actual costs of the performances that it measures. This, however, creates a Catch-22 problem. As the array of performance indicators narrows, the indicators cover less of each university's total performance, which in turn makes the measurement of institutional performance less reliable and performance funding less influential. Context is crucial in appreciating the complexity of this problem. With one exception, no Canadian province or American state allocates more than 3.4% of its total funding for post-secondary education through performance funding. Some allocate as little as 1%. It is difficult to imagine any manipulation of an array of performance indicators that could realistically match the performance measured with the actual costs of that performance. According to the Rockefeller Institute's surveys of performance funding, this problem fits the old adage about the weather: 'Everybody talks about it, but no one does anything about it.' Not one of the stakeholder groups surveyed – from state governors and legislators to deans and chairs of faculty senates – thought that the amount of funding allocated by performance funding was too large. The almost unanimous consensus was that funding was too small, but the surveys also report no plans to increase the allocation (Serban 1997). In some cases it has become smaller (Burke and Minassians 2003).

What lessons can we learn from trial and error? As the Rockefeller Institute reported on the basis of its annual surveys, about 25% of the American states that deployed performance funding have since abandoned it (ibid.). Sweden, the Netherlands, and Australia introduced various versions of performance funding, only to either abandon them or change them fundamentally. Australia, which is an example of replacement instead of abandonment, ended up with an arrangement that was basically performance budgeting instead of performance funding. Under that arrangement, a uniform national system of performance indicators was replaced by a system that allows each institution to select and declare its own performance indicators in periodic *performance agreement* negotiations with government.

An examination of the experience of the American states that installed performance funding and later discontinued it, and of those states that in the same period kept it in place, indicates some factors that lead to success or failure. A very important conclusion was that performance funding worked in jurisdictions in which the performance indicators emphasized quality, and did not work where the emphasis was on efficiency (Burke and Modarresi 2000). Efficiency was particularly problematic in terms of the measurement of administrative cost and faculty workload (Burke 1997).

The track record of performance funding is good when the following conditions are met:
• Performance indicators are carefully chosen, definitive, and neither too numerous nor too few.
• Institutional diversity is preserved.
  Government priorities are stable and for the long term.
• Funding is realistic relative to the expected performances.
(Stein 1996, Ewell 1998, Burke and Modarresi 2000).

What is interesting about this list is that it could apply just as aptly to formula funding generally as to performance funding specifically (Serban 1998, Lang 2005). Some performance funding schemes comprise performance indictors that are virtually identical to those that one would expect to find in a composite funding formula. The list that follows is drawn from the performance funding program used by the State of Texas (Ashworth 1994):
• Number of undergraduate degrees   @$97.64
• Number of course completers   @$4.41
• Number of minority students   @$51.48
• Number of minority graduates   @$449.99
• Number of graduates in top 50%   @$312.45
  on GRE, LSAT, MCAT tests
• Number of tenure track faculty in   @$333.33
  in lower division courses

This is not the complete list of performance indicators used in the Texas performance funding program, but it is indicative of the types of indicators used, and of the precision of the funding assigned to each indicator. If the 'if it walks like a duck, swims like a duck, and quacks like a duck, it's a duck' test were applied to the Texas performance funding program, it could just as aptly be called formula funding as performance funding.

The detail of the Texas scheme is important for more than reasons of precision. It allows a university to use the performance indicators for purposes of strategy and planning as well as budgeting, because the financial outcomes of responding to the various indicators can be forecast. This provides the stability and long-term perspective that effective performance funding requires. If one objective of performance funding is to modify institutional behaviour more or less permanently, a stable and long-term connection between funding and performance is essential.

This type of funding – whether one labels it performance funding or formula funding – has another dimension that sometimes, despite its effectiveness, makes it less attractive to government. In some jurisdictions governments and funding agencies are becoming wary of incentive and performance funding. There are two reasons for this: one political and one financial. The political reason is that this form of funding, some governments are beginning to realize, can work in two directions. If a specific performance target is set, is visibly measurable by a performance indicator, and is financed by earmarked funding, the effects of inadequate funding, as well as institutional performance, can be measured. In other words, the government's performance as a funding agent becomes visibly measurable too. More to the point, it may just as easily become a political liability as an asset.

The other reason is that a tight, realistic, and predictable fit between performance indicators and performance funding generates what amounts to entitlement funding. In other words, the more successful performance funding in this form is in terms of raised institutional performance, the more it costs. Open-ended funding schemes make governments nervous, especially those in tight fiscal circumstances (Wildavsky 1975, Blakeney and Borins 1998). This perhaps explains the growing preference that the Rockefeller Institute's surveys reported for performance budgeting over performance funding, The preference is significant. In the institute's 2003 survey, states were asked about the likelihood that they would adopt either performance funding or performance budgeting in the future. Only five states said that it was 'likely' that they would adopt performance funding, while 13 said that performance budgeting would be their likely choice (Burke and Minassians 2003). A few said they might adopt both.

Since it was government that initiated the interest in performance funding, it should not be surprising that, after 20 years of deployment, it is government that is most satisfied by the track record so far. Universities are the least satisfied, mainly because of the intrusions that performance funding makes into their autonomy, and because of the lack of symmetry between the economic assumptions about performance indicators and performance funding and the actual facts of university cost structures and functions. Other stakeholders – system administrators, governing boards, 'buffer' agencies – are in between. At all levels, there is concern that performance funding promotes monocultures that undermine diversity. This concern, it is important to note, arises when performance funding works, not when it doesn't. Given the fundamental objectives of performance funding, performance funding works when universities respond to it by modifying their behaviours and, ideally, by internalizing the priorities and causal relationships that the intersections of performance indicators and performance funding represent. We know that universities often do not respond in these ways, and why. The response seems to have been greatest in those jurisdictions in which performance funding was not preceded by formula funding or some other form of objective, systematic budgeting for higher education. South Carolina is the American jurisdiction that has used performance funding the most; its budgeting processes prior to the introduction of performance funding were highly political and incremental. As the president of one university in the state said about the pre-performance funding era, 'As long as I can remember, legislators financed higher education by poking money through a hole in the fence' (Schmidt 2002). The degree of satisfaction with performance funding is thus relative, depending on the alternatives to it available.

The Future of Performance Funding

The future of performance funding for colleges and universities is easier to foresee generally than specifically. Generally, it is not likely that governments will or should become less interested in accountability, with which performance funding is often closely associated. Nor, given the track record, is it likely that many more jurisdictions will turn to performance funding. There is such a plethora of performance indicators from which governments can choose – the number is literally in the hundreds – that it is not probable that new and better measurements will be devised.

There is no reason to expect that, again generally, those jurisdictions that have already deployed performance funding will allocate more money through it. Performance funding that is installed to change institutional behaviour by incentive is expensive. This might not appear to be the case at first glance, since relatively small percentages of public funding for colleges and universities flow through this type of funding device. But the small percentage is indicative of the point: funding for the institutional performances that incentive funding is supposed to engender is often too small to provide the intended incentives. The result is that colleges and universities sometimes ignore the incentives or find them too costly to comply with. This is not likely to change because, whether for reasons of globalization and economic theory or of lack of wealth, public funding for higher education is declining in many jurisdictions in which performance funding is in use. The decline in public funding often is accompanied by increases in other forms of funding, usually higher tuition fees. One result is that governments are in some cases becoming minority partners in the financing of colleges and universities. Public grants are becoming public subsidies to institutions that are more autonomous out of necessity as the institutions are forced to rely more and more on alternative sources of funding. This trend will further weaken the impact of performance funding on institutional behaviour. At the same time it may strengthen the role of accrediting agencies because, in terms of accountability, they have broader audiences. Some performance funding schemes already use accreditation standards as indicators.

These developments in the scale and role of public funding might lead to three specific changes in the shape of performance funding, jurisdiction by jurisdiction. First, enrolment-based performance indicators will become more prevalent because they most closely reflect the role of public funding as a subsidy to ensure student accessibility, and because other types of formula funding usually imply a higher degree of financial responsibility than governments either can or wish to assume. Second, performance funding will allow more permutations and combinations among performance indicators institution-by-institution in order to respect institutional autonomy and promote diversity over isomorphism. For example, in a given jurisdiction, there might be a smaller array of core or compulsory indicators and a larger array of indicators from which institutions may choose according to their missions, mandates, and priorities. Third and last, if tuition fees continue to rise, performance funding may revert to one of its original roots: accountability by means of student choice within a regulated market. Some American states have already moved in the direction of what is sometimes called *performance reporting* (Burke and Minassians 2003). Other than a new terminology, performance reporting is simply the deployment and wide publication of performance indicators without any connection to funding. The indicators are not new. What is new is their broad and universal propagation. In a sense, performance reporting may essentially be a movement of government into what has so far been the private-sector world of journalistic surveys and rankings that have been very successful commercially. One does not have to spend much time examining the statistical detail of, say, the *U.S. News & World Report* annual surveys to realize that their indices are very similar – sometimes identical – to performance indicators. That examination will also show that the system of 'weights' by which some magazines place institutions in ranked order are similar to the priorities that governments place among performance indicators.

Finally, there are some voices that are beginning to argue that public systems of higher education are becoming too big, too highly centralized, and too complex to be managed successfully by anyone (Callan 1994, MacTaggart 1998, Gaither 1999, Berdahl 2000). Gary Rhoades (2000) characterized this as 'managerial myopia.' James March (1994) used the phrase 'limited rationality' to describe the inability of large, centralized organizations to make universally competent decisions. Public universities, specifically because they are public, are typical of what Scott (1998) called 'complex inter-dependencies' that cannot easily be reduced to the schematic system-wide visions that performance funding often represents. These views may lead to three changes in performance funding. Two have already been discussed: fewer compulsory performance indicators and more discretionary indicators that can better matched to different institutional roles, and the disconnection of performance indicators from funding. The third is a retreat from the imposition of system-wide 'best practices' by the use of performance indicators as benchmarks. Ironically, the strongest incentive for universities to seek best practices systematically may not be the addition of performance funding specifically but the reduction of funding generally.

References

Alstete, J.W. *Benchmarking in Higher Education: Adapting Best Practices to Improve Quality*. Washington: ASHE-ERIC, 1995.

Altbach, Philip. 'The Costs and Benefits of World-Class Universities.' *Academe*, June 2004, 1–5.

Ashworth, Kenneth. 'The Texas Case Study.' *Change*, November/December 1994, 9–15.

Ben-David, Joseph. *American Higher Education*. New York: McGraw-Hill, 1972.

Berdahl, Robert. 'A View from the Bridge: Higher Education at the Macro-Management Level.' *Review of Higher Education* 24:1 (2000), 103–12.

Birnbaum, Robert. *Management Fads in Higher Education*. San Francisco: Jossey-Bass, 2000.

– *Maintaining Diversity in Higher Education*. San Francisco: Jossey-Bass, 1983.

Blakeney, Allen, and Sandford Borins. *Political Management in Canada*. Toronto: University of Toronto Press, 1998.

Bottrill, Karen, and Victor Borden. 'Examples from the Literature.' *New Directions for Institutional Research* 82 (Summer, 1994), 107–19.

Burke, Joseph. *Performance Funding Indicators: Concerns, Values, and Models for Two- and Four-year Colleges and Universities*. Albany: Nelson A. Rockefeller Institute of Government, 1997.

Burke, Joseph, and Henrik Minassians. *Performance Reporting: 'Real' Accountability or Accountability 'Lite': Seventh Annual Survey*. Albany: Nelson A. Rockefeller Institute Government, 2003.

Burke, Joseph, and Shahpar Modarresi. 'To Keep or Not to Keep Performance Funding: Signals from Stakeholders.' *Journal of Higher Education* 71:4 (2000), 432–53.

Burke, Joseph, Jeff Rosen, Henrik Minassians, and Terri Lessard. *Performance Funding and Budgeting: An Emerging Merger: The Fourth Annual Survey*. Albany: Nelson A. Rockefeller Institute of Government, 2000.

Callan, Patrick. 'The Gauntlet for Multicampus Systems.' *Trusteeship*, May–June 1994.

Clark, Burton R. *Creating Entrepreneurial Universities*. Oxford: Pergamon, 1998.

Darling, A.L., M.D. England, D.W. Lang, and R. Lopers-Sweetman. 'Autonomy and Control: A University Funding Formula as an Instrument of Public Policy.' *Higher Education* 18:5 (1989), 559–84.

Dill, David. 'Effects of Competition on Diverse Institutional Contexts.' In Marvin Peterson, David Dill, and Lisa Mets, eds, *Planning and Management for a Changing Environment*, 88–105. San Francisco: Jossey-Bass, 1997.

El-Khawas, Elaine. 'Strong State Action but Limited Results: Perspectives on University Resistance.' *European Journal of Education* 33:3 (1998), 317–30.

Ewell, Peter. 'Achieving High Performance: The Policy Dimension.' In William Tierney, ed., *The Responsive University*, 120–61. Baltimore: Johns Hopkins University Press, 1998.

Frederiks, Martin, and D. Westerheijden. 'Effects of Quality Assessment in Dutch Higher Education.' *European Journal of Education* 29:2 (1994), 181–200.

Gaither, Gerald, ed. *The Multicampus System: Perspectives and Prospects*, 8–40. Sterling, Va.: Stylus, 1999.

Gaither, G., B. Nedwek, and J. Neal. *Measuring Up: The Promises and Pitfalls of Performance Indicators in Higher Education*. Washington: ASHE-ERIC, 1994.

Hossler, Don, Jack Schmit, and Nick Vesper. *Going to College: How Social, Economic, and Educational Factors Influence the Decisions That Students Make.* Baltimore: Johns Hopkins University Press, 1999.

Just, Richard. 'Rankophile: In Defense of the *U.S. News & World Report* College Rankings.' *The American Prospect*, 18 September 2002.

Lang, Daniel. 'Formulaic Approaches to the Funding of Colleges and Universities.' In Nina Bascia et al., eds., *International Handbook on Educational Policy.* Manchester, UK: Springer, 2005.

– 'Responsibility Center Budgeting and Management at the University of Toronto.' In Douglas Priest et al., eds, *Responsibility-Centered Budgeting Systems in Public Universities*, 109–36. Northampton: Edward Elgar, 2002.

– 'Similarities and Differences: Measuring Diversity and Selecting Peers in Higher Education.' *Higher Education* 39:1 (2000), 93–129.

Lang, Katherine, and Daniel Lang. '"Flags and Slots": Special Interest Groups and Selective Admission.' *Canadian Journal of Higher Education* 32:2 (2002), 103–42.

Layzell, Daniel, and J. Kent Caruthers. 'Budget and Budget-Related Policy Issues for Multicampus Systems.' In Gerald Gaither, ed., *The Multicampus System: Perspectives and Prospects*, 110–27. Sterling, Va.: Stylus, 1999.

MacTaggart, Terrence. *Seeking Excellence through Independence.* San Francisco: Jossey-Bass, 1998.

March, James. *A Primer on Decision Making.* New York: Free Press, 1994.

Marginson, Simon. *Markets in Education.* St Leonards, NSW: Allen & Unwin, 1997.

McColm, Marjorie. 'A Study of Performance Funding of Ontario CAATs.' EdD thesis, University of Toronto, 2002.

McDonogh, Patricia. *Choosing Colleges.* Albany: SUNY Press, 1997.

McDonogh, Patricia, et al. 'College Rankings: Who Uses Them and With What Impact?' Paper presented at the Annual Meeting of the American Educational Research Association, March 1997.

Neave, Guy. 'The Evaluative State Reconsidered.' *European Journal of Education* 33:3 (1988), 264–84.

Pike, Gary. 'Measuring Quality: A Comparison of *U.S. News* Rankings and NSSE Benchmarks.' *Research in Higher Education* 45:2 (2004), 193–203.

Rau, Einhard. 'Performance Funding in Higher Education: Everybody seems to love it but does anybody really know what it is?' Paper presented at the EAIR 21st Annual Forum, Lund University, Sweden, 1999.

Rhoades, Gary. 'Who's Doing It Right? Strategic Activity in Public Research Universities.' *Review of Higher Education* 24:1 (2000), 41–66.

Schmidt, Peter. 'Most States Tie Aid to Performance, Despite Little Proof That It Works.' *Chronicle of Higher Education*, 22 February 2002, 21–2.

Schmidtlein, Frank. 'Assumptions Underlying Performance-based Budgeting.' *Tertiary Education and Management* 5 (1999), 159–74.

Scott, James. *Seeing Like a State: How Certain Schemes to Improve the Human Condition Have Failed*. New Haven: Yale University Press, 1998.

Sedaie, Behrooz. 'Economic Literacy and the Intention to Attend College.' *Research in Higher Education* 39:3 (1998), 337–64.

Serban, Andreea. 'Precursors of Performance Funding.' In Joseph Burke and Andreea Serban, *Performance Funding for Public Higher Education: Fad or Trend?* 15–24. San Francisco: Jossey-Bass, 1998.

– *Performance Funding for Public Higher Education: Views of Critical Stakeholders*. Albany: Nelson A. Rockefeller Institute of Government, 1997.

Spence, Michael. 'Signaling in Retrospect and the Informational Structure of Markets.' Nobel Prize Lecture, Stockholm, Sweden, December 2001.

Stein, R.B. 'Performance Reporting and Funding Programs.' In Gerald Gaither, ed., *Performance Indicators in Higher Education: Current Status and Future Prospects*. College Station: Texas A&M University Press, 1996.

Taylor, Barbara, and William Massy. *Strategic Indicators for Higher Education*. Princeton: Peterson's, 1996.

Taylor, Barbara, Joel Meyerson, and William Massy. *Strategic Indicators for Higher Education: Improving Performance*. Princeton: Peterson's, 1993.

Wildavsky, Aaron. *Budgeting: A Comparative Theory of Budgetary Processes*. Boston: Little, Brown, 1975.

Public Funding, Markets, and Quality: Assessing the Role of Market-Based Performance Funding for Universities

ANDREW GREEN AND EDWARD IACOBUCCI*

> A strong competitive and collaborative environment with resources comparable to those in competing university sectors will be the most powerful influence on quality and should receive primary attention in building the quality of Ontario's university sector.[1]

David Smith, former principal of Queen's University, ends his report on quality measures and enhancement in Ontario universities with a strong statement about the benefits of competition and collaboration. He argues that the incentives from competition in the university sector must be 'sufficiently strong' to promote quality.[2] Universities that compete in the markets for students, professors, and donations will find themselves pushed to provide high quality. Our essay picks up on this theme in exploring how governments can use markets in designing funding systems for universities that provide useful incentives. Markets work directly in providing incentives to universities, in that, for example, a university that does not attract any students will not last long. But markets can also provide valuable information to governments in establishing incentives around the allocation of public monies. We argue that once the benefits of markets are taken into account and their risks mitigated, government incentive-based funding using, at least in part, information from markets has an important role in quality enhancement.

Placing incentives for quality at the centre of our analysis implies that some other potentially relevant policy considerations are set aside. Indeed, consider the fundamental question of whether public funding should disproportionately go to universities that are struggling with respect to quality, or to universities that are prospering. Cogent arguments are available to support either approach. An argument that more funding should go to underperforming universities is that the marginal social benefit of a dollar spent at a lower-level university would, all things being equal, be greater than the marginal benefit of spending a dollar at a successful university. One could analogize to sprinters. Spending a thousand dollars to improve the speed of the best sprinter in the world might possibly improve that individual's time by a tiny fraction of a second, while spending that money on a slow sprinter may improve his or her time more significantly. On average, a sprinter society would be more productive if significant resources were allocated to slower runners. One could also argue that concentrating social resources in a small handful of elite institutions is inconsistent with a society's commitment to equitable treatment of all its citizens.

On the other hand, the assumption of a declining marginal benefit of spending as merit increases implicit in the above example could well be wrong. Spending a dollar at an underperforming institution could be less productive given its poor quality than similar spending at a well-run institution. For example, having two first-class scholars in a field at one university could produce better results than the combined efforts of the first-class scholars if they were working at different institutions. That is, there could be increasing returns to investment in first-class institutions; excellence begets excellence.

Without resolving these arguments, we take it as a starting point for our analysis that incentives matter. This implies that governments should allocate at least a portion of public funding on the basis of merit. If poorly performing universities were just as likely or more likely to receive public funding, it would create perverse incentives given that low quality is much easier to achieve than high quality. This is not to say that other concerns, such as equity, do not push for a portion, even a large portion, of public funding to be allocated on a more equal basis. Rather, we simply take it as given that there is a role for some incentive-based funding, and ask how market-based mechanisms are useful in designing such funding.

In our view, a fruitful place to start in examining the role of incentive-based funding of universities is to review why this is an important question for policy-makers. Government policy-makers do not even ask how best to motivate restaurants to offer good food and service, yet the question of how best to provide incentives to universities has generated considerable debate. A response, at least in the Ontario context, to this conundrum is that universities are public; therefore incentives are a public matter. This is true, but is in our view at least edging towards tautology. It is fundamental in thinking about the role of incentives to universities to ask why it is that universities are not run like any other enterprise that sells goods to the public.

Our approach in this essay will be first to review the incentive schemes that are generally relied upon in the private sector. Section 1 presents an overview of the various market mechanisms that provide incentives to individuals, at least those at senior management levels, in the corporate context. Section 2 discusses how market-based incentives could be applicable in the university sector. Some generally available incentive mechanisms in the private sector are clearly inapt in the university sector, but others may be more useful, as this section emphasizes. Section 3 discusses various shortcomings of market-based incentive structures for universities. There are clearly some problems with the markets on which we propose to place some reliance. Still, as we discuss, this is insufficient reason to reject their application altogether. The essence of our essay is to discuss privately available market-based incentive devices and to show why the appropriate set of these devices for application in the university setting is smaller, but far from empty. Many of the concerns about markets in the university sector are either unrelated to quality or more appropriately addressed through other instruments. In order for market-based public funding of universities to enhance university quality, it is important to be clear about what it can and should try to accomplish and what can be better dealt with in other ways. Section 4 draws on the analysis of both the benefits and dangers of markets in this setting to suggest some ways in which markets can play a tangible role in designing public incentive-based funding.

1. Market-Based Incentives in the Private Sector

In order better to understand the dilemma facing governments seeking to provide incentives to public universities, it is helpful to consider what instruments the private sector relies on to motivate workers.[3] Most economic activity in market economies is organized through corporations. Corporations, whether closely held family firms with a handful of shareholders or large publicly traded companies, rely heavily on markets to motivate executives and employees. In a closely held corporation the principal employees often are also significant shareholders. To the extent that the firm succeeds in the marketplace in which its products compete, the principals benefit either through the capital gains in the value of their shares or through higher dividends. Similarly, in public corporations, senior executives are generally compensated at least in part with company stock. Awarding executives with stocks provides them incentives to increase the value of the stock. Awarding stock in a publicly traded company is an ideal kind of incentive pay. The value of a share is the present value of all profits accruing to shareholders over the life of the corporation. This value is precisely what shareholders want maximized, thus increasing pay when shares increase in value provides incentives in precisely the direction shareholders want. Moreover, while there is a debate about how well share prices in publicly traded corporations reflect the 'true' value of a share, it is usually acknowledged that shares do a good, if not always perfect, job of reflecting public information about the value of a share.[4] After all, they are traded by literally thousands of shareholders, each of whom has an economic interest in having at least a basic understanding of what value will accrue to the share over time. Share-based incentives thus not only are aimed at exactly the right target, but also accurately reflect the direction of the corporation at any point in time.

This is not to say that share-based incentives are a panacea in the private sector. There are several limitations on the efficacy of share-based compensation. For one, to give an executive the full incentives to maximize the value of the corporation, it would be necessary to give her 100% of the shares. Both because individuals are wealth-constrained and risk-averse, giving one person 100% of the shares is often not feasible. Indeed, even giving her a large number of shares will expose her to significant risk given that share prices are affected by many matters beyond the agent's control, such as macroeconomic phenomena. As a result, optimal contracts between risk-averse managers and diversified (and thus risk-neutral) shareholders would only rely in part on incentive pay.[5] Shareholders cannot therefore be confident that managers face perfect incentives to maximize the value of the corporation, as opposed to pursuing other self-interested objectives. Nevertheless, paying senior managers with shares helps provide useful incentives.

Notice that the discussion has focused on senior managers. Only senior managers systematically can be expected to make decisions that strongly increase share prices. Paying custodial staff with shares is highly unlikely to provide useful incentives, but is certain to expose the staff to undiversified and thus costly risk. However, this is not to say that share incentives do not affect the motivations of lower-level employees. Since senior managers affect, and through their compensation schemes are affected by, share price, senior managers have an incentive to provide incentives to those below them in the corporate hierarchy, who in turn have incentives to motivate those below them and so on. Senior managers will typically strive to provide the optimal combinations of targets (e.g., sales targets, profit targets, clean premises), bonuses, and fixed pay. In many cases optimal incentives are provided by a fixed wage and the threat of termination, or of foregone promotions and raises. Whatever incentives are struck, it is important to recognize that they are usually structured in the shadow of the stock-based incentives motivating senior managers.

Another market-based form of incentive that helps motivate managers arises from the participation of the firm in a product marketplace.[6] Corporations sell goods or services in competition with other firms. If senior managers do not do a good job themselves, or if they do not do a good job in motivating lower-level employees, then the corporation will not compete effectively in product markets and the viability of the firm will be in doubt. Since managers generally like to keep their jobs, perhaps because of the value of firm-specific human capital that would be lost to them if the firm were to fail, product market competition disciplines managers.

There are other market-based incentives confronting senior managers. Managers may wish to earn a reputation for being good managers, since they are rewarded for this reputation by competition over their services from other corporations.[7] There is also the 'market for corporate control.'[8] This is the market for the acquisition of control of a public corporation. If a manager performs poorly, stock price drops and an acquiror may seek to buy the shares, oust incumbent management, improve corporate performance, and realize gains on the acquired shares.

2. Market-Based Incentives in the University Sector

Shareholder Incentives

It is immediately obvious that some important market-based incentives are not currently available in the university context. In Ontario, universities are public and do not have shares. Share-based compensation, while ideal in much of the private sector, is currently impossible in the university sector. But this begs the question: why are universities not publicly traded? If we are worried about providing incentives to universities, should we consider privatizing universities, publicly listing them, and paying university employees with stock? The answer is no.

While there may be a wide variety of reasons against the conversion of universities into for-profit, publicly traded corporations, in our view compelling evidence is found in the marketplace itself: even in jurisdictions where private universities flourish, such as the United States, it is rare for institutions of higher learning to be structured as for-profit corporations. While there are a variety of possible reasons for this choice of organizational form, an important factor is the risk of opportunism. A key starting point for any analysis of non-profit corporations is Hansmann's pioneering article about non-profit corporations.[9] He emphasizes that the defining characteristic of a non-profit is not that they do not make operating profits; they can and do. Rather, the key is that non-profit corporations face a 'non-distribution constraint': any excess of revenues over expenditures cannot be distributed to the corporation's 'owners,' unlike in a for-profit corporation, where profits are distributed to shareholders. Hansmann suggests that the non-distribution constraint exists as a check on opportunism by the non-profit corporation. In particular, he suggests that choosing the non-profit corporate form may reassure customers/donors that certain kinds of opportunism are foreclosed. A donor to a for-profit educational corporation would worry that rather than using the donated funds to improve the quality of education, the corporation may simply distribute the funds to shareholders. Similarly, students may be concerned that a university will take their tuition money and distribute it to shareholders rather than commit to providing a high-quality education. Quality is not easily amenable to contract and students are therefore vulnerable to opportunistic behaviour by a university.

Thus, private universities tend to be non-profit corporations because donors and students may be concerned that their donations or fees will simply be diverted to shareholders rather than put towards improving/subsidizing education. Such an analysis suggests that valuable incentives based on share value, including the market for corporate control, will be of little use in the university context.

Product Market Competition

This is not to say that markets are irrelevant to a university's incentives. The university, as pointed out, competes both in attracting students and in attracting donations. Product market competition can be a valuable source of incentives in the private sector since if corporations cannot compete effectively, they will eventually run out of money; similarly, setting aside government subsidies, if a non-profit university cannot attract tuition revenue or donations, it too runs out of resources. But even without a private corporation becoming insolvent, product markets are helpful in conveying information about the quality of management to their overseers.[10] If a board of directors, or a controlling shareholder, observed that the corporation was consistently losing money in the product market at the same time that other firms in the market were earning handsome profits, it would be alerted to the possibility that its managers are not doing a particularly good job. Analogously, the informational cues from the markets for donations and for students can be useful indicators of the performance of a university.

There may be good reason to take an approach to promoting quality in universities based on students' choices. First, while there are limitations on students' information that we discuss further in section 3, students often have better information than government does about their own preferences.[11] To the extent there is a trade-off for a student in terms of job opportunities versus teaching quality or research or facilities, she is in a better position to make these decisions.

Second, individuals may have better information than the government does about the job market and future job prospects in different areas.[12] If so, and if universities are permitted to respond to these demands, consumer choice promotes greater flexibility in university programs, pushing universities to expand or develop programs that respond to these new demands. In such cases, flexibility and diversity enhances welfare, particularly in a rapidly changing environment in which it may be difficult for central administrators to adapt quickly and accurately.[13] Barr argues that therefore 'decisions should be taken not through central planning but as a result of choices by all the major stakeholders – students, universities, employers and government.'[14]

With respect to the donor market, universities and donors can take several steps to ensure that the donation is linked to a particular educational initiative that a university is pursuing. At a basic level, we have discussed how universities adopt the non-profit corporate form in part better to reassure investors that the donated funds will be directed to the purpose of the donation. In addition, donors could conceivably enter into legally enforceable contracts with donee institutions. For example, a donor could offer money to a university in exchange for a promise to construct a new building and name it after the donor. On the assumption that donors seek to maximize the educational impact of their donations, the decision of a donor to donate to a particular educational institution provides valuable information about the quality of that institution.

There are important qualifications to this analysis. First, individual donors may not be motivated by educational objectives that society as a whole would share. For example, they could be interested in supporting an institution with a radical religious view similar to their own. Alternatively, they could be interested in the publicity and attention associated with a large donation rather than the actual use of that donation.[15] (We note, however, that the 'warm glow' of publicity attendant on a donation to a high-quality prestigious university may exceed that for a second-rank school. That is, a prestige objective is not necessarily inconsistent with quality.) But as long as donors are on average motivated in part by educational quality, then the market for donors provides some feedback about the quality of the donee university. Second, there may be limits on the ability of donors to assess the quality of universities, which we discuss in section 3.

Managerial Markets

Competition for managers in universities is likely to work differently from competition for managers in the private sector. Where there are shareholders who stand to gain materially from any increase in profits, these shareholders have incentives to hire and provide optimal incentives to first-rate managers. In the university setting, and in the non-profit sector more generally, there is no person or group who has a legal right to pocket profits, and thus no person or group with a material interest in appointing and providing optimal incentives to first-rate managers.

There are, however, important ways in which the managerial market can work in the academic setting. First, both boards of governors (or their equivalents) at universities and university managers are likely to be motivated by something other than material returns from their positions. As others have pointed out, managers at non-profit institutions often share the goals of the enterprise.[16] They may aim at such goals as improved quality of education and increased access to education.[17]

Second, simply because markets for managers are likely to operate differently within the university sector from the private sector is not reason to conclude that managerial markets do not provide potentially important sources of incentives. There are two ways of thinking about managerial markets and incentives. One is to recognize that even if managers are intrinsically motivated by ideology, this does not preclude provision of material incentives as well. (Indeed, a university manager motivated solely by educational excellence could refuse a salary increase on condition that it be diverted to educational purposes.) If managers at universities were provided incentive pay, this could help motivate them to provide quality. Of course, there would be a difficulty in crafting a metric of quality that motivates the manager appropriately. But assuming incentive pay were feasible, there is another sense in which the managerial market could provide incentives. If pay were higher the more meritorious the manager, better qualified managers would be attracted by job openings. There could emerge healthy competition among universities for managers that would itself provide useful incentives. That is, incentive-based pay would increase pay for competent managers, and higher pay would invigorate incentives of managers to be noticed by the marketplace.

Summary of Market Mechanisms and University Incentives

To summarize, stock-based incentives, which are the centrepiece of incentives in the private sector, are unavailable in the university setting. But this does not preclude the operation of other market-based forms of incentives. Product market competition, while not perfect, will take place with respect to both donors and students. And incentive pay in managerial markets can also be useful in motivating incumbent managers and in attracting meritorious university managers in the future. We turn now to a discussion of the limitations on these market mechanisms in the context of universities.

3. The Limits of Markets

We have suggested that product market competition can be useful in providing information to governments about the quality of a university. But there are clearly some shortcomings of market-based incentives for universities. Product markets may suffer from a range of imperfections, including the presence of important externalities, information problems facing both students and donors, and capital market imperfections that distort demand for university education.

Public Goods and Externalities

Assume for a moment that students have perfect information about the quality of education at a particular institution and about their goals in life, and individuals' funds were not a concern. Students will make choices based on their preferences and their information. It is clear that university education provides private benefits – that is, benefits directly to the individual students. The private economic returns (higher life-time earnings) are high, although such returns vary according to both the discipline and level of education.[18] There are also private non-economic returns to education including better health, personal growth, and fulfilment.[19] If individuals can assess these private returns, they can make reasoned choices about the relative costs and benefits of attending a particular university themselves.

However, there may be broader social benefits of (or positive externalities to) universities that are not captured in the private decisions of individual students. First, research at universities may have broad public benefits. To the extent students do not take excellence or productivity of the research of a university's faculty into account in deciding which institution to attend, a pure market-based system will not reward excellence in research and hence it will be under-provided.[20] The existence of these social benefits appears to provide a reason for public funding for universities, but this does not necessarily imply that the funding should not be based on student choice. Whether or not students value research quality raises an age-old question about whether research and teaching are complements or substitutes. It is at least arguable that institutions with excellent reputations for research also tend to attract the best students; that is, that students view teaching and research as complementary.[21] If so, then the information from students' choices is valuable feedback about the institution's research and teaching quality. In addition, it could lead to valuable diversity across types of universities – with some focusing on teaching and research and some on teaching alone.[22] If students do not or insufficiently value research, there is a case for public funding, but that funding should address the issue of under-provision of research.[23] While there are concerns about the rigid and increasingly government-directed nature of research funding,[24] it is at least conceivably easier to establish research funding based on quality than a broad-based attempt to judge the quality of an institution.

Second, there may also be benefits to the public from students pursuing certain courses of study that are not captured by a focus on jobs or individual demand. At lower levels of education (primary and second-ary school), this may include basic concepts of citizenship.[25] At the post-secondary level, many of the basic elements of such citizenship benefits would likely be in place. However, there may be other public benefits such as greater understanding of the political system, of his-tory, of philosophical views of the world or of other cultures that the individuals would not otherwise be exposed to and are not priced in the market or readily appropriable by individuals. Society may benefit from research and study in such areas, such as through the enhance-ment of deliberative democracy.[26] These broader social benefits are very hard to identify and especially hard to quantify.[27]

Third, there can be economic benefits to society in terms of increased economic growth and standard of living. Such benefits may stem from individuals with higher education being more productive on average and causing a 'spill-over' effect that raises the productivity of those around them. It could be, for example, that a collaboration of educated individuals is more productive, even controlling for the cost of the investment in education, than the collaboration of an educated and a less educated individual.[28]

These latter two forms of social and economic benefits not captured by individual students suggest a role for government in subsidizing higher education. However, they do not necessarily point to a need to provide those funds directly to universities as opposed to students. Product markets themselves, or public funding based on information from product markets, may still be able to promote quality even where externalities are important.

Information

There are a number of informational problems that may arise in either donors' or students' ability to assess the quality of post-secondary education as well as the aspects of post-secondary education that are important to them.

Poor Information about Quality

Product markets for university education may not work well where donors or students have poor information about the quality of universi-ties or programs. However, even if information among donors or stu-dents is imperfect, their decision to attend or donate to a university will presumably turn at least in part on information about that institution's quality. Students and donors will consult alumni, guidance counsellors, universities themselves, newspaper rankings, and so on in order better to inform themselves about the experience they can anticipate.[29] Admittedly, these sources may be flawed. For example, the *Maclean's* survey of universities has been criticized for attempting to rank universities as opposed to simply providing relevant information.[30] The Dean of the Wharton School of Business has recently criticized international rankings of business schools by news services on the basis that schools distort the information they provide to these services to improve their ranking.[31] But if donors and students value information about quality, there will be sources that on average are helpful, which in turn implies that student choices convey information about quality. The solution to poorly designed rankings may lie in more rankings, such as in the United States, where there are a plethora of rankers of colleges and universities.

As long as students are on average better than random in discerning quality, then their decision to attend a university says something about its quality. Similarly with donors. Success in the competition for students and donors will imply something about the quality of the university.

It is important to appreciate that imperfect information could vary across types of students. Individuals with highly educated families or in communities with a high degree of individuals with higher education may have better information about the quality of different institutions than individuals without such connections.[32] In addition, imperfect information may vary across programs. Individuals entering undergraduate programs may have poorer information about the quality of programs, institutions, and job-market prospects than individuals entering either graduate or professional programs. To the extent university education is a search good (individuals can get information on quality prior to entering the program) or an experience good, the market for reputation may be more finely tuned at the graduate and professional levels, where individuals have a better understanding of universities and what quality entails.

If there are systematic variations in the information of different students about certain kinds of programs, however, this does not undermine the case for reliance on student and donor choices. Rather, these issues potentially point to a greater role for government in subsidizing information dissemination.[33] If information flaws exist in markets, better to remedy the information deficiencies to the extent they can be corrected than to ignore the market altogether.

Poor Information about the Value of Higher Education

Individuals may not enter university because they do not have any experience with or understanding of the benefits of higher education. These information problems may be worse for students from low-income backgrounds who may not have family members with higher education.[34] Again, this issue does not necessarily suggest that the market for students is irredeemably flawed. Rather, it creates an argument for greater outreach programs to under-represented communities. It may also point to an increase in the use of grants for such students where there are income-contingent loan programs in place in conjunction with deregulated tuition. It does not mean, in and of itself, that the government needs to design mechanisms to fund universities and tie the funding to quality measures.

A related, though separate, concern is that those who do enter university may not have a clear picture of what they want to do – either because they have not experienced a range of options or because they are focused on short-term rather than longer-term returns. If the initial decisions are biased in a particular direction (such as towards more technical occupations), universities may under-provide the alternatives. However, there is no reason to suppose that for many choices (especially those related to more tangible economic benefits), students cannot take account of the scope of options available at a particular institution. It also points to ensuring that there is collaboration between universities such that individuals can transfer to where preferred programs are being offered.[35] Again this seems somewhat more blunted as one moves from undergraduate to graduate and professional schools, and as individuals develop a better understanding of the course they wish to choose in life.

Cost Issues

Cost issues, either from tuition or cost of living, surrounding markets for universities raise both issues of fairness and of efficiency. University education promotes equality of opportunity, and a sense of fairness militates against distribution of spaces within a market for universities based on the ability to pay. In addition, there may be two important flaws of capital markets that threaten to create inefficiencies in a regime that places significant reliance on student choice. First, unlike the case in which a person borrows in order to invest in physical capital that she can offer as collateral to the lender, a borrower seeking to invest in education cannot offer her human capital as collateral. Consequently, it is difficult to borrow to invest in human capital. This makes it difficult, particularly for an undergraduate with little in the way of a credit history, to borrow in order to finance an education.[36] Second, there are shortcomings in insurance markets that affect education. Individuals are risk-averse. The value of an education, while it may be high in expected terms, will have a large variance across individuals. At the time of choosing to invest in education, a student faces considerable risk about the value of her education, risk which is costly. However, complete insurance is not available against future earnings for obvious moral-hazard reasons (once insured, the student would have little incentive to work hard). Both of these capital market imperfections hinder the operation of the market for students, since students may be reluctant or unable to pay the full cost of their education. Allocating places to students solely on the basis of willingness-to-pay would not attract the highest-quality students.[37]

While we cannot discuss the equity and efficiency concerns about the cost of an education in detail in this paper, considerable work has been done in attempting to devise programs to overcome these issues by offering funding to students directly, rather than to universities. In particular, income-contingent loans can permit governments to aid individuals in obtaining funding for university education in the context of higher tuition fees. Such loan programs could, for example, be combined with a substantial grant program to aid those who may otherwise be dissuaded from attending university due to the 'sticker shock' from the size of the potential debt.[38]

Instituting such a program of income-contingent loans and grants while deregulating tuition incorporates fairness concerns in a manner that preserves the market for quality in university education. It can permit individuals with the willingness *and* ability to attend university to choose where to study. Such choice can provide universities with the incentive to increase quality in order to attract students.[39]

4. Connecting Public Funding, Markets and Competition

There are a variety of ways that government can establish incentives for universities to provide high quality.[40] We suggest that our analysis of markets points towards tentative conclusions about the role for government in improving university's incentives for quality. Government should

- enhance market competition in the university sector;
- provide some funding directly to universities; and
- tie a portion of this funding to market-based indicators.

Enhance Market Competition

Competition is essential for raising the quality of education at universities. A theme of this paper is that competition can be fostered in the market for students or donors. A significant step that government can take to increase quality is therefore to increase reliance on and the functioning of these markets. Such action would include improving the flow of information on differences between universities and increasing information and outreach to individuals in under-represented groups.[41] It would also include deregulating tuition, but in combination with programs designed to ensure that individuals have funding to participate in the market, so that university education is not limited simply to those with the highest willingness-to-pay. A beneficial structure appears to be providing such funding to the student through income-contingent loan programs combined with a program of grants.

Provide a Portion of Public Funding Directly to Universities

As section 3 points out, however, not all funding may be able to follow the student. For example, there may be social benefits (perhaps related to research or broader social or economic benefits) that students do not take into account in their decisions. While not a focus of this essay, concerns about equality of opportunity may also militate against exclusive reliance on incentive funding.[42] It is therefore important to consider how public funding directly to universities can provide incentives to provide high quality.

Focus on Market Based Indicators

Taking as given that some public funding is directly granted to universities, and not allocated to universities indirectly through student choice, does not preclude a role for markets in helping the government establish incentives to provide high quality. If feasible, governments could simply establish programs that provide more funding the higher the measured quality of the university.[43] While we would not reject a possible role for direct measures of quality, we do note that these schemes have encountered significant problems. For example, it is very difficult for governments to design indicators to measure quality, and once they do, the indicators can take on a life of their own.[44] As the indicators will not in all likelihood measure 'quality' directly, institutions may attempt to 'game' the system by focusing on improving the indicators to increase funding without increasing quality. Further, these indicators can be extremely expensive to administer – both for the government and the individual institutions being assessed. The UK appears to provide an example of such costs, with incentive-based systems there leading to considerable administrative costs, and some gaming of the funding system.[45] As an example of the latter concern, Smith reports that in the UK '[i]t is said that appointments of faculty with impressive curriculum vitae are sometimes hurriedly made to meet [a quality review's] deadline, without sufficient consideration of the broader needs of a department.'[46]

Market-based indicators of quality, however, avoid some of these problems. Product market competition for donors and students may be attenuated in the shadow of direct public funding to universities, but only to the extent that the public monies themselves do not depend on competitive results. If public funding were allocated in part on the basis of signals from success in competitive markets for donors and students, then clearly these markets would have an indirect effect on university incentives. It may also reduce the costs of administering the system.

It is noteworthy that Ontario has historically relied on signals from these markets in allocating funding. With respect to the donor market, Ontario has adopted significant funding programs that depend on signals from donor markets. Most importantly, it has occasionally adopted matching programs pursuant to which the province matches donations that universities realize from private donors. There are clearly incentive aspects of such programs. First, they provide a greater incentive for a donor to give to a university since the marginal impact of the donation is greater when combined with the provincial matching grant. Second, they provide a greater incentive for universities to make an effort to solicit donations since the marginal return on a donation is greater given the matching grant. But it is perhaps not always appreciated that there is a powerful informational aspect to the government's reliance on matching grants. Matching grants automatically result in the government allocating more resources to universities best able to attract private donations. Public funding turns on signals from the donation market. This generally increases a university's incentives to improve quality, since higher quality will attract donors interested in contributing to educational excellence, which in turn will also attract public monies.[47]

Ontario also relies on competition for students, but does so in a relatively weak way. Higher-quality universities, all things equal, will have greater demand from students. The province weakly captures information from the market for students in allocating funding by giving universities a per-student capitation payment.[48] This only faintly harnesses information from the student market, however, given that universities do not set tuition so as to clear the market.[49] Rather than setting tuition fees such that there is nobody demanding a spot at the university at that tuition level, universities set tuition such that there is excess demand. This lower-than-clearing price could be relatively low because of regulation, as it is in Ontario, or it could be lower than the clearing price so that universities assure themselves of attracting high-quality students.[50] Rather than allocating spots solely on the basis of willingness to pay, universities combine willingness to pay and merit. As a consequence, since most every university has excess demand for spots at the existing tuition level, information from the enrolment numbers at an institution is unlikely to say much about the relative quality of the university. Both mediocre and excellent universities are likely to have excess demand. This is particularly so in Ontario, where tuition fees are regulated at very low rates.

Ontario, when it established matching programs, wisely relied on signals from donation markets in allocating resources, but in setting a capitation fee the government fails to glean much information from competition for students. In our view, more information about university quality could be available from a closer examination of the nature of demand for an institution. In what follows we assume that willingness-to-pay is not the sole criterion for allocating university spots, but rather that government programs, such as income-contingent loans, are in place in order to ensure that every qualified student could afford to go to university. We have noted that a simple head count of students attending university may not convey much about the intensity of student demand for a university. It might then be suggested that looking at the number of applications would be instructive about student demand. While this may have potential, we are sceptical. Given that there is some cost to applying to a university, either because of an application fee or even because of time and effort, applicants who do not anticipate acceptance at a very selective university may choose not to apply, but this does not imply that they would not have gone to that university if they could have obtained a spot.

We suggest that examining student quality is likely to convey better information about students' perception of the quality of an institution than a head count or the number of applications it receives. Because of regulation, and/or because universities are concerned about the quality of their students, tuition fees do clear the market in Ontario; universities rely on student quality to allocate spots. It is therefore sensible to look at student quality to draw inferences about student demand, and in turn to draw inferences about university quality from student demand. Students will on average be attracted to better schools. Universities allocate their spots on the basis of the students' ability. A measure of the demand for a university is therefore found in the quality of its students.[51]

If an Ontario university can attract a student that could get a spot in every other Ontario university, it is probable that the student views this university as being of relatively high quality. Conversely, if a student can only get into one university, her decision to attend that university says nothing about her perceptions of that university's relative quality. As a result, a university with higher average quality incoming students will on average be of higher quality. Structuring funding to universities not only on the basis of capitation, but also on the basis of the actual quality of their students would capture information from the student market about students' perceptions of university quality. Further, it would not interfere with the quality signals from the market and would not be costly to implement in terms of either administration costs (for the government and schools) or gaming. It may also be appropriate to create competition among programs, not just among universities. Allocating funding to particular programs at different schools on the basis of student demand would enhance local incentives to improve quality. For example, allocating public funding to philosophy departments on the basis of student demand would provide some market-based incentives to encourage these programs to excel, while not requiring such departments to obtain funds purely through a market that may not fully value their social benefits.

Some qualifications are in order. Students may not have good information about quality, may (but may not) view teaching and research as substitutes rather than complements, and moreover may choose schools on the basis of something other than educational quality, such as geography. As noted above, however, as long as students are on average motivated to attend high-quality universities, student demand as measured by the quality of students is a valuable signal of university quality. In addition, measuring student quality may not be easy, as any university admissions committee will confirm.[52] Variance in grading standards across high schools, for example, makes mere reliance on incoming averages a dubious measure of quality. Such variance points to the need to reconsider standardized exit exams from high school.[53] But there are some other objective criteria available, like performance on standardized aptitude tests such as the LSAT. These may be helpful in informing the government about university quality.

We have suggested that Ontario could do more in harnessing the informational content of donor and student choices in their respective marketplaces. The managerial market for university administrators is likely also to stand some improvement. Like corporations, universities could reward presidents for gains realized in the donor and student markets. But it is not clear what role government can or ought to play directly here. If the government can establish background funding rules that reward universities for high quality, this should in turn spur boards at universities to find ways of motivating their managers to improve quality. As noted above, since there are no shareholders in public universities, there is no group of people who are affected in a pecuniary way by the success of the university in the marketplace or in obtaining quality-based funding. However, we would be wary of governments directly intervening to improve managerial incentives. First, just as members of universities' boards do not have a pecuniary incentive to get managerial incentives right, neither do provincial politicians or bureaucrats.[54] Second, it is more likely that university board members understand the educational context better than individuals in government. Moreover, they are on average likely to be more committed to education given their choice to dedicate time to an educational institution. For these reasons, even if there are gains to be had from changing managerial incentives at a university, we would stress the role of incentives for the university as a whole and allow these in turn to operate to spur the provision of incentives to university administrators.

5. Conclusion

In conclusion, let us summarize both what we have said and some of what we have not said. We have not said that there is no place for allocating some, even a considerable amount, of public funding across institutions regardless of merit. There may be efficiency reasons (e.g., similar marginal productivity across institutions even if average productivity is unequal) and equity reasons for spreading the wealth. But we have stressed that incentives matter and that as a result it makes sense to have at least a portion of public funding allocated on the basis of quality.

With respect to the subset of public funding that is allocated on the basis of quality, we have not rejected the possibility that governments should canvass explicit indicators in order to reward quality. We have said, however, that relying on explicit indicators is costly and sometimes misleading, and that either in place of or in addition to such programs governments can learn much from the operation of markets. Capital markets are not likely to prove useful; universities are not likely to succeed as for-profit institutions. But product markets can be more influential than they have been to date in Ontario universities. Not only do these markets directly discipline universities, but governments can use information from the markets to allocate public funding. Ontario could look to the quality of incoming students as a measure of students' estimate of quality. It could look, as it has in the past, to donor choices as well in order to gather information about quality. While market-based incentive schemes are far from a complete response to concerns about quality – indeed they have several shortcomings, as we have discussed – they are valuable tools for governments seeking to promote quality in post-secondary education.

Notes

* Faculty of Law, University of Toronto
1 D.C. Smith, 'How Will I Know If There Is Quality?' (Report on Quality Indicators and Quality Enhancement in Universities: Issues and Experiences, Council of Ontario Universities, 2000), 33.
2 Ibid.
3 For surveys of incentive compensation issues in the private sector, see P. Milgrom and J. Roberts, *Economics, Organization and Management* (Upper Saddle River: Prentice-Hall, 1992), chap 12; E.M. Iacobucci with M.J. Trebilcock, *Value for Money: Executive Compensation in the 1990s* (Toronto: C.D. Howe Institute, 1996); and E.M. Iacobucci, 'The Effects of Disclosure on Executive Compensation,' *University of Toronto Law Journal* 48 (1998), 489.
4 See, e.g., E. Fama, 'Efficient Capital Markets II,' *Journal of Finance* 46 (1991), 1575.

5 See, e.g., B. Holmström, 'Moral Hazard and Observability,' *Bell Journal of Economics* 13 (1979), 74.

6 See, e.g., O. Hart, 'The Market Mechanism as an Incentive Scheme,' *Bell Journal of Economics* 14 (1983), 366.

7 See E. Fama, 'Agency Problems and the Theory of the Firm,' *Journal of Political Economy* 88 (1980), 288.

8 H. Manne, 'Mergers and the Market for Corporate Control,' *Journal of Political Economy* 73 (1965), 110.

9 H. Hansmann, 'The Rationale for Exempting Nonprofit Organizations from Corporate Income Taxation,' *Yale Law Journal* 91 (1980), 54. See also H. Hansmann, *The Ownership of Enterprise* (Cambridge: Harvard University Press, 1996).

10 See, e.g., D. Harris et al., *Cases, Materials and Notes on Partnerships and Canadian Business Corporations*, 4th ed. (Toronto: Thomson-Carswell, 2004), 214–16.

11 N. Barr, *The Economics of the Welfare State*, 4th ed. (Oxford: Oxford University Press, 2004), 323.

12 Ibid.

13 N. Barr, 'Higher Education Funding,' *Oxford Review of Economic Policy* 20:2 (2004 [henceforth 2004a]), 264. See also D. Cameron, 'The Challenge of Change: Canadian Universities in the 21st Century,' *Canadian Public Administration* 45:2 (2002) 145 (discussing the desirability of diversity).

14 Barr (2004), 329.

15 See, e.g., E. Posner, *Law and Social Norms* (Cambridge: Harvard University Press, 2000) (arguing that charitable donations can signal the donor's type to potential trading partners).

16 See, e.g., S. Rose-Ackerman, 'Altruism, Nonprofits and Economic Theory,' *Journal of Economic Literature* 34 (1996), 701.

17 G. Winston, 'Subsidies, Hierarchy and Peers: The Awkward Economics of Higher Education,' *Journal of Economic Perspectives* 13:1 (1999), 13.

18 C. Riddell, 'The Role of Government in Post-Secondary Education in Ontario,' Research paper no. 29, Ontario Panel on the Role of Government (2003) (canvassing estimates of the significant private returns to higher education) and D. Laidler, 'Renovating the Ivory Tower: An Introductory Essay,' in D. Laidler, ed., *Renovating the Ivory Tower: Canadian Universities and the Knowledge Economy* (Toronto: C.D. Howe Institute, 2002) (arguing that the returns to undergraduate education are high, with some exceptions such as for fine arts for males, but the returns to graduate education are low and possibly negative).

19 Riddell (2003), Barr (2004), and Laidler (2002).

20 Laidler (2002) (noting the possible existence of societal spill-overs from research, but arguing that there is reason to doubt that they exist in some cases based on empirical research).

21 J. Chant, comments at Higher Education in Canada conference (John

Deutsch Institute, Queen's University, February 2004): 'Evidence suggests, however, that many students themselves value university research' (5).

22 Chant (2004) and Cameron (2002).

23 Chant (2004).

24 D. Laidler, 'Incentives Facing Canadian Universities: Some Possible Consequences' (Higher Education in Canada conference, 2004) (discussing the risks in the focus of current research funding on research in science and technology) and Chant (2004) (discussing the shift in the role of research funding agencies in Canada from granting agencies focused on potential for significant contribution to knowledge to research managers specifying the research that is valuable).

25 See discussion in M.J. Trebilcock and E.M. Iacobucci, 'Privatization and Accountability,' *Harvard Law Review* 116:5 (2003), 1422.

26 See A. Green, 'Equality of Opportunity and University Education' in this volume for a discussion of the impact of university education on democratic decision-making.

27 Riddell (2003) (discussing private benefits such as increased health and personal development and broader or public benefits such as improved outcomes for children of educated parents, reduced criminal activity, enhanced 'social cohesion,' such as increased civic participation, smaller social inequalities, and lower levels of reliance on public transfers) and Laidler (2002).

28 Laidler (2004) discusses the differing impact of university education on the level, as opposed to the rate of growth, of productivity. See also, for example, Laidler (2002) (discussing the potential role of universities in fostering growth in the standard of living by raising the productivity of workers and by generating spill-overs such as from the creation and dissemination of new ideas) and Riddell (2003) (discussing the empirical evidence relating education and economic growth arising from innovation [dynamic externalities] and from interactions between educated workers and others [knowledge spillovers]).

29 For example, R. Mueller and D. Rockerbie, 'Do the Maclean's Rankings Affect University Choice? Evidence for Ontario' (Higher Education in Canada conference, 2004), find that after controlling for a range of factors, *Maclean's* rankings of universities have a significant impact on excess demand across types of universities as measured by the entry grades of first-year students. The impact varies across programs with the largest impact for medical/doctoral universities, then comprehensive universities, followed by primary undergraduate universities. Further, many universities such as University of Toronto are developing a range of publicly available performance indicators (University of Toronto, 'The Choice for a Generation: Investing in Higher Education and Ontario's Future,' University of Toronto submission to the Rae Review, November 2004).

30 See, e.g., S. Page, 'Rankings of Canadian Universities, 1995: More Problems in Interpretation,' *Canadian Journal of Higher Education* 26:2 (1996), 47,
discussing problems with 'rank' data for universities. However, it may be
that deregulating tuition will lead to a demand for more and better information from rankings (Laidler [2004]).

31 However, the Wharton School still provides some information to these
services. Gordon Pitts, 'Are Business Schools Fudging Their Numbers?'
Globe and Mail, 17 November 2004, B3.

32 Barr (2004a).

33 Ibid.

34 Barr (2004). See also R. Finnie, E. Lascelles, and A. Sweetman, 'Who Goes?
The Direct and Indirect Effects of Family Background on Access to Post-
Secondary Education' (Higher Education in Canada conference, 2004) on
the positive relationship between family background and participation in
post-secondary education.

35 Smith (2000).

36 See Barr (2004a).

37 Ibid.

38 See, e.g. M. Trebilcock, R. Daniels, A. Green, and R. Hrab, *Creating a
Human Capital Society for Ontario*, Staff Report, Ontario Panel on the Role
of Government (March 2004), Barr (2004a) and Riddell (2003) on income-
contingent loans and grants to students.

39 It may, however, point to the need for government to engage in the distribution of such funding, as universities may use such programs to price
discriminate among students. Winston (1999).

40 B. Jongloed and H. Vossensteyn, 'Keeping Up Performances: An International Survey of Performance-Based Funding in Higher Education,' *Journal
of Higher Education Policy and Management* 23:2 (2001), 127 (surveying
government higher education funding policies in 11 OECD countries).

41 Jongbloed and Vossensteyn (2001) (arguing governments are increasingly
requiring universities to generate more information to improve stakeholder and student decisions).

42 See Winston (1999); Barr (2004a) (discussing the potential need to consider
both distribution and efficiency).

43 Jongbloed and Vossensteyn (2001) (finding that the OECD countries
surveyed tended to employ performance-based funding, although the
proportion of such funding is generally low with countries relying on
more than one measure and on a negotiating process).

44 Janice Gross Stein, *The Cult of Efficiency* (Toronto: Anansi Press, 2001) and
Michael Trebilcock, *The Prospects for Reinventing Government* (Toronto: C.D.
Howe Institute, 1994).

45 See, e.g., Smith (2000) (reviewing considerable administrative costs involved with quality assessment in the UK).

46 Smith (2000), 23.

47 For similar reasoning with respect to the role of tax deductions for charitable donations, see S. Levmore, 'Taxes as Ballots,' *University of Chicago
   Law Review* 65 (1998), 388: 'The tax deduction essentially casts the government as a financing partner, with taxpayer-donors serving as intermediar-
   ies or agents who choose the providers of, or indeed the very existence of,
   certain services. In an important sense, private contributions are matched
   by the government through the charitable deduction.'

48 The Honourable Robert Rae, *Higher Expectations for Higher Education*
   (Discussion paper, 2004, available at www.raereview.on.ca) (providing
   a summary of the current funding model). See also D. Leyton-Brown,
   'Demystifying Quality Assurance' (Higher Education in Canada conference, 2004) (discussing the current systems in place in Ontario for quality
   assurance).

49 Further, simple per-capita funding provides universities with the opportunity to cross-subsidize courses – that is, accept students into lower-cost
   courses and shift excess funding to higher-cost areas (such as those requiring laboratories and equipment). This cross-subsidization may not be an
   issue in terms of the base level of funding (and may be attenuated by
   deregulating tuition such that students can decide not to attend universities that excessively cross-subsidize). However, it does not give much
   confidence in terms of incentives for quality. Chant (2004).

50 Winston (1999).

51 Mueller and Rockerbie (2004) discuss how the excess demand in the
   market for university admissions at current tuition levels may be cleared
   by student quality (as measured by GPAs). They find that excess demand
   for an institution leads to increased entrance standards (and GPAs).

52 S. Mizrahi and A. Mehrez, 'Managing Quality in Higher Education
   Systems via Minimal Quality Requirements: Signaling and Controls,'
   Economics of Education Review 21 (2002), 53, advocate basing funding on
   the minimum entrance standards set by an institution. However, such
   standards may lead to gaming of admission standards and neglect the
   information provided by actual entrance quality.

53 Trebilcock, Daniels, Green, and Hrab (2004).

54 See Trebilcock and Iacobucci (2003).

PART IV

Building Excellence: Graduate and Research Support

Post-secondary Education and Research: Whither Canadian Federalism?

DAVID M. CAMERON*

> There is in every country a constitutional morality which must be
> observed if a tolerant and democratic polity is to survive.'
> — J.A. Corry[1]

The question posed in this paper is the following: What are the implications for Canadian federalism of recent federal government initiatives in post-secondary education in general and research in particular?

The Evolution of Federal Involvement in Post-secondary Education and Research[2]

The federal government has been directly involved in supporting research in Canadian universities since the First World War and the establishment of the National Research Council (NRC) in 1916. This was, in fact, the first direct contact between the federal government and Canada's universities, and it came about more by dint of circumstance than by design. The NRC was established to promote industrial research in aid of the war effort, but it was quickly and ineluctably drawn into support for university-based research, including the training of graduate students. The reason was quite simple. Then, as now, Canada's private-sector capacity for research and development was limited and universities provided a willing receptor for federal aid. Provincial governments have seldom challenged the federal role in university-based research and graduate training, tacitly accepting federal primacy. Federal spending on research, however, remained relatively modest. It would take another world war before it reached the $1 million mark. [Ed: See Wolfe, pp. 327–334.]

The Second World War gave rise to a further expansion of federal involvement in universities, this time in support of returning veterans. The federal government not only covered their full tuition but also provided a weekly allowance and paid a grant on behalf of each veteran to the receiving university as well. The result was that university enrolment more than doubled, peaking at over 80,000 in 1947, with veterans making up a third of the total.

Universities managed to accommodate the influx of veterans mostly through temporary means, renting space, increasing class sizes, and shortening the time required to complete a degree. They also took advantage of the attendant relationship with the federal government to argue for continuing federal support. In 1951 the Massey Commission endorsed this argument and the prime minister, Louis St Laurent, almost immediately accepted it. Federal grants would be paid at the rate of fifty cents per capita, divided among the provinces in proportion to population and paid to universities and colleges in each province in proportion to enrolment. The grants would subsequently be increased, to $1 per capita in 1956, and to $5 in 1965, just before the federal government changed the scheme profoundly, substituting transfers to the provinces for grants to universities.

That change had its roots in the decision by the premier of Quebec, Maurice Duplessis, to bar Quebec universities from accepting federal grants after 1952, even though he had allowed them a year earlier. The two governments remained deadlocked on that issue until 1959 when, after the death of Duplessis and the defeat of St Laurent's government, an accommodation was finally reached. It involved a significant retreat by the federal government and the first instance of a province 'opting out' of a wholly federal program with equivalent compensation. What happened in 1965 was essentially that all provinces were now to be treated the same as Quebec. Federal grants to universities would cease, to be replaced by a new fiscal arrangement with the provinces. If the federal government seemed to be retreating from its direct involvement with universities, the same was certainly not the case with respect to research.

The fiscal arrangement that was to run from 1966 to 1972 was designed to assure the provinces of federal transfers equal to half of what provinces spent on post-secondary education. This was to be accomplished through an equalized transfer of tax points plus cash, if necessary. It turned out to be very necessary indeed, as post-secondary expenditures by the provinces exceeded all expectations. By 1972, when the arrangement was extended for another five years, the federal government found it necessary to impose a 15% cap on annual increases in its cash transfer.

Meanwhile, research was beginning to appear on the radar screen of federal public policy. Two studies had been launched in 1967. One was co-sponsored by the Science Council and the Canada Council, and headed by Dr John Macdonald, the former president of UBC. It reported in 1969. The second study was launched by the Senate and headed by Hon. Maurice Lamontagne. It issued the first volume of its report in 1970. Not surprisingly, the Macdonald report was more respectful of university autonomy, but both argued for a major expansion of federal support for research. Macdonald argued for more comprehensive coverage of university research, to include all academic disciplines. That recommendation would eventually lead to the reorganization of the federal granting councils in 1976, redefining the mandate of the NRC, expanding the mandate of the Medical Research Council (MRC), which had been separated from the NRC in 1960, and creating two new councils, the Natural Science and Engineering Research Council (NSERC) and the Social Sciences and Humanities Research Council (SSHRC). Meanwhile, Senator Lamontagne's argument that a national science policy should be driven by federal policy objectives and not by the interests of scientists led almost immediately to the establishment of the Ministry of State for Science and Technology (MOSST) in 1971.

By 1976 and the expiry of the federal-provincial fiscal arrangements the need to regain control of federal expenditure commitments had gained the upper hand. For the 1977–82 period, a new federal approach was introduced. Post-secondary education, along with hospital insurance and medicare, were characterized as 'established programs,' to be supported by what amounted, at least in the case of post-secondary education, to a wholly unconditional transfer to the provinces. The transfer, known as Established Programs Financing (EPF), was partly in the form of cash and partly tax points, initially at least in equal proportions. The key change was that federal transfers would no longer be tied to provincial expenditures. Moreover, the transfer really had nothing to do with post-secondary education at all. It was completely unconditional except, perhaps, in the eyes of some federal officials. Then, in 1983, the post-secondary component of EPF, but not the two health-related components, was limited by the '6 and 5' restraint program.

Several provinces had begun to take an interest in promoting research within their universities. Alberta had been an early entrant into this field, and its Heritage Foundation, established in 1979, gave a considerable boost to medical research in that province's two major universities and associated hospitals. Quebec entered the field as early as 1969 with the creation of the Institut national de la recherche scientifique (INRS) within the Université du Québec. A general program of sponsored research was launched shortly thereafter with the establishment of a program known as Formation de chercheurs et action concertée (FCAC). In 1983 this program would be reorganized under a separate agency known as the Fonds pour la formation des chercheurs et l'aide à la recherché (Fonds FCAR). Ontario entered the field with a significant move in 1986, establishing a Premier's Council and a $1billion fund to support research and technology. Within the year the first seven 'centres of excellence' were designated under this initiatiave.

Ontario's initiative caught the eye of the new federal prime minister, Brian Mulroney. What was increasingly being recognized was the potential contribution of research, both pure and applied, to economic development and productivity. The initial federal steps were tentative and not always successful, but they clearly marked the beginning of a new era in federal policy, an era that would lead incrementally to a dramatic transformation of the federal role in research and post-secondary education, and one that would raise fundamental questions about the future of Canadian federalism.

The Mulroney initiatives began with the ill-fated matching-funds program, launched in 1986. It tied future increases in granting-council support to matching contributions from private industry. The program was so broad in its definition of terms that universities were quickly able to reach the limit of increased federal funding of $380 million over four years. The Senate committee on national finances doubted the program had any significant impact in terms of increasing private-sector support for university research.

Then came the much more successful Networks of Centres of Excellence (NCEs) program, launched in 1989. This was a direct copy of Ontario's Centres of Excellence initiative. It started with fourteen projects recommended by both international and Canadian panels of experts, and involved scientists from thirty universities as well as government agencies and the private sector.

A third initiative by the federal government was the creation of a full-blown Department of Industry, absorbing MOSST and part of the former

Department of Regional Industrial Expansion. The federal government finally seemed to be ready to take research, and the science and technology that sustains it, seriously. But it would take the resolution of the chronic debt and deficit situation before further progress was forthcoming. And that resolution would shake the very foundations of Canadian federalism.

The centrepiece of the federal government's deficit-reduction strategy was unveiled in the 1995 budget. And it was a stunning illustration of the oft-forgotten truth that what the federal government giveth, the federal government can taketh away. In this case it took away some $6 billion from the provinces. It did so by first rolling EPF and the Canada Assistance Plan (CAP) into a single envelope, called the Canada Health and Social Transfer (CHST). Post-secondary education was not even mentioned in the name. Post-secondary education became an easy target for provinces left to pick up the program pieces after the federal cuts. Tuition fees, for example, were quickly allowed to double as a share of total university revenues.

The provinces set about to repair some of the damage, demanding both restitution of the cuts and meaningful constraints on the future use of the federal spending power. The result, embodied in the 1999 Social Union Framework Agreement (SUFA), went a long way towards achieving the first objective (the rest would be added in the 2004 health accord), but made little progress on the second. Indeed, SUFA embodied formal acceptance by the provinces of the federal government's right to spend money in areas of provincial jurisdiction.

> The use of the federal spending power under the Constitution has been essential to the development of Canada's social union. An important use of the spending power by the Government of Canada has been to transfer money to the provincial and territorial governments. These transfers support the delivery of social programs and services by provinces and territories in order to promote equality of opportunity and mobility for all Canadians and to pursue Canada-wide objectives.
>
> Conditional social transfers have enabled governments to introduce new and innovative social programs, such as Medicare, and to ensure that they are available to all Canadians.[3]

Since SUFA contained no binding dispute-resolution mechanism, the whole framework agreement is really only a statement of intent. But its intent is clear and powerful: the constitutional division of powers has now been subsumed under the spending power of Parliament. And, of course, it was precisely because of this intent that Quebec refused to sign the agreement.

On the other side of the federal divide, however, the 1995 cuts in transfers to the provinces quickly helped to reverse the pattern of chronic deficit and rising debt. Within three years the federal government was running a surplus and paying down its debt. And while health care has been the major beneficiary of the new-found federal largesse, post-secondary education, research, and graduate study have received a healthy chunk of federal money. The list of federal initiatives is an impressive one, at least in terms of the money spent and committed, if not always in terms of their overall impact.

Federal Spending and Program Initiatives

The first of these initiatives was the 1997 introduction of the Canada Foundation for Innovation (CFI). The CFI is designed to support research infrastructure, including major equipment, facilities, and installations, in Canadian universities, hospitals, and colleges. It was established with an initial endowment of $800 million, which was subsequently increased to $3.65 billion. The funding is slated to last until 2010. A distinguishing feature of the CFI is the way it is designed to lever substantially greater funds than its own endowment. The foundation provides only 40% of the cost of an approved project, with the rest coming from private or provincial agencies or corporations. As a result, the actual impact of the foundation is two and a half times the amount invested by the federal government, bringing the total funding for infrastructure to over $9 billion.

The CFI addressed a real problem for Canadian universities. At the same time, it confirmed the federal government's pre-eminence in financing university research. And it did so by reinforcing attempts to shift that research in favour of the applied, and especially patentable, end of the research scale.

It also exposed a particular problem for universities in Atlantic Canada, for whom access to private-sector funding was limited if not unavailable, and whose provincial governments were even more severely strapped for funds than elsewhere. The solution to that problem was found through the Atlantic Canada Opportunities Agency, a federal body responsible for economic development in the Atlantic region. It has some $300 million available specifically for the purpose of providing the funds necessary to contribute to the matching contribution required by the CFI.

The federal government used the same organizational device – a private foundation – to create its second major initiative. This was the Canadian Millennium Scholarship Foundation (CMSF), which was set up with an endowment of $2.5 billion, and designed to last for ten years. Despite the name of the foundation, only a small proportion of its payments to students (5%) are true scholarships, based on merit. The remaining 95% are bursaries, based on need.

Conceived in obvious haste, the foundation suffered from considerable confusion as to its true intent. The legislation setting it up stated its purpose as improving access to post-secondary education, but when introducing it the then finance minister, Paul Martin, indicated its purpose was to reduce student debt. The two are clearly not the same. Besides this initial confusion as to purpose, the foundation got itself tangled up in overlapping federal and provincial student aid arrangements, with the result that much of the federal bursaries simply displaced existing provincial student aid. The net benefit to students has been a good deal less than the federal contribution to the foundation.[4]

Both the CMSF and the CFI, as independent foundations, have been roundly criticized by the Auditor General.[5] The burden of her criticism has been that as private corporations spending public funds, they violate the principles of responsible government and public accountability. Peter Aucoin has also been critical of these foundations, and for many of the same reasons: 'These foundations are privately governed by a board of directors ... As board members of an independent corporation, their obligations are to promote and protect the interests of the corporation. Accordingly, ministers cannot issue directives to their appointees. By the same token, ministers are not accountable for the performance of their appointees.'[6]

Another foundation of a slightly different character was announced in February of 2002. This was the Pierre Elliot Trudeau Foundation, established with an endowment from the federal government of $125 million. It will operate under an independent board of directors and its primary purpose will be to 'award internationally competitive doctoral fellowships, similar in value and stature to the Rhodes, so that Canadian universities will continue to attract the very best students from our own country, and around the world.'[7] Up to 25 fellowships will be awarded annually, three-quarters of them to Canadians. The awards will all be in the humanities, broadly defined. In addition, up to five mid-career awards will be granted each year to Canadian scholars who have already earned international reputations. Finally, additional stipends will be paid to a small number of individuals working in the areas of public policy, law, and academia who are involved in areas identified as central to the themes being pursued by the foundation. The fellowships and awards are intended to serve as a lasting memorial to the former prime minister.

Another federal initiative had been announced in 1999, and confirmed in legislation a year later. This involved the transformation of the Medical Research Council, one of the federal government's three granting councils, into the Canadian Institutes of Health Research. This was accompanied by an initial doubling of federal funds for health-related research, which would subsequently be increased further, along with support for the other granting councils. The concept of health 'institutes,' clearly borrowed from the United States, will allow the government's support of health research to be concentrated in thirteen distinct lines of research, each easily identified as a priority for Canadians.

That same year saw the establishment of yet another federal initiative, this time with the creation of the Canada Research Chairs (CRCs). Funding for this program is to come in the form of annual appropriations over a five-year period, at a total cost of some $900 million. It is intended to support the hiring of 2000 professors, half at a senior level, known as Tier 1 Chairs and funded at a total of $200,000 annually, and the other half at more junior levels, known as Tier 2 Chairs and funded at a total of $100,000 each.

Considerable controversy surrounded the way in which these chairs are to be allocated among Canadian universities. Every university gets at least one chair, except for institutions formally affiliated with a larger university. But after that, the chairs are distributed in proportion to each university's share of research grants awarded by the three granting councils. The government did intervene when it came to dividing the chairs among the three councils. The humanities and social sciences, which would have qualified for approximately 12% of the chairs on the basis of their share of research grants, were actually awarded 40% of the chairs. The health sciences were allotted 34% and the natural sciences and engineering 45%. Still, there were complaints that the humanities and social sciences should have received more.

The CRC program reveals how artificial the distinction between research and teaching can sometimes be. While these are formally characterized as research chairs, those appointed are expected to teach as well. Moreover, each appointment is approved through a process established by the federal government and ultimately answerable to it. It brings the federal government's acknowledged pre-eminence in research into close proximity with what has always been perceived as the domain of universities and provincial governments, namely teaching. Universities applying for a CRC are required to submit a detailed plan for approval by a 'college of reviewers' operating under a steering committee of federal officials.

The CRCs are intended to at least partially address a looming shortage of professors in Canadian universities. This shortage is anticipated as the result not only of the growth in student numbers, especially in Alberta, BC, and Ontario, but also the pending retirement of the cohort of professors hired in the 1960s and 1970s. A third factor was the observed tendency of some of Canada's most promising scholars to be lured away by prestigious American universities.

In 2001 the federal government took what might well turn out to be one of its most significant steps in terms of promoting the effectiveness of Canada's research effort. For the first time, it began to recompense universities for the indirect costs of sponsored research. The reason this is so important is that it finally addresses, if not yet fully, what amounted to a tax on success. Ever since research grants were first introduced in 1916 the federal government has covered only direct costs, leaving universities (or provincial governments) to pick up the indirect costs (most administrative expenses, heat, light, depreciation, and professors' salaries). The upshot is that universities were penalized in direct proportion to their success in attracting sponsored research grants. It is hard to imagine a more counter-productive strategy. The move was initially a tentative one, involving a one-time payment of $200 million for 2001–2. The 2003 budget increased the amount to $225 million and put it on an annual basis.

The one serious qualification in this program is that the calculation of indirect costs is inversely related to the value of research undertaken in each university. Thus, universities doing relatively little research have a higher proportion of their research expenditures reimbursed as indirect costs, as compared with more research-intensive universities. There may be some logic to this based on the actual marginal costs of supporting relatively small research enterprises, but as a strategy for encouraging success it leaves much to be desired.

One final initiative completes this rather impressive list of federal programs in support of research and graduate study. This was the introduction in 2003 of the Canada Graduate Scholarship Program, under which 2000 masters and 2000 doctoral scholarships will be offered through the three granting councils. The program will be phased in over a three-year period and will be fully operational by 2006. Masters fellowships will carry a stipend of $17,500, while doctoral fellowships will be worth a handsome $35,000 each. Interestingly, this time 60% of the awards will be administered by SSHRC.

The emerging federal strategy for post-secondary education and research came into sharper focus with the publication in 2002 of the white paper entitled 'Canada's Innovation Strategy.' This was a joint product of Industry Canada and Human Resources Development Canada (now Human Resources and Skills Development Canada), and actually came out as two documents, one from each department. The papers set out an ambitious set of goals intended to move Canada into the top rank of countries in terms of competitiveness in the global knowledge economy, and to take the steps necessary for Canadians to acquire the skills and attitudes appropriate to an innovative society.

By 2010, according to this strategy, Canada should rank among the top five countries in the world in research and development, and rank among the world leaders in terms of its share of private-sector sales from innovations. To get there federal investments in R&D will have to at least double, while the per-capita value of venture-capital investment will have to match that in the United States.[8] By the same target date, every high school graduate should have the opportunity to attend some form of post-secondary education, and at least 50% of those in the 25 to 64 age group should have completed a degree or diploma. Moreover, the number of masters and doctoral students should increase by 5% each year.[9]

The white paper constituted a direct challenge to Canada's post-secondary community. Speaking as the collective voice of universities, or at least of their presidents, the AUCC responded with 'A Strong Foundation for Innovation: An AUCC Action Plan,' announcing that Canada's universities 'are ready and willing to build on their already impressive contribution. They are eager to perform more research, to produce even more highly-qualified graduates, and to play an even more central role in empowering their communities through knowledge and innovation.'[10] Indeed, the AUCC accepted all of the specific targets set out in the Innovation Strategy, noting, however, that this would require substantially increased resources.

In November of 2002 the AUCC and the federal government consummated the deal by jointly signing a 'Framework of Agreed Principles on Federally Funded University Research.' The framework agreement confirmed the AUCC's acceptance of the federal targets and, in turn, announced that the federal government 'is responsible for providing the necessary levels of investment in university research to achieve these aims.'[11]

This by no means exhausts the list of recent federal initiatives in the field of post-secondary education and research. There have been others, including improvements to the Canada Student Loans Program, introduction of the Canada Learning Bond, and enhancement of the Canada Education Savings Grant.

Whither Canadian Federalism?

In his 2000 Killam lecture, Robert Prichard discussed a number of the above federal innovations and concluded that they constituted a new paradigm in federal support of higher education. 'Over the past five years,' he said, 'we have witnessed major policy changes which have substantially transformed the federal role and which have significant implications for Canadian higher education and research.' Moreover, he continued, these changes 'are very much for the better.'[12]

One year later, using the same forum, John Evans, another of Toronto's distinguished presidents, elaborated on the same theme. 'The thesis of this Killam Lecture' he said, 'is that'

> universities are undergoing a transformation triggered by what I shall call the Public Research Contract. The Contract is between governments and the universities. It involves longer-term commitments by both parties. For government it is a much higher level of investment than previously provided to Canadian universities for their traditional role in the creation and transmission of knowledge. For universities the commitment is economic and social return on public investment, and particularly, jobs and wealth created in Canada. It entails new levels of accountability to perform at international standards of excellence, to use efficiently substantial public funds, and to promote commercialization of the resulting intellectual property.[13]

If we are witnessing a paradigm shift in federal support of higher education and research, under a new 'public research contract,' what are the implications for Canadian federalism? And what are the broader implications of such changes in federalism for J.A. Corry's idea of constitutional morality?

There is no doubt that the last few years have witnessed a fundamental transformation in both the style and substance of Canadian federalism. Buoyed by the current fiscal imbalance, the federal government has been able to pour money into selected areas, most of which fall under provincial legislative jurisdiction. Health, post-secondary education and research, along with cities (or communities) and early childhood development, are the current favourites. Most of these initiatives rest on the somewhat dubious foundation of the federal spending power. This may be sufficient in the case of research, which has long been accepted as a de factor shared jurisdiction. But the current federal initiatives are reaching well beyond research per se to touch most aspects of post-secondary education.

What is missing in this new regime are two critical partners. If there is to be a new paradigm or public research contract or, with apologies to the current adviser to the premier and minister, what might even be called a new social contract, is evidence of buy-in by the whole university community and of provincial governments. Universities are not hierarchical institutions, and their faculties will not be taken in new directions by command. Yet Canadian universities are now almost everywhere organized into trade unions which have the right to negotiate many of the policy issues that lie at the heart of this new paradigm. Similarly, the governance of Canadian universities, again almost everywhere, falls under provincial jurisdiction. There is a limit to how far the spending power can go in transforming the character of universities.

The absence of provincial participation is particularly troublesome, since even with respect to the spending power of Parliament a province can easily neutralize federal initiatives, as we saw clearly in the case of the Millennium Scholarships and the problem of federal payments displacing provincial funds for student aid.[14] The question here is conceptually simple. It may, of course, be much more difficult to deal with in practice. The question is whether the provinces share the same objectives for post-secondary education and research as the federal government. If they work at cross-purposes, universities may, at best, see the benefits of federal aid diminished or negated by provincial cuts or conflicting priorities. And even if a province does share the federal government's objectives, where are the mechanisms for achieving this coordination?

The Social Union Framework Agreement of 1999 promised a new era of 'collaborative federalism,'[15] but if that agreement provides any indication of what the future holds in story, there is little reason for optimism. It seems unlikely that a grand solution can be found for this problem of coordination, that any new mechanism can somehow transform divergent provincial and institutional interests into common purposes and common goals. The more prudent course may be to not even try. Why not, instead, champion the virtues of diversity and channel resources to where they actually achieve demonstrated success?

For this to occur, the federal government must first get its own ducks in a row. By that I mean that it must resist more forcefully the temptation to compromise its objectives in order to satisfy demand for pieces of the distributive pie. Of course, to do this it has to be clear about what those objectives are. But if they are to embrace the new knowledge-based economy, to promote excellence in frontier research, and to increase commercial applications – as current policy statements suggest – then a more single-minded strategy is required. One of the best examples of the kind of strategy required is contained in the Canada Research Chairs. Here chairs are awarded in proportion to demonstrated success in winning research competitions. We need more policies that reward success. Yet even here the objective was compromised, if only partially, by guaranteeing every university at least one chair. An even more convincing example is the Millennium Scholarship Foundation, which serves no clear purpose and, in fact, has been defended on grounds quite distinct from those set forth in the legislation establishing it. But perhaps the best example of conflicting objectives is the treatment of the indirect costs of research. The decision to accept responsibility for such costs, after all these years, is certainly to be commended. But the way it was done, with payments inversely related to the actual success of a university in attracting research support, severely limits its potential effectiveness.

A greater challenge falls to the provinces. Where do they want to position themselves and their universities? Will they passively allow their universities and other research institutions to compete for federal dollars within the financial framework of equity-based funding formulae, or will they actively promote a culture of excellence and reward those institutions that strive successfully to achieve it? Provincial governments do have a choice here. Inaction is always a choice. Where does Ontario stand on this issue?

The greatest challenge of all falls to individual universities, for they are the ones that must ultimately embrace change. Governments, federal and provincial, can help or hinder, but the universities themselves must determine the course they will steer. What kind of university will succeed in the new knowledge economy? I close with lessons gleaned from a study of five European universities, all of which had transformed themselves into what Burton Clark called 'entrepreneurial universities.' An entrepreneurial university, he argued, is one that 'on its own, actively seeks to innovate in how it goes about its business. It seeks to work out a substantial shift in organizational character so as to arrive at a more promising posture for the future.'[16] By way of contrast, Clark described the conventional university, one that may be more familiar to Canadian readers: '"Underfunding" becomes a constant. Traditional university infrastructure becomes even more of a constraint on the possibilities of response. If left in customary form, central direction ranges between soft and soggy. Elaborate collegiate authority leads to sluggish decision-making: 50 to 100 and more central committees have the power to study, delay, and veto. The senate becomes more of a bottleneck than the administration.'[17]

Clark identified five characteristics which all of the entrepreneurial universities in his study shared in common. First, they all had what he called a strong steering core, a leadership group with the capacity to steer the institution. Their leadership was exercised not through control, but rather through shared values and operating procedures. The second characteristic was an 'enhanced development periphery' consisting of new units which undertake new lines of interdisciplinary enquiry, often in cooperation with industry. Third, these universities all managed to diversify their funding bases, seeking new sources of funds and thus freeing themselves from the vagaries of government grants. Fourth, the entrepreneurial university maintained its commitment to its heartland departments, sharing resources across the whole institution, with some units more dependent than others on traditional sources of revenue. Finally, a common but necessary characteristic was a shared culture of innovation. Significantly, he found, this culture was not the inspiration of one great person, but rather a shared, unifying vision that encompassed and transformed the whole institution.

We have clearly abandoned any adherence to classical federalism. The federal government is now deeply involved in many aspects of post-secondary education and especially research. Moreover, it is an involvement designed, if somewhat hesitantly, to lead universities in the direction of competitive excellence and innovation. The challenge to the federal government comes down to how thoroughly it will pursue that objective, or how much it will compromise it in pursuit of equity objectives. The challenge to the provinces is even greater. Will they join the federal government and pursue complementary policies? Or will they stay out of the way, accepting a residual role in support of universities? Or, finally, will they work at cross-purposes, seeking to frustrate federal initiatives? In the end, however, the fundamental choices have to be made by individual universities. The real challenge to governments is to get their signals straight. That is probably the best we can hope for in terms of constitutional morality.

Notes

* Department of Political Science, Dahhousie University
1 J.A. Corry, 'The Uses of a Constitution,' in *The Constitution and the Future of Canada*, Special Lectures of the Law Society of Upper Canada (Toronto: Richard De Boo Ltd, 1978), 2.
2 This section is based on David M. Cameron, *More Than an Academic Question: Universities, Governments, Public Policy in Canada* (Halifax: IRPP, 1991), 59–291.
3 'A Framework to Improve the Social Union for Canadians,' included as an appendix in Tom McIntosh, ed., *Building the Social Union: Perspectives, Directions and Challenges* (Regina: Canadian Plains Research Centre, 2002), 115.
4 Harvey Lazar et al., *Canadian Millennium Scholarship Foundation: Evaluation of the Foundation's Performance, 1998–2002* (Kingston: Institute of Intergovernmental Relations, Queen's University, 2003).
5 Two reports by the Auditor General addressed concerns related to these independent foundations. See Canada, Office of the Auditor General, *Report to the House of Commons, November 1999* (Ottawa: Public Works and Government Services Canada, 1999), chap. 23, 'Involving Others in Governing: Accountability at Risk.' See also Canada, Office of the Auditor General, *Report to the House of Commons, April 2002* (Ottawa: Public Works and Government Services Canada, 2002), chap. 1.
6 Peter Aucoin, 'Independent Foundations, Public Money and Public Accountability: Whither Ministerial Responsibility as Democratic Governance?' in *Canadian Public Administration* 46:1 Spring 2003, 12.
7 Allan Rock, 'Speaking Notes for Allan Rock Minister of Industry in the House of Commons: the Pierre Elliott Trudeau Foundation Fellowship' (Ottawa, 20 February 2002), 1.
8 Industry Canada, 'Achieving Excellence: Investing in People, Knowledge and Opportunities,' in *Canada's Innovation Strategy* (Ottawa: Industry Canada, 2002).
9 Human Resources Development Canada, 'Knowledge Matters: Skills and Learning for Canadians,' in *Canada's Innovation Strategy* (Ottawa, HRDC, 2002).

10　Association of Universities and Colleges of Canada, 'A Strong Foundation for Innovation: An AUCC Action Plan' (Ottawa: AUCC, July 2002), 2.

11　Government of Canada and Association of Universities and Colleges of Canada, 'A Framework of Agreed Principles on Federally Funded University Research' (Ottawa, 18 November 2002), 2.

12　J. Robert Prichard, 'Federal Support for Higher Education and Research in Canada: The New Paradigm,' *2000 Killam Annual Lecture* (Winnipeg, 2000), 4.

13　John R. Evans, 'Higher Education in the Higher Education Economy: Towards a Public Research Contract,' *2001 Killam Annual Lecture* (Montreal, 2001), 9–10.

14　See Lazar et al., *Canadian Millennium Scholarship Foundation*, 30–2.

15　See Ian Robinson and Richard Simeon, 'The Dynamics of Canadian Federalism,' in James Bickerton and Alain-G. Gagnon, *Canadian Politics*, 3rd ed. (Peterborough: Broadview Press, 1999), 256–60.

16　Burton R. Clark, *Creating Entrepreneurial Universities: Organizational Pathways of Transformation* (Paris: IAU Press, 1998), 4.

17　Ibid., 131.

Anchors of Creativity: How Do Public Universities Create Competitive and Cohesive Communities?

MERIC S. GERTLER AND TARA VINODRAI

1 The Public University as an Anchor of Creativity

Universities have long been viewed as crucial to the processes of learning, innovation, and knowledge creation, and this is more important now than ever before. Given that universities are key institutions for knowledge production, integration, and inclusion, it is crucial to ask ourselves: what role do institutions of research and graduate education play in enabling regions, provinces, and the nation to attract and retain talented people, thereby contributing to wider goals of competitiveness and social inclusion?

This paper begins by outlining the recent literature on regional economic development, innovation, and the role of the university in anchoring the competitiveness and cohesion of communities. The university is viewed as a key institution that enhances competitiveness by connecting city-regions (and nations) to global flows of knowledge and talent. Furthermore, universities build social inclusion and cohesion by creating more diverse and tolerant communities and society. However, this is a virtuous circle, since diverse and tolerant communities in turn help to build stronger universities. Through this process, the university acts as an anchor for creative thinking and activity within the economy. Building on these arguments, we present recent evidence on how well Ontario and Canada measure up in terms of their ability to attract and retain two particular forms of talent: graduate students and scholars from around the world. Finally, we conclude by identifying the opportunities and challenges that face public policy-makers as they consider how to build excellence in graduate education and research at our public universities

2 Creativity and Innovation

There is a well-established and extensive literature on cluster-based regional economic development and on regional and national innovation systems that provides insight into the role of universities in a knowledge-based economy.[1] This literature suggests that regions (and nations) support the growth of innovative and dynamic industries and clusters through the provision of general and specialized infrastructure. An instrumental component of this knowledge infrastructure includes a well-developed education and research system comprised of universities, colleges, and research institutes.

In general, this literature promotes a somewhat narrow view of the role of the university in the community, in which the university is typically seen as a 'knowledge factory.' The university produces knowledge and technologies that are then transferred from the university to the private sector through technology-transfer centres, incubators, R&D partnerships, university-industry alliances, commercialization programs, and spin-off firms. These local interactions between firms and other institutions are crucial to economic competitiveness, since it is through these interactions that cutting-edge research is transformed into commercially viable products or processes leading to prosperity for both firms and regions. Scholars of innovation studies have documented the successes (and failures) of developing technologies and commercializing research through these types of government-supported programs and initiatives, as well as demonstrating how the university generates knowledge spillovers to other parts of the regional economy.[2] Unquestionably, there is an important role for the university in bolstering the competitiveness of regions, provinces, and the nation through these types of initiatives. However, the role of the university must be seen in its wider societal context. As a key institution in a knowledge-based economy, the university plays multiple roles, reaching well beyond this narrow view of the university as 'knowledge factory.'

3 Local and Global Flows of Talent and Knowledge

More recently, this literature has recognized that technology transfer does not just occur through formalized programs and mechanisms. An equally, if not more important, role for the university is to facilitate the indirect transfer of technology and flow of knowledge through producing well-educated talent for the local (and national) labour market. An abundance of local highly skilled workers is often cited as one of the most important factors for the success and dynamism of locally based clusters and regional innovation systems.

This local flow of talent and knowledge-transfer facilitated by the university is often complemented by global flows of talent and knowledge. Recent research demonstrates that the most dynamic and innovative places are those that have *both* strong local interaction (collaboration and competition between firms and institutional actors) as well as strong linkages to other sites of knowledge and innovation around the globe.[3] The most successful places are those that combine a *rich local milieu*, where knowledge circulates with relative ease across disciplinary, organizational, and firm boundaries, with a *high degree of openness and interaction* with other innovative clusters and dynamic places. Again, the university – through its research and graduate programs – has a crucial role to play in facilitating the global flow of knowledge. The university's research networks and linkages connect city-regions, provinces, nations, and their clusters to global knowledge flows.

Saxenian provides a compelling account of how these global flows of knowledge enhance the dynamism of Silicon Valley.[4] In Silicon Valley, a large number of top researchers and students come from other countries seeking an open and supportive university environment in which to work or study. Many foreign students who sought higher education in the Valley's pre-eminent research institutions stay to work for local firms, gaining experience and accessing the many social and professional networks in the Valley. Subsequently, many of these 'immigrant entrepreneurs' start up their own companies either in the Valley or in their 'home country.' However, even those who leave the Valley to return to their home country tend to maintain connections to the Valley through strong transnational social and business networks. This results in technology and knowledge transfer to places such as Bangalore, India, and Hsinchu, Taiwan, but also provides business opportunities for firms in the Valley alongside local job creation in both locales. Rather than processes of brain drain or brain gain, there is an ongoing process of 'brain circulation' characterized by continuous flows of ideas, knowledge, and people between institutions and firms that enrich both the Valley *and* the regions of origin. This leads Saxenian (2000: 267) to suggest that the competitiveness of regional and national economies is 'derived from [their] openness and diversity – and this will be increasingly true as the economy becomes more global ... [therefore], we need to encourage the continued immigration of skilled workers, while simultaneously devoting resources to improving education and training for native workers.'

These arguments concerning the importance of openness and diversity are echoed in the recent work of Richard Florida and his colleagues.[5] Florida argues that highly educated labour ('talent') – one of the most important inputs to the production of goods and services in a knowledge-based economy – is drawn to places that already have a critical mass of creative people and activities. Those places that are best able to attract and retain the most talented people will be those that are the most open, diverse, and tolerant and that have a rich quality of place.[6] The ability to attract creative people and to be open to diverse groups of people of different ethnic, racial, and lifestyle groups provides distinct advantages to regions in generating innovations, growing and attracting competitive industries and clusters, and spurring economic growth. In this view, the most successful and dynamic communities will be those with a social environment that is open to creativity and diversity of many kinds.

It is worth considering what institutions are important in creating these communities. In other words what helps to anchor creativity in certain places more than others? Which institutions are important and how are they important? The work of Saxenian, Florida, and others points to the university as a critical institution in this process. The university plays a number of interrelated roles, acting to generate, attract, and retain highly skilled talent while at the same time contributing to the creation of open and tolerant places, which, in turn, helps to create the necessary conditions for attracting and retaining talent, thereby making the entire process mutually reinforcing. In other words, the university has a much *wider role* to play in the community that reaches well beyond simple technology transfer. The precise contours of this process are discussed below.

First, the university plays an important role in shaping the quality of place and fostering openness and tolerance in the community. Crucial to this process is the ability of the university to create a social environment that is open to dialogue and debate, tolerant of different viewpoints, and accessible to many different social, ethnic, and cultural groups (locally, nationally, and internationally). In other words, the university has a role in reducing 'barriers to entry' and working towards social inclusion.

Second, the university acts as a talent magnet by making places attractive to highly skilled research talent. In addition to providing an open, diverse setting, there are other aspects that attract talent to particular institutions and locales. A critical mass of researchers in a particular place signals some very important qualities and characteristics of the university: a rich portfolio of current and future research and collaboration opportunities; and the opportunity to learn from peers engaged in exciting work at the leading edge of one's discipline. This ability for the university to generate 'buzz' around a series of research initiatives in turn attracts more graduate students and other researchers, as well as opening the door to potential linkages with firms and other collaborators, thereby making the process self-reinforcing.[7] Additionally, a university setting where there is a diverse range of research activities also provides the opportunity for cross-disciplinary learning through interaction with researchers in other fields, often leading to unexpected synergies and outcomes.

Finally, strong research-intensive universities with graduate programs also tend to have strong undergraduate teaching programs that attract domestic and foreign students alike. Graduates of these programs are most likely to stay if there is an attractive social environment (e.g. open and tolerant), which – in turn – provides a substantial advantage to the region. The presence of these deep pools of talent is also attractive to firms who locate to take advantage of being proximate to high-quality university facilities and researchers, as well as to a source of newly minted and well-educated talent. This secondary ability to attract both firms and talent should not be overlooked, as it is crucial to the continued competitiveness of firms and regions.

The above discussion highlights the wider role that the university plays in shaping the quality of place and fostering the openness and tolerant environment necessary for both economic competitiveness and social cohesion in contemporary society. In a recent article in the *Harvard Business Review*, Richard Florida warns that the current geopolitical conditions in the United States pose a serious threat to the creation of new ideas and knowledge that often come with an open, diverse, and tolerant society.[8] Significant new barriers to entry are beginning to impede the ability of foreign talent to enter the country, either for work or study. Florida (2004: 128) identifies students as the 'canaries of the talent mine,' and as such they are 'a leading indicator of global talent flows. The countries and regions that attract them will have a leg up on retaining them and also on attracting other pools of foreign talent.' There is mounting evidence that the flow of international talent into the US is slowing or subsiding. For example, a recent study by the Institute for International Education reports that the number of foreign students enrolled in institutions of higher education in the United States declined for the first time in more than 30 years. The reasons cited for this decline include 'real and perceived difficulties in obtaining student visas (especially in scientific and technical fields), rising U.S. tuition costs, vigorous recruitment activities by other English-speaking nations, and perceptions abroad that international students may no longer be welcome in the U.S.'[9] This will become a significant advantage as other countries – including Canada – continue to invest in higher education and maintain open and diverse environments that are more attractive to foreign talent.

4   How Do Ontario and Canada Measure Up?

Canada has maintained a global reputation for being an open, diverse society that provides a foundation for building success. Florida and his colleagues construct a Global Creative Class Index (GCCI) to demonstrate the relative standing of countries around the world in terms of the proportion of their work force currently working in creative fields. Canada ranks 8th, behind Ireland (1), Netherlands (2), Australia (3), New Zealand (5) and the United Kingdom (7), but ahead of the United States (11), Sweden (12), Switzerland (14), and Denmark (15). Canada's performance must be at least partially attributed to the role of universities in providing the undergraduate and graduate education necessary for work across a variety of creative occupations, from architecture, design, and fine arts to engineering, sciences, and computer programming.

Recent evidence on cities in Ontario and Canada serves to underscore this point.[10] Gertler et al. conducted an analysis of 309 cities in the United States and Canada and evaluated them using a series of measures of talent, diversity, creativity, and technology. Their results revealed a strong correlation between the level of creativity (the 'bohemian index' as measured by the proportion of the labour force in artistic occupations) and talent (the proportion of the population with a university-level degree) (figure 1). However, cities in Ontario (and Canada) appeared to lag behind US cities, having relatively low levels of university-level education, a finding that is consistent with other studies.[11] A strong relationship also existed between levels of creativity and technology-based employment; the local presence of a critical mass of creative and cultural activity seems to enhance the ability of city-regions to

Table 1   16 largest North American cities (1 million or more)

	Talent	Mosaic Index	Bohemian Index	Tech Pole Index
San Francisco	3	5	6	1
Washington	1	11	5	2
New York	9	6	2	5
Boston	2	13	12	4
Los Angeles	27	4	1	3
Seattle	6	19	11	6
Toronto	**24**	**1**	**4**	**15**
San Diego	12	8	16	11
Denver	4	27	8	9
Chicago	13	12	19	8
Dallas	11	17	17	7
Ottawa	**10**	**9**	**14**	**23**
Atlanta	7	31	15	12
Minneapolis	5	35	9	16
Vancouver	**31**	**2**	**3**	**29**
Montréal	**43**	**7**	**10**	**13**

Source: Gertler, M.S., Florida, R., Gates, G., and Vinodrai, T. 2002. Competing on Creativity.

generate knowledge-intensive employment (figure 2). These relationships between talent, creativity, and technology-based employment were as strong as or stronger than those for US cities.

However, what is most striking is the degree of diversity in Canadian cities (as measured by the proportion of the population that is foreign-born). At the national level, 17.2% of Canada's population is foreign-born as compared to 8% in the United States. Canada's largest cities (two of which are in Ontario) perform exceedingly well compared to their US counterparts, all ranking in the top 16 cities, primarily on the merit of their high rankings for levels of diversity and creativity (table 1). This performance on measures of diversity and creativity is typical of Ontario's cities in general. Ontario's cities are remarkably diverse and open, especially when compared to other North American cities of approximately the same size (table 2). This suggests that Ontario's cities, many of which are home to at least one university, have a high degree of openness to newcomers. The superb performance of city-regions in Ontario and Canada on measures of diversity and creativity suggests that these regions possess the underlying social and cultural assets on which to build successful local economies.

Table 2   Ontario's cities: North American rank by population

	Talent	Mosaic Index	Bohemian Index	Tech Pole Index
Population more than 1 million (43 cities)				
Toronto	24	1	4	15
Ottawa	10	9	14	23
Population 500,000 to 1 million (39 cities)				
Hamilton	35	2	18	37
Population 250,000 to 500,000 (68 cities)				
Kitchener	46	3	15	15
London	28	6	18	26
Oshawa	67	11	36	54
St Catharines–Niagara	66	8	27	58
Windsor	52	5	49	63
Population less than 250,000 (159 cities)				
Sudbury	142	16	128	120
Thunder Bay	125	6	103	76

Source: Gertler, M.S., Florida, R., Gates, G., and Vinodrai, T. 2002. *Competing on Creativity*.

5 Global Flows of Talent to Ontario and Canada

So far our discussion has identified the university as one of the central actors in creating competitive and cohesive communities. It does so in both direct and indirect ways that rely on the interrelationships between creativity, competitiveness, and cohesion.[12] Overall, universities – especially research-intensive universities with strong graduate programs – have a critical role to play in producing talent, as well as in attracting and retaining talent – both foreign and domestic. Moreover, these institutions are instrumental in influencing the quality of place, so crucial to creating the environment necessary to these processes. Finally, these processes are mutually reinforcing and reflexive. As identified above, one of the key roles for the university is to attract and retain talent both locally and globally. As such, we turn now to an analysis of Ontario's – and Canada's – performance in attracting foreign talent to

Table 3   Sources of global talent: Country of origin for foreign students

Ontario		Canada		United States	
Country	%	Country	%	Country	%
China	20.3	China	15.2	India	13.9
Korea	15.4	Korea	15.0	China	10.8
United States	7.5	United States	9.2	Korea	9.2
Hong Kong	6.1	Japan	8.0	Japan	7.1
Japan	5.4	France	4.9	Canada	4.7
Top 5 (total)	54.7	Top 5 (total)	52.3	Top 5 (total)	45.7

Source: Citizenship and Immigration Canada. 2003. *Foreign Students in Canada, 1980–2001*; Institute for International Education, 2004. *Open Doors 2004: International Students in the U.S.*

its universities. We begin by reviewing the most current data on foreign students in Canada. We then consider the ability of Ontario and its universities to attract and retain international researchers and scholars.

5.1 Sources of Global Talent: Graduate Students

It should be noted from the outset that, while attracting foreign talent is an important role for the university, this should not undermine the key role that universities play in educating and training Canadian students – a vital source of talent for local and national labour markets. This is especially true at the undergraduate level. The Council of Ontario Universities reported that, in 1999, 44% of undergraduate students came from the local area and another 47% came from elsewhere in Ontario. Only 5% came from elsewhere in Canada and 4% came from other countries.

However, graduate education has a global reach. Ontario's universities attract graduate students from across Canada, as well as from around the world. The distinctly more international flavour of graduate education can be seen at the University of Toronto, where 20.2% of graduate students are international compared to only 7.8% of undergraduates (figure 3). Certainly, at the University of Toronto, where 30% of doctoral-stream students come from other countries, the contribution of foreign students cannot be underestimated.[13] Similarly, other Ontario universities have a considerable international presence within their graduate programs: University of Waterloo (23.4%), McMaster University (17.6%), University of Western Ontario (14.8%), University of Ottawa (11.9%).[14]

While Ontario and Canada draw foreign students from across the globe, a high proportion are accounted for by only a handful of countries (table 3). In Ontario, with the exception of the United States, these are all Asian countries, with 20.3% of foreign students coming from China.[15] The most striking difference between Canada and the United States is the significantly higher proportion of students from India seeking higher education in the United States. And while Canada and the United States each appear in the other's list of major sources of foreign students, there is almost double the proportion of US students in Canada than vice versa.

5.2 Attracting and Retaining Global Talent: Graduate Students

Over the past two decades, Canada has witnessed a substantial increase in the number of foreign students who come to study at the post-secondary level (figure 4). In 1980, slightly fewer than 20,000 foreign students were issued visas to study in Canada. By 2001, this number had increased more than three-fold to over 75,000 foreign students. This high rate of growth is even more remarkable when compared to the United States. Figure 5 compares the change in the number of foreign students studying at post-secondary institutions in Canada and the US for the period between 1980 and 2003. The number of foreign students is indexed to 100 in the base year (1990) to facilitate comparisons, since the United States has a much larger number of foreign students in absolute terms. The growth in the number of foreign students in Canada – while cyclical – has far outpaced that in the United States. The recent downturn in the number of foreign students in the US coincides with a time when Canada has experienced extraordinarily high levels of growth. This further reinforces our position that Canada demonstrates a greater degree of openness compared to our southern neighbour and that this presents a significant opportunity for Ontario and Canada.

Between 1980 and 2001, Canada's regions (Atlantic Canada, Quebec, Ontario, the Prairies, and British Columbia) experienced substantial increases in the number of university-level foreign students (figure 6). However, there are significant differences in the pattern of growth between Canada's regions. Atlantic Canada and the Prairies experienced steady growth throughout the period. By 2001, British Columbia had more than five times as many university-level foreign students than in 1980. In Quebec there was a three-fold increase in the number of university-level foreign students over this same period. However, Ontario experienced a very different – and far less consistent – pattern of change. The total number of university-level foreign students reached a peak of almost 14,000 in 1982 before experiencing decline until 1987. Ontario's number of foreign students began to increase again until 1992 before declining to a level below Quebec's in the mid-1990s. Since 1995, Ontario has witnessed a sharp increase in its number of university-level foreign students.

Overall, Ontario's position has been declining relative to other regions of Canada. This is evident when we examine the share of Canada's university-level foreign students accounted for by each region (figure 7). Both Quebec and British Columbia increased their share of university-level foreign students, while Ontario saw its share decrease dramatically from over 50% in the early 1980s to less than 30% in the mid-1990s. Ontario's share has only rebounded slightly since then. During the 1990s, most of the decline in Ontario's foreign student enrolment was borne out in graduate programs (figure 8). The level of international participation in undergraduate education remained fairly consistent throughout the 1990s, dipping only slightly in the mid-1990s. Taken together this has meant that most of the fluctuations observed in Ontario's intake of foreign students have been at the graduate level.

Ontario's declining position relative to Quebec and British Columbia is also evident in the trends for Toronto, Montreal, and Vancouver (figure 9). While Toronto, Montreal, and their institutions attracted similar numbers of university-level foreign students from the 1980s to the early 1990s, there is a clear divergence between the two cities after that time. Montreal continued to experience large increases in the number of foreign students, along with Vancouver. Toronto experienced a decline through the early 1990s and has only recently experienced resurgence in the number of foreign students. Toronto's share of Canada's university-level foreign students has declined from a high of 20.3% in the early 1980s to 13.9% in 2001. These three cities act as Canada's portals to the rest of the world: they are the point of entry for a very high proportion of Canada's immigrants.[16] It is therefore somewhat surprising that Toronto, which has the highest proportion of foreign-born residents and receives the most immigrants, should attract such a low proportion of foreign students. During this same time period, Toronto's share of Ontario's university-level foreign student population increased from 38.9% to 43.8%. Toronto's increased provincial share combined with its declining national share suggests that the rest of Ontario is lagging even more in its ability to attract and retain foreign talent.[17]

There is only limited evidence on the retention of graduate-level talent by Canadian universities and communities. A pilot survey conducted by Statistics Canada in partnership with the University of Toronto and the Université de Montréal provides us with some insight. The *Survey of Earned Doctorates* (SED) conducted in 2002–3 revealed that while there were some variations between disciplines, 58.4% of earned doctorates at the University of Toronto had already secured a place to study, do research, or work upon completion of their degree. Of those with secured plans, 68.5% planned to stay in Canada upon graduation, while 19.2% planned to go to the United States; the remaining 12.3% intended to go elsewhere internationally.[18] The issue of attracting and retaining graduate-level talent (upon completion of their degree) is also considered in the next section, which addresses the attraction and retention of scholars in the university system.

5.3 Attracting and Retaining Global Research Talent

The data on the attraction and retention of foreign research talent are quite limited. However, we place our discussion of Ontario's (and Canada's) ability to attract top researchers within the growing public-policy concern over the outflow of highly skilled workers from Canada to other destinations, especially the United States. Finnie (2001) provides some useful estimates of Canada's ability to attract and retain highly qualified professionals.[19] He finds that the net outflow of talent to the United States has been quite small, especially when considered in historical perspective. However, outflows to the United States exceeded inflows to Canada for highly educated workers. For example, between 1990 and 1997 the ratio of outflows to inflows for university professors was 2.1 to 1. However, for other highly educated groups such as physicians this ratio was high, at 18.7 to 1. Researchers have shown that the inflow of highly educated immigrants to Canada between 1990 and 1996 exceeded the outflow of emigrants to the United States by a 4 to 1 margin.[20] Using a unique data set created from tax records, Finnie (2002) traces both the exit and return of migrants to the United States[21]. He shows that emigration is quite small (0.01% of the population) and began to slow in the late 1990s. And while return rates were generally low, they had increased substantially in recent years, and those with higher incomes were more likely to return. This may suggest a process of brain circulation akin to that described by Saxenian (2000).

We also assess Ontario's ability to attract foreign research talent by examining the characteristics of Ontario's university professors. Figure 10 shows that 41.5% of Ontario's university professors are foreign-born, compared to only 29.1% of the employed labour force. This suggests that Ontario has enjoyed past success in attracting foreign talent. However, as figure 11 shows, most of these professors immigrated to Canada prior to 1981 and do not reflect more recent waves of immigration. Figure 10 also shows that slightly less than 25% of university professors and the employed labour force have a language outside of Canada's two official languages as their mother tongue, indicating a certain degree of diversity within Ontario's university research community. One last measure to assess the diversity of research talent at the university is to examine the proportion of visible minorities. It also acts as a measure of the openness of the university. Only 14.5% of Ontario's university professors are visible minorities as compared to 18.1% of Ontario's employed labour force. Looking at this in more detail (figure 12), we can see that there are some striking differences between Ontario's professors and the employed labour force. Ontario's universities still have some work to do in order to attract and retain a diverse and talented pool of researchers.

6 Creativity, Competitiveness, Cohesion: Challenges for Public Policy

The analysis and argument put forth in this paper suggests that public universities – especially those with strong graduate and research programs – can act as anchors in the creative economy and are crucial institutions in making Ontario a socially cohesive and globally competitive place. In this way, the university can be an integral part of a strategy to place Ontario – and Canada – on the talent map. To build excellence and invest in research-intensive universities and their graduate programs is to invest in the communities in which they are located. The university can act as a catalyst for economic development, but – more importantly – the university is also a crucial actor in making places more open and diverse, thereby contributing to wider goals of social inclusion and cohesion within Canadian society.

The discussion and evidence in this paper present both opportunities and challenges for Ontario. Ontario begins from a position of strength relative to its North American peers given its performance on measures of diversity and creativity. Ontario and Canada are particularly well placed to take advantage of the current geopolitical climate in the United States. There is some documented evidence to suggest that Canadian universities are already benefiting from this in terms of higher levels of applications from foreign students, especially to professional, masters, and doctoral-stream programs.[22]

Despite Canada's favourable performance relative to the United States in terms of the growth of the number of foreign students enrolled in higher education, Ontario's position relative to Quebec and British Columbia has declined steadily over the past 20 years. Ontario's commitment to attracting foreign graduate students appears to have wavered over the past two decades at the same time that other provinces have actively sought to attract foreign students. It is clear that a stronger commitment to this aspect of graduate education is needed, and should be based on a deeper understanding of how the attraction of foreign talent can advance the goals of social inclusion, competitiveness, and connecting our local economies to global knowledge networks. This also represents an opportunity for Ontario to reconsider its model for supporting graduate education, to make it more accessible to both foreign and domestic students regardless of social background.

Ontario needs to build on the success of recent (or renewed) programs that have been designed to attract foreign scholars and retain potentially mobile Canadian scholars, as well as bolster the research capabilities of universities and their researchers. For example, the Canada Research Chairs (CRC) program has funded the appointment of 207 international researchers (15%) and 188 expatriate researchers (14%) out of a total of 1348 chairs created since its inception in 2000.[23] Other investments and funds such as the Canadian Foundation for Innovation (CFI), the Ontario Innovation Trust (OIT), the Ontario Research and Development Challenge Fund (ORDCF), and the Premier's Research Excellence Awards (PREA), coupled with reinvestments in the major funding councils (SSHRC, CIHR, NSERC) that fund basic research, have been critical to much of Ontario's recent successes.

More often than not, research-intensive universities rely on having strong graduate programs. They are two sides of the same coin and should be thought of as being inextricably linked and mutually reinforcing. Therefore, it is of great importance to recognize the relationship between research and graduate education and that both of these critical areas of public policy evolve in mutually reinforcing ways. The investment in developing the strength of research-intensive universities reaches well beyond a simple, linear technology-transfer model and represents an investment in the competitiveness and cohesion of communities, the province, and the nation.

We must ask ourselves: what are the necessary and sufficient conditions under which Ontario can compete in an increasingly global field? The answer lies in developing places with fertile environments to foster creativity and social cohesion, but that are also open and interactive on a global scale. Places that have dynamic research centres open to flows of talent and knowledge will be the likely candidates for success in a knowledge-based society. Ontario has the necessary building blocks: an open, diverse society and strong research institutions. However, there is also strong evidence to suggest that Ontario's universities are not funded at an appropriate level to match the growing demands for a highly skilled and educated workforce, and are seriously lagging behind other provinces in Canada.[24] It is only with government support and public funding for the expansion and upgrading of graduate education and research institutions that the *necessary and sufficient* conditions will be met for the future prosperity of Ontario and its communities.

Notes

* Department of Geography and Munk Centre for International Studies, University of Toronto

1 See Porter, M.E. (2000) Locations, clusters, and company strategy, in Clark, G.L., Feldman, M. and Gertler, M.S., eds., *The Oxford Handbook of Economic Geography*. Oxford: Oxford University Press, pp. 253–74.

2 Zucker, L.G., Darby, M.R., and Brewer, M.B. (1998): Intellectual human capital and the birth of U.S. biotechnology enterprises. *American Economic Review*, 88: 290–306.

3 Bathelt, H., Malmberg, A., and Maskell, P. (2004): Clusters and knowledge: local buzz, global pipelines and the process of knowledge creation. *Progress in Human Geography* 28: 57–77.

4 Saxenian, A. 1999. *Silicon Valley's New Immigrant Entrepreneurs*. Public Policy Institute of California. San Francisco, California. See also Saxenian, A. 2000. 'Networks of Immigrant Entrepreneurs.' In C-M. Lee et al., eds. *The Silicon Valley Edge: A Habitat for Innovation and Entrepreneurship*. Stanford, California: Stanford University Press.

5 Florida, R. 2002. *The Rise of the Creative Class*. New York: Basic Books;

Florida, R. 2002. 'Bohemia and economic geography,' *Journal of Economic Geography*, 2(1): 55–71; Gertler, M.S., Florida, R., Gates, G., and Vinodrai, T. 2002. *Competing on Creativity: Ontario Cities in North American Context*. A report to the Institute for Competitiveness and Prosperity, and Ontario Ministry of Enterprise, Opportunity and Innovation, Toronto, Ontario.

 6 See Donald, B. and Morrow, D. 2003. Competing for Talent: Implications for Social and Cultural Policy in Canadian City-Regions, a report prepared for Strategic Research and Analysis, Canadian Heritage, Ottawa, Ontario.

 7 See Storper, M. and Venables, A.J. 2004. 'Buzz: face-to-face contact and the urban economy.' *Journal of Economic Geography*, 4: 351–370.

 8 Florida, R. 2004. 'America's looming creativity crisis.' *Harvard Business Review*, 82 (10): 122–136.

 9 Institute for International Education. 2004. *Open Doors: Report on International Educational Exchange*. New York. [Available from http://opendoors .iienetwork.org]

10 Gertler, M.S., Florida, R., Gates, G., and Vinodrai, T. 2002. *Competing on Creativity: Ontario Cities in North American Context*. A report to the Institute for Competitiveness and Prosperity, and Ontario Ministry of Enterprise, Opportunity and Innovation, Toronto, Ontario. [Available at www.competeprosper.ca]

11 Bowlby, J.W. 2002. *Post-Secondary Educational Attainment in Canada and the United States in the 1990s*. Applied Research Branch Strategic Policy Technical Paper Series T-02-2E. Ottawa: Human Resource Development Canada.

12 Elsewhere Gertler (2004) has argued that these relationships are also crucial to the economic prosperity and the enhanced quality of life in Canadian cities. See M.S. Gertler. 2004. *Creative cities: What are they for, how do they work, and how do we build them?* Background paper prepared for the Canadian Policy Research Network. Ottawa, Canada. [Available from http://www.cprn.ca/en/doc.cfm?doc=1083]

13 University of Toronto, 2004. *The Choice for a Generation: Investing in Higher Education and Ontario's Future*. Submission to the Honourable Bob Rae, Advisor to the Premier and the Minister of Training, Colleges and Universities on Postsecondary Education.

14 Office of Institutional Planning & Budgeting, University of Western Ontario. 2004. *Western Facts 2003–04*; Planning and Analysis, McMaster University. 2004. *University Data Manual 2002/03*; Institutional Research and Planning, University of Ottawa. 2004. *Number of Students by Canadian Status*; Institutional Analysis and Planning, University of Waterloo. 2004. *Self-serve report generator.*

15 Due to data availability and comparability with US data, these statistics include all post-secondary students, regardless of level or program.

16 For recent evidence, see Gertler, M.S. (2001) 'Urban economy and society in Canada: flows of people, capital and ideas,' *Isuma: The Canadian Journal of Policy Research*, 2, no. 3, 119–30.

17 We could speculate that despite the performance of Ontario's communities on measures of diversity, there may not always be a critical mass, established community, or ample opportunities for highly skilled talent in these centres. See Levitte, Y.M. and Silverman, E. 2004. *(Wasted) talent? Exploring Richard Florida's argument about the relationship between human capital and regional growth in college towns.* Paper presented at the Association of Collegiate Schools of Planning, Portland, Oregon. October 21–24, 2004.

18 Office of the Vice-President and Provost, University of Toronto. 2004. *Performance Indicators for Governance: Annual Report.* [Available at http://www.provost.utoronto.ca/English/Reports.html]

19 Finnie, R. 2001. 'The brain drain: myth and reality – what it is and what should be done.' *Choices: Institute for Research on Public Policy,* 7(6): 3–29.

20 Zhao, J., Drew, D., and Murray, S. 2000. 'Brain drain and brain gain: the migration of knowledge workers to and from Canada.' Education Quarterly, 6(3): 8–35.

21 Finnie, R. 2002. *Leaving and coming back to Canada: evidence from longitudinal data.* School of Policy Studies Working Paper 32, Queen's University, Kingston, Ontario.

22 Drolet, D. 2004. 'Many universities report big jumps in foreign enrolment.' *University Affairs* [Accessed at http://www.universityaffairs.ca/issues/2004/jan/news_1.html]; Office of the Vice-President and Provost, University of Toronto. 2004. *Performance Indicators for Governance: Annual Report.* [Available at http://www.provost.utoronto.ca/English/Reports.html]

23 Canada Research Chairs. 2004. *Recruitment of Chairs from Within and Outside of Canada.* [Accessed at http://www.chairs.gc.ca/web/media/stats/recruitment_e.asp]

24 University of Toronto, 2004. *The Choice for a Generation: Investing in Higher Education and Ontario's Future.* Submission to the Honourable Bob Rae, Advisor to the Premier and the Minister of Training, Colleges and Universities on Postsecondary Education.

Figure 1   Talent and creativity in North American cities

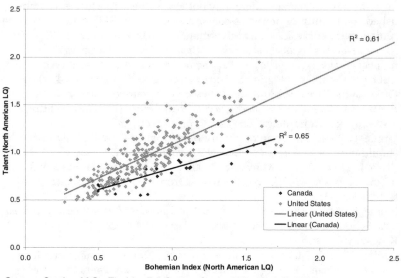

Source: Gertler, M.S., Florida, R., Gates, G., and Vinodrai, T. 2002.
Competing on Creativity.

Figure 2   Technology and creativity in North American cities

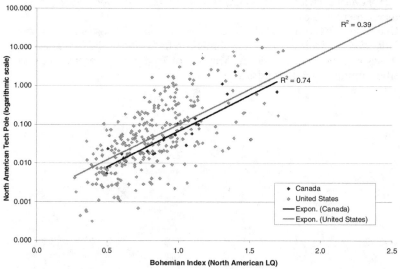

Source: Gertler, M.S., Florida, R., Gates, G., and Vinodrai, T. 2002.
Competing on Creativity.

Figure 3   Sources of Talent: Where do University of Toronto
students come from?

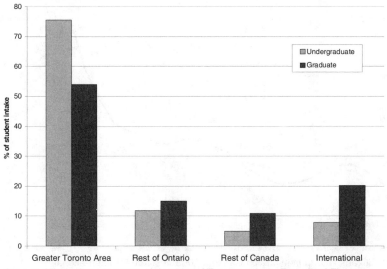

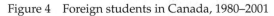

Source: Office of the Provost, University of Toronto. 2003. *Facts and Figures.*

Figure 4   Foreign students in Canada, 1980–2001

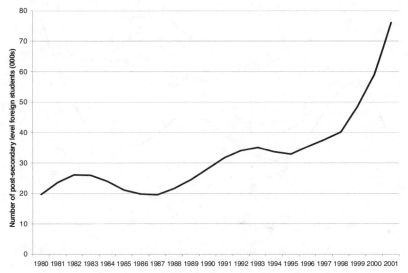

Source: Citizenship and Immigration Canada. 2003. *Foreign Students in Canada,
1980–2001.*

Figure 5   Foreign students in Canada and the United States (1990=100)

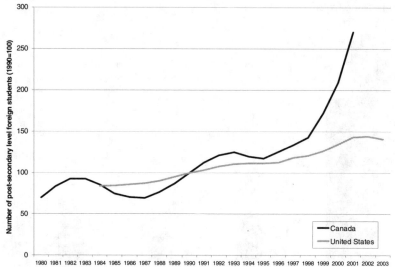

Source: Citizenship and Immigration Canada. 2003; Institute for International Education, 2004.

Figure 6   Foreign students in Canada by region, 1980–2001

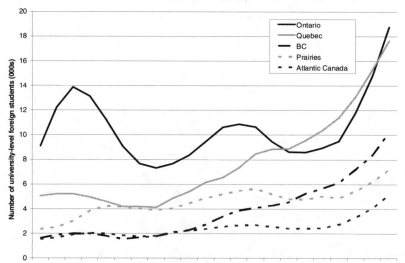

Source: Citizenship and Immigration Canada. 2003. Foreign Students in Canada, 1980–2001

Figure 7   Share of foreign students in Canada by region, 1980–2001

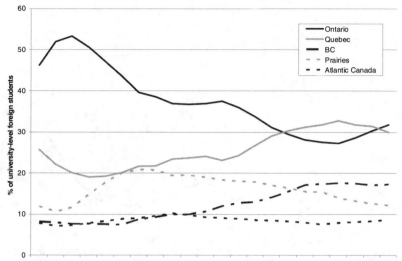

Source: Citizenship and Immigration Canada. 2003. *Foreign Students in Canada, 1980–2001.*

Figure 8   Foreign students in Ontario, % full-time enrolment, 1990–9

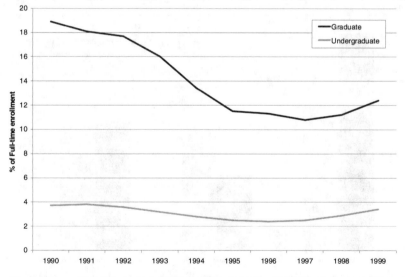

Source: Council of Ontario Universities. 2001. *Facts and Figures: A Compendium of Statistics on Ontario's Universities.*

Figure 9   Foreign students in Toronto, Montreal, and Vancouver, 1980–2001

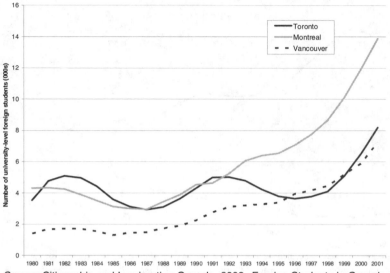

Source: Citizenship and Immigration Canada. 2003. *Foreign Students in Canada, 1980–2001.*

Figure 10   Characteristics of Ontario's university professors, 2001

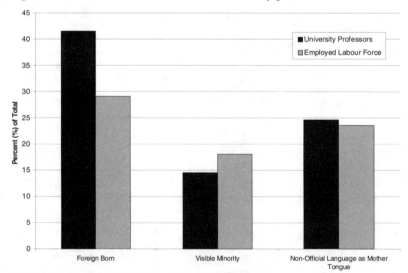

Source: Statistics Canada. 2001. *Census of Population.*

Figure 11   Year of immigration for Ontario's foreign-born professors, 2001

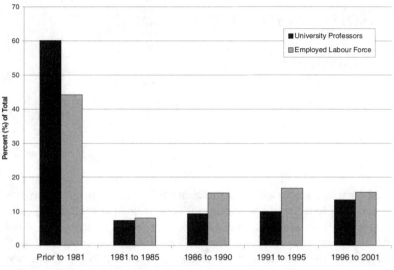

Source: Statistics Canada. 2001. *Census of Population*.

Figure 12   Visible minority status of Ontario's university professors, 2001

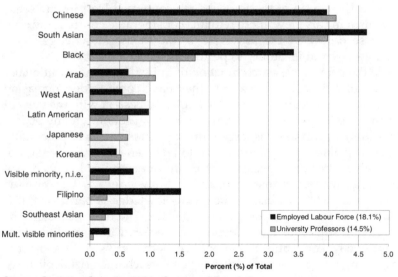

Source: Statistics Canada. 2001. *Census of Population*.

Innovation and Research Funding: The Role of Government Support

DAVID A. WOLFE*

The shift to more knowledge- and research-intensive production has been a defining feature of the industrial economies for the past decade and a half. As this shift has gained momentum, governments have become more preoccupied with the policies required to support it and, in particular, with the role of the university. A survey in *The Economist* several years ago provided a unique conception of the role of the university in the knowledge-based economy, 'not just as a creator of knowledge, a trainer of young minds and a transmitter of culture, but also as a major agent of economic growth: the knowledge factory, as it were, at the centre of the knowledge economy.'[1] Despite the sense of optimism in this view, there remains considerable controversy over the precise nature of the university's role in the knowledge-based economy – or even its ability to perform this role.

While the primary research function of universities has traditionally been the conduct of basic research, they have come under increasing pressure in recent years to expand this role. Consistent with the view of universities as 'knowledge factories' for the new economy, many policy-makers view universities as largely untapped reservoirs of potentially commercializable knowledge waiting to be taken up by firms and applied. Universities are expected to generate more applied knowledge of greater relevance to industry, to diffuse knowledge, and to provide technical support to industry. Once this knowledge is harnessed, it is hoped, it will fuel innovation within the firm, thereby increasing its productivity, stimulate the emergence of regional industrial clusters, and, indirectly, contribute to national economic growth. In short, the changes impacting the university system are characterized by three trends: the linking of government funding for academic research and economic policy; the development of more long-term relationships between firms and academic researchers; and the increasing direct participation of universities in commercializing research.[2] This shift partly reflects the decline in the proportion of in-house basic research funded by industry, especially in the US, but it is also the result of a parallel expectation on the part of government that their investments in basic research will produce a direct and increasing economic return.[3]

The adoption of this overly mechanistic view of the process by which basic scientific research is transformed into economically valuable products risks placing an unacceptable set of demands on universities – ones that they are not well equipped to meet. The task of transferring knowledge from universities to industries has proven far more complex than the perspective of the knowledge factory assumes. The basic assumptions about the role of universities in economic development, upon which many of the decisions about government funding for research in the higher education sector are based, need to be re-examined in light of our current understanding of the innovation process in the knowledge-based economy. Assumptions about the public goods character of scientific knowledge and basic research, and concerns about the problem of appropriability with university-generated intellectual property belie the level of sophistication and scientific knowledge required by firms in order to make use of this knowledge. At the same time, the correlation between basic research and generalized economic and social benefits is not a linear one, and is therefore difficult to measure. Clearly there is a need for a more nuanced and contextualized understanding of the actual role that universities play in economic development in order to clarify the rationale for continued government funding for research and graduate training in the universities.

This paper briefly contrasts the rationale underlying the traditional linear model of science and technology development and funding for basic research with more recent evolutionary ones. An over-reliance on the commercialization of basic research and the licensing of intellectual property is short-sighted and illustrates a lack of understanding of how basic research in universities contributes to the broader process of economic development. Instead, the social and economic benefits of basic research depend on the absorptive capacity of firms to make use of the scientific knowledge that is generated. The transfer of knowledge from universities is highly localized, and is underpinned by the pool of tacit knowledge that is shared across robust personal networks of highly qualified personnel, including academic researchers and scientists working in industry. The role of government is critical in supporting the process of basic research in universities at both the federal and provincial levels, but policy at both levels of government tends to be hindered not only by problems of jurisdictional overlap and duplication, but also by the erosion of core funding, coupled with unrealistically targeted expectations for the applicability of basic research. Ultimately, while government funding expands the pool of technological opportunities available for firms to draw upon in their process of innovation and offers institutional support to these firms as they draw from such pools, public support for university-based research should best be seen as an investment in generating and sustaining a learning capability that promotes the formation of skills, networks, and a capacity for technological problem-solving on the part of a society.

The Role of Universities in the Knowledge-Based Economy: Linear vs. Evolutionary Perspectives

There is a popular belief that public investment in basic science can translate directly into sustained economic and social benefits, and most studies of the social and private rate of return to publicly funded research stress the positive rates of return. Despite assertions about the role of knowledge in the emerging economy, the exact relationship between public support for scientific research and the level of economic performance and social well-being remains primarily a matter of affirmation. There are several reasons for this uncertainty relating to the nature of knowledge, government programs, and the innovation process. The postwar consensus on the benefit of investing in basic research failed to produce a clear methodological or empirical approach for determining its benefits. The 'social contract' for science, forged in the aftermath of World War II, saw society willing to fund massive investments in basic research in the expectation of long-term economic benefits, while leaving the principal research institutions, the universities, autonomous in the conduct of that research. The social contract for science implied a high degree of autonomy for the realm of science, vigorously reinforced by the 'boundary work' of the scientific community itself; it afforded 'expert' status to the role of scientists in the exercise of judgment about most matters relating to the conduct of scientific investigations and the application of the resulting knowledge; and it privileged the role of the universities and other public research organizations as the principal site for the conduct of scientific research, although these arrangements exhibited considerable variation across national innovation systems.[4]

Underlying this view of the social contract for science was the 'linear model' of innovation that supported the development of postwar science policy in the US. The model defined the relationship between basic research and more applied forms of technology development as a linear one, involving the progression through a sequence of steps leading eventually to product development – the final stage involving the systematic adoption of research findings into useful materials, devices, systems, methods, and processes. In the idealized linear model, the innovation process commences with basic research conducted without any thought of potential application that leads to discoveries. These discoveries, in turn, open up the possibility of potential applications that are pursued, usually by firms, through applied research, development, design, production, and marketing. The latter stages in this sequence lead to the successful commercialization of the resulting products and processes.[5]

But the essential elements of the social contract for science have been subject to increasing strain in the past two decades as the linear model of innovation has become open to question. These developments are a consequence of major shifts in the relationship between the university and other constituent parts of the national innovation system.[6] The traditional justification for the public funding of basic research is that it expands the amount of information available for firms to draw upon in their technological activities, but this view largely underestimates the substantial effort and costs needed by users to take advantage of this information. Inherent in this rationale for public support of basic research is the danger of confusing the notion of science as a public good (i.e., codified, published, easily reproducible) with science as a free good (i.e., costless to apply as technology). The difficulty with the pure-information theory of basic research is that the commercial value or application of scientific findings is not always immediately evident. In one of the final reports issued before its untimely demise, the US Office of Technology Assessment noted numerous examples of key scientific discoveries whose commercial application could not fully be conceived of at the time of their discovery – the widespread adoption of lasers took decades to advance from their initial discovery in the laboratory to their practical application in communication systems, medical devices, and consumer electronics. The difficulty with exploiting this type of research lies in determining commercially viable applications of the new discovery and developing the necessary engineering.[7]

A more accurate understanding of the relationship between those institutions in the innovation system that conduct basic research and those that exploit and develop its commercial potential requires a sophisticated framework for analysing the character of the institutional and interpersonal linkages between universities and firms and, in turn, how those linkages contribute to knowledge transfers between the two. An alternative approach to analysing the economic benefits that flow from knowledge transfer focuses on the properties of knowledge not easily captured by the informational view associated with early work on the economics of basic research and the linear model. Scholars working in the evolutionary tradition characterize knowledge as dynamic and often unarticulated, and argue that firms must invest substantial resources of their own to perceive the economically valuable aspects of knowledge and capture the economic benefits that flow from it. This view shifts attention from the applicability of knowledge to the processes that enable a firm to successfully absorb and apply that knowledge.[8]

A great deal of confusion arises in the literature over exactly what it is that firms draw from public sources – information or knowledge.[9] In many innovation surveys, these terms are used interchangeably and, for many firms, the distinction between information and knowledge is an academic one. However, the difference between information and knowledge is important for understanding the role played by publicly funded basic research. The traditional justification for government-funded basic research relied on the public-good qualities of information.[10] However, the evidence deduced from the relevant studies indicates that what firms draw upon is not information per se, but knowledge. Understanding information almost always requires knowledge. Conventional approaches to the issue of knowledge flows frequently treat knowledge itself as a universally available commodity, virtually as a free public good, and knowledge transfer as a commercial and legal transaction between clearly defined agents. This perspective flies in the face of evidence from a growing number of sources that successful knowledge transfer depends on the type of knowledge involved, and how it is employed. Individuals and organizations require a complex set of skills and must expend considerable resources to both absorb and understand information. Without these investments, firms would be unable to make use of the information available to them. In this respect, information only becomes codified knowledge (and therefore valuable and useful) when users have the skills and capabilities to make sense of it.[11]

The shift to a more knowledge-based economy embodies a number of changes in both the production and application of new scientific knowledge that have critical implications for the processes of knowledge transfer. One of the most significant of these changes involves the relation between the codified and tacit dimensions of knowledge. The dramatic expansion of the higher education sector and the increased funding for research associated with the postwar contract for science have generated substantial increases in scientific and research output which largely take the form of codified knowledge, transmitted relatively easily between researchers through published scientific papers and formal presentations. But as the stock of scientific knowledge has grown and become more widely accessible through electronic and other means, the relative economic value of that knowledge is diminished by its sheer abundance. Often access to the key elements of the knowledge base depends upon the second or tacit dimension. Following the work of Michael Polanyi, tacit knowledge here refers to knowledge or insights which individuals acquire in the course of their scientific work that is ill defined or uncodified and that they themselves cannot articulate fully. It is highly subjective and often varies from person to person. Furthermore, individuals or groups working together for the same firm or organization often develop a common base of tacit knowledge in the course of their research and production activities. This common base of tacit knowledge arises from the internal procedures and the heuristic techniques developed by firms in the process of applying new scientific knowledge to improve existing products and processes or develop new ones.[12]

This underscores the centrality of learning for the innovative process. Lundvall, among others, argues that the knowledge frontier is moving so rapidly that access to, or control over, knowledge assets affords merely a fleeting competitive advantage. It may be more appropriate to describe the emerging paradigm as that of a 'learning economy,' rather than a 'knowledge-based' one. He argues that innovation is a *social process* triggered by consumers (or users) who engage in a mutually beneficial dialogue and interaction with producers. In this way, users and producers actively *learn* from each other, by 'learning-through-interacting.' Such a process involves a capacity for localized learning within firms, among firms that deal with each other, and between firms and the supporting infrastructure of research institutions that constitute a critical component of the national or regional innovation system. Learning in this sense refers to the building of new competencies and the acquisition of new skills, not just gaining access to information or codified scientific knowledge. In tandem with this development, forms of knowledge that cannot be codified and transmitted electronically (tacit knowledge) increase in value, along with the ability to acquire and assess both codified and tacit forms of knowledge, in other words, the capacity for learning.[13]

Analysing this process from the perspective of the firm, Cohen and Levinthal argue that the process of knowledge transfer from universities and research institutes is strongly conditioned by the capabilities of firms. Firms need to build an internal knowledge base and research capacity to effectively capture and deploy knowledge acquired from external sources. The ability to evaluate and utilize outside knowledge is largely a function of the level of prior, related knowledge within the firm, including basic skills or even a shared language, but may also include knowledge of the most recent scientific or technological developments in a given field. These abilities collectively constitute a firm's *'absorptive capacity.'*[14] The overlap between the firm's knowledge base and external research allows the firm to recognize potentially useful outside knowledge and use it to reconfigure and augment its existing knowledge base. Research shows that firms which conduct their own R&D are better able to use externally available information. This implies that the firm's absorptive capacity is created as a by-product of its own R&D investment. A key implication of this argument is that firms require a strong contingent of highly qualified research scientists and engineers as a precondition of their ability to absorb and assess scientific results, most frequently recruited from institutions of higher education. The members of this scientific and engineering labour force bring with them not only the knowledge base and research skills acquired in their university training, but often, more importantly, a network of academic contacts acquired during their university training.

This underlines Keith Pavitt's oft-repeated point that the most important source of knowledge transfer is person-embodied. Pavitt stresses that scientific and technological knowledge often remains tacit, that is, embodied in the knowledge, skills, and practices of the individual researcher. Building on the above argument, Pavitt maintains that the most effective mechanism for knowledge transfers between research institutions and commercial firms is through the flow of researchers. Policies that attempt to direct basic research towards specific goals or targets ignore both the considerable indirect benefits across a broad range of scientific fields that result from the training of highly qualified personnel in institutions of higher education and the kind of unplanned discoveries that invariably result from the conduct of basic research.[15] This view reinforces the idea of knowledge as the capacity to acquire and apply research results, rather than as an end in itself. In this perspective, knowledge is the ability to put information to productive use. It provides the basis for understanding new ideas and discoveries and places them in a context that enables more rapid application. The development of such internalized or 'personal knowledge' requires an extensive learning process. It is based on skills accumulated through experience and expertise. It also emphasizes the learning properties of individuals and organizations. Of crucial importance are the role of skills, the networks of researchers, and the development of new capabilities on the part of actors and institutions in the innovation system.[16]

The role played by networks in the process of knowledge transfer has been the focus of a great deal of research which indicates that firms and industries link with the publicly funded science base in a variety of ways. These links often are informal. Faulkner and Senker studied the nature of public-private sector linkages in three areas – biotechnology, engineering ceramics, and parallel computing. Their research indicates that good personal relationships between firms and public-sector scientists are the key to successful collaboration between the two sectors. Personal relations build up understanding and trust, leading to long-term contractual relationships.[17] Other researchers stress the positive role that government-funded research plays in generating new forms of social interaction among actors in the innovation system. Bridging institutions, such as provincial and national Centres of Excellence in Canada or Engineering Research Centers in the US, provide institutional mechanisms to embed and support interaction and facilitate knowledge flows between universities and industry.[18] This networking capacity is essential for tapping into the shared intelligence of both the individual firm and the research organization, as well as a collectivity of firms within a given geographic space.

The preceding discussion suggests that the relationship between publicly funded research and the innovation process is far more complex than assumed by many recent public-policy pronouncements about the role of the higher education sector in the commercialization of scientific research. While the shift in policy perspective was partly stimulated by a questioning of the assumptions underlying the linear model, it has yet to be replaced with a more complex and realistic appreciation of the way in which knowledge flows between universities and industry. As

Fumio Kodama and Lewis Branscomb argue, '[D]isappointment awaits those who expect quick results from university-based high-technology strategies for industrial renewal. First-rank research universities can and most often do make a large and positive contribution to economic performance, regionally and nationally. But to understand the effects we should not focus on the style and content of the transactions with firms but rather look at the university as a pivotal part of a network of people and institutions who possess high skills, imagination, the incentive to take risks, the ability to form other networks to accomplish their dreams.'[19]

The Role of Universities in Economic Development: Knowledge Spillovers, Networks, and Highly Qualified Personnel

Among the key contributions that publicly funded universities make to economic growth in the knowledge-based economy are the performance of research and the training of highly qualified personnel, both of which are sustained by networks and social interaction; universities act both as a primary source of 'knowledge workers,' as well as the key factor of production – knowledge itself. The preceding discussion emphasizes the fact that knowledge transfers between universities and their partners are highly personalized and, as a consequence, often highly localized. This underscores the significance of geographical proximity for the process of knowledge transfer. Proximity to the source of the research is important in influencing the success with which knowledge generated in the research laboratory is transferred to firms for commercial exploitation, or process innovations are adopted and diffused across researchers and users.[20] The proximity effect of knowledge transfer provides a strong clue as to why universities are increasingly seen as an essential element in the process of local and regional economic development, especially in knowledge-intensive industries, such as information and communications technology or biotechnology. A critical issue involves the question of which of the university's central roles in the knowledge-based economy – the performance of scientific research or the training of highly qualified personnel – exert the dominant influence on the process of regional economic development.

Many studies of the economic benefits of publicly funded research highlight the role of skilled graduates as the primary benefit that flows to firms from the government's investment in scientific research. New graduates, who have had the opportunity to participate in the conduct of basic research, enter industry equipped with training, knowledge, networks, and expertise. They bring to the firm knowledge of recent scientific research, as well as an ability to solve complex problems, perform research, and develop ideas. The skills developed through their educational experience with advanced instrumentation, techniques, and scientific methods are extremely valuable. Students also bring with them a set of qualifications, helping set standards for knowledge in an industry. Senker suggests that graduates bring to industry an 'attitude of the mind' and a 'tacit ability' to acquire and use knowledge in a new and powerful way.[21] Nelson also notes that academics may teach what new industrial actors need to know, without actually doing relevant research for industry. Basic techniques in scientific research are often essential for a young scientist or technologist to learn to participate in the industrial activities within the firm.[22] Gibbons and Johnston's research in the 1970s demonstrated that students provide a form of benefit that flows from research funding.[23] Studies by Martin and Irvine in the 1980s also showed that students trained in basic research fields, such as radio astronomy, move into industry over time and make substantial contributions.[24] Our own research on the experience with Ontario programs to promote international collaborative research, as well as university-industry partnering, suggests that the movement of doctoral and post-doctoral students into industry frequently provides the most effective method for transferring research results from the laboratory directly to industry. These benefits are often difficult to anticipate or measure, yet the evidence indicates that students bring a wide range of skills and techniques to industry. They enable firms to increase their base of tacit knowledge and expand into new activities.[25]

Firms also indicate that students fresh from their educational experience bring to the firm an enthusiasm and critical approach to research and development that stimulates other members of the research team. Over the entire career of the new hire, the skills acquired in their education and research experience are valuable and often serve as a precursor to the development of more industry-related skills and knowledge that appear over time. This point was strongly underscored by Mike Lazaridis, the founder, president, and co-CEO of Waterloo-based Research in Motion in his presentation to the fourth annual Re$earch Money Conference in Ottawa:

> The number one reason to fund basic research well and with vision is to attract the very best researchers from around the world. Once here, they

can prepare Canada's next generations of graduates, masters, PhD's and post-doctorates, including the finest foreign students. All else flows from this ... If you really want to understand commercialization, all you have to do is attend convocation at your local university. At mine, the University of Waterloo, we celebrate – yes celebrate – the passage of the next generation of students into the economy and society twice each year. Armed with cutting edge technology from around the world, the latest tools, the latest techniques and processes learned from their work under the very best researchers, they graduate with much fanfare and go on to build the industry, institutions and society of our country.[26]

There is a critical need to maintain, support, and strengthen this crucial link between student training and government-funded basic research. Students provide a key transfer mechanism for the benefits of public-sector funding to be channeled into industry and the broader society. This provides the most compelling justification for combining the conduct of both basic research and graduate training in the same research-intensive institutions.

A number of recent studies have also identified the finding and retaining of talent as a critical factor influencing the development of clusters and the growth of dynamic urban economies. Locations with large talent pools reduce the costs of search and recruitment of talent – they are also attractive to individuals who are relocating because they provide some guarantee of successive job opportunities. Recent research into the concentration of high-tech activity indicates that a concentration of high-technology employment is the most important factor in promoting local academic knowledge transfers.[27] In Richard Florida's interviews, numerous executives confirmed that they will 'go where the highly skilled people are.' Highly educated, talented labour flows to those places that have a 'buzz' about them – the places where the most interesting work in the field is currently being done. One way to track this is through the inflow of so-called 'star scientists,' or by tracking the in-migration of tomorrow's potential stars (post-docs). In their path-breaking research on the geographic concentration of the US biotechnology industry, Zucker and Darby document the tendency of leading research scientists to collaborate more within their own institutions and with firm scientists located close by. As a consequence, 'where and when star scientists were actively producing publications is a key predictor of where and when commercial firms began to use biotechnology.'[28]

Another approach, employed by Florida and colleagues, utilizes a more broadly defined measure of 'talent,' and documents its strong geographical attraction to the presence of other creative people and activities locally.[29] In-bound talented labour represents knowledge in its embodied form flowing into the region. Such flows act to reinforce and accentuate the knowledge assets already assembled in a region. Ultimately, the most valuable contribution that universities make to this process is as providers of highly skilled and creative members of the labour force and attractors of talent. Learning processes are eminently person-embodied in the form of talent. According to Florida, 'universities ... are a crucial piece of the infrastructure of the knowledge economy, providing mechanisms for generating and harnessing talent.'[30]

Thus, the role of public policy in stimulating economic development, particularly as it applies to the research-intensive universities, is critical. The current national research initiative on the growth and development of industrial clusters across Canada, conducted by members of the Innovation Systems Research Network, provides compelling evidence of the central role played by the presence of a 'thick labour market' in grounding individual clusters in a specific geographic location – and the essential role that research-intensive universities play in feeding the supply of talent to those thick labour markets. On balance the public interventions which have the most enduring effect in sustaining the process of local economic development are those that strengthen the research infrastructure of a region or locality and contribute to the expansion of its talent base of skilled knowledge workers.[31] These points were strongly emphasized in a recent report prepared for the Ontario government.

> Basic university research advances fundamental understanding and provides a substantial rate of economic return through the preparation of a highly skilled workforce, contributing to the foundation of many new technologies, attracting long-term foreign (and domestic) investment, supporting new company development and entrepreneurial companies and participating in global networks. Government funding is the primary support for virtually all investment in truly frontier university research.[32]

Government Funding of Research in the Post-Secondary Sector

Despite unequivocal assertions about the role of knowledge in the new economy and the critical role that universities play, responsibility for, and the appropriate funding levels of, basic research remain a matter of some contention in this country. Growing awareness of the link between the level of basic research activity and the process of economic development, as well as the shift to a more knowledge-based economy, has raised the profile of post-secondary research among provincial governments over the past two decades. The pressing need to define a clearer role for the province with respect to post-secondary research strategy has been compounded by the growing incursion of the federal government into the post-secondary education (PSE) sector and a blurring of the traditional roles and responsibilities of the federal and provincial governments with respect to post-secondary education and research. Education has been the exclusive jurisdictional responsibility of the provinces since Confederation, but since the creation of the National Research Council in 1916, the federal government has played a direct and ever more active role in supporting research and development activities across the country, including the mandate to finance research activities within the post-secondary sector. For much of the postwar period, this implicit division of responsibility between the two levels of government was maintained. Through the evolving role of the federal granting councils, from the 1950s to the 1970s, the federal government assumed responsibility for funding most of the direct costs of sponsored research in the PSE sector and some graduate training through the provision of fellowships; but not for the overhead costs incurred to support that research, nor the cost of the infrastructure and equipment needed to conduct it. This was the presumed responsibility of the provinces, to be financed out of the funds available for core operations or, in some cases, out of special envelopes established for that purpose. [Ed: See Cameron, pp. 277–282.]

Federal involvement in financing post-secondary education expanded dramatically with the passage of the Post-Secondary Education Financing Arrangements Act in 1967, which introduced a post-secondary education transfer from the federal government designed to help the provinces respond to the rapid rise in the demand for post-secondary education, while respecting provincial sensitivities over their jurisdiction in the education field.[33] The level of financial contributions to the operating costs of post-secondary institutions declined subsequently after the shift from a shared-cost funding formula to a block funding formula in the Established Program Financing (EPF) Act in 1977.[34] Federal contributions to post-secondary research expenditures also increased with the expansion of the role of the Medical Research Council, the transfer of responsibility for research funding in the natural sciences and engineering from the National Research Council to a new council, NSERC, and for the social sciences and humanities from the Canada

Council to SSHRC in 1976. The extent of overlap and duplication in the financing of research in the PSE sector grew during the 1980s, when many of the provinces perceived a lack of strategic direction in the research funded by the federal granting councils and stepped into the gap with their own programs to support targeted research through measures such as the Centres of Excellence program in Ontario, the Action Structurante program in Quebec, the Alberta Heritage Fund, and a number of others. The confusion over their respective roles and responsibilities was further compounded in the late 1980s with the establishment of the federal Networks of Centres of Excellence program, a direct imitation of the Ontario program. While the result has been beneficial in terms of the amount and quality of the research funded in the PSE sector, it is more confusing from a policy perspective.[35]

Funding levels for post-secondary education and research suffered a setback in 1995 as the creation of the Canada Health and Social transfer reduced the amount of funding for operations available to post-secondary educational institutions and the federal budget also targeted the three federal granting councils for expenditure reductions. The trend in research funding was reversed in 1997 with the introduction of the first of several new federal programs aimed directly at the PSE sector. Since that point the contribution of these new federal initiatives, combined with the introduction of a number of new provincial programs, have greatly strengthened the research capacity of post-secondary institutions, including the research and teaching hospitals, within the province.[36]

The rapid introduction of new program initiatives in this field by both the federal and provincial governments has given rise to a pervasive sense of overlap, duplication, and competition between the two levels of government. In a seminal work for the Ontario Economic Council in 1977, Richard Simeon suggested that there are many reasons why both levels of government compete in a variety of policy areas. The first is constitutional – rarely are areas of constitutional jurisdiction neatly compartmentalized. As noted above, while education proper is unequivocally an area of provincial jurisdiction, the federal government has played a primary role in research funding since 1916. In the areas of research and graduate education, this distinction loses most of its relevance. In addition, citizens and narrower stakeholder communities make demands on governments for the delivery of services with little respect for the niceties of constitutional divisions of power. This has clearly been the case with the dramatic increase in targeted federal interventions in the area of post-secondary education and research since 1997. The growth in overlapping areas of jurisdiction and blurred responsibilities results in a general problem of what Simeon, following the Government of Ontario, termed 'entanglement.'[37] Entanglement takes several forms, including duplication of programs (clearly the case with the creation of both federal and provincial centres of excellence in the late 1980s), fragmentation (a long-standing issue with respect to the assumption of responsibility for research overheads), incursion (some might view the Canada Research Chairs program in this light), and spillovers (an ongoing and persistent program for the provinces, particularly in Atlantic Canada since the creation of the Canada Foundation for Innovation).

The degree of entanglement between the federal and provincial governments in the funding of university-based research has produced some perverse spillover effects in the past two decades. The shift from shared-cost funding for post-secondary education to a block funding formula with the negotiation of the EPF Agreement in 1977, and the gradual imposition of limits on spending increases under the EPF transfers by the federal government in the 1980s, imposed serious constraints on the fiscal resources available to the provinces. While they compensated for some of this reduction with their own revenues, part of the reduction was inevitably passed on to the post-secondary sector itself. Combined with the lack of federal support for the indirect costs of research, and only limited provincial funding for this envelope, the universities responded to this fiscal constraint by charging many of the overhead costs of research, including secretarial assistance, computer services, photocopying, and phone, fax, and courier services back to the research grants themselves. As Al Johnson's report to the federal Secretary of State noted in 1985, this was a perverse way of shifting part of the overhead expenses back onto the senior level of government, but at the cost of diminishing the actual amount of research that could be purchased with the grants from the federal agencies.[38]

The degree of fragmentation and incursions in post-secondary research and graduate education was further exacerbated with the creation of the Canada Foundation for Innovation and the establishment of the Canada Research Chairs program. It is arguable that both initiatives could have been supported more effectively through a generalized increase in the federal level of transfer payments to the provinces for the operating costs of post-secondary education. This transfer could have taken the form of increases in the existing Canada Social Transfer, or it could have come in the form of a new Canada Education Transfer, such as that proposed by the president of the Canadian Federation of the Humanities and Social Sciences in a brief to the federal government in 2003.[39] The creation of a CET with funding levels that included both adequate support for the operating costs of the universities and the increases provided by the introduction of the CFI and CRC programs would have left the provincial governments and the universities with much greater autonomy in the allocation of these funds between research and graduate education and between basic and targeted research.

The federal government decision to increase its support for post-secondary education through moving the funds off budget into separate endowments (a budget strategy soundly criticized by the Auditor General of Canada) has increased the amount of funding available to the universities for research; but it has done so in a manner that blurs the traditional line demarcating provincial responsibility for post-secondary operating costs and federal responsibility for research. Arguably, the requirement of matching funds to qualify for CFI investments has compelled the provinces to increase the amount of financing available for the universities, but in a manner that has generated considerable confusion in provincial policy – witness the successive introduction of the Ontario Research and Development Challenge Fund, the Ontario Innovation Fund, the Ontario Innovation Trust, the Ontario Innovation Institute, and, finally, the Ontario Research Fund – which have created greater uncertainty and instability for the universities with respect to the amount of funding available to them.

The end result is the absence of a clear delineation of roles and responsibilities in the area of post-secondary research policy, and the lack of an institutionalized mechanism for monitoring the consequences of the fragmentation and spillovers outlined above. This area of jurisdictional entanglement seems marked by little advance consultation between the two levels of government, and no efforts to anticipate the consequences of new initiatives by one level for the other. Similarly, the presence of duplicate sources of funding in some targeted areas of research activity raises the possibility that a suboptimal distribution of research funding may result from the lack of monitoring and coordination (although this assertion is contested by the granting councils). In an era of constrained resources, there is clearly a compelling need for more effective monitoring and coordination of all elements of the post-secondary research system on the part of both levels of government.

The blurring of the respective roles of the federal and provincial governments also raises a related question of the response by the universities and the research community. To a large extent, the universities (and the province) have defined their role in the research field in a reactive fashion, letting the federal government define research programs (and sometimes priorities) and then ensuring that the research community within their respective institutions was supported in its efforts to obtain the maximum portion of the available funds. To date, the Province of Ontario has developed its own agenda with respect to post-secondary research policy in fits and starts – displaying great innovation in the 1980s with the creation of the University Research Incentive Fund, the Centres of Excellence, and the Premier's Council Fund. More recently, however, it has proceeded in a more reactive fashion that has deteriorated at times into relative confusion, particularly with respect to the issue of how it would meet the requirement of matching funds for the CFI program.

For their part the universities have been finally compelled to enter into a more focused planning process by the requirement of producing strategic plans to justify their requests for funding under both the CRC and CFI programs, but this has negative consequences from the perspective of both research priorities and provincial policy. In the first place, it reinforces the trend in evidence since the 1980s towards more targeted and applied research funding at the expense of the broader-based support for basic research provided by the granting councils. Second, given the degree to which research and teaching are integrally related within the university, it gives the federal government significant leverage over the allocation of both research and *teaching* priorities within the universities. Given the extent to which the ability to provide first-class research facilities in conjunction with an offer of a teaching position is essential to attract world-class researchers to Canada, both the CFI and CRC secretariats have assumed a high degree of influence in determining not only research priorities, but *teaching* ones as well in Ontario universities.

The trend towards more targeted and applied research recalls some of the critical issues raised in the first half of this paper. This growth of targeted funding has occurred in the context of increasingly constrained funding for both general operating costs and basic research. It must be recognized that this shift may have negative consequences in the long term from the perspective of research policy for the post-secondary sector. In general, there is a growing sense in both the US and Canada that the emphasis on targeted funding for applied research at the PSE level, coupled with a decline in the basic research role of some of the key corporate laboratories, is jeopardizing the long-term status of basic research. A white paper on basic research published by *R&D Magazine* in the US echoed this warning. It noted the growing concern among both R&D managers in industry and research administrators in universities that the shift away from basic research and a more long-term focus towards more commercially relevant research with a shorter time horizon is drying up the pool of scientific knowledge that can feed future innovations.[40] This concern was echoed even more forcibly in a report on information technology research to President Clinton in 1999:

> During the past decade both industry and Government have altered the balance between basic research and the later stages of technology development and commercialization. At the same time, major corporations have cut back on basic research expenditures, shifting staff from centralized laboratories to operating divisions where applied work is closely tied to commercial products and processes. In both the public and private sectors, the interacting reasons are 1) downward budget pressures, 2) increased focus on mission and 3) the inefficiency of transitioning long-term research to near-term product ... [T]his restructuring came at a high price: a serious decline in basic research activities.
>
> It is time to swing the pendulum back in the other direction and to strike a proper balance. We need more basic research – the kind of groundbreaking, high-risk/high-return research that will provide the ideas and methods for new disciplinary paradigms a decade or more in the future. We must make wise investments that will bear fruit over the next forty years.[41]

In Canada this problem has been compounded by a decline in funding available from the granting councils relative to the increase in the number of worthy research proposals going unfunded for lack of resources. The question of the appropriate balance between the funding of basic research and that for targeted and applied research should rank high on the list of priorities for any consideration of university research and graduate education policy. Given the primary responsibility of the provinces for post-secondary education, it is an area of jurisdiction that they can ill afford to abdicate by default. The preceding discussion suggests compelling reasons for provinces to assume a greater role in formulating post-secondary research policy. Given the growing overlap between the actions of the two levels of government and the inevitable relationship that exists between the core funding of post-secondary education and its research activity, what is the unique role that the provinces should play with respect to post-secondary research? The integral connection between the educational role of the post-secondary sector and its research role provides one justification for the provinces to elaborate their own policy approach. Further support is provided by the growing body of evidence that links the strength and vitality of university research capability with a dynamic, innovative capacity in regional economies. Given this evidence and the increasing importance of both basic and applied research policy in a knowledge-based economy, there is an obvious need for the province to assume a more effective leadership and coordinating role in setting university research policy.

There are a number of elements of post-secondary research policy that could be considered. The most pressing area of concern is that of the spillovers created by the lack of coordination and integration of federal and provincial policy in this area. The lack of coordination means that the current allocation of funds for post-secondary research activities may be less than optimal in a number of respects: in terms of the distribution of available funds between direct research costs, support for graduate training, indirect or overhead costs, and the costs of infrastructure and equipment; in terms of the distribution of funds between longer-term basic research and more intermediate or medium-term targeted research; and in terms of the distribution of funds across different areas of research activity. Consideration of these issues should be a central focus of a reinvigorated provincial effort to review its support for university-based research and graduate education.

Within the provincial government, there is a clear division of responsibility between post-secondary education and economic development. Provincial policy towards post-secondary research support has been aligned more closely with the latter than the former, reflecting the fact that it has primarily been of a targeted and applied nature. Furthermore, other provincial ministries, such as agriculture, have a defined research mission and capability of their own. The result is a lack of coordination with respect to research and graduate education inside the provincial government itself. As the potential economic value and benefit of university-based research activity is recognized more widely, it becomes essential to ensure that research policy is coordinated across the respective ministries of the provincial government. This represents an additional challenge in this area.

Conclusion: The Role of the Research University in Economic Development

Talk of a knowledge-based economy is more than just a convenient turn of phrase. Government-funded basic research is a critical source of investment for developing a society's learning capabilities. Government funding expands the technological opportunities available for firms to draw upon as they go about developing new products and processes. It supports the training of students, who, upon entering industry, transfer their skills and knowledge about science and technology into the private sector. Given the localized nature of the innovation process, government support for basic research fosters the creation of dynamic agglomerations of firms around centres of higher education and sustains the growth of untraded interdependencies among these parts of the innovation system.

The strength and vitality of universities remains essential for growth in the knowledge-based economy. Universities perform vital functions both as generators of new knowledge through their leading-edge research activities and as trainers of highly qualified labour. As most research universities will attest, the two functions are integrally linked, and when they are most effective they contribute strongly to regional economic growth and development. As such, they provide an essential part of the infrastructure that local and regional innovation systems draw upon. But it is important to be clear about the precise role they play. Strong research-intensive universities feed the growth of their local economies by expanding the local knowledge base and providing a steady stream of talent to support the growth of firms. They also serve as magnets for investments by leading or anchor firms, drawing them into the cluster to gain more effective access to the knowledge base and *local buzz*. Recent policy initiatives which aim to elevate the commercialization of technology to equal status with research and teaching as mandates of the university fundamentally miss this point. Universities must also be a vital part of the local 'economic community' by building the region's social capital and taking a leadership role in activities designed to enhance the region's absorptive capacity. Continued public support for both the teaching and research mandates of the university are essential if universities are to succeed in these roles and contribute to the growth of their local and regional economies.

Notes

* Professor of Political Science and Co-Director, Program on Globalization and Regional Innovation Systems, Centre for International Studies, University of Toronto. This paper draws upon research previously conducted with Ammon Salter and Matthew Lucas. Allison Bramwell provided admirable research assistance in the preparation of the paper. However, responsibility for all errors or omissions rests with the author alone.

1 Peter David, 'The Knowledge Factory: A Survey of Universities,' *The Economist*, 4 October 1997, 4.

2 Henry Etkowitz and Andrew Webster, 'Entrepreneurial Science: The Second Academic Revolution,' in *Capitalizing Knowledge: New Intersections in Industry and Academia*, ed. Henry Etkowitz, Andrew Webster, and Peter Healey (New York: SUNY Press, 1998).

3 Richard S. Rosenbloom and William J. Spencer, 'The Transformation of Industrial Research,' *Issues in Science and Technology*, Spring 1996, 68–74. Cf. also Richard S. Rosenbloom and William J. Spencer, eds, *Engines of Innovation: U.S. Industrial Research at the End of an Era* (Boston: Harvard University Press, 1996).

4 Ben R. Martin, 'The Changing Social Contract for Science and the Evolution of Knowledge Production,' in *Science and Innovation: Rethinking the Rationales for Funding and Governance*, ed. Aldo Geuna, Ammon J. Salter, and W. Edward Steinmuller (Cheltenham, UK: Edward Elgar, 2003).

5 Harvey Brooks, 'The Evolution of US Science Policy,' in *Technology, R&D, and the Economy*, ed. Bruce L.R. Smith and Claude E. Barfield (Washington: The Brookings Institution and the American Enterprise Institute, 1996), 21; and Donald E. Stokes, *Pasteur's Quadrant: Basic Science and Technological Innovation* (Washington: Brookings Institution Press, 1997), 10–11.

6 David A. Wolfe, 'Commentary on Part I: The Evolving Research Environment,' in *Science and Innovation: Rethinking the Rationales for Funding and Governance*, ed. Aldo Geuna, Ammon J. Salter, and W. Edward Steinmuller (Cheltenham, UK: Edward Elgar, 2003).

7 US Congress, Office of Technology Assessment, *Innovation and Commercialization of Emerging Technology* (Washington: US Government Printing Office, 1995), 43.

8 Giovanni Dosi, 'Sources, Procedures and Microeconomic Effects of Innovation,' *Journal of Economic Literature* 26 (September 1988), 1120–71.

9 This argument draws upon David A. Wolfe and Ammon J. Salter, 'The Socio-Economic Importance of Scientific Research to Canada,' discussion paper prepared for the Partnership Group on Science and Engineering (Ottawa, 1997). Cf. also Ammon J. Salter and Ben R. Martin, 'The Economic Benefits of Publicly Funded Basic Research: A Critical Review,' *Research Policy* 30 (2001), 509–32.

10 Richard R. Nelson, 'The Simple Economics of Basic Scientific Research,'
    Journal of Political Economy 67 (1959): 297–306; Kenneth Arrow, 'Economic
    Welfare and the Allocation of Resources for Invention,' in *The Rate and
    Direction of Inventive Activities*, ed. Richard R. Nelson (Princeton: Princeton
    University Press, 1962), 609–25.

11 Paul Nightingale, 'Knowledge in the Process of Technological Innovation:
    A Study of the UK Pharmaceutical, Electronic and Aerospace Industries,'
    doctoral dissertation, Science Policy Research Unit, University of Sussex,
    Brighton, 1997.

12 Michael Polanyi, *Personal Knowledge: Towards a Post-Critical Philosophy*
    (New York: Harper & Row, Harper Torchbooks/Academy Library, 1962).
    See also Richard R. Nelson and Sidney G. Winter, *An Evolutionary Theory of
    Economic Change* (Cambridge, Mass.: Belknap Press, 1982), 76–82.

13 Bengt-Åke Lundvall and Björn Johnson, 'The Learning Economy,' *Journal
    of Industry Studies* 1:2 (December 1994), 23–42; Bengt-Åke Lundvall, 'Why
    the New Economy Is a Learning Economy,' DRUID Working Paper no. 04-
    01 (Copenhagen 2004); and Peter Maskell and Anders Malmberg,
    'Localised Learning and Industrial Competitiveness,' *Cambridge Journal of
    Economics* 23 (1999), 167–85.

14 Wesley M. Cohen and Daniel A. Levinthal, 'Absorptive Capacity: A New
    Perspective on Learning and Innovation,' *Administrative Science Quar-
    terly* 35 (1990), 128–52.

15 Keith Pavitt, 'What Makes Basic Research Economically Useful?' *Research
    Policy* 20 (1991), 109–19; Nathan Rosenberg, 'Why Do Firms Do Basic
    Research (with Their Own Money)?' *Research Policy* 19 (1990), 165–74: cf.
    also National Academy of Engineering, *The Impact of Academic Research on
    Industrial Performance* (Washington: National Academies Press, 2003), 42,
    47–8.

16 The findings of a number of recent studies employing both survey re-
    search methodology and qualitative interview techniques strongly rein-
    force the perspective that a key aspect of the process of knowledge transfer
    from universities and research institutes is that it occurs through personal
    connections and that the knowledge being transferred is thus 'tacit' and
    'embodied.' To deploy university-generated knowledge in a commercial
    setting, firms need to capture both its tacit, as well as its more explicit, or
    codified, component. Faulkner and Senker explored the relationship from
    the perspective of the innovating organization, focusing on its knowledge
    requirements and trying to develop a better understanding of the knowl-
    edge flows from academia to industry. While the findings differ slightly
    by industry, they conclude that partnering with universities contributes
    most to firm innovation through an exchange of tacit knowledge and that
    the channels for communicating this knowledge are often informal. Such
    informal linkages are both a precursor and a successor to formal linkages,

and many useful exchanges of research materials or access to equipment take place through non-contractual barter arrangements. The flexibility inherent in such arrangements promotes the goodwill between partners that supports more formal linkages. For this argument see Jacqueline Senker, 'Tacit Knowledge and Models of Innovation,' *Industrial and Corporate Change* 4:2 (1995), 425–47; and W. Faulkner and J. Senker, *Knowledge Frontiers: Public Sector Research and Industrial Innovation in Biotechnology, Engineering Ceramics, and Parallel Computing* (Oxford: Clarendon Press 1995).

17 Faulkner and Senker, *Knowledge Frontiers*.
18 National Academy of Engineering, *The Impact of Academic Research*, 59–60.
19 Fumio Kodama and Lewis M. Branscomb, 'University Research as an Engine for Growth: How Realistic is the Vision?' in *Industrializing Knowledge: University-Industry Linkages in Japan and the United States*, ed. Lewis M. Branscomb, Fumio Kodama, and Richard Florida (Cambridge, Mass.: MIT Press, 1999), 16.
20 See Maryann P. Feldman, 'Location and Innovation: The New Economic Geography of Innovation, Spillovers and Agglomeration,' in *The Oxford Handbook of Economic Geography*, ed. Gordon L. Clark, Maryann P. Feldman, and Meric S. Gertler (Oxford: Oxford University Press, 2000), James D. Adams, 'Comparative Localization of Academic and Industrial Spillovers,' *Journal of Economic Geography* 2 (2002), 253–78; and Anthony Arundel and Aldo Geuna, 'Proximity and the Use of Public Science by Innovative European Firms,' *Economics of Innovation and New Technology* 13:6 (2004), 559–80.
21 Senker, 'Tacit Knowledge and Models of Innovation.'
22 Richard R. Nelson, *Understanding Technical Change as an Evolutionary Process* (Amsterdam: Elsevier Science Pub. Co., 1987).
23 M. Gibbons and R. Johnston, 'The Role of Science in Technological Innovation,' *Research Policy* 3 (1974), 220–42.
24 Ben Martin and John Irvine, *Foresight in Science: Picking the Winners* (London: Pinter, 1984).
25 David A.Wolfe, 'Networking among Regions: Ontario and the Four Motors For Europe,' *European Planning Studies* 8:3 (2000), 267–84; David A. Wolfe and Matthew Lucas, 'Investing Knowledge in Universities: Rethinking the Firm's Role in Knowledge Transfer,' in John de la Mothe and Dominique Foray, eds, *Knowledge Management in the Innovation Process: Business Practices and Technology Adoption* (Amsterdam: Kluwer Academic Publishers, 2001), 173–91; Matthew J.W. Lucas, 'Bridging a Cultural Divide: Strengthening Similarities and Managing Differences in University–Industry Relations,' PhD dissertation, University of Toronto, 2005.
26 Mike Lazaridis, 'The Importance of Basic Research,' *Re$earch Money* 18:18 (2004), 8.

27 Attila Varga, 'Local Academic Knowledge Transfers and the Concentration of Economic Activity,' *Journal of Regional Science* 40:2 (2000), 289–300.

28 Lynne G. Zucker and Michael R. Darby, 'Star Scientists and Institutional Transformation: Patterns of Invention and Innovation in the Formation of the Biotechnology Industry,' *Proceedings of the National Academy of Science* 93 (November 1996), 127–9. Cf. also Johanne Queenton and Jorge Niosi, 'Bioscientists and Biotechnology: A Canadian Study,' paper presented at the 3rd European Meeting on Applied Evolutionary Economics, University of Augsberg, Germany, 9–12 April 2003, for a modification of the research methodology and its application to Canadian data.

29 Richard Florida, *The Rise of the Creative Class: And How It's Transforming Work, Leisure, Community and Everyday Life* (New York: Basis Books, 2002); and Meric S. Gertler, Richard Florida, Gary Gates, and Tara Vinodrai, *Competing on Creativity: Placing Ontario's Cities in North American Context*, report prepared for the Ontario Ministry of Enterprise, Opportunity and Innovation and the Institute for Competitiveness and Prosperity (Toronto, 2002). Cf. also Meric S. Gertler and Tara Vinodrai, 'Anchors of Creativity: How Do Universities Create Competitive and Cohesive Communities,' in this volume.

30 Richard Florida, 'The Role of the University: Leveraging Talent, Not Technology,' *Issues in Science and Technology*, Summer 1999, 72.

31 David A. Wolfe and Meric S. Gertler, 'Clusters from the Inside and Out: Local Dynamics and Global Linkages,' Special Theme Issue on Clusters and Local Economic Development, *Urban Studies* 41:5 (2004), 1055–77; Jérôme Doutriaux, 'University-Industry Linkages and the Development of Knowledge Clusters in Canada,' *Local Economy* 18:1 (2003), 63–79; David A. Wolfe, ed., *Clusters Old and New: The Transition to a Knowledge Economy in Canada's Regions* (Montreal and Kingston: McGill-Queen's University Press for Queen's School of Policy Studies, 2003); David A. Wolfe and Matthew Lucas, eds, *Clusters in a Cold Climate: Innovation Dynamics in a Diverse Economy* (Montreal and Kingston: McGill-Queen's University Press for Queen's School of Policy Studies, 2004)

32 Heather Munroe-Blum, *Growing Ontario's Innovation System: The Strategic Role of University Research*, report prepared for the Ontario Ministries of Colleges, Training and Universities, Energy, Science and Technology, and the Ontario Jobs and Investment Board, (Toronto, 1999), 14.

33 Parliamentary Tax Force on Federal-Provincial Fiscal Arrangements, *Fiscal Federal in Canada* (Ottawa: Supply and Services Canada, 1981), 38–9.

34 A.W. Johnson, *Giving Greater Point and Purpose to the Federal Financing of Post-Secondary Education and Research in Canada*, report prepared for the Secretary of State of Canada, (Ottawa, 1985), 2. These developments are discussed at greater length in the paper by David M. Cameron, 'Post-secondary Education and Research: Whither Canadian Federalism?' in this

volume. It is important to keep in mind that a significant portion of the expenditures on research activities in the PSE sector are funded out of the universities' own operating funds.

35 For a broader overview of trends in Ontario's innovation policy during this period, cf. David A. Wolfe, 'Harnessing the Region: Changing Perspectives on Innovation Policy in Ontario,' in *The New Industrial Geography: Regions, Regulation and Institutions*, ed. Trevor J. Barnes and Meric S. Gertler (London and New York: Routledge, 1999), 127–54. A more detailed analysis of the role of the PSE sector within Ontario's innovation system is provided in Heather Munroe-Blum, *Growing Ontario's Innovation System*.

36 For a more comprehensive discussion of the specific federal and provincial programs, see the contribution by David M. Cameron to this volume. I have examined recent trends in federal and provincial science and technology policy at greater length in David A. Wolfe, 'The Role of Cooperative Industrial Policy in Canada and Ontario,' in *Competitive Industrial Development in the Age of Information: The Role of Cooperation in the Technology Sector*, ed. Richard J. Braudo and Jeffrey G. MacIntosh (London and New York: Routledge, 1999), 30–63.

37 Richard Simeon, 'The Federal-Provincial Decision Making Process,' in *Intergovernmental Relations: Issues and Alternatives 1977* (Toronto: Ontario Economic Council, 1977), 26–9.

38 A.W. Johnson, *Giving Greater Point and Purpose*, 16. This perverse effect was finally corrected with the introduction of federal funding to cover the indirect costs of research, in exchange for a commitment from the AUCC to support a greater commercialization effort on the part of the universities. As noted above, this growing emphasis on commercialization may overlook the real nature of the contribution that university-based research makes to economic development.

39 Doug Owram, *Discussion Paper on the Proposed Canada Social Transfer*, prepared for and presented to the Joint Meeting of the Government Caucuses on Social Policy and Post-Secondary Education and Research, Ottawa, 3 November 2003.

40 R&D Magazine Online, *Basic Research White Paper*, http://www.rdmag.com/BRWP/index.html.

41 President's Information Technology Advisory Committee, *Information Technology Research: Investing in Our Future*, Report to the President (Washington: National Coordination Office for Computing, Information and Communications, 29 February 1999).

Post-secondary Education and Ontario's Prosperity

JAMES MILWAY*

In carrying out its mandate to measure and monitor Ontario's competitiveness and prosperity relative to other North American jurisdictions, the Institute for Competitiveness & Prosperity has identified the importance of post-secondary education in realizing our prosperity potential. In this paper we review Ontario's competitiveness and prosperity relative to a group of peer jurisdictions in North America, identify the importance of productivity as the key driver of our prosperity gap relative to these peers, and review the importance of our under-investment in post-secondary education to productivity.

Ontario's Prosperity Gap versus North America's Leading Economies

Ontarians should be proud of the economic strength of our province. As we compare prosperity in Ontario to other significantly sized jurisdictions around the world, we see that Ontario is among the world's leaders. In fact, compared to countries that have half of Ontario's population or greater, we have the second highest GDP per capita. We trail only the United States. Among the regional powerhouses of Europe, the four motors of Baden Württemberg (Germany), Cataluña (Spain), Lombardia (Italy), and Rhône-Alpes (France), Ontario stands first in GDP per capita.[1] The challenge we face as Ontarians is to build on our strengths to improve our competitiveness even further and close the prosperity gap we have identified with leading US states.

As the Institute has highlighted over the past three years, in competitiveness and prosperity Ontario lags behind the leading jurisdictions within North America. It is heartening to out-perform economies outside North America, but the true benchmark of our potential is the

Figure 1   GDP per capita for Peer States and Provinces C$ 2003

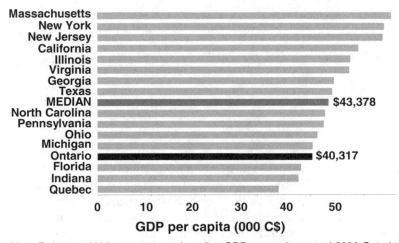

GDP per capita (000 C$)

Note: Estimated 2003 peer state and median GDP per capita; actual 2003 Ontario and Quebec GDP per capita used.
Source: Statistics Canada; US Department of Commerce, Bureau of Economic Analysis; OECD PPP indices; Institute for Competitiveness & Prosperity Analysis

results achieved by jurisdictions with a similar endowment of natural resources, legal and administrative frameworks, development history, culture, and attitudes. For this comparison, we have focused on the states and provinces within North America that have half of Ontario's population or greater, or more than 6 million people. This criterion yields a set of 15 other jurisdictions – 14 states and Quebec – as a peer group against which we assess Ontario's competitiveness and prosperity.

Against this North American peer group, Ontario's performance is not as positive as against the international group. In GDP per capita for 2003, we stand 13th out of 16 (figure 1). This is the same standing as in 2001. In 2002 we actually moved up two spaces, ahead of Ohio and Michigan, as the US was coming out of its recession; however, we reverted to 13th in 2003. This translates into a prosperity gap (the difference between Ontario's and the median GDP per capita) of 7.1% or $3,061[2] versus the median of the peer jurisdictions. The prosperity gap represents lost potential for Ontarians. We are less successful than our US counterparts in adding value to natural, physical, and human resources.

As recently as 1988 we had no prosperity gap relative to our US peers. But through the 1990s, the economic growth of the peer states outstripped Ontario, and by 2000 the gap reached $4,811 per capita.

Since then it has declined, primarily as the result of US economic sluggishness rather than through Ontario achieving a new economic trajectory.[3] Our challenge is to return to a median status, which we have set as an objective for Ontario in the next decade. To achieve median status among the most competitive economies in the world is an ambitious goal.

Still, it is worth striving for. If Ontarians were able to overcome this prosperity gap, the average Ontario household's annual after-tax disposable income would rise by $6,755. Families would be able to choose among several meaningful spending options. For example, among mortgage holders, more than half their annual payments ($11,043) would be covered. Among renters, more than 80% of their average annual bill of $8,193 would be covered. The increased disposable income could cover renovation costs of $5,474 among those who renovate. Ontarians could increase their recreational spending (currently $3,914 per household) significantly. Many could choose to invest more in their RRSP contribution (currently $3,950 per contributing household in Ontario).

In addition, closing the prosperity gap would generate $13.7 billion in tax revenues for the federal and provincial governments in Ontario. This additional tax revenue would enable the two levels of government to address funding issues in health care, education, and social services more adequately than they can today.

Lower Productivity: The Largest Source of Our Prosperity Gap

To clarify the source of the prosperity gap, we use a framework for disaggregating the gap into four measurable elements of our GDP per capita (figure 2):

- The demographic **profile** in a jurisdiction – the percentage of the population that is of working age and can therefore contribute to economic prosperity
- The **utilization** of the working-age population – the percentage of the working-age population who are seeking (participation) and succeeding in finding work (employment)
- The **intensity** of work – the number of hours workers on average spend on the job
- The **productivity** of the workforce – the success in translating working hours into products and services of value to customers in Ontario and around the world.

Figure 2   Measurable elements of GDP per capita

Prosperity		Profile		Utilization		Intensity		Productivity
GDP per capita	=	Potential labour force / Population	x	Jobs / Potential labour force	x	Hours Worked / Jobs	x	GDP / Hours Worked
				• Participation • Employment				• Cluster mix • Cluster content • Cluster effectiveness • Urbanization • Education • Capital investment • Productivity residual

Source: Adapted from J. Baldwin, J.P. Maynard, and S. Wells (2000), 'Productivity Growth in Canada and the United States' *Isuma* 1:1 (Spring 2000), Ottawa Policy Research Institute.

To provide further insight into productivity we examine six of its sub-elements:

- the mix of our industries into traded clusters, local industries, and natural resources
- sub-industries that make up our clusters of traded industries
- the productivity strength of our clusters of traded industries
- the degree to which our population lives in urban centres
- the educational attainment of our population and its impact on productivity
- the degree to which physical capital supports the productivity of workers
- effectiveness with which we generate value based on the platform created by all of the other sub-elements – the residual value.

The most significant contributor to the prosperity gap is productivity (figure 3). We discuss each measurable element in turn.

Labour supply factors – Profile, Utilization, and Intensity – have a limited impact on our prosperity gap

Our work demonstrates that Ontarians are investing adequate work effort for matching US prosperity. By this we mean that Ontarians seek and secure hours of work at nearly the same level as our peers.

Figure 3   Productivity and Ontario's prosperity gap

Median GDP per capita*	$43,378
Ontario's GDP per capita*	$40,317
Prosperity gap	−$3,061

Elements of Prosperity Gap – Impact on GDP per capita

Profile		+$987
Utilization		
– Participation	+1,321	
– Employment	−253	+1,068
Intensity		+145
Productivity		
– Mix of clusters	+1,906	
– Cluster content	+489	
– Cluster effectiveness	−1,748	
– Urbanization	−3,765	
– Education	−907	
– Capital investment	−808	
– Productivity residual	428	−5,261
Prosperity Gap		−$3,061

Note: '+' indicates Ontario advantage versus peer state median; '−' indicates disadvantage
* of 16 peer jurisdictions (see figure 1)
Source: Task Force on Competitiveness, Productivity & Economic Progress, Realizing Our Prosperity Potential, 3rd annual report, November 2004, 16

First, we have a demographic *profile* that represents an advantage for Ontario versus the median peer state. We have 67.2% of our population between the ages of 16 and 64, compared to 65.6% in the peer jurisdictions. This higher percentage of our population at working age translates to a potential advantage of $987 per capita in GDP (figure 3). In other words, if Ontario equalled the peer states on every factor but profile, our GDP per capita would be $987 higher than that of the peer jurisdictions.

Utilization of the potential labour force represents another advantage for Ontario. Ontario has a higher percentage of its working-age population actually seeking work (69% compared to 66.8% for the peers). Similarly to the way we calculate the impact of demographic profile (i.e., holding all other factors constant between Ontario and the median of the peer jurisdictions), this equates to a $1,321 per capita advantage for Ontario. However, Ontario's economy tends to be less capable of generating employment opportunities for people who are available for and interested in working. Thus our employment rate[4] tends to be slightly lower than in the peer states (a 93.2% employment rate versus 93.8% for the peers in 2003). This under-performance in employment accounts for $253 of the prosperity gap. The net effect of these participation and employment results is that Ontario's out-performance in utilization was worth $1,068 in GDP per capita.

Based on 2003 results of the Ontario-US **intensity** difference (33.4 hours worked per week in Ontario versus 33.3 hours in the US), we can attribute to this factor a positive impact on the prosperity gap of $145 per capita from Ontarians' working more hours than their US counterparts.[5]

Profile, utilization, and intensity have a net positive effect on the prosperity gap. By working more and longer than our counterparts in the peer states Ontarians achieved a $2,200 per capita advantage versus the peer states. However, as we see next, we are less productive than our counterparts during the hours in which we are working.

Lower productivity accounts for the largest share of our prosperity gap

We assess six sub-elements of productivity to determine the impact of this key driver of the prosperity gap.

Cluster mix and cluster content in Ontario contribute positively to our productivity. We conclude that high-performing clusters are an important element of closing our prosperity gap with our US peer group. Traded industries are those that are typically concentrated in specific geographic areas and sell to markets beyond their local region. Research by Michael Porter of the Harvard-based Institute for Strategy and Competitiveness has shown that clusters of traded industries achieve higher levels of productivity (as represented by wages) and innovation. In addition, the presence of traded clusters in a region has a spillover effect in that they typically generate opportunities for increased success of the local economy. The 'tide' of traded clusters raises the prosperity level for both local and traded industries, and everyone benefits.

Drawing on Porter's methodology, the Institute has determined that fully 39.9% of employment in Ontario is in clusters of traded industries, versus 32.3% among the peers. Ontario's strength in business services, financial services, education and knowledge creation, and automotive, for instance, has created an attractive mix of clusters of traded industries. Our analysis of Ontario's *cluster mix* estimates a $1,906 per capita advantage over the peers. This benefit is derived from higher output than would be likely if Ontario's mix were the same as the peers' mix.[6]

Sub-clusters make up each cluster of traded industries.[7] As with clusters, there are wage and productivity differences across sub-clusters. One of the issues being discussed by business analysts and economists is 'hollowing out.' Some observers believe that Canada is losing the high value-added component of its industries, as head offices and decision-makers relocate outside the country. As we analyse the sub-clusters that make up our clusters of traded industries and compare these with the mix in the US, we conclude that the impact of *cluster content* on GDP per capita is a $489 advantage for Ontario.

Our weaker clusters are a significant part of the Ontario's productivity gap. While Ontario has an excellent mix of clusters, their productivity is much lower than that in the peer states. We estimate that this lower productivity in our clusters of traded industries reduces Ontario's GDP per capita by $1,748 per capita versus the peer states.'[8] In other words, while our mix and content of clusters provides a potential benefit to prosperity of $2,395 per capita, we do not realize this potential, as our lack of cluster strength costs Ontarians $1,748 per capita.

Relatively low urbanization is a significant contributor to the prosperity gap. The Institute has synthesized current research by Canadian and other urban geographers and economists[9] that linked urbanization, innovation, learning, and urban policy. We found that the increased social and economic interaction of people and firms, the cost advantages of larger-scale markets, and a diversified pool of skilled labour all improve productivity in urban areas.[10] The interplay of these factors promotes innovation and growth in an economy. Canada's lower degree of urbanization hurts our productivity compared to the US.

There is a positive relationship between degree of urbanization[11] and the labour productivity of the 50 states and 10 provinces. For Ontario, it includes our 11 largest cities, ranging in size from Toronto to Kingston. Our analysis indicates that we have a $3,765 per capita disadvantage against the US. This makes low urbanization the largest negative contributor to Ontario's productivity gap.

Lower educational achievement weakens our productivity. Most economists agree that the level of education attained across the workforce is an important determinant of the 'quality' of an economy's human capital. Our analyses reinforce the positive correlation between productivity and wages.[12] Economic studies also show repeatedly that individuals' earnings increase with their level of education.[13] In fact, the best single predictor of personal income is level of educational attainment. Canada's under-performance in educational attainment, mainly at post-secondary levels, translates into a negative impact on GDP per capita of $907 per capita. As one example of this under-attainment, only 31% of Ontario managers (as defined by Standard Occupational Classifications)[14] had a university degree in 1996, versus 46% in the US. More recent results are not available for the United States, but by 2001 Ontario's results had barely improved to a university-degree attainment rate of 33%.

Capital under-investment is a drag on productivity growth. Our underinvestment in machinery and equipment in Ontario compared to levels in US peer states[15] slowly erodes the amount of our capital stock compared to that in the US. This erosion in turn reduces the productivity of our labour and hence our prosperity. For Ontario, we estimate this under-investment to be worth at least $808 per capita in lost productivity and prosperity. Later, we discuss further this under-investment and its possible causes, including the higher tax burden on capital.

The remaining gap of $428 relates to lower effectiveness. We have been able to account for the impact of profile, utilization, and intensity on prosperity, as well as for the effects of several elements of productivity. The gap that remains is related to productivity on the basis of like-to-like cluster mix and strength, urbanization, education, and capital intensity. In sum, Ontario is less effective than the peer states in converting our natural, physical, and human resources into goods and services.

In the balance of this paper we focus on the importance of education, particularly post-secondary education, for increasing Ontario's productivity and decreasing its prosperity gap.

Ontario's Underinvestment in Post-secondary Education

The key challenge for the Institute has been to determine the important factors that drive the productivity and prosperity gap with our peer jurisdictions. We have been seeking answers to the question 'What are the important drivers in strengthening our capacity for innovation and upgrading?' To help guide our analysis and recommendations for Ontarians, the Institute developed the AIMS framework. AIMS is built on an integrated set of four factors:

- **Attitudes** towards competitiveness, growth, and global excellence. Our view is that an economy's capacity for competitiveness is grounded in the attitudes of its stakeholders. To the extent that public and business leaders believe in the importance of innovation and growth, they are more likely to take action to drive competitiveness and prosperity. Our previous research indicates that, in general, Ontarians' attitudes towards competitiveness, risk taking, innovation, and other related issues hardly differ from their US counterparts in the public and business community.[16]
- **Investments** in education, machinery, research and development, and commercialization. As businesses, individuals, and governments invest for future prosperity they will enhance productivity and prosperity. Our work indicates that relative to our peer-state counterparts, Ontarians under-invest in human and physical capital.
- **Motivations** for hiring, working, and upgrading as a result of tax policies and government policies and programs. Taxes that discourage investment or labour will reduce the motivations for investing and upgrading. Our research indicates that taxes, especially on capital, are a factor in our under-investment.[17]
- **Structures** of markets and institutions that encourage and assist upgrading and innovation. Structures, in concert with motivations, form the environment in which attitudes are converted to actions and investments. Our work here indicates that a significant factor behind our under-investment is that our market structures are not as competitive and supportive as in the peer states, and consequently our businesses and individuals invest less for future prosperity.[18]

We turn to the investment factor, particularly investment in education.

Post-secondary education has significant economic impact

Investment in education affects productivity and prosperity throughout our society. Most researchers who have analysed Canada's and Ontario's productivity challenge conclude that education is an important part of the solution. A more educated and better-trained labour force creates more value. Studies show repeatedly that individuals' earnings increase with the level of education. In fact, the best single

Figure 4   Returns to Education, 1997

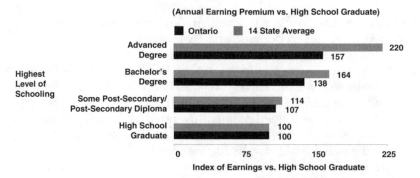

(Annual Earning Premium vs. High School Graduate)

■ Ontario   ■ 14 State Average

Source: Institute for Competitiveness & Prosperity based on Baker and Trefler, 'The Impact of Education and Urbanization on Productivity,' www.competeprosper.ca

predictor of personal income is level of education. The best advice parents can give their children is to stay in school. Every extra year of school and each additional degree raise income prospects for individuals (figure 4). While the economic returns from each level of education are higher in the US than in Ontario, the data indicate a significant increase in earnings from advanced education in the province.

For businesses, the increased availability of skilled workers, researchers, and managers is a critical benefit of post-secondary education. For all of us, the ideas that spill out of universities improve and create products, services, and processes and lead to new companies and whole new industries.

Investment in education by Ontarians trails that in peer states

Our review of Ontario's investment in education shows that we under-invest relative to our peer group and that this under-investment is more pronounced as we move through the educational system. Our analysis includes funding from all public and private sources. On a per capita basis, Ontarians invest competitively with the peer group in primary and secondary schools (86% of US rates) and in colleges (87%). But university spending is at a much lower rate – 49% of US spending per capita. On a per student basis, the spending disparities widen in primary and secondary schools (85% of US rates) and colleges (68%), since Ontario has proportionately more of its population enrolled as students in these levels. In effect, higher per capita investments do not go as far

Figure 5   Ontario spending as % of US total expenditure 1995–9, C$ (2000)

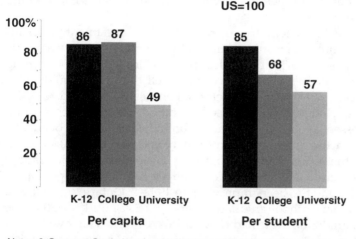

Notes & Sources: Capital and operating expenditures; auxiliary enterprises excluded for college and university for consistency; US data for all US; expenditure includes public and private institutions at all levels

K–12: Statistics Canada, CANSIM II #4780014 (expenditure); Education in Canada 2000 (enrolment); National Center for Education Statistics 1996–2002, tables 30, 162–4 (expenditure), tables 2 & 37 (enrolment)

College: CAAT data only, Ontario Ministry of Training Colleges & Universities, College Financial Information System (expenditure and enrolment) adjusted to exclude non-diploma training and apprenticeship and international students; US public and private 2-year institutions, National Center of Education Statistics, Digest of Education Statistics 2002, tables 330–57 (expenditure), tables 200–1 (enrolment)

University: Statistics Canada, CANSIM II Table #4780008 (expenditure), Education in Canada 2000 (enrolment); US data for public and private 4-year institutions, National Center for Education Statistics, Digest of Education Statistics, tables 330–57 (expenditure), tables 200–1 (enrolment)

at the level of spending per student. At the university level, because of our lower participation rate, the spending on a per student basis narrows, but is still only 57% of the US rate (figure 5).

Primary and secondary education investment shows mixed results

In its Working Paper 3, the Institute concluded that through the 1990s, while our investments in primary and secondary education remained flat, investments by our peer group grew.[19] As a result, Ontario fell from 6th place in per capita spending in 1992–3 to 15th in 1999–2000 – behind all peer states.[20]

It is difficult to be definitive on whether this investment pattern is worrisome or not. The results achieved by Ontario's primary and secondary school systems are better than those achieved in our peer group of states. As Ontario's rank in investment fell through the mid-1990s, there is no evidence that relative achievement results declined. It is also possible to conclude that the increased education spending in peer-group states addressed an obvious weakness – both the overall level of and the disparities in achievement – in their primary and secondary education.

Through the 1990s, Ontario's rank in the percentage of Grade 9 students who ultimately graduate on time has been in the upper half of its peer group and has been improving. In 1992–3, Ontario's public and private secondary school graduation rate was 73%. By 1999–2000, the high school graduation rate had risen to 78%. Ontario's rank within the peer group of US states rose from eighth in 1992–3 to second in 1999–2000, with only New Jersey having a higher success rate (86%).

Ontario students also perform well on standardized tests. Their results are generally on a par with students' scores across the country and exceed those of students in the US (table 1). In addition, the disparity of results across schools is significantly lower in Ontario than in the United States, indicating our success at providing a better-quality education for a broader range of students. The results do point out that there is room for improvement in Ontario given the better results in Alberta and Quebec.

Conversely, while the province performs well at graduating students on time, the Institute is concerned about whether post-secondary students' aspirations are competitive with those of peer states' students, since a smaller percentage of Ontario high school graduates are university bound. Compared to the peer group median, the difference is minimal: 28% of Ontario Grade 9 students were enrolled in university five years[21] later, versus 32% for the median of the 14 states. When colleges are also considered, Ontario outperforms the median and most states in the peer group: 50% of Ontario compared to 40% in the peer group.[22]

More significantly, however, in several of the leading peer-group states, university enrolments far exceed Ontario's – Massachusetts 45%, New Jersey 44%, Pennsylvania 40%, and New York 33%. Given the increased productivity from higher levels of education, this difference is a barrier to overcome if we are to close the prosperity gap.

Our concern about students' aspirations is highlighted in findings

Table   1 OECD PISA Results, 2000

Country/Province	Reading	Math	Science
International	**500**	**500**	**500**
United States	**504**	493	499
Ontario	533	524	522
Atlantic	**514**	**510**	**510**
Quebec	536	550	541
Prairies	529	529	525
Alberta	*550*	*547*	*546*
British Columbia	538	534	533
Canada	534	533	529

Note: Bold numbers indicate a statistically significant (95% confidence limit) lower score relative to the corresponding Ontario score. Bold italics indicate a statistically significant higher score.
Source: Institute for Competitiveness & Prosperity based on 'Measuring Up: The Performance of Canada's Youth in Reading, Mathematics and Science,' OECD PISA (Programme for International Achievement) Study – First Results for Canadians Aged 15

from a recent report by the Canada Millennium Scholarship Foundation,[23] indicating that 50% of Canadian students, who score in the top 40% on standard achievement tests, including PISA, do not attend post-secondary school. These findings reinforce our view that Ontarians need to be more successful in encouraging high school graduates to pursue a post-secondary degree, especially since the study uncovered that it was students' attitudes – and not financial barriers – that dissuaded them from attaining higher levels of education.

In fact, tuition fees are not the major deterrent to students considering pursuing post-secondary education. A recent Statistics Canada study shows that over the past decade, the post-secondary participation rate gap between the students from low- and high-income families has actually narrowed. Further, when high school graduates were asked the main reason for their decision not to go on to college or university in a study by the Canada Millennium Scholarship Foundation, 77% of respondents listed a non-financial reason.[24]

Ontarians' Lag in Post-secondary Education Investment and Attainment

The lower rate of investment in university education by Ontarians can also be seen in the difference in graduation rates between Ontario and the US (figure 6). Ontario trails the US in degrees conferred per thou-

Figure 6   Degrees Conferred per Thousand Population, 1999–2000

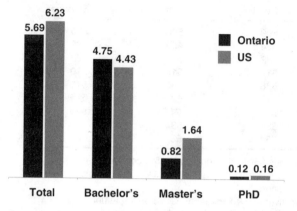

Source: Statistics Canada Educational Databases; CANSIM II; US Department of Education, National Center for Education Statistics

sand population by 8.7% (5.69/1000 vs. 6.23/1000). Although at the bachelor's level we actually outperform the US, at the master's and PhD levels we produce graduates at half the rate they do.

This finding is consistent with the recurring theme in our work – Ontario investment matches peer states' spending to increase prosperity to a point, but then trails off as advanced investments are required.

In its Working Paper 6, *Reinventing Innovation and Commercialization Policy in Ontario*, the Institute for Competitiveness & Prosperity found that Ontario has more science and engineering graduates per capita than the US. However, Ontario's advantage in degrees conferred is entirely at the bachelor's level; for graduate degrees conferred, the US has outperformed Ontario by 40%.[25]

This theme recurs when we analyse the educational attainment of the managers and CEOs of our businesses. As stated above, our managers have lower educational attainment overall, and in business specifically, than do those in the US; only 31% of our managers possess a university degree, versus 46% of US managers. As well, CEOs of our largest corporations tend less to have formal business education at the graduate level. We believe it is reasonable to conclude that the more highly educated our managers, the more likely they are to think innovatively and strategically and to operate more effectively. Given that the US confers twice as many business degrees as Ontario, it is hard to avoid the logical connection between the lower educational attainment of our managers and CEOs and the level of prosperity the US has achieved. Our lower level of human-capital resources means that we are less able to create the specialized support for competitiveness necessary for innovation and upgrading.

As we noted earlier, Ontarians' attitudes towards competitiveness and innovation do not differ significantly from those of their counterparts in the peer states. However, we found one significant attitudinal difference. In the survey, we asked respondents among the public and the business community what advice they would give to young people on the level of education they should attain. Relative to their US counterparts, the Ontario public and the business community are more likely to recommend a college diploma as the highest level of education to receive; their counterparts in the peer group are more likely to recommend a bachelor's or graduate degree.[26]

This advice to Ontario's youth runs counter to the economic realities of the returns to education we described above. It also runs counter to results in Ontario's secondary schools. Our high school students are better prepared for post-secondary education based upon their higher achievement scores on international standardized tests,[27] as well as their higher high school graduation rates. These findings reinforce our view that more Ontarians are capable of pursuing a post-secondary degree at the bachelor's level and beyond. Our challenge is to encourage more high school graduates to pursue a college diploma before entering the work force; to encourage more college graduates to consider pursuing a university degree; and to encourage more university graduates to consider pursuing a post-graduate degree.

Our under-investment in post-secondary education is worrisome, since those with higher levels of education earn more over their lifetimes and our economy benefits more from their knowledge and capabilities. We all lose out when individual Ontarians fall short of their educational potential. Raising educational aspirations and increasing investment in education at all levels by individuals, businesses, and governments are important ways to increase productivity. We think that stakeholders in Ontario's prosperity should be encouraged as a high priority to increase their investment in education.

Tuition freezes result in under-investment in post-secondary education

One way to increase investment and accessibility in post-secondary education would be to lift the current freeze on post-secondary tuition. Current policy is driven by the observation that reducing prices on

Figure 7   Average tuition vs. university participation rates (2000), Canada, by Province

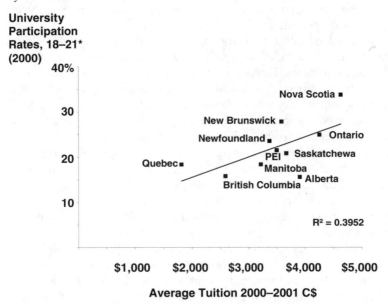

University Participation Rates, 18–21* (2000)

Average Tuition 2000–2001 C$

*18–21 for all provinces except Québec and Ontario, where it is 19–22.
Source: Statistics Canada (tuition), Association of Universities and Colleges of Canada (participation rates)

most goods and services increases demand. The logic is that if tuitions are lower more students will want to attend college or university. But this logic ignores supply factors. If universities and colleges are constrained in the amount of funding they have available to create spaces for students, they will create fewer places. In most instances, where prices are controlled output is reduced. Rent controls and their impact on apartment supply is a well-known example.

We see evidence of this effect across Canada. Those provinces that have controlled tuition the most have lower university accessibility (figure 7). British Columbia is the best example. Its long-time NDP government suppressed tuition to about 75% of the average Canadian level. In the spring of 2002, the BC Liberals finally set BC free. The result of the legacy of tuition suppression: its university system puts onto the market 56% of the university spaces per student-aged resident of Ontario, with its maligned tuition 23% above the Canadian average. Only 16% of high school seniors in British Columbia had university spaces in 2000, thanks to the previous BC government's policy of 'enhancing' accessibility through low tuition. As Anne Dowsett-Johnson pointed out in this year's *Maclean's* university ratings, only BC students with an average greater than 80% have a shot at a spot in any BC university.

Meanwhile, in 2000 there were spaces for 34% of graduating high school seniors in Nova Scotia, where tuition rates were the highest in Canada. As Roger Martin, dean of the Rotman School of Management at the University of Toronto and chairman of the Institute for Competitiveness & Prosperity observed, 'Suppressing tuition puts the supply of spaces at the whim of politicians because universities don't have a revenue source with which to build spaces without the largesse of politicians. And for politicians, regardless of what they say, trading-off the long term benefit of having a greater proportion of university-educated citizens for short term burning needs like health care, infrastructure, and social programs is a daily habit for them.'[28]

This relationship is observed internationally. In European countries like Denmark and Germany, where university education is tuition-free, accessibility is the lowest in the industrialized world: 66% of Canada's and 55% of America's. By restricting tuitions, governments reduce the amount of money invested in post-secondary education and thereby reduce accessibility.

Conclusion

The Institute for Competitiveness & Prosperity is encouraging Ontarians to aspire to close our prosperity gap with the world's most prosperous economies. A critical element to closing this gap is for Ontario governments, businesses, and individuals to invest more in our future prosperity, and this includes investment in post-secondary education. We are recommending that by 2012

- the Ontario Government work with other stakeholders in post-secondary education to match peer-state investment per student in post-secondary education and to halve the shortfall in graduate degrees and business degrees per thousand population;
- businesses match the level of managerial educational attainment achieved in the peer states; and
- individuals increase their educational aspirations and halve the gap with their counterparts in the peer states in donations per capita to educational institutions at all levels.

Notes

* Executive Director, Institute for Competitiveness & Prosperity.
1 In 2001, per capita GDP in Canadian dollars was: Ontario, $38,068; Lombardia, $35,191; Baden-Württemberg, $30,609; Rhône-Alpes, $28,596; Cataluña, $26,978. Source for Four Motors GDP per capita: Eurostat database, available at http://epp.eurostat.cec.eu.int
2 Unless otherwise stated, all dollar figures are in 2003 constant Canadian dollars using Purchasing Power Parity (PPP) conversion rates.
3 Task Force on Competitiveness, Productivity & Economic Progress, *Realizing Our Prosperity Potential*, 3rd annual report, November 2004, 14
4 By 'employment rate' we mean the number of people employed, 16 and over, as a percent of the labour force, 16 and over.
5 State-level data are not available. Canadian intensity data are from the Productivity Program Database of Statistics Canada. US data are from unpublished US Bureau of Labor Statistics, total hours and employment series, which adjusts the BLS Current Employment Survey for agriculture, public administration, and self-employment. We have used these data as published by the Centre for the Study of Living Standards, www.csls.ca.
6 It is important to note that our measure focuses on the mix of clusters only. It estimates the productivity performance we could expect in Ontario if each cluster were as productive as its US counterpart. As we showed in the Institute's Working Paper 5 (*Strengthening Structures: Upgrading Specialized Support and Competitive Pressure*, July 2004), Ontario's clusters are less productive than their counterparts in the peer states (see pp. 25–8).
7 Institute for Competitiveness & Prosperity, *A View of Ontario's Clusters of Innovation*, April 2002, 18–20.
8 See *Realizing Our Prosperity Potential*, 18, for more detail.
9 Institute for Competitiveness & Prosperity, *Missing Opportunities: Ontario's Urban Prosperity Gap*, June 2003, 11.
10 Ibid., 20.
11 Urbanization is defined as the percentage of population living in Census Metropolitan Areas (CMAs) in Canada and Metropolitan Statistical Areas (MSAs) in the US. Differences in the definitions of the two concepts have been adjusted for.
12 Task Force on Competitiveness, Productivity and Economic Progress, *Closing the Prosperity Gap*, November 2002, 27.
13 For a literature review of the rates of returns to education and results of their own calculations, see F. Vaillancourt and S. Bourdeau-Primeau (2002), 'The Returns to University Education in Canada, 1990 and 1995,' in D. Laidler, ed., *Renovating the Ivory Tower: Canadian Universities and the Knowledge Economy*, C.D. Howe Institute Policy Study no. 27.
14 Institute for Competiveness & Prosperity, *Reinventing Innovation and Commercialization Policy in Ontario*, October 2004, 40.

15 Task Force on Competitiveness and Prosperity, *Closing the Prosperity Gap,* 36, and *Investing for prosperity,* November 2003, 25.
16 Institute for Competitiveness & Prosperity, *Striking Similarities: Attitudes and Ontario's Prosperity Gap,* September 2003
17 *Realizing our Prosperity Potential,* 32–6.
18 Institute for Competitiveness & Prosperity, *Strengthening Structures: Upgrading Specialized Support and Competitive Pressure,* July 2004.
19 *Missing Opportunities: Ontario's Urban Prosperity Gap,* 30.
20 This pattern does not change much when looked at on a per student basis. Recent data on private-school spending in US states are not available, but comparisons of Ontario public and private spending to US national results do not differ dramatically from comparisons of public-to-public spending.
21 Four years later for US students.
22 *Investing for Prosperity,* 23–4.
23 Canada Millennium Scholarship Foundation, 'Ready or Not? Literacy Skills and Post-Secondary Education,' September 2003.
24 Canada Millennium Scholarship Foundation, 'Why Don't They Go On? Factors Affecting the Decisions of Canadian Youth Not to Pursue Post-Secondary Education,' 2001.
25 *Reinventing Innovation and Commercialization Policy in Ontario,* 30–1.
26 *Striking similarities: Attitudes and Ontario's Prosperity Gap,* 36.
27 Ibid., p. 22
28 Roger Martin, 'A bright light on a bad strategy,' *Globe and Mail,* 18 May 2004.

The University Research Environment

JOHN R.G. CHALLIS,* JOSÉ SIGOUIN,* JUDITH
CHADWICK,* AND MICHELLE BRODERICK†

In this paper we shall provide a brief analysis of the strengths, weak-nesses, opportunities, and challenges for the research environment in Canadian universities, particularly from the standpoint of the Province of Ontario. We shall draw upon examples from the University of Toronto, in the belief that the general principles have applicability across the provincial and national system. We shall argue that the research-inten-sive universities occupy a special place in the Canadian higher educa-tional system, and that Canada has a requirement for a handful of research universities that are truly world class by any measure. The economic impact of university-based research is substantial, both di-rectly in terms of jobs for students, fellows, technicians, faculty, and administrative and support staff, and indirectly. The ripple effect of research at the University of Toronto contributes at least another billion dollars annually to the economy. We shall argue that university re-searchers complement and in part underpin the teaching mission of Canadian universities at both the graduate and undergraduate level. Finally, we shall argue that the federal and provincial government initiatives in support of the research enterprise over the past five to seven years have had a tremendous impact and have altered the inter-national perspective of Canadian universities to one where they are regarded as being highly desirable and supportive institutions. This position has taken time to become established. The trick now, as politi-cal priorities change, is to sustain that early momentum, the levels of

* Office of the Vice-President, Research and Associate Provost, University of
  Toronto
† Office of the Vice-President and Provost, University of Toronto

productivity, and international reputation. As Canadian universities continue to evolve in their research activities, they will need to resolve the competing demands of research in the interests of new knowledge, and research that aligns with commercialization objectives established through industrial and political innovation agendas.

We have endeavoured to evaluate different metrics that characterize the research environment, and to establish appropriate research performance markers that allow benchmarking against international peers. Clearly one measure is represented by the research funding input to the institution. Output measures include commercialization metrics, measures of publications and citations, national and international honours, and contributions to public policy and societal good. Others include the training of highly qualified personnel, graduate students, post-doctoral fellows, and specialists in a variety of areas. We recognize that none of them is ideal, nor is any one of them satisfactory for a broad spectrum of investigative disciplines. We continue to seek appropriate measures, particularly for colleagues in the arts and humanities, where traditional indicators of publications, citations, and commercialization outcomes have much less meaning than in the sciences.

The magnitude of the research enterprise at the University of Toronto is substantial. The 'University' includes nine independent, affiliated teaching hospitals and the federated universities, and is spread across three campuses: UT Mississauga, UT Scarborough, and, downtown, UT St George. Total research expenditures in fiscal 2002–3 were approximately $560 million per annum. If one adds targets at 40% for recovery of academic salaries and 40% recovery of the indirect costs of research, the total research enterprise is almost $1 billion annually. In other words, at the University of Toronto we conduct approximately $3 million of research each day. This level of activity exceeds the budgets of CIHR (base plus Canada Research Chair component approximately $650 million), Science and Engineering Research Canada (NSERC, $700 million), and the Social Sciences and Humanities Research Council ($200 million). It is slightly greater than the annual budget of the National Research Council. The level of research funding at the University of Toronto has risen progressively over the last twenty years from approximately $100 million per annum in 1982–3 to the current figure (figure 1). The funding curve flattened during the difficult period of the mid-nineties, but then showed an accelerated increase with the introduction of new Federal and Provincial research funding programs beginning in 1997–8. The proportions of budget attributable to the

Figure 1   Research Funding Trend – Two Decades in Current Dollars,
University of Toronto, Including Affiliates

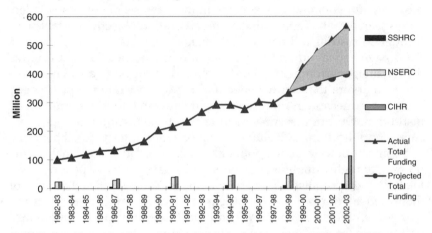

Note: Projected total funding values were forecasted based on 1982–3 to 1998–9
values.

tri-councils have decreased overall from approximately 50% in 1982 to
30% in 2002 (figure 2). The amounts of monies from SSHRC and NSERC
have remained relatively stable over the past fifteen years, whereas
almost a doubling has occurred in the amounts of money from CIHR
between 1999 and 2002–3, coincident with the dramatic increase in
funding for the Canadian Institutes of Health Research.

The introduction of new provincial and federal funding programs,
beginning with the announcement of the Canada Foundation for Innovation (CFI) in 1997 has changed radically the research landscape in
Canadian universities and research institutes. The range of different
programs and opportunities is truly impressive and the combination of
personnel support through the Canada Research Chair program, infrastructure support through CFI, start-up and operating support (CFI and
tri-council sources respectively), graduate student support (Premier's
Research Excellence Awards), and recognition of the need to provide
indirect costs have produced an atmosphere of enlightenment and enthusiasm for research across the country. These programs place the
Canadian research enterprise at a distinct advantage in the international recruitment of scholars from overseas. This circumstance has
been exacerbated by Homeland Security measures in the United States
Post 9/11, visa requirements, and security demands.

Figure 2   Research Funding by Source, University of Toronto and Affiliates

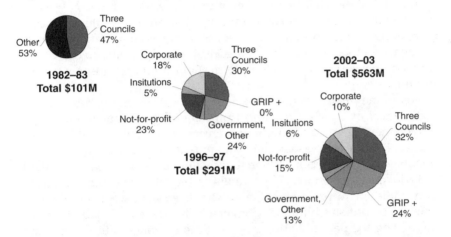

In health research the increase in funding available with the transformation of the old Medical Research Council of Canada to the new Canadian Institutes of Health Research has been dramatic. The *CIHR Act* was passed in 2000; the 13 virtual institutes began activity in January 2001. At that time the total CIHR funding was $339 million, spread across the four pillars of population health, health services, clinical research, and biomedical research. By 2003–4, the budget had increased to $576 million. Proportionate increases in population health and health services research were 500% and 600% respectively. Support for biomedical research had increased by almost $200 million over this period, a 200% increase. CIHR was able to combine strategic, targeted initiatives through its Institutes, with core individual investigator-based discovery programs. The introduction of training grants and call for applications in that area, in 2001, was a watershed in Canadian health research. Fifty-one applications were funded in the first round of competition, with partnerships from a wide variety of provincial, private-sector, and not-for-profit organizations. The increase of funding available in CIHR has inevitably created increased application pressure. Hence, although the actual number of grants funded has increased dramatically, the success rate has declined marginally. The President and Council have worked hard to sustain an acceptable level of success (approximately 30%). This has become the envy of colleagues in the United States and in parts of Europe. In addition to an increase in the absolute number of grants funded, the average value of open operating grants has risen from $92,000 per annum in 2000–1 to $106,000 per annum in 2003–4. This is consistent with the President's stated objective of achieving levels of research funding that are truly internationally competitive. This position, however, will require rapid attainment of the goal of a total budget exceeding $1 billion, the ability to carry over funds from year to year, and long-term stability and commitment to the funding base.

Across the provinces there has been a modest increase, consistently, in the level of research funding from federal government sources to universities. There was a dramatic increase between the periods 1995–7 and 2001–3, for the reasons cited previously, coincident with the introduction of new programs. When these values are expressed in constant 2003 dollars, indexed to 1977–79 total funding, the increased support to universities in the province of Ontario has been less than that in Alberta, Quebec, or British Columbia. Conversely, the increase in federal funding during the period 2001–3 was particularly marked in Alberta and Quebec (figure 3). This pattern is clearly evident in figure 3b. Provincial funding in Ontario has lagged dramatically behind that in Alberta and British Columbia, and is somewhat less than in the province of Quebec. It is particularly noticeable that provincial support to universities in Alberta was three–fold higher, expressed in this way, than in Ontario during the period 2001–3. This remarkable growth has provided a magnet attracting new colleagues to Alberta.

The time-trend analysis of research funding from the federal granting councils, expressed in constant 2002 dollars, indexed to 1980–1, shows a similar pattern (figure 4). Funding to universities in Quebec, Alberta, and British Columbia is consistently higher than funding to universities in Ontario. Indeed, the Ontario university system has remained relatively constant over this period of time, whereas each of the other three major provinces have shown approximately three-fold increases, when the data are expressed this way. There are several reasons that may underlie these different trends, but in particular it is noticeable that in at least two of these provinces, Quebec and Alberta, there are strong provincial research programs that provide recruitment and start-up monies for outstanding colleagues, particularly in the health sciences. British Columbia, through the Michael Smith Foundation, has recently joined this elite group. The differences illustrated in figure 4 show clearly the need for strong provincial funding of research-intensive universities in the province of Ontario if we are to avoid falling further behind other provinces.

Figure 3   Total Research Funding Universities in Constant 2003 Dollars, Indexed to 1997–9

(a) From Federal Government Sources

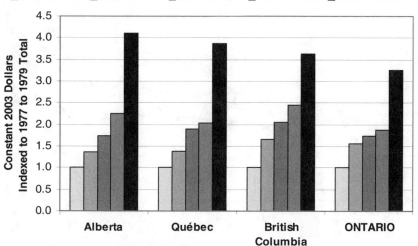

(b) From Provincial Sources

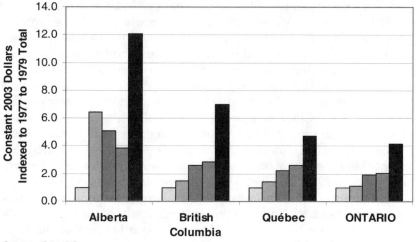

Source: CAUBO

Figure 4   Research Funding from the Tri-Councils to Universities in Constant 2002 Dollars, Indexed to 1980–1

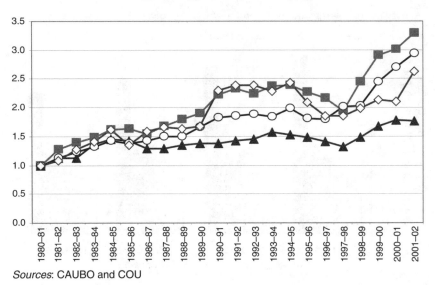

Sources: CAUBO and COU

What are the provincial programs that have made such a difference to colleagues in Ontario? These include the Ontario Research Development and Challenge Fund (ORDCF, introduced in 1997), the Premier's Research Excellence Award (PREA, introduced in 1998), the Ontario Innovation Trust (OIT, introduced in 1999), and the Research Performance Fund (RPF, introduced in 2000). Figure 5 shows the cumulative investment in leading Ontario universities from these different funds.

Monies from OIT have been crucial to provide provincial matching support for awards made available from CFI, and the CFI match to the Canada Research Chair program. The availability of these monies has allowed Ontario universities to attract rising stars and distinguished colleagues to this province and has sent a message worldwide that this province is supportive of university-based research and values intensely this activity. In 2004, the Liberal government of Ontario announced that these programs had been terminated and would be repackaged in a new Ontario Research Fund. At this writing, details of the Fund and its administration are not available. However, one hopes that the total money available will be not less than the sum of the current constituent

Figure 5   Ontario Government Research Infrastructure Programs,
1997–2004

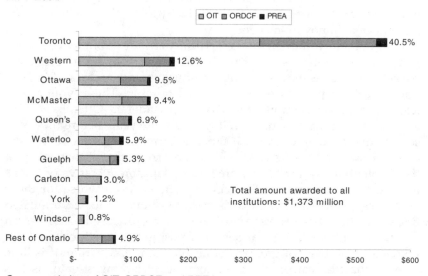

Source: websites of OIT, ORDCF, and PREA

funds. Further, it will be crucial to assure flexibility in the areas of
research supported by the Fund, in a manner that allows universities to
recruit in a way consistent with their own strategic plans, rather than
simply with a government agenda based around commercialization
opportunities. These matching monies from the province (whether they
are regarded as matching or as leverage) have allowed Ontario universities to maximize opportunities afforded through the new federal programs previously, and it seems likely that they will be crucial to realize
opportunities from future federal initiatives.

It is perhaps important that in Alberta, Quebec, and British Columbia
the major provincial funding agency has been established at arm's
length from government, whereas the new Ontario Research Fund appears to be destined for administration within the Ministry of Economic
Development and Trade. Given that reality it is not surprising that early
discussions around the administration of the Fund focused on its use in
particular commercialization foci related to materials, information technology, life sciences, the environment, and nanotechnology. University
administrators have argued strongly for a broadening of these criteria
to include the social sciences and humanities, and to include areas of

basic science where the commercialization opportunities of research might not be immediately apparent. Nevertheless, it is those areas from which fundamental new knowledge is likely to arise that will drive the pipeline of an innovation agenda.

The availability of these funds is crucial in the development of career pathways of colleagues at our universities. Our younger investigators are getting older as they take longer to finish their degrees, and embark upon extended periods of post-doctoral training. These 'young' colleagues have to be committed to a career in academia. Often faced with a significant personal debt load, it will be some years before they earn salaries greater than even $40,000 per annum and then move into the ranks of assistant professors. It is of concern, perhaps, that many of these potential new academics are finding far more lucrative positions in industry or commerce. This circumstance is even worse for those graduates of medical school with substantial debt loads accumulated through years of first- and second-level undergraduate education, often combined with an additional period of post-graduate education. With potential debt loads of greater than $100,000 at graduation, it is little wonder that the career of an academic clinician-investigator is less attractive today than it might have been some years ago. The lifestyle sacrifices may not seem worthwhile.

Start-up monies available through provincial awards and federal leverage are clearly crucial to provide infrastructure and operating support for young investigators. These colleagues require the availability of start-up monies and assistance in generating their first peer-review research awards, and the renewal of those awards. They will thereby be faced with an extraordinary complexity of grant deadlines and opportunities. Indeed, one might argue that in some areas there are simply too many deadlines and too many different competitions and announcements. For example, a young entry-level faculty member in medical genetics might, within the space of five months, be required to write applications for a CFI New Opportunity, a not-for-profit sector operating and personnel support, a CRC Tier II award, addendum, and OIT-CRC submission. He or she will have two opportunities in that period for submission to the CIHR individual operating grants competitions, and potentially opportunities to apply to a CIHR Institute–specific strategic initiative, and an award from Genome Canada. Our young investigators spend 30% or more of their time writing grants and rewriting the same grant; their colleagues then spend another 30% of *their* time reviewing the grants that have been submitted. It seems that this is an extraordinarily unproductive use of time. Our young investigators should be doing more research, and our mid-career reviewers would welcome the time in their laboratories or in the library. There is a real need and opportunity in this country to develop a common curriculum vitae, a common grant application, a common entry portal and review process. There is an obvious opportunity to coordinate applications for infrastructure, salary, and operating and indirect costs. We applaud the early discussions of the prime minister's science advisor, Dr Arthur Carty, and the presidents of the Research Councils to establish such a process. We recognize that to do so will not be easy. However, to achieve such an objective would be a watershed moment in Canadian, and indeed in international, science.

It is pertinent here to comment on the profile of research funding as a function of faculty age. This relationship is important given that tri-council support in Canada is crucial, not only as the gold standard for research funding, but as the dictator of the numbers of Canada Research Chairs and the allocation of indirect costs to our universities. At the University of Toronto, colleagues in the 45 to 55 age group are the recipients of the majority of CIHR funding, and there is a decline in total CIHR funding in later age groups. However, at SSHRC and at NSERC the pattern is quite different. Here, it is colleagues between 50 and 65 who hold the lion's share of council support. As these members of the professoriate retire (if, indeed, they do retire) we shall need very clearly to increase the level of funding for younger colleagues in order to maintain our market share of tri-council support. We shall need to do that in order to maintain our share of Canada Research Chairs and of federal indirect costs for research. One anticipates that other universities across the country may be in a similar position. For those that are not, however, the population dynamics of our professoriate might offer an unexpected windfall.

The introduction by the federal government of the indirect-costs program was an extraordinarily important initiative. For every dollar of direct costs awarded by the tri-councils, it costs the universities $0.50 to $0.60 to create and support the research environment necessary for the conduct of the research. Without indirect costs the only source of those monies was the core university operating grant, which would otherwise have been used in the support of undergraduate education. Thus, one strong argument to expand the indirect-costs program is that, indirectly, it enhances availability of resources for undergraduate education.

The provision of indirect costs in Canada from the central government has been tied to tri-council support, and the ability to increase indirect costs has been tied to a commercialization formula. There are clear implications from these relationships. First, our university Vice-Presidents, Research preach to our colleagues, 'Apply to the tri-councils; that is essential for your university to sustain Canada Research Chairs and to generate indirect costs.' In so doing, applicants may be persuaded not to seek support from the not-for-profit sector or from other government sources. Furthermore, agencies within the not-for-profit sector may fail to provide indirect costs on the assumption that these flow directly from the federal government, and are not necessary. Clearly this argument fails to appreciate the way in which these monies are utilized, and the real costs of the conduct of research. It is absolutely crucial that the monies available for indirect-costs recovery should accrue to reach at least 40% of the direct costs of research, and this is particularly true at Canada's larger research-intensive universities. The formula that was established by AUCC for the allocation of indirect costs ensured that a higher proportion would be paid on the first $100,000 and the next $900,000 of research monies accrued. Hence, smaller universities are already recovering indirect costs at 60% to 80% of the direct cost value, whereas at the University of Toronto we recover, on average, only 18.4% of these monies. Across the country, the median recovery of indirect costs is already 60%, but that occurs to the disadvantage of those very universities where the research enterprise is most developed.

The indirect-costs formula was established in a manner that monies for hospital research activities flowed through the affiliated university. The effect of this partitioning has been to further disadvantage research-intensive universities and their affiliated teaching hospitals. This situation is particularly severe at the University of Toronto, with its nine fully affiliated teaching hospitals, which lose in aggregate approximately $3-plus million annually in indirect costs, to which they would have been entitled were they to have been regarded as distinct entities. Clearly, this should be the time to reconsider the manner in which the program is operated. A far simpler and equitable model would be to guarantee a base level of indirect cost support for smaller universities, and then above a floor value of, say $1 million, flow indirect costs directly with grants from the tri-councils. This would allow central government to show how these monies are being utilized directly in support of research. It would also establish strongly the principle of the

Figure 6   University Operating Grants and Research Funding in Ontario in Constant 2003 Dollars, per FTE Student, Indexed to 1987–8

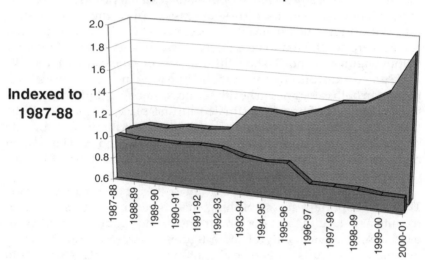

importance of indirect costs to those other agencies and sources of research funding that currently have been reluctant to recognize their necessity.

These monies, of course, not only support research but allow reallocation of resources in order to enhance the overall university enterprise, including teaching. Our researchers are also our teachers, and often among our very best teachers. Our researchers are key to the provision of new undergraduate research programs that might provide the impetus for a new student to consider a lifetime career of investigation. At the University of Toronto, federal personnel research awards support 10% to 15% of our faculty. This support buttresses the decline in the university operating grant. Figure 6 shows how, as the operating grant has declined over the last 20 years, research expenditures, including salary support for the research-focused professoriate, have increased.

These divergent patterns have meant that the ability of the university to sustain its faculty complement has come to depend increasingly, not on the operating grant, but on the soft money provided through *research* career awards. If that funding for research from federal and/or provincial sources were not available, our universities would have fallen into decline at a much earlier stage.

We would like briefly to mention output performance measures. A traditional area of assessment of university research productivity is that of publications and citations. These are easier to measure in the sciences than in the humanities. In health sciences in particular, publications and citations are considered to be a reasonably robust measure of research output. Figures 7a and 7b show the numbers of publications for public AAU universities and G10 institutions. The inset includes private institutions. In both categories in health sciences, among public universities, the University of Toronto is situated in first place, just ahead of the University of Washington and UCLA. With the addition of the private universities, the University of Toronto ranks second to Harvard in numbers of publications, and third to Harvard and Johns Hopkins University in numbers of citations.

We are continuing to refine and evaluate these performance metrics. They are important in establishing the university's reputation as it recruits new faculty, post-doctoral trainees, and graduate students. In particular, the availability of these figures is important in attracting international recruits, and especially international graduate students to a university. Often, the best way of judging a truly 'international' university is in its ability to attract international graduate students and post-doctoral fellows. We need to build, within Canada and within Ontario, a scholarship program that supports and nurtures these highly skilled individuals, many of whom may wish to remain in Canada in the longer term, and make life-long contributions to our economy and society.

At the University of Toronto we have also placed great importance on faculty recognition through national and international awards. Within Canada these would include Steacie Awards and Fellowships in the Royal Society of Canada. Internationally, these would include Fellowships in the American Academy of Arts and Sciences, the National Academy of Sciences, and the Royal Society of London and, of course, the Nobel Prize. Canadian universities in general have a wonderfully qualified professoriate, the stars of which are often not recognized proportionately through such international honours. We need to nominate colleagues for such awards, and then explain the value of such awards to politicians and to the general public. It seems axiomatic that an explanation of the international value of a particular piece of univer-

Figure 7   Health Sciences – Top 10 Public AAU and G10 Institutions,
1998–2002

(a) Number of Publications

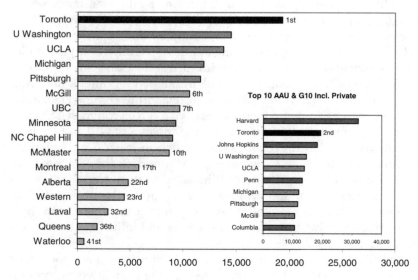

(b) Number of Citations

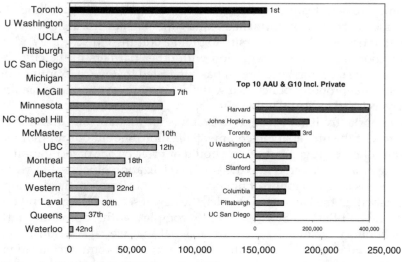

Source: Institute for Scientific Information (ISI)

sity research should contribute to enhanced understanding of the importance of research in general to a lay audience and to the general public.

Finally, we have begun to consider commercialization outcomes as an indication of the effectiveness of university research activity. These are discussed elsewhere in this symposium by other speakers, and we will refer here briefly to our ongoing studies. Overall, it is apparent that the pre-eminent standing of universities such as the University of Toronto in scholastic achievement, measured through publications and citations, is not reflected in our standing in relation to commercialization activities. We have assessed indicators such as gross commercialization revenues, and numbers of new licences compared to G10 and US peer institutions. Ontario universities have much to learn from American institutions such as the University of Washington, the University of Minnesota, and the University of Illinois. It is our position that issues around commercialization will be paramount as the universities of Ontario consider their evolution. Already, our government funding is being linked to commercialization outcomes and influences the universities' strategic plans.

The University of Toronto has recently commissioned a report on its commercialization activities, conducted for the past 20 years through the University of Toronto Innovation Foundation. The report team was chaired by former Industry Minister the Honourable John Manley. The Manley review team has charged this university with matching its commercialization performance to its fundamental research achievement. It has asked the university to build a culture of disclosure and to seek coordination and integration with other partners in the city, including the teaching hospitals. It has suggested that we re-examine our intellectual property policy in a way that is more favourable to faculty inventors and indicates university support for commercialization activity. Importantly, it has asked us to examine the fundamental question of the role of the university in commercialization. Should our role simply be one of revenue generation, or should our role be one of facilitation in taking new information into the commercialization pipeline, but without necessary expectation of financial reward? In Toronto, the developments within the Discovery District, the new research facilities, and the Medical and Related Sciences (MaRS) complex, with 1.5 million sq. ft. of laboratory incubator space, are a signal that we take seriously the opportunities to link universities, innovation, and commercialization. Developments such as MaRS will afford partnerships between universities, venture capitalists, and the private sector. They will also facilitate linkages between clusters and between groupings of universities to build their commercialization enterprise and relationships. These developments will, over the next few years, facilitate the evolution of industry partnerships with universities on university campuses. In turn, these nodes of university-industry activity should provide an environment that is conducive to further training opportunities in basic research, linked to commercialization outcome and application, in technology transfer, and in industrial application. We believe that Canadian universities will face their most demanding and challenging, yet exciting, opportunities, as they develop relationships with the business sector. Such relationships are not without threat to the university, yet surely are entirely consistent with our mandate of knowledge acquisition and information translation and transfer.

We have tried here to summarize some aspects of the importance of research at Canadian universities. In this brief article we have illustrated some of the challenges that Canadian universities face in seeking adequate research funding, and emphasized some of the extraordinary opportunities for Canadian universities in the future. That future is very much around advocacy, facilitation, differentiation, and integration of our research enterprise in a way that will ensure that our universities are recognized as key players in the economies of our cities, provinces, and country in the twenty-first century.

PART V

Governing the System: New Modes for Promoting Accountability, Transparency, and Responsiveness

The Governance of Public Universities in Australia: Trends and Contemporary Issues

V. LYNN MEEK AND MARTIN HAYDEN*

This chapter presents an overview of the governance of public universities in Australia. It begins with a brief history of developments during the past 50 years. This account is important in providing a context for the second part of the chapter, in which contemporary issues related to the governance of Australia's higher education system are addressed.

The chapter is written with the needs of a Canadian readership primarily in mind. For this reason, matters of fine detail are omitted and there is more of an emphasis upon historical developments than would normally be required. Throughout the chapter, references are made simply to the 'Commonwealth,' that is, the government elected to the federal parliament in Canberra, and the 'States,' that is, the governments elected to the six State and two Territory parliaments in Australia[1] – these are the equivalent of provinces in Canada. As in Canada, the Australian federal structure involves the sharing of powers between two levels of government. In Australia, though, the Commonwealth is the dominant level of government across a wide range of areas. This dominance is especially evident in relation to Australian higher education.

There are many useful introductions available in relation to higher education in Australia.[2] In brief, it is a national system of 39 universities, 37 of which are public universities in the sense that they have traditionally relied upon public funds for their existence.[3] It is a relatively homogeneous system, that is, all universities offer programs across a wide range of disciplinary and professional fields, all are entitled to offer awards up to the PhD level, there is no formal stratification of institutions,[4] and there is no formal streaming of students.

Australia's universities are relatively autonomous – each has a governing Council with powers that permit a high level of independence in the accreditation of academic programs and the management of resources. Each Council is accountable under State or Commonwealth[5] legislation for discharging governance responsibilities. Australia's universities receive about 40% of their funds from the Commonwealth (this figure increases to 56% if calculated to include transfer payments from the collection by the Commonwealth of Higher Education Contribution Scheme charges to students).[6] The remaining funds come mainly from fee-paying Australian and international students, from research activities and from returns on the investment of capital assets. About 18% of Australians have a university degree, which compares favourably with the OECD average of 14%, but is below levels for the United States (27%), Norway (25%), the Netherlands (20%) and Canada (19%).[8] Rapid growth in student numbers is an enduring characteristic of the system. Over the period 1991–2000, for example, there was a 30% increase in student numbers – among domestic students the growth rate was 19%, while among overseas students the growth rate was 223%. A contemporary feature of the system is its growing dependence upon fee income from overseas students. Approximately 23% of all students are international students – which is considerably higher than for nearly all OECD countries.[8] In addition, therefore, to serving the higher education needs of an Australian community of 20 million people, the system is now also responding on a fee-for-service basis to the higher education needs of many overseas communities, principally in Asia. In 2002 international education was Australia's third-largest services export earner.[22]

Historical Setting

By the late 1930s, each of the six State capital cities in Australia had its own university.[10] These universities were developed separately and functioned largely in isolation from one another. There was virtually no movement of students between them. Members of academic staff were recruited from Britain, or were Australians who had gained their qualifications in Britain. Though an Australian Vice-Chancellors' Committee was established in 1920, there was little or no sense prior to the Second World War of a national system of higher education in Australia. Universities, like all other forms of public education, were solely the responsibility of the States.

The war resulted in an unprecedented injection of Commonwealth funds into universities. More importantly, it raised public awareness about the social and economic value of science and technology. Shortly after the war, the Commonwealth established the Australian National University for the purposes of furthering research and postgraduate study. In 1949, the State of New South Wales established a second university in Sydney, with a focus on technology.[11]

Over the period from 1949 to 1972, a coalition of conservative parties formed successive Commonwealth governments. During this period, the Commonwealth contributed strongly to the growth of higher education. In the mid-1950s, a committee appointed to inquire into the future of Australian universities recommended that the Commonwealth should become more involved in the affairs of universities, particularly with regard to finance and development, and that an Australian Universities Grants Committee should be established to advise the Commonwealth on university matters, including funding. In 1959, the Commonwealth established the Australian Universities Commission – the first statutory education authority established in Australia for the purposes of acting as a 'buffer' between higher education and government. By 1960 there were ten universities in Australia.[12]

In 1961, another committee appointed by the Commonwealth to inquire into the future of higher education recommended the creation of a new sector, comprising colleges of advanced education, as an alternative to the further expansion of the university sector. Colleges were differentiated from universities by their function: vocational and teaching-oriented colleges on the one hand, and academic and research-oriented universities on the other. These new institutions came into existence in 1965. The binary system was to remain in existence until 1988.

In 1972, the Labor party was elected to form the Commonwealth government – the first Labor government since 1949. It implemented a sweeping range of social and economic reforms before its untimely replacement in 1975 by a conservative government. In the field of higher education, two decisions implemented in 1974 had far-reaching consequences for higher education. The first was to abolish student tuition fees for all higher education courses. The second was a decision that the Commonwealth should accept nearly all of the financial responsibility for higher education from the States. The latter decision changed irreversibly the extent of Commonwealth influence on higher education.

During the 1970s, the colleges of advanced education progressively shed many of their responsibilities in the sub-diploma fields of education and assumed a more prominent role in providing degree-level and post-graduate programs. A Technical and Further Education sector, supported by the States, developed to fill the vacuum. By 1977, the Commonwealth had three statutory education authorities acting in a 'buffer' capacity – a Universities Commission, a Commission on Advanced Education, and a Technical and Further Education Commission. In 1977, the Commonwealth established the Commonwealth Tertiary Education Commission (CTEC) to replace these three authorities. Its brief was to ensure 'balanced and co-ordinated development' across the three sectors of tertiary education.[13] By 1978, there were 19 universities, 70 smaller colleges, and almost 400 quite small Technical and Further Education colleges.[14]

In 1978, another committee appointed by the Commonwealth to inquire into higher education addressed, amongst other things, the possible rationalization of the system – though there was no suggestion of the need to replace the system's binary structure. Its recommendations resulted in a lengthy consultative process In 1981, the Commonwealth pre-empted the consultative process by announcing abruptly that, as a cost-saving measure, 30 colleges of advanced education had to amalgamate or else receive no further Commonwealth funding. By 1983 the higher education system comprised 19 universities and 47 colleges of advanced education.

In 1983, a Labor government was re-elected, and it remained in power until 1996. In 1985, the Commonwealth Tertiary Education Commission conducted a review of the efficiency and effectiveness of the tertiary education system and recommended important modifications to the system, but not any change to its tri-sectoral structure. In 1987, the Commission suggested the creation of yet another committee, this time to review the binary structure of higher education. By this time, the Commonwealth was interested in more radical reforms. In 1987, it abolished the Commission and transferred its advisory (but not its coordinating) role for higher education to a new advisory committee called the Higher Education Council. The Commission's coordinating role was transferred to the Department Employment, Education and Training (DEET), a new 'super department' established by merging a range of other departments and authorities. Universities and colleges were now required to negotiate directly with the Commonwealth through DEET, rather than through a 'buffer' body.

In 1988, the Commonwealth abolished the binary distinction between universities and colleges, and replaced this structure with a 'unified national system' of 35 universities, created through amalgamations with existing universities and the enactment of State legislation to establish new universities.[15]

In 1989 the Commonwealth introduced the Higher Education Contribution Scheme (HECS), requiring all students to make an equal contribution (of less than 20%) to the average cost of their studies – with an option to defer payment of the contribution until they entered employment and were earning above a threshold level of income. This initiative was a significant innovation that has subsequently been copied in many other parts of the world. Its precursor was a Higher Education Administrative Charge, introduced in 1986, which imposed a small charge on all students. The significance of the Administrative Charge is that it ended Labor's opposition since 1974 to a user-pays system for funding higher education. The HECS initiative in 1989 was combined with the removal of restrictions on universities from enrolling fee-paying overseas students and the introduction of a variety of provisions to deregulate the system. Universities were made more accountable for their expenditure of Commonwealth grants, and there was an indication of intent to introduce performance-based funding to the system. Further changes were made in 1994 to expand fee-paying options for domestic students seeking to undertake postgraduate courses.

In 1996, a Liberal/National conservative coalition was elected to government, and has remained in power since then. The Commonwealth budget statement in 1996 introduced significant new cost-saving changes to higher education, including an increase in the HECS charge (requiring a contribution of 20% of the average cost of studies), the introduction of three different HECS payment bands, the setting of a substantially lower income threshold for the repayment of HECS, the introduction of an option for fee-paying domestic students to undertake undergraduate courses, and the phased removal of government financial support for post-graduate coursework enrolments. In addition, the Commonwealth signalled the reduction of operating grants to universities by 5% over three years, and indicated that it would provide no financial supplementation for academic salary increases.

In 1998, a Committee appointed by the Commonwealth to report on higher education financing and policy simply restated the policy perspectives of the government. On the matter of funding, for example, the Committee argued: 'The present funding framework does not assist, or provide incentives for, institutions to manage effectively. Governance structures hamper management and there are no incentives for institutions to be aware of their costs or to minimise them.'[16] Also in 1998, restrictions on the ability of universities to charge fees to domestic undergraduate students were further lifted. Universities were now permitted to enrol up to 25% of domestic undergraduate students in a course on a full-fee-paying basis. In fact, less than 1% of domestic undergraduate students ever took advantage of this option, though in some individual high-demand courses the rate of take-up may have been two or three times higher than this.

In 1999, a fully performance-based funding approach was introduced for research and research training in Australian universities. It was consolidated in 2001 with the introduction of a national competitive research-grants system, the establishment of the Australian Research Council as an independent statutory authority responsible for the national allocation of research funds, and the provision of a substantial boost to research spending under a policy entitled *Backing Australia's Ability*.

In 2000, there were further changes to HECS that raised the contributions students were required to make to approximately 32% of the average cost of studies.

In 2002, the Commonwealth Minister for Education, Science and Training conducted a review of the higher education sector to determine areas in need of further change. The review involved the production of a series of discussion papers, followed by extensive consultation with universities, student groups and other stakeholders. A conclusion reached was that 'the current arrangements for funding universities were not sustainable and would, in the longer term, lead to an erosion of the excellent reputation of our universities.'[17] This conclusion was not interpreted as implying that the Commonwealth should be investing more heavily in Australia's university system. Rather, it was the basis for the Commonwealth arguing that the users of the higher education system, that is, students, should be paying more – and that even more efficiencies within the system were required.

Late in 2003, the Commonwealth approved an extensive package of higher education reforms for implementation from 2005, including provisions permitting public universities to enrol up to 35% of domestic students in a course on a full-fee-paying basis, introducing a new loans program to enable all domestic full-fee-paying students to borrow funds to finance their studies, and making additional Commonwealth funding for individual universities conditional upon compliance with prescribed governance protocols and the provision of choice for staff in relation to participation in industrial agreements. The reforms also provided for further expansion of the number of Commonwealth-funded places in higher education over coming years, and for the establishment of a number of specific programs to allocate funds to specific target areas in higher education (for example, improvements in the quality of teaching and curriculum, increased participation in higher education by Indigenous peoples, and incentive schemes to encourage workplace reforms consistent with Liberal-National coalition policies on labour market deregulation).

Importantly, significant changes were made to HECS, for implementation in 2005. The three different payment bands approved in 1996 'to reflect more appropriately the balance of public and private returns to higher education, the relative costs of courses and the earning potential of graduates in particular fields'[18] were retained. The low-cost band included Arts, Social Science, Education, and Nursing. The high-cost band included Law, Medicine, and Dentistry. From 2005, universities were to be permitted (except in two national priority areas, Nursing and Education) to add a premium of up to 25% to the charge imposed within these HECS bands. Approximately one-half of all universities have opted to impose the premium, which has not been popular with students. The stated intention for this Commonwealth's policy was that 'As student contribution levels vary between courses and higher education providers, higher education providers will become more competitive in terms of cost and quality, and will focus more on what is important to students.'[19] Students continue to have a choice of paying their contribution up-front upon enrolment (thereby receiving a 20% discount) or later on through the income-tax system once their income reaches a threshold level.[20]

A further change of long-term significance to the system is that from 2005 the Commonwealth will fund approved target student loads for each university across a range of twelve funding clusters, with the largest contribution per equivalent full-time student load going to Agriculture (A$15,996) and the smallest to Law (A$1472). This change sharpens the focus of the contract between the Commonwealth and individual universities. It also means that the Commonwealth will be better placed to determine funded student load profiles across the system.

An undertaking given in the 2003 budget statement that the Minister would review the cost-adjustment indexation mechanism for universities has yet to be addressed by the Commonwealth. Since 1996, the

Commonwealth has not been applying a realistic cost-adjustment in-dexation mechanism to higher education, resulting in a steady decline in real levels of public expenditure on higher education. It is estimated that in 2003, for example, the shortfall in funding for universities in terms of what they should have received from the Commonwealth had an appropriate index been applied was as much as 10%.[21]

Contemporary Issues in Higher Education Governance

In selecting contemporary issues in higher education governance for discussion in the remaining part of this chapter, consideration has been given to striking a balance between, on the one hand, the gravity attached to certain issues by various stakeholders in Australian higher education and, on the other hand, the need to address topics identified as being of interest to a review of the design and funding of the post-secondary education system in Ontario. The issues selected for consid-eration attempt to meet both sets of needs.

1. From New Public Management to Neo-Liberalism: The Increasing Importance of the Market

Commonwealth approaches to the management of higher education in Australia have changed markedly over the past two decades. The pe-riod from the mid-1980s to the mid-1990s was one in which precepts of *new public management* impacted forcefully on higher education. Since then, *neo-liberalism* has become the dominant public-policy ideology. A trend that is clearly evident over the period is the increasing reliance on the market as a mechanism for decision-making about higher educa-tion. The system of public universities is no longer thought about as being 'publicly supported,' but is instead regarded as being 'publicly subsidized.' The normative question is, At what point does this trend go too far? The weight of opinion within the sector, as expressed by bodies such as the Australian Vice-Chancellors' Committee, is that the trend has already gone far enough.

In 1983, after eight years in opposition, Labor returned to power with a strong desire to portray itself as a sound and responsible economic manager. A particular commitment was the reform of the public ser-vice. In 1984, an initial wave of legislation was enacted to increase ministerial control of the public service and introduce merit-based processes for appointments to senior levels of the service. In 1987, following its re-election, a second phase of reform was initiated. In a move clearly intended to allow direct ministerial control over the implementation of social and economic policy, the number of independent statutory authorities in existence was slashed and many of their functions were given back to departmental heads, reporting directly to ministers. These measures were implemented in the belief that 'for many purposes government departments have the decided advantage of making the relevant Minister directly responsible for the effectiveness and efficiency of administration and of saving costs through the use of long established administrative machinery.'[22] One authority that was quickly 'axed' following the 1987 elections was the Commonwealth Tertiary Education Commission.

The approach to public-service management adopted by the Commonwealth at the time was by no means unique to Australia and has been labelled *new public management*. The approach entails 'a preference for market mechanisms of governance, more business-like management of public agencies, the minimisation of public bureaucracy, a focus on clear responsibility and accountability for results and the empowerment of consumers of governments services.'[23] It did not take long for this approach to affect universities. From 1989 onwards, universities were required to negotiate directly with the Commonwealth for resources and were made more directly accountable for the expenditure of their Commonwealth grants. University managers were prevailed upon to adopt the tools of *new public management*, including mission statements, performance indicators, outcomes-based evaluation processes, systems for continuous improvement, and so on. Universities began to be discussed using market analogies. Vice-chancellors came to be widely referred to as chief executive officers. Academic staff willing to undertake executive and senior management functions within universities began to be offered attractive salary packages for doing so. A rhetoric about students as consumers became widespread. The trend was fuelled by the parallel development after 1989 of a market-oriented approach to the recruitment of fee-paying overseas students. A national process of institutional quality reviews implemented by the Commonwealth from 1993 to 1995 provided further strong reinforcement – in large part because of the emphasis placed upon being able to produce documentation that provided evidence of the existence of a vision, mission, goals, performance indicators, and client feedback.

In 1996, following the Liberal/National coalition's return to government, a new and additional dynamic became evident – the coalition's all-pervading commitment to the ideology of *neo-liberalism*, that is, a public policy agenda characterized by the desire to extend market relationships and private ownership to all areas of social and economic activity. Its principal manifestations in higher education since 1996 have included a marked increase in the extent to which students are being made responsible for the cost of their studies, a heightened expectation of accountability by universities to the Commonwealth for their expenditure of operating and other specific Commonwealth grants, an increased tendency for the Commonwealth to provide funds tied to specific priorities or intended to be spent in particular ways that support the social and economic priorities of the government, and an increase in the level of pressure on universities to be entrepreneurial in the pursuit of resources required to remain financially viable. A further manifestation is a preoccupation by the Commonwealth with the progressive elimination of all forms of collective bargaining by the major national union representing university employees, and with workplace-based reforms to employment practices that will result in increased efficiencies in the utilization of public funds.

It is in relation to the funding of higher education that one of the most significant manifestations of *neo-liberalism* is to be found. Australian higher education is predominantly 'public' – there are 37 public universities and only two private universities, both quite small. The system's public status derives from the fact that its assets are publicly owned and that it has always been publicly funded. Since 1988, however, and particularly since 1996, there has been a marked diversification in the funding base of the system. In 2003, for example, the system received only 40% of its funds in the form of Commonwealth grants. In 1989, by comparison, the system received 70% of its funds in the form of Commonwealth grants.[24] Further, the value in constant dollars of the Commonwealth's operating grant for higher education fell each year over the period from 1996 to 2002.[25] An indication of how these trends, particularly since 1996, are linked with *neo-liberalism* is provided by the fact since 1996 there has been a substantial growth in Commonwealth subsidies for private-schools in Australia. Approximately one-third of all school students in Australia attend a private school. Over the period from 1996 to 2000, Commonwealth funding per university student fell by 19.2%, but Commonwealth funding per private-school student increased by 21.4%.[26] The Commonwealth's obvious support for private education is evident in these figures. Its record in relation to public higher education suggests strongly that it would prefer to see the system privatized. The Commonwealth is providing increasingly generous public subsidies to private higher education providers, and it has even indicated tacit support for the presence of private overseas universities in Australia.

The effects of *neo-liberalism* on Australia's public universities will be better understood over coming years as the range of Commonwealth initiatives announced in 2003 are implemented from 2005 onwards. It is evident, however, that *neo-liberalist* ideology has already resulted in a striking deterioration in teaching and research infrastructure over recent years, with consequent adverse effects on the quality of academic life for staff and students. Staff-to-student ratios in universities are also deteriorating; there is an increasing reliance upon casual academic staff appointments; academic salary levels as a proportion of average weekly earnings are in steady decline; and there is a reduced range of opportunities for academic staff to engage in research. At the same time, universities have proved themselves to be remarkably resourceful in finding new non-government sources of funding, particularly from the sale of services overseas and from the commercialization of research. No doubt, the additional scope for them to earn more revenue from increased HECS rates and from fee-paying domestic students will confirm their resourcefulness. As the Australian Vice-Chancellors' Committee has warned, however: '[T]he direct fee income paid by students and their families can never be a complete substitute for investment by the government in the infrastructure and resources (human and capital) that is fundamental to ensuring quality outcomes in teaching and learning.'[27] More broadly, there is concern that the premises of *neo-liberalism* are incompatible with the nature and purposes of universities. A university system that is 'expected to behave like ordinary profit-seeking businesses, utilising corporate management practices, serving consumers in markets, seeking measurable productivity improvements and producing services with controllable quality attributes' may not be addressing its core values and purposes.[28]

2. New Sensitivities in Commonwealth-State Relations: Issues of Control and Ownership

Historically and constitutionally, public education in Australia is a matter for the States. As a consequence, the States have a wide range of responsibilities for Australia's public universities. These include legislative control, ownership of land and capital assets, controls on the use of terms such as 'university' and 'degree,' as well as a range of statutory requirements relating to industrial matters and the governance of individual institutions, including the appointment of governing councils.[29] Since 1974, however, when the States ceded financial responsibility for higher education to the Commonwealth, the Commonwealth has been the dominant partner affecting the growth, structure, and processes of the sector, though its power has never been absolute because of the wide range of legislative and proprietorial responsibilities of the States. Most recently, a debate has been triggered by a suggestion from the deputy premier of New South Wales, Australia's most populous State, that full responsibility for all 11 of that State's universities should be handed over to the Commonwealth. While other States and the Australian Vice-Chancellors' Committee promptly opposed the proposal, the Commonwealth minister has expressed an interest in the idea. The issue of Commonwealth-State responsibilities for universities is once again in the limelight. Any change from the existing situation of shared responsibility by both levels of government for higher education would have a dramatic effect on university governance.

In 1991, State and Commonwealth ministers of Education considered but rejected the option of allocating full responsibility for higher education to the Commonwealth. A working-party report accepted by the ministers stated: 'Although this model is consistent with the national interest, it was recognised that universities also have a role to play in contributing to State economic and social development, particularly in the provision of a skilled workforce. Further, the interfaces of the higher education system with State-based school, TAFE and training systems necessitate a degree of State involvement in higher education policy and planning processes.'[30] The ministers agreed that higher education should be classified as a Shared Responsibility Program, requiring effective Commonwealth-State consultative processes, simplified and efficient funding and accountability systems, and a more uniform approach to financial management and other controls on higher education institutions. The Commonwealth would retain primary responsibility for funding higher education, but the States should be able to develop their own priorities within the framework of national priorities, and they should continue to have legislative responsibility for the establishment and oversight of higher education institutions and the maintenance of standards through controls on the use of terms such as 'university' and 'degree.' A process for streamlining payments by the Commonwealth to universities was also agreed upon. Instead of the

Commonwealth paying university operating grants to the States, which then passed the funds on to individual universities according to Commonwealth specifications, under a new arrangement, implemented in 1993, the Commonwealth would pay the operating grants directly to the universities. At the time, some States were 'concerned that direct payments may alter the relationship between the Commonwealth, States and institutions, and undermine the capacity of the States to fulfil their Constitutional responsibility for education.'[31] These concerns were, however, in the minority.

During the past decade, expenditure by the States on higher education has been modest, never moving much above 1.5% of total higher education revenues. Since 2001, however, the proportion of university funds received from the States has been increasing. In 2002, for example, the proportion was 4%[32] – and the trend since then has been upwards. This sharp increase in financial support from the States for universities has been more pronounced in some States, notably Queensland, Western Australia, and Victoria, than in others. Individual States have ambitious plans to promote economic and social innovation in the context of an increasingly competitive global knowledge-based economy, and universities are regarded as being critical partners in these initiatives. The States also have an interest in universities because of their importance as a destination for larger and larger proportions of young people completing the final year of school, and because universities are necessary as partners in addressing labour-market shortfalls in the number of trained teachers and nurses – the States are primarily responsible for providing employment opportunities in these professional areas.

The States also have an interest in shared Commonwealth/State approaches to accreditation and quality assurance in higher education. This was the topic for discussion at a meeting of the State and Commonwealth ministers in 2000, when they agreed to a set of national protocols for the establishment of new universities, and to the establishment of an Australian Universities Quality Agency (AUQA). The Agency, which came into existence in 2001, is responsible to Commonwealth and State ministers for promoting, auditing, and reporting on quality assurance in Australian higher education. It conducted its first institutional audits in 2002. Further audits have been undertaken since then – at a rate of seven to eight universities per year. These audits have as their focus the quality-assurance processes of a university, rather than the quality of teaching and research. By 2005, all universities will have been audited, and then the cycle of institutional audits will begin again. The audit process is an important mechanism for accountability within the Australian higher education system. Transparency is provided by the publication of all institutional audit reports.[33]

Universities, as independent statutory bodies, are accountable to the State in which they have been established for their financial administration and audit. While requirements vary from State to State, universities are generally required to produce an annual report for tabling in the relevant State parliament, and they must also produce audited financial statements and performance information for consideration by the relevant State minister. Universities are subject to State regulations in relation to undertaking commercial activities, and they may not dispose of assets, especially land, without approval of the relevant State authorities.

Universities are also accountable to the Commonwealth. The main instrument of accountability to the Commonwealth is the 'educational profile,' a document produced annually to provide a basis for funding decisions for the following year. The document requires (a) details of strategic planning, (b) a Research and Research Training Management Report, (c) data on the allocation of funded student load to places in courses, (d) a capital asset management plan, (e) an equity plan, (f) an Indigenous education strategy, and (g) a quality-assurance and improvement plan. In practice, funding decisions are made on the basis of a historical input-based funding model, and very little turbulence occurs within the system as a consequence of unexpected reallocations of student load. The new arrangement of funding student load within cluster groups will provide the Commonwealth with considerably more transparency than in the past regarding the load distributions within universities. It may eventually result in an increase in the incidence of load-shifting between universities by the Commonwealth.

Universities are responsible to the Commonwealth for the provision of audited financial statements for the previous calendar year. They must also provide annual statistical returns, and separate acquittal statements are required for all Commonwealth grants made for specific purposes.

Though it is not entirely clear what the motivation was for the deputy premier of New South Wales to offer to transfer all responsibility for State-based universities to the Commonwealth, it is inconceivable in the current environment that most States would be willing to transfer ownership of these valuable assets to the Commonwealth without the guarantee of substantial compensation. It is equally inconceivable that an arrangement whereby some States handed over all responsibility, but not others, would be stable for long. The sector itself is unlikely to be enthusiastic about any transfer of ownership given the Commonwealth's current ambivalence to the importance of providing strong financial support for a public system of universities in Australia. The fact that the States have ownership rights in relation to the system is placing a powerful check on the Commonwealth's desire to control the system.

3. Institutional Governance: An Area of Increasing Political and Institutional Interest

There has been a remarkable increase of interest in university Councils during the past decade. There was a time when Councils were largely invisible, addressing at a leisurely pace the need to provide final approval to university documentation and to address prudential considerations related to the plans brought forward by the administrative machinery of the university. This situation has dramatically changed. University Councils are becoming the focus of increased interest within universities because of the importance of the decisions they are increasingly being required to make. They are also becoming of considerable political interest, especially to the Commonwealth, because of the considerable delegation of authority to them by the States.

Except in the case of the Australian National University, Councils derive their authority from State legislation. The legislation provides them with considerable scope to affect the management, academic profile, and internal quality-assurance processes of a university. Of special importance is that, as trustees for the State, they can buy property, form companies, enter into partnerships, approve and grant academic awards, and, most importantly, appoint the vice-chancellor. Since 1995, when the first substantial report was produced on university Councils, various official documents have catalogued perceived weaknesses. That first report identified the need for them to have, amongst other things, an explicit set of responsibilities, a threshold level of professional knowledge and skills commensurate with the task of governing complex institutions, a strategic focus in their deliberations, and a more refined sense of their role in relation to asset and risk management.[34] Also identified was the need for university Councils to be smaller in size, preferably with 10 to 15 members, for external members to out-number internal members, and for potential external members to be identified through an independent professional process.

Since that report, Councils have engaged in a process of reform that has resulted in smaller memberships of about 21, on average, and increased thoroughness in the selection of external members.[35] Examples of 'best practice' are being widely produced, and annual conferences are now routinely being convened to facilitate benchmarking across universities. There are, nonetheless, perennial problems affecting Councils. Within the past few years, for example, there have been well-publicized instances of factionalism within Councils and of intense conflicts between Councils and the senior academic management of universities. Further, there are continuing expressions of concern that Councils are not well equipped to respond promptly and decisively to change, and that Council members have a great deal of difficulty in being properly informed about not only the operations of a university but also about the activities of its controlled entities.[36] Membership of university Councils in Australia remains a form of honorary public service. In some States, members of the State parliament are appointed as members. In most States, the membership includes a chancellor (as chair), a deputy chancellor, the vice-chancellor, the chair of the Academic Board or Senate, a group of members appointed by the Council itself, a group of members appointed by the State, and a small group of members elected by university staff members and students.

Because Councils appoint (and can dismiss) the vice-chancellor, they have a pervasive influence on the culture of a university. This influence has for a long time gone unnoticed in most university communities. Recent celebrated cases of Councils acting decisively to dismiss their vice-chancellors have provided a reminder of the strength of the latent power of a Council. Most recently, Councils have been in the public limelight because they have had to sign off on important decisions affecting the welfare of students and the financial health of their institution. It has been for Councils to decide, for example, whether or not to charge the premium of an additional 25% on the HECS rates for students. Councils have had to decide whether or not to admit fee-paying undergraduate domestic students, and, if so, in what proportions. These decisions have attracted extraordinary attention, no doubt because they have touched a raw nerve with students, who are spending longer hours in paid employment than ever before in order to meet their living expenses. A recent national survey reported, for example, that seven out of every ten students at university were in paid employment during university semesters – an increase by about one-half since 1984.[37] Among full-time students, the average number of hours worked by those in paid employment during a semester was 15.5 hours per week – a three-fold increase since 1984. About 20% of respondents in such paid employment reported that work adversely affected their study 'a great deal,' and about 10% reported that they 'frequently' missed classes because of in-semester paid employment.

In 2003, the Commonwealth introduced a statement of National Governance Protocols for Higher Education, with which universities must comply in order to secure additional Commonwealth funds.[38] These identify generically the main responsibility of university Councils and require that individual members of Councils should be aware of their duties. Of note is a requirement that Councils must make available a program of induction and professional development for its members, and that the size of the Council must not exceed 22 members.

A continuing issue with university Councils concerns the matter of who owns universities.[39] Though at one level this question invites speculative thinking, at another level – that is, in trying to resolve whose interests should primarily be considered in making decisions at a Council meeting – the question is quite practical. Technical considerations are mainly influential in instances where a decision is one requiring the assessment of risk against a given set of standards, for example, published accounting standards. Many decisions are not so technical, however. In deciding about the appointment of new members, for example, even though there are general prescriptions about the matter in the National Governance Protocols, considerations related to the needs of the many stakeholders in a university need to be pondered. Is there an obligation to make a decision in light of the value of the university to the Commonwealth, the State, the university community, the regional community, or the world community? These are matters that relate to notions of ownership of a public university.

4. System Governance: Direct Ministerial Control

A recent Commonwealth discussion paper on higher education governance states: 'Over the years Australia has experimented with "buffer" bodies responsible for making decisions on the allocation of student places and funding, or for advising the Government on policy. Australia does not currently have such a body.'[40] This statement reflects a serious loss of memory: Australian higher education had almost three decades of experience with 'buffer' bodies in higher education – from 1959 until 1987. What the statement is really expressing is a complete disinterest on the part of the Commonwealth in ever again having a 'buffer' organization between it and universities. The reasons for this disinterest, while they may relate to the perceived deficiencies of the Commonwealth Tertiary Education Commission during the years immediately prior to its demise in 1987, more likely reflect a desire on the part of the Commonwealth to be able to exercise direct ministerial control over universities whenever it is considered appropriate. Somewhat contradictory, however, is the fact that in 2001 the Commonwealth established the Australian Research Council as an independent statutory authority to act in a 'buffer' capacity between it and the universities in relation to research and research training. Research is not the main area of public expenditure on higher education, however, and in any case decision-making by the Council must take place within a framework prescribed by Commonwealth policies, which include the creation of national research priority areas and further enhanced competition and selectivity in research funding both within and between universities.

One of the major challenges of a 'buffer' organization between the Commonwealth and the universities is that it must also accommodate the needs of the States. The Commonwealth Tertiary Education Commission, during its existence from 1977 to 1987, developed a complex system of 'consultative arrangements' that allowed it to respond to both levels of government. Marshall describes these as follows:

At the beginning of each triennium state authorities and institutions prepared forward proposals which were presented to the relevant sectoral council for consideration. The reports of the three councils were then worked into a comprehensive policy statement by CTEC which was known as Volume 1. Volume 1 was submitted to the Commonwealth Minister for Education who consulted with her state counterparts before taking a final proposal to the cabinet table. The decisions made by cabinet were termed the 'guidelines' and constituted CTEC's policy directives. The guidelines became the subject of further negotiation between the Commission, the advisory councils and other bodies before specific measures were finalised in Volume 2 which outlined the implementation programme.[41]

This complex process of consultation resulted in protracted negotiation and meant that decisions, when finally taken, were the product of a considerable amount of compromise. Marshall reports that the process worked well for many years because it 'fostered a stable and predictable policy environment' and was 'internally flexible,' and because for many years the Commission had 'a monopoly of funding, expertise and authority.' During the early 1980s, this monopoly was challenged. First, the Commonwealth became convinced that the higher education system could contribute more effectively and directly to national goals than was happening under the Commission's supervision. Second, other agencies, including government ministries and other statutory authorities, developed a view that the higher education system was important to the realization of their organizational goals, and so new, disparate, and complex pressures from within government came to bear upon the Commonwealth's 'guidelines' issued to the Commission. Third, the Commission itself became overloaded with intractable demands, such as having to restrain the growth of new funded places in higher education because of budgetary constraints imposed by the Commonwealth, while at the same time seeking to achieve equity goals through improvement in the participation rates of disadvantaged groups. Finally, the lengthy consultation process that was once a source of stability and strength became cumbersome against the background of a pressure for rapid political change.

Though the prospects of re-establishing a statutory authority like the Commission to act in a 'buffer' capacity between the Commonwealth and universities now seem remote, there are strong supporters of the return of such a body. One of these, the founding chair of the Commission, has proposed establishing such a body 'to promote the plurality of priorities among universities, to ensure their institutional independence, and to provide the Commonwealth Government, the universities themselves and the wider public with a source of objective advice on university matters.'[42] It is of interest that New Zealand, a nation that shares much in common with Australia, has recently established a Tertiary Education Commission with a mandate to implement the government's tertiary education strategy, allocate funds to tertiary education organizations, and advise the government on policies. The Commission, a statutory authority, has a board of eight Commissioners with backgrounds that are broadly representative of the range of public stakeholders in tertiary education.

Conclusion

This chapter has sought to present an overview of the governance of public universities in Australia. It has located this overview within the context of the system's historical development. A characteristic of the story not explicitly addressed in this chapter but nonetheless critically important is the extent to which reformist ministers at the Commonwealth level have sought to leave their mark. Ministerial ambitions continue to be constrained, however, by a curious feature of the Australian higher education system whereby responsibility for public universities is shared between the Commonwealth and the States. A critical issue for the future will be the willingness of the States to cede all of the responsibility, not just the financial responsibility, for public universities to the Commonwealth.

An even more critical issue concerns the need for points of view in addition to the Commonwealth's that have an influence on the policy debate. A feature of the past decade is the extent to which the current Liberal/National coalition government is single-handedly reshaping Australia's public university system according to the ideology of *neo-liberalism*. As a consequence, the system is becoming rampantly market-oriented and increasingly utilitarian. It is the case that, as Professor Peter Karmel, the founding chair of the former Commonwealth Tertiary Education Commission, has observed, 'Commonwealth policy appears to have been built on assumptions about the nature and purposes of universities that, at the very least, are debatable.'[43] It is regrettable, though, that there is now no proper set of inclusive advisory structures that provide a forum for this debate. The Commonwealth's approach is increasingly to interpret its political mandate as an endorsement to pursue a single vision. Ironically, as more and more of Australia's public universities are weaned off Commonwealth financial support – some already receive less than 20% of their total revenues from the Commonwealth, the stage is set for them to begin to reject Commonwealth control of their activities. The consequences of this kind of development are unpredictable. As argued above, it is doubtful that the Commonwealth will ever again restore a 'buffer' body like the former Commonwealth Tertiary Education Commission to allow a distancing of the system from the changing fashions of politics, or to bring cohesiveness to the system. In the absence of such a body, however, new ways will need to be found to enable Australia's public universities to continue to be valued for their contribution to the public good. In this regard, the Australian system of public universities may have a good deal to learn from Canadian experience.

Notes

* Professor Meek is Director of the Centre for Higher Education Management and Policy, University of New England, Australia; Professor Hayden is Professor of Higher Education and Head, School of Education, Southern Cross University, Australia.
1 The States are New South Wales, Victoria, Queensland, South Australia, Western Australia, and Tasmania, and the Territories are the Australian Capital Territory and the Northern Territory.
2 See, for example, Brendan Nelson, *Higher Education at the Crossroads: An Overview Paper* (Canberra: Commonwealth Department of Education, Science and Training, 2002). See also the Australian Vice-Chancellors' Committee web site at http://www.avcc.edu.au/content.asp?page=/universities/overview.htm.
3 In the case of 36 of these universities, their assets are also publicly owned. In the case of one public university, the Australian Catholic University, the Catholic church owns the assets but the Commonwealth government is the main source of funds. The two private universities, Bond and Notre Dame, are quite small.
4 There is a quite pronounced informal stratification. The eight longer-established universities comprise a grouping of research-intensive universities. Five former city-based Institutes of Technology comprise a grouping of technology-based universities.
5 The only university now established under Commonwealth legislation is the Australian National University.
6 Australian Vice-Chancellors' Committee, *Key Statistics on Higher Education* (Canberra: AVCC, 2003), table A21.
7 Commonwealth Department of Education, Science and Training, *Setting Firm Foundations* (Canberra: Commonwealth Department of Education, Science and Training, 2002), 23–4.
8 Commonwealth Department of Education, Science and Training, *Students 2003: Selected Higher Education Statistics* (Canberra: Commonwealth Department of Education, Science and Training, 2004), summary tables (i).
9 Australian Vice-Chancellors' Committee, *Key Statistics on Higher Education*, table D7.
10 The Universities of Sydney, Melbourne, Adelaide, Queensland, Tasmania, and Western Australia.
11 Initially called the New South Wales University of Technology, and now called the University of New South Wales.

12 The University of New England was established in 1954, having received its independence from the University of Sydney. In 1958, Monash University became Melbourne's second university.

13 Neil Marshall, 'End of an Era: the Collapse of the "buffer" Approach to the Governance of Australian Tertiary Education,' *Higher Education* 19 (1990), 147–67.

14 The universities had a total of about 160,000 enrolments; the colleges had about 150,000 enrolments – mainly undergraduate; and the Technical and Further Education colleges had about 850,000 enrolments – 95% of them part-time.

15 In the early 1990s one of the merged institutions dis-amalgamated, thus adding one more university to the public system. In 2000 another university was created when a university-affiliated institution received full university status, resulting in the current number of 37 public universities.

16 Review of Higher Education Financing and Policy (West Committee), 'Learning for Life: A Policy Discussion Paper (Canberra: Commonwealth Department of Employment, Education, Training and Youth Affairs, 1997), 89.

17 Brendan Nelson, *Higher Education: Report for the 2004–2006 Triennium* (Canberra: Commonwealth Department of Education, Science and Training, 2004), 3.

18 Commonwealth Department of Education, Science and Training, *Setting Firm Foundations*, 7. The HECS contribution levels for 2004 are A$3768 per annum for arts and humanities, justice and legal studies, social science and behavioural science, visual and performing arts, education and nursing; A$5367 per annum for mathematics and computing, other health sciences, agriculture and renewable resources, built environment and architecture, science, engineering and processing, and administration, business, and economics; and A$6283 per annum for law, medicine and medical science, dentistry and dental services, and veterinary science. The currency conversion is AUD$1 = CAD$0.93.

19 Commonwealth of Australia, *Information for Commonwealth Supported Students 2005* (Canberra: AusInfo, 2004), 6.

20 From 2005, the income threshold at which HECS repayments commence will be $35,001. The rate applied to HECS repayment income at this level will be 4%. The rate will increase to 8% at an income level of $65,000 and above.

21 Australian Vice-Chancellors' Committee, 'Indexation: Maintaining the Value of Our Investment in Universities,' *Pursuing the Vision for 2020 – AVCC Election Issue 1* (Canberra: AVCC, 2003), 1.

22 B. Williams, 'The 1988 Paper on Higher Education,' *Australian Universities' Review* 2 (1988), 2.

23 S. Zifcak, 'Managerialism, Accountability and Democracy: A Victorian Case Study,' *Australian Journal of Public Administration* 53:3 (1997), 107.

24 Australian Vice-Chancellors' Committee, *Key Statistics on Higher Education*, table A21.

25 Ibid., table A1.

26 David Phillips, *Independent Study of the Higher Education Review*, Stage 1 Report (Byron Bay, NSW: Phillips Curran, 2002), 31.

27 Australian Vice-Chancellors' Committee, *Public Under-Investment in Higher Education* (Canberra: AVCC, 2001), 2.

28 Peter Karmel, 'Higher Education at the Crossroads: Response to Ministerial Discussion Paper,' Individual submission 14: 2. Accessible at http:// www.backingaustraliasfuture.gov.au/submissions/crossroads/ crossroads1.htm.

29 The exception is the Australian National University, which derives its statutory authority from an act of the Commonwealth parliament.

30 Working Party on Higher Education, *Report to the Australian Education Council* (Canberra: Australian Government Publishing Service, 1991), 5.

31 Ibid., 14.

32 Australian Vice-Chancellors' Committee, *Key Statistics on Higher Education*, table A21.

33 Details about the Agency, including copies of institutional reports, are available from the Agency's web site: http://www.auqa.edu.au/.

34 Higher Education Management Review (Hoare Committee), *Report of the Committee of Inquiry* (Canberra: Australian Government Publishing Service, 1995).

35 Commonwealth Department of Education, Science and Training, *Meeting the Challenges: The Governance and Management of Universities* (Canberra: Commonwealth Department of Education, Science and Training, 2002), 17.

36 Ibid., 17–18.

37 Michael Long and Martin Hayden, *Paying Their Way: A Survey of Australian Undergraduate Student Finances, 2000* (Canberra: Australian Vice-Chancellors' Committee, 2001).

38 See http://www.dest.gov.au/highered/governance/nat_gov_prot.htm.

39 Lynn Meek and Fiona Wood, *Higher Education Governance and Management: An Australian Study* (Canberra: Department of Employment, Education, Training and Youth Affairs, 1997).

40 Nelson, *Higher Education at the Crossroads*, 5.

41 Marshall, 'End of an Era,' 150.

42 Nelson, *Higher Education at the Crossroads*, 14.

43 Karmel, 'Higher Education at the Crossroads.'

Deliberative Democracy: The Role of Educational Research in Educational Policy

JANE GASKELL*

The Rae review has already had a positive impact on the university system, by stimulating debate about and raising the profile of post-secondary education. Of course we expect even more impact over the next months, but demonstrating that the issues are fascinating and of critical importance for the well-being of the province, the country, and ultimately the globe is a good start. In this paper, I will argue that keeping such debate going is a critical issue for the well-being of the post-secondary education system.

This section of our proceedings concerns the question of intermediary bodies, the thorny issue of the appropriate relationship between government and the post-secondary system of education. The governance structure must recognize a delicate balance between government's responsibility for the public good and traditions of university autonomy, in a changing context in which the colleges play a critical role, the nature of important knowledge in the workplace is changing, and enrolments as well as costs and expectations are increasing.

Public universities and colleges depend on governments for the major part of their revenue; their mission is the public good. The state has a legitimate role in interpreting and holding them accountable for that public good. At the same time, traditions of university autonomy and self-government, and the ability of universities to differentiate themselves in order to exploit their particular histories and resources, have been the strength of the system. No Canadian government has shown the appetite to run a post-secondary system of education centrally. No university in Ontario wants to opt out of the public system. We are in this together.

The Rae report points to intermediary bodies in the US, where a plethora of models exist, and in the UK, where a very centralized and detailed system of regulation is in place. In the Australian system, as Meek and Hayden report in this volume, a federal intermediary body, the Tertiary Education Commission, was abolished in 1987. The Australian context is also very different from that in Canada, with more federal involvement, and more centralization. Looking abroad is important, but Canada has a distinct set of traditions, shaped by our federal-provincial relations, our British and French traditions, and our particular politics.[1]

This paper begins with an overview of the intermediary bodies that have been set up in Canada, providing an analysis of their dilemmas and a history of their evolution. It then turns to their role in stimulating analysis of the system and developing relationships that allow for conversation, negotiation, and compromise. This becomes an argument for the creation of a permanent body whose mandate avoids the political tasks better carried out by governments, universities, colleges, or other interested parties. The permanent body becomes a site for the production of research, analysis, and discussion about the system, a way of enhancing democratic deliberation.

My argument draws on what has been written about intermediary bodies, some conversations with those involved, and my own experience of the difficulties and rewards of carrying out educational research in this country.

The Politics of Intermediary Bodies in Canadian Higher Education

Governments use both regulations and financing to affect the operation of universities; they must make decisions about how to allocate scarce resources and about which forms of regulation are most appropriate. All of these decisions are contested. There will be winners and losers; those who agree and those who object. For governments, one attraction of intermediary bodies is political. Perhaps an intermediary body will be able to resolve these intractable political problems to the satisfaction of all the parties involved. Perhaps it will deflect political pressures to a place where discussion is easier and compromise more acceptable. Perhaps it will take governments off the hook for the difficult trade-offs and decisions that must be made, or make more legitimate the decisions that are taken.

For universities, the political attraction of an intermediary body is the perceived barrier it provides to government 'interference'; that is, government decisions that will restrict universities' autonomy and have a negative impact on their funding. These bodies also promise universities an increased ability to represent their interests, both to government and to the general public. Our voices will be heard; our issues will be understood. Universities have been well represented on most intermediary bodies; they therefore offer the promise of increased self-regulation within a framework that provides legitimacy.

These conflicting political goals and expectations put intermediary bodies in a difficult and often thankless position. McGuinness et al. say:

> By definition, the role is to be caught in the middle, to serve as a 'suitably sensitive mechanism' for handling the interaction between demands of society and the internal values and priorities of the academy. From the perspective of colleges and universities, the board should serve as a buffer against inappropriate external intrusion and should advocate the needs of higher education to the state and the broader society. From the perspective of the public and the state political leadership, the board should transmit the priorities of the broader society to the academy, be a force for change and a protector of the broad public interest. In the best times, the role is to be a constructive, mediating force between often contradictory perspectives. But in more times than not, it is to be vilified by one side or the other, occasionally ignored altogether and sometimes crushed in the middle.[2]

The history of Canadian intermediary bodies reveals a plethora of models, whose success depends on their particular form, in their particular context. Few have survived for long. Most were formed as the post-secondary education system expanded, before governments developed ministries of advanced, post-secondary, or university education, and before universities developed sophisticated lobbying efforts and established secretariats. Most have been abolished, or reformed to become much less powerful than they were. British Columbia, Alberta, Saskatchewan, and Ontario abolished the councils they set up and did not replace them. The Maritime provinces created a commission that continues to exist, though its powers are strictly limited by provincial jurisdiction as well as by university prerogatives. Nova Scotia's advisory board on colleges and universities replaced the much more powerful and extensively staffed Nova Scotia Council on Higher Education (NSCHE) in 2000. Manitoba replaced its University Granting Council in 1996 with a council on post-secondary education designed to 'plan and coordinate,' to approve programs but not fund them. Quebec alone continues to have a *conseil* with considerable independence, offering broad advice on university policy to the government.

David Cameron starts his discussion of the introduction of intermediary bodies in Canadian university education with the comment that 'Canadian university leaders ... were devoted to the myth of the University Grants Committee in Britain, with a passion that bordered on the unseemly. Its attraction derived from the prospect of continued public support coupled with protection from government direction.' He concludes, however, that 'most intermediary agencies fell short of the ideal, frustrating governments because they could do little to force coordination of university programs and activities, and frustrating the universities because they could not extract sufficient funds from government.'[3]

Each province has its own story, and we are most interested in Ontario in this place, at this time. The first intermediary body in Ontario was an informal advisory committee appointed by Premier Frost in 1958 to make recommendations on funding universities. The committee consisted of eleven members, all closely associated with universities. It became the Committee on University Affairs (CUA) and was involved in enrolment forecasting, doing research on the demographics of education in the province. The committee enlisted the services of Bob Jackson, professor of educational research at the University of Toronto and, a few years later, first director of the Ontario Institute for Studies in Education. He had proved his worth to Bill Davis, then minister of education, by determining how many children would be entering kindergarten over the next few years. Jackson's projections for higher education panicked the CUA, who hired an economist with excellent knowledge of the education system, John Deutsch, to check the figures and come up with a plan. The government accepted Deutsch's report although his figures proved to be wrong, and enrolment fell short of expectations for a while.[4] Bill Davis now says, 'from my standpoint, it worked quite well ... It provided an excuse to beat up on the minister of finance.' CUA provided useful advice for the government on financing and the allocation of capital funds, and an external body had more credibility with the treasury than bureaucrats from the Ministry of Education.

As the system expanded, and university–government relations became strained in Ontario, the government increased its own ability to analyse and direct policy, setting up the Department of University Affairs in 1964. The government adopted formula financing in 1967 to alleviate the political pressure from an increasing number of universities and their political representatives. The Council of Ontario Universities (COU), made up of the university presidents, also set up the Ontario Council of Graduate Studies (OCGS) to regulate graduate programs (and avoid more government regulation).

In 1974, the government set up the Ontario Council on University Affairs (OCUA), with a new mandate: to provide advice on the global funding needed by the university system, its allocation to institutions, the approval of programs eligible for funding, and other policy matters referred to it by the minister. Its twenty members were appointed by government, and its chair was Stefan Dupré, a well-respected university figure with the confidence of both the government and the universities. OCUA engaged in system planning 'on terms decreed or confirmed by the minister and consented to by the universities themselves.' There was no legislation; all parties started with confidence in the system. Although Dupré describes his mandate as keeping both the universities and the government 'honest,' he was creative in his efforts to increase funding to the universities. According to Axelrod,[5] Dupré 'secured from the government an explicit statement of its funding objectives for higher education, which included: offsetting inflationary trends, maintaining existing levels of service, and accommodating expected enrolment increases. The OCUA critically parsed these statements, and added a goal of its own: the need to maintain the financial viability of the university system. It costed each of these objectives and found the operating grant shortfall between 1974 and 1976 to be some $16 million.' This was at a time when the federal government was reducing its support, and, despite the best efforts of OCUA, financing in Ontario failed to keep up with what universities wanted. George Connell points out that although the government did not accept OCUA's recommendations on the overall envelope, it did accept their recommendations for how it should be divided, with 'disastrous consequences.' In 1979, OCUA reported that the Ontario system stood 'at the brink of serious trouble.'

Over its lifetime, OCUA failed to ensure that increases in funding matched increases in student enrolment. During the twenty years of OCUA's existence, Ontario moved from being a leader in university funding to being the worst province in Canada in dollars per FTE student. On OCUA's watch, various commissions called for more funding and a stronger OCUA to resolve conflicts in the system.[6] This increased articulation of the system's needs ('the more the merrier,' according to Dupré) had no effect.

From 1985 to 1990, the Peterson government put a renewed emphasis on the role of universities in global competitiveness, relasing reports such as *Competing in the New Global Economy* and *People and Skills in the New Global Economy*. However, funding did not keep pace, despite a new provincial Centres of Excellence program and some enrolment growth funding.

The NDP government from 1990 to 1995 added to the agenda for universities an emphasis on accessibility, social equity, and transferability between colleges and universities. It introduced the social contract, which attempted a dramatic government incursion into the direct operation of universities. Targeted and conditional government grants increased. Increasingly, the government was setting priorities, and by 1993, only 60% of operating income came through the BIU formula, down from 75% in 1985.[7]

The Conservatives' Common Sense Revolution reduced funding further, increasing targeted funding while granting more autonomy to universities in fee setting. The Conservatives also abolished OCUA, and it has not been reinstated. At a time when the government was reducing expenditures and wanted change, the Conservatives argued that OCUA was costing money and standing in the way. Moreover, the Council had little support from the university sector. OCUA had undertaken a major review of funding in 1994–5 that was unpopular with most universities. And, as one university president put it, 'The OCUA was a constant excuse for inaction and added zero value ... As a result of highly political appointments in the Rae era, it was filled with individuals representing special interests and had too few members supporting the cause of higher education itself. It had become just another publicly subsidized critic of the universities and took the government off the hook.'

The history of CUA and OCUA does not suggest that intermediary bodies are effective in realizing the university's desire for increased funding and increased self-regulation. It is not clear how these bodies have helped governments with the politics of change, although at some moments respected members of OCUA brokered compromise. The politics of education have evolved since these bodies were put in place to become more differentiated, with a stronger state, a more elaborate and sophisticated university sector, and more representation from colleges, students, and the broader public.

In this environment, it is difficult to see that an intermediate body could be perceived as apolitical. It is equally difficult to see that it would be appropriate for government to hand over power to an unelected group of appointees. There remains, however, a continued hankering for an intermediary body that will represent universities to government and protect them from interference. Axelrod, after reviewing the incursions of government into university autonomy over recent years, calls for an intermediary body that will 'forge a system-wide resolution,' while ensuring that 'the government's reach into institutional life would be contained.'[8]

There are other lessons from other provinces. Most provinces have instituted, then abolished, intermediary bodies, as the ideal of what they might be collided with the reality of what they actually were. An extensive review is beyond the bounds of this paper, but the experiences of British Columbia and Nova Scotia are instructive.

In British Columbia, the Universities Council of British Columbia (UCBC) was established in 1974 by the NDP, after a report by Walter Young, professor of political science at University of Victoria, recommended a more powerful intermediary agency 'for the reconciliation of public accountability with university autonomy and to ensure a greater sensitivity to social needs in the development of university education.'[9] The council advised the minister of post-secondary education on the allocation of grants and capital funding, and the approval of new programs. Initially the council served as an advocate of the universities, and its recommendations were accepted by the universities and approved by governments. Although it began at a time when the government was increasing funding, by the early 1980s, the Social Credit government effected large reductions (5% cuts to base funding, two years in a row) at a time of high inflation, and bypassed the council on some key program decisions in relation to a university hospital at UBC, and engineering programs at Simon Fraser University and University of Victoria. Things fell apart. As Cameron comments, '[F]rom the beginning the new agency played a remarkably passive role ... the universities could be forgiven if they sometimes questioned the value of the new arrangement.'[10] As one observer reports:

A decade later it still existed and its influence had become negative in every way. Its existence made it illegitimate for universities to interact with government directly and UCBC put more energy into trying to psych out what increase/decrease government wanted to make in the grant (so it could determine its asking price accordingly) than it put into advocating for higher education. Soon after David Strangway's arrival as president, he invited UCBC to meet with the senior executive at UBC. The vice-chair actually fell asleep during David's presentation at the table in the social suite. That was the beginning of the end for UCBC!

The university presidents went to Victoria in 1987 to ask the government to abolish UCBC and save the money. The council was eliminated, and a new minister of post-secondary education worked productively with the universities. Funding for universities increased, because the government's own polling indicated that university funding had been cut too deeply.

Nova Scotia provides an example of perhaps the most active and challenging intermediary body in Canada's university system. NSCHE was set up in 1992 to 'rationalize' the system of higher education in a province that had more small universities than any other. Universities had poor relationships with each other, and none of them worked well with the government. Costs were high.

The council was set up with 'executive authority and discretionary powers over funding in order to ensure that university planning, programming, and resource allocation are performed in the context of a provincial university system.'[11] Janet Halliwell, former chair of the federal Science Council, became chair and CEO of the council.

The NSCHE brought about significant changes in the structure of the universities in Nova Scotia, targeting the areas of education, engineering, and computer science. It had to work to keep the confidence of the government, and some university presidents were unhappy with the decisions that were taken. The political pressures that played through and around the council were fierce. It discharged its responsibilities by reviewing programs, talking to and consulting experts, and doing research. After four years Halliwell left the council, at a time when it was reconsidering its mandate. After that, the council lost a good deal of its power. Today, Halliwell comments that these bodies will not have longevity, and that appointments are crucial: 'A few bad appointments will just wreck it.' When she left, she reflected on her tenure:

> Some would focus on the structural aspects such as our confirmation of the continued existence of relatively small, differentiated institutions, the signing of the Dalhousie-TUNS merger agreement ... the strengthening of our system of teacher education ... the establishment of a system vision and policy context for Nova Scotia universities that recognizes our distinctiveness from the rest of Canada; but I would contend that the most powerful and profound change has been in the improved relationships

between government and universities. From attitudes of frustration and often hostility on both sides four years ago has emerged a more mature understanding of the legitimate roles and responsibilities of both government and universities and a sense of partnership in forging the future of this province together.[12]

The legacy of the NSCHE, we might conclude, was as much about relationships as structural change, and due as much to the way the premier and university presidents had engaged with the process as with the specific recommendations of the council. Politics must be negotiated whatever the structures; good relationships make things happen. While an intermediary body may improve relationships and understanding at a particular point in time, it is no panacea.

The simple conclusion is that intermediary bodies have promised more than they can deliver. The illusion of an intermediary body that will make the right decisions still tends to trump the reality of what intermediary bodies have been able to accomplish. As one informant put it, 'Everyone is in favour of intermediary bodies except those who have actually worked with them.' While this is a bit harsh, especially for the early days of some intermediary bodies, in today's environment a targeted task force is more likely to be useful than a permanent advisory council.

The Information Functions of an Intermediary Body

Behind the desire for an intermediary body lies a desire for correct decisions, outside politics. Surely an expert group, an arm's-length body, a buffer, will be able to supersede the nasty politics of the real governments we elect. While this opting out will not do, the argument for intermediary bodies may have a lot to do with expertise and information. Governments need information in order to use financing and regulation effectively: How will financial aid policies affect admissions? How will funding for new places in nursing affect other programs in hospitals? How will a reduction in grants affect class size? An intermediary body promises expertise that is not available inside government and will help with effective policy-making.

It is not just the government that wants better information. OCUFA's argument to the Rae commission for an intermediary body emphasizes that 'it would build a solid base of research for debate and decision-making, expanding higher education information gathering activities.' Trebilock and Daniels, in this volume, mention the necessity of getting more information about universities out to students. And as the work of universities is knowledge building, more research in the neglected area of post-secondary education will help them fulfil their mandate. Universities must make an intellectual commitment to examining their own mission and processes, just as they make a commitment to research and teaching in their various disciplines and fields.

Within the history of intermediary bodies lies an untold story of educational research. All intermediary bodies have had an impact on how information about post-secondary education is achieved, shared, and used. Governments have been aware of how complex, difficult, and contested knowledge and beliefs about higher education are. They have been aware of their inability to get it right. Arm's-length bodies have often delivered expertise: statistics, studies, knowledge, conversation, the building of relationships based on inquiry and a quest to understand. The system can use a good deal more systematic and ongoing inquiry. While I am not convinced we need a decision-making body that attempts to fly above the political fray, I am convinced we need more information that can be used in political discussion – information that will have an impact, if it is well researched and if it has a political constituency to champion it.

Ontario needs a new body that is structured to pursue important knowledge for the post-secondary education system, to share it widely, to discuss it, and to motivate people to produce more knowledge and understanding, in order to staff the ministry, the leadership of universities and colleges, and the interest groups concerned with the future of higher education in this province. While this happens every few years, as commissions such as Rae's are set up, as reports are written and debated, we need to invest in a continuing process of analysis and adjustment to inform the politics that will continue to flow around higher education, and that cannot and should not be replaced.

Throughout recent provincial debates about the impact of tuition increases, the role of community colleges, the effectiveness of different forms of financial aid, the nature of income-contingent repayment schemes, the impact of post-secondary education on the economy, and other critical issues, I have been struck by the lack of evidence brought to bear on the arguments. This book is a counter-example, and it has brought together scholars from across campus to think seriously about the university. But in a sea of speculation and political posturing about education, we need more evidence to debate, compare, critique, and generally inform the discussion.

Research in and on education has not been well developed in Canada.

Although faculties of education were established in universities at the turn of the century, they have not, by and large, fared well in the university environment. There is no undergraduate degree in higher education, and undergraduate education by and large pays for faculty members and graduate programs. Few study higher education at the graduate level; leaders in higher education have degrees in other areas. Higher education is not, then, a big seller in the university market. Most faculties of education have no one who studies higher education. At OISE/UT we have a relatively large program, with a total of six and a half FTE faculty members. This is not enough to create the expertise the province needs to fuel a debate that affects us all so profoundly. 'The marginal, fragile nature of higher education as a field of inquiry in Canada'[13] has meant that there is no robust body of knowledge that is shared and has been widely debated.

What has emerged in Canada is 'a complex arrangement of federal and provincial government departments and agencies, interest groups, scholarly associations, academic departments, institutional researchers and individual scholars which compromise a loosely coupled collection of research communities.'[14] The *Maclean's* rankings are taken to be indicators of quality. The *Globe and Mail* carries out research on student satisfaction. The Institute on Productivity, based in the Rotman School of Management at U of T, has provided the most frequently quoted data on the impact of tuition policy and the levels of graduate enrolment in Ontario. While I applaud *Maclean's*, the *Globe*, and the Institute for their initiative and interest in education, this is not an adequate research base for policy. Where is the investment in a policy institute that examines educational policy in the way we examine health policy or economic productivity?

Intermediary bodies have been responsible for a good deal of the policy research that has been carried out on higher education. In the 1960s, when our story of intermediary bodies starts, Jackson's research on the demographics of education was crucial. The CUA did extensive further work on enrolment forecasting, with mixed results. Research on education was important in mainstream economics and sociology at the time, perhaps because of the rapid changes that were taking place, and the research money that was made available by governments to explore the issues. John Porter's important book examining educational achievement and access in Canada, *The Vertical Mosaic*, came out in 1965. Raymond Breton, Robert Pike, and others in sociology pursued the question of class, gender, and ethnic inequality in access to university.

The Economic Council of Canada was publishing studies on educational policy. Human capital theory was developed and elaborated in economics. The relation between education and economic development was debated. The Atkinson Foundation funded surveys of educational aspiration and achievement. There was money for research; there was interest in the academy.[15]

Research on education became less central in the social sciences thereafter. Stefan Dupré, a fine academic, does not recall referring to much in the way of books or articles on higher education in his work at OCUA. He consulted with institutional researchers at the universities, and had good working relations with analysts at COU and in the government. He was particularly concerned with getting university financial information. And, as he says about enrolment forecasting, 'Boy, were we ever wrong,' though he had consulted extensively.

Later, OCUA hired research staff, several of whom have PhDs from OISE/UT. The annual reports of the OCUA, however, make little mention of research, though they document forms of educational reasoning about university education in Ontario over twenty years, along with useful statistics and contextual information. Decisions on programs and funding are justified by data provided by universities, by reviewers' comments, by program documents, and by the opinions of the members of the council and its committees. A 1991 recommendation on the level of graduate stipends, for example, says: 'Council believes there is ample need and student demand to warrant the funding of additional awards. Council also believes that such additional awards should be targeted to particular needs.'[16] The report provides tables on application rates, success rates, and faculty retirements by discipline. There are many, many more examples for scholars interested in the development of the system.

The NSCHE also had a remarkable record of research over four years. Thirty-one publications came out of the council, on issues ranging from the capacity of the system to the roles and responsibilities of governing boards in Canadian universities, to new approaches to financing universities. A number of these were produced by university-based researchers and graduate students; they went beyond descriptions of the provincial system. Janet Halliwell, who now works for SSHRC, describes the research as 'a fragment of what I had hoped,' but characterizes the opportunity to create it as 'a wonderful power of the Council.'

Intermediary bodies, lobby groups, and governments have produced research of various kinds on higher education. Much of it is very useful, but its association with particular groups tends to undermine its credibility with others. Much is statistical and descriptive: funding, enrolment, and graduation rates. Data for quality assurance are increasingly available, as are data on student satisfaction, research productivity, and class size. An analysis of the work of the research staff at the Rae commission could tell us a good deal about what kinds of analysis are seen to be important and timely. Comparative research – across provinces and across the world – is increasingly important as we look for new ideas in relation to student aid, tuition, student exchange, student services, and research. Analysis of best practices is becoming more common. And rigorous analytic research on how the system is working should be the basis on which all the rest depends.

Research has an underlying politics and this becomes clear in education, as it does in all public policy research. The hankering for objective information is a legacy of the Enlightenment, and it is illusive. The scientist who is neutral, outside politics, has no axe to grind, and can see with the sophisticated lenses of social theory has much to offer, but does not always inform the questions of the day. No research can address the entirety of any issue, much less a controversial and complex one, as any interesting policy issue is. No single viewpoint, however well informed, is adequate to the task of definitely characterizing social reality. Researchers must simplify and define a frame of reference and a series of questions in order to do their research. Policy research is undertaken by people with values and assumptions that will be reflected in the research questions they ask and the methodology they employ.[17]

There is a widespread belief that increased knowledge leads to increased agreement and more cooperation. This is certainly not true; more research can mean clarifying the arguments for different positions and it can lead to clearer conflict. But democracy requires debate and difference.

To be effective, then, a research body must have independence from any particular political position. It must allow freedom of expression, welcoming research that starts from the premises of many different policy arguments. It must be aware of the politics of an issue, ensuring that different policy positions get their research due. This is what universities do best. Investment in a research institute on post-secondary education, associated with a university, representing in the institute's governing body stakeholders of all persuasions, and employing researchers from different disciplinary backgrounds would increase the capacity of the province to produce an excellent, responsive, and high-quality post-secondary system. The research the institute carried out would be politically disparate, peer reviewed, and thoroughly tested through debate. Through this process, the institute would attain the legitimacy it needs to be influential. Rather than being a neutral 'buffer,' it would explicitly engage debate.

The details of such a research institute would have to be worked out in some other forum. There are models of post-secondary institutes around the world, but Ontario could claim global leadership with a serious investment. The beginnings exist already. Ontario has a group of fine scholars. We have an international community of graduate students. We could build conferences, seminars, graduate programs, and professional development programs for leadership in post-secondary education. We could create the research and scholarship that would make Ontario the centre of a world-wide discussion of universities. It's a better investment than another political intermediary body.

Conclusion

Ontario has a well-regulated system of university education, using a variety of instruments including enrolment targets, funding envelopes, performance indicators, OCGS reviews, periodic internal reviews, and the accreditation of professional programs. These systems can be critiqued, amended, and reformed. They will be and they should be.

Politics is the art of making choices about how and when this will happen. Accountability for those choices should be clear, not confused by a body that does not have the power to achieve its ends but takes the pressure off those who should be held responsible – both universities and government.

We have a host of partnerships, lobby groups, and associations concerned with the post-secondary system, and they have different views of where the system should be heading. They interact with one another, both formally and informally; discussion among them must be informed to be useful. This kind of debate, along with good relationships that encourage compromise, discussion, and accountability, is what democracy is all about. It should not be limited to periodic provincial commissions.

Effective government requires a civil service with a sophisticated understanding of the post-secondary system and a commitment to the public good. Effective post-secondary institutions require public-spirited leadership and the capacity for reflective self-analysis. An institute that carried out world-class research on post-secondary education and, through the education of graduate students and policy-makers, increased our capacity for research and informed discourse, would make an enormous contribution to the future of education in Ontario.

Notes

* Dean, Ontario Institute for Studies in Education, University of Toronto
1 Jones makes the argument for the distinctive nature of the Canadian system in a variety of publications. See, for example, Jones et al., 'Arrangements for Co-ordination.'
2 McGuinness et al., *State Postsecondary Education.*
3 Cameron, *More Than an Academic Question,* 154.
4 This paragraph draws from Cameron, *More Than an Academic Question,* 97–102.
5 Axelrod, 'Public Policy.'
6 Fisher, *Committee on the future role of Universities in Ontario,* 1981; Bovey, *The Commission on the Future Development of the Universities of Ontario,* 1984; Stubbs, *The Report of the External Advisor to the Minister of Colleges and Universities on the Future Role and Function of the Ontario Council on University Affairs and its Academic Advisory Committee,* 1988. Since the early 1980s the OCUA has assumed responsibility for advising the government on such matters as funding new undergraduate professional or similar programs, and authorizing out-of-province institutions to offer degree programs in Ontario.
7 George and McAllister, *Expanding Role,* quoted in Axelrod, 'Public Policy.'
8 Axelrod, 'Public Policy.'
9 Cameron, *More Than an Academic Question,* 201.
10 Ibid.
11 This is from a letter from Kontak, principal assistant to the premier, to Thomas McInnis, chairman of the policy board, in November 1991.
12 Halliwell, speaking notes.
13 Jones, 'Research on Higher Education,' in Sadlak and Altbach, eds, *Higher Education Research,* 204.
14 Ibid.
15 In retrospect, the interest was mainly in analysing numbers in sociology and economics. The absence of political analysis contributed to the inadequacies of the way policy was developed.
16 OCUA, *Eighteenth Annual Report,* 220.
17 Gaskell, 'Policy Research and Politics' and Cohen and Lindblom, *Useable Knowledge.*

Bibliography

Axelrod, Paul. 'Public Policy in Ontario Higher Education from Frost to Harris.' Paper presented at the Canadian History of Education conference, May 2003.

Bovey, *The Commission on the Future Development of Universities in Ontario*, 1984.

Cameron, David. *More Than an Academic Question: Universities, Government and Public Policy in Canada*. Halifax: Institute for Research on Public Policy, 1991.

Cohen, David, and Charles Lindblom. *Useable Knowledge: Social Science and Social Problem Solving*. New Haven: Yale University Press, 1979.

Gaskell, Jane. 'Policy Research and Politics' *Alberta Journal of Educational Research*. 36:4 (1988), 403–17.

George, Peter, and James A. McAllister. *The Expanding Role of the State in Canadian Universities: Can University Autonomy and Accountability Be Reconciled?* Toronto: Council on Ontario Universities, 1994.

Government of Ontario. *Competing in the New Global Economy*. Toronto: Government of Ontario, 1988.

– *People and Skills in the New Global Economy*. Toronto: Government of Ontario, 1988.

Jones, Glen. 'Research on Higher Education in a Decentralized Academic System: The Case of Canada.' In Jan Sadlak and Philip Altbach, eds, *Higher Education Research at the Turn of the New Century*. Paris: UNESCO, 1997.

Jones, Glen, Michael Skolnik, and Barbara Soren. 'Arrangements for Coordination between University and College Sectors in Canadian Provinces: 1990–1996.' *Higher Education Policy* 11 (1998), 15–27.

McGuinness, A.C., R.M. Epper, and S. Arredondo. *State Postsecondary Education Structures Handbook*. Denver, Col.: Education Commission of the States, 1994.

Ontario Council on University Affairs (OCUA). *1991–92 Eighteenth Annual Report*. Toronto: OCUA, 1993.

Porter, John. *The Vertical Mosaic*. Toronto: University of Toronto Press, 1965.

Stubbs, John O. *The Report of the External Advisor to the Minister of Colleges and Universities on the Future Role and Function of the Ontario Council on University Affairs and Its Academic Advisory Committee*. July 1988.

Public Universities and the Public Interest: The Compelling Case for a Buffer between Universities and Government

What does autonomy mean in the context of a public university? From whom is the university autonomous? Typically, this autonomy is defined in relation to government intervention in academic programs, and in the past was associated with preserving academic freedom.[1] More recently, questions of autonomy have extended to a range of government-sponsored regulatory instruments.[2] From this autonomy vantage, government interference with universities may be seen as motivated by short-term horizons and partisan inclinations or demonstrating insensitivity to the unique context of universities. What makes a 'public university' public? It is not simply that public funds are disbursed to these institutions or that they are established by statute, but rather that public universities exist in order to advance the public interest. It falls to government to preserve and promote the public interest. The rationales for government involvement in post-secondary education are well accepted and flow from the government's guardianship over public-interest values (citizenship and civic virtues, pursuit of knowledge, accessibility of social mobility, etc.)[3] From this accountability vantage, universities may appear disconnected from these public-interest goals unless close governmental supervision is maintained. While both government and universities are dedicated to promoting the public interest in post-secondary education, their differing vantages on the issues cannot easily be reconciled.

What distinguishes public universities from private universities is also what complicates the tensions around autonomy and accountability with government – if the defining quality of a public university is its advancement of the public interest, and both those universities and the government of the day owe an obligation to act in the public interest, how are differences of opinion over the interpretation of the public interest to be resolved? These differences of opinion may arise internally to government (e.g., between the minister responsible for universities and the rest of Cabinet, between political staff and civil servants, etc.), internally to universities (e.g., between faculty, staff, students, and the administration, among faculties, units, and divisions, etc.), or between government and universities. The public interest, in this sense, is not a definable set of static directives, but rather a framework within which internal and external dialogues about the appropriate and desirable aspirations for the university may take place. To say that public universities exist to advance the public interest is also to make a participatory claim on whose voices will be considered legitimate in such a dialogue and a stakeholder claim on whose vested interests must be considered.

In this brief paper, I examine the relationship between governments and public universities from a public-interest perspective. My focus is not on the rationale for government involvement nor on the desirability of various regulatory instruments, both of which are canvassed elsewhere in this conference, but rather on the balance between autonomy and accountability. I conclude that the public interest would not be served either by direct government intervention in university affairs nor by authority over university affairs being completely devolved to the universities themselves. The proper balance between autonomy and accountability must address the interests of both universities and governments, but should not be unilaterally determined by either. I argue that there is a compelling case in this setting for a buffer agency to both help find and implement the proper balance – this requires an arm's-length body which has a legitimate public interest mandate, and which is controlled neither by the government nor by the universities.

This paper will be divided into four sections. In the first I consider the possibilities and limits of direct governmental oversight over universities. In the second section I explore the more decentralized approach of relying on internal university governance for oversight. In the third section I examine the potential of a buffer agency which would serve as an intermediary between governments and universities. Finally, in the fourth section, I sketch an approach to the interdependence of and interaction between these three forms of oversight. Most of the examples cited in this paper are drawn from Ontario. This is both the jurisdiction with which I am most familiar and a jurisdiction now receiving significant attention in light of the post-secondary review. I believe most if not all the dilemmas explored, however, apply more broadly in Canada. Indeed, the overarching tension between autonomy from and accountability to government represents a universal characteristic of public universities in all welfare states. That said, a comparative analysis among provinces or other welfare states lies beyond the scope of this study.[4]

1. The Possibilities and Limits of Governmental Control

The relationship between government and universities has always been complex. Indeed, from a legal standpoint, the defining characteristic of universities is their autonomy from government control. This issue reached the Supreme Court of Canada in *McKinney v. University of Guelph* when it considered a challenge by university faculty and librarians to mandatory retirement under the *Charter of Rights and Freedoms*.[5] The *Charter's* applicability is limited to 'government action.' In concluding as a preliminary matter that the affairs of universities would not be subject to scrutiny as government action within the meaning of the *Charter*, Justice La Forest observed: 'It is evident from what has been recounted that the universities' fate is largely in the hands of government and that the universities are subjected to important limitations on what they can do, either by regulation or because of their dependence on government funds. It by no means follows, however, that the universities are organs of government.'[6] La Forest J. added, 'Though the legislature may determine much of the environment in which universities operate, the reality is that they function as autonomous bodies within that environment.'[7] While this may be true, the line between government influence over operations and government control over policy is not always easy to draw.

Canada has a long history of governmental involvement in public universities. As Craig Riddell has observed, 'All Canadian jurisdictions are characterized by extensive government involvement in the provision and financing of post-secondary education.'[8] As David Laidler has emphasized, '[T]he resources needed to create, maintain, and expand Canadian universities have, from the outset, come predominantly from government ... In Canada, when governments feel short of funds ... and cut back on university spending, the reduction impinges on the whole sector, not just one segment of it.'[9] Provincial governments, of course, were once far more involved in university affairs. For example, Martin Friedland's *The University of Toronto: A History* details the proactive role of premiers of Ontario and Cabinet in deciding on the hiring of faculty well into the nineteenth century.[10] In fact, legislation creating greater self-government for the University of Toronto through a governing board in the nineteenth century was sparked not by the recognition that government should have an arm's-length relationship with universities, but rather by the recognition that self-government would preserve governmental influence at the expense of religious denominational institutions which then controlled many universities.[11]

The tradition of government supervision of public universities is reflected in the fact that public universities in Canada were, with some notable exceptions, statutory creations. The University of Toronto was established by the Ontario legislature in 1859. Other universities were created out of specialized educational bodies under the direct control of the province, such as the University of Guelph. Provincial statutes set out the universities' powers, functions, privileges, and governing structure. While these statutes affirm governmental stewardship over university affairs, they also, by their terms, recognize that each university is an autonomous institution, where most significant authority over academic development is vested in a governing board or senate. Some empowering statutes also provide for specific objectives for universities,[12] but most provide for what I would term a general public-interest authority relating to the advancement of learning and dissemination of knowledge for the betterment of society. To give one example, the *York University Act*, provides that its objects are '(a) the advancement of learning and the dissemination of knowledge; and (b) the intellectual, spiritual, social, moral and physical development of its members and the betterment of society.'[13] While these acts affirm the university's mission and establish a structure of internal governance and authority, they are silent on the relationship between those universities with government. Because Canadian jurisdiction rejected the American model of a single centralized and unified system of universities (e.g., the University of California has campuses throughout the state), one must speak not of a single relationship between the government and the public university system but of multiple relationships between the government and individual institutions (18 universities in Ontario). The inefficient and unwieldy prospect of managing multiple institutional relationships lends to the logic and efficiency of a mediating buffer agency discussed below.

While the motivations for particular government programs and initiatives may vary, traditionally, direct government involvement in university life has come in three related forms: (a) funding schemes; (b) regulatory requirements, and (c) policy development.[14] I will briefly touch on each in turn.

(a) Funding

The methods, timing, and adequacy of government funding of public universities has been extensively explored by others. Increasingly, funding has been tied to targeted government priorities. This may be done in several ways. A portion of the funding may be set aside to disburse according to results of performance indicators (Ontario's Key Performance Indicators is one example, though it accounts for less than 1% of the operating grants provided to universities from the Ontario government. Or, new funding could be made available targeted to specific programs or initiatives. Another form of tying funding to government priorities is to cap expenditures on specific programs. Such a cap in Ontario has applied to new graduate programs. Funding implements policy preferences in a global sense as well. As the Ontario government has reduced its funding relative to university expenditures, this has compelled universities to seek funding from other sources, principally through tuition revenues (separately regulated by the province) and charitable donations.

The government has also tied its funding for post-secondary education to an accountability framework which is intended to promote the achievement of the following objectives: (1) program quality, (2) access, (3) responsiveness to changing educational needs, and (4) cost-effectiveness in the delivery of programs and services and sound financial management.[15]

(b) Regulatory Requirements

Universities are enmeshed in a variety of regulatory relationships with government. In addition to operating grants to universities and special program funding, both of which come with regulatory requirements (including issuing audited financial statements, etc.), government sets the parameters within which universities may set tuition levels. Government also regulates various aspects of facilities and physical-plant development. Government oversees a range of programs designed to benefit students, including funding for accessibility to disabled students, and student loans and grants, among others. Universities, of course, must also comply with a host of other governmental rules, ranging from labour relations laws to environmental regulations, from compliance with the *Human Rights Code* to compliance with municipal building codes.

Another important regulatory dimension to the government–university relationship relates to the process by which the ministry of Training, Colleges and Universities approves academic programs for funding. The ministry does not impose qualitative standards for approving new programs but does ensure that any institution seeking approval meets the institution's own quality standards and that these standards are objectively set. Additional criteria for ministry approval relate to the institution's ability to manage and finance the program and prior approval of the program (if a graduate program) by the Ontario Council for Graduate Studies (OCGS), part of the Council of Ontario Universities (COU) discussed below. While some provincial governments review the academic quality of a program directly (e.g., BC and Alberta), in Ontario it is the eligibility of a program for public funding that is subject to government approval, not the authority of a university to offer the program.

These regulatory relationships give rise to dense and often onerous reporting requirements imposed on universities. Reporting requirements between Ontario universities and the Ontario government include reporting on enrolment target agreements, audited financial statements, capital-plan investment reports, facility-renewal program reports, Ontario Student Opportunity Trust status reports, Access to Opportunity Program reports, Ontario Graduate Scholarship in Science and Technology reports, bilingualism grants reports, tuition-fee set aside reports, tuition-fee monitoring reports, accessibility funding for students with disabilities reports, quality-assurance fund reports, audited OSAP compliance reports, reports on special purpose grants, graduate surveys, new program approval submissions ... the list goes on.[16] These reporting requirements are, of course, over and above the extensive reporting requirements of governing boards to the university community itself.

The regulatory relationship between governments and universities is inextricably bound up in their funding relationship, but extends beyond it as well. Notwithstanding the complexity of this relationship, accountability generally continues to be understood in a linear and one-dimensional fashion – primarily as rules established by government as a condition of providing universities with funding, or as a condition of their authority to operate and grant degrees, to which recipient institutions must demonstrate compliance through reporting and audits.[17] This formalistic approach to regulatory compliance tends to overemphasize those aspects of university life which can be quantified and verified (e.g., enrolments, graduation rates, budgets), while underemphasizing more subjective aspects of university affairs which resist quantification (e.g., teaching excellence, acquiring critical thinking and analytic skills, excellence in research, enriching civic values and promoting a learning society, etc.).

(c) Policy Development

Government involvement in universities relates not only to funding and regulatory requirements but also to substantive policy aspirations. Governments see themselves not simply as funding universities but as investing in particular policy outcomes. Typically, these outcome-related interests hark back to the rationales for government intervention in post-secondary education discussed at the outset of this paper – economic benefits and skills training and benefits of social mobility, civic engagement, and accessibility. Here, government policy mingles with the qualitative standards set by universities themselves. For example, by targeting funding to growing computer science programs through its Access to Opportunities Program (ATOP) initiative, the Ontario government was able to demonstrate a policy initiative to capture public interest in the 'new economy,' rise to a challenge from industry to 'double the pipeline' of IT professionals, and encourage university responsiveness to market demands.[18]

Concerns over government interference in the day-to-day operations of Canadian universities have become an increasingly familiar refrain in the university setting.[19] Part of this trend is driven by politics and the desire to reap political capital from the success of universities. Part is driven by fiscal pressures on government and the desire to decrease operating grants or increase the value of existing operation grant moneys. Part is driven by reports from provincial auditors and others critical of the accountability of universities. Part, finally, is driven by broader public sector trends, whether 'new public management' strategies or neo-liberal restructuring.

Should government develop its own minimum standards of quality or aspirations to excellence in post-secondary education? Is government well placed to articulate such standards? Even if developed, can such standards be imposed on universities without compromising their autonomy? These questions are beyond the scope of this paper and dovetail with the discussion of performance indicators to be taken up in a separate paper.[20] Here again, however, the advantages of a buffer agency appear clear. Such an agency would be ideally placed to develop standards for the post-secondary system, but in a fashion sensitive to various institutional cultures and the distinctive challenges of the university context.

To conclude, government involvement in university affairs through funding, regulation, and the pursuit of policy is both broad and deep. The breadth and depth of this involvement, however, necessarily impairs the autonomy of public universities to identify and pursue their own priorities in the public interest.

2. The Possibilities and Limits of University Governance

The 1993 Ontario Task Force Report, *University Accountability: A Strengthened Framework*, recognized that universities' own governance structures should represent the 'primary and most effective locus of institutional accountability' for universities, as they would be able to address 'the legitimate interest of the government in holding the institution responsible for its use of public funds.[21]

Most universities have a bicameral structure of internal governance, dividing up responsibilities over governance and management to a board,[22] and decisions over academic programs and related matters to a senate.[23] Through governance institutions such as a university's board, various constituencies in the university community find representation, including faculty, staff, students, and alumni. The senate typically serves as a representative body for a university's diverse faculties, departments, and units. Thus these bodies serve at once to advance the public-interest mandate of universities, to demonstrate accountability to the university community, and to reflect, through the range of reporting requirements discussed above, accountability to the government.

University policies and practices to provide oversight over the affairs of its units, divisions, and faculties are sophisticated and extensive and beyond the scope of a study. However, because universities do have extensive internal accountability measures, they may be justifiably sceptical of the need for extensive external accountability measures (beyond external oversight over the proper functioning of internal accountability measures). The Council of Ontario universities' submission to the post-secondary review captures this tension in its articulation of how universities should demonstrate accountability to government: 'Universities acknowledge the need to demonstrate accountability for the public funding they receive, and to demonstrate accountability to all their various stakeholders and funders, but assert that an accountability framework for universities must reflect their status as autonomous institutions, the overall diversity of the system and the evolving differentiation of universities as they develop strong missions and mandates appropriate to their particular size, location and role in Ontario. Universities should be judged against these particular missions and the strategic plans put in place to ensure that each university contributes to Ontario's economic and social development.[24]

Furthermore, apart from its role in external accountability, the government also exercises significant influence over internal accountability in public universities. The government is involved in this internal governance framework in several ways. First, the establishment of these governance structures, their composition and authority, all derive from statutory sources over which the government retains supervisory jurisdiction. Second, provincial governments have established additional standards to which internal governance structures must comply (e.g., requiring conflict-of-interest guidelines). Finally, provincial governments themselves typically appoint a proportion of board members. In the University of Toronto, for example, which has a unicameral system of governance consisting of an elected 50-member body known as the Governing Council, the composition is designated as follows: Twenty-five members of the Governing Council are from within the university: 12 teaching staff, 8 students, 2 administrative staff, the president, and 2 senior officers appointed by the president. The other 25 members consist of 16 appointees of the provincial government, 8 elected alumni, and the chancellor, who is also elected by the alumni. The Governing Council annually elects a chair and vice-chair from among the members appointed by the province.

The accountability of such governing bodies is often complex. They must represent and enjoy the confidence of the university community (faculty, staff, students, and alumni), reflect the diversity of the university's mandate, and maintain a relationship with the city, town, or region where the university is situated. Because of their differing structures and disparate operating environments, it is difficult to aggregate the sum of these internal structures. Thus, while the importance of external accountability to the government from particular universities may be debatable, the importance of government's own accountability for the post-secondary sector as a whole is clear, and requires aggregate measures on all universities.

3. The Need for a Buffer Organization

While direct governmental involvement and decentralized university authority each fulfils a part of a public-interest mandate, I conclude that neither governments nor universities may advance the public interest in post-secondary education alone. It is as a complement to the public-interest mandate of governing bodies of universities and as an extension of the public-interest mandate of government over the post-secondary system of education that the need for and value of a buffer agency is most apparent.[25] Buffers can shield government from the distorting effects of being required to intervene directly in disparate institutions, while at the same time shielding universities from governmental meddling.[26]

There are many examples of buffer agencies in the university sector in North America, Europe, Australia, and beyond. Too often, the desire to create a buffering entity between a public organization and government simply establishes a different and cumbersome bureaucracy to navigate. Worse, as the example of the United Kingdom's 'Quality Assurance Agency' suggests, buffer agencies with a mandate to evaluate academic performance to which funding is tied can trigger perverse incentives.[27]

Ontario's prior experience with buffer agencies represents in my view a cautionary tale.[28] Following the recommendation of a 1972 Commission on Post-Secondary Education in Ontario, the government established the Ontario Council on Universities Affairs (OCUA). While there was consideration given to investing this buffer agency with authority over admission standards and the authority to establish or terminate programs, in the end it was created as an advisory body.

In 1996, the Ontario government disbanded OCUA along with a host of other advisory bodies (including the Ontario Law Reform Commission), ostensibly as a cost-saving measure.[29] At the time of its demise, OCUA had an annual budget of $800,000, seven in-house staff, and a council of 20 – members of the public, students, and representatives from government, faculties, and administrations – the council met monthly, and wrote advisory memoranda that were subsequently released publicly. According to Stefan Dupré, who happened both to serve as the first chair of OCUA in 1974 and was interim chair in 1996 when it was shut down, 85% of the council's recommendations had been accepted by successive provincial governments. While the proportion of recommendations accepted may have been accurate, this masks the central criticism of OCUA, which was that its recommendations for global funding increases were routinely ignored while its recommendations for allocations of funding to various parts of the university sector were often accepted. When asked about the decision to scrap OCUA, Dupré observed, 'As a former professor of public administration, I know that all government bodies are necessarily transient.'[30] This, in the end, is perhaps the most salient point. Even if a buffer agency enjoys success, its continued existence depends on governmental support. Unless a buffer agency has formal or informal means at its disposal to resist government pressure, then it is unlikely to serve its purpose effectively.

Another model of buffer agency is one made up not of government and community appointees, but of appointees from the public universities themselves. The Council of Ontario Universities (COU) is an example of this form of stakeholder-led buffer agency.[31] Originally known as the Committee of Presidents of the Universities of Ontario (CPUO), the organization was formed in 1962 in response to a need for institutional participation in educational reform and expansion. The committee was later enlarged to include two representatives from each member and associate institution: the executive head (university president, principal, or rector) and an academic colleague appointed by each university's senior academic governing body. In 1971, the committee changed its name to the Council of Ontario Universities. The COU describes its activities as ranging from 'issues management to information management' and from 'leadership on collective issues to general operational support for our member institutions, committees and affiliates.' The Council views itself as a venue both for addressing public policy expectations of greater accountability while supporting institutions' traditional rights of autonomy and self-regulation.[32]

The COU also engages in a variety of regulatory activities as well, which include quality assessments of academic programs. For example, the Ontario Council Graduate Studies unit appraises every graduate program offered in Ontario on seven-year cycles and all publicly assisted universities in Ontario are bound not to implement or offer graduate programs which are not approved. The appraisal includes elements of self-study requirements, peer review, and external judgment.[33] In describing the motivation behind quality assurance programs, David Leyton-Brown observes:

Quality assurance measures of various kinds have arisen for two principal reasons. Universities for many years have been concerned to ensure and enhance the quality of their educational programs ... After all, even the best of programs can be made even better, and continuous quality improvement is a distinguishing feature of the most renowned programs and institutions in the higher education community. However, that purpose is often in tension with the other driving force behind the recent increase in quality assurance processes in many jurisdictions – namely the increasing government pressure for public accountability. Governments in many countries are pressing for demonstration that their funding for higher education is well spent, that desired outcomes are achieved, and that quality is assured. Accountability purposes can lead to celebration or defence of the status quo, rather than the active search for change and improvement.[34]

With the post-secondary review, fresh calls for a revamped buffer agency structure have been issued, notably by the Ontario Confederation of University Faculty Associations (OCUFA), which supports a return to the OCUA model. OCUFA's report contends, 'Such a council could achieve greater accountability of the university system to the public. It would build a solid base of research for debate and decision-making, expanding higher education information-gathering activities currently undertaken by the Ontario government and the Council of Ontario Universities, while giving faculty, staff, students, administrators and the broader community a forum to participate in the shaping of the future of institutions of enormous importance to the province's future.[35] Michael Doucet, the head of OCUFA, commented upon the release of the report that '[t]he university system is too important to the future of the province to be held hostage to too much political ideology.'[37] But how is 'political ideology' to be distinguished from legitimate policy preferences of the government of the day? While it is unclear that a buffer organization would find such questions less daunting, such an organization would be best placed to address these questions.

Still another model of the buffer organization is the Social Sciences and Humanities Research Council of Canada (SSHRC), an arm's-length federal agency that promotes and supports university-based research and training in the social sciences and humanities. Created by an act of Parliament in 1977, SSHRC is governed by a 22-member council that reports to Parliament through the Minister of Industry. SSHRC funding supports individual researchers as well as university-based programs across the country. Its base budget for 2004–5 is $230 million, as determined by Parliament. SSHRC reports to Parliament annually on how it disburses its funds, but has autonomous authority to set its priorities, policies, and funding programs and to make granting decisions. One of SSHRC's most ambitious programs has been its Canada Research Chairs (CRC) program, which has a total budget of $900 million over five years and aims to establish 2000 research chairs at universities in Canada. Eligibility for the program hinges on a university's success in securing SSHRC and other grant funding.

Finally, one may see the role of the Provincial Auditor as a further example of a buffer agency with an oversight mandate. In Ontario, the Provincial Auditor as a legislative office has significant independence from the government of the day. The Provincial Auditor also has expertise reviewing other areas characterized by autonomous bodies receiving government funding (for example, auditing public expenditures on courts). The oversight of the Provincial Auditor usually encompasses the financial and accounting practices of public institutions, but more recently has embraced more controversial 'value for money' audits in a range of social-policy spheres. These types of audits, while sometimes methodologically suspect, may constructively extend the reach of the Provincial Auditor to assessing the success of government performance indicators, tracking, and results. The role of the Provincial Auditor, in other words, is not so much to serve as an intermediary between governments and universities but to act as an arm's-length check on the objectives, policies, and activities of each. This is a different but essential buffer role in the public universities' sector.

While buffer agencies may come in various forms (and may focus in varying combinations on the financial, academic, or governance aspects of universities), the form used to create a buffer agency cannot guarantee its effectiveness. Without a new vision of the relationship between government and universities oversight is likely to mean simply more paperwork. I now turn to sketching some principles which I believe ought to guide the new vision.

4. Toward a Shared Public-Interest Mandate for Government and Universities

In a post-Enron, post–sponsorship scandal era, one tends to equate oversight with independent auditing. Audits, to be sure, have a role to play, and in an era of value-for-money auditing, even that role is not without its agendas and controversy. I would like to focus, however, on relationships of oversight based on a shared public trust and multiple perspectives on how that public trust should best be discharged. Both the concept of a shared public trust and the concept of a pluralist approach to oversight warrant brief elaboration.

(a) Public Trust

Both government and universities have duties to promote the public-interest through the post-secondary education system – yet each has distinctly different perspectives and capacities to bring to bear on discharging this public-trust obligation. The success of their relationship, I would suggest, depends not only on clear, mutual expectations regarding roles and responsibilities, but also on the principle of a shared public trust. This public trust, in turn, should be the foundation for the trust which governments and universities nurture in each other and the basis for the trust both nurture in the public through their collaboration. As Glenny and Dalglish have observed, writing in the American context:

> In the long run, however, institutional autonomy rests primarily on the amount of trust that exists between state government and institutions of higher education. That trust colors relationships between the two sectors so much that talk of the marginal effects of legal status pale into something close to insignificance by comparison ... There are too many ways that state government can assert controls over institutions of higher education, whatever their legal status, to permit confidence in an institution's ability to operate with complete or even marginal autonomy. The power of the University to protect itself, and the academic values it is assumed to have, from political and bureaucratic interference rests primarily on public trust and confidence.[37]

As school boards, police boards, and public-health authorities demonstrate, buffer organizations can constructively diffuse the partisan implications of operational decisions and provide better responsiveness to specific areas of significant stakeholder and public concern than could direct government decision-making.[38] A buffer organization not only could facilitate the development of relationships of mutual recognition and trust between universities and government, but also could develop better relationships between universities, as they would not have to compete for special governmental attention.

(b) Pluralism

Both autonomy and accountability, I would suggest, are advanced by a pluralist approach to oversight of the government–universities relationship. As discussed above, universities' own structures of internal governance, government's own ministerial policy-making and implementation of performance-based funding, and the various approaches to buffer organizations suggest there are multiple lenses through which to view the activities and achievements of universities, each of which is legitimate and valuable. There are distinct advantages to a pluralist approach to the oversight relationship, including a buffer organization, which include additional checks against error and bias, fuller information and deeper analysis, greater public awareness and transparency, and, finally, depoliticization.[39]

Beyond such advantages, pluralist approaches to oversight involving buffer organizations also raise additional concerns, which include

1 Where is the first or ultimate point of contact for concerned members of the university community, or concerned members of the public to have input?
2 Where does the buck stop? Who has ultimate authority for the success of the public universities system?
3 How will a buffer organization ensure that multiple oversight does not mean multiple bureaucracy, regulatory reporting, and compliance costs?
4 How will the proper legislative authority, capacity and budget for a buffer organization be assured?

If the benefits of the pluralism principle are to be reaped, these concerns must be addressed through the design and implementation of a buffer organization. Beyond emphasizing the need for any buffer organization to be sensitive to the concerns of all parties but lie at arm's length from each, it is beyond the scope of this paper to explore the particular aspects of a buffer organization which might best address these concerns. In Ontario, previous attempts at such a buffer organization (OCUA) and existing forms of analogous bodies (COU) would presumably represent the point of departure. The purpose of such an organization would be, at a minimum, to build on the capacities and perspectives both of government and universities, develop standards or benchmarks where desirable, identify best practices, provide oversight, and serve as a venue for dialogue on public values in the university system.

Given the historic tendency of buffer organizations in Ontario to over-promise and under-deliver, it may well be advisable to task a new buffer organization with a modest and readily attainable set of objectives to start, and to let it build up legitimacy and buy-in from both governmental and university quarters. Such an approach would be consistent with calls for a research and analysis based organization which would refrain from expressly taking a role in policy-making.[40] Another approach would be to envision a buffer organization with responsibility for monitoring and reporting on the implementation of a task force such as the post-secondary review's recommendations. Eventually, however, for a buffer organization to fulfil a public-interest mandate, it will have to add its own credible voice to the broader discussion on the purposes and aspirations of a public university.

Conclusion

In this paper I have emphasized the public-interest and public-trust dynamics of public universities as a framework within which to view the relationship between public universities and government. I briefly analysed the possibilities and limits of governmental intervention in public universities and of universities' own governance mechanisms. I concluded with an exploration of and argument for a buffer organization. In closing, I believe that government and universities, because of the need to balance autonomy and accountability and the need for coherence in addressing the challenges and opportunities now facing post-secondary education, should look outside their own horizons for new institutional forms capable of best advancing their shared commitment to the public-interest.

Notes

* Faculty of Law, University of Toronto. I am grateful to Harry Arthurs, Ian Clarke, Andrew Green, and Edward Monahan for constructive discussions during the drafting of this paper. I am also indebted to Pekka Sinervo and Janice Gross Stein for their comments on the paper during the conference presentation. I wish to thank Leslie Zamojc for her superb research assistance on this paper.
1 Some scholars have asserted that university autonomy may not always have been so instrumentally conceived. Glenny and Dalglish, for example,

argued, 'The conception of the autonomous university really anteceded any perception of the function or utility of that kind of independence. Autonomy was not then seen as a means of insulating the university from outside interference or meddling; it was simply a social fact, a state of being, a given on the basis of which the organizational structure and traditions of the university developed.' See Lyman A. Glenny and Thomas K. Dalglish, *Public Universities, State Agencies and the Law: Constitutional Autonomy in Decline* (Berkeley: Center for Research and Development in Higher Education, University of California, 1973), 9.

2 For discussion, see Terrence J. MacTaggart et al., *Seeking Excellence through Independence: Liberating Colleges and Universities from Excessive Regulation* (San Francisco: Jossey-Bass, 1998).

3 In this volume of papers, see Ronald J. Daniels and Michael J. Trebilcock, 'Towards a New Compact in University Education in Ontario,' section 1. In broad terms, the authors identify three rationales for government intervention in post-secondary education: positive externalities (i.e., civic virtues and citizenship values), paternalism (i.e., students may not be sufficiently informed to make rational choices), and equality-of-opportunity goals.

4 For a review of provincial initiatives, see Peter J. George and James A. McAllister, 'The Expanding Role of the State in Canadian Universities: Can University Autonomy and Accountability be Reconciled?' Council of Ontario Universities, Discussion series, Issue no. 3, 1994. For an insightful look at the Australian approach to the autonomy/accountability tension in the setting of public universities, see Martin Hayden and Lynn Meek's contribution to this volume: 'The Governance of Public Universities in Australia: Trends and Contemporary Issues.'

5 [1990] 3 S.C.R. 229.

6 Ibid., 272.

7 Ibid., 274.

8 W. Craig Riddell, 'The Role of Government in Post-Secondary Education in Ontario,' paper prepared for the Panel on the Role of Government, October 2003, http://www.law-lib.utoronto.ca/investing/reports/rp29.pdf, p. 7.

9 David Laidler, ed., *Renovating the Ivory Tower: Canadian Universities and the Knowledge Economy* (Toronto: C.D. Howe Institute, 2002), 5.

10 M. Friedland, *The University of Toronto: A History* (Toronto: University of Toronto Press, 2002), 113–25. See also David M. Cameron, *More than an Academic Question: Universities, Government and Public Policy in Canada* (Halifax: Institute for Research on Public Policy, 1991), 26.

11 Friedland, *The University of Toronto*, 64–73.

12 Those terms may also reflect clear policy goals. For example, the *University of Ontario Institute of Technology Act, 2002*, S.O. 2002, c.8, provides that the objects of the university are

(a) to provide undergraduate and postgraduate university programs with a primary focus on those programs that are innovative and responsive to the individual needs of students and to the market-driven needs of employers;

(b) to advance the highest quality of learning, teaching, research and professional practice;

(c) to contribute to the advancement of Ontario in the Canadian and global contexts with particular focus on the Durham region and Northumberland County; and

(d) to facilitate student transition between college-level programs and university-level programs.

13 *York University Act*, 13–14 ELIZABETH II, 1965, s.4.

14 I am here focusing on provincial government involvement in universities. The federal government also plays a significant role as a funder of universities, but this is almost entirely indirect. The federal government subsidizes tuition through its Millennial Scholarships and other financial aid, and subsidizes university operating grants through transfers of cash and tax points to the provinces. The federal government, as a practical matter, does not retain control over how these funds are disbursed by the provinces. Finally, through SSHRC, the federal government subsidizes a vast array of research through direct funding of academics. The recent Canada Research Chairs program, administered through SSHRC, is likely the most direct influence the federal government has had over the academic priorities and performance of universities.

15 This accountability framework is discussed in the Ontario Provincial Auditor's Report in 2001 – see 4.13, 'Accountability Framework for University Funding' at http://www.auditor.on.ca/english/reports/en01/413e01.pdf, pp. 335–7.

16 This list is drawn from appendix A to Council of Ontario Universities, *Proposed University Accountability Framework*, 15 November 2004.

17 For a discussion and critique of this approach to accountability, see Rod Dobell, 'The Role of Government and the Government's Role in Evaluating Government: Insider Information and Outsider Beliefs,' paper for the Panel on the Role of government, August 2003, 53.

18 The Ontario government introduced ATOP in 1998 and committed $150 million to the creation of 17,000 new spaces for computer science and engineering. Funding was subsequently increased and the target number of spaces expanded. Universities, in order to access ATOP funding, had to match the amount of money of their request. An advisory board for ATOP was established with John Roth, then CEO of Nortel, as its chair. The ATOP example is a cautionary tale. Many universities participated and thousands of new spaces in computer science departments and engineering faculties were created and faculty hired. With the downturn in the

high-tech sector beginning in 2000–1, however, a sharp downturn in computer science enrolments occurred. For discussion, see Heather Jane Robertson, David McGrane, and Erika Shaker, *For Cash and Future Considerations: Ontario Universities and Public-Private Partnerships*, Canadian Centre for Policy Alternatives (September 2003), at http:// www.policyalternatives.ca/publications/.

19 See Riddell, 'The Role of Government.' This issue is neither new nor novel – it was also of concern a decade ago. See George and McAllister, 'The Expanding Role of the State.' See also Peter C. Emberley, *Zero Tolerance: Hot Button Politics in Canada's Universities* (Toronto: Penguin, 1996), 1–20.

20 See contribution to this volume by Andrew Green and Edward Iacobucci.

21 *University Accountability: A Strengthened Framework*, 35.

22 Including the appointment of a president, appointing, promoting, terminating teaching staff and university officers, granting and terminating tenure, fixing duties and salaries of officers and employees, planning and implementing the physical development of the university, establishing and collecting tuition fees, regulating conduct of university community members, and establishing rules and regulations over university affairs, including making by-laws and compliance with governmental legislation and regulations. For discussion of these roles and responsibilities, see *Proposed University Accountability Framework*, 5–6

23 Including the establishment and modification of curricula and programs, determining standards of admission, governing exam-writing and grading, hearing and determining appeals from decisions of faculty, granting degrees and other awards, and coordinating long-range academic planning. See ibid., 7.

24 Ibid., 2.

25 In Ontario, calls for such a 'buffer' approach date back at least to the 1950s. In 1958, the Advisory Committee on University Affairs in Ontario was one of the first attempts at a mediating body to assess university needs. The 1972 Report of the Commission on Post-Secondary Education in Ontario, entitled *The Learning Society*, was one of several to recommend this approach (p. 108). For discussion, see Ontario Confederation of University Faculty Associations, *Overdue for Renewal: Pulling Ontario's Universities Together by Bringing an Improved Council on University Affairs Back to Life* (September 2004), research report series, vol. 5, No. 5.

26 I am grateful to Harry Arthurs for this observation.

27 These are alluded to in Daniels and Trebilcock (see note 4), section 4, under 'Public Money and Performance Funding.'

28 For a general review of the Ontario experience, see Paul Axelrod, *Scholars and Dollars: Politics, Economics and the Universities of Ontario, 1945–1980* (Toronto: University of Toronto Press, 1982). For a history of OCUA, see

Edward J. Monahan, 'University–Government Relations in Ontario: The History of a Buffer Body, 1958–1996,' *Minerva* 36 (1998), 347–66.

29 Lynda Hurst, 'Clear-cut mandate: A zealous Tory MPP has no qualms about felling active agencies along with deadwood,' *Toronto Star*, 15 July 1996, C1.

30 Quoted ibid.

31 The following description of the COU is drawn from its website, http://www.cou.on.ca/_bin/home/aboutCouncil.cfm, and its submission *Proposed University Accountability Framework* (note 16).

32 The COU's mission statement states: 'The Council of Ontario Universities (COU) represents the collective interests of 18 member institutions and two associate members. Its mandate is to provide leadership on issues facing the publicly funded universities, to participate actively in the development of relevant public policy, to communicate the contribution of higher education in the Province of Ontario, and to foster co-operation and understanding among the universities, related interest groups, the provincial government and the general public.' See www.cou.on.ca. See also Ian D. Clark, 'Advocacy, Self-Management, Advice to Government: The Evolving Functions of the Council of Ontario Universities,' paper presented to the Oxford Roundtable on Education Policy, 2 Aug. 1999; and Edward J. Monahan, *Collective Autonomy: A History of the Council of Ontario Universities 1962–2000* (Toronto: University of Toronto Press, 2004).

33 D. Leyton-Brown, 'Demystifying Quality Assurance,' paper prepared for the Conference on Higher Education in Canada, John Deutch Institute, Queen's University, Kingston, 13–14 February 2004, 10–12. Undergraduate program reviews in Ontario are undertaken by way of auditing a university's own policies and practices for quality assurance of undergraduate programs. This oversight function is performed by the Ontario Council of Academic Vice-Presidents (OCAV), which in turn delegates this role to the Undergraduate Program Review Audit Committee (UPRAC).

34 Ibid., 3.

35 'Overdue for Renewal: Pulling Ontario's Universities Together by Bringing an Improved Council on University Affairs Back to Life,' OCUFA Research Reports 5:5 (Sept. 2004), 3–4.

36 Colin Perkel, 'Profs want advisory council; They say putting universities in hands of bureaucrats leaves them open to political interference,' *Hamilton Spectator*, 7 Sept. 2004, A11.

37 *Public Universities, State Agencies and the Law*, 152.

38 This point is asserted and elaborated more fully in Colleen Flood and Duncan Sinclair, 'Steering and Rowing in Health Care: The Devolution Option?' Paper for the Role of Government Panel, September 2003, 13.

39 I discuss the advantages of pluralism in oversight in an analysis of the policing sector in Ontario in L. Sossin, 'The Oversight of Executive Police

Relations in Canada: The Constitution, the Courts, Administrative Processes and Democratic Governance,' commissioned by the Ipperwash Inquiry, June 2004.
40 See, for example, the recommendation for a research centre in Jane Gaskell, 'Deliberative Democracy: The Role of Educational Research in Educational Policy' in this volume.

PART VI

Enhancing Accessibility: Normative Foundations for Income-Contingent Grant and Loan Programs

Higher Education Funding

NICHOLAS BARR

I. INTRODUCTION

Higher education matters. No longer only a consumption good enjoyed by an élite, it is an important element in national economic performance. So it is no accident that the numbers in higher education have increased in all advanced countries. However, a mass, high-quality university system is expensive and competes for public funds with other imperatives.

Though in part about the British reforms announced in 2004, the paper is general in its application. It starts with some background issues. Section II sets out lessons from economic theory, largely rooted in the economics of information. Section III considers lessons from country experience, which complement and illustrate the theoretical analysis. Section IV assesses the 2004 Higher Education Act in England against the backdrop of the previous two sections, on the assumption that the legislation going through Parliament at the time of writing is not substantially changed. The concluding section considers the unfinished agenda.

Some caveats about what the paper is not about. The emphasis on funding does not imply the crude fallacy, against which Wolf (2002) rightly cautions, that increased spending automatically increases economic growth. The quality of higher education and its ability to adapt to changing economic conditions are critically important, and central to later arguments that market forces do a better job than central planning in matching the skills of graduates with their own preferences and the demands of the labour market.

Second, the concentration on the economic importance of higher education does not diminish the pursuit of knowledge for its own sake, nor downplay the centrality of academic freedom, nor deny that for many people getting a degree has important consumption benefits and is not simply an investment in their career. Third, the paper focuses on the finance of teaching, setting to one side the issues raised by research funding (on which see McNay, 1999; Roberts, 2003). Fourth, it is rooted in economic theory, but is not quantitative. Finally, though country experience is discussed, this is not a comparative paper.

(i) Background Issues

Higher education matters, first, because of the nature of technological change. Though it can reduce the need for skills (e.g. computers are increasingly user-friendly), it mostly increases the demand for skilled workers. Amplifying the trend, skills date more quickly and need to be replenished. The 'information age' can be taken to mean a need for education and training that is larger than previously, more diverse, and repeated, in the sense that periodic retraining is required.

Demographic change offers a second reason for expansion. The rising proportion of older people foreshadows increased spending on pensions, medical care, and long-term care. Part of the solution is to increase output sufficiently to meet the combined expectations of workers and pensioners. If workers are becoming relatively more scarce, the efficient response is to increase labour productivity. Demographic change is thus an argument for additional spending on investment in both technology and human capital.

Two debates shed light on implicit assumptions which often underpin opposing arguments. The first is about the nature of higher education, which can be characterized in terms of two stylized models.

- In the 'Anglo-American' model, policy sees higher education as heterogeneous, regards this as proper, and encourages diversity, varied forms of provision, and quality comparisons between them.
- In the 'Scandinavian model,' policy is based on the assumption that institutions are homogeneous, and therefore treats them equally and regards all programmes as equal.

This paper argues that the second model, whatever its merits, is incompatible with mass higher education, and that funding should therefore support a diverse, decentralized system. That line of argument is supported by the theoretical discussion in section II.

The second debate is about ability to pay. There is agreement that this should be a central element in policy design, but disagreement about how it should be measured. Should it be based on current income – i.e. on where people start? The strategy to which this leads is support for people whose family is poor, even if recipients end up becoming rich. Or should ability to pay be based on future income – that is, on where people end up? This approach leads to finance based on income-contingent loans or graduate taxes, with more generous support, *ex post*, where someone derives little financial benefit from his or her degree.

Section II argues that the second approach is correct for people who are well informed. Thus support for the generality of students should derive from a mix of tax funding and income-contingent loans (i.e. loans with repayments calculated as x per cent of the borrower's subsequent earnings). However, there is a socioeconomic gradient in the extent to which people are well informed, so that children from disadvantaged backgrounds may not even think of going to university. For such people, the first approach may be required.

Policy objectives
Higher education in Britain faces three widely agreed problems.

- Universities have too few resources: real funding per student almost halved in the 20 years to 2000 (Greenaway and Haynes, 2002, Figure 1).
- Student support is inadequate (Callender and Wilkinson, 2003).
- Access is unequal. In 2002, 81 per cent of children from professional backgrounds went to university; the comparable figure for children from manual backgrounds was 15 per cent (UK Education and Skills Select Committee, 2002, p. 19).

There is also widespread agreement about two core objectives: strengthening quality and diversity, both for their own sake and for reasons of national economic performance; and improving access, again for both efficiency and equity reasons. At least in the UK, therefore, the argument is less about what policy is trying to do than about the best way of doing so.

(ii) Blind Alleys

Before proceeding, it is helpful to clear the undergrowth by considering a series of often-asserted propositions.

Higher education is a basic right and should therefore be free.
The assertion that access to higher education is a right is a value judgement that commands widespread agreement. But it does not follow that higher education must be free. We all agree that food is a basic right, yet competitive supply at market prices is uncontentious. The equity objective is not free higher education, but a system in which no bright person is denied a place because he or she comes from a disadvantaged background.

In arguing for free higher education, however, people are reaching towards an important point: there is a strong case for making higher education *free at the point of use*. The arrangements set out below are designed to make that possible.

It is immoral to charge for education.
The same arguments apply. It is immoral (in my view) if people with the aptitude and desire are denied access to higher education because they cannot afford it; it is also immoral if underfunded earlier education means that they never even aspire to university. Similarly, it is immoral if someone is malnourished. But that is not an argument for making food free for everyone, including the rich; rather, it argues for income transfers so that everyone can afford a healthy diet.

Making something free for everyone can be justified in efficiency terms, where market failures make consumer choice problematic, and in equity terms, where the commodity is consumed by everyone – for example, school education and health care. As discussed below, higher education conforms with neither criterion. As a result, taxpayer subsidies are regressive and, as already noted, free higher education has done badly on access.

Elitism has no place in higher education.
Argument often blurs two separate elements. Many people, including me, agree with the value judgement that *social* elitism is wrong – social background *per se* should not influence access to the best universities. In contrast, *intellectual* élitism is both proper and desirable. The best musicians and athletes are chosen precisely because of their abilities, irrespective of whether their background is poor (Pele) or middle class (Tiger Woods). There is nothing inequitable about intellectually elite universities. The equity objective should be a system in which the ability of the brightest students to study at the most intellectually demanding universities is unrelated to their socioeconomic background.

Graduates pay for their higher education through income tax.
It is sometimes argued that higher education should be wholly tax funded because graduates earn more than non-graduates and therefore pay for their higher education through subsequent higher income tax payments. There are three counter-arguments.

- Income tax raises only one-quarter of government revenue and is paid by many more non-graduates than graduates: 82 per cent of working-age adults in the UK do not have a degree (OECD, 2002, Table A3.1a).
- Suppose a person with a degree pays an additional £100,000 in tax, of which £20,000 is deemed to pay for his higher education. By implication, he therefore pays £80,000 towards the National Health Service, schools, etc. – less than the £100,000 contributed to those services by someone with identical lifetime income who has not been to university. This is horizontally inequitable.
- If the argument is that the taxpayer gets a 'good deal' by paying for people's investment in higher education, the same logic says that the US taxpayer should pay all Microsoft's development costs.

A further argument against sole reliance on taxpayer funding is a practical one. There are limits to taxation, not least because of political pressures, which collide with other priorities for public spending. Thus it is no accident that real funding per student declined sharply over the years as UK student numbers increased.

II. LESSONS FROM ECONOMIC THEORY

Economic theory offers three strong lessons for financing higher education (for fuller discussion, see Barr, 2001a, chs 10–13): the days of central planning have gone; graduates should share in the costs of higher education; and well-designed student loans have core characteristics.

(i) Lesson 1: The Days of Central Planning Have Gone

Present arrangements
Central planning of UK universities has increased considerably since the mid-1970s. The problem has not been academic freedom, but reduced economic freedom through price control, quantity control, and heavily bureaucratic quality control.

Price control. UK universities are free to set fees for non-EU undergraduates and for all postgraduates. For UK and other EU undergraduates, fees were forbidden until 1998; since then, universities have been required to charge a flat fee (£1,150 in 2004/5), i.e. the same for all subjects at all universities. It is illegal to charge more and illegal to charge less.

Quantity control. Universities in England and Wales contract with the Higher Education Funding Council for England to teach a specified number of students. Though those controls have varied, universities have been penalized for recruiting fewer students than their quota and for recruiting too many.[2]

Monitoring quality. Universities are rightly held accountable for their receipt of public funds and rightly subject to quality control in the interests of consumer protection. However, the specific methods, notably the regime to assure teaching quality in the late 1990s, have been roundly criticized.[3]

The following analysis argues that central planning is no longer feasible and, separately, that it is not desirable.

Central planning of higher education: no longer feasible

The literature on the communist system (see Kornai, 1992, ch. 9) distinguishes extensive and intensive growth. The former refers to an era when surplus inputs, notably agricultural labour, could be brought into the industrial sector, characterized by rapid growth in the Soviet Union in the 1930s. Intensive growth, when surplus inputs had been used up, depends on technological advance and more efficient use of inputs. Central planning was not able to cope with the more complex problems that arose when inputs became scarce and with more advanced technology, as manifested by declining, and in some countries negative, growth rates in the 1980s and 1990s.

The analogy with higher education is instructive. Forty years ago, with a small university system offering degrees in a limited range of subjects, it was possible, as a polite myth, to assume that all universities were equally good and hence fund them broadly equally. Today there are more universities, more students, and much greater diversity of subjects. As a result, the characteristics and the costs of different degrees at different institutions vary widely, so that institutions need to be funded differentially. In principle, this could be done by an all-knowing central planner. In practice, the problem is too complex. A mass system in an increasingly complex world needs a funding mechanism which allows institutions to charge differential prices to different costs and missions. Central planning is no longer feasible.

Central planning of higher education: undesirable
Prices give signals to buyers and sellers. In contrast with communist central planning, the OECD countries all have mixed economies in which most resources are allocated by the market.

However, markets can fail – information failures being key – giving a robust case for public provision of health care and school education (see Barr, 2004, or, more briefly, Barr, 1998). Consider the following stylized facts about health care: consumers are imperfectly informed because much health care is highly technical; treatment is frequently not by choice but because of an external event, such as breaking a leg; and there is often only limited choice about the type of treatment. Much of the efficiency case for the National Health Service is based on these facts. With food, the story is different. We are generally well informed about what we like and about its costs, and there is considerable choice over how we meet those needs. These *technical* differences start to explain why we ensure access to health care by giving it to people (largely) free; with food, in contrast, we ensure that a person has access to nutrition by paying her a pension and letting her buy her own food at market prices.

In the case of school education, small children are not well informed; attendance is compulsory, so that education is consumed by all young people; for younger children, the range of choice about content is constrained; and a case can be made in terms of social cohesion for providing all children with a similar educational experience. These arguments and others provide a compelling case for publicly funded and publicly organized schools.

Higher education contrasts strongly. Students are generally well informed and can and should be made better informed. The process is assisted because going to university can be anticipated (unlike finding a doctor to deal with injury after a road accident), so that students have time to acquire the information they need, and time to seek advice. Second, people can choose whether or not to go to university – it is precisely that fact that has made taxpayer-funding of higher education so regressive. Finally, the choice of which subject to study and at which university is, quite properly, large and growing.

It can be argued that students are well informed, or potentially well informed, and hence better able than planners to make choices which conform with their own interests and those of the economy. To maintain otherwise is to argue that even with extensive regulation, students (the best and the brightest, by assumption) are unable to choose sensibly. The argument of well-informed choice is central, and underpins the efficiency case for variable fees in section II(v). It implies that price signals will be useful and hence that competition will improve welfare by making universities more responsive to the preferences of students and the needs of employers.

Though that proposition is robust, two caveats are discussed below. First, students from poorer backgrounds might not be fully informed, with implications for access generally and debt aversion in particular. Second, though the approach gives a greater role to students, employers, and universities in making choices about subject, content, and mix, it does not imply unrestricted markets. Rather, the analysis points to regulated markets.

(ii) Lesson 2: Graduates Should Share in the Costs of Higher Education

There are strong qualitative arguments that higher education creates benefits to society above those to the individual – benefits in terms of growth, social cohesion and the transmission of values (Bynner and Edgerton, 2001; Bynner *et al.*, 2003), and the development of knowledge for its own sake. Those arguments suggest that taxpayer subsidies to higher education should be a permanent part of the landscape. Quantifying those benefits, however, entails a series of difficulties, not least because it is hard to separate the effects of education from other determinants of a person's productivity.[4] Thus the division of costs between the taxpayer and the graduate – like the definition of poverty – has no definitive answer.

In contrast, there is much firmer evidence of the substantial private returns from a degree (e.g. Blundell *et al.*, 2000). Such estimates are based on data for an earlier, smaller cohort of graduates, suggesting that increased numbers may drive down those returns. But Blundell *et al.* rightly point out that the demand for graduates is also increasing. To the extent that demand and supply increase broadly in step, there is no reason why private returns should fall.

In sum, there is limited quantitative evidence of external benefits and robust evidence of private benefits. The latter suggests that it is efficient that graduates bear some of the costs. In that case, however, the design of student loans becomes critical.

(iii) Lesson 3: Well-designed Student Loans Have Core Characteristics

Discussion thus far argues for a graduate contribution for the following reasons.

- It is efficient in microeconomic terms because of the private benefits of a degree and, given earlier arguments, because price signals in higher education are useful.
- It is necessary for fiscal reasons, given the high cost of mass higher education and competing fiscal pressures, such as population ageing and combating social exclusion.
- It improves equity by reducing the regressivity of a system in which the degrees of mainly better-off people are paid for by people who on average are less well off.

This section argues that graduate contributions should be based on student loans which have income-contingent repayments, charge a rational interest rate, and are large enough to cover tuition charges and realistic living costs.

Income-contingent repayments
I have argued for many years (Barr, 1989), as have others before me (Friedman, 1955; Peacock and Wiseman, 1962; Prest, 1962; Glennerster *et al.*, 1968) that student loans should have income-contingent repayments, i.e. repayments calculated as x per cent of the borrower's subsequent earnings, collected alongside income tax or National Insurance contributions, until the borrower has repaid. There are both efficiency and equity arguments for that position.

Problems with conventional loans. It is useful to use a conventional loan – for example, to buy a house – as a benchmark. The loan will have a fixed duration (e.g. 25 years) and a positive interest rate. Monthly repayments are entirely determined by three variables: the size of the loan, its duration, and the interest rate. Apart from adjustments reflecting changes in the interest rate, the monthly repayment is fixed.
   Buying a house is a relatively low-risk activity.
(a) The buyer generally knows what he is buying, having lived in a house all his life.
(b) The house is unlikely to fall down.
(c) The real value of the house will generally increase.

(*d*) If income falls, making repayments problematic, he has the option to sell the house.

(*e*) Because the house acts as security for the loan, he can get a loan on good terms.

For these reasons, the market provides home loans. The contrast with lending to finance investment in human capital – for example, a university degree – is sharp.

Demand-side problems. Earlier discussion concluded that university students are well informed (element (*a*)). However, some people, particularly from poor backgrounds, may be poorly informed, an issue taken up in section II(v). In addition, all borrowers face risk and uncertainty because (*b*), (*c*), and (*d*), though true for housing, are less true for investment in skills. A qualification can 'fall down,' because a borrower may fail his exams. He still has to make loan repayments, but without the qualification that would have led to the increased earnings from which to make those repayments. Separately, even well-informed students face risk: though the average private return to investment in human capital is positive, there is considerable variation about that average. Finally (element (*d*)), someone who has borrowed to acquire a qualification, but then has low earnings and high repayments does not have the option to sell the qualification, further increasing exposure to risk.

For all these reasons, borrowing to finance investment in human capital exposes the borrower to more risk and uncertainty than borrowing to buy a house. The problem arises for all borrowers, and most acutely for those from poorer backgrounds. As a result, borrowing to finance investment in human capital will be inefficiently low.

Supply-side problems. Lenders also face risk and uncertainty. If I borrow to buy a house, the house acts as security. If I am unable to repay, the lender can repossess the house, sell it, and take what he is owed. Deliberate default is not a problem: though I could disappear, I could not take the house with me. For both reasons, loans are available on good terms. An analogous arrangement with human capital would allow the lender, if I default, to repossess my brain, sell it, and take what he is owed. That being ruled out, lenders have no security: they face uncertainty about the riskiness of an applicant – whether the person will acquire the qualification and whether their subsequent earnings will allow him or her to repay – and therefore charge a risk premium.[5] A risk premium assessed by a well-informed lender is efficient (analogous to higher automobile insurance premiums for bad drivers). But since lenders are not well informed about the riskiness of an applicant, they face incentives to cherry pick, i.e. to find ways of lending only to the best risks, analogous to private medical insurance. An obvious way to do so is to lend only to students who can provide security, e.g. a home-owning parent. The resulting lending will be inefficiently low.

Thus conventional loans lead to inefficiently low borrowing and lending. They are also inequitable. The various efficiency problems impact most on people from poor backgrounds, women, and ethnic minorities, who may be less well informed about the benefits of a qualification and therefore less prepared to risk a loan. In addition, these groups are likely to be on the wrong end of cherry picking.

The case for income-contingent loans. Income-contingent repayments have a profound effect in ways that are not widely understood (Barr, 1991, 2001a, ch. 12). Low earners make low or no repayments. People with low lifetime earnings do not fully repay. A larger loan (or a higher interest rate) has no effect on monthly repayments, which depend only on the person's income; instead, a person with a larger loan will repay for longer.

In efficiency terms, income-contingent loans are designed explicitly to protect borrowers from excessive risk; in equity terms, they assist access because they have built-in insurance against inability to repay. Following through the consumption-smoothing analogy, we pay National Insurance now to finance our pension later; income-contingent graduate contributions are the mirror-image.[6]

A rational interest rate

Well-designed loans have income-contingent repayments. They should also charge a rational interest rate. However, many schemes incorporate an interest subsidy whose aim is to promote access by preventing excessive debt. The aim is commendable, but blanket interest subsidies will not achieve it. Like many price distortions, they cause inefficiency and inequity. Current UK arrangements, like those in some other countries (e.g. Australia), charge a zero real interest rate.

The first resulting problem is cost. In the UK, about one-third of all money lent to students is not repaid because of the subsidy, partly because loans extend over a long duration, and partly because of arbitrage (i.e. students who do not need the loan nevertheless borrowing as much as they are allowed and putting the money into a savings account to make a profit). Second, the subsidy impedes quality because student support, being politically salient, crowds out the funding of universities. Third, it impedes access: loans are expensive, therefore rationed and therefore too small.

Finally, interest subsidies are deeply regressive. They do not help students (graduates make repayments, not students). They help low-earning graduates only slightly, since unpaid debt is eventually forgiven. They do not help high-earning graduates early in their careers: with income-contingent loans, monthly repayments depend only on earnings; interest rates only affect the duration of the loan. Thus the major beneficiaries are successful professionals in mid-career, whose loan repayments are switched off earlier because of the subsidy (for fuller discussion, see Barr, 2003, section 4.3).

The discussion thus far leads to the question of what interest rate is efficient. The simplest arrangement would charge the government's cost of borrowing. If all students repaid in full, this would make it possible for the loan to stand on its own feet. In practice, however, there will be losses because of low lifetime earnings, early death, etc. – such non-repayment being a deliberate design feature of income-contingent loans. The taxpayer could cover those losses, as currently in the UK. Alternatively, the cohort of borrowers could cover at least some of the loss through what is, in effect, a form of social insurance. In New Zealand in the 1990s, for example, the interest rate on student loans was set about 1 per cent above the government's cost of borrowing, thus, according to official estimates, covering about half the loss on the portfolio, the taxpayer covering the remaining loss.[7] There is also a case, discussed in section II(v), for interest subsidies targeted at low earners.

Large enough to cover tuition fees and realistic living costs
Loans are an instrument for consumption smoothing. Where there are no distortions such as interest subsidies, the amount people choose to borrow should not be strongly constrained. An implication is that loans should be large enough to cover tuition fees and realistic living costs, resolving such problems as student poverty, excessive reliance on expensive credit-card debt, long hours spent earning money, and/or forced reliance on family support. A ceiling on borrowing each year and on the number of years for which a student may borrow would offer protection against improvidence.

Entitlement to a loan that covers all costs is not an argument against earning opportunities or family support, but for allowing individuals to make choices in the face of an efficient budget constraint (for fuller discussion, see Barr, 1993). A rational interest rate – another price signal – is thus central to ensuring adequate student support.

(iv) The Balance between Market and State

As discussed in section II(i), the case against central planning does not mean, and should not mean, that government is marginalized.

Part of the government's role is to empower demand:

- as partial funder of higher education, not least because of its external benefits;
- as organizer of student loans, to provide a mechanism for individual consumption smoothing in the face of the capital-market imperfections discussed earlier;[8]
- as promoter of access. Options for consumption smoothing may be sufficient for people who are well-informed, but further action, including grants and other activities discussed in section II(v), is necessary for those who are not.

On the supply side, government has a role:

- as regulator, to ensure that satisfactory quality assurance is in place. Consumers may be well-informed, but that does not mean that they are perfectly informed, justifying quality assurance for reasons of consumer protection. But this task does not necessarily mean a state-run bureaucracy (Brown, 2000). A minimalist approach would require universities to publish timely, accurate performance data on their web sites – for example, the destinations of its recent graduates – giving prospective students the information they need to vote with their feet;[9]
- as setter of incentives. In addition to targeting resources at particular individuals for reasons of access, government properly sets incentives in other ways. It can target resources at particular subjects. Even if we agree that students and employers are well informed, that does not deny government the right to have views about subject mix. It can be argued that subjects such as accounting, law, and economics can look after themselves. But governments might wish to target additional resources at subjects such as classics,

music, or drama, or (a perennial worry of governments) at engineering. Government might also wish to target resources at particular
institutions for reasons of regional balance.

One further set of incentives – the degree of competition – requires
separate discussion. At one extreme, the government could intervene
only minimally on the supply side. Universities would compete for
students; those attracting large numbers flourish and expand, those
failing to do so go to the wall. Universities, however, are not the conventional firms of economic theory: they do not make a homogeneous
product; they do not maximize profit; and the 'product' is not well
defined (see Winston, 1999). Thus red-in-tooth-and-claw competition is
not the best environment for higher education. But this is not the only
approach. The more government ties funding to specific subjects or
institutions, the less powerful is competition – in the extreme, mim-
icking a system of central planning. Competition is more usefully
thought of as a continuum, from completely unconstrained (law of the
jungle) to 100 per cent constrained (pure central planning), or any-
where in between.

The approach thus allows intervention to foster both distributional
and educational objectives. The system can be as redistributive as desired; and the degree of competition is a policy variable, with different
answers possible for different subjects. The resulting system is efficient,
because outcomes are determined not by a single, dominant – and often
badly informed and ineffective – arm of government, but by the inter-
acting decisions of students, universities, and employers, subject to
transparent influence by government. Particularly with complex mass
systems of higher education, this approach is more likely than central
planning to achieve individual and national objectives.

(v) A General Funding Strategy

The preceding analysis points to a strategy with three elements: variable fees (i.e. prices) assist the efficient allocation of resources within
higher education; well-designed loans provide consumption smoothing, thereby assisting efficient allocation over a person's life cycle; and
measures to promote access improve equity.

Leg 1. Variable fees
Universities should be free to vary their tuition fees, though, as discussed later, there is a case for a ceiling. Students should be helped to

pay through Legs 2 and 3, discussed below. Charges should be deferred: thus graduates make repayments, not students.

Variable fees – not least because they are so contentious in Europe (though taken for granted in the USA) – require careful justification.

The efficiency case. A major conclusion of the theoretical argument in section II(i) is that price signals are useful in higher education, improving efficiency and, through competition, making the system more responsive to student and employer preferences.

Resources are misallocated if students face no price signals between subjects. Employers want people with quantitative skills and computer literacy. Both mathematics and engineering graduates have these skills, but one degree is considerably more expensive than the other. In the absence of price signals, students are indifferent; the taxpayer is not.

The same is true of the choice of university: a well-taught cheaper course at a local university might well suit a student better than a more expensive course; there are gains for the student, the taxpayer, and (through increased competition) the higher education system if the student can give the right signal in responding to the price mechanism.

As well as distorting demand, fixed prices also have adverse effects on the supply side. Price ceilings erode incentives to improve quality (whose costs cannot be covered by price increases); price floors erode incentives to increased efficiency (whose benefits cannot be appropriated through lower prices). Flat fees, including zero fees, are both a floor and a ceiling, and thus particularly inimical to efficiency gains.

These arguments are rooted in the economics of information, not in ideology. The argument that price should have no effect on a student's choice of subject or university is wrong because it uses a price subsidy to pursue equity objectives. This is inefficient and, as argued shortly, also inequitable.

The previous paragraphs relate to microeconomic efficiency. A second efficiency aspect is more macroeconomic, in that variable fees make funding open ended. With flat fees, the Treasury controls the funding envelope. If tax funding falls (for example, because of the competing claims of nursery education and health care), so does university income – the example of Australia, discussed later, being a case in point. With variable fees, in contrast, funding is open ended. Universities have at least some autonomy over their income stream.

The equity case. Perhaps counter-intuitively, variable fees are not only more efficient than flat fees, but also fairer, notably by facilitating redistribution from better-off to worse-off. One of my earliest newspaper articles criticized the 1974 Labour government for restoring universal milk subsidies. The aim was to help the poor, but the subsidy was worth more to the middle class because they drank more milk. Much more progressive to have charged an unsubsidized price and used the resulting savings to increase pensions, child benefit, and poverty relief.

Variable fees replace the former strategy, price subsidies for milk, by the latter, income transfers targeted at particular people. The strategy has two elements.

- Variable fees introduce higher charges for those who can afford them (note that with income-contingent loans, 'can afford' refers to a person's earnings as a graduate, not to family circumstances while a student).
- Redistributive policies help poor people to pay those charges.

To an economist, these elements are staggeringly familiar: the first, a price increase, represents a movement *along* the demand curve. Taken alone, this element would harm access. However (*a*) the fees are deferred (Leg 2, below), and (*b*), there are targeted transfers to groups for whom access is fragile (Leg 3). This moves their demand curve *outward*.

Thus the strategy is deeply progressive. It shifts resources from today's best-off (who lose some of their fee subsidies) to today's worst-off (who receive a grant) and tomorrow's worst-off (who, with income-contingent repayments, do not repay their loan in full).

As well as redistributing between people, variable fees facilitate redistribution between institutions. With flat fees or tax funding, the volume of resources going to the sector is fixed by government, so that prestigious universities and local institutions compete for the same pot of money in a zero sum game. Variable fees start to address this gridlock.

Third, variable fees are directly fairer. Flat fees force someone going to a small local university to pay the same fee as someone going to an internationally renowned one. This is inequitable. With the milk subsidy, at least everyone got broadly the same quality of milk. In countries with a diverse higher education system, charging everyone the same fee is more like taxing beer to subsidize champagne.

A fourth part of the equity puzzle arises if a country controls fees for home students but allows greater freedom for overseas students. In the UK context, this causes a problem that was both predictable and predicted:

> A further impediment to access is the incentive to discriminate against British students. A flat fee will continue the erosion of quality at the best universities, which face the biggest shortfalls in funding. British students could suffer in one of two ways. The quality of the best institutions might fall; though British students could still get places, the quality of the degree would be less. Alternatively, the best institutions will largely stop teaching British undergraduates (for whom they receive on average £4,000 per year) and will use the fees from foreign undergraduates (around £8,000 per year) to preserve their excellence. The government is considering trying to prevent British universities from charging additional fees to UK/EU students. ... [This] ends up harming the very people it is aimed at helping. (Barr and Crawford, 1998, p. 80)

Variable fees, by reducing or eliminating the price differential, avoid such discrimination.

The resulting landscape. Each university sets a fee for each of its degrees, though, for the reasons set out in section III(i), subject to a maximum. Fees would be influenced by the level of demand for each degree and by its cost. Demand would be influenced by educational factors (the university's reputation for teaching, completion rates, subsequent destinations, and employment rates) and by broader aspects (ancient buildings, access to the city centre).

Under such a system, economics at Oxford might charge a higher fee than classics, with potential adverse effects on staff–student ratios in classics and on the ability of students from poor backgrounds to afford economics. These are valid worries in a pure market system. That, however, is not the model to which economic theory points. The major continuing role of government was discussed earlier, notably in promoting access and through its ability to target resources at particular subjects, for example classics. The result is a market that can make beneficial use of price signals, but a regulated market. In an English context, universities will have more freedom, but constrained by the Higher Education Funding Council, the Access Regulator, and the fees cap.

Why not fees decided by government? As argued in section II(i), with a mass and diverse higher education system, the problem is too complex for a central planner to decide the different efficient price for each degree at each university. Why not flat fees that rise over time? As argued above, this is equivalent to a simultaneous price floor and price ceiling.

Variable fees alone, however, would impede access – hence the other two legs of the strategy.

Leg 2. A well-designed loan scheme

Loans should have income-contingent repayments and should charge an interest rate broadly equal to the government's cost of borrowing. The full loan should be large enough to cover tuition fees and realistic living costs, and all students should be eligible for a full loan, i.e. entitlement should not be income tested. As a result, higher education is free at the point of use, unless students choose to pay in part through earning activities or family support. With a rational interest rate, there is no major distortion to such choices.

Some amplification is needed about interest rates. The default rate should be related to the government's cost of borrowing. However, if someone has extended spells out of the labour force, his or her loan can spiral upwards. In terms of strict rationality that should not matter, since repayments will never exceed x per cent of monthly earnings; and if the person never fully repays that is not a problem. But in practice, large nominal debts worry people. Thus, though there is a strong case against blanket interest subsidies, there are good arguments for targeted subsidies, discussed below, for people with low earnings or out of the labour force.

Leg 3. Action to promote access

At this stage we return to the debate about whether ability to pay should be assessed relative to a student's current income, i.e. where he starts from, or his future income, i.e. where he ends up? The latter is philosophically appealing, and it is therefore sometimes argued (a) that income-contingent loans have built-in insurance against inability to repay and, to that extent, are a no-lose bet, and therefore (b) that provided loans are large enough to make higher education free at the point of use, such loans are all that is needed. Leg 2 is sufficient.

If all students were well informed, that argument would be strong, and consumption smoothing through income-contingent loans would be all that is necessary. But not all potential students are well informed. In particular, if they underestimate the benefits of higher education and/or overestimate the costs, it might be rational for them, *given what they know*, to be unwilling to take out a loan. This is the origin of so-called debt aversion.

Addressing the problem requires measures to tackle exclusion which, it can be argued, has three roots: financial poverty, information poverty, and poor school education.

Measures to address financial poverty should be wide-ranging.

* An income-tested stipend for children above the minimum school leaving age would encourage them to complete school.
* An income-tested grant should cover some or all costs at university. There are advantages in offering full scholarships to first-year students from poor backgrounds, who may not be well informed about whether they are well suited to university. By the end of their first year they are no longer badly informed and, if doing well, are more prepared to finance the rest of their degree, at least in part, through a loan.
* Both policies could be supported by financial incentives to universities to widen participation, and by extra resources to provide additional intellectual support at university for students from disadvantaged backgrounds.

A second set of money measures supports access by offering assistance for people with low incomes after graduation.

* Targeted interest subsidies could freeze the real value of debt of people with low earnings, including people who are unemployed.
* People with low lifetime earnings could be protected by writing off any loan not repaid after (say) 25 years.
* The loans of workers in the public sector could be progressively written off. In the UK, 10 per cent of the loan of new teachers in shortage subjects is written off for each year in the state system. That scheme could be extended to other groups.
* People caring for young children or elderly dependants could be granted loan remission – for example, 10 per cent of outstanding debt for each year caring for a pre-school child and 5 per cent per year if the child is of school age.

Information poverty, the second strategic impediment to access, is inadequately emphasized. Action to inform school children and raise their aspirations is therefore critical. The saddest impediment to access is someone who has never even thought of going to university.

Finally, problems of university access cannot be solved entirely within the higher education sector. More resources are needed earlier in the system, not least because of the growing evidence (Feinstein, 2003) that the roots of exclusion lie in early childhood.

III. LESSONS FROM COUNTRY EXPERIENCE

Country experience supports the strategy just discussed.[10]

(i) Financing Universities: Lessons about Fees

Three lessons should be pondered: fees relax the supply-side constraint; big-bang liberalization is politically destabilizing; but no liberalization is also a mistake.

Fees relax the supply-side constraint
The funding of higher education faces a paradox. Large taxpayer subsidies can create supply-side constraints because of the desire to contain public spending. Where qualified students have no automatic entitlement to a place, the constraint takes the form of a view (typically by the Treasury) about student numbers. The result can be a high-quality system, but one which turns away qualified applicants. In countries where students have a right to a place, cost containment impacts mainly on quality. In contrast, in countries which offer less public funding per student (e.g. the USA), there are no externally imposed supply-side constraints. Unless limited taxpayer funding is sufficiently redistributive, however, students from lower-income backgrounds will be deterred from applying. Thus high subsidies can harm access on the supply side, but their absence can harm it on the demand side. This is the dilemma which Legs 2 and 3 of the strategy are designed to alleviate.

Table 1 shows public and private spending on higher education in OECD countries, and also participation rates. Given the differences in country systems and in definitions, comparisons should not be pushed too far. However, in a range of countries (Australia, New Zealand, Korea, and (from other data sources) Canada and the USA), high private spending goes along with high participation rates. A few countries combine high participation with little private spending, notably Finland and Sweden, but only because those are the two countries with the

Table 1   Spending on Tertiary Education and Participation Rates, OECD

| | Spending as % of GDP, 2000 | | | |
	Public	Private	Total	Net entry rate 2001[a]
Australia	0.8	0.7	1.6	65
Austria	1.2	0.0	1.2	34
Belgium	1.2	0.1	1.3	32
Canada	1.6	1.0	2.6	n.a.
Czech Republic	0.8	0.1	0.9	30
Denmark	1.5	0.0	1.6	44
Finland	1.7	0.0	1.7	72
France	1.0	0.1	1.1	37
Germany	1.0	0.1	1.0	32
Greece	0.9	negligible	0.9	n.a.
Hungary	0.9	0.3	1.1	56
Iceland	0.8	0.0	0.9	61
Ireland	1.2	0.3	1.5	38
Italy	0.7	0.1	0.9	44
Japan	0.5	0.6	1.1	41
Korea	0.6	1.9	2.6	49
Mexico	0.8	0.2	1.1	25
Netherlands	1.0	0.2	1.2	54
New Zealand	0.9	n.a.	0.9	76
Norway	1.2	negligible	1.3	62
Poland	0.8	n.a.	0.8	67
Portugal	1.0	0.1	1.1	n.a.
Slovak Republic	0.7	0.1	0.8	40
Spain	0.9	0.3	1.2	48
Sweden	1.5	0.2	1.7	69
Switzerland	1.2	n.a.	1.2	33
Turkey	1.0	negligible	1.0	20
United Kingdom	0.7	0.3	1.0	45
United States	0.9	1.8	2.7	42
OECD average	0.9	0.9	1.7	47

Notes: [a] The net entry rate is based on the probability of a 17-year-old entering higher education for the first time by the age of 30. n.a. = not available. Numbers do not always add up, due to rounding.
Source: OECD (2003).

highest public spending on higher education – levels that might be unsustainable given other budgetary demands and international competitive pressures.

What matters is not only the total amount of private spending, but also how it is determined. With flat fees, government controls total funding. If fees go up and public spending on higher education declines, all that happens is a change in balance between public and private funding. In 1989, Australia introduced centrally-set tuition fees to address a funding crisis. Over the years, fee income increased but tax funding fell back. By 2000, the system was back in crisis, leading to reform, announced in 2003, partially liberalizing fees.

Big-bang liberalization can be politically destabilizing
In 1992, New Zealand introduced twin reforms: fees set by universities, with no constraint on fee levels; and student loans which (*a*) had income-contingent repayments, (*b*) charged a positive real interest rate related to the government's cost of borrowing, and (*c*) covered all fees and realistic living costs.

On the face of it, these arrangements were close to the strategy outlined above, but mistakes were made. First, reform was to some extent big-bang. Student loans were new, and fees, though not new, were fully liberalized. Second, though the system included targeted interest subsidies for low earners, more could have been done. In addition, the third leg of the strategy – active measures to promote access – was not strongly emphasized. Fourth, and equally important, the politics were not handled well: the government treated reform as an event not a process and, having implemented the reforms, stopped campaigning for them; in particular, the government did not do enough to explain to students and parents the considerable advantages of income-contingent repayments. As a result, when nominal student debt rose over the years, worried middle-class parents created political pressures. The scheme was diluted in 2000 (for assessments, see Larocque, 2003; McLaughlin, 2003).

Without liberalization quality and access suffer
The opposite policy direction – no liberalization – is equally a mistake. 'Free' higher education or low fixed fees create two problems. Quality suffers because the education budget has to compete with other budgetary imperatives; and, within the education budget, universities compete with nursery education, school education, and vocational training. As a result, real funding per student declines.

Access also suffers. If places are scarce, it will disproportionately be middle-class students who get them; and if places are not scarce, the need to finance a mass system typically means that resources for the pro-access strategy are limited.

(ii) Student Support: Lessons about Loans

This section focuses on four lessons: income-contingent loans do not harm access; interest subsidies are expensive; positive real interest rates are politically feasible; and the design of the student loan contract matters.

Income-contingent loans do not harm access
Australia introduced a system of income-contingent loans in 1989 to cover a newly introduced tuition charge, and thus offers the longest historical record. Chapman (1997; see also Chapman and Ryan, 2003) notes the increase in overall participation since 1989 and finds, superimposed on that trend, that women's participation grew more strongly than men's, and that the system did not discourage participation by people in the lowest socioeconomic groups. Similarly, though participation by Maoris and Pacific Islanders needs continuing work (McLaughlin, 2003, p. 37), participation in New Zealand since the introduction of fees has increased for all groups.

There are two sets of reasons why we should expect these results. First, the income-contingent mechanism is designed explicitly to reduce the risks borrowers face. Second, fees supported by loans free resources to promote access.

A recent study emanating from Statistics Canada offers empirical support for the overall strategy in section II(v). Canada liberalized fees (Leg 1) in the early 1990s with no changes to Legs 2 and 3. Predictably, access suffered. In the mid-1990s, the loan limits on the student loan scheme were raised, with knock-on increases in other forms of loan and student support. Again, predictably, access improved, notwithstanding that the Canadian loan scheme is not income-contingent. The report concluded that:

> There is a clear positive correlation between parental income and university attendance, and this correlation ... became stronger during the mid-1990s when tuition fees began increasing significantly. This change reflected declines in participation rates of youth from middle income families. ... The correlation, however, declined during the latter half of the decade reflecting rises in participation of those from the lowest income groups. This pattern is consistent with the fact that the changes in the Canada Student Loans Program raising the maximum amount of loan occurred only after tuition fees had already begun to rise. (Corak *et al.*, 2003, p. 14)

Interest subsidies are expensive
Simulations by Barr and Falkingham (1993, 1996) found that for every 100 the government lends, only about 50 is repaid. Of the missing 50, 20 is lost because some graduates have low lifetime earnings and so never repay their loan in full, and 30 is not repaid because of the interest subsidy. In other words, the interest subsidy converts nearly one-third of the loan into a grant. Sales of student debt by the UK government in the late 1990s offer independent evidence. The debt was sold for about 50 per cent of its face value. Official estimates suggest that of the missing 50, about 15 was because of low lifetime income, etc., and 35 because of the interest subsidy. The evidence is compelling because the two sets of results are independent, the latter with a market test.

New Zealand offers parallel evidence. A government elected in 1999 acted early on a manifesto commitment. It introduced an interest subsidy in the form of a zero *nominal* interest rate while a student was still at university (previously a real interest rate was charged from the time the student took out the loan). In addition, the real interest rate charged after graduation was frozen at somewhat below its previous rate. The impact of these changes was startling. Previously, according to official estimates, of every 100 that was lent, 90 would be repaid. As a result of the changes, it was estimated that only 77 out of every 100 would be repaid (New Zealand Ministry of Education, 2002, p. 7). The change is so expensive precisely because the subsidy to students while still at university applies to *all* students. A key message is that seemingly small adjustments can be very expensive.

Not least for these reasons, an official inquiry, echoing the discussion in section II(iii), concluded:

> Participation goals should continue to be supported through a Student Loan Scheme with income-contingent repayments as at present. The Commission believes, however, that the current policy of writing off interest on loans for ... students while they are studying is not an effective use of the government's resources. While this policy has decreased the length of time taken to repay loans after graduation, it has also led to an increase in the number of students taking out loans and in the overall level of student debt. To compound matters, the policy has made it possible for learners to borrow money and invest it for private gain (arbitrage). Consequently, the Commission believes that this policy should be discontinued – or that, as a minimum, the incentives for arbitrage should be removed. Any savings ... should be reinvested in the tertiary education system and be used for the benefit of students. (New Zealand Tertiary Education Advisory Commission, 2001, p. 14)

Positive real interest rates are feasible
In the Netherlands and Sweden (and, no doubt, elsewhere), as in New Zealand until the changes in 2000, a real interest rate is charged from the moment the student takes out the loan, both matters which are taken for granted. As noted earlier, with income-contingent loans a higher interest rate does not increase a graduate's monthly repayments, only the duration of the loan.

Contract design is important
International labour mobility is high and, with EU enlargement, likely to increase, raising questions about potential default if a person emigrates. In Australia, loan repayments are part of a person's tax liability, so that someone outside the Australian tax net has no liability to make repayments. With interest subsidies this is a costly error. In the UK, in contrast, there is an explicit loan contract which includes the collection of repayments through the tax system, but does not exempt a person outside the UK from making repayments. Clearly, default and administrative costs are higher for people working abroad, but the effect is not large. Certainly there is no question of emigration causing a repayment black hole.

IV. THE 2004 REFORMS IN THE UK

(i) Assessment

Reforms in 1998 brought in income-contingent loans, for which loud cheers.[11] Beyond that, however, the system had serious problems (Barr and Crawford, 1998; Barr, 2002):

- central planning continued;
- fees were introduced, set by central government and the same for all subjects at all universities, and fees were an upfront charge, since there was no loan to cover them;
- loans displayed serious design problems – they were too small to cover realistic living costs (let alone fees), and incorporated an interest subsidy;
- on the access front, the 1998 reforms abolished the previous system of grants which partially covered a student's living costs.

I strongly support the UK reforms of 2004 because they address most of these problems (see Barr, 2003). They simultaneously conform with the strategy in section II(v), based on economic theory, and accommodate the main lessons from country experience. Other countries had attempted to move in the same direction for the same reasons (Commonwealth of Australia, 1998; New Zealand Ministry of Education, 1998), but were unable to move forward for a variety of reasons, not least political opposition.

Leg 1. Tuition fees
From 2006, the reforms replace the upfront flat fee with a variable fee between 0 and £3,000 per year. Within those limits each university can set the fee for each of its courses. Students can pay the fee upfront or take out a loan. In the latter case, the student loans administration pays the fee directly to the university, whose financial position is therefore independent of how students choose to pay their fees.

As discussed earlier, variable fees improve efficiency by making funding open-ended, hence increasing the volume of resources going to higher education and, by strengthening competition, improve the efficiency with which those resources are used. Both trends are assisted by appropriate regulation, for example the cap on the maximum fee.

The equity advantages of variable fees were also discussed earlier. They contribute to access by redistributing from better-off to worse-off; they facilitate redistribution from universities with more market power to those with less; they are directly fairer, in that students do not have to pay the same fee at a small local university as at an internationally famous one; and they reduce discrimination against home students if there is a differential between home and overseas fees.

Alongside these advantages of principle, the fees regime also draws on international experience by liberalizing fees, but not completely. The fees cap is crucial in this context. It should ideally be high enough (*a*) to pay the best universities the rate for the job and (*b*) to bring in competition, but low enough (*c*) to ensure that the new regime is politically sustainable by giving students and parents time to adjust, and (*d*) to give universities time to put in place management suitable for a competitive environment.

Leg 2. Loans
The 1998 reforms introduced income-contingent loans, but they did not cover tuition fees and were too small to cover realistic living costs. The 2004 reforms improve the system by extending loans to cover tuition

fees and by increasing the loan for living costs. They also raise the threshold at which loan repayments start: from 2006, graduates will repay 9 per cent of earnings above £15,000 per year, up from £10,000.

From the point of view of the student, the situation is little different from the days of 'free' higher education: their fees are paid on their behalf, and money is paid into their bank accounts to cover living costs. From the point of view of the graduate, the arrangements are like a system financed out of income tax, except that the repayments (*a*) are only made by people who have been to university and benefited financially and (*b*) do not go on forever.

Notwithstanding public anxiety, these repayments should not be exaggerated. The taxpayer will continue to pay the bulk of the costs of higher education. And a loan of (say) £20,000 should not be daunting compared with other expenditure: over a 40-year career, a typical current graduate will pay (in cash terms) about £850,000 in income tax and National Insurance contributions,[12] and will spend about £½ million on food. As an alternative comparator, it is possible to pay off £10,000 of student debt in about 10 years by giving up a smoking habit of 20 cigarettes per day (Barr, 2003, para. 84). Part of the problem is that people continue to conflate credit-card debt (rightly a concern to parents), with income-contingent loan repayments.

In one important respect, however, the loan arrangements conform neither with theory nor country best practice – the 2004 reforms continue the interest subsidy.

Leg 3. Action to promote access
Grants to cover at least part of living costs, abolished in 1998, will be restored. From 2006, students from poor backgrounds will be entitled to a grant of £2,700 per year, in addition to a loan;[13] and universities charging fees of £3,000 will be expected to provide students from poor backgrounds with bursaries of at least £300 per year to help to pay those fees. The intention is that no student from a poor background will be made worse-off by the reforms.

The Act also brings in an Access Regulator, whose formal task is to ensure that institutions have satisfactory plans to widen access as a *quid pro quo* for charging higher fees. Those plans can include scholarships for students from poor backgrounds; importantly, they can also include outreach to schools to improve the information available to schoolchildren.

(ii) Remaining Issues

In sum, the arrangements, which are intended to come fully into effect in 2006, bring in additional resources and strengthen competition, both of which contribute to quality, and redistribute from better- to worse-off, contributing to access. Those desirable features do not, however, mean that the scheme is perfect.

Fees
The desirability of a cap on fees was discussed earlier. Some commentators argue that the cap is too low and/or that it will be kept at £3,000 for too long (roughly the life of a Parliament). This is a balancing act. If the cap is too high, it risks destabilizing the system politically, but if it is too low for too long, most universities will charge the maximum, approximating a system of flat fees. The result would be to reintroduce closed-ended funding and to restore central planning by the back door.

Loans
Notwithstanding the improvements, loans display continuing problems. The interest subsidy is expensive and regressive. In addition, the reforms raised the threshold at which graduates start to make repayments. The change reduces the repayments of all graduates, hence increases the average duration of repayment, and hence increases the leakage caused by the interest subsidy.

Digging more deeply, matters are even worse. Student loans are currently off-budget. Thus eliminating the interest subsidy yields saving only off-budget. Redirecting those savings towards larger grants (for example) would involve on-budget spending; that is, would increase measured public spending.

What is needed, therefore, is a twofold reform: eliminating the blanket interest subsidy and replacing it by a targeted subsidy; and bringing loans on-budget for reasons of rational public budgeting.[14] These reforms would make it possible to offer somewhat larger loans, and to offer all students a full loan; they would also free considerable resources for pro-access policies.

Access measures
More could be done to protect low-earning graduates as described in section II(v); for example, targeted interest subsidies, loan-write-off for

some public-sector workers, and loan remission for people undertaking caring activities.

A second area of potential progress is to address public concerns by improving information. Some of these worries are that:

- the new system will leave students with large debts;
- higher participation will lower the return to getting a degree;
- student debt will make it harder to get a mortgage;
- variable fees are inequitable;
- variable fees will harm access;
- variable fees will create a two-tier system;
- it is morally wrong to charge for higher education.
- this is the start of a slippery slope.

Some of these concerns have been discussed in this paper. For responses to the others, see Barr (2003, paras 121–30).

V. THE UNFINISHED AGENDA

Economic theory and practical experience offer solutions to avoidable problems: (*a*) unsustainable public spending; (*b*) public spending which is hijacked by the middle class; (*c*) loans absent, or badly designed, so that they bring in few, if any, extra resources; (*d*) economic constraints on universities, which reduce incentives to efficiency; and (*e*) specific design features that are costly (interest subsidies), administratively demanding (income testing), or both.

These are widespread in OECD countries, though (*b*) and (*d*) are less of a problem in countries which allow variable fees. They also occur elsewhere: an account of Latin America reported that

Most of the public institutions ... have argued that low or no tuition fees have provided greater equality of educational opportunity by providing greater access. ... Such reasoning is simply incorrect ... the overwhelming public subsidy has been and continues to accrue to students from middle and high-income families. (Lewis, 1999)

The policy in section II(v) is designed as a strategic whole explicitly to address these problems. Each of the elements – deferred variable fees, income-contingent loans, and active measures to promote access – can be crafted in various ways and with differing weights, to reflect differences in national objectives and different constraints. Broadly, the strategy is applicable to any country which can do an effective job in collecting income tax – and hence student loan repayments.

The three elements offer a benchmark against which countries could assess future policy directions. The USA, for example, does well on Leg 1 (variable fees) but less well on Leg 2 (loans are not income-contingent, nor collected as a payroll deduction, and generally attract an interest subsidy) and Leg 3 (where scholarship arrangements can be criticized both for parsimony and complexity). Canada, too, might consider action on the second leg. Australia has recently moved partially to liberalize fees under Leg 1, but its loan scheme, though with income-contingent repayments collected by the tax authorities, does not cover living costs for most students, and continues to include a blanket interest subsidy. New Zealand came close to getting all three elements right in the 1990s but was burnt by moving too fast. Most countries in mainland Western Europe and in the Nordic countries have yet to address fees under Leg 1, and with few exceptions, have work to do on the loans front.

In these Western countries, the unfinished agenda has more to do with politics and administration than with policy.

- In many of the European countries, tuition fees for higher education are a no-go area – a Nordic education minister used the word 'taboo.' The British government showed considerable courage in addressing these serious political obstacles. Other governments will have to do the same, sooner or later. Their task should be made easier by the example of countries such as England, Canada, Australia, and New Zealand.
- Greater public understanding both of the centrality of higher education and of the nature of income-contingent repayments has thus far been slow in coming, and merits continuing effort.
- International cooperation in collecting loan repayments (discussed briefly in Barr, 2001a, ch. 14) requires attention with increasing urgency as international labour mobility increases both generally and within the wider EU.

Outside the OECD a challenge that continues to haunt commentators is how to design a loan scheme which mimics income-contingent repayments in poorer countries with a large informal sector and only limited capacity to collect income tax. This is, perhaps, the greatest challenge of all.

Notes

Originally published in *Oxford Review of Economic Policy* 20:2 (2004); © Oxford University Press and the Oxford Review of Economic Policy Limited 2004; reprinted with permission.

1 This paper draws on Iain Crawford's and my 15-year collaboration (see Barr and Crawford, 2005), on assistance from Colin Ward and his team at the Student Loans Company on factual matters and administrative feasibility, and on work by the three of us advising the Hungarian government. I am also grateful for helpful comments from Howard Glennerster, Michael Shattock, the editors, and an anonymous referee, and for help on factual matters from officials at the New Zealand Ministry of Education.

2 'Prince William's university has been fined £175,000 for attracting too many students. Applications ... leapt by 45 per cent after it was revealed that the prince planned to start his studies there last autumn. However, higher education funding rules penalize universities that exceed their recruitment targets.' (*Independent* (London), 29 March 2002)

3 A prized possession is the photograph I took of the 14 filing cabinets of material for the 3½ day visit to assess LSE's teaching of politics in October 2000.

4 The screening hypothesis argues, first, that education beyond a basic level does not increase individual productivity and, second, that firms seek high-ability workers but are unable, prior to employing them, to distinguish them from those with low ability. Individuals, therefore, have an incentive to make themselves distinctive by some sort of signal. According to the screening hypothesis, post-primary education fills exactly that function: it gives a signal to prospective employers. Just as an individual's good health may be due more to a strong constitution than to medical care, so, according to this view, is productivity the result of natural ability rather than post-primary education.

5 The problem is compounded by adverse selection; see Barr (2001*a*, pp. 177–8).

6 It was for this reason that my first specific UK proposal (Barr, 1989) argued that income-contingent repayments should be an add-on to National Insurance contributions, an idea originally suggested by Mervyn King.

7 In New Zealand the Student Loan Scheme Act 1992 requires that the Student Loan Scheme interest rates be set annually and that, in determining the rates, the Governor-General has regard to, but shall not be bound by: 'the movements, as determined by the Government Statistician, that have occurred in the Consumers Price Index in the year to the 30th day of September immediately preceding the making of the regulations' and 'the costs to the Crown of the Student Loan Scheme, including the cost of Government borrowing in the year to the 30th day of September immedi-

ately preceding the making of the regulations'. In the later 1990s, the interest rate was based on the 10-year bond rate.

8 See Palacios (2004) for a proposed arrangement for private income-contingent loans.

9 Students themselves are an important source of information. Student satisfaction is not all that matters, but that is not a reason for ignoring it. The 2004 UK legislation includes help for student organizations in gathering relevant information.

10 For a survey of higher-education finance in different countries, see UK Department for Education and Skills (2003).

11 Repayments were 9 per cent of income above £10,000 per year.

12 Dearden *et al.* (2004) estimate payments of income tax and National Insurance contributions of £330,000. Their figure is lower than mine mainly because it (*a*) covers a shorter time period, (*b*) is in real terms, and (*c*) starts from a lower starting salary. The point is not the exact number, but that loan repayments are small relative to income tax and National Insurance contributions.

13 Students receiving the maximum grant are entitled to a somewhat reduced loan.

14 For more detailed discussion of targeted interest subsidies and a critique of the Education Department's position, see Barr (2003, paras 104–20); see also UK Education and Skills Select Committee (2003).

References

Barr, N. (1989), *Student Loans: The Next Steps*, Aberdeen University Press for the David Hume Institute and the Suntory–Toyota International Centre for Economics and Related Disciplines, London School of Economics and Political Science.

– (1991), 'Income-contingent Student Loans: An Idea Whose Time Has Come,' in G.K. Shaw (ed.), *Economics, Culture and Education: Essays in Honour of Mark Blaug*, Cheltenham, Edward Elgar, 155–70; reprinted in Barr (2001*b*, Vol. III, 583–600).

– (1993), 'Alternative Funding Resources for Higher Education,' *The Economic Journal*, **103**(418), 718–28; reprinted in C.R. Belfield and H. M. Levin (eds), *The Economics of Higher Education*, The International Library of Critical Writings in Economics 165, Cheltenham and Northampton, MA, Edward Elgar, 534–44.

– (1998), 'Towards a "Third Way": Rebalancing the Role of the State,' *New Economy*, **4**(2), 71–6.

– (2001*a*), *The Welfare State as Piggy Bank: Information, Risk, Uncertainty, and the Role of the State*, London and New York, Oxford University Press.

– (ed.) (2001*b*), *Economic Theory and the Welfare State, Vol. I: Theory, Vol. II: Income Transfers, and Vol. III: Benefits in Kind*, Edward Elgar Library in

Critical Writings in Economics, Cheltenham and Northampton, MA, Edward Elgar.

- (2002), 'Funding Higher Education: Policies for Access and Quality,' House of Commons, Education and Skills Committee, *Post-16 Student Support*, Sixth Report of Session 2001–2002, HC445, London, The Stationery Office, Ev 19–35, available at http://econ.lse.ac.uk/staff/nb

- (2003), 'Financing Higher Education in the UK: The 2003 White Paper,' House of Commons Education and Skills Committee, *The Future of Higher Education, Fifth Report of Session 2002–03, Volume II, Oral and written evidence*, HC 425–II, London, the Stationery Office, Ev 292–309, available at http://econ.lse.ac.uk/staff/nb

- (2004), *The Economics of the Welfare State*, 4th edn, Oxford, Oxford University Press, and Stanford, CA, Stanford University Press.

- Crawford, I. (1998), 'The Dearing Report and the Government's Response: A Critique,' *The Political Quarterly*, **69**(1), 72–84.

- (2005), *Financing Higher Education: Lessons from the UK*, Routledge.

- Falkingham, J. (1993), 'Paying for Learning,' Welfare State Programme, Discussion Paper WSP/94, London, London School of Economics.

- (1996), 'Repayment Rates for Student Loans: Some Sensitivity Tests,' Welfare State Programme, Discussion Paper WSP/127, London, London School of Economics.

Blundell, R., Dearden, L., Goodman, A., and Reed, H. (2000), 'The Returns to Higher Education in Britain: Evidence from a British Cohort,' *The Economic Journal*, **110**(461), F82–99.

Brown, R. (2000), 'The New UK Quality Framework,' *Higher Education Quarterly*, **54**(4), 323–42.

Bynner, J., and Egerton, M. (2001), *The Wider Benefits of Higher Education*, London, Higher Education Funding Council.

- Dolton, P., Feinstein, L., Makepeace, G., Malmberg, L., and Woods, L. (2003) *Revisiting the Benefits of Higher Education*, London, Higher Education Funding Council.

Callender, C., and Wilkinson, D. (2003), '2002/03 Student Income and Expenditure Survey: Students' Income, Expenditure and Debt in 2002/03 and Changes since 1998/99,' Research Report 487, Nottingham, Department for Education and Skills.

Chapman, B. (1997), 'Conceptual Issues and the Australian Experience with Income Contingent Charges for Higher Education,' *The Economic Journal*, **107**(442), 738–51.

- Ryan, C. (2003), 'The Access Implications of Income Contingent Charges for Higher Education: Lessons from Australia,' Australian National University, Centre for Economic Policy Research, Discussion Paper No. 463, April.

Commonwealth of Australia (1998), *Learning for Life: Review of Higher Education Financing and Policy: Final Report*, Canberra, AGPS.

Corak, M., Lipps, G., and Zhao, J. (2003), 'Family Income and Participation in Post-secondary Education,' Statistics Canada, Family and Labour Studies Division, Analytical Studies Branch, Research Paper No. 210, Ottawa.

Dearden, L., Fitzsimons, E., and Goodman, A. (2004), *An Analysis of the Higher Education Reforms*, Briefing Note No. 45, London, Institute for Fiscal Studies, available at http://www.ifs.org.uk

Feinstein, L. (2003), 'Inequality in the Early Cognitive Development of British Children in the 1970 Cohort,' *Economica*, **70**(277), 73–98.

Friedman, M. (1955), 'The Role of Government in Education,' in A. Solo (ed.), *Economics and the Public Interest*, New Brunswick, NJ, Rutgers University Press, 123–44.

Glennerster, H., Merrett, S., and Wilson, G. (1968), 'A Graduate Tax,' *Higher Education Review*, **1**(1), 26–38; reprinted in Barr (2001b, Vol. III, 570–82), and in *Higher Education Review* **35**(2), 25–40.

Greenaway, D., and Haynes, M. (2002), 'Funding Higher Education in the UK: The Role of Fees and Loans,' *The Economic Journal*, **113**, F150–66.

Kornai, J. (1992), *The Socialist System: The Political Economy of Communism*, Princeton, NJ, Princeton University Press.

Larocque, N. (2003), *Who Should Pay? Tuition Fees and Tertiary Education Financing in New Zealand*, Wellington, Education Forum, available at http://www.educationforum.org.nz/documents/publications/who_should_pay.pdf

Lewis, D. (1999), 'Latin America Must Raise Fees to Help Poor,' *Times Higher Education Supplement*, 11 June.

McLaughlin, M. (2003), *Tertiary Education Policy in New Zealand*, Fulbright Report, available at http://www.fulbright.org.nz/voices/axford/docs/mcLaughlin.pdf

McNay, I. (1999), 'The Paradoxes of Research Assessment and Funding,' in B. Little and M. Henkel (eds), *Changing Relationships between Higher Education and the State*, London, Jessica Kingsley.

New Zealand Ministry of Education (1998), *Tertiary Education in New Zealand: Policy Directions for the 21st Century*, White Paper, Wellington, Ministry of Education.

– (2002), *Annual Report: Student Loan Scheme*, Wellington, Ministry of Education.

New Zealand Tertiary Education Advisory Commission (2001), *Shaping the Funding Framework: Fourth Report of the Tertiary Education Advisory Commission: Summary Report*, Wellington, Tertiary Education Advisory Commission, November, available at http://www.teac.govt.nz/fframework.htm

OECD (2002), *Education at a Glance, 2002*, Paris, Organization for Economic Cooperation and Development.

– (2003), *Education at a Glance: OECD Indicators 2003*, Paris, Organization for Economic Cooperation and Development.

Palacios, M. L. (2004), *Investing in Human Capital: A Capital Markets Approach to Student Funding*, Cambridge, Cambridge University Press.

Peacock, A., and Wiseman, J. (1962), 'The Economics of Higher Education,' *Higher Education: Evidence – Part Two: Documentary Evidence*, Cmnd 2154-XII, 129–38, London, HMSO.

Prest, A. R. (1962), 'The Finance of University Education in Great Britain,' Higher Education: Evidence – Part Two: Documentary Evidence, Cmnd 2154-XII, 139–52, London, HMSO.

Roberts, G. (2003), *Review of Research Assessment: Report to the UK Funding Bodies*, Bristol, Higher Education Funding Council for England.

UK Department for Education and Skills (2003), *Higher Education Funding – International Comparisons*, London, Department for Education and Skills, available at http://www.dfes.gov.uk

UK Education and Skills Select Committee (2002), *Post-16 Student Support*, Sixth Report of Session 2001–2002, HC445, London, The Stationery Office, available at http://www.parliament.uk

– (2003), *Post-16 Student Support: Government response to the Sixth Report from the Education and Skills Select Committee, Session 2001–2*, Second Special Report of Session 2002–3, HC440, London, The Stationery Office, available at http://www.parliament.uk

Winston, G. C. (1999), 'Subsidies, Hierarchy and Peers: The Awkward Economics of Higher Education,' *Journal of Economic Perspectives*, **13**(1), 13–36.

Wolf, A. (2002), *Does Education Matter: Myths about Education and Economic Growth*, London, Penguin Books.

Student Financial Aid: The Roles of Loans and Grants

ROSS FINNIE*

Why do governments provide loans to post-secondary students? The fundamental reason is that some individuals lack the funds they need to pay for their schooling and loans are an obvious source for that financing, but private lending institutions are generally reticent to loan to students because they (or their families) may not be able to provide the necessary collateral and a student's capacity to repay a loan in the post-schooling period is inherently uncertain. In the absence of a government-run loans system there will be limited lending to students, a general under-investment in post-secondary education, and access is likely to be particularly restricted for individuals from lower-income families. To serve both economic efficiency and equity goals, governments around the world operate student loan systems.[1]

Governments also provide student grants (defined here to include need-based scholarships and bursaries and other kinds of non-repayable support), which have the effect of not only (like loans) providing students with the money they need to meet their direct schooling costs and related living expenses, but also of increasing the incentives to invest in higher education by effectively decreasing the student's share of the costs of the investment.

The general goal of this paper is to identify in a precise fashion the effects of loans and grants on access to post-secondary education, to compare the effects and effectiveness of these two forms of assistance, and to identify some general rules on how they should be combined in student financial aid systems.

The paper begins by outlining a simple choice model of post-secondary participation and describing how loans and grants affect individuals' participation decisions by helping them overcome financing constraints and by shifting the net benefits of the schooling by reducing its effective cost to the student. It then makes the case for loans (over grants) for addressing financing/liquidity barriers on equity, efficiency, and fiscal grounds. The role of grants is then discussed, with their natural function being to make higher education a more attractive investment for individuals from disadvantaged backgrounds – while also helping overcome any financing barriers as a matter of course. This is followed by a discussion of loan subsidies and the establishment of some general principles for determining when and how loans should be subsidized, including both 'back-end' and 'front-end' assistance. Given that loans typically have a grant element associated with any subsidies provided, while grants help overcome the credit constraints upon which loans are targeted, the paper then attempts to provide some general rules for the use of loans, loan subsidies, and 'pure' grants in any full student assistance system. It concludes with an application of these principles as embodied in a recent proposal for reforming the student financial system in Canada.

Student loans should probably constitute an important part of any student financial aid system, and this is increasingly the case in practice as governments around the world attempt to expand and improve their higher education systems and in many cases shift the costs of post-secondary education from taxpayers to students and contain the costs of student support programs. Yet grants also continue to be used extensively, especially for individuals from lower socio-economic backgrounds. The existing literature tends, however, to be characterized by relatively vague discussions of exactly how loans and grants affect individuals' participation decisions and largely ignores how the two sources of support typically become intrinsically entwined in terms of their financing and subsidy effects. The aim of this paper is to drill more deeply into the student loan and grant instruments and to establish a framework for discussions of how they should be combined in any complete student financial aid system.[2]

1. How Grants and Loans Affect Post-Secondary Access

A useful starting point for discussions regarding student financial aid is the standard economist's approach of considering post-secondary education as an investment, whereby individuals decide whether or not to go to university (or college) by weighing the benefits and costs of doing so. On the benefits side are higher expected future earnings and other improved career opportunities, other enhancements of the individual's future quality of life, and any other benefits gained from the schooling, including any enjoyment derived from the education experience itself (i.e., its 'consumption value'). On the costs side are tuition fees and other direct costs (books, computers, etc.), as well as foregone earnings.

Students thus pursue post-secondary studies if (a) they perceive that the benefits outweigh the costs, and (b) they have the means of paying the associated out-of-pocket expenditures, including both the direct costs of the schooling and living costs. That is, they choose to participate in post-secondary education if the schooling is deemed worthwhile and they face no 'liquidity constraint' (or 'credit' or 'financial' constraint – the terms are used interchangeably) in doing so. In short, they both *want* to go, and are *able* to go.[3]

This said, two other conditions must be met before a student's *demand* for post-secondary education is translated into actual *participation*, or enrolment: the system must have a place for the student, and (related) the student must possess the marks and pass any other entry criteria for being admitted. For the remainder of these discussions, however, the focus will be on how student financial aid affects the *demand* for post-secondary education, leaving these other issues – central as they are to any more general discussion of participation in the post-secondary education system – to other venues.[4]

Different forms of student aid affect the demand for post-secondary education in different ways. The two principal types are loans and grants (the latter taken here to include scholarships, bursaries, and other non-repayable awards).

Grants affect the demand for post-secondary education by operating through both of the two principal factors that determine individuals' participation decisions as just described. First, by putting money into the hands of students, they help individuals overcome any liquidity or financing constraints they may face. Second, because the money is given and does not have to be repaid, grants reduce the effective cost of the education to the student and thus increase its net return. Both influences will tend to increase the demand for post-secondary education among recipients.

Student loans have different effects on post-secondary participation decisions. Like grants, they help provide the money individuals need to pay their schooling-related expenses and thereby overcome financing constraints. But unlike grants, loans do not generally change the costs of the schooling or its rate of return – precisely because the money is lent, not given. The effects of loans on the demand for post-secondary school-ing may, therefore, potentially be strong and direct (i.e., to the degree liquidity constraints are binding), but will never be as powerful as an equal amount of money given in the form of grants.

To the extent a student loan is subsidized, however, it may also possess the characteristics of a grant, because such subsidies can reduce the effective cost of the schooling, thus affecting the rate of return and influencing participation decisions through this path as well.[5] In par-ticular, student loans are, in practice, very often interest-free while students are in school, and this can represent a major subsidy (even if it is often not recognized as such).[6] Any covering of default costs represents another kind of subsidy, as is assistance provided for those experiencing difficulty in repayment more generally.

But although loans begin to resemble grants to the degree they are subsidized, the subsidy is never as great as it is with a grant as long as at least a portion of the loan is paid back. Furthermore, some kinds of loan subsidies act principally to offset the costs of the borrowing, including those related to the risks of the loan being excessively burdensome if the student's future income is lower than anticipated (or the debt load higher), as well as other kinds of 'debt aversion.' Such 'loan-facilitating subsidies' do not, therefore, necessarily decrease the true overall costs of the schooling, and as a result do not change the net returns of the investment – or the student's schooling decision – in the same way as grants or loan subsidies, which do reduce the student's effective school-ing costs.

Having outlined the ways in which grants and loans affect the de-mand for post-secondary education, we now turn to the cases for each of these kinds of support.

2. The Cases for Loans and Grants

As described above, the basic case for student loans is quite simple. Loans permit students for whom post-secondary education is a desir-able and worthwhile investment to finance that activity by tapping into their own (expected) future income flows to meet the required up-front expenditures. Providing student loans is thus an important function of governments, because opening up opportunities for higher education in this way is appropriate on both equity and efficiency grounds. First, by reducing the financial barriers that potentially stand in the way of the schooling, its direct benefits are made more accessible to a wider population of individuals, especially those from lower-income families who would have particular difficulty coming up with the required financing. And second, by expanding the schooling option to all those for whom the investment is most worthwhile – and thus (generally) 'productive' – rather than just those who can pay for it, there will be an increase in the quality (productivity) of the pool of individuals with higher education, which is especially important to a nation's economic efficiency and competitiveness in the new knowledge-based economy.[7]

But if grants can also provide the funds students need to meet their schooling costs and are likely to have an even greater effect on access since they also reduce the costs of the investment borne by the individual and thus make it more attractive, as described above, why would loans ever be preferred to grants? There are three main reasons for favouring loans over grants.

The first argument is an entirely fiscal one. The simple arithmetic is that a given amount of government spending on student financial assistance will generally go much further when put into loans rather than grants, precisely because in most cases at least some of the money is paid back and can thus effectively be recycled. A loan system can, therefore, provide a greater number of students with more money for any given amount of government spending: than can a set of grants, perhaps by a factor of three, four, five, or even more, depending on the degree of subsidy in the loan system, administration costs, and other related factors.

It thus follows that to the degree the relevant access problem is one of individuals being prevented from gaining access to post-secondary education due to credit constraints – that is, individuals want to go to school but they lack the money to do so – loans will generally be the more effective vehicle for delivering student financial aid. Especially in times of scarce government dollars, this is an important practical consideration.

The second argument in favour of loans over grants rests on equity considerations. Post-secondary education has a strong individual investment component which is generally characterized by a very favourable rate of return, and it can thus be argued on grounds of fairness that students should be expected to pay their loans back out of their future earnings, which in turn derive to a significant degree from the investments in their schooling which the loans make possible.[8]

In short, it is the individual student who undertakes the schooling, it is the individual student who is the principal beneficiary of that schooling, and so, it can be argued, it is the individual student who should pay for the schooling – those payments effectively coming out of future earnings in the case of a loan system. This argument is strengthened by the fact that post-secondary graduates tend to earn higher than average incomes, and are thus 'wealthy' relative to the average taxpayer in a lifetime perspective.[9]

The final argument for loans over grants is grounded in the concept of economic efficiency. It has been explained above how student loans can ensure that those for whom post-secondary education is a worthwhile investment can obtain the financial means to make those investments and then pay those loans back out of future earnings. Grants can, in contrast, by their very nature of reducing the net costs of schooling cause individuals for whom schooling is *not* a worthwhile personal – or social – investment to undertake it precisely because a grant makes it 'cheap.' Grants can thus result in an *over*-investment in post-secondary education on the part of at least some recipients (i.e., the benefits do not justify the costs at the social level – even though it makes sense for the individual to undertake the schooling in the face of the reduced costs faced).

These constitute the principal arguments for loans over grants. But what, alternatively, is the case for grants over loans? Grants are most appropriately used precisely where the net returns to education *should* be boosted in order to encourage members of certain targeted groups to invest in higher education, and this can only be achieved by *giving* money with no obligation to repay, even if this makes it an inherently more expensive form of aid. Such interventions may, again, be justified on what might be classed as both equity and efficiency grounds.

The 'efficiency justification' (which also has equity elements) relates to situations where individuals for whom post-secondary education is in fact a worthwhile investment in (objective) benefit-cost terms might choose not to undertake the schooling in the absence of a grant because they underestimate the benefits or overestimate the costs, because they apply inordinately high subjective discount rates to the benefits, because they undervalue higher education or its associated benefits for 'cultural' reasons, or because they are otherwise deterred from investing in the education they 'should.'

One policy option might be to deal with these problems directly by correcting any erroneous perceptions, or 'educating' individuals with regard to the benefits of higher education (see below in the context of loan subsidies), or otherwise helping individuals see the wisdom of undertaking the favourable investments they face. A grant will, on the other hand, change the actual benefit-cost ratio of the schooling, and thereby increase the incentives to undertake the investment, thus causing more individuals to do so. Using grants in this manner would be especially appropriate, and feasible on a practical level, where the under-investment problem exists along certain identifiable characteristics, such as family income, which can become the criteria for grant eligibility.

In terms of more full-blown equity considerations, grants can also be used to improve the incentives for certain disadvantaged individuals to undertake higher education even when the schooling is not necessarily a worthwhile investment in strict benefit-cost terms, perhaps because the individuals in question are less well prepared for the schooling, precisely owing to their disadvantaged background. That is, a grant can again – in lowering the costs of the schooling to the individual – make it worthwhile for the individual to undertake the schooling when this would not otherwise be done in the absence of the grant. Awarding grants to this end is again especially feasible on a practical level, and probably most justifiable on grounds of fairness, when the disadvantages deemed worthy of being counteracted can be identified in terms of observable characteristics, such as family income.[10]

In practice, these equity and efficiency justifications (as defined here) will often go together hand in hand, as individuals from disadvantaged groups will typically face objectively less attractive benefit-cost calculations because they are less well prepared for higher education, and also more likely to be less oriented towards choosing higher education even when it might actually represent a good investment in objective terms – although in principle, different amounts of grant might be required to overcome each of these factors.

The money awarded in the form of a grant can also, of course, help overcome any financing barriers, but it is useful to recognize that the argument for issuing a grant may hold even in cases where the targeted individuals do not actually face such a financing constraint and would in fact able to pay for the schooling even in the absence of any financial support – the problem being that they would choose not to do so for the sorts of reasons just described (which constitute the fundamental justification for awarding grants rather than loans).

The general cases for loans and grants have now been established. Loans should be used when the principal problem is the need to help students overcome credit constraints – that is, to help those who *want* to pursue advanced schooling be able to do so, whereas grants should be used when individuals need the cost-reducing (and net benefit-increasing) incentives that grants embody to make them *want* to engage in higher education.

The two forms of aid are, however, fundamentally entwined, since grants can help overcome financing constraints and thus do at least some of the job that loans could otherwise do, while student loans are often subsidized, which effectively makes them a mix of loan and grant, and thereby affects the incentives to invest in schooling, which is the principal domain of grants. We begin to address these inherent overlaps in the next section by looking at the issue of when loans should be subsidized and the form those subsidies should take, before turning in the following section to the issue of how loans, loan subsidies, and pure grants should be assembled together in any overall student financial aid package.

3. Loan Subsidies

General subsidies for post-secondary education are typically grounded in the idea that higher learning has external benefits – that is, some of the returns to the schooling are realized by society as a whole rather than by the individual alone. This is one of the principal reasons used to justify setting tuition fees at levels which do not cover the full costs of the schooling, as practised in most developed countries.[11] Going beyond such general subsidies, we have discussed in the preceding section the case for grants, which (as discussed here) represent a form of subsidy targeted on specific groups, such as those from disadvantaged backgrounds (or others); the intention being to increase the incentives of the targeted individuals to undertake higher education, such interventions are justified on efficiency or equity grounds. In this section we concern ourselves with a different set of subsidies – those targeted neither on the general student population nor necessarily on 'disadvantaged' students, but rather on student borrowers as a group. The questions we address are: Why, when, and how should student loans be subsidized?[12]

Back-End Loan Subsidies

We begin with 'back-end' subsidies, defined here as those provided in the repayment (post-schooling) period. The first, clearest, and strongest case can be made for helping students whose loan payments represent excessive burdens because their incomes are low relative to their debt loads. Such assistance provides not only direct benefit to those actually facing the hardship, but in doing so also offers an implicit insurance plan which benefits *all* borrowers, including those who never receive the assistance.[13]

This kind of assistance effectively allows the loan system to better do its basic job of getting funds into the hands of students by reducing the risk – which represents an important part of the cost – of the borrowing. In short, individuals who might hesitate to take out a loan to finance their schooling out of concern that they would face significant hardship were they to have lower-than-expected future earnings (or higher debt loads) would be more willing to borrow in the presence of such an implicit insurance scheme. This kind of assistance thus helps alleviate what we might call 'risk-based debt aversion.'[14]

Such assistance would be of particular benefit among those with the greatest chances of facing excessive debt loads (including those more likely to have lower earnings in the post-schooling period), and those for whom the consequences of any such excessive debt burdens would be more serious (such as individuals from lower-income families who would be less likely to receive support in such circumstances).

Practical design issues regarding this kind of back-end loan support would generally involve deciding what constitutes an 'excessive' debt burden and determining the precise form the aid should take, including the amount of the assistance, how long it should continue, how much it should consist of abating current payments ('interest relief') versus reducing the principal owed ('debt reduction'), and so on. The central design principle is simply that the aid should take into account the individual's debt load and post-schooling income, thus targeting the assistance on those who are truly 'needy' in the sense of facing hardship with their loans in the repayment period. Simplicity and ease of use would also be important real-world design issues.

This concept of assistance in repayment is directly related to the well-known notion of income-contingent repayment (ICR), because ICR in some sense simply represents a particular form of this kind of back-end loan support whereby payments are geared to the individual's income according to an established formula, typically collected through the income tax system.[15] Whereas a 'mortgage'-style loan consisting of fixed payments may be seen as one extreme form of repayment system and ICR another (Barr [1993]), any system which provides assistance in repayment or which otherwise adjusts payments to an individual's particular circumstances in the post-schooling period effectively represents a movement away from the former and towards the latter – or what we might call a 'quasi-ICR' (Finnie and Schwartz [1996]) or 'income sensitive' repayment system. The relative merits of these different approaches – quasi-ICR and 'income sensitive' systems versus a purer ICR system – will depend on the complexity of the associated design issues, the relative administrative costs, and other such factors.

While the particular form of assistance offered in repayment is open to discussion, what is effectively beyond debate is that any student loan system (or delayed fee-payment system) not possessing back-end subsidies (or related forms of 'risk pooling') of this general type will be lacking an important manner of reducing the risks of borrowing and thereby realizing the potential of the loan system (explicit or implicit as in the HECS system) to meet students' financial needs – and thus of advancing the potential of the loan system to improve educational opportunities, particularly among those from lower-income families.

Equally important to recognize is that while such assistance does represent a form of subsidy in the way discussed by Barr (1993) and others (see the relevant note above), the primary purpose of this kind of subsidy should only be to neutralize the costs of borrowing (its risk component in particular), and thus not affect the net costs, net returns, or incentives to undertake the schooling. In short, the subsidy should only make the loan system work better – allowing those who need the money to undertake any worthwhile schooling investments.[16]

Front-End Loan Subsidies as General Schooling Subsidies

The other general manner in which loans may be subsidized is 'upfront' (or at the 'front end'), which we can define as either at the point the loan is taken out or otherwise while the individual is still in school. Under what conditions would such subsidies – such as making loans interest-free (or interest-subsidized), replacing them partly or even fully with grants (thus in the limit making them no longer loans), or adding additional subsidies/grants to the amounts borrowed – be appropriate? It is worth identifying the possibilities if only to try to understand where existing systems might lie in this respect, as well as to think about what changes should perhaps be made or how new systems should be structured.

One potential set of reasons might be essentially the same as those

suggested earlier for awarding grants more generally. Individuals requiring loans may, for example, generally tend to (also) overestimate
the costs or underestimate the benefits of schooling and thus generally
under-invest in higher education as much as they 'should.' Or they
might – again 'also' (i.e., in addition to needing loans) – be disadvantaged in some general manner, such as being less well prepared for
higher education, which reduces the actual net benefits of any schooling investments made and thus again reduces their schooling rates as
compared to those not facing such disadvantages. In such cases, subsidizing loans (e.g., a general interest subsidy or adding an explicit grant
component) could be a relatively expedient manner of delivering support where it was deemed appropriate – for essentially the same equity
or efficiency reasons discussed previously.

In short, loans could be a vehicle for delivering the same sort of
support for the same reasons as the pure grants discussed earlier. It
should, however, be carefully considered as to why subsidies justified
on these grounds should be attached to loans in such an automatic
fashion, rather than allowing loans and grants/subsidies (including
those subsidies attached to loans) to be kept more separate in order to
deliver each kind of support in the optimal amounts to different kinds
of individuals in different kinds of situations. If some borrowers, in
particular, do not require or merit subsidies/grants on these grounds
whereas others do, then attaching subsidies to loans in this manner will
not be as efficient, or fair, as separating the different classes of borrowers and delivering grants/subsidies only to those who need/merit them
– in which case we are simply back to the general rule of awarding
grants where they are appropriate, awarding loans where they are
appropriate, and keeping the two separate, as previously suggested as
a general strategy for awarding student financial aid.

Front-End Loan Subsidies to Overcome 'Debt Aversion'

A second set of conditions under which up-front loan subsidies might
be warranted is where potential borrowers are 'debt averse.' Since the
meaning of this term is often unclear, it might be worth attempting to
define it with some precision. One general definition of debt aversion
might be situations where individuals are unwilling to take out loans to
finance their post-secondary schooling even though they know the
schooling represents a good investment *and* it could be facilitated by the
loans in question. That is, the two conditions for choosing to invest in

higher education presented earlier are met – and hence grants per se are not required – but individuals are unwilling to borrow to finance their (worthwhile) investments.

With that general definition of debt aversion established, let us consider some specific forms it might take. 'Risk-based debt aversion' was defined above as referring to situations where individuals are unwilling to borrow out of concern that debt burdens in the post-schooling period could turn out to be excessive if earnings are lower than anticipated or accumulated borrowing is higher. But in such cases the problem would – as described earlier – be best addressed more directly by providing interest-relief and debt-reduction programs in the post-schooling period, a fully income-contingent repayment system, or some other form of targeted back-end support, not broad up-front subsidies.

A second, more extreme form of debt aversion – what might be called 'value-based debt aversion' – could occur where individuals are unwilling to borrow as a matter of principle, perhaps owing to personal, religious, class-based, or other culture-related values. To be clear, this definition implies that individuals will not borrow even though the borrowing facilitates a worthwhile investment, and risk is not the issue.

In such cases, the policy options would seem to be (1) to try to change individuals' attitudes towards borrowing – at least insofar as it concerns investments in higher education, (2) to identify and provide such credit-constrained debt-averse individuals with subsidies (or even complete grants) while others are not so favoured, (3) to provide subsidies (or pure grants) to all those needing financial support to pursue their studies, or (4) to accept such risk aversion and its attendant effects on post-secondary participation as something the government cannot, or should not, address.

The first option is similar to the ones offered above regarding comparable information problems, and seems similarly laudable at least as a starting point. The second option would appear to be inequitable, difficult to operationalize, and run the potential risk of generating undesirable incentives (as individuals attempt to qualify as subsidy/grant receivers). The third option carries the same disadvantages of grants relative to loans for the fiscal, equity, and efficiency reasons discussed above. The fourth option will depend on societal norms, the level of tolerance for different cultures and attitudes, and related factors.

Nevertheless, if – at last in principle – this sort of debt aversion did exist in a widespread manner among those needing financial assistance to meet their schooling costs, up-front loan subsidies, adding pure grant components to loans, or, more likely (since it is a matter of *principle* we are talking about here), providing all assistance in the form of grants rather than loans might in fact be required to provide students with the financing they need. Implementing such subsidies would involve some serious policy design challenges, however, including identifying to what extent and perhaps among which groups (if more specific targeting were considered) this kind of debt aversion – which is inherently difficult to identify – existed.

Returning to the last policy option (essentially doing nothing), such loan subsidy-grant strategies might also present a potential dilemma at the level of principles: should this kind of debt aversion in fact be accepted as grounds for providing subsidies? After all, it is (by definition) a problem of attitude, and beliefs, not an objective barrier. To the degree it was a general social (e.g., class-based) phenomenon among a well-defined group of individuals (e.g., those from lower-income families), then one of the subsidy strategies might make sense. Beyond such neatly aligned circumstances, it is hard to imagine coming up with a practical policy to deal with this kind of debt aversion.

Furthermore, we might well question how widespread such debt aversion based on this sort of fundamental principle could be such in advanced economies which are so credit-oriented in general – and especially when the borrowing in question here is to finance the best and most important investment most individuals would ever make.

A third form of debt aversion might be referred to as 'sticker price debt aversion,' which could be defined as situations where potential students are deterred from borrowing because the total debt expected to be accumulated over a given year or an entire schooling career somehow *seems* 'excessive' – and this even though the schooling investment is worthwhile, and the aversion comes from something other than the actual risks of excessive debt burdens associated with borrowing (i.e., the first kind of debt aversion defined above) or some absolute opposition to borrowing in principle (the second kind of debt aversion).

Once those other kinds of debt aversion are allowed for, however, this third type becomes difficult to precisely identify, but may exist nonetheless, perhaps because students are simply not used to borrowing, especially the sorts of larger sums that might be needed to finance their schooling.[17] At least part of this kind of debt aversion would, however, seem to be closely related to the same sort of information problems noted above, especially if it in fact stemmed from overestimated debt loads or underestimated future earnings flows – in which case it would again be more directly addressed by correcting any such erroneous information. Additional loan subsidies (or pure grants) would then presumably be required only to the degree those more simple, direct, and ultimately more efficient and equitable measures did not deal (completely) with the problem. Simply familiarizing students with the general concept of borrowing – especially borrowing for an investment that is likely to pay them substantial returns over their lifetimes – might represent another simple yet effective policy option.[18]

In the end, however, if this particular form of debt aversion did in fact deter individuals from borrowing for their own benefit, was extensive, and could not be addressed in any of these other ways, it might in fact be appropriate to provide up-front loan subsidies (or pure grants) – although consideration should be given to the fact that such subsidies would again carry the attendant equity, efficiency, and fiscal disadvantages of grants relative to loans previously discussed.

Other kinds of debt aversion could perhaps be defined – and any attempts to do so would provide a useful contribution to the related policy discussions, since identifying the specific nature of the alleged problem would presumably help focus discussions and lead to the most appropriate policy options.

4. Student Loans and Grants and Complete Financial Aid Packages

Given the fundamentally different functions of loans and grants, the different financial needs of different students with respect to overcoming financing constraints versus more fundamental disadvantages in their preparation for higher education and associated attitudes, and the different equity, efficiency, and fiscal implications of each kind of aid, the fullest student financial aid system should probably include an integrated system of loans and grants, including both up-front and back-end loan subsidies for the latter, as appropriate. To consider what integrated packages should look like, it is worth reviewing the different functions and effects of loans and grants.

Student financial aid systems have two basic purposes. The first is to help students overcome credit constraints which stand in the way of their making the schooling investments they want to make – that is, the investments are worthwhile in benefit-cost terms and recognized as such, but the individuals lack the money to pay for those investments (including living costs). The second purpose is to boost the net returns of the educational investment so that certain individuals who would not undertake the investment in the absence of the aid because the investment is not worthwhile in net benefit terms, or is not *perceived* to be worthwhile, do so once the financial assistance is factored in. In both cases, levelling the higher education playing field for those from different socio-economic backgrounds by making available the optimal type and amount of aid will improve schooling outcomes in terms of efficiency and equity goals.

Loans are more suited to the credit-constraint problem because they can deliver considerably more support for a given amount of government spending, because they recognize the personal-investment nature of the schooling investment and the generally regressive nature of non-repayable assistance (i.e., grants), and because they do not (in general) distort individuals' benefit-cost decisions in a way that can cause some individuals to undertake the schooling simply because it is made less costly (even though it is inherently not a worthwhile personal/social investment). Grants are, conversely, best suited for shifting individuals' schooling decisions in order to cause recipients to undertake schooling when they would otherwise not do so in the absence of the support.

The different objectives, and effects, of loans and grants are therefore at least conceptually separable and can lead to an optimal mix of the two policy instruments – relieving credit constraints with loans, providing subsidies with grants.

The two kinds of aid are, however, more inextricably intertwined than this dichotomization suggests. On the one hand, loans are usually subsidized, thus making them part-loan and part-grant. Conversely, by putting money in students' hands, grants help individuals overcome credit constraints (i.e., meet schooling-related costs) in addition to shifting the net benefits of the individual's investment. There is, furthermore, often overlap in the individuals upon whom the different kinds of aid are targeted – typically including those from the middle- or lower-income families who may need help overcoming financial barriers that stand in the way of the investment, or who merit subsidies that improve the returns to schooling.

Further complicating these aid issues are the related empirical issues. Stated most generally, it is typically difficult to identify precisely where and how financial aid dollars should be spent in order to improve access and advance various equity and efficiency goals in the most effective manner (i.e., which kinds of aid help most?). For example, although loan systems can get more money into the hands of more students for a given level of government spending, grants may be sufficiently effective in increasing participation among certain types of targeted individuals so as to make their greater cost worthwhile, at least in some cases. It all depends on the underlying elasticities – how individuals respond to an increase to the amount of loan money available versus what happens as grants are expanded – in addition to how well the different forms of aid can be effectively targeted on their intended recipient groups.

We might, however, hazard a few general principles in terms of the design of student financial aid systems in general – at least in terms of equalizing the opportunities for pursuing post-secondary education. First, given the two different purposes, and effects, of loans and grants, most student financial aid systems should probably include both kinds of aid.

Second, loans should generally focus on helping individuals overcome any credit or financing barriers that stand in the way of their schooling, while any loan-based subsidies should be geared to making the loan system work better, such as counteracting any debt aversion that might prevent individuals from taking out loans that make sense in terms of the investments they permit. Grants should, in contrast, be used to provide the extra incentives required to encourage certain types of individuals to undertake schooling where justified on equity or efficiency grounds – whether or not, or to what degree, they are borrowers.

In such an integrated system, it would be expected that some students would receive loans, some grants, and some both – depending on the relative importance and distribution of the financing-constraint barrier versus the more fundamental disadvantages individuals may face, particularly as pertaining to their family backgrounds. The final mix of loans and grants will depend on the extent of the competing underlying needs, the effectiveness of each kind of aid in terms of addressing the two different kinds of access problems, the resources available, the general political environment, and other factors.

It thus makes sense to start with grants – at least conceptually. Once grants are correctly targeted, any remaining liquidity constraints could be addressed with loans, subsidized as appropriate. The art in the program design will be in determining the optimal applications of grants and loans, and making them fit into a coherent overall package.

5. Conclusion: An Application to the Canadian Student Aid System

Finnie, Usher, and Vossensteyn (forthcoming) propose an integrated student financial aid system for Canada based on the general principles described above, distilled into a form which would have the additional attribute of fitting relatively easily into existing financial aid structures, thus obviating the need for more wholesale reform and presumably conforming to prevailing Canadian values regarding student financial assistance. It begins by calculating students' financial needs, essentially estimating the money individuals need to pay their direct schooling costs plus living expenses after factoring in expected contributions on the part of the student and his or her family. This assessed need, which represents the potential financial barrier to the individual's schooling, would represent the individual's student financial-aid package, which would be delivered with a combination of loans and grants.

In the baseline proposal, the first $5000 (CAN) would be provided in the form of loans, the rest in grants – this in a context where financial aid packages would generally range up to around $12,000 CAN (about $9600 US at current exchange rates) for those with low family incomes who left home to go to university. Such a loans-first approach would require students to contribute the first dollars to their education, thus ensuring certain efficiency properties with respect to the investment (i.e., it is not made 'too' inexpensive), but would also cap loans at reasonable amounts (thus addressing general 'debt aversion' problem and otherwise not saddling individuals with 'excessive' loan burdens). Grants would make up the rest of the package, and would thus be implicitly targeted on individuals from lower-income families (who would be assessed to have greater overall financial need precisely due to the limited expected parental contributions), for whom such subsidies are likely to have the greatest effect in terms of overcoming various background effects which constitute the sort of non-financing barriers to post-secondary participation discussed in this paper.

The main loan system would be interest-free during school principally in order to (further) counteract any general debt-aversion problems and – perhaps more importantly in a political sense – to conform to established Canadian practices in this respect (although the extent of those subsidies should perhaps be debated). A parallel unsubsidized loan program would be introduced for students whose parents did not provide the assumed level of support, or for students who were not able to come up with their own expected contributions, with lending permitted up to the maximum of those amounts.

The main loan system would include substantial back-end subsidies targeted on those whose loan payments were high relative to their incomes in the post-schooling period (which should be relatively uncommon given the borrowing limits established above), while we leave open the possibility of adopting an explicit income-contingent repayment system, run through the tax system. These subsidies (like the up-front loan subsidies at least in part), would exist essentially to make the loan system work more effectively by addressing any risk-based debt aversion.

The particular parameters of this system are open to discussion, as are even some of its basic structures (e.g., grants could be front-loaded), but it seems reasonable in terms of attempting to use loans and grants in a coherent manner to improve access to post-secondary education in Canada in an efficient and equitable manner. In short, loans would be focused on helping individuals overcome any financing constraints that might stand in the way of a worthwhile schooling investment. Loan subsidies would be designed principally to make the loan system better accomplish that function by counteracting any general sort of debt aversion that might exist. Pure grants would be focused on shifting the net benefits of the schooling investment for those facing more funda-mental disadvantages, while also of course helping overcome credit constraints. (Additional grants focused on specially disadvantaged groups, such as aboriginals, would be layered on top of this system.)

Different designs might be proposed, but having a clearly enunciated set of goals and using the different policy levers available in a coordi-nated fashion to meet those different goals in this sort of way would seem to represent a good general approach, the principles of which could be adapted for other countries.

Notes

* School of Policy Studies, Queen's University. This paper draws from joint work with Saul Schwartz, Alex Usher, and Hans Vossensteyn, to whom various intellectual debts are owed. Comments offered by Usher, and David Ploquin on earlier versions of this paper are also appreciated. The author's work on student financial aid and related topics has, over the years, been supported by Statistics Canada, Human Resources Develop-ment Canada, and the C.D. Howe Institute, and those contributions are also gratefully acknowledged, although these organizations should not in any way be implicated in the present paper. A lengthier and more detailed version of this paper is found in Finnie (2004).

1 See Barr and Crawford (1998), Chapman (1997), Mankiw (1986), and others for general discussions of these principles.

2 Student financial assistance can come in other forms (e.g., tax credits and savings subsidies) and have other goals, including promoting the independence of students from their parents, providing general subsidies to the costs of post-secondary education to students and their families beyond those required to ensure access, putting money into the hands of students so that the system might be more responsive to their preferences, encouraging student effort and performance, and more. This paper, however, focuses on loans and grants, which are the principal forms of student financial aid in most countries (and to which most other forms of aid can effectively be reduced in one way or another), and on the access goal which typically represents the first and foremost objective of any student financial aid system.

3 See Cameron and Taber (2004) and Keane (2002) for more formal representations of this kind of model, but the basic elements are consistent with those just described.

4 See Finnie (forthcoming) for a discussion of the role of capacity as well as demand-side factors in determining who gains access to post-secondary education.

5 As Barr (1993) states: 'Subsidised loans are a mixture of loan and implicit grant; the source of support is in part the student himself [i.e., paid out of future earnings] and in part the taxpayer (if it is the state which pays the subsidy)' (724).

6 A full-interest subsidy means that the real value of the loan falls over time with the rate of inflation (i.e., the value of the money that the student repays is less than the value of the money borrowed) – effectively reducing the student's cost of schooling. These issues are returned to below.

7 It is worth noting that 'education for its own sake' is also facilitated by a student loans system, as cash-strapped individuals again obtain the money they need to pay for their schooling to be repaid out of future income flows – even if those future flows are not the primary reason for the investment, and even if those flows are not particularly enhanced by the schooling.

8 See Vaillancourt and Bourdeau-Primeau (2001) for recent evidence on the returns to post-secondary education in Canada and a review of the existing literature.

9 These equity arguments are typically offered from all sides of the political spectrum – from 'left' and 'right' alike. A recent justification that has been offered for grants is that in a progressive tax system post-secondary graduates support higher education through their higher taxes. This is false reasoning. Although a well-functioning progressive tax system does in fact redistribute income (and wealth) from the rich to the poor, such transfers serve to finance *all* government activities, and any particular transfer back to the better-off segment of the population (such as post-secondary

graduates) simply represents a partial undoing of the equalizing effects of the tax system.

10 Grants can also be used to meet other participation-related policy goals, such as providing incentives for students to enter certain 'non-traditional' fields of study (such as the grants Canadian women receive to enter the natural sciences and engineering at the graduate level). Our focus here, however, is on strategies aimed at evening opportunities at a more general level, such as encouraging individuals from low-income families to go to university.

11 The basic idea is that students will under-invest in post-secondary education from a social perspective if they consider only the private benefits of the schooling. A general tuition subsidy will thus encourage individuals to invest beyond that point. See Barr (1993), among others, for general discussions of this principle, including discussions of the difficulties involved in estimating the social returns to higher education.

12 We do not address here the issue of using subsidized tuition fees as a means of improving access. The issue is discussed in many other places (e.g., Barr (1993), Chapman (1997), and Finnie and Schwartz (1996) and Finnie (2001, 2002) for the Canadian context.) The general conclusion in the literature is that because reduced tuition fees essentially deliver the same benefit to all students, whether they need the assistance or not (i.e., rich and poor alike), they represent an inefficient means of delivering student aid where it is truly needed, while possessing the same equity, efficiency, and fiscal disadvantages discussed above regarding the advantages of loans over grants.

13 See Barr (1993) and Chapman (1997) for discussions of these issues, the latter in the context of Australia's HECS income-contingent repayment system, which provides a means for students to pay their fees in the post-schooling period rather than up front.

14 This form of debt relief can be contrasted with 'loan remission,' a particularly Canadian form of assistance which forgives loans based only on total accumulated borrowing (over the course of a year or an entire program), without regard to the individual's current (or future) income level, thus treating those for whom the debt is a greater or lesser burden in the same way. Canada also has, however, a set of debt-reduction and interest subsidy programs which have more attractive – and more efficient – risk-reduction properties of the kind discussed here.

15 See Barr (1993), Chapman (1997), Krueger and Bowen (1993), Nerlove (1975), Friedman and Kuznets (1945), and Mankiw (1986), among others, regarding ICR. In some cases, including the best-known Australian and New Zealand cases, ICR has been presented as a means of introducing new fees so that students can bear a greater share of the costs of their education, but this need not be the case. ICR can instead be thought of as

any income-sensitive payment scheme which can apply to conventional loans taken out in the traditional, explicit fashion, as implemented in the UK in recent years; to deferred fee payments (with no 'loan' as such taken out) as in the Australian HECS system or as about to be adapted in the UK; or to any other kind of future payment obligations (Finnie and Schwartz [1996]).

16 See Finnie (2004) for the more technical aspects of this proposition.

17 The individual would have to possess an attitude along the following lines: 'The schooling is a worthwhile investment for me. The loan permits that investment. I am confident I won't face any excessive debt burdens after school. And I am not opposed to borrowing (for education) in principle. Still, it seems like a lot to borrow, and therefore I won't.'

18 Students are, after all, often exposed to this kind of 'education,' especially as they approach graduation, as banks, car companies, and others line up to convince them of the benefits of borrowing in order to finance current consumption out of future income.

References

Barr, Nicholas. 1993. 'Alternative Funding Resources for Higher Education.' *The Economic Journal* 103:418, 718–28.

Barr, Nicholas, and Iain Crawford. 1998. 'Funding Higher Education in an Age of Expansion.' *Education Economics* 6:1, 45–70.

Cameron, Stephen V., and Christopher Taber. (2004). 'Estimation of Educational Borrowing Constraints Using Returns to Schooling.' *Journal of Political Economy* 112:1, pt 1, 132–82.

Carneiro, Pedro, and James Heckman. 2002. 'The Evidence on Credit Constraints in Post-Secondary Schooling.' *The Economic Journal* 112, 705–35.

Chapman, Bruce. 1997. 'Conceptual Issues and the Australian Experience with Income Contingent Charges for Higher Education.' *The Economic Journal* 107:442, 738–51.

Dynarski, Susan. 2002. 'The Behavioural and Distributional Implications of Aid for College.' *American Economic Review* 92:2, 279–85.

Finnie, Ross. Forthcoming. 'Access and Capacity in the Canadian Post-Secondary Education System: A Policy Discussion Framework.' In Paul Anisef and Robert Sweet, eds., *Preparing for Post Secondary Education: New Roles for Governments and Families*. Montreal: McGill-Queen's University Press; also published as a Queen's University School of Policy Studies Research Paper.

– 2004. 'Student Financial Aid: The Roles of Loans and Grants.' Queen's University School of Policy Studies Discussion Paper.

– 2002. 'Student Financial Assistance in Canada: The Need for More Loans.' *Journal of Higher Education and Policy Management* 24:2, 155–70.

– 2001. 'Measuring the Load, Easing the Burden: Canada's Student Loan

Programs and the Revitalization of Canadian Postsecondary Education.'
Toronto: C.D. Howe Institute Commentary no. 155.

Finnie, Ross, and Saul Schwartz. 1996. *Student Loans in Canada: Past, Present and Future*. C.D. Howe Institute: Toronto.

Finnie, Ross, Alex Usher, and Hans Vossensteyn. 2004. 'Meeting the Need: A New Architecture for Canada's Student Financial Aid System.' Presented at the Higher Education in Canada conference held at Queen's University, Kingston, 13–14 Feb. 2004, sponsored by the John Deutsch Institute for the Study of Economic Policy, and forthcoming in Charles Beach, Robin Boadway, and Marvin McInnis, eds, *Higher Education in Canada* (Kingston: John Deutsch Institute, McGill-Queen's University Press, forthcoming). Also published by the Institute for Research on Public Policy, *Policy Matters* 7:6 (2004), 48 pp.

Friedman, Milton, and Simon Kuznets. 1945. *Income from Professional Practice*. New York: NBER.

Greenaway, D., and M. Hayes. 2003. 'Funding Higher Education in the UK: The Role of Fees and Loans,' *The Economic Journal* 113:485, F150–66.

Heller, Donald. 1997. 'Student Price Response in Higher Education: An Update to Leslie and Brinkman.' *Journal of Higher Education* 68:6, 624–59.

Jackson, G.A., and G.B. Weathersby. 1975. 'Individual Demand for Higher Education.' *Journal of Higher Education* 46:6, 623–52.

Junor, Sean, and Alexander Usher. 2002. *The Price of Knowledge*. Montreal: Canada Millennium Scholarship Foundation, Research Series.

Kane, Thomas J. 2001. 'College-Going and Inequality: A Literature Review.' Paper prepared for the Thomas Sage Foundation.

Keane, Michael P. 2002. 'Financial Aid, Borrowing Constraints, and College Attendance: Estimates from Structural Estimates.' *American Economic Review* 92:2, 293–7.

Krueger, Alan B., and William G. Bowen. 1993. 'Income-contingent College Loans.' *Journal of Economic Perspectives* 7:3, 193–201.

Mankiw, N. Gregory. 1986. 'The Allocation of Credit and Financial Collapse.' *Quarterly Journal of Economics*, August.

Nerlove, Mark. 1975. 'Some Problems in the Use of Income-Contingent College Loans.' *Journal of Political Economy* 83:1, 157–83.

Vaillancourt, François, and Sandrine Bourdeau-Primeau. 'The Returns to Education in Canada: 1990 and 1995.' In David Laidler, *Renovating the Ivory Tower: Canadian Universities and the Knowledge Economy*, 215–40. Toronto: C.D. Howe Institute.

Public and Private Benefits in Higher Education

ARTHUR RIPSTEIN*

Discussions about funding for post-secondary education eventually turn to the question of who pays. Central questions concern the likely effects of various proposals: will higher tuition be a bar to accessibility, making education the privilege of those who can afford it, and deterring those who can't?[1] Or will it increase accessibility by creating more spaces and transferring money from those who can pay to those who cannot?[2] The facts are contested, and competing views claim that the truth is on their side. Yet both sides can't be right.

There's another, equally important debate about funding. In this debate, opposed views about tuition levels both claim to occupy the high ground of justice. Those who want tuition frozen or reduced argue that post-secondary education is a public good. It provides the reflective and skilled people that society needs, and both justice and efficiency require that everyone get an equal chance to participate in it. If tuition is prohibitively high, both public goals will be frustrated. The best students will not be the ones who are educated, and opportunities will be unfairly distributed. Those who favour increasing tuition argue that education confers a substantial private benefit on those who receive it, a benefit that other people do not receive. Justice requires that those who receive a disproportionate benefit pay for it.

Each side appeals to a principle that is beyond dispute. The first says, roughly, that fair equality of opportunity requires that as society reproduces itself across generations, it must offer the benefits of higher education to everyone who is capable of acquiring them. The other one, put equally roughly, says that if some people receive a scarce benefit, but others don't, those who receive it should pay for it. People who expect to derive substantial benefits are free to do so, but they have no business asking for public subsidies.

In this debate, both sides are right. Post-secondary education falls squarely under each principle. It's a necessary part of society's moral task of reproducing itself across generations in a way consistent with the equality of all citizens. It's also a benefit that is conferred differentially, creating further opportunities and benefits for those who receive it. Even if its opportunities are open to all, not everyone either takes or receives the same advantage of the opportunities offered. Those who do benefit get advantages that other people don't.

Both sides are also wrong if they claim to offer a full account of higher education. Quite apart from questions about who pays, an exclusive focus on either aspect – public good or private benefit – distorts its importance in our society. An exclusive focus on the private benefits of education distracts attention from the role of universities as custodians of cultural heritage, and also fails to acknowledge the important ways in which they contribute to the health and success of society as a whole, making life better even for those who don't participate directly.[3] It also overlooks the synergies between research and teaching, which have almost nothing to do with imparting marketable skills. An exclusive focus on the public benefits distracts attention from the fact that students get to choose what to study, what parts of the cultural heritage to explore, and what to do with what they have learned. Post-secondary education is nothing like military conscription, or even like a volunteer army, and no student should experience their first term as the equivalent of boot camp.

If both sides are right, there has to be some way of bringing the two intuitive ideas of justice together in a way that takes account of both of their claims. I want to argue that to take proper account of both principles in the case of post secondary education, we need a system in which the public pays for the public benefits provided by higher education, but each person pays for the private benefits that they, in particular, receive. I will make a proposal about how these components can be sorted out, as well as a proposal about when they can be sorted out.

The Division of Responsibility

Modern democracies are sometimes described as 'welfare states,' making it sound as though their primary job is to see to it that there citizens are happy or at least content with their lot. That picture is more misleading than illuminating, both as a description of the basic activities of modern liberal states and as a prescription for what justice demands of them. It's better to think of modern democracies as resting on what the late John Rawls called a 'division of responsibility' between society and the individual.[4] Rawls suggested that society as a whole has the responsibility to ensure that everyone has the basic abilities and protections they need to be able to choose their own path in life, and a public culture that enables them to do so. That responsibility requires public provision of a wide range of services and benefits to citizens, including both pure public goods, such as waste-treatment facilities, the protection of the environment, the supply of police services, and national defence,[5] and goods such as health care and basic education that contribute to the ability of all citizens to decide what kind of lives they wish to lead. Most of these goods are provided more or less unconditionally.[6] Your claim to medical treatment does not depend on your ability to pay for it. It also doesn't depend on how you came to need it. Maybe you should have gotten a flu shot, but if you get seriously ill with the flu because you didn't, you get treated anyway.

Public provision of health care shows the sense in which the state's main business isn't making people content, let alone happy. Other things may matter to you more than your health – maybe you would rather skip an expensive medical treatment that will extend your life and take a fraction of what it would have cost to spend as you see fit, perhaps on a spectacular vacation. Public provision doesn't work that way. You receive treatment, or some form of voucher you can use only for treatment, rather than receiving the cash to spend in whatever way would make you happiest. The focus on provision of particular goods and services doesn't reflect a paternalistic distrust of the poor judgment people might exercise in spending their money. Nor does it express contempt for the particular choices that people are likely to make. Instead, it is a reflection of the basic requirements of justice under a division of responsibility. Society's task is not to see to it that you are happy, or that you succeed in your ambitions. Instead, its obligation is to see to it that you will have the wherewithal to make what you will of your own life.[7] That requires both meeting your needs and securing conditions in which you can set your own purposes.

The other side of the division of responsibility is that if public provision is in place, each individual has a special responsibility for his or her own life. Nobody is entitled to demand an extra share of social resources just because they happen to want something particularly badly. They also can't demand extra resources, or limitations on the fundamental freedoms of others, on the grounds that their chosen path in life is more valuable or important than those of others.[8] The problem with those demands isn't that they are controversial, but that demanding more is inconsistent with the responsibility each person has for their own life.

The special responsibility that each person has for his or her own life also provides an important role for markets. Markets enable people to decide what to do with their lives and abilities, and to decide what to do in light of the choices of others. People offer each other incentives to do the things they want them to do. Freedom entitles each person to decide which incentives to offer others – what to buy – and how to respond to the incentives others offer – how hard to work, and whether to do something interesting or lucrative. One of the opportunities opened up by market society is the freedom to use liberties and abilities to acquire income and wealth, subject to the claim of society as a whole to tax income and wealth as needed to sustain its responsibility of providing adequate resources and opportunities to all.

The division of responsibility generates each of the two principles that animate debates about tuition, and specifies the appropriate domains for their application. In most cases, the domains are separate. The first principle governs things that everyone gets, whether directly or indirectly; the second those that people seek out and acquire differentially. The second principle governs most other things, which go to those who pay for them on the basis of their ability and willingness to pay.

It's difficult to imagine a tolerable social life organized around only one of these principles. Leaving everything to the market would make each person's life prospects depend too much on contingencies of birth and health; distributing everything centrally would prevent people from taking responsibility for their own lives.

The distinction between these two principles cuts across the question of whether government should be in the business of *producing* particular goods. Whether the private sector or the state is a more effective provider of certain goods doesn't speak directly to the question of who should pay for them. The two principles of just distribution are silent about who produces what, because they concern who receives and who pays for various things. Governments have at various times run airlines, coal mines, and gas stations, each of which charged their customers for their products. At other times governments have contracted out the provision of essential services. There may be no general answer to the question of which arrangements work best, just a series of specific answers about specific services. These questions can only be answered under the cold gaze of efficiency: what is likely to produce the best result at the lowest cost? The answers to those questions don't tell us which things should be provided to all.

Higher Education and the Division of Responsibility

Higher education straddles the division of responsibility between society and the individual. Educating a significant proportion of the public provides benefits to everyone, by enabling economic development and innovation, and by ensuring the articulate citizenry that democracy demands. For those who are educated, it provides the further benefits both of a broader array of options and, no less important, broadened horizons of understanding.

For all of its public benefits, post-secondary education is not something that is actually provided to everyone. When it is provided, it doesn't get delivered to everyone in the same way, in the way that primary and secondary education, health care, and clean water are supposed to be. At most, higher education is supposed to be available to all those who are capable of participating in it. Participation rates in Ontario are in the neighbourhood of 40%. It may be a matter of some concern to lag so far behind some countries with very high participation rates – Finland at 56.1%, for example – but even Finland doesn't approach universal participation in post-secondary education. The model of education cannot be assimilated to the model of health care, where everyone gets to participate, at least if they wait in line long enough. Not everyone who applies to college or university gets in, no matter how long they wait in line, and those who do get 'in' to very different institutions face different offerings, and, within those institutions, take advantage of different options available to them in different ways and to different degrees. Those differences in institutional structure, offerings, and even quality are not imperfections in the system. They are strengths. It is a good thing that students can choose the type of institution they wish to attend and also good that institutions have some choice about the type of students they want and the programs they offer.[9]

This range of choices already marks a sharp contrast with things for which public provision is required. If sewage treatment systems vary in their reliability or quality, or are only available to some people, we have both a public health disaster on our hands and a pressing issue of justice. If vaccinations are only available to people living in urban areas, that raises a problem of justice too. If elementary schools in wealthy neighbourhoods get more resources than those in poor ones, that is an issue of justice. In each of these cases, society's ability to sustain itself across generations on terms of justice is called into question. Those who are excluded from basic services are wronged by the system that fails to give them the basic things they need. They will also probably experience high-minded talk about a 'culture of responsibility' as a mask for injustice, because they are told to 'take responsibility' for their lives but denied the means they need for taking it.

Post-secondary education is nothing like that. It may be that ideally we would have a participation rate of close to 100% in post-secondary education. But nobody would advocate a system in which there was 100% participation at any given institution or in any particular program at a particular institution, let alone at the graduate or second-entry level.

The variation in offerings and the unavoidable use of criteria for selecting students raise the first question about justice in higher education: how can something be a public good that is provided as a matter of justice if it isn't provided to everyone? Post-secondary education isn't a basic need in the way that primary and secondary education are. Instead, it is a public good because an educated public is a benefit to everyone, even if they are educated in different ways and to different degrees. Everyone benefits when society has skilled and educated people. The provision of that public benefit doesn't require either that everyone have a particular skill or level of education, or that any particular person have any particular level of skill and education. Part of society's mandate under the division of responsibility is to see to it that there are people who are well enough educated to carry out the various parts of society's tasks.

Higher education is also a public good in another sense. Although receiving post-secondary education isn't a matter of entitlement in the way that primary education is, the opportunity to participate in it is one. Both justice and efficient provision of educated people requires that everyone has a fair opportunity to participate. It would be unjust to exclude people from a chance to develop their power simply because they couldn't afford to pay. It would also be unwise to limit the pool of people to be educated on the basis of ability to pay, since it is so obviously not a reliable indicator of ability to learn.

Reproducing society across generations on terms of justice also requires that higher education be dedicated to the pursuit of excellence, in both research and teaching. The pursuit of excellence is a benefit to society as a whole, even in those cases when the aim is not achieved. Most of the public benefits of post-secondary education only accrue when the quality is high, and accrue in proportion to quality. Although the monetary costs of low-quality education are lower, the real costs are high. Over the short term, students pay those costs, in the form of fewer spaces, larger classes, less intensive instruction, and loss of research faculty. In the longer term, the public also pays, by getting graduates with both less training and less of the things that education brings to a democracy.

It may be that some of the *private* benefits of post-secondary education could be acquired with low-quality education. Some of those private benefits may be the result of differentiation – imagine a society where employers prefer people with a diploma even if the training they receive is of such indifferent quality that it doesn't enable them to do their jobs any better.[10] The purpose of publicly funded education isn't to lead to that sort of differentiation, but to provide people who are very good at the things that they do, and a society can only provide that by providing access to high-quality education.

The social benefits of higher education require that different people benefit to different degrees. Gifted students have a broader range of choices, and success opens up further opportunities. These differences reflect the public benefits. As a society, we need people with a wide range of different types of education and training. We can't realize that benefit if everyone receives the same training, and we can't realize it justly if the decisions about who gets into which programs are left to anything other than a combination of individual choices and promise in relation to a particular program. Nobody can be required to take a post-secondary program that doesn't interest them, and if more people want to take a program than it can accommodate, the choice is supposed to be made on the basis of suitability for the program.[11] It's easier to say what doesn't count as part of suitability than to say what does. In particular, wealth, or as some private universities politely call it, 'legacy' status, is not part of what qualifies a person for admission to an institution or program. Wealth-based admissions aren't just unfair to those who are excluded on the basis of their financial status. In a society where markets allocate most goods, people are excluded from lots of things on just that basis: houses, cars, and dinners in restaurants are allocated primarily on the basis of wealth. However much some people might complain about this, objections to market provision overlook the specific problem with having access to post-secondary education depend on wealth – the way that it frustrates one of the purposes of public provision. In order to provide the educated workforce and the educated public necessary for economic growth and informed public debate, those who are selected must be selected on the basis of criteria relevant to those public purposes. Family wealth isn't a serious candidate for such a criterion.

Assessing Private Benefits

Because it is differentially distributed, post-secondary education also provides differential private benefits. Society as a whole may need engineers, people with good writing skills, doctors, lawyers, and so on. Society also requires excellence in those things. Those who are chosen to do each of these jobs both get the personal benefits of additional education and the longer-term financial benefits that follow education. Those benefits are well documented, and it would be disingenuous to pretend that if they are benefits to society as a whole, they can't also be benefits to those receive them. They flow to those who receive them in a way that they don't flow to anybody else, so that public benefits are provided by giving particular people additional powers for making their own way in the world, powers that aren't provided to everyone.

How much private benefit does someone receive from a particular level of education? There are lots of statistical measures, most of which focus on such things as life expectancy and income earned, treating these as an implicit proxy for improved welfare. One fascinating artefact of these measures is the surprising (though on reflection not) result that, on average, students who do an undergraduate degree in philosophy do better financially those who do undergraduate degrees in more 'practical' disciplines.[12] Does this mean that the benefits of a philosophy education are significantly private, so that philosophy students should be charged a higher tuition fee for their investment than students who major in such low-paying subjects as commerce?

We usually think of economic benefits in a way that makes no direct contact with ideas about welfare. Instead, we focus on realized value. Any sane tax system thinks about talents in this way, for example. If you have a beautiful singing voice, but use it only to sings songs to your children, you don't have to pay tax on the happiness that you receive, or pay a gift or estate tax on the happiness that your children receive from it. If you take that same beautiful voice and sing with the Canadian

Opera Company, you must pay tax on any income you earn. Why treat these cases so differently? After all, in the first case you make yourself or your children happy; in the second you make the paying patrons of the opera happy. If we cared about welfare, it might be a better idea to encourage you to make other people happy by making you pay the tax on what you could do for others, even if you don't. But neither your welfare not other people's is at issue here. The difference is that in the first case you simply enjoy something, whereas in the second case you turn it into a resource that you use in order to acquire further resources. It's not that there's anything wrong with using it that way. It's just that you have turned your talent into an asset that the state can tax to support its legitimate activities. It can tax you, even though it can't force you to sing – it can't, for example, assess the likely market value of your voice and require you to pay the tax that you would owe if you marketed your talent, effectively requiring you to do just that on pain of bankruptcy. The problem is not just that this would be impractical or intrusive, or even that it would effectively enslave those with talents, forcing them to deploy them in the most efficient way.[13] These problems are just symptoms of the way a talent tax is at odds with the division of responsibility. Your abilities are yours to use as you see fit; your special responsibility for how your life goes entitles you to use them in ways that are unproductive. Others can offer you monetary inducements to use them in ways that make them happy – that's essentially what a market does – but the division of responsibility requires that you get to decide.[14] Only the realized value of your assets is taxable, or, to put the same point more precisely, your voice is only an asset in the relevant sense if you realize its value.

The example of your beautiful voice shows the problems with some familiar ways of thinking about the talents that you develop with the help of others, notably the publicly funded post-secondary education system. The idea that students should be made to pay the probable market value of their education is like the idea that you should be forced to pay the tax on the income that you would have earned had you decided to become a successful opera singer.[15] Or, to take another example, making you pay for the welfare gain from your education would be like making the price you pay for a car depend on how happy it is likely to make you. Happiness taxes, like talent taxes, would be an administrative nightmare, but that isn't the only thing wrong with them. Your obligation to pay for a private asset is part of your special responsibility for your own life. If you gain a valuable resource which you use to gain economic advantage, you can be asked to pay for it.

Post-secondary education provides other benefits. It will expand your horizons, introduce you to people you would not otherwise have met, enliven your imagination, and sharpen your intellect.[16] Those benefits, like the benefits of singing in the shower or to your children, are not private benefits of the sort that anyone has any right to make you pay for, or make you deploy to guarantee that they bear fruit. You no more need to pay for them than for the benefits you get from clean water, the enforcement of the criminal law to protect you, and the various other publicly provided services that make your life better in various ways. They also increase your life expectancy and probably your income. You don't need to pay for them because they are provided to you in the process of providing them to society, because the only way they can be provided is by providing them to particular people. The only way that you have to pay for them is the way you pay for the public provision of public benefits – through the tax system, on the basis of the income you earn.

The private benefits that come from the realization of education as an asset redound to you in particular in a different way. The income you generate through the exercise of your publicly acquired skills is a measure of the private benefit you receive. Income is a poor proxy for welfare, but the ability to earn income isn't a proxy for the private benefit of education: it just is that private benefit. That private benefit is something that you can be made to pay for.

You don't know how valuable a private asset you will receive when you decide to enrol in a program, begin, or even complete your studies. You only know once you have actually brought your education to market. How much benefit you get is a function both of the opportunities that are available to you, and of the particular way in which you decide to bring it to market: whether, for example, you want to work in industry or for a non-profit organization; whether you want to use a legal education to do corporate work or to try to preserve wetlands. Or someone may want to use a humanities degree to write novels, something that can be either very lucrative, or very not-lucrative, with very little middle ground in between. Again, what you plan to do and what you end up doing may not turn out to be the same thing. It is the private benefit you realize that you should be made to pay for, not the ones you seek or that you could realize.

The issue here is not just that you don't know in advance what asset you will realize through your education. Calculating the expected value of an asset in conditions of uncertainty is straightforward enough. Instead, the value of the asset depends upon what you decide to make of it. Any sensible way of calculating the asset value of your education in advance would be inconsistent with the idea that you are free to choose what to do with your abilities, including the ones you acquire through your education. If you choose to turn your education into an asset, and succeed, then you should pay for it. If you don't turn it into an asset, or if you turn it into a sort of half-asset, then you pay that proportion of its cost.

Pricing the benefit is complicated by the fact that things that are publicly provided don't have a market price. The supply of education isn't controlled by aggregate demand for it. Since provision is public, the level of provision is set either by the Legislature or a particular institution. How much does it cost? Whatever it cost to provide the skills that you turned into a private benefit. The cost of that provision turns out to include some of the costs of the way in which it is provided. To take a simple example, even if you have perfect grades and test scores, so that your application takes no time to process, you still need to pay your proportionate share of the cost of running the admissions process. More generally, you need to pay some proportion of their share of operating the university as a whole, even if you never set foot in any buildings that are used by some of the programs that it offers. There is no natural way to disaggregate the various costs of the provision of private benefits that the university engages in, no natural way to measure the exact amount of private benefit that students receive because their professors talk to colleagues in other disciplines, for example. There is also no natural way to disaggregate the costs of training a student who goes on to make a lot of money from the costs of training the student who doesn't. If half of the graduating class makes a lot of money, then the price of the private benefit they have received includes covering part of the cost of educating their classmates, because they got the private benefit they did through the provision of the entire education system.[17]

It would be naive to pretend that a properly functioning and funded system of post-secondary education will somehow dissuade all students from viewing their education as a commodity. Some students aspire to be wealthy, stylish, or successful, and will choose their education based upon the prospect of a large income. Nobody thinks that governments or universities should stop trying to attract promising students by drawing attention to the increased lifetime earnings an education can bring. A free society has to let people make their own choices in life, including engaging in self-seeking behaviour. If people want to view higher education in narrowly careerist terms, probably nothing will stop them, and it may be that nothing should stop them. But the point of making them pay for the assets they realize isn't that they thought of their education in that way all along, but that they realized the value of an asset. If they view it that way, then they should be required to pay for the career benefits that they receive – just as everybody else should. They should not be required to pay for the career benefits that they seek, just the ones they receive.

The division of responsibility is an abstract way of thinking about social life, but it has significant implications for institutional design. An ideal system would have full public provision of post-secondary education, with only retroactive payment for the private benefits received, on the basis of the private benefits received. Prohibitive up-front costs are objectionable if they deter academically qualified students from enrolling. That would undermine fair equality of opportunity and produce a less talented pool of graduates.[18] Back-end costs are another matter. They can be high for those who earn high incomes as a result of their education. On this model, the total debt a graduate owes is tied to the private benefit realized, on the grounds that people should be made to pay for private benefits that they receive through public education. Income earned is an appropriate measure of private benefit gained, because earning power is the private benefit.

Because it makes provision for debt relief, this model isn't subject to the familiar objections to those models of income-contingent debt repayment that simply extend the amortization period to ensure that nobody's annual debt payment exceeds a fixed proportion of their income. The objections assume that those with smaller incomes pay more over the long term because the interest costs escalate as the amortization period grows.[19] If earnings set the total amount owed, as well as the repayment schedule, those objections have no purchase. Those who earn less, whether because of career choice or bad luck don't just get more time to repay: they have less to pay for.

No single institution is likely to be in a position to implement such a system, because of concerns about start-up costs, defaults, and so on. A province-wide or national system is more manageable. One possible mechanism is to use a progressive income tax, which we already have, to collect taxes that go into the general revenue pool, and then have a portion of them flow back into the education system. In principle, progressive taxation is a good way of raising money for the public component of higher education, even if higher education has tended to lose out when it competes with primary and secondary education, let alone health care. Even if we assume away that problem, total income earned isn't a particularly good measure of the extent to which someone has turned their education into an asset. Loans with back-end debt relief for those who earn less than the typical projected income from a particular degree or program are more promising. Any such program would need to be set up in such a way that students could realistically be expected to understand that they are taking on debt only conditionally, so that the amount that they have to pay for their education depends on how much they earn from it. Making financial aid programs understandable raises difficult issues of communication, but those are not issues of justice.[20]

Such a program is within reach, institutionally and politically. A substantial increase in government funding and student aid is needed to provide the public component of education at an acceptable level of quality. But there aren't any alternatives that don't require a significant infusion of public money. Setting up system of loans with debt relief is also manageable. With such a system in place, nominal tuition could be allowed to rise. Considered in the abstract, debt is neither good nor bad. Nothing is gained by focusing on the average amounts owed unless we know who owes what amount, and what assets were gained by acquiring it. Debt that covers the cost of a private benefit received is probably good on balance, even though debt where no private benefit is received is bad. The solution is to address debt where it is a problem, not to eliminate it where it isn't.

Implementing such a system could be done in a variety of ways. The simplest modification of the current system would require more public funding for the public aspects of education, and higher tuition, coupled with forgivable loans, to cover the private benefits. One consequence of implementing it this way would be that students who could afford to would get a discount by paying upfront, because they could avoid paying interest on the debt they expected to accumulate. This isn't a serious objection on grounds of justice. Anyone who did so would be getting a discount on the probable private benefit, not the public benefit. In return they would effectively decline the right to debt relief if they earned less than they expected. That wouldn't relieve them of the need to cover the cost of the private benefit they expect to receive, including the cost of debt relief to other students. These are matters of detail, and minor details at that. The key issue about post-secondary education is not how students from wealthy families will pay for it, but making sure that students from poor ones can.

Student loans and student debt have gotten a bad reputation, especially among students. The prospect of an enormous debt is terrifying, and any debt looks enormous when you are living on a tight budget with uncertain prospects ahead, even if you know, statistically, that most Canadians carry mortgages far in excess of their student debt, and that your income will be greater than average. The answer to these concerns isn't to pretend that they aren't real, but to set up an institutional mechanism that assures students that they only need to pay for the income they earn.

Notes

* Faculty of Law and Department of Philosophy, University of Toronto. I am grateful to Benjamin Alarie, G. Bruce Chapman, Sujit Choudhry, Ron Daniels, Abraham Drassinower, Andrew Green, Gopal Sreenivasan, and Karen Weisman for comments and discussion.

1 See, for example, the arguments offered by the Canadian Federation of Students at http://www.cfs-fcee.ca/reviewrae/english/.

2 Aaron Edlin and Ian Ayres make this argument in 'Why Legislating Low Tuitions for State Colleges Is a Mistake: They Just Subsidize the Rich,' available at http://writ.news.findlaw.com/commentary/20031030_ayres .html.

3 Treating education as a commodity may also invite students to view themselves as consumers rather than learners in a way that may, paradoxically, deprive some of many of the benefits of post-secondary education, including depriving them of many of the private benefits that would accrue to them if they thought about it in less consumerist terms.

4 John Rawls, 'Social Unity and Primary Goods,' in Samuel Freeman, ed. *John Rawls Collected Papers* (Cambridge, MA: Harvard University Press, 1999), 359–87.

5 Public health provisions are sometimes thought of in economic terms as 'non-excludable' public goods, where market provision is simply not feasible because those who are unwilling to pay still reap the benefit. The division of responsibility casts public provision in a different light: even if it were possible to provide public health measures in a way that excludes those unable to pay for them, it would be unjust for a society to do so,

because everybody needs them in order to have a chance at a decent life. The same point applies to police services. Everyone is entitled to them because they are a precondition of a decent life.

6 Any conditions that are attached to their provision are usually explicable as related to the prevention of readily foreseeable forms of abuse of unconditional provision.

7 I assume here that public provision takes place through the state, and that the state's primary duties are to its citizens, rather than being owed in the first instance to every human being. The best discussion of these issues is Michael Blake, 'Distributive Justice, State Coercion, and Autonomy,' *Philosophy and Public Affairs* 30:3 (2001).

8 If the state supports valuable cultural activities that wouldn't survive the pressures of market society, the only rationale consistent with the division of responsibility is one of securing a qualitatively distinctive cultural context for individual choice. See Ronald Dworkin, 'Can a Liberal State Support Art?' in *A Matter of Principle* (Cambridge, MA: Harvard University Press 1986), 221–33.

9 Part of the public mission of university education includes seeing to it that the best qualified students are admitted, and another part requires that institutions be able to assess the relevant dimensions of merit among their applicants based in part on their more general academic and scholarly priorities.

10 There may be some public benefit derived directly from the screening function of stiff admission requirements, which stream people who have met earlier requirements into more demanding positions. If so, that screening could be done by simply having admissions committees, and disbanding the research and teaching aspects of higher education.

11 What counts as suitability may be controversial – people may debate the extent to which, for example, increasing the representation of the historically under-represented is part of the purpose of the program.

12 Carol Marie Cropper, 'Philosophers Find Their Degree Pays Off in Life and Work,' *New York Times*, 26 Dec. 1997; Thomas Hurka, 'How to Get to the Top: Study Philosophy,' *Globe and Mail*, 2 January 1990, available at http://thereitis.org/displayarticle633.html.

13 Ronald Dworkin, *Sovereign Virtue* (Cambridge, MA: Harvard University Press, 1999), 99.

14 It follows that the division of responsibility is inconsistent with any analyzis that carries the idea of a market inward to conclude that your decision to sing to your children must be analysed as spending some of your resources to 'purchase' happiness for them.

15 Or the same amount discounted by the small likelihood of success.

16 It may also increase your life expectancy in a way that doesn't correlate with any of the other benefits it brings you. I leave this out of my analysis,

partly because I suspect some pre-selection goes on, and also because I suspect life expectancy correlates heavily enough with income that it is not really an independently measurable factor. Insofar as it correlates with income, we don't need to measure it. Insofar as pre-selection goes on, the solution is obviously to make post-secondary education more accessible to those with health difficulties.

17 Those costs in turn include the overall costs of running a university. For example, professional education differs from apprenticeship and training in its dependence on strong research departments in the arts and sciences. Within a given institution, the same factors may apply in the opposite direction. As a result, the costs can only be assessed relative to the institution as a whole, and by the institution itself.

18 The role of tuition in blocking social mobility is less than certain. Comparisons across jurisdictions are notoriously unreliable, but evidence suggests that in countries in which tuition is free, students from wealthy families are much more likely to participate in higher education than students from poor ones. For depressing details, see David Duff and Benjamin Alarie's contribution to this volume. Obviously many other things need to be done to encourage participation, including at the primary and secondary school level.

19 These complaints are articulated at http://www.cfs-fcee.ca/html/english/campaigns/index.php.

20 One issue that bridges justice and communication is the choice of words: debt is relieved, not forgiven: those who earn less than expected from their degrees haven't done anything wrong for which they require forgiveness. They have acquired less, so pay less for it.

Access to Public Universities: Addressing Systemic Inequalities

MELISSA S. WILLIAMS*

The modern university stands in a complex relationship to its surrounding society. The core function of the university remains its traditional one – fostering the highest possible level of human knowledge and understanding, and transmitting that knowledge to future generations. Yet contemporary universities – or 'multiversities,' as some call them – do and should serve a wide array of social purposes. In generating new knowledge through research, they also function as an engine of social and economic development. In educating students, they also create informed citizens and enable social mobility. In training society's leaders and professional classes, they serve as gatekeepers for the roles that profoundly affect the shape of society as a whole. In supporting applied as well as primary research, they contribute to the efficacy of individuals and institutions across virtually every domain of social practice. With the performance of these social functions comes a great responsibility. The words of former Harvard University President Derek Bok, written over twenty years ago, remain equally pertinent today:

> [U]niversities have an obligation to serve society by making the contributions they are uniquely able to provide. In carrying out this duty, everyone concerned must try to take account of many different values – the preservation of academic freedom, the maintenance of high intellectual standards, the protection of academic pursuits from outside interference, the rights of individuals affected by the university not to be harmed in their legitimate interests, the needs of those who stand to benefit from the intellectual services that a vigorous university can perform. The difficult task that confronts all academic leaders is to decide how their institution can respond to important social problems in a manner that respects all of these important interests.[1]

The university's responsibilities to society are mirrored by society's responsibilities to the university. First and foremost, society has an obligation to respect and protect academic freedom against the temptation to distort knowledge to advance a partisan political agenda, or to obstruct knowledge that runs counter to dominant opinion. Second, the profound public interest in the generation of knowledge, both as a source of economic prosperity and for the improvement of social practices, gives rise to a public responsibility to provide financial support to universities. This responsibility is especially acute in our emerging knowledge-based economies.

Third, in a democratic society there is a strong public responsibility to educate all citizens, both in order to ensure that they have the skills necessary to be contributing members of society, and to ensure that they possess the capacity to participate as well-informed members of a political community. Of course this does not mean that every citizen should receive a post-secondary education. Not every citizen has the academic ability or the disposition to pursue higher education. But the principle of democratic equality entails that the opportunity to pursue post-secondary education – and to reap the social and economic benefits of that education – should be open to all citizens on fair and equal terms. If we assume that natural intellectual talents are distributed more or less evenly across all segments of the population, it follows logically that a purely meritocratic distribution of participation in higher education would produce equal participation rates across all these segments. Ideally, differences of class or income, gender, 'race,' place of residence, language, religion, ethnicity, physical ability, and sexual orientation should have no impact on the distribution of higher education in a democratic society. As the philosopher John Rawls famously expressed this idea, such differences are 'arbitrary from a moral perspective,' and have no proper place in the just distribution of individuals' chances of fulfilling their life goals.[2]

The good news is that, for some population segments, the goal of fair equality of opportunity in achieving an undergraduate university education has been fully realized in Canada. Although women were wholly excluded from universities through most of the nineteenth century, and were underrepresented through most of the twentieth, by the end of the 1990s women's university enrolment had surpassed that of men. Women now constitute 55%, and men 45%, of full-time university students.[3] Further, notwithstanding evidence of ongoing discrimination against visible minorities in the sphere of employment, their participation rates in higher education are not below the average for the population as a whole. Indeed, both Canadian-born visible minorities and those born abroad participate at a significantly higher rate than do non-racialized groups.[4]

For some other social segments, however, inequalities in university education persist. Family income is a major predictor of a student's likelihood of attending university. Students from high-income families were more than twice as likely to attend university as students from low-income families in the period between 1993 and 1998.[5] The gap between Aboriginal and non-Aboriginal Canadians is even more striking. The 2001 census shows that among individuals aged 25 to 34, 7.8% of persons reporting Aboriginal identity had completed a university degree, in contrast to 27.6% of the general population in this age group. Although the number of Aboriginal university graduates has been growing rapidly in recent years, there is still an enormous educational disparity.[6] Other population segments that are underrepresented in higher education include students from rural and remote areas, students with disabilities, and sole-support mothers.[7]

Why should increased access to university education for underrepresented groups be a key priority for a democratic society? In order to fully address this question, it is necessary to introduce the concept of *systemic inequality* (sometimes also referred to as structural discrimination). Systemic inequalities are those that are reliably reproduced over time along the lines of social group differences even in the absence of patterns of overt or intentional discrimination on the part of identifiable social agents. Such group-patterned inequalities extend *across an array of social domains*, including income, education, social status (including cultural affirmation or stigmatization), health, life expectancy, infant mortality, and representation in political institutions. Moreover, systemic inequalities tend to be *intergenerational* patterns of group-structured difference. Where systemic inequalities are in place, inequalities in one social domain generate inequalities in other social domains and interact dynamically to reproduce themselves over time and across generations.[8]

In the case of post-secondary education, for example, it is easy to see how these dynamics can work. Because low-income individuals are less likely to pursue higher education, their average lifetime earning potential is less than that of students from middle- and upper-income families. Moreover, one of the most important determinants of an individual's propensity to pursue a university education is whether he or she has a parent with a university degree.[9] This can create a 'vicious cycle' that reproduces both educational underachievement and low earning potential from one generation to the next. Moreover, income inequality is highly correlated with other forms of social inequality. It is well established, for example, that individuals' health status is positively correlated with income.[10] An individual's life chances over all, then, are powerfully affected by the income status of the family she or he happens to be born into. The social contours of group-patterned intergenerational inequality, in other words, confer social status on individuals at birth – according to characteristics that are 'arbitrary from a moral perspective.' Such a circumstance clearly contradicts the principle of fair equality of opportunity as a pillar of democratic society.

This example highlights the pivotal place of universities in the overall structure of social inequality. Because higher education so profoundly affects individuals' lifetime earning potential,[11] *the social pattern of access to post-secondary education necessarily functions either to reinforce or to weaken existing systemic inequalities*. Where access to higher education for historically underrepresented groups is increased, and where the boundaries of those groups coincide with patterns of systemic inequality, the long-term consequence will be to ameliorate group-patterned inequality – not only within a single generation, but across generations. Conversely, where access to higher education remains slanted in favour of the well-off, patterns of systemic inequality will be reproduced. Indeed, in a knowledge-based economy, where higher education yields greater and greater advantages to those who pursue post-secondary education, an unchanged pattern of access to university will not only reinforce but will likely amplify existing structures of social and economic inequality.

For these reasons, it makes sense to consider universities as part of what Rawls calls 'the basic structure of society': '[T]he primary subject of justice is the basic structure of society, or more exactly, the way in which the major social institutions distribute fundamental rights and duties and determine the division of advantages from social cooperation ... Taken together as one scheme, the major institutions define men's rights and duties and influence their life-prospects, what they can expect to be and how well they can hope to do.'[12] Of course, it is not the primary function of universities to rectify patterns of systemic inequality. Nonetheless, a societal commitment to the ideal of fair equality of opportunity entails a corollary commitment to ensure that the distribution of access to higher education functions to ameliorate systemic inequalities rather than to reinforce or amplify them, wherever these goals are consistent with the core purposes of the university.

If we maintain a steady focus on the impact of access to higher education on systemic inequalities, what follows for public policy? Which methods of financing university education are most effective at enhancing access for educationally disadvantaged students? Can the goal of ameliorating systemic inequality be reconciled with the other purposes of the university system, including the adequate funding of university programs and the affordability of university for middle-income students?

In what follows, I will attempt to address these questions with a particular emphasis on the accessibility of university education to low-income and Aboriginal students. Although the societal interests in addressing other forms of educational disadvantage are also strong, constraints of time and space force me to focus on these two categories of students.

With respect to low-income students, I suggest that Canadian universities should proceed warily in introducing further tuition increases, even if such increases are accompanied by income-contingent loan programs. The experience of the United States, where tuition increases have negatively affected access for low-income students and minorities, should serve as a cautionary tale for Canadians. In particular, this experience tells the *political* story that as it becomes more difficult for middle-income families to send their children to university because of high tuition, political pressures intensify to introduce financial relief for middle-income students. The public costs of higher education balloon, and governments respond by finding ways to limit spending: cutting grant aid in favour of loans and shrinking direct transfers to institutions in favour of individual student aid. The result is impaired access for the neediest students and a diminished capacity for universities to increase net revenues through tuition increases. Avoiding this dynamic would entail strongly redistributive grant programs to offset the impact of increased tuition on needy students. Yet because the class of needy students grows with every tuition increase, the margin of increased net revenue to universities from each tuition increase will gradually narrow. Taken together, these considerations suggest that there may be a limit to tuition increases as a solution to universities' underfunding.

With respect to Aboriginal students, I argue that improved access depends on carefully tailoring programs to overcome cultural as well as material barriers. Given the extremity of the systemic inequalities confronting Aboriginal people in Canada, continued improvements in access to university should be a top priority for educational reform.

Access for Low-income Students: A Natural Limit on Tuition Increases?

Across North America, tuition fees for both public and private universities have risen dramatically over the last two decades. Several factors appear to contribute to these increases, and it is difficult to reach a generalizable conclusion as to which is the most important.[13] First, the cost of providing a high-quality education has increased. The importance of supporting cutting-edge research; the need to provide an increasing array of support services to students; an increasingly competitive market for top faculty; the high cost of addressing years of deferred maintenance on universities' physical plant; the rising costs of technology; investment to encourage technology transfers that build on primary research; the demographic and social trends that have generated increasing enrolments: these forces make running high-quality educational institutions more costly than in the past. Second, higher education competes with other spending priorities in public sector budgets, and during this period many governments have cut spending on universities in favour of health care (and, in the United States, on prisons). In the face of budget cuts, universities have turned to tuition increases to meet their rising costs.[14]

Over all, tuitions in Canadian universities increased markedly during the 1990s. Between 1990 and 2004, average undergraduate tuition across Canada increased from $1,464 to $4,172, or by 185%.[15] In the first half of the 1990s, government-funded student assistance declined by approximately 20% in real terms even as tuitions were rising, reducing the number of grants available and increasing limits on student loans. This trend was reversed in 1994, however. Both the federal government and the provinces (especially Ontario) introduced new grant and loan-remission programs, with the result that total government expenditures on student assistance nearly doubled in the latter half of the decade.[16] The gap between grant support and student loans that increased substantially beginning in 1992 appears to have narrowed in recent years, but the funding system as a whole is tilted much more heavily toward loans than at the beginning of the 1990s.[17] The clear result of this shift to student loans is a dramatic increase in student indebtedness at graduation from a four-year university program: students' average indebtedness increased from \$10,800 in 1990 to \$21,200 in 2001, or almost double.[18]

Although the price elasticity of demand for higher education is relatively low as compared with most consumer commodities, education economists agree that the market for higher education is characterized by a downward-sloping demand curve: other things being equal, demand decreases as price increases.[19] Nonetheless, economists have further shown that the price elasticity of demand decreases as income increases. That is to say, individuals in upper-income categories are less responsive to an increase in the cost of higher education than are those in lower-income categories.[20] The poorer the student, the more likely he or she will be deterred from pursuing a university education by the rising cost of that education, or encouraged to attend by the reduction of net costs.

In the complex world we live in, however, other things are not equal. The 1990s were a period in which tuitions rose at a fast pace at the same time that other social trends pressed demand for higher education upward. These trends did not change the basic downward-sloping shape of the demand curve, but they did function to shift the curve upward: although demand for higher education is still price-responsive, students are willing to pay more for it than they were willing to pay in earlier decades. Most important among these trends is the shift toward knowledge-based economies, where the return to individuals of the investment in higher education increases. There is a growing wage premium for university graduates, and rising participation rates express students' rational response to this phenomenon. Women's increasing participation in higher education has also generated a significant upward pressure on enrolments. Finally, since one of the strongest predictors of a student's attendance at university is whether his or her parents have a university education, the growing participation of historically underrepresented groups – lower-income families and minorities, in particular – has an intergenerational 'snowball' effect.[21] The net result of these trends is that, for the period in question, the demand curve as a whole has shifted out.[22] Because of these complexities, the negative relationship between tuition and participation rates has been unsettled. For example, a recent cross-national comparative study sponsored by the Canada Millennium Scholarship Foundation finds that the empirical evidence on the relationship between tuition and enrolment is quite mixed. Jurisdictions that introduced or increased tuition did not necessarily experience declining enrolment, and those that decreased or froze tuition did not necessarily experience increasing enrolments.[23] Wide variations in the extent of redistributive programs aimed at low-income students further complicate the relationship between tuition and participation. In short, although there are cases where increasing enrolments have accompanied increasing tuition, they do not establish a statistically significant positive correlation between tuition and participation.[24]

In the United States, however, several recent studies have shown that tuition increases have had a disproportionate impact on low-income students. Thomas Kane shows that even as overall enrolments rose despite tuition increases, participation rates for low-income students slowed.[25] In a study of increases in tuition in Massachusetts during the 1980s and the 1990s, Kane found that the gap in participation between upper- and lower-income students grew as tuition increased. Even more troubling, he found that the enrolment decline among lower-income Black students was significantly more pronounced than the decline among lower-income white students during this period.[26] One explanation of these growing participation gaps may be the fact that the percentage of family income required to pay the net (post–financial aid) costs of a post-secondary education grew significantly during the 1990s in the United States. As Douglas Heller shows, this percentage was higher for lower-income than for upper-income students, and for minority students as compared with white students. Thus, those groups that have been chronically underrepresented in higher education were disproportionately burdened by rising tuition.[27]

This negative impact of rising tuition on educationally disadvantaged groups in the United States cannot be understood without attending to the changing structure of student assistance programs during this period. Again, the picture is complex, but it is possible to make some general observations. First, there has been a major shift in the funding structure of financial aid from grants to loans. The federal Pell Grant program covered 84% of students' costs of attending a four-year public university in the mid-1970s, but now covers only 42% of those costs; the slack has been taken up by loan programs.[28] The pressure of increasing tuition on middle-income families has also led to federal, state, and institutional funding programs that are not need-based, including both subsidized and unsubsidized loans, tax credits or deductions, and merit-based scholarships. The eligibility requirements for federally subsidized loan programs were relaxed in 1978 by the *Middle Income Student Assistance Act*, which produced a rapid and sustained increase in student borrowing, and a resulting increase in the amount of public expenditures on loans. Although grant spending also increased during this period, it did so at a much slower rate than spending on loans. By the end of this process, spending on loans exceeded grant spending by a considerable margin. As Michael Mumper notes, 'While Congress was spending more each year on students, it was shifting subsidies away from the most needy to often considerably less needy middle-income students.'[29]

Tax credits and unsubsidized loans, which also add to public expenditures on higher education, enhance the affordability of university for middle-income families, but they do little or nothing to improve access for low-income families.[30] Further funds have been injected into student assistance in the form of new merit-based scholarships, which tend disproportionately to benefit middle- and upper-income students. Meanwhile, the rolling back of affirmative action programs through the 1990s also diminished minority students' access to higher education. The net result is that the participation gap between low-income and upper-income students has grown over recent decades.[31] Mumper concludes: 'The emergence of this new generation of federal and state student aid programs has helped to undermine the goal of equal opportunity that characterized the earlier programs. These are explicitly not need-based programs. Instead, they are designed to make higher education more affordable to middle- and even upper-income families. There is substantial evidence that these programs are creating a future in which government spending on student aid is ever increasing and yet the access available to lower-income students is ever diminishing.'[32]

In Canada, rising tuition has also been accompanied by a substantial increase in total government spending on student aid. Indeed, in the decade since 1994 this spending has doubled in real terms.[33] And as in the United States, this increase in aid has taken the form of a massive expansion in loan programs and a reduction in grant programs. Borrowing limits in subsidized loan programs were increased, with the result that student borrowing increased by 70% in a period of two years, while the value of student grants decreased. The growth in student borrowing halted in the late 1990s, both because many students had reached borrowing limits and because stricter eligibility criteria were introduced in some provinces. Another important parallel to the American experience is an increase in federal expenditures on higher education through tax credits and relief from capital gains and interest taxes through the Registered Education Savings Plan program. In fact, the latter is currently the fastest-growing federal tax expenditure on higher education. Several provinces also offer tax credit programs to recent graduates.[34] These tax credit programs are not need-based, and tend disproportionately to benefit middle- and upper-income families and graduates. In the latter half of the decade, the creation of the Canada Millennium Scholarship Foundation, new income-contingent loan repayment programs, and grant-sustaining programs such as Ontario's matching grants for private donations to institutional student assistance restored some of the need-based funding that had been eroded early in the decade.

The overall picture of federal and provincial governments funding for higher education must also take into account direct transfers to institutions as well as aid to individual students. Here, the story is clear: direct transfers to institutions declined 15% during the 1990s, with the largest decreases concentrated at the federal level and in Ontario.[35] Taking institutional transfers, government tax expenditures (tuition credits and subsidized savings programs), and student aid expenditures together, we see that over the course of the 1990s there was a major restructuring in the way that governments fund higher education, with a large increase in the proportion of funds spent on support to individuals and a decline in institutional transfers. Within the category of financial support for individual students, both need-based and non-need-based funding has increased. But whereas need-based funding has increased by a little less than 50%, non-need-based expenditures have more than doubled.[36] It remains to be seen how these trends will play out over the coming years.

Despite important similarities in the changing structures of government spending on student aid in the United States and Canada, there is a signal difference in the impact on low-income and minority students: rising tuition has not deterred educationally disadvantaged students in Canada from pursuing a university education. Although there are persistent participation gaps between low-income and upper-income students, participation for all income groups increased until the mid-1990s. More to the point from the standpoint of systemic inequality, the rate of participation for low-income students increased throughout the decade. Although the correlation between income and university attendance increased in the first half of the decade, when tuitions began rising, it actually *declined* in the latter half of the decade because of rising enrolment among the lowest income groups.[37] Available studies do not appear to focus on the relationship between this shift in the correlation between income and attendance and student financial aid, but it is worth noting that it *coincided with the introduction of new need-based funding, especially in the form of grants*, such as the Canada Millennium Scholarship program. This would appear to reinforce the common observation that grant support targeted toward the neediest students is the surest route to increasing the likelihood that they will attend university.[38]

So far, then, Canadian governments' student funding programs appear to have prevented tuition increases from negatively affecting access to university for low-income students. Yet there are reasons to believe that it would be *a mistake to infer that tuitions can continue to rise indefinitely without negatively affecting access*, even with redistributive grant programs in place. Most importantly, a 2004 study shows that the diminishing correlation between income and access to university is in part an artefact of *declining participation rates among middle-income students*, those who come from families with incomes between $25,000 and $100,000 per year. In short, the increasing costs of higher education appear to have had the greatest impact on middle-income students, as reflected in much higher levels of indebtedness and declining participation among this population. It is worth noting, in particular, that the participation rate of the second-lowest income group (families earning between $25,000 and $50,000), fell below that of the lowest income group in 1997, the most recent year in which data are available.[39]

In this light, the experience of the United States may be a cautionary tale about tuition increases for Canadians who are concerned about sustaining access to university for all students regardless of family income. The American story may, in fact, be best understood as follows: As tuition increases, the financial pressures on students from middle-class families intensify. These difficulties translate into *political* pressures to increase government support to enable these families – who are the most numerous and whose votes determine election outcomes – to send their children to university. Government expenditures on student aid for the middle class therefore increase. Eligibility for subsidized loans is extended to higher income groups, and tax credits are introduced to relieve the pressure on the middle class. Because these benefits flow to an ever-increasing segment of the population, government expenditures on higher education increase dramatically. Yet other spending pressures persist, especially in the field of health care, and over time governments are forced to make difficult spending choices. The political gains from maintaining and enhancing supports for middle-class families to send their children to university far outweigh the losses of cutting generous transfers to low-income students, and governments can rightly claim that they are spending more on higher education even as they reduce need-based grant funding. Over time, cuts in aid to the neediest students make it increasingly difficult for them to afford a university education. These students therefore forgo a university education in favour of less-expensive vocational colleges, or simply opt out of higher education altogether. The net result of these dynamics is that the higher education system reinforces (and possibly amplifies) existing patterns of systemic inequality. While it would be foolish to attribute growing income inequality in the United States to the changing structure of higher education funding, it is sensible to suppose that these changes may be a contributing factor.[40]

If this is story is correct – as it appears to be in the American case – it implies that there may be a natural limit on the degree to which public university tuition can be increased without a negative impact on accessibility for low-income students.[41] Subsidized loan programs such as income-contingent repayment schemes can go some distance toward making a university education affordable for middle-income students. But as the cost of these programs increases, governments will be hard pressed to maintain the strongly redistributive grant programs that foster access for low-income students. The recent decline in participation among lower-middle-income students may be a 'canary in the mine' signaling that university tuitions are already nearing their natural limit. Further increases will intensify pressures on the core of the middle class. The cost of a university education as a proportion of household income will continue to increase, as will the ratio of students' average indebtedness at graduation to their average expected incomes. Indeed, a December 2004 study sponsored by the Canada Millennium Scholarship Foundation shows that a university education is already less affordable in Canada than in the United States, where affordability is read as the proportion of family household income required to cover tuition and living costs.[42]

Although it is reasonable to maintain current rules whereby universities redistribute a portion of increased tuition revenues in the form of grants to the neediest students, as in Ontario, there will be pressure to raise the level of income eligibility, such that the class of 'needy students' gradually expands to include more and more middle-income students as tuition rises. Otherwise, middle-class resentment of transfers to lower-income students will tend to grow. Whether relief for these students comes from additional government expenditures on student aid or from the universities themselves, the likely result is that net university resources will not be significantly enhanced by tuition increases beyond a certain limit. As they have already shown, governments are likely to offset the increasing costs of student aid with cutbacks in direct transfers to institutions. Thus the pressures on the university finance system as a whole will be to raise the threshold of eligibility for redistributive student aid, and to cut back on the per-student amount of such aid to keep overall costs in check. Over time, it seems likely that that this will negatively affect the amount of support available for low-income students, and hence their ability to pursue a university education.

I do not claim to have established the empirical validity of this narrative, which would require careful and sustained study across a range of cases. If it turns out to be correct, however, what follows for tuition and financial aid policies – again, keeping our eyes on the broader issue of systemic inequalities?

First, baseline tuitions for public universities should be benchmarked to median family income or per capita GDP.[43] Where this benchmark should be set – what the appropriate percentage of median income should be – is a question best left for economists. But the basic intuition is that once tuition rises above a certain percentage of middle-class income, political pressures will rise to expand government expenditures on student aid in order to render a university education affordable for the middle class, driving up public spending on education at the expense of other policy priorities and eventually creating pressures to correct this trend through education cutbacks. A tuition policy linked to median income would avoid these political spirals. For students whose families fall below the median income, tuition subsidies should be provided so that the effective net tuition fee does not exceed the percentage of household income required of the median family. Such subsidies could take the form of outright grants, or they could take the form of variable tuition rates.

It is important to acknowledge that from the standpoint of equity a flat tuition rate set as a constant percentage of median household income is not ideal. Low-income families must spend a higher percentage of their incomes on basic necessities, so even if they were not paying a higher percentage of their incomes for tuition than middle-income families, the impact of tuition payments on their quality of life would be considerably greater. This constitutes a good reason for higher tuition subsidies for needier families. At the other end of the spectrum, tuition fees set according to median family income offer a significant discount to upper-income families, who would of course be spending a much smaller percentage of their income on tuition. To correct for this, tuitions could be set at a price that upper-income families will bear, and subsidies offered to middle-income families to arrive at the desired net cost of tuition as a percentage of total income. It is important to note, however, that the percentage of total tuition revenues necessary to achieve this result would increase with the price of tuition. Thus universities would reap a diminishing margin of revenue increase with every increase in tuition, and at some point this margin would reach the vanishing point.[44]

Second, maximum student indebtedness should be benchmarked to students' average expected income within a designated period after graduation. While it is perfectly fair to expect students to contribute to the cost of their education, since they benefit from the income dividend that generally accompanies a university degree, it would not be economically rational for them to invest more in their educations than they could expect to reap within a reasonable period after graduation. As many others have argued at length, income-contingent loan repayment programs therefore make a great deal of sense both from the standpoint of efficiency or economic rationality as well as from the standpoint of equity.[45] Yet this does not mean that income-contingent loans should be provided without limit. The price of an undergraduate education should not be a lifetime of debt burden; nor should the income advantage of a university education be erased by debt payments beyond a limited number of years.[46] The appropriate percentage of post-graduation income assignable to debt repayment, and the precise duration of a 'reasonable period after graduation,' are partly economic and partly political or socio-cultural questions.

Two further points follow from these claims: (a) For those whose income falls below the average expected for their graduation class, they should receive debt relief (whether in the form of income-contingent repayment schemes or through outright forgiveness of a portion of their debt); and (b) once the 'reasonable period' has expired, and a student has met payment obligations throughout that period, the remaining loan should be cancelled. If the maximum debt load is defined at too high a level, the cost of these different forms of loan forgiveness (which are effectively *post hoc* grants) will become so expensive for the public purse as to set into motion the political dynamics described above. If it is defined too low, public subsidies to financial aid exceed the level that is necessary to enable widespread access to university.

Third, assessments of financial need must cover the actual cost of living as well as tuition obligations. The difference between this total need assessment and total available resources (including family contributions and student loans within the limits described above, plus a limited amount of paid term-time employment) should be covered by grants. In some jurisdictions, need assessment formulae have not kept pace with inflation or the rising cost of living. In Ontario, for example, the cost of living estimates used by the Ontario Student Assistance Program have not been increased since 1994 and are not sensitive to the higher-than-average cost of living in some cities. When students' actual needs are not met through a combination of parental contribution and loans, they must turn to paid employment to make ends meet. Working during term-time is not necessarily a detriment to students' overall educational experience, and work experience can be an asset when students enter the competitive job market. Yet when students work above a certain number of hours per week, their studies suffer and they are more likely to drop out than students who are not working. There is evidence that low-income students are more likely to work beyond the advisable limit (which appears to be approximately 10–15 hours per week) than students from other income categories. A financial aid system geared toward accessibility for students across all income groups should therefore include mechanisms for closely monitoring students' paid employment and providing grant relief when students are overworking in order to meet basic needs.[47]

Fourth, where class-based debt aversion deters students from borrowing up to the reasonable maximum discussed above, students should receive additional grant support to encourage them to attend university. It is empirically well established that low-income students are more risk averse when it comes to borrowing for higher education than are middle- and upper-income students.[48] In part, this flows from an information gap: lower-income students are less likely to be aware of the individual returns of investment in higher education than are students from better-off backgrounds. In part, as noted above, students' inclination to pursue university is shaped by their own social and cultural experience. Students whose parents have attended university are more likely to attend. Not only does the experience of a close family member increase awareness of the employment opportunities that a university education can provide, it also increases one's appreciation for the idea that higher learning is a worthwhile pursuit for its own sake as well as for instrumental reasons. Further, students from low-income backgrounds may have less confidence in their ability to complete a university degree than those from other backgrounds. This uncertainty may make them wary of taking on debt they fear they will not be able to repay if they do not complete their programs and therefore cannot compete for the higher-paying jobs available for university graduates. Finally, lower-income students may be less likely to trust governments and universities to stand by commitments for *post hoc* debt relief.[49] In the face of these understandable sources of risk aversion, a higher education policy that seeks to ameliorate rather than to reinforce systemic inequalities will provide grant support to encourage qualified low-income students to attend university.

Access for Aboriginal Students: The Importance of Targeted Programs

Patterns of systemic inequality do not appear spontaneously. The institutional and societal structures that reproduce inequality over time and across social domains have a history. Sometimes that history includes explicit policies of state-sponsored exclusion and domination toward particular groups. In these cases, the scale and scope of enduring patterns of group-structured inequality is a matter not only of distributive justice, of which fair equality of opportunity is a key component. For cases of historical injustice, confronting systemic inequalities is also a matter of remedial justice, a social responsibility to redress the legacies of a morally indefensible past.

To engage in a thorough discussion of the relationship between historical injustice and ongoing patterns of systemic inequality would take me far beyond the purposes of this essay.[50] What is beyond dispute, however, is that the current patterns of social and economic inequality along the lines of Aboriginal identity in Canada flow from the past practices of the state. These practices include the forcible relocation of indigenous peoples from their traditional homelands to economically unviable reserves;[51] the system of residential schooling; and legal prohibitions on the maintenance of indigenous languages and cultural practices.[52] Patterns of ongoing systemic inequality for Aboriginal peoples are equally clear. No matter which measure of social and economic well-being one uses, Aboriginal people are uniformly worse off than other Canadians. While the average Canadian has a life expectancy of seventy-two years, for example, the average Aboriginal person lives

fifty-four years. The infant mortality rate for Aboriginal persons continues to exceed that of non-Aboriginal Canadians by a considerable margin: in 1991, the general Canadian infant mortality rate was eight per
thousand births, while for the Aboriginal population it was thirteen per
thousand.[53] Average family income for status Indians (those registered
as Indians under the Indian Act) is about half that of the average
Canadian family, and income disparity is increasing. In short, 'Aboriginal people have five times the rate of child welfare [dependency], four
times the death rate, three times the violent death, juvenile delinquency,
and suicide rate ..., and twice the rate of hospital admissions of the
average Canadian population.'[54]

As noted above, this pattern of inequality is replicated in the sphere
of higher education, especially at the university level. It is greatly
encouraging that the rate of Aboriginal university enrolment has been
increasing more quickly than for other demographic groups, and increasing numbers of Aboriginal students are going on for post-graduate
and professional study. While higher education is not a 'silver bullet'
solution to the problem of systemic inequality for Aboriginal persons or
any other disadvantaged group, there are positive signs that we are
moving in the right direction.

At the same time, there is ample reason not to be complacent. The
barriers between Aboriginal students and university remain high.
Because of extensive poverty within Aboriginal communities, many
Aboriginal students face all of the challenges that confront low-income
students in general. Since many Aboriginal communities are remote
from urban centres, Aboriginal students also confront the same obstacles as rural students in general, who (as noted above) are also
underrepresented at the university level. A disproportionate number of
Aboriginal students are also single parents, and so they confront all the
challenges distinctive to that social position.

To add to all this, many Aboriginal students find the cultural and
social climate of the university extremely alienating. In the words of the
Royal Commission on Aboriginal Peoples:

> Many [education and training] programs ignore Aboriginal perspectives,
> values and issues and give scant attention to the work environment in
> which students will use their professional knowledge and skills. In the
> informal culture of the institution, there may be little or no affirmation of
> Aboriginal identity, and the environment may replicate the negative fea-
> tures that [lead] students to drop out of school ... Aboriginal support

systems – peer networks, family activities, financial, personal and academic counseling, or daycare services – may not be in place. The lack of institutional readiness to develop these supports is a significant deterrent to the completion of programs for students who do enroll. Lack of Aboriginal control, strongly evidenced in the education of children and youth, is also encountered in the education of adults.[55]

A recent study sponsored by the Canada Millennium Scholarship Foundation documents the challenges confronting Aboriginal students very well. I will not duplicate these findings here, but strongly recommend this report to those who are concerned to combat systemic inequality for Aboriginal students through the higher education system.[56] Instead, let me simply emphasize the study's findings about what we have learned so far about the 'best practices' for preparing and encouraging Aboriginal students for university.

First, 'access programs' – programs oriented toward preparing Aboriginal students for the transition to post-secondary institutions – are highly effective. These programs often focus on 'non-traditional students' whose social and educational background leave some gaps in the skill set they need in order to be successful in university. They provide intensive academic advising, housing assistance, child care, guidance on adjusting to an urban setting, and career counselling. A crucial element of their success in meeting the needs of Aboriginal students is that they also create a culturally welcoming environment through connections to Aboriginal cultural centres on campus and beyond and to Aboriginal Studies programs. The province of Manitoba has been especially successful in creating effective access programs for Aboriginal students; the Transitional Year Programme at the University of Toronto also emphasizes access for Aboriginal students and is noted for its successes.[57]

Second, Aboriginal institutions – those created and designed by Aboriginal scholars and leaders – enable the delivery of higher education in modalities that are conscious of and responsive to Aboriginal cultures. One of the most well-developed institutions thus far is the First Nations University of Canada, which collaborates with the University of Regina in providing university-level education for Aboriginal students. The result is that Aboriginal enrolment at the University of Regina is proportionate to the Aboriginal population in the province of Saskatchewan. Other excellent examples include the Native Law Centre at the University of Saskatchewan and the Indigenous Governance

Program at the University of Victoria, both of which are training grow-ing numbers of Aboriginal post-graduate students and have curricula rich with indigenous content. As these examples suggest, one of the most promising routes for increasing access for Aboriginal students is to create partnerships between mainstream universities and Aboriginal communities, whether through the creation of autonomous Aboriginal institutions or by enabling Aboriginal leadership within existing insti-tutional boundaries. The defining elements of successful programs in-clude: the recruitment and involvement of Aboriginal community leaders (including elders) and Aboriginal faculty in the design and implemen-tation of programs; curriculum content that expresses or is sensitive to Aboriginal cultures, including the availability of training in Aboriginal languages; and adequate financial and community supports to prevent social isolation and to meet basic needs for housing, transportation, and child care.

Finally, creating a positive cultural environment for Aboriginal stu-dents requires not only putting supports in place for them, but also educating non-Aboriginal faculty, students, and staff about Aboriginal culture and the presence of Aboriginal students in the university com-munity. The cultural ignorance and insensitivity of non-Aboriginal com-munity members creates a hostile environment for Aboriginal students which direct services for these students cannot, by itself, correct. Robust support for Aboriginal cultural activities on campus, and building vis-ible and well-resourced centres for Aboriginal students, can increase the general community's awareness of Aboriginal culture. The Aborigi-nal Longhouse at the University of British Columbia, for example, serves both as a hub of Aboriginal activities on campus and an architec-tural celebration of Aboriginal culture.[58]

In short, increasing access for Aboriginal students is not only a matter of making university affordable for them, though of course this is a necessary condition. It is equally important to create programs that are specifically targeted at making universities hospitable environments for Aboriginal learning. A university, as the gateway to post-graduate and professional training, is at least one component of the leadership that so many Aboriginal communities need. Given the extremity of Aboriginal peoples' current marginalization in contemporary Cana-dian society, continued improvements in the formation of programs targeted toward Aboriginal students should be a top priority for reform in higher education.

Notes

* Department of Political Science, University of Toronto
1 Derek Bok, *Beyond the Ivory Tower: Social Responsibilities of the Modern University* (Cambridge: Harvard University Press, 1982), 88.
2 John Rawls, *A Theory of Justice* (Cambridge: Harvard University Press, 1971), 74.
3 Sean Junor and Alexander Usher, *The Price of Knowledge: Access and Student Finance in Canada* (Canada Millennium Scholarship Foundation, 2004 [cited 27 Nov. 2004]); available at http://www.millenniumscholarships.ca/factbook/en/. See chap. 2, 39.
4 Jean Lock Kunz, Anne Milan, and Sylvain Schetagne, 'Unequal Access: A Canadian Profile of Racial Differences in Education, Employment and Income' (Toronto: Canadian Race Relations Foundation, 2000), 16. Note, however, that the category 'visible minority' is not further disaggregated. There may be significant differences in participation rates across visible minority groups, but the data do not enable us to ascertain whether or not this is the case. Because of concerns that certain minority populations may be at risk of educational disadvantage or under-performance, there is a strong argument to be made for the collection of more differentiated data in order to target these groups for support. This is a controversial issue, as some fear that the collection of such data reinforces rather than dissipates social distinctions among groups. Such concerns underlie recent debates over the collection of academic performance data by racial group in the Toronto District School Board. Toronto's school trustees narrowly passed a motion to gather the data. See Susan O'Neill, 'School Board to Track Race Data,' *Inside Toronto*, 19 Nov. 2004 [cited 27 Nov. 2004]); available at http://www.insidetoronto.ca/to/annex/story/2355259p-2726572c.html. It is also important to acknowledge that many new immigrants to Canada are unable to find employment within the field of their expertise, or commensurate with their levels of training and education. Elizabeth McIsaac, 'Immigration in Canadian Cities, Census 2001: What Do the Data Tell Us?' *Policy Options*, May 2003, 58–63.
5 Nineteen per cent of 18- to 21-year-olds from families in the lowest income quartile attended university between 1993 and 1998, whereas 39% of students from the highest quartile attended. The participation gap between the two middle quartiles is higher than that between the two lowest quartiles. Junor and Usher, *The Price of Knowledge*, 49 and table 2.V.2.
6 Statistics Canada, *Education in Canada: Raising the Standard* [cited 27 Nov. 2004]; available at http://www12.statcan.ca/english/census01/products/analytic/companion/educ/canada.cfm. Thirty-eight per cent of Aboriginal persons between the ages of 25 and 34 had not completed high school in 2001, in contrast with 23% of the general population. The gap between

Aboriginal and non-Aboriginal Canadians who had completed a vocational college program was less glaring: 15.1% and 19.7%, respectively.

7 Rae Commission on Higher Education, *Higher Expectations for Higher Education: A Discussion Paper* (Government of Ontario, 2004 [cited 27 Nov. 2004]); available at http://www.raereview.on.ca/en/default.asp?loc1=home, p. 13.

8 For a classic study of inter-domain patterns of gender inequality, see Susan Moller Okin, *Justice, Gender, and the Family* (New York: Basic Books, 1989).

9 Kelly Foley, *Why Stop after High School? A Descriptive Analysis of the Most Important Reasons That High School Graduates Do Not Continue to PSE* (Canada Millennium Scholarship Foundation, 2001 [cited 26 Nov. 2004]); available at http://www.millenniumscholarships.ca/en/research/foley_en.pdf, p. 24.

10 See, e.g., John Wildman, 'Modelling Health, Income and Income Inequality: The Impact of Income Inequality on Health and Health Inequality,' *Journal of Health Economics* 22: 4 (2003), 521–38.

11 Michael Paulsen, 'Recent Research on the Economics of Attending College: Returns on Investment and Responsiveness to Price,' *Research in Higher Education* 39:4 (1998), 471–89. Paulsen also finds that unemployment rates among university graduates are significantly lower than among those who only completed high school.

12 Rawls, *A Theory of Justice*, 7.

13 For an overview of the upward pressures on tuition in the United States, see Michael Mumper, 'The Paradox of College Prices: Five Stories with No Clear Lesson,' in D.E. Heller, ed., *The States and Public Higher Education Policy: Affordability, Access, and Accountability* (Baltimore: Johns Hopkins University Press, 2001), 39–63.

14 Tuition has become an increasing percentage of revenues for public institutions in the United States since the early 1980s, from 16% in 1981–2 to 24% in 2001–2. Michael Mumper, 'The Future of College Access: The Declining Role of Public Education in Promoting Equal Opportunity,' *Annals of the American Academy of Political and Social Science* 585 (2003), 101.

15 Statistics Canada, *University Tuition Fees* (Statistics Canada, 2004 [cited 26 Nov. 2004]); available at http://www.statcan.ca/Daily/English/040902/d040902a.htm.

16 Junor and Usher, *The Price of Knowledge*, 161, 166.

17 Ibid., figure 4C.II.1, p. 162.

18 Ibid., figure 5.II.3, p. 186.

19 Watson Scott Swail and Donald E. Heller, *Changes in Tuition Policy: Natural Policy Experiments in Five Countries* (Canadian Millennium Foundation, 2004 [cited November 29, 2004]); available at http://www.millenniumscholarships.ca/en/research/tuition_e.pdf.

20 Paulsen, 'Recent Research on the Economics of Attending College,'

pp. 483–4; Larry Leslie and Paul Brinkman, *The Economic Value of Higher Education* (New York: Macmillan, 1989); Thomas Kane, 'Rising Public College Tuition and College Entry: How Well Do Public Subsidies Promote Access to College?' Working Paper no. 5164, National Bureau of Economic Research (1995); Donald E. Heller, 'The Effects of Tuition and State Financial Aid on Public College Enrollment,' *Review of Higher Education* 23:1 (1999): 65–89.

21 See esp. Donald E. Heller, 'Trends in the Affordability of Public Colleges and Universities: The Contradiction of Increasing Prices and Increasing Enrolment,' in Donald E. Heller, ed., *The States and Public Higher Education Policy: Affordability, Access, and Accountability* (Baltimore: Johns Hopkins University Press, 2001), 26–30.

22 *Ibid.*, figure 1.13, p. 30.

23 See generally Swail and Heller, *Changes in Tuition Policy*.

24 This calls into question recent claims that there is a positive correlation between participation and tuition prices. See, e.g., Roger Martin, 'A Bright Light on a Bad Strategy,' *Globe and Mail*, 18 May 2004: 'Throughout the industrialized world, accessibility is strongly positively correlated with the level of tuition – the higher the tuition, the greater the accessibility on average.' Despite some effort, I have been unable to find any economic analysis that establishes a statistically significant positive correlation between tuition and participation.

25 Kane, 'Rising Public College Tuition.'

26 Cited in Michael Mumper, 'The Future of College Access,' p. 102.

27 Heller, 'Trends in the Affordability of Public Colleges and Universities,' 24–5. Another study also shows that 'increases in net tuition have impaired access and choice principally for students from low-income families.' Michael S. McPherson and Morton Owen Schapiro, 'Financing Undergraduate Education: Designing National Policies,' *National Tax Journal* 50:3 (1997), 557–71. The evidence suggests that low-income students who qualify for university admission are shifting to lower-cost vocational colleges instead: 'It appears that in many states the only financially viable option for many students from lower-income families is to live at home and attend the local community college. It is no criticism of the education offered at community colleges to note that these lower-income students are being denied options that are available to their more affluent peers.' Ibid., 559–60.

28 Preston H. Smith and Sharon Szymanski, 'Why Political Scientists Should Support Free Public Higher Education,' *PS Online*, October 2003, 700.

29 Mumper, 'The Future of College Access,' 103.

30 The estimated cost of tax credit programs introduced in the 1990s is $41 billion over the first five years, already as much as is spent on the Pell Grant program. Ibid., 108–9.

31 Ibid., 107.

32　Ibid., 111.

33　Junor and Usher, *The Price of Knowledge*, 161.

34　Ibid., 167–71.

35　Ibid., 174.

36　Ibid., figure 4C.VI.4, p. 180

37　Miles Corak, Garth Lipps, and John Zhao, *Family Income and Participation in Post-Secondary Education* (Institute for the Study of Labour, 2004 [cited 27 Nov. 2004]); available at ftp://repec.iza.org/RePEc/Discussionpaper/dp977.pdf, pp. 5, 29–30.

38　See, e.g., Mumper, 'The Future of College Access,' 115.

39　Ibid., 29–30 and 55, figure 9.

40　Income inequality has been growing in the United States since the mid-1960s, though the greatest increases took place in the 1980s. Between 1990 and 2001, the Gini coefficient (the standard measure of income inequality) in the United States increased from .396 to .435, or by almost 10%. United States Census Bureau, 'Gini Ratios for Families, by Race and Hispanic Origin of Householder: 1947 to 2001' [cited 27 Nov. 2004]; available at http://www.census.gov/hhes/income/histinc/f04.html.

41　This claim applies only to tuition for four-year undergraduate degree programs. The relevant factors for graduate and professional-school tuition are significantly different than for undergraduate education, and I do not address them here.

42　Watson Scott Swail, *The Affordability of University Education: A Perspective from Both Sides of the 49th Parallel* (Educational Policy Institute, 2004 [cited 8 Dec. 2004]); available at http://www.educationalpolicy.org/pdf/Affordability.pdf. See also Karen Birchard, 'Higher Education in Canada Is Not as Affordable as Many Assumed, Study Concludes,' *Chronicle of Higher Education*, 1 Dec. 2004.

43　For an argument along similar lines, see Arthur M. Hauptman, 'Reforming the Ways in Which States Finance Higher Education,' in D.E. Heller, ed., *The States and Public Higher Education Policy: Affordability, Access, and Accountability* (Baltimore: Johns Hopkins University Press, 2001), 79–80

44　For an econometric analysis of the conditions under which tuition increases can benefit needy students, see David C. Rose and Robert L. Sorenson, 'High Tuition, Financial Aid, and Cross-Subsidization: Do Needy Students Really Benefit?' *Southern Economic Journal* 59:1 (1992), 66–76. They find that although it is theoretically possible for rising tuitions to increase access for low-income students, in practice this possibility has not been realized because universities use increased tuition fees to subsidize other institutional functions. '[W]hile institutions that appear to inflate their tuition do make larger financial aid awards, their awards are not large enough to reduce the average net price paid by needy students' (74). They also find that university administrators and faculty members tend to be important beneficiaries of high tuition (75). Similarly, a 1993 study of public universities in the US found that increases in tuition were not usually accompanied by offsetting increases in student aid. M. Mumper and J. Anderson, 'Maintaining Public College Affordability in the 1980s: How Did the States Do?' *Journal of Education Finance* 19 (1993), 183–99, cited in Paulsen, 'Recent Research on the Economics of Attending College,' 480.

45 See, e.g., Nicholas Barr, 'Higher Education Funding,' *Oxford Review of Economic Policy* 20:2 (2004), 264–83.

46 A substantial number of American university graduates report that they have delayed purchasing a home, and some have indicated that they have delayed having children, because of the burden of student debts. Garance Franke-Uta, 'The Indentured Generation,' *The American Prospect* 14:5 (2003), A23. In Canada, the rate at which students repay their educational loans has been decreasing in recent years, as debt loads increased. Ross Finnie, 'Student Loans: Borrowing and Burden,' *Education Quarterly Review* 8:4 (2002).

47 One study showed that whereas 80% of low-income students who work under 15 hours per week complete their degrees, more than half of those who work more than 35 hours per week drop out. Smith and Szymanski, 'Why Political Scientists Should Support Free Public Higher Education,' 700. In general, students from less well-off backgrounds are more likely to work than those from more affluent backgrounds, and appear to be working longer hours than they used to. There is also evidence that working beyond a certain limit takes a toll on academic performance. Claire Callendar, 'Fair Funding for Higher Education: The Way Forward,' in Annette Hayton and Anna Paczuska, eds, *Access, Participation and Higher Education* (London: Kogan Page, 2002), 75–6. Thus term-time work may help to explain the fact that, on average, '[s]tudents from affluent backgrounds are more likely to persist and graduate from [university] than are students with low SES backgrounds.' Therese L. Baker and William Velez, 'Access to and Opportunity in Postsecondary Education in the United States: A Review,' *Sociology of Education* 69, Special Issue on Sociology and Educational Policy: Bringing Scholarship and Practice Together (1996), 91. See also Brenda Little, 'UK Institutional Responses to Undergraduates' Term-Time Working,' *Higher Education* 44 (2002), 357. The percentage of Canadian university students who work part-time increased from about 21% in the early 1980s to about 34% in 2001. The percentage of students working full-time has remained fairly constant during this period, at less than 10%. Corak, Lipps, and Zhao, *Family Income and Participation in Post-Secondary Education*, 29, figure 5.

48 See Barr, 'Higher Education Funding,' 275.

49 The social capital literature shows a positive relationship between income

status and social trust in advanced industrial democracies. See, e.g., Robert Putnam, *Bowling Alone: The Collapse and Revival of American Community* (New York: Simon and Schuster, 2000); Ronald Inglehart, 'Trust, Well-Being, and Democracy,' in M.E. Warren, ed., *Democracy and Trust* (Cambridge: Cambridge University Press, 1999), 88–120.

50 For a more extensive discussion of these connections, see Melissa S. Williams, *Voice, Trust, and Memory: Marginalized Groups and the Failings of Liberal Representation* (Princeton: Princeton University Press, 1998), esp. chap. 6.

51 For a brilliant study of this history in the context of British Columbia, see Cole Harris, *Making Native Space: Colonialism, Resistance, and Reserves in British Columbia* (Vancouver: UBC Press, 2002).

52 See, e.g., Royal Commission on Aboriginal Peoples, *Report of the Royal Commission on Aboriginal Peoples* (Ottawa: Royal Commission on Aboriginal Peoples, 1996), esp. vol. I, chap. 10.

53 Although this gap has been narrowing in recent decades, there has been a disturbing rise in Aboriginal neonatal mortality since 1988. See James S. Frideres and Rene R. Gadazc, *Aboriginal Peoples in Canada* (Toronto: Pearson, 2001), 66, 71.

54 Ibid., 74.

55 Royal Commission on Aboriginal Peoples, vol. III, chap. 5.

56 Canada Millennium Scholarship Foundation, *Aboriginal Peoples and Post-Secondary Education: What Educators Have Learned* (2004 [cited 27 Nov. 2004]); available at http://www.millenniumscholarships.ca/en/research/aboriginal_en.pdf.

57 For a discussion of the Manitoba programs, see ibid., 24–6. See also Eileen M. Antone, 'Aboriginal Students in the Transitional Year Programme at the University of Toronto,' in K.S. Braithwaite, ed., *Access and Equity in the University* (Toronto: Canadian Scholars' Press, 2003), 165–79.

58 See ibid., 38. The Longhouse web site is located at http://www.longhouse.ubc.ca/longhouse.html [cited 29 Nov. 2004].

Education, Equity, Economics: Can These Words Be in the Same Title?

ARTHUR SWEETMAN

Democratic societies face many challenges in making decisions about allocating resources across alternative needs, for example, between health care and higher education. It has been well known since at least Arrow (1951), and discussed in some circles since the Marquis de Condorcet (1785), that, in general, voting cannot uniquely aggregate underlying individual preferences into a single decision.[1] Hence, the outcome of a vote reflects both the particular voting mechanism employed and the individual preferences of the voters.

Still, decisions are made in democratic societies and a set of normative theories have developed to describe and/or proscribe approaches to the questions at hand. Similarly, economists have developed concepts that help to clarify various aspects of the decision-making process. This paper provides a very basic discussion, from an economics perspective, of various viewpoints on some of these approaches with reference to educational access and funding. Clearly, these ways of thinking about the world sometimes conflict, and one theory and/or concept sometimes applies to a particular issue more readily than another. After surveying the relevant concepts, I take an eclectic strategy (some would say an inappropriate strategy, since I alternate between world views that can be at odds with each other) and employ alternative rationales to address a few diverse questions that are relevant to post-secondary access. The set of questions addressed is meant to be broad and representative of larger sets of issues, and is meant to promote discussion as much as offer possible implementation strategies.

1. Views on Equity

Economists usually begin by noting that there is frequently a trade-off between equity and efficiency; enhancing equity in post-secondary access, therefore, may have real costs and make all of society less well off materially. Reducing equity is frequently defined as reducing the variance, or some measure of the spread, of some outcome of interest. However, it can also refer to altering the distribution of access to some good or service so as to increase the outcomes of an under-represented party. While a trade-off does not always follow from such actions – sometimes increasing equity improves efficiency – it is important to be aware of any costs that are being generated. Most often, and most relevant, the costs follow from disincentives associated with redistribution, social insurance, and/or similar equity-enhancing government activities. One broad area of economics concerned with equity and allocation issues is sometimes called social choice, which combines philosophical underpinnings with economic aspects of social decision-making.[2]

It is also worth noting that most observers agree, in theory if not in practice, that even severe inequality does not, on its own, justify government intervention. Government action must be expected to be able to improve the situation. It is not unheard of for government programs to have deleterious impacts on their intended beneficiaries, or on others in the community. See, for example, the discussion by Smith and Sweetman (2002) of impacts in the context of employment training programs.

While not discussing them in any depth, I begin by recognizing three distinct and very widely known philosophical approaches to equity and redistribution, and one pragmatic alternative to the first two approaches. The three are first introduced to many economics students in the very common first-year undergraduate economics text by Mankiw et al. (1999, chapter 20) as utilitarianism, liberalism, and libertarianism. Utilitarianism (associated with Jeremy Bentham, John Stuart Mills, and a host of others) is interested in maximizing individual levels of satisfaction or utility. Liberalism, as it is called in that textbook, follows in part from the ideas of John Rawls and suggests that social decisions should be made behind a 'veil of ignorance,' as if each person were equally likely to obtain each initial endowment of resources, and each possible set of preferences. Rawls extends this idea under the assumption that people are extremely risk averse and arrives at a criterion that maximizes the endowment of the worst-off individual. Much 'social choice' economics is (usually implicitly) associated with these two world views, though the application may be quite distinct from that envisioned by those named above as being associated with each approach. For example, many economists appear not to find it credible that people are as risk averse as Rawls seems to believe. However, both these approaches support redistribution to make society more satisfied/ better off and frequently support what is called welfarism.[3]

An opposing voice to these first two approaches, not presented in first-year texts of which I am aware, but which appears to be very common in practice, is termed 'extra-welfarism.' It is discussed at some length in the health-economics/health-policy literature (see Hurley 2000 for a survey). This approach is more communitarian (or dictatorial/ paternalistic/maternalistic) in that, unlike welfarism, it does not concern itself with what individuals might choose of their own accord but seeks to maximize some decision-maker's objective. For example, it might seek to maximize health, or high school completion rates, without (much) regard for individual preferences.[4]

Libertarianism, associated with Robert Nozick, is an alternative approach. It rejects the idea of society having any ownership of the output of production that would justify redistributing individual resources, and argues instead for ensuring that the allocation process is (or the many processes of society are) 'fair' and evenly enforced. Equality of opportunity, and private ownership, are central features of this approach.

Although not emanating from Nozick, and standing quite independent of libertarianism, two concepts of 'fairness' or equity are worth considering at this point. These concepts, used most commonly in the economic field of public finance, are 'vertical' and 'horizontal' equity. Boadway and Kitchen (1999, 53) summarize horizontal equity, saying that 'a tax [or subsidy] is said to be horizontally equitable if two persons who have the same level of well-being before the tax [or subsidy] is imposed still have the same level of well-being after it is imposed.' This is not to say that a horizontally equitable tax cannot alter the relative wealth of taxpayers; redistributing from high to low income implies making the high-income person worse off and the low-income person better off. However, these two persons are not in the same situation before the tax is imposed. (Of course, well-being has to do with more than only income.) In considering education, the same principle applies to subsidies; two students who are in the same situation prior to a loan or subsidy should be in the same situation after.

This concept can be interpreted broadly. It supports, for example, indexing tuition fees so that students in different years face the same real (i.e., after inflation) price for the same education. Similarly, it raises questions about intergenerational equity when tuition is raised dramatically so that the pre-tuition increase generation receives a generous subsidy for their studies from the public purse, while the next receives no subsidy or a very small one. This problem is made more severe when debt financing is employed to subsidize the first generation's subsidy. Then the non-subsidized generation has to pay their own full (or nearly full) costs and contribute to the previous generation's debt payments. Clearly, horizontal equity is not satisfied; of course, other intergenerational transfers may have a counterbalancing effect.

Vertical equity is concerned with how to treat individuals with different levels of well-being and is tied to the issue of how progressive the tax and transfer system should be. Much research suggests that behavioural responses to taxes and transfers place important limits on the degree of redistribution that is possible.[5] See Boadway and Keen (2000) and Boadway and Kitchen (1999) for discussions of the issues.

2. A Few Relevant Economic Concepts

Externalities are usually defined as the benefits or costs not fully taken into account by a decision-maker in the decision-making process. (Note that 'fully take into account' is much stronger than 'be aware of' – it is not enough to simply know that a potential cost or benefit exists.) Their existence implies that what appears to be an optimal decision from a private agent's perspective is not the optimal one for society as a whole since not all the costs and benefits are taken into account.

A slightly expanded definition is sometimes, however, more appropriate and best described with an example. A decision-maker may be aware of all the costs and benefits for the various parties that will follow from a decision. Further, the decision-maker may take these costs and benefits into account in making that decision so as to create the maximum net benefit for society. However, if the winners never actually compensate the losers, a type of externality can still be said to have followed from the decision in that there are some individuals with uncompensated costs.

In the context of decisions regarding access to post-secondary education, the more limited definition applies to the individual potential applicant who does not take into account that there are, an average, substantial benefits (and some costs) to society. I will not address the 'spill-overs' of individual education to the broader society in any detail since they are addressed by Riddell in this volume. The usual 'solution' is to recognize that education, or at least some people's education, should be subsidized by society.

However, if the latter, more expansive, definition is employed, then some quite interesting issues arise, especially if post-secondary institutions, or provincial governments, are seen as the decision-makers. If tax revenue from non-post-secondary attendees is used to fund a benefit for those who attend, then an externality is created if the former group is not compensated.

Finally, it is important to understand what many consider to be the largest externality of education, that is, the development and dissemination of knowledge that leads to advances in technology and practice, and in our social and cultural fabric.[6] As discussed further below, education is arguably foundational to both the technological side of advanced societies, and the democratic process.

Financial liquidity constraints exist if a person who would go to post-secondary studies is prevented from doing so because of an inability to access the required financial resources. This funding issue is broader than simply not having sufficient funds for tuition and includes all direct costs of education (but not the opportunity cost). A person who has access to some, but insufficient, financing is still liquidity constrained. Although in popular discussion these ideas are commonly confounded, at least at a conceptual level, if not so easily in practice, the concept of a liquidity constraint needs to be differentiated from the costs of education and borrowing since they have different policy levers.

First, a person who has access to financing may elect not to attend a post-secondary institution because the direct costs are too high to make it worthwhile. Second, a person may elect not to attend because, while financing is available, the interest rate on the loan is too high. Of course, the first and second issues here really need to be considered as a pair. A high tuition may be acceptable if the interest rate is low enough, while a low tuition may not be low enough if borrowing charges are sufficiently high.[7] While price and borrowing cost issues are important and clearly influence post-secondary attendance decisions, they are not the same as the extreme issue of liquidity constraints.

If the 'true' expected costs and benefits of education were known and accounted for (i.e., all potential externalities are internalized), and a person had access to loans at the 'socially correct' interest rate, then that person might still elect not to attend, citing excessive tuition and/or the high cost of financing. This is not a liquidity constraint, but a reasonable decision in the face of the true costs and benefits of post-secondary education. In practice, people probably do not face the 'right' prices or interest rates, but those are different issues from liquidity. Liquidity constraints justify providing loans for the 'true' costs at 'true' interest rates (adjusted for taxation). Other motivations, such as externalities or moral imperatives, are required to justify subsidizing the costs and/or borrowing rates.

Risk aversion and information asymmetries abound in the educational decision-making process. Debt aversion seems to be related to the combination of these problems. First, individuals may not understand the magnitude of the benefit that accrues, on average, to those who pursue higher education. Even the private return, which is easier to measure than the social one (and by definition smaller, given that both are positive), is very substantial (see Riddell and Sweetman 2000). Second, individuals, especially those from disadvantaged backgrounds, may be risk averse and disinclined to take the risk associated with higher-education investment or may not understand its value. Dicks and Sweetman (1999) show that differences in ethnic-group-level educational outcomes can take three or four generations to converge in Canada. Further, even if potential students also realize the average benefit, they understand that there is substantial variance around that average. This can cause under-investment relative to that that which should be optimally undertaken.

At a minimum, there is a need for information about the true costs and benefits, and the range of costs and benefits, associated with higher education. Moreover, since governments should be risk neutral in this environment they can also offer forms of educational insurance, such as income-contingent loans, to increase attendance to its optimal level and distribution. Subsidies can also be justified. However, interventions using this justification should recognize that potential students also have private information. For example, many have a better sense of their chances of completing post-secondary education than does the government.

Hysteresis is a word brought into the economics lexicon from engineering and physics. It implies that history, or the path taken, continues to matter after the particular path is travelled. There is sometimes a particular focus on the persistence of effects resulting from idiosyncratic or chance events. In considering policy and the procedures around post-secondary access, path dependence is clearly crucial, especially for those on the margins of access. Many potential post-secondary students are not accepted into university and college at all, or not into their program of choice. For those individuals on the margin of acceptance, access is life-altering and can have massive implications for not only standards of living, but a host of other issues throughout their lives (it can even, on average, impact the duration of life – see Riddell in this volume); further, the effect may also alter their children's outcomes.

Many who have served on post-secondary admissions committees would concur, I believe, that the quality of the information on which decisions are made is not always very good and that there is, therefore, an element of randomness in the process. Riddell (2003) speaks to the relevance of good information at the secondary level for improving procedural fairness in access to post-secondary education.

3. A Few Recent Findings from Economics

A few recent findings in the economics literature are relevant to this discussion since they affect the way the issue is framed. Some of these are discussed by Riddell in this volume.

3.1 Is the Return to Higher Education Higher?

First, the idea that students who drop out of school/do not pursue college have a low economic rate of return to education has been challenged recently. This is relevant to equity, but also to efficiency. It appears to be commonly believed that those who 'ought' to have the resources required to attend college and undergraduate post-secondary learning focused on them are those who are the most academically able. This is operationalized by ranking applicants according to marks/GPA and then, starting from the top of the list, admitting students until the number of available spots is filled. However, as summarized by Card (1999, 2000), there is consistent evidence from several countries suggesting that the 'causal' labour-market return to education is at least as large, and quite possibly larger, for those who, for example, want to drop out of high school but are forced by compulsory schooling legislation to attend, or those (primarily from disadvantaged backgrounds) who attend because they face particularly low costs due to the proximity of a post-secondary institution. This suggests that the economic return to some types of remedial programs is much higher than understood previously. However, Warburton and Warburton (2002) show that not all types of remedial training programs have significant impacts.

Unfortunately, we do not understand these relationships with any precision. Further, there is no evidence on how far this argument can be pushed, but it seems unlikely that it applies to research-oriented programs. They have a different motivation, and a different set of externalities.

Note that while the evidence is not comprehensive, it has a strong interpretation and is not about correlations, but about 'causality' defined in the same way as it would be for random assignment trails in medical research (see Smith and Sweetman 2002). It is this causal impact that matters for formulating policy. It is not that those with high levels of education obtain high levels of earnings, health, and other outcomes, but that those outcomes are higher than they would have been without the education that matters in justifying investments. It is the impact (value-added) of the policy/education that matters. Graduates may have strongly positive outcomes, but low impacts, if they would have had similar outcomes even in the absence of their schooling. Other graduates may have poor outcomes, but substantial impacts, if those individuals would have had very poor outcomes had they not pursued their education.

3.2 Field of Study

The focus of much economic research on education ignores post-secondary field of study and similar details of higher education, and focuses on simple measures such as years of schooling or degrees obtained. Recent work by McBride and Sweetman (2003) looks at post-secondary field of study and finds (perhaps unsurprisingly) that many of the generalizations about levels of education do not follow automatically once detailed fields of study are recognized. In particular, while community college graduates may, on average, have poorer outcomes than university graduates, some college fields of study have superior earnings and related outcomes than some university ones. Average earnings are higher, and social benefit receipt lower, among trades and technology graduates from community college than among university graduates from some humanities, social sciences, and related fields. Although post-secondary education is about much more than earnings, this part of the story needs to be more fully communicated.

That the economic returns to various fields of study differ has implications for income-contingent financing and graduate-tax frameworks. Relatedly, it raises questions about whether governments should be primarily interested in equalizing the costs of education. Of course, since these field of study results are correlational and not causal, it is not clear what fraction of the differences in earnings across fields represents the causal impacts of education, and what fraction represents earnings differences following from, for example, compensating differentials reflecting the characteristics of jobs, or the economic structures of jobs (e.g., economic rents following from monopolies).

3.3 Innovation and Economic Growth

There is an increasing understanding of the role of knowledge generation in economic growth and the improvement of standards of living over time. And, of course, knowledge generation relies crucially on higher education. See Riddell in this volume or Sweetman (2002) for a fuller discussion of the issues, which are not discussed here. Further, an older tradition in economics points to the importance of entrepreneurship and innovation among a very small fraction of the population as making crucial contributions to social and economic growth and generating massive externalities. Together, these views strongly support vibrant graduate programs that in turn support advanced study leading to technological and social progress, and economic growth leading to increases in well-being.

Taken together, these three findings from the economics literature point to the complexity of the post-secondary system and remind us about how little we really know. Still, where do we go from here?

4. Conclusions, Discussion, and Recommendations

1. Overall, there is support for some redistribution/subsidization in an effort to improve equity if one follows a welfarist, or even a non-welfarist, approach. Although there is less support from a libertarian perspective, it, along with the others discussed, can still be interpreted to support redistribution in an effort to maximize the wealth of society by alleviating externalities as long as there is compensation (although Nozick might disagree). It is hard to argue against some redistribution to solve under-investment problems where there are clear social benefits and compensation.

Redistribution is perhaps the central normative issue in public policy regarding post-secondary access (and much of what government does). Although some particular (secondary) externalities may be generated by government actions to improve access, the benefits to society of taxing broadly to support some individuals pursuing post-secondary education is almost universally thought to be worthwhile, since other, larger externalities are alleviated and broader issues of equity are addressed. Nevertheless, redistribution implies cross-subsidization and it is crucial to understand exactly who is subsidizing whom.

It is particularly worthwhile to contrast the graduate tax, proposed by Carmichael, with income-contingent loans as discussed by Barr (in this volume, and see articles in Beach, Boadway, and McInnis 2004). One (perhaps the) essential difference is who is doing the subsidization. In most formulations income-contingent loans have a subsidy that derives from all taxpayers, and graduates pay more only inasmuch as they have, on average, high incomes. In contrast, a graduate tax keeps all of the cross-subsidization within the group of post-secondary attendees, with high graduates who realize high earnings subsidizing low-earning ones and no educational subsidy from non-attendees (though research might be subsidized). In effect, it can be thought of as a form of insurance that students offer to each other, although it might well not be actuarially fair given what we know about predicting individual earnings and earnings potential by fields of study. Income-contingent loans, on the other hand, can motivate redistributing educational costs from low-earning graduates to all of society by pointing to the externalities that are created.

2. While the evidence on the causal impacts of education is not as detailed and precise as one might like, it suggests an empirical regularity. It seems likely that, on average, individuals who would drop out of high school, or would be unlikely to attend a post-secondary institution in the absence of financial incentives or other inducements have substantial economic and social returns to that education. At the post-secondary level, community colleges typically provide this type of programming and it is frequently focused on those from disadvantaged backgrounds. (See Finnie, Lascelles, and Sweetman 2004 for an analysis of the effect of family backgrounds on post-secondary attendance.) Together, this suggests the need for a strong community college system. Further, research on post-secondary fields of study shows that, for example, community-college-level trades and technology, and health profession, fields have remarkably high private economic returns.

However, many of the greatest spill-overs or externalities in terms of economic and social growth built on technological and cultural advances appear to accrue from higher education, especially graduate education at the masters and PhD levels. In the long (and even the medium) term, the associated accumulation and dissemination of knowledge has substantial implication for the overall well-being of society and it is hard to overestimate its importance.

3. Unless one has a strongly extra-welfarist approach, we need to recognize that post-secondary education need not be a good investment for everybody. Well-informed students facing the 'true' costs and benefits might well decide that pursuing post-secondary education is not in their best interest. However, as discussed above, the fact that the economic returns to attending is so high for those who would drop out implies that either non-economic issues tilt strongly in the other direction, or that decisions are not being made well. Many observers believe the latter and suggest that information problems are crucial.

Providing education and information to pre-post-secondary students to facilitate their decision making seems crucial. Although conducted in the United States, a survey by Betts (1996) suggests that even first-year undergraduates know shockingly little about the connection between their education and the labour market, especially in relation to field of study. This suggests an important role for government. Moreover, it reinforces the idea that good decisions require potential post-secondary students to face the 'true' costs and benefits of their decisions, even though they are made under uncertainty. This does not rule out subsidies, but they are best made explicit, not hidden, and well targeted.

4. A major contribution of the libertarian view is to make us focus more closely on the fairness of post-secondary processes. If we are to take post-secondary education seriously, and are concerned about equity, then the post-secondary system must look carefully at the equity implications of its own administrative and decision-making processes. They need to be 'squeaky clean.' The hysteretic nature of post-secondary admission decisions makes this all the more important.

An example of a crucial process with important equity implications is admissions. Anyone who has looked at university admissions, including applications for graduate studies, is all too aware of the poor quality of the information available for decision making. Since enrolment is limited – that is, some applicants are denied admission while others are accepted – it is crucial that admissions decisions be the best possible and based on good information. There has recently been a reform and standardization of high school report-card formats in Ontario, which attempts to improve information flows, and Riddell (2003) points to the need for consistent measures to allocate post-secondary spaces both more efficiently and more equitably.

In contrast to the reforms at the secondary level, university transcripts remain difficult to interpret. A reform of this information device would be very helpful for the graduate-studies admissions process. In particular, class averages or means, and quantiles of each class's mark distribution (e.g., 25th and 75th percentiles), where class size is sufficiently large, would be valuable standards. However, Anglin and Meng (2000) point to more difficulties. Grade inflation, which they observe to be substantial in Ontario universities, makes interpreting marks a challenge. Further, the rate of change appears to differ across fields of study, and perhaps universities. Universities appear to not be overly concerned about equity in the sense of process, or do not take themselves very seriously.

5. Following from the randomness that appears to result in the admissions process, a broader ethical question arises, especially in the presence of subsidies. Is it horizontally equitable that some individuals are subsidized to attend multiple programs at the same level of post-secondary education while others are denied access? While some education is cumulative, and that is not at issue here, some repetition also appears to occur. In some contexts this is not an issue, but given the combination of subsidization, random elements in admission, and limited access, the case for ongoing subsidization is not straightforward. This is an interesting issue for debate.

6. Finally, it is worth looking closely at who is subsidizing whom, and at the appropriate degree of subsidy. Issues of vertical and horizontal equity are common in post-secondary funding, but are frequently not addressed very clearly. Partly this results from the complexity of the system and our corporate ignorance regarding the magnitude of various externalities and causal impacts. However, for example, the intergenerational aspects of many funding decisions have the potential to be sizeable. Current students are being asked to carry a very large burden of the costs of their post-secondary education, without being excused from carrying a share of the burden of the education of earlier generations who were heavily subsidized. This is an area where much more research and discussion is required.

Notes

* Queen's University, School of Policy Studies
1 Of course, if voters hold only limited classes of preference types then voting can uniquely aggregate preferences.
2 Note that the adjective 'social' in economics should almost always be taken to mean 'of society,' not 'socialization.' Hence, social choice looks at the choices societies make.
3 Some economists, however, note the limitations of these approaches, pointing out that interpersonal utility comparisons are not possible. Much of Nobel laureate Amartya Sen's early work has looked at this issue.
4 Ontario's recent Panel on the Role of Government's final report takes a decidedly welfarist perspective for the most part, but then also advocates increasing the compulsory schooling age, which is clearly extra-welfarist. The report recognizes the contradiction, but is sensible enough to allow it to exist in the pursuit of good public policy. To alleviate conflicts of interest, it should be declared that Sweetman (2003) is the Panel's underlying research paper that argues for increasing the compulsory schooling age.
5 Of course, the economic and legal incidence of taxes/subsidies are not believed to coincide in most cases, since all sides of a market adjust to their existence.
6 Interestingly, and perhaps sadly, the Ontario Postsecondary Review mandate as articulated on page 5 of the Review discussion paper does not extend to research. It is clear that the authors of the paper and the mandate are aware of research, since on the same page the paper mentions that the commercialization and research agenda is being studied independently. Although there may be disciplinary differences, at least for universities it is not clear how easily teaching and research can be separated in designing a system. It is also unclear how easily the two activities can be separated at the level of the individual student and faculty member. If this omission from the mandate is not at least indirectly addressed, it is not clear that any sensible advice can be provided by the Review with respect to system design.
7 Formally, what matters is the net present value of the investment in education. This combines not only the relevant price, stream of benefits, and borrowing interest rate, but the timing of each.

References

Anglin, Paul M., and Ronald Meng. 2000. 'Evidence on Grades and Grade Inflation at Ontario's Universities.' *Canadian Public Policy* 26:3, 361–8.
Arrow, Kenneth. 1951. *Social Choice and Individual Values.* New York: Wiley, 1951.
Beach, Charles M., Robin W. Boadway, and Marvin McInnis, eds. 2004. *Higher*

Education in Canada. John Deutsch Institute, Queen's University. Kingston: McGill-Queen's University Press.

Betts, Julian R. 1996. 'What Do Students Know about Wages? Evidence from a Survey of Undergraduates.' *Journal of Human Resources* 31(1), 27–56.

Boadway, Robin W., and Michael Keen. 2000. 'Redistribution,' In *Handbook of Income Distribution*, vol. 1, 753–72. Ed. A.B. Atkinson and F. Bourguignon. Amsterdam: North-Holland.

Boadway, Robin W., and Harry M. Kitchen. 1999. *Canadian Tax Policy*. 3rd ed. Toronto: Canadian Tax Foundation.

Card, D. 1999. 'The Causal Effect of Education on Earnings.' In *Handbook of Labor Economics, Volume 3A*. Ed. O. Ashenfelter and D. Card. Amsterdam: North-Holland.

– 2000. 'Estimating the Return to Schooling: Progress on Some Persistent Problems.' NBER Working Paper 7769, June.

Condorcet, Marquis de. 1785. *Essai sur l'Application de l'Analyse aux Probabilités des Décisions Rendue à la Pluralitté des Voix*. Reprinted, New York: Chelsea Publishing Co., 1973.

Dicks, Gordon, and Arthur Sweetman. 1999. 'Education and Ethnicity in Canada: An Intergenerational Perspective.' *Journal of Human Resources*, 34(4), 668–96.

Finnie, Ross, Eric Lascelles, and Arthur Sweetman. 2004. 'Who Goes? The Direct and Indirect Effects of Family Background on Access to Post-Secondary Education.' Statistics Canada, Analytical Studies Research Paper.

Finnie, Ross, Alex Usher, and Hans Vossensteyn. 2004. 'Meeting the Need: A New Architecture for Canada's Student Financial Aid System.' IRPP Policy Matters, 5(7), 3–47.

Hurley, Jeremiah. 2000. 'An Overview of the Normative Economics of the Health Sector.' *Handbook of Health Economics*, vol. 1. Ed. A.J. Culyer and J.P. Newhouse. Elsevier Science.

Junor, Sean, and Alexander Usher. 2002. *The Price of Knowledge*. Montreal: Canada Millennium Scholarship Foundation, Research Series.

Mankiw, N. Gregory, Ronald D. Kneebobe, Kenneth J. McKenzie, and Nicholas Rowe. 1999. *Principles of Microeconomics*. 1st Canadian ed. Toronto: Harcourt Brace.

McBride, Stephan, and Arthur Sweetman. 2003. 'Immigrant and Non-Immigrant Earnings by Postsecondary Field of Study.' In *Canadian Immigration Policy for the 21st Century*, 413–62. Ed. C.M. Beach, A.G. Green, and J.G. Reitz. John Deutsch Institute for the Study of Economic Policy. Montreal and Kingston: McGill-Queen's University Press.

Panel on the Role of Government. 2004. 'Investing in People: Creating a Human Capital Society for Ontario.' Ontario.

Postsecondary Review, Ontario. 2004. 'Higher Expectations for Higher Education: A Discussion Paper.'

Riddell, Craig. 2003. 'The Role of Government in Post-Secondary Education in Ontario.' Background Paper for the Panel on the Role of Government in Ontario.

Riddell, W.C., and A. Sweetman. 2000. 'Human Capital Formation in a Period of Change.' In *Adapting Public Policy to a Labour Market in Transition*, 85–142. Ed. W.C. Riddell and F. St-Hilaire. Montreal, QC: Institute for Research in Public Policy.

Smith, Jeff, and Arthur Sweetman. 2002. 'Improving the Evaluation of Employment and Training Programs in Canada.' Prepared for HRDC's conference 'From Theory to Practice.' Paper available at http://www11.hrdc-drhc .gc.ca/edd-doc/fttp/conf_paper.shtml.

Sweetman, Arthur. 2003. 'Ontario's Kindergarten to Grade 12 Education System: Some Thoughts for the Future.' Panel on the Role of Government, Ontario, Research Paper 25.

– 2002. 'Working Smarter: Productivity and Education.' In *The Review of Economic and Social Progress: Productivity*, 157–80. Ed. K. Banting, A. Sharpe, and F. St-Hilaire. Montreal and Ottawa: CSLS and IRPP.

Warburton, William, and Rebecca Warburton. 2002. 'Should the Government Sponsor Training for the Disadvantaged?' In *Towards Evidence-Based Policy for Canadian Education*, 69–100. Ed. P. de Broucker and A. Sweetman. Kingston: McGill-Queen's University Press.

An Income-Contingent Financing Program for Ontario

BENJAMIN ALARIE AND DAVID DUFF*

In a report released earlier this year entitled *On the Edge: Securing a Sustainable Future for Higher Education*,[1] the OECD identified a number of challenges facing public colleges and universities internationally. These challenges include rapid growth in enrollment and research activity, declining state funding, unsustainably low levels of infrastructure investment, and greater competition among institutions.[2] Post-secondary education in Ontario is not immune from these concerns.[3] Provincial operating grants per student have declined by 25% in real terms over the past decade. Over the same period, enrollment has grown significantly. As a result, the government's share of university operating costs has decreased from 70 to 50%. In order to make up the difference, student contributions have had to nearly double to 45% of university operating costs.[4] From 1989–90 to 2003–4, tuition fees for undergraduate students in Ontario rose dramatically, increasing from approximately $2,000 to almost $5,000 (in 2003 dollars).[5] Tuition increases have been even larger in professional programs like dentistry, medicine, and law.[6]

Although the positive externalities associated with higher education favour substantial government support,[7] sound arguments also favour student contributions to the costs of post-secondary education – based both on the private benefits obtained[8] and the regressive impact of general subsidies for higher education.[9] At the same time, the central role that higher education performs as a vehicle for social mobility and the general reluctance of private lenders to finance individual investments in higher education suggest that governments also have an important role to play in the area of student assistance – ensuring that higher education is accessible to all students on the basis of merit, irrespective of financial ability.[10] Given how tuition fees have increased over the last decade in Ontario, the need for a well-designed student assistance program is more important than ever.

Among many proposals for a restructured student aid system,[11] one of the most promising is to replace existing 'mortgage-style' student loans with a financing arrangement involving repayment obligations that depend on the student's income after graduation.[12] To the extent that this 'income-contingent' approach reduces the risk to borrowers with respect to their investments in higher education, it will likely lessen the reluctance that students exhibit with respect to such borrowing. Moreover, where funding covers both the direct costs of higher education (tuition and ancillary fees, books and supplies) as well as living expenses, income-contingent financing programs may enhance accessibility by making higher education effectively free at the point of purchase – offsetting the 'sticker shock' associated with increased tuition fees as well as living costs which generally exceed the direct costs of higher education. Finally, collection through the income tax should reduce the incidence of nonpayment and dramatically lessen the costs of administering student financial aid.

This article proposes an income-contingent financing program (ICFP) for Ontario[13] to replace the current system of mortgage-style loans, automatic debt remission, and interest and debt relief available under the Ontario Student Assistance Program (OSAP). Part 1 reviews the current system of government-provided student aid in Ontario, providing an essential foundation for our subsequent proposal for an ICFP. Part 2 examines the experience with ICFPs in Australia, New Zealand, Sweden, and the UK, in order to derive lessons relevant to the design of an ICFP for Ontario. Part 3 considers the essential features of an ICFP, canvassing the competing arguments and making specific recommendations informed by our review of the current system in Ontario and the international experience with ICFPs. Part 4 concludes.

1. Student Financial Aid in Ontario

In order to finance investments in post-secondary education, students rely on a number of sources, including personal income and assets, parental and/or spousal contributions, private borrowing, institutional assistance, tax credits, and government-provided loans and grants.[14] In Canada, federal and provincial governments spent over $2 billion on student aid in 2000–1,[15] with expenditures divided roughly equally between direct grants and interest subsidies on student loans.[16] In Ontario, provincial government spending on student aid was $234 million in 2002–3, most of which was devoted to a grant program designed to reduce debt loads after graduation.[17]

The combination of federal and provincial grant and loan programs in Ontario and other provinces makes the current system of government-provided student aid seem dauntingly complex.[18] Indeed, the Ontario Government's guide for student assistance in Ontario describes a variety of grant and loan programs, including grants and loans for full-time students, grants and loans for part-time students, bursaries and grants for students with disabilities, federal and provincial grants for students with dependants and child-care costs, as well as other types of bursaries and grants.[19] For most post-secondary students in Ontario, however, financial assistance depends on three of these programs: an integrated Canada-Ontario student loan for full-time students, a federal bursary provided by the Canada Millennium Scholarship Foundation, and Ontario Student Opportunity Grants that reduce debt loads after graduation. In addition, the federal and provincial governments operate interest-relief and debt-reduction programs for low-income graduates unable to make regular payments on their loans.

The following sections review the key features of government-provided student assistance in Ontario, considering the administration of grants and student loans, eligibility for student aid, the amount of assistance that is made available to eligible students, the reduction of student debt through the Ontario Student Opportunity Grant program, the repayment of student loans, interest-relief and debt-reduction programs for graduates who are unable to make regular loan payments, and procedures for dealing with graduates who default on their loans or declare personal bankruptcy.

A. Administration

Administrative responsibility for student assistance in Ontario is shared between two bodies: the Ontario Student Assistance Program (OSAP), a branch of the Ontario Ministry of Training, Colleges and Universities; and the National Student Loan Service Centre (NSLSC), a private service provider operating under contract with the federal Department of Human Resources and Skills Development. While OSAP administers student assistance programs for the federal and provincial governments, processing applications, assessing eligibility and assistance, and providing for the release of funds, the NSLSC processes loan documents, arranges for funds to be deposited in students' bank accounts, and administers loan repayments as well as interest-relief and debt-reduction programs.[20] Funds for grants and loans are provided directly by the federal and provincial governments.[21]

In order to obtain financial assistance, a student must first submit an application to OSAP,[22] which assesses eligibility and need based on the information provided by the student, subject to verification and audit,[23] and determines the amount and composition of financial assistance. For students studying in Canada, grant cheques and loan certificates are distributed through each institution's financial aid office after students have registered.[24] Loan certificates are submitted to the NSLSC, which requires students to complete a loan agreement and arranges for funds to be deposited in students' bank accounts. Under the Canada-Ontario Integrated Student Loan system, the federal government provides 60% of the funds for each student loan while the provincial government pays 40%.[25] Where a student qualifies for a bursary from the Canada Millennium Scholarship Foundation, the amount of this federal grant is deducted from the Ontario portion of the integrated loan.

After graduation, students who have received student loans are required to 'consolidate' these loans and set up a repayment schedule with the NSLSC, which administers both the repayment of loans as well as interest-relief and debt-reduction programs offered by the federal and provincial governments. When a loan is in arrears for a lengthy period, however, the NSLSC relinquishes its role to the federal and provincial governments, at which point the file is referred to a collection agency.[26]

B. Eligibility

To apply for student assistance in Ontario, a student must satisfy four initial conditions.[27] First, the student must be a Canadian citizen, a permanent resident (i.e., landed immigrant), or a protected person under the *Immigration and Refugee Act*. Second, the student must be a resident of Ontario, meaning that the student has lived in the province for at least 12 consecutive months immediately before applying without attending a post-secondary institution on a full-time basis. Third, the student must be enrolled in, or qualified to enroll in, an approved program at an approved post-secondary institution.[28] Fourth, except for part-time students who are eligible for federal loans and specific types of federal and provincial grants, the student must be enrolled in a program lasting at least 12 weeks, and must take at least 60% of a full course load.[29]

Even if all four of these conditions are satisfied, however, students may nevertheless be denied financial assistance if they (i) fail to meet the academic requirements to continue in their program of study; (ii) have defaulted on a previous student loan; (iii) are under investigation for breaching the terms and conditions under which assistance is received; (iv) have loan overpayments for two or more academic years; (v) have received other government assistance for post-secondary studies; or (vi) have provided income information to OSAP that differs significantly from income reported to the Canada Revenue Agency.[30] In addition to these restrictions, financial assistance for each program is limited to the normal duration of the program plus one year, and aggregate financial assistance is capped at 340 weeks of study (10 academic years), increased to 400 weeks for doctoral students and 520 weeks for students with disabilities.[31]

C. Available Assistance

For students who are eligible for government-provided financial assistance, the amount of assistance is generally determined by an assessment of financial need, subject to a maximum amount for each week of study.[32] Need is assessed according to a four-step procedure, involving (i) a determination of the student's category; (ii) an assessment of student costs; (iii) a calculation of available resources; and (iv) the subtraction of available resources from assessed costs. Maximum amounts depend on the student's category and academic program.

In order to assess student costs, students are first grouped into six categories: (i) single dependents living at home; (ii) single dependents living away from home; (iii) single independents living at home; (iv) single independents living away from home; (v) students who are married or in a common-law or same-sex relationship; and (vi) single parents.[33] Students living at home are assumed to have lower costs than students living away from home, while married students and students with children or other dependents are assumed to have higher costs than single students. Dependent and married students are assumed to obtain financial support from parents and spouses, while independent students are assumed to receive no such support. In Ontario, students are considered independent of their parents if they are married or in a common-law or same-sex relationship, are divorced or widowed, have one or more dependents, have been in the workforce for two or more years, or have been out of secondary school for at least four years.

Student costs include direct costs of post-secondary education (tuition and ancillary fees, books and supplies) as well as living expenses (including travel expenses and child-care expenses where applicable). For tuition and ancillary fees, assessed costs are capped at $2,250 per term ($2,675 for co-op programs), which corresponds to regulated fees for most undergraduate programs.[34] For books and supplies, assessed costs are limited to $3,000 for each study period. Monthly living allowances are $391 for single students living at home, $937 for single students living away from home, $1,212 for single parents, $1,799 for married students, and an additional $500 for each dependent.[35] In addition to these amounts, students who are living away from home may add to their assessed costs up to $1,200 for two trips home per year, while students with children may add amounts for child-care expenses.[36] Surprisingly, given significant differences in housing costs in different locations, there is no adjustment for these variations in expected living costs.

Available resources are calculated by taking into account the student's personal income (including scholarships) and assets, parental income for dependent students, and spousal income and assets for students who are married or living in a common-law or same-sex relationship. Contributions from pre-study income depend on amounts earned and living expenses, but are in the range of $1,600 to $2,200 for students living at home and $25 to $600 for students living away from home.[37] Expected study-period income is also included to the extent that it exceeds $50 per week of study, as is scholarship income over $3,500.[38] Savings and assets are also added to available resources, subject to exceptions for personal vehicles and registered retirement savings plans (RRSPs).[39]

Expected parental contributions are determined in the following manner.[40] No contribution is required if combined parental income is below an after-tax minimum of $30,000 for a two-person family (plus $5,000 for each additional family member). For parents with a combined after-tax income between $30,000 and $40,000, expected contributions are $100 plus 5% of after-tax income exceeding $30,000. Parents with a combined after-tax income exceeding $40,000 are expected to contribute 45% of the first $3,000 of after-tax income above the threshold, 60% of the next $3,000, and 75% of all income above this amount.

For students who are married or living in a common-law or same-sex relationship, partners are deemed to make contributions based on their assets and income. Asset contributions are determined according to the same rules that apply for the student's own assets. The partner's contribution on the basis of income comes from the following formula: [(Ontario minimum wage) × (average number of weekly work hours) × (4.3) – (the partner's monthly taxes)] × (number of months in the study period).[41] Where the student's partner is also a student, no income contribution is deemed.

Although assessed need is calculated by subtracting available resources from assessed costs, available assistance is limited to maximum amounts for each week of study. For single students with no dependents, this maximum is $275/week ($9,350/year) for full-time students enrolled in a publicly funded Canadian college or university or an approved private post-secondary institution, and $165/week ($5,610/year) for students enrolled in an approved post-secondary institution outside Canada, an approved private post-secondary institution or private degree-granting institution in Ontario on a probationary status, or an approved hair-styling school in Ontario.[42] For students who are married, living in a common-law or same sex relationship, or who are sole-support parents, the maximum available assistance is $500/week ($17,000 per year) for full-time students enrolled in a publicly funded Canadian college or university or an approved private post-secondary institution, and $165/week ($5,610/year) for students enrolled in an approved post-secondary institution outside Canada, an approved private postsecondary institution or private degree-granting institution in Ontario on a probationary status, or an approved hairstyling school in Ontario.[43] These limits have not been increased since 1994.

For students with the highest assessed need, up to $3,000 of the maximum annual amount is available in the form of a bursary provided by the Canada Millennium Scholarship Foundation. Other grants are available for financially needy students, disabled students, and students with dependents and child-care expenses.[44] Aside from these grants, student loans represent the remainder of a student's financial assistance package.

D. Debt Remission

In addition to grants that students may receive during the course of their studies, Ontario also provides grants after graduation, designed to reduce the amount of debt that students accumulate from each year of study. Under the Ontario Student Opportunity Grants (OSOG) program, each graduate is automatically eligible for a grant that reduces the outstanding amount of their Canada-Ontario Integrated Student Loan to $7,000 for each two-term year of an academic program or $10,500 for each three-term year of an academic program. In order to qualify for the grant, a student must have negotiated an integrated loan in an academic year, received a loan that exceeds $7,000 for a two-term academic year (or $10,500 for a three-term academic year), enrolled in a full-time program for two terms, and completed the academic year. Although described as a grant program, OSOG is more accurately characterized as a loan forgiveness or debt remission program, since grants are not paid to the student directly but reduce the amount of student loans.

E. Repayment

No interest is payable on student loans while students are enrolled in full-time studies.[45] When students complete their studies or cease studying full-time, however, interest on student loans begins to accrue. Six months later, students must begin to repay their loans.

Canada-Ontario Integrated Student Loans are mortgage-type loans. As such, payments depend on the applicable interest rate, the balance outstanding, and the repayment or amortization period. The standard repayment period is 10 years, although students may negotiate shorter or longer amortization periods when they make repayment arrangements.[46] Students have a choice of paying interest at a floating rate of prime plus 2.5% or a fixed rate of prime plus 5%,[47] and have the option to switch from floating to a fixed rate at any point during the repayment period. Repayment terms are negotiated with the NSLSC, which students must contact after graduation in order to set up a repayment schedule.

F. Interest Relief and Debt Reduction

Depending on the circumstances, students experiencing difficulties making payments on student loans may make use of three different types of relief. First, students may ask the NSLSC to extend the repayment period for up to 15 years, thereby lowering monthly payments.[48] Second, students who are unemployed or have low incomes may apply for interest-relief for six-month periods, up to a maximum of 30 months (54 months if the student has also increased the loan repayment period to 15 years and has completed studies within the past five years).[49] Finally, students who have been out of school for five years and have obtained interest relief for 30 months or more may be eligible for 'Debt Reduction in Repayment' should monthly loan payments exceed an 'affordable payment' based on family size and gross family income.[50] Under this combined federal and provincial program, students may receive a one-time debt reduction of up to $10,000 or 50 per cent of their outstanding loan balance (whichever is lower) and two subsequent debt reductions of up to $5,000 each.[51]

G. Default and Bankruptcy

Students are considered to have defaulted when they miss payments for three consecutive months.[52] In this circumstance, the NSLSC ceases to administer the loan and the federal and provincial governments may report the student's default to a credit bureau and refer the file to a collection agency. Where collection is unsuccessful, governments may also direct the Canada Revenue Agency to withhold the student's income tax refund and apply the proceeds against the amount owing.[53] Borrowers who are in default are barred from obtaining further student aid (including Ontario Student Opportunity Grants) and are denied in-school interest-free status on loans until accrued interest is paid and six consecutive monthly payments are made.[54]

Bankruptcy is a more serious process than default, in which a debtor seeks to clear existing obligations to creditors because of an inability to pay. Under federal legislation introduced in 1998, student loans survive declarations of personal bankruptcy that are made within ten years of graduation. Borrowers who declare personal bankruptcy may nevertheless apply for interest-relief and debt reduction programs.

2. Income-Contingent Financing Programs Internationally

Several developed countries have introduced and implemented ICFPs in the past 20 years. The most prominent of these programs were those introduced in Australia, New Zealand, Sweden, and the UK. The following sections briefly review the design features of each these ICFPs and canvass the available evidence relating to the experience each country has had as a result with accessibility to higher education.

A. Australia

Leading up to the mid-1970s, Australian post-secondary institutions had charged tuition fees roughly comparable to those prevailing at Ontario universities.[55] In 1974, in what eventually proved to be a failed initiative to improve minority group participation in post-secondary education,[56] tuition fees were eliminated entirely. The no-tuition policy was partly abandoned in 1987 when the Commonwealth government introduced an administration charge of A$250 per student per year to help defray the costs of higher education (albeit in a minor and mostly symbolic way).[57] In January 1989, the Labor Party reintroduced substantial tuition fees in conjunction with the launching of the 'Higher Education Contributions Scheme' (HECS), the first national ICFP for post-secondary education.[58] Since being introduced, the parameters of HECS have been amended several times, most notably in 1997, and further changes have been announced and are on the way for 2005.

In 1989, tuition fees were set at a flat rate of A$1,800 per student per year, regardless of the course of study or institution attended.[59] These tuition fees were indexed for inflation and could be repaid in two ways. The first was to pay up front at a significant discount, which was initially set at 15% and later increased to 25%.[60] The second way was to defer all payments until after graduation, at which point repayments were income-contingent. Loan funds were available for tuition fees, but not for living expenses. The balance owing was indexed for inflation, so the nominal amount to be repaid would increase from year to year, but no real interest accrued. Provision was made for repayments to be collected at rates varying from 1 to 3% of income through the income tax system, administered by the Australian Tax Office. No repayments were required of those earning less than A$22,000 annually (in 1989 dollars).[61] Evidence suggests that since 1989 the collection costs (not including other administration costs) have amounted to just 1% of the annual HECS collections.[62] Payments are collected until a student's debt is completely repaid, but there is no set schedule that must be met. If a student dies before repaying completely, the debt is forgiven. All students have the option to make voluntary early repayments that attract a 15% bonus.

Reforms to HECS taking effect in 1997 increased prescribed tuition fees, which varied by course of study but not by institution. Three tuition bands replaced the original flat tuition rate. These same three bands continue to apply, though the rates charged have increased. For

2004 tuition fees are: (i) Band 1: A$3,768 (Arts, Humanities, Social Studies and Behavioural Sciences, Education, Visual and Performing Arts, Nursing, Justice and Legal Studies); (ii) Band 2: A$5,367 (Mathematics, Computing, other Health Sciences, Agriculture, Architecture, Sciences, Engineering, Administration, Business and Economics); and (iii) Band 3: A$6,283 (Law, Medicine, Medical Science, Dentistry, Dental Services and Veterinary Science).[63] The 1997 reforms allowed institutions to enroll students who would not be counted for the purposes of the provision of Commonwealth institutional grants and who would also not qualify for participation in HECS. These students pay a tuition fee set independently by the institution and are limited to 25% of enrollees. The set of 1997 reforms have been justifiably criticized on the basis that they retained central planning, in that prices continue to be set by the Commonwealth government, and on the additional grounds that the reforms in effect allow less-able students from relatively wealthier families preferential (unsubsidized) access to elite institutions.[64]

Despite the 'study now, pay later (if you can)' innovation of HECS for undergraduates, from 1989 to 2001 graduate students had to pay tuition fees up front. In January 2001, however, the Australian government announced a program inspired by HECS to assist graduate students – the Postgraduate Education Loan Scheme (PELS). PELS operates similarly to HECS, with loans being made available in respect of all tuition fees (but not living expenses), and income-contingent repayment through the income tax system on essentially the same terms as HECS.

Beginning in January 2005, HECS and PELS are being repackaged with some changes under the auspices of what is being called the 'Higher Education Loan Programme' (HELP). HELP is composed of three separate initiatives, HECS-HELP (the new name for HECS), FEE-HELP (the new name for PELS), and OS-HELP (an overseas studies assistance initiative). Although the general scheme has not changed dramatically, one interesting development is that upfront payments of tuition will no longer need to be all-or-nothing. So long as upfront payments exceed the minimum threshold of A$500, partial upfront payments will be accepted and students credited with a 20% prepayment bonus (down from the 25% bonus that current upfront payments attract). On the back end, voluntary early repayments will attract a 10% bonus as of January 2005 (down from the current more generous 15% bonus).

For 2005–6, no HECS repayments are required of those whose 'HELP Repayment Income' (HRI) is below A$36,185. HRI is defined by the

Australian Taxation Office as 'Taxable income plus any net rental losses, total reportable fringe benefits amounts and exempt foreign employment income.'[65] For those with incomes ranging from A$36,185 to A$67,200, the repayment rates range progressively from 4 to 7.5%. For those whose HRI exceeds A$67,200, the repayment rate is 8%. As was true of the original design, it remains the case that the amount owing is indexed to inflation and the real rate of interest charged is zero.

Given HECS's novelty and the fact that 15 years have elapsed since the Commonwealth of Australia introduced the scheme, it should come as no surprise that the intense interest of observers has led to several studies evaluating the country's experience with the program. In a 2003 paper, Bruce Chapman argues that there are four main lessons that can be drawn. First, he argues that HECS has proved to be surprisingly inexpensive to implement and administer. Current figures suggest that total administration costs (not just collection costs) amount to 2–3% of the amount collected per year. Second, HECS successfully collects a considerable amount of revenue – approximately 20% of higher education expenditures. Third, the program has not led to any discernable change in the composition of the student body. More specifically, there is no evidence that choices regarding post-secondary education have been impaired for socio-economically disadvantaged students. Lastly, enrollment in higher education has grown by about 50% since 1989 (though this growth cannot be attributed solely to the influence of HECS, since enrollment grew dramatically over the course of the 1990s in most developed countries). The one major caveat to the conclusion that the Australian experience has been a positive one that should be emulated elsewhere is that the administrative success of a system like HECS inevitably turns on the efficiency of a jurisdiction's tax system.[66]

In a recent study aimed at more directly investigating and assessing the accessibility impacts of HECS, Chapman and co-author Chris Ryan conclude that '[T]he socioeconomic composition of the higher education student body changed somewhat between 1988 and 1993 in Australia, with the main change being the relative increase in participation by individuals in the middle of the wealth distribution… In the period after the [1997] modifications to HECS, there [were] apparently no differences between the proportionate increases in the participation of all socioeconomic groups. Further, while there was a slight across-the-board decrease in the intentions of secondary students concerning university participation, in the next year enrolment intentions rebounded to their previous level for all socioeconomic groups.'[67]

Chapman and Ryan sum up their findings by remarking that 'the introduction of income-contingent charging systems for higher education has the potential to protect the access of the disadvantaged.'[68] The accessibility findings are consistent with Chapman's earlier work, as well as with studies by others examining the Australian experience with HECS. In a 1999 study sponsored by the Australian Department of Education, Training, and Youth Affairs, Les Andrews concluded that '[w]hile students from low SES backgrounds are under-represented in higher education institutions this is a long term concern which has not worsened following the introduction and changes to HECS over the past decade.'[69] Consistently with the other studies, Hans Vossensteyn and Eric Canton found in 2001 that the socio-economic characteristics of the Australian post-secondary student population did not change in representativeness following the reintroduction of tuition fees in 1989 or with the 1997 reforms.[70]

B. New Zealand

Prior to 1990, New Zealand students paid only nominal fees for post-secondary education.[71] That year, tuition fees of NZ$1,250 per year per student were introduced for all courses of study and at all institutions. Two years later, New Zealand followed Australia's 1989 lead by introducing an ICFP of its own – the 'Student Loan Scheme' (SLS). The SLS provides income-contingent loans for tuition fees charged by public post-secondary institutions. Contemporaneously with the introduction of the SLS in 1992, tuition fees were deregulated, which resulted in considerable increases in tuition fees for most programs. Despite these increases, and consistent with the experience in other developed countries, the 1990s witnessed a dramatic surge in enrollment. By 2002, the tuition fees charged for undergraduate arts programs ranged from NZ$2,950 to NZ$3,880; the fees for law ranged from NZ$3,480 to NZ$3,850; and for medicine, from NZ$9,180 to NZ$9,646.[72] In response to political pressure associated with these increases, the government initiated a 'voluntary' fee-stabilization program in 2001, whereby institutions agreed not to increase tuition fees in exchange for an offsetting increase in government funding.[73] The fee-stabilization program ended in 2003, and the government announced a new 'fee maxima' initiative. This program, now implemented, established a hard cap for undergraduate tuition fees, but allows increases of up to 5% annually provided a program's fees are below the published maxima.[74]

In addition to tuition fees, SLS funds are available to full-time students for course-related costs (such as books) ranging up to NZ$1,000 per year, and for living expenses at a rate of NZ$150 per week. Though not strictly part of the SLS, the 'Student Allowances Scheme' (SAS) operates in parallel with the SLS and provides income-tested grants to students to assist in meeting living expenses. The SAS grants available depend on parental income, and can range up to NZ$164.16 weekly for students who are over 25, studying full time away from home, and whose parents have low incomes.[75]

SLS collections are managed through the income tax system by Inland Revenue. The income threshold below which no repayments are required is currently NZ$16,172.[76] The rate of repayment on income beyond the income threshold is 10%. The SLS indebtedness of non-residents is repaid on a 15-year mortgage-style schedule of predetermined repayments of principal and interest that applies regardless of income.

Interest on all outstanding SLS balances begins accruing as soon as funds are drawn, and is calculated daily. The interest rate on SLS loans has remained at 7% since 1999, which reflects a real interest rate ranging from 3.1 to 6.2% (the 'base interest rate') and an allowance for inflation ranging from 0.8 to 3.9% (the 'interest adjustment rate').[77] Although not the case when the SLS was introduced, a change of government in 2000 and political pressure led to the introduction of a series of complicated interest abatement measures.[78] Students studying full-time or those studying part-time having income below a certain threshold are eligible for complete interest abatement. Those no longer studying are eligible for 'base interest write-offs' (i.e. no real interest will accrue) if income does not exceed the repayment threshold. Provision is also made for what is termed a 'base interest reduction,' which limits the amount of real interest charged on a loan to a maximum of 50% of the income-contingent repayment obligation for that year.[79] Bruce Chapman and David Greenaway have reported that the Inland Revenue's costs of administering the SLS at one point reached nearly triple that of HECS in Australia, which in retrospect was largely the result of a rocky start in administering the complicated interest abatement provisions.[80] The recently published 2004 figures demonstrate that the net administration costs of the SLS now amount to 3% of collections; in this respect New Zealand's administrative experience with the SLS is now essentially the same as Australia's with HECS.[81]

With the important exception of the complicated and costly interest rate abatement measures, the SLS has generally been regarded as a success by commentators in administrative (if not always in political) terms.[82] Notwithstanding this administrative success, some genuine representation issues remain, particularly with regard to the participation of Maori and Pasifika Peoples in post-secondary education. However, there are encouraging signs that these groups are increasing their use of the SLS in both absolute and relative terms.[83] Between 1992 and 1999, Maori and Pasifika Peoples increased their participation rates in New Zealand post-secondary education by 24% and 28%, respectively.[84]

C. Sweden

Swedish universities do not charge tuition fees, although there are nominal student union fees at most universities that range from SEK 150–400 ($27–$70).[85] The Swedish National Board of Student Aid administers the country's student financial aid program, which is intended to assist students in meeting their living expenses while they are studying (further loan funds are also available for certain non-tuition academic costs).[86] The first 35% of a student's funding, SEK 593 per week (about $103), is the basic amount of support and is paid as a grant to all who qualify for funding. A higher grant representing 82% of the total amount, SEK 1,414 per week (about $245), is available for those who demonstrate greater need. The means-testing takes into account only the income of the student (i.e., not that of the student's parents or spouse).[87] Provided a student maintains an adequate level of academic performance (student performance is reported by universities directly to the National Board), he or she remains eligible for the loan and grant program for up to six years.

Until 2001 student loans were repayable on an income-contingent basis at the rate of 4% of earnings, provided an individual's income exceeded a minimum threshold.[88] Since 2001, however, student loans have been repayable on a fixed schedule determined by regulation, depending on various factors including the student's age; for most students the repayment term is 25 years. It is not entirely clear what precipitated the abandonment of the ICFP, though at least one commentator has suggested that it may be related to the high rate of emigration of Swedish post-secondary graduates.[89] The available evidence suggests that approximately 15% of graduates leave the country.[90] The repayment schedule is not a conventional annuity; rather repayments trend upward and are greater towards the end of the schedule. Interest accrues immediately upon loan funds being received, and is calculated at a rate equivalent to the government's average cost of borrowing for the previous three years. Any balance outstanding upon a student's death or upon an individual reaching his or her 68th birthday is forgiven.

It appears that despite the considerable measures in place to ensure the financial accessibility of Swedish post-secondary education – there being no tuition fees and generous support for living expenses – the student population is drawn disproportionately from higher socioeconomic groups. According to a report prepared last year by the Swedish National Agency for Higher Education, 'There is a relatively high degree of social skew in the recruitment of students to higher education. The probability that an individual from a well-off white collar family will go on to higher education is six to seven times greater than that an individual from a working class background will do so.'[91] That socio-economic factors play a significant role in higher education participation in Sweden is surprising, since there are no tuition fees and basic grants exceeding $100 per week are paid for a student's living expenses (even for students from affluent families). As with the Australian experience in abandoning tuition fees from 1974 to 1987, it appears that affordability is not generally a binding constraint on the participation of students from less-affluent socio-economic backgrounds in higher education in Sweden.

D. United Kingdom

Following the Dearing Report,[92] released in July 1997, the funding of higher education in the UK has changed considerably, in the main consistently with the report's 93 recommendations for improving the provision of higher education.[93] Among the most dramatic changes was the introduction of a means-tested tuition fee of £1,000 (now standing at £1,150) for students in all programs and at all institutions. For the current academic year, if a student's parents' residual income amounts to less than £21,475, tuition fees are waived entirely; if parental income exceeds £31,973, full fees are assessed.[94] Another important change following the Dearing Report was the introduction of an ICFP. Student loans are intended to cover those tuition fees not forgiven as a result of means-testing, plus provide some contribution towards living expenses. The maximum loan amount available for students for 2004–5 is £4,095 for students living away from home, £5,050 for students living in London away from home, and £3,240 for students living at home. Outstanding balances increase in nominal terms to keep pace with inflation, but no real interest rate is charged. The rate of repayment is 9% of all income in excess of £10,000 per year. A Higher Education Grant was introduced for students beginning their studies in 2004. The grant is worth up to £1,000, depending upon parental income. For students with family income of £15,200 or lower, the maximum grant is awarded. Partial grants are available for students whose family income ranges from £15,200 to £21,185. With students whose family income exceeds £21,185, no Higher Education Grant will be awarded.[95]

Beginning in 2006, students will be able to defer the payment of their tuition fees directly by taking a 'fees loan' ranging up to the full tuition. Tuition fees are also being deregulated such that institutions will be free to charge any rate for tuition, subject to a hard cap of £3,000.[96] Outstanding balances will continue to be adjusted for inflation and will accrue no real interest charges.[97] Students from low-income families will be entitled to grants of up to £2,700, in addition to loan funding. Universities charging the maximum tuition fees of £3,000 will need to ensure that students from low-income families are provided with bursaries of at least £300 per year, so that when these bursaries are combined with the grants, tuition fees will be completely covered. It has been announced recently that the threshold annual income for repayment of income-contingent loans will be increasing from £10,000 to £15,000 beginning in 2006.

Although the UK's ICFP has been around only since 1998, several studies have already attempted to discern its impact on accessibility to post-secondary education. The preliminary results are somewhat discouraging. In recent empirical work, a group of researchers from the London School of Economics investigated the impact of the introduction of tuition fees and other responses to the Dearing Report on the socio-economic characteristics of students participating in UK post-secondary education.[98] They examined the trend in the likelihood a university student was from a poor neighbourhood and the role of family background.[99] The results showed, encouragingly, that children from all socio-economic backgrounds were considerably more likely to be enrolled in higher education in 2001 as compared to 1994, despite the introduction of tuition fees.[100] However, the increase in participation over the period for students from more privileged backgrounds exceeded the increases realized by poorer students. The authors argue that the relative affordability of post-secondary education likely has only a small *direct* effect on participation and that 'much of the impact from social class on university attendance actually occurs well before entry,' although they acknowledge the possibility that students from poorer backgrounds might anticipate poor accessibility of higher education and therefore exert themselves on their studies less intensely.[101]

Sveinbjörn Blöndal, Simon Field, and Nathalie Girouard found that '[i]n the United Kingdom, the replacement of grants by loans and the introduction of tuition fees has left the social class mix of entrants to universities unchanged, and the proportion of ethnic minority entrants and women slightly higher than before.'[102] According to a 2001 report by the UK Department for Education and Employment, students from more- and less-affluent backgrounds have taken on loans at approximately the same rate. The Department for Education and Employment found that a consistent proportion of students, regardless of position on the socio-economic spectrum, reported worries about taking on study-related debt. The upshot, if these conclusions are accurate, is that debt aversion does not particularly disadvantage those from less-affluent families. The same study concluded also that some ethnic minority students are more reluctant to take out loans than average; however, this does not appear to result in lower rates of participation in post-secondary education in the UK for these ethnic groups.[103]

The experience of the UK in accessibility terms is consistent with findings from Australia, New Zealand, and Sweden, where higher tuition fees coupled with ICFPs led to nearly no discernable impact on the socio-economic composition of the student body. One promising result common to both the New Zealand and the UK experience is that ICFPs appear to be associated with greater participation in higher education by certain ethnic minorities.

3. Designing an Income-Contingent Financing Program for Ontario

There is a strong case that post-secondary education should be free at the point of use in order to maximize accessibility.[104] But equity arguments similar to those supporting the idea that higher education should be free at point of use imply that it should not be free afterwards.[105] An income-contingent financing program (ICFP) provides an attractive way to facilitate the achievement of both goals. The essential feature of an ICFP is that payments are not fixed, as they are with mortgage-style loans, but vary according to an individual's post-study income.[106] For this reason, ICFPs lower the risk of student borrowing, making it more likely that students will invest in higher education.[107] More importantly, as Nicholas Barr explains, by making payments contingent on post-studying incomes, ICFPs effectively charge participating students for their post-secondary education according to the future income benefits that they receive from this education as well as their ability to pay after graduation.[108] As a result, he observes, an ICFP functions much like an income tax on graduates, with the important difference that payments are 'switched off' when the graduate repays the full amount of the balance outstanding.[109]

As a type of income tax, the design of an ICFP necessarily involves many of the same questions that must be addressed for income taxes more generally: Whose income is subject to the tax? What amounts are properly included in computing income and what, if any, amounts may be deducted? What percentage or percentages of income should have to be paid as tax? And below what income level, if any, should no tax be payable? In tax policy terms, these questions concern the tax unit, the tax base, the tax rate or rates, and the exemption or threshold. As a student assistance program, however, an ICFP must also address many of the same questions that are involved in a mortgage-style student loan program: Who is eligible for financial assistance? What level of assistance is available? At what rate should interest accrue on balances outstanding? How long should payment obligations last? And what, if any, interest relief or debt reduction assistance should be available? A further issue, which is common to both income tax and student assistance aspects of an ICFP concerns the administration and collection of payments. The following sections discuss the essential elements of an ICFP, considering student assistance aspects, income tax aspects, and the administration and collection of payments.[110]

A. Student Assistance Design Considerations

The lynchpin among the student assistance design considerations is determining how subsidies should be delivered through an ICFP (if at all). To the extent that any student financial aid program is subsidized, funds will need to be rationed in some way because demand for funding will exceed supply. The current design of OSAP embodies a number of subsidies, including interest rate subsidies while students are studying, debt remission measures through OSOG, and interest and debt relief provisions for those with low earnings in the post-study period. In the case of OSAP, the resulting rationing has led to inadequate borrowing limits and troubling deemed parental and spousal contributions (which are regularly not actually received).[111] This has in turn led to impaired accessibility for students whose needs exceed the borrowing limits or whose parents or spouses do not contribute the amount deemed.

There is thus a trade-off between providing subsidies through an ICFP – even if these subsidies are intended to enhance the accessibility of education for those who pass the test for the subsidized (but rationed) financing – and providing unsubsidized (or, in any event, much less subsidized) funding to all students to the extent they demand it. While incorporating the use of subsidies into the design of an ICFP may make it more politically saleable, it also introduces rationing and access complications.[112] One way to address this rationing problem is to design an unsubsidized ICFP which contains few constraints on borrowing up front, and explicitly target subsidies to those who are most in need through separate initiatives. Even if this approach proves not to be administratively convenient when it comes time to implement Ontario's ICFP, this separation may prove conceptually helpful at the design stage.

1. Eligibility

The current system of student aid in Ontario requires students to satisfy various residency and program requirements in order to be considered eligible to receive student financial aid in Ontario through OSAP.[113] It also limits financial assistance for each program to the normal duration of a program plus one year and aggregate financial assistance to 10 academic years or longer for doctoral students and students with disabilities. For the most part, we see no reason why these eligibility criteria would not also be appropriate to serve as the gatekeepers to the ICFP program envisioned here.

That said, a shift from mortgage-style loans to income-contingent financing might require some rethinking of maximum limits if (as we recommend below) annual limits are relaxed and students are able to fully finance the direct and indirect (living) costs associated with higher education. Although a market interest rate discourages students from obtaining greater financing than they actually need for their education, those who accumulate substantial ICFP balances might be unable to repay these amounts from post-study earnings. While this result might be considered acceptable, on the basis that assistance will be directed to those who need it most, it might also put the ICFP at financial risk –

requiring substantial subsidies from general tax revenues. For this reason, it might be necessary to consider a shorter eligibility period, such as the six-year limit in Sweden.[114] Alternatively, the system might adopt a maximum dollar amount that might vary according to the student's age and/or academic program – diminishing as the student's age increases and increasing for academic programs with higher prospects of future income.[115] Whichever approach is adopted, the existence of maximum limits on income-contingent financing suggests a continuing need for other forms of student assistance such as grants and bursaries that are targeted to students with unmet needs.

2. Available Assistance
One of the most important issues in the design of an ICFP concerns the amount of funding that should be made available to students. The interests of maximizing accessibility suggest that a brief answer is that the amount of funding available should be that which meets a student's requirements while he or she is studying, effectively making higher education free at point of purchase.[116] Three issues arise in determining a student's requirements: (i) eligible expenditures, (ii) available resources, and (iii) maximum annual amounts.

Under the current system of student aid in Ontario, eligible expenses include tuition fees, ancillary fees, books, supplies, and living expenses. Tuition and ancillary fees are capped at an amount which corresponds to regulated fees for most undergraduate programs,[117] books and supplies are capped at $3,000 per year, and living expenses are based on six student categories which account for different living arrangements and family responsibilities. For the most part, we see no need to change these rules under an ICFP. To the extent that the introduction of an ICFP is accompanied by a deregulation of tuition fees, however, eligible costs should include actual tuition fees without any limits.[118] Finally, we would favour an additional adjustment to eligible living expenses to reflect differences in the actual cost of living in different regions – as is the case in the UK, where students living in London are assumed to have higher living costs than other students.

With regard to available resources, current rules for student assistance take into account the student's personal income (including scholarships) and assets, parental income for dependent students, and spousal income and assets for students who are married or living in a common-law or same-sex relationship. This means-testing is made necessary by the interest-rate subsidy in current student loans, since students without financial need would otherwise borrow at below-market rates. Under an ICFP with a market rate of interest, by contrast, students have no economic incentive to obtain more financing than they actually need.[119] In principle, therefore, it should be possible to do away with all means testing, allowing students to finance all direct and indirect (living) expenses associated with higher education, irrespective of their income or assets, or those of their parents or spouses. Given the substantial administrative costs associated with means testing, this would be a significant advantage of an ICFP with market interest rates.

In practice, however, a market interest rate based on the government's costs of borrowing is likely to be lower than the rate at which many students could borrow, suggesting that some attention to available resources is advisable. For two reasons, however, contributions based on parental income and spousal income and assets should be abandoned: first, studies strongly indicate that presumed contributions are often not made, leaving students in poverty and causing significant barriers to access; second, even where these contributions are made, they are often made only under conditions (e.g., with respect to program selection) that undermine personal autonomy.[120] As well, requiring contributions from personal assets is probably not worth the administrative effort, since many students have little in the way of personal assets, those who do are unlikely to seek assistance at market rates, and information on personal assets is not readily verifiable from tax returns. As a result, assessments of available resources should be limited to personal income, including scholarship income. For this purpose, we see no need to depart from current rules requiring specific contributions from pre-study earnings, study-period earnings, and scholarships.

A final issue concerns the existence of a maximum annual limit on allowable assistance, which is currently set at $9,350 for full-time students in Ontario – an amount that was last increased in 1994. If this cap was appropriate in 1994, it is certainly inadequate today, given increases in living expenses and tuition fees in particular.[121] More generally, one might question the need for any annual limit beyond actual assessed expenses less assessed resources.[122] To the extent that some such cap is considered necessary, however, it should be substantially increased to reflect current reality.

3. Interest Rates
Subsidized interest rates are the most common subsidy incorporated into the design of ICFPs internationally[123] and, like most untargeted

subsidies, are generally undesirable.[124] The current practice whereby students pay no interest until they have completed their studies diminishes the incentives students have to borrow only what they need. This explains in large part the tight rationing and deeming of parental and spousal contributions under the current student assistance regime. If a fundamental goal of a student financial aid program is promoting accessibility, then tight rationing must be relaxed. An obvious way to lessen rationing is to reduce subsidies. Consequently, there is a strong case for unsubsidized interest rates. Interest rate subsidies can result from the delayed onset of interest obligations – for example, only after a student finishes his or her studies – or from a below-market interest rate being imposed on outstanding balances. Both types of subsidies should be resisted in the design of an ICFP for Ontario.[125]

Delving a little deeper into what an unsubsidized rate of interest would mean in the context of an ICFP demonstrates that the inquiry cannot end with an assertion in favour of an unsubsidized rate. One option would be to attempt to determine the riskiness of the average student borrower and charge a single rate of interest in an attempt to reflect the average risk. This 'average riskiness' approach appears to be the one currently taken in Ontario. Students have the option of repaying their OSAP loans at a variable rate of interest at prime plus 2.5% or at a fixed rate of interest plus 5%. However, not all student borrowers present the same risks to government lenders. Students in professional programs, such as medicine, dentistry, and law, have much better earnings prospects and will be more likely to repay financial assistance than student borrowers in, say, the fine arts.[126] Even students studying in the same programs at different institutions in many instances have vastly different repayment prospects. The three tuition bands in the Australian system are based in part on the polite myth that all institutions provide programs that are of equal value to students.[127] If one accepts the proposition that student repayment prospects will vary from program and program, then a natural question arises whether these differences should be accounted for through varying interest rates (or, for example, whether such differences should be reflected only through varying tuition fees).[128] An advantage of risk-rating is that programs would have an incentive to improve their students' income prospects after graduation. The competitive pressure to improve upon incomes would ensure that programs set on providing graduates with the skills and abilities demanded by the labour market would be rewarded with more attractive borrowing terms for students.[129] Because students studying at private institutions would not be cross-subsidized by students elsewhere, risk-rating programs would also facilitate freer entry of private institutions into post-secondary education, as there would be little reason to restrict entry by private institutions. In addition, allowing students to access funds up front would allow students to finance a privately provided education more easily than is currently the case, which would have the added benefit of facilitating access to innovative private institutions. Risk-rating by program might therefore promote a post-secondary system that is more competitive, invigorated, and more responsive to the demands of labour markets.[130]

Risk-rating programs is not without potential problems. All the arguments that suggest that interest rates should vary by program would also suggest that especially talented or motivated students should be entitled to borrow at lower interest rates (since they should not be forced to cross-subsidize less-talented or less-motivated students).[131] More perniciously, the same arguments would suggest that students who are subject to discrimination in labour markets (e.g. females, handicapped individuals, members of ethnic minorities, and, taken to an extreme, those shorter or less attractive than average, or the morbidly obese)[132] should pay higher rates of interest. Even if distinctions in interest rates on the basis of ethnicity, gender, or these other grounds were prohibited, if programs were risk-rated on the basis of labour market experience post-graduation, then programs would have an incentive to admit students expected to have the best *ex post* earnings prospects – those who are least disadvantaged (or, equivalently, the most advantaged). Another potential problem is that programs would have an incentive to encourage graduates to pursue careers yielding private benefits at the expense of careers in the public interest. Students would then be tempted to use a program's risk-rating as a proxy or signal of the program's quality. Anticipating this behaviour on the part of students, employers could be expected to use the program's risk-rating as a signal of student quality.[133] This implicit understanding about which programs attracted the best students (and thus attracted the most employer attention) would then be self-reinforcing. The best students would be the ones being admitted to the 'best' programs, which would lead inexorably to a situation of 'have' and 'have-not' programs, which might be inconsistent with the aspirations of public post-secondary education.

The foregoing suggests that while in theory the optimal approach would be to charge each student a tailored risk-adjusted interest rate, based on personal characteristics or on the basis of the experience of previous graduates from a particular program (or a combination thereof), this is probably not desirable due to the undesirable incentives it would engender at the program level and for the pernicious discriminatory impacts such risk-rating would have for females and for those from disadvantaged ethnic groups (and others). While any number of calculations might support the selection of one real interest rate or another to reflect the average riskiness of student borrowers, the current rate for student loans offers a clue. Since the current prime rate is 4.25%,[134] the variable rate option is 6.75% (2.5% greater than the prime rate). Because the latest CPI figures suggest that inflation is running at approximately 2.3%,[135] the current real rate of interest on student loans is about 4.45%. This suggests that an interest rate representing the 'average risk' of students through an ICFP, with its many advantages on the administration and collections front,[136] would perhaps be a slightly lower real interest rate of 4%.

4. Length of Payment Term

Aside from subsidized interest rates, another common way of delivering subsidies through an ICFP is by forgiving the amount outstanding at a certain date (e.g., 25 years following the commencement of the repayment period, or upon the borrower reaching a certain age, such as the standard retirement age). While the basic parameters for ICFP payments should be designed to recover most ICFP balances within a reasonable period of time (e.g., 25 years or the graduate's working life),[137] there is no reason why payment obligations should cease at this time if individuals have balances outstanding. On the contrary, since an ICFP bases the level of periodic payments on an individual's ability to pay, no individual will be subjected to undue hardship as a result of having to satisfy payment obligations, as is often the case with large mortgage-style student loans that are repayable over relatively short terms such as 10 years. Those with very large ICFP obligations will never be called upon to make larger payments than they can afford to pay, in accordance with the conventional formula. As a result, artificially limiting the payment term would tend to benefit those who remain capable of paying toward the accumulated cost of their education plus a reasonable rate of interest. It also creates perverse incentives to minimize income, particularly around the designated time when payment obligations cease.

With reasonable parameters for income-contingent payments, most participants will discharge their ISFP balance during their lifetimes. For those who do not, however, because they die young, their lifetime earnings are low, or their balance is large, it must then be determined whether ICFP obligations cease at death or convert into conventional debts that attach to the deceased's estate. In our view, the logic of an ICFP favours the former approach: to the extent that an ICFP 'taxes' participants based on their ability to pay and the benefits that they receive from higher education in the form of increased lifetime earnings, these principles are satisfied by income-contingent payments during the individual's lifetime but not after death. Nor does death create the same opportunities for strategic behaviour as one might expect with a repayment term limited to 25 years or the age of retirement, since few individuals can be expected to pursue this option to avoid income-contingent payments.

5. Interest Relief and Debt Reduction

Under an ICFP, payment obligations vary with income and are designed to be affordable given an individual's ability to pay. For this reason, additional interest relief and debt reduction programs, as exist in the current student aid system in Ontario, would seem to be unnecessary in an ICFP.[138] For individuals who would discharge their ICFP balances during their lifetimes, these measures simply shorten the payment period. For individuals who would leave an unpaid ICFP balance at death, they provide this relief earlier. If periodic payments are contingent on the individual's income, however, it is not clear why either of these responses is warranted.[139] On the contrary, the same reasons that favour a market interest rate and repayment until the amount outstanding is satisfied or the participant dies also militate in favour of precluding the possibility of interest relief and debt reduction.

B. Income Tax Design Considerations

Under an ICFP, the payments to discharge outstanding balances are contingent on post-study income. As a result, these payments function much like a temporary income tax that ceases when outstanding balances are repaid. This section considers the manner in which this tax should be designed, considering the choice of the tax unit, the definition of the tax base, and the specification of rates and a non-taxable threshold.

1. Tax Unit

The choice of a tax unit determines whose income is subject to the tax. With an individual tax unit, income tax applies to the income of each individual. A spousal or family tax unit, by contrast, aggregates the income of spouses or families (however defined) before computing the amount of tax payable. While the US federal income tax aggregates the income of married couples, and the French income tax applies to aggregate family income,[140] federal and provincial income taxes in Canada apply to each individual's income.[141] Tax-delivered benefits like the federal Goods and Services Tax Credit and the Canada Child Tax Benefit, however, are based on aggregate spousal income and phased out as this combined income increases. Similarly, interest relief and debt reduction programs under the current financial aid system depend on the combined income of the borrower and the borrower's spouse, common-law partner, or same-sex partner. Which approach should be adopted under an ICFP?

Although a spousal unit makes considerable sense if the purpose of a program is to deliver benefits on the basis of need, the logic of an ICFP suggests that repayment should be contingent on the individual student's post-study income rather than the combined income of this individual and his or her spouse. If a key justification for an ICFP is that it taxes participants according to their ability to pay and the income benefits that they receive from higher education, it makes sense to tax the individual who obtained financial assistance to pursue this education rather than the spouse with whom this person resides. Nor should the income-contingent character of the repayment be regarded as a benefit that should only be available to persons in need, but as a basic term for repayment that generally affects only the duration of this repayment rather than the aggregate amount of the payment. Further concerns with a spousal unit are the economic barriers that it could create for long-term relationships with heavily indebted graduates, and the disincentive that it would create for graduates to engage in less-remunerative activities like public service or child rearing. Finally, integration with the existing income tax (discussed below) would be greatly facilitated if the ICFP were to adopt the same unit as the federal and provincial income taxes.

2. Tax Base

The tax base of an income tax may be defined as the amount to which the rate or rates of tax are applied in order to determine the amount of tax payable. More specifically, the tax base includes 'all of the rules respecting the measurement of income, including exemptions and deductions, as well as inclusions.'[142] Although the concept of income may seem straightforward, it is defined by a multitude of provisions in contemporary income tax statutes and is a subject of recurring policy analysis.[143]

As a general rule, tax policy analysis favours a broad or comprehensive definition of income on the basis that this provides the best measure of each taxpayer's relative ability to pay.[144] In Canada, however, federal and provincial income taxes, most of which employ the same tax base,[145] are based on a 'source concept' of income which includes only certain kinds of receipts – excluding, for example, lottery winnings, gifts and inheritances, and other windfalls.[146] Other tax rules encourage specific kinds of behaviour through exemptions and deductions – exempting, for example, half of all capital gains, half of the gain on most employee stock options, and the first $500,000 of lifetime gains on the sale of a private corporation or a family farm; and allowing individuals to deduct contributions to registered pension plans (RPPs) and registered retirement savings plans (RRSPs). Under bilateral tax treaties, moreover, Canada may also exempt certain kinds of income that are earned in other countries. What definition of income should an ICFP employ?

As with the choice of a tax unit, integration with the existing income tax may favour a definition of income for ICFP purposes that corresponds with the definition used in the federal and provincial income taxes. Since this definition captures most forms of earned income, moreover, it is arguably consistent with the aim of an ICFP to tax participants according to the future incomes they derive from their higher education. If repayments are to depend on each individual's ability to pay, however, the standard definition of taxable income may be deficient. In Australia, for example, the concept of income for the ICFP adds to the tax concept of taxable income 'net rental losses, total reportable fringe benefits amounts and exempt foreign employment income.'[147] Likewise in Canada, an ICFP could use an adjusted concept of income that would add specific amounts to taxable income. A possible model for this purpose might be the adjusted income tax base employed for the federal Alternative Minimum Tax. Precisely which amounts should be added requires more detailed consideration than we can provide here.

3. Rates and Threshold

A final issue in the design of an ICFP repayment regime concerns the rate or rates at which payments should be assessed and the income threshold, if any, below which no amount should be payable. These questions are intimately connected, since a threshold effectively defines an initial rate bracket for which the contribution rate is zero. The choice of a threshold also affects the rates at which payments must be calculated if expected ICFP balances are to be discharged within a reasonable period of time.[148] For the purpose of this discussion, we assume that the threshold and rates should be designed to recover most ICFP balances within a period of 30 years.

Beginning with the question of a non-taxable threshold, two principles might apply. First, one might argue that payments should be required when participants earn more than average incomes earned by individuals who have not attended post-secondary education. While this approach corresponds with one interpretation of the benefits from higher education, it ignores the consumption benefits that students enjoy from studies, most often perhaps from programs that yield lower economic returns after graduation. Alternatively, as with an income tax more generally, it is arguable that a threshold should be established to exempt a minimum amount of income that is necessary for basic subsistence. In Canada, non-refundable personal credits currently exempt the first $8,012 of taxable income at the federal level and $8,043 in Ontario.[149] These levels, however, have been widely criticized as unrealistically low, and might reasonably be increased to the $10,000 to $15,000 range. For the purpose of this discussion, we assume a threshold of $12,500.

Above this threshold, payments could be computed at a single flat rate or at progressive rates that increase as income levels increase. The arguments for a single flat rate emphasize potentially adverse incentive effects if progressive payments are added to already progressive income tax rates. For the most part, however, empirical studies question the extent to which progressive income taxes affect labour supply.[150] In the case of an ICFP, moreover, progressive rates have a greater impact on the pattern of payments over time than on aggregate payments – imposing lower burdens on recent graduates with lower incomes and higher burdens as earnings increase over time. Progressive rates also reflect the insurance aspect of an ICFP – requiring lower proportionate contributions from graduates with relatively low incomes and higher proportionate contributions from graduates with relatively higher incomes. For the purpose of this discussion, we assume a 5% contribution rate on income from $12,500 to $27,500, and a 10% contribution rate on income above $27,500.

Assuming a base income equal to the average earnings of an Ontario university graduate in 2003 of $42,100,[151] a real interest rate on ICFP balances of 4% per year, and real income growth of 2% per year, the hypothetical threshold and rates that we have imagined define various payment schedules based on the ICFP balance at graduation. With a balance of $20,000, for example, which approximates the average student debt of graduates with bachelor's degrees in 2003,[152] payments would cease before the end of ten years. Increasing the ICFP balance to $60,000 (roughly three times the average university graduate student debt in 2003) would increase the payment period to approximately 30 years. Consider the same system applied to a representative Ontario college graduate in 2003, who earned $29,400 in the year following graduation[153] and carried student debt of $13,100.[154] If all the other assumptions remain the same, this representative graduate will take just over 13 years to satisfy his or her ICFP obligations. If instead the student had a balance of $30,000 on graduation, the corresponding time to discharge the ICFP balance would be just under 30 years.

These calculations suggest that an ICFP is feasible with the rates and brackets that we have assumed and a real interest rate of 4%, and that even relatively large balances of $60,000 for university graduates or $30,000 for college graduates would be discharged over the course of a graduate's career. Moreover, while graduates who carry the largest ICFP obligations at graduation and earn below-average incomes during their careers might never discharge their ICFP balances, this does not suggest that the ICFP idea is a failed one, but rather that the ICFP is working as intended. Indeed, the key advantage of an ICFP is to only require payments when individuals can afford to pay them.

C. Collection and Administration Considerations

The practical advantages of having an ICFP administered as part of the income tax system are enormous. First, since payments function as a form of income tax, it makes sense to rely on the well-established legal rules and administrative processes that already exist for collecting general income taxes. Second, given these legal rules and administrative processes, collection through the income tax is much more difficult to avoid or evade than collection through a separate administrative agency – particularly where employees are subject to tax withholding at source, as in Canada. Third, withholding at source allows for rapid adjustments to ICFP payments as an individual's circumstances change. Finally, administration through the regular income tax promises dramatic reductions in the costs of collecting ICFP payments. In Australia and

New Zealand, where payments are collected through the income tax, administrative costs are only 2 to 3% of amounts collected.

In Canada, income taxes are levied by federal and provincial governments, although the federal government alone (through the Canada Revenue Agency) collects personal income taxes in all provinces but Quebec, under tax collection agreements with each province.[155] Under these tax collection agreements, provincial income tax must be levied on the same income tax base as the federal income tax, meaning that the provincial definition of taxable income must correspond to the federal definition. As a result, while payments under a provincial ICFP could be collected by the federal government, the concept of income for this purpose would have to follow the federal definition. Given the substantial administrative advantages to collection through the income tax, this limitation would seem to be a reasonable price to pay.

More seriously, however, subsection 92(2) of the *Constitution Act, 1867* limits provincial taxing authority to direct taxation within the province, and (consistent with this constitutional limitation) section 2601 of the federal *Income Tax Regulations* limit provincial income taxes to individuals who are resident in the province on December 31. As a result, while payments under a provincial ICFP could be collected with provincial income tax on participants residing in Ontario on December 31 of each year, they could not be collected from participants residing in other provinces. Nor could they be collected from participants who have emigrated from Canada. Although payments from these participants might be collected through a separate administrative agency, high levels of mobility within Canada suggest that this solution would preclude many of the advantages associated with collection through the income tax. For this reason alone, therefore, it would be best to coordinate the introduction of a provincial ICFP with the federal government in order to ensure that payments could be collected from participants who are residents in other provinces.[156] Collection from participants who leave Canada would be more difficult, but could be accomplished by requiring emigrants to file Canadian tax returns until they discharge their ICFP balances, or by converting ICFP balances into mortgage-style loans upon emigration.

4. Conclusion

Post-secondary education in Ontario is at a crossroads. In the discussion paper of the post-secondary review, Bob Rae aptly remarks that higher education in the province is 'on the edge of the choice between steady decline and great improvement.'[157] One of the ingredients necessary for a thriving post-secondary system is for institutions to have access to adequate funding – preferably both private and public. There are strong arguments supporting the idea that the most attractive way of drawing on both private and public sources of funding is through a well-designed ICFP. This article has attempted to outline the features that such an ICFP should take based on the design features already embodied in Ontario's student financial aid programs and the experience of other jurisdictions – Australia, New Zealand, Sweden, and the UK.

The good news is that a well-designed ICFP is feasible for Ontario. Moreover, the experience of Australia, Sweden, and the UK predicts that an ICFP will probably have insignificant impacts on accessibility for low socio-economic students, and potentially positive impacts on accessibility for those from disadvantaged ethnic groups, as has been the experience in New Zealand and the UK. In addition, many of the administrative features of an ICFP are already embodied in the current OSAP arrangements. For example, the federal and provincial governments are already the lenders for student loans, meaning that an ICFP will not supplant private lending that is merely guaranteed by government (as would have been the case earlier in OSAP's history). The current system also contains various interest relief and debt reduction provisions that an ICFP would simply replace by explicitly income-contingent repayment at affordable levels.

The ability of Ontario's public post-secondary education system to overcome the various challenges recently identified by the OECD would improve dramatically with the introduction of a well-designed ICFP. Ontario students would benefit from dramatically enhanced access to post-secondary education, and the province's system of higher education would be well poised to play the leading role it has previously assumed in Canada, guiding the country's public colleges and universities towards great improvement and a new era of productivity, excellence, and international competitiveness.

Notes

* Faculty of Law, University of Toronto. We are indebted to Lauren Cappell for research assistance.
1 Organization for Economic Cooperation and Development (OECD), *On the Edge: Securing a Sustainable Future for Higher Education* (2004).

2 Ibid., 11–12.
3 See, for example, Ronald J. Daniels and Michael J. Trebilcock, 'Towards a New Compact in University Education in Ontario' (November 24, 2004).
4 See Council of Ontario Universities (COU), A Vision for Excellence: COU Response to the Postsecondary Review Discussion Paper (October 29, 2004), 4.
5 Sean Junor and Alex Usher, The Price of Knowledge 2004: Access and Student Finance in Canada, (Montreal: Canada Millennium Scholarship Foundation, 2004), 118.
6 Ibid., 120–1 (documenting real increases of 300% or more).
7 These societal benefits are both economic and intangible, including increased tax revenues and economic growth as well as broader cultural advantages resulting from a more educated citizenry. See Nicholas Barr, The Economics of the Welfare State, 3d ed. (Oxford: Oxford University Press, 1998), 325–7.
8 These private benefits are twofold, including the consumption value of education itself and the private economic returns associated with post-secondary education. For studies documenting substantial private returns to higher education in terms of reduced unemployment and higher incomes, see David A.A. Stager, Focus on Fees: Alternative Policies for University Tuition Fees (Toronto: Council of Ontario Universities, 1989); Harry M. Kitchen and Douglas Auld, Financing Education and Training in Canada (Toronto: Canadian Tax Foundation, 1995), 88–92; David A.A. Stager, 'Returns to Investment in Ontario University Education, 1960–1990, and Implications for Tuition Fee Policy' (1996), 36:2 Can. J. Higher Education 1; François Vaillancourt and Sandrine Bourdeau-Primeau, 'The Returns to University Education in Canada, 1990 and 1995,' in David Laidler, ed., Renovating the Ivory Tower: Canadian Universities and the Knowledge Economy (Toronto: C.D. Howe Institute, 2002); Kelly Ann Rathje and J.C. Herbert Emery, 'Returns to University Education in Canada Using New Estimates of Program Costs' in Laidler, supra; Sveinbjorn Blondal, Simon Field, and Nathalie Girouard, 'Investment in Human Capital through Upper-Secondary and Tertiary Education' (2002), 34 O.E.C.D. Econ. Stud. 41; and W. Craig Riddell, The Role of Government in Post-Secondary Education in Ontario, paper prepared for the Panel on the Role of Government in Ontario (15 October 2003), 42–8.
9 Since students attending post-secondary educational institutions are disproportionately drawn from affluent backgrounds and more likely to receive higher incomes after graduation, general subsidies for higher education are apt to benefit a more affluent group than the taxpaying public from which the revenues for these subsidies are obtained. This effect is offset to the extent that the overall incidence of taxes is progressive. For evidence on the socio-economic background of persons attending post-secondary educational institutions in Canada, see Sean Junor and

Alex Usher, *The Price of Knowledge 2004: Access and Student Finance in Canada* (Montreal: Canada Millennium Scholarship Foundation, 2004), 53–6 (documenting a positive relationship between parental income and participation in higher education). For evidence on the overall incidence of taxes in Ontario, see Ontario Fair Tax Commission, *Fair Taxation in a Changing World* (Toronto: University of Toronto Press, 1993), 182 (reporting that the incidence of all taxes in Ontario is largely proportional over all income groups, while federal taxes are moderately progressive over the first six income deciles, roughly proportional over the next three deciles, and slightly progressive for the last decile).

10 On different rationales for student assistance, some favouring loans and others grants, see Ross Finnie, 'Student Financial Aid: The Whys, Whens, and Hows of Loans and Grants,' in this volume. On the demand and supply side market failures that impede efficient borrowing for higher education, see Nicholas Barr, *The Welfare State as Piggy Bank: Information, Risk, Uncertainty, and the Role of the State* (Oxford: Oxford University Press, 2001), 175–8.

11 See, e.g., Ross Finnie, Alex Usher, and Hans Vossensteyn, 'Meeting the Need: A New Architecture for Canada's Student Financial Aid System' (February 2004); and H. Lorne Carmichael, 'How Best to Fund Post-secondary Education: A Graduate Tax?' (February 2004).

12 For a detailed explanation of this approach by a leading contemporary advocate, see Barr, *The Welfare State as Piggy Bank*, 179–90. For an early proposal to finance professional student tuition fees on this basis, see Milton Friedman and Simon Kuznets, *Income from Independent Professional Practice* (National Bureau of Economic Research, 1945). For another early proposal to extend this approach to all students, see Milton Friedman, 'The Role of Government in Education,' in Robert A. Solo, ed., *Economics and the Public Interest* (New Brunswick, NJ: Rutgers University Press, 1955).

13 Various terms are used to describe ICFPs, such an 'income-contingent loans' or 'income-contingent debt repayment.' We prefer to steer clear of terms such as 'loans' and 'debt' for the simple reason that the program we envision will provide for the automatic suspension of repayment (with the prospect of eventual forgiveness) for those without adequate income to repay.

14 For a detailed survey of these various sources, see Junor and Usher, *The Price of Knowledge 2004*, 181–272.

15 Ibid., 249. Of this amount, the federal government accounted for approximately 60%. Ibid., 252.

16 Alex Usher, *Who Gets What? The Distribution of Government Subsidies for Post-Secondary Education in Canada* (Toronto: Educational Policy Institute, 2004), 5, reporting that Canadian governments collectively spent $943 million on the cost of servicing student loans, and $1.07 billion on grants and debt remission programs. In recent years, aggregate expenditures on

loans have declined to approximately $700 million, as student borrowing has declined. Junor and Usher, *The Price of Knowledge 2004*, 253.

17 Canada Millennium Scholarship Foundation, 'Focus on: Ontario' (November 28, 2004), available at http://www.millenniumscholarships.ca/en/research/pok_on.htm#_ftn1.

18 Finnie, Usher, and Vossensteyn, *Meeting the Need*, 2. See also Junor and Usher, *The Price of Knowledge 2004*, 181. This complexity is increased by changes to federal and provincial student assistance programs over the last decade – moving from a system in which private financial institutions issued loans to one in which loans are issued directly by the federal and provincial governments. This part reviews only the current student assistance regime in Ontario.

19 Ontario Student Assistance Program (OSAP) and Canada Student Financial Assistance (CSFA), *Setting Out: Information about Financial Assistance for Postsecondary Students 2004–05* (Thunder Bay: Queen's Printer, 2004), available at http://www.canlearn.ca/nslsc/multimedia/pdf/CA_ON_guide0405.pdf.

20 Ibid., 5.

21 Direct financing by the federal and provincial governments has existed only since 2001. Before 1995, private financial institutions issued loans that were guaranteed by the federal and provincial governments. From 1995 to 2000, instead of acting as guarantor, the federal and provincial governments paid a 5% risk premium on the aggregate value of loans for which repayments commenced during the year. Finnie, Usher, and Vossensteyn, *Meeting the Need*, 5.

22 This application can be completed online at http://osap.gov.on.ca/eng/eng_osap_main.html.

23 OSAP and CSFA, *Setting Out*, 6. Among other kinds of information subject to verification, OSAP cross-references and verifies all income information with the Canada Revenue Agency. Ibid., 11.

24 For students studying outside Canada, documents are sent directly to the student.

25 Junor and Usher, *The Price of Knowledge 2004*, 195.

26 OSAP and CSFA, *Setting Out*, 34.

27 Ibid., 12 (full-time students) and 19 (part-time students).

28 According to the OSAP guide to financial assistance in Ontario: 'Most programs offered by Ontario public universities and colleges of applied arts and technology are approved for funding.' Ibid., 12.

29 This percentage is reduced to 40% for students with a permanent disability.

30 OSAP and CSFA, *Setting Out*, 13.

31 Junor and Usher, *The Price of Knowledge 2004*, 185.

32 For part-time students, financial assistance is based on family income rather than assessed need, and capped at a maximum amount for each academic year. OSAP and CSFA, *Setting Out*, 17–21.

33 Junor and Usher, *The Price of Knowledge 2004*, 187. Students are considered to be living in a common-law or same-sex relationship if they have lived together in a conjugal relationship for three years or as a couple are the natural or adoptive parents of a child.
34 Ontario allows graduate programs and selected undergraduate programs (e.g. medicine and law) to levy higher tuition fees. These 'additional cost recovery' programs are required to provide additional financial assistance to students who qualify for government-provided student aid, covering tuition and ancillary fees above the maximum amounts recognized for government-provided student aid. OSAP and CSFA, *Setting Out*, 11.
35 Junor and Usher, *The Price of Knowledge 2004*, 189.
36 Ibid., 188. For married students, child-care expenses are capped at $40/week per child for families with one or two children, and increased to $80/week for the first two children for families with three or more children. For sole-support parents, child-care expenses are capped at $83/week per child for families with one or two children, and increased to $166/week for the first two children for families with three or more children.
37 Ibid., 190.
38 Ibid.
39 Ibid. As a general rule, students need not include personal vehicles worth less than $5,000, nor $2,000 of RRSP savings for each year since the student graduated from secondary school.
40 Ibid., 191.
41 Ibid., 193.
42 OSAP and CSFA, *Setting Out*, 10.
43 Ibid.
44 See ibid., 26–8.
45 Students who obtain loans for part-time studies are required to pay interest while in school. Junor and Usher, *The Price of Knowledge 2004*, 184. For an excellent illustration of the value of the in-school interest subsidy, see ibid., 205.
46 Ibid., 212.
47 Ibid.
48 OSAP and CSFA, *Setting Out*, 34.
49 Junor and Usher, *The Price of Knowledge 2004*, 213. Details on the Ontario Interest Relief Program are available at http://osap.gov.on.ca/eng/not_secure/ir.htm.
50 See the description of Ontario Debt Reduction in Repayment, available at http://osap.gov.on.ca/eng/not_secure/DRR.htm. For the purpose of this calculation, income is broadly defined to include non-taxable amounts such as lottery winnings.
51 Junor and Usher, *The Price of Knowledge 2004*, 213.
52 Ibid., 214.
53 OSAP and CSFA, *Setting Out*, 35.

54 Junor and Usher, *The Price of Knowledge 2004*, 214.
55 Stager, *Focus on Fees*, 121.
56 See D.S. Anderson, R. Boven, P.J. Fensham, and J.P. Powell, 'Students in Australian Higher Education: A Study of Their Social Composition since the Abolition of Fees' (1980); D.S. Anderson and A.E. Vervoorn, 'Access to Privilege: Patterns of Participation in Australian Post-Secondary Education' (1983); and Committee on Higher Education Funding, 'Report of the Committee on Higher Education Funding' (Australian Government Publishing Service, 1998).
57 Stager, *Focus on Fees*, 121.
58 See Barr, *The Welfare State as Piggy Bank*, 208; Bruce Chapman, 'Conceptual Issues and the Australian Experience with Income Contingent Charges for Higher Education' (1997) 107 *Economic Journal* 738; and Commonwealth of Australia, *Learning for Life: Review of Higher Education Financing and Policy* (Canberra, 1998).
59 Stager, *Focus on Fees*, 121–2.
60 See Bruce Chapman and Chris Ryan, 'Income Contingent Financing of Student Charges for Higher Education: Assessing the Australian Innovation' (May 2002), Centre for Economic Policy Research, Australian National University, Discussion Paper no. 449, 6.
61 Kim Jackson, 'Parliamentary Library of Australia E-Brief: The Higher Education Contribution Scheme' (updated 12 August 2003), available at http://www.aph.gov.au/library/intguide/SP/HECS.htm.
62 Barr, *The Welfare State as Piggy Bank*, 209.
63 See 'Fact Sheet 5' from 'Our Universities: Backing Australia's Future' (March 2004), available at http://www.backingaustraliasfuture.gov.au/fact_sheets/5.htm.
64 Barr, *The Welfare State as Piggy Bank*, 208.
65 See Australian Taxation Office, 'Higher Education Contribution Scheme (HECS) repayment schedule and rates,' at http://www.ato.gov.au/.
66 Bruce Chapman and Chris Ryan, 'The Access Implications of Income Contingent Charges for Higher Education: Lessons from Australia' (April 2003), Centre for Economic Policy Research, Australian National University, Discussion Paper no. 463, 4.
67 Ibid., 28.
68 Ibid.
69 Les Andrews, *Does HECS Deter? Factors Affecting University Participation by Low SES Groups* (Canberra: Department of Education, Training and Youth Affairs, August 1999), 25.
70 See Hans Vossensteyn and Eric Canton, 'Tuition Fees and Accessibility: The Australian HECS,' in Sdu Uitgevers, ed., *Higher Education Reform: Getting the Incentives Right* (2001).
71 Norman Laroque, 'Who Should Pay? Tuition Fees and Tertiary Education Financing in New Zealand' (Educational Forum, 2003), 15.

72 Ibid., 16.
73 Ibid., 37.
74 See New Zealand Ministry of Education, Ministry of Social Development & Inland Revenue, *Student Loan Scheme: Annual Report* (October 2004), 13–14.
75 See New Zealand Ministry of Social Development, 'How Much Will I Get,' available at http://www.studylink.govt.nz/financial-assistance/student-allowance/how-much-will-i-get.html.
76 *Student Loan Scheme: Annual Report*, 11.
77 Ibid., 56.
78 See Barr, *The Welfare State as Piggy Bank*, 212.
79 *Student Loan Scheme: Annual Report*, 58.
80 Bruce Chapman and David Greenaway, 'Learning to Live With Loans? Policy Transfer and the Funding of Higher Education' (2003), paper presented at the Internationalisation and Policy Transfer Conference, Tulane University, 11–12 April 2003; available at http://www.tulane.edu/~dnelson/PolTransConv/Chapman-Greenaway.pdf.
81 In 2004 the SLS had net administrative costs of NZ$15.9 million on collections of NZ$509.5 million. See *Student Loan Scheme: Annual Report*, 59–60.
82 Chapman and Greenaway, 'Learning to Live With Loans.' 14.
83 See *Student Loan Scheme: Annual Report*, 23–4.
84 New Zealand Ministry of Education, *Student Loan Scheme Report* (Wellington, 1999).
85 Swedish Institute, 'Fees and Costs' (accessed 21 Nov. 2004), available at http://www.sweden.se/templates/SISCommonPage____4962.asp.
86 The Swedish National Board of Student Aid's website is at http://www.csn.se. This description of the Swedish student financial aid program draws heavily from the contents of the website as of 21 November 2004.
87 See Barr, *The Welfare State as Piggy Bank*, 207–8.
88 Ibid.
89 See Panu Poutvaara, 'Educating Europe' (January 2004), CESifo Working Paper Series no. 1114, 4.
90 See K. Eklund, 'Jakten på den försvinnande skatten' (1998), SNS Förlag, Stockholm, cited by Poutvaara, ibid.
91 National Agency for Higher Education, *The Changing Face of Higher Education in Sweden* (May 2003), 21.
92 The Dearing Report was issued by the committee set up by the UK government in early 1996 and chaired by Sir Ron Dearing. See National Committee of Inquiry into Higher Education, *Dearing Report* (1997).
93 Though by no means were all the recommendations followed.
94 See Department for Education and Skills, 'Student Support FAQ' (accessed 21 Nov. 2004), available at http://www.dfes.gov.uk/studentsupport/faqs.shtml.

95 Ibid.

96 See Nicholas Barr, 'Higher Education Funding' (2004) 20(2) *Oxford Review of Economic Policy*, 279.

97 Ibid., 280.

98 Fernando Galindo-Ruedal, Oscar Marcenaro-Gutierrez, and Anna Vignoles, 'The Widening Socio-economic Gap in UK Higher Education' (June 2004), Centre for the Economics of Education, LSE, available at http://www.lse.ac.uk/collections/pressAndInformationOffice/PDF/HigherEducationPaperJuneAmended.pdf.

99 Ibid., 3.

100 Ibid., 18.

101 Ibid.

102 Sveinbjörn Blöndal, Simon Field and Nathalie Girouard, 'Investment in Human Capital through Upper-Secondary and Tertiary Education' (2001) *OECD Economic Studies* no. 34, 77; citing Universities and Colleges Admissions Service, *Statistical Bulletin on Widening Participation* (2000).

103 Ibid., citing UK Department of Education and Employment, *Social Class and Higher Education* (2001).

104 See Barr, 'Higher Education Funding,' 266.

105 See the discussion in the introduction to this paper.

106 The term 'post-study' is used rather than 'post-graduation' because students who attend college or university but do not graduate still have to make repayments on the amount borrowed.

107 Barr, *The Welfare State as Piggy Bank*, 184.

108 Ibid., 185–6.

109 Ibid., 219. In a sense, the 'graduate taxes' sometimes advocated as a way of financing post-secondary education are simply a special case of ICFP in which the income tax imposed on graduates does not end when one has already paid for one's education.

110 For useful references on the design of an ICFP, see Congressional Budget Office (CBO), *Issues in Designing a Federal Program of Income-Contingent Student Loans* (Washington: CBO, 1994); and Barr, *The Welfare State as Piggy Bank*, 188–90.

111 See Barr, *The Welfare State as Piggy Bank*, 205.

112 For a general discussion of these issues, see Ross Finnie, 'Student Financial Aid.'

113 See the discussion in part 1.A, above.

114 A six-year limit would probably allow almost all students who have not gone on to graduate or professional programs (who should be given additional time) sufficient opportunity to complete their studies, and would deter students from progressing unreasonably slowly.

115 See, e.g., CBO, *Issues in Designing a Federal Program*, 19.

116 See Barr, *The Welfare State as Piggy Bank*, 185, 188.

117 As explained in part 1, 'additional cost recovery' programs with deregulated tuition fees must provide additional financial assistance to students who qualify for government-provided student aid, covering tuition and ancillary fees above the maximum amounts recognized for government-provided student aid.

118 Under this proposal, the ICFP would assume the student assistance function that is currently farmed out to 'additional cost recovery' programs with deregulated fees. To the extent that governments assume this function through an ICFP, financial assistance obligations for 'additional cost recovery' programs could be dropped, allowing institutions to allocate higher fees as they wish. In exchange, of course, governments could reduce subsidies to these institutions in order to finance increased student assistance in the form of grants as well as the ICFP.

119 See Barr, *The Welfare State as Piggy Bank*, 189.

120 See ibid., 205–6 (adding that deemed parental and spousal contributions 'are likely to affect women more seriously than men, especially women from particular cultural and ethnic backgrounds, and thus have potential gender and ethnic effects that deter access'). See also Ross Finnie, 'Student Loans, Student Financial Aid and Post-secondary Education in Canada' (2002), 24 *Journal of Higher Education Policy and Management*, 165 (reporting on data suggesting that many students whose families have incomes above current loan cut-off levels are in fact receiving little or no parental support).

121 Finnie, Usher, and Vossensteyn, *Meeting the Need*, 8.

122 We have already suggested that an ICFP may require an aggregate maximum on allowable assistance.

123 For example, in Australia and the UK no real interest is charged on outstanding balances. New Zealand has an appropriate interest rate, but the various interest-rate abatement provisions mean that most students and many graduates are not charged interest. See part 2.

124 See Barr, *The Welfare State as Piggy Bank*, 189. The one type of untargeted subsidy that is unproblematic is a subsidy paid to reflect the positive externalities associated with a student's education. However, this subsidy is effectively achieved through direct subsidies to post-secondary institutions and tuition fees which do not reflect the full costs of the relevant academic program.

125 See Barr, 'Higher Education Funding,' 270–1 (arguing for an interest rate pegged to the government's cost of borrowing).

126 This is evidenced by the fact that each of the major Canadian banks has a student loan program aimed at professional students. CIBC, Royal Bank of Canada, Bank of Nova Scotia, TD CanadaTrust, National Bank of Canada, and Bank of Montreal all have special borrowing terms for

students in professional programs, with lines of credit maximums ranging up to $150,000 and interest rates at the bank's prime lending rate.

127 The term 'polite myth' to describe a similar phenomenon can be attributed to Nicholas Barr, 'Funding Higher Education: Policies for Access and Quality' (2002), House of Commons, Education and Skills Committee, Post-16 Student Support, Sixth Report of Session 2001–2, HC445 (TSO, 2002), 2; available at http://econ.lse.ac.uk/staff/nb/Barr_Selcom020424.pdf.

128 Economic theory suggests that students will assess programs based on the total private costs and benefits. Thus, if students know that a certain program leads to greater private benefits, they will be willing to pay more, all else the same. Decreasing the interest rate applicable to any financing would not change the maximum amount a student would be willing to pay to take a certain program, but would mean that the program could capture some of this excess willingness to pay by charging higher tuition.

129 But remember that interest rate savings might not be passed on to students, but might be captured by the program through higher tuition fees, leaving the overall cost of the program the same (or only slightly lower). To the extent that a lower risk-rating is used by students as a signal of program quality, programs might *more* than offset the interest rate savings through higher tuition rates to capitalize on the value of the associated signal.

130 Again, for the reasons above, only well-performing programs are apt to be better off financially; students might not be.

131 Indeed, whenever talented or motivated students are forced through participation in an ICFP, there will be at least a minor adverse selection problem, whereby high-performing students will avoid being on the wrong end of a program involving cross-subsidization. For a discussion of the problems associated with such cross-subsidization, see Marc Nerlove, 'Some Problems in the Use of Income-contingent Loans for the Finance of Higher Education' (1975) 83(1) *Journal of Political Economy*, 157.

132 See Barry Harper, 'Beauty, Stature, and the Labour Market: A British Cohort Study' (2000) 62 *Oxford Bulletin of Economics and Statistics* 771 (finding that higher earnings are positively correlated with attractiveness and height, but negatively correlated with obesity).

133 This is the 'screening hypothesis' of higher education, which has been developed in the economics literature. For an early treatment, see Kenneth Arrow, 'Higher Education as a Filter' (1973) 2(3) *Journal of Public Economics* 193. For empirical criticisms of the screening hypothesis, see Richard Layard and George Psacharopoulos, 'The Screening Hypothesis and Returns to Education' (1974) 82(5) *Journal of Political Economy* 985.

134 See, for example, TD CanadaTrust, 'Today's Rates: Prime Rate' (29 Nov. 2004), available at http://www.tdcanadatrust.com/Numbers/prime.jsp.

135 See Statistics Canada, 'Latest Release from the Consumer Price Index' (23 Nov. 2004), available at http://www.statcan.ca/english/Subjects/Cpi/cpi-en.htm.

136 Discussed below in part 3.B.3.

137 See the discussion in part 3.B.2.

138 For a contrary argument, see Barr, 'Higher Education Funding,' 274–5.

139 The only justification, as Barr seems to suggest, is that students may regard ICFP balances as real debts, and be unwilling to obtain financing unless these further measures are available. See ibid., 274 ('in practice, large nominal debts worry people. Thus, although there is a strong case against blanket interest subsidies, there are good arguments for targeted subsidies ... for people with low earnings or out of the labour force') .

140 See Louise Dulude, 'Taxation of the Spouses: A Comparison of Canadian, American, British, French and Swedish Law' (1985), 23 *Osgoode Hall Law Journal* 67.

141 Notwithstanding this choice of an individual unit, a number of adjustments recognize spousal and other family relationships. See the discussion in David G. Duff, *Canadian Income Tax Law* (Toronto: Emond-Montgomery, 2003), 18–29.

142 Peter W. Hogg, Joanne E. Magee, and Ted Cook, *Principles of Canadian Income Tax Law*, 3rd ed. (Toronto: Carswell, 1999), 145.

143 For a brief introduction to the concept of an income tax base and its basic definition in Canadian income tax law, see Duff, *Canadian Income Tax Law*, 35–59.

144 See, e.g., Henry C. Simons, *Personal Income Taxation: The Definition of Income as a Problem of Fiscal Policy* (Chicago: University of Chicago Press, 1938); and Canada, *Report of the Royal Commission on Taxation* (Carter Commission Report), vol. 3 (Ottawa: Queen's Printer, 1966). For other useful discussion, see Boris I. Bittker, 'A "Comprehensive Tax Base" as a Goal of Income Tax Reform' (1966–7), 80 *Harv. L. Rev.* 925; Richard A. Musgrave, 'In Defense of an Income Concept' (1967), 81 *Harv. L. Rev.* 44; Jonathan Pechman, 'Comprehensive Income Taxation: A Comment' (1967), 81 *Harv. L. Rev.* 63; Charles Galvin, 'More on Boris Bittker and the Comprehensive Tax Base: The Practicalities of Tax Reform and the ABA's CSTR' (1968), 81 *Harv. L. Rev.* 1016; Boris I. Bittker, 'Comprehensive Income Taxation: A Response' (1968), 81 *Harv. L. Rev.* 1032; and Victor Thuronyi, 'The Concept of Income' (1990), 46 *Tax L. Rev.* 45.

145 Under federal-provincial tax collection agreements, the federal government collects provincial income taxes on behalf of participating provinces provided that they adhere to the same income tax base as the federal income tax. All provinces but Quebec have signed on to these agreements for the collection of personal income tax.

146 See Duff, *Canadian Income Tax Law*, 36–49.
147 Australian Taxation Office, 'Higher Education Contribution Scheme (HECS) repayment schedule and rates.'
148 The higher the threshold, the higher the rates must be in order to ensure that ICFP balances are discharged within a reasonable period of time. In contrast, a lower threshold allows for ICFP balances to be paid down in a reasonable period of time with lower rates.
149 Federal and provincial income taxes provide numerous other non-refundable credits as well as some refundable credits, but these depend on specific relationships (e.g., spouses or common-law partners), characteristics (e.g., disability), or expenses (e.g., medical expenses).
150 For a useful summary of these studies, see Neil Brooks, 'Flattening the Claims of Flat Taxers' (1998), 21 *Dalhousie Law Journal*, 342–8.
151 See Usher and Junor, *The Price of Knowledge 2004*, 309.
152 Ibid., 282.
153 Ibid., 309.
154 Ibid., 282.
155 See the brief discussion of these agreements in Vern Krishna, *The Fundamentals of Canadian Income Tax* (Toronto: Carswell, 2004), 9–10.
156 The integration of provincial and federal student loans through the Canada-Ontario Integrated Student Loan Program is another good reason why a provincial ICFP should be coordinated with the federal government.
157 Bob Rae, 'Higher Expectations for Higher Education: Working Through the Possibilities' (2004), 2.

Timing the Payment of Tuition to Enhance Accessibility: A Graduate Tax?

H. LORNE CARMICHAEL[*]

There are many issues facing the post-secondary education sector in Ontario, but the greatest passion seems to be generated by the problem of accessibility. Student leaders complain that the opportunity for a university education that should be available to all qualified high school graduates is in fact given only to those whose family wealth is sufficient to cover the costs, or to those who are willing to take on a large load of debt.

There are several policy instruments that could be used to enhance accessibility. The most popular among students and some faculty is a pure public subsidy. We should, it is argued, tax the general public and use the money to set the student's portion of the cost of instruction to zero. Needless to say this option is not so popular with taxpayers, the majority of whom did not go to university, and do not expect their children to go either. Taxpayers in Canada, through the governments they elect, have made it abundantly clear that their priority is access to a quality health care system – not a quality university system.

This places universities and potential students in a critical situation, as the need for more funding is acute. There is essentially no chance that tuition levels will be reduced, and indeed it is likely that tuition will have to rise even further if the system is to be maintained. How can universities maintain and enhance accessibility under these circumstances?

This paper outlines the argument for a graduate tax. Such a tax in practice would look a great deal like an income-contingent student loan (ICSL), and to be most efficient would require the same level of cooperation from government in its collection. But it has the advantage that prospective students are never presented with a fixed amount that must be repaid, and so are never subject to 'debt aversion.' In addition, a graduate tax is more equitable than an ICSL both in its treatment of university students versus non-students, and within the group of students themselves. Under the graduate tax, those students who get a greater financial return from their education also pay more for it. In essence, the program would ask the public to take an equity interest in the success of its most talented scholars.

The paper begins with a brief discussion of the optimal tax treatment of investments in post-secondary education. Standard considerations of equity and efficiency suggest that there should be a significant public subsidy to education, quite apart from the external benefits that may be realized when society educates some of its brightest young people. The rest of the paper outlines the case for raising the remaining money from students through a graduate tax.

Readers familiar with the Economics of Education will find little that is new in this paper, and indeed there are few ideas here that can even be called recent. The problem of funding post-secondary education has received steady attention from economists, and the work has been surveyed already in several places (Barr 1993; Greenaway and Haynes 2003). My hope is that this paper will make some aspects of the problem and at least one of the solutions accessible to a wider audience.

Tax Treatment of Investments in Education[1]

It seems fair that the tax system should treat investments in education in the same way it treats investments in physical capital. This will also ensure that taxes do not distort individual choices between various investments. The most basic principle of fair and efficient taxation is simply that the cost of an investment be deductible against future income. To see why, assume we have a very simple investment that costs an amount C in period one and some time later (period two) is expected to return the total benefit R. The cost must be paid out of after-tax savings.

If an individual just puts her money in the bank over this period, she would earn interest at the rate r. Thus her savings would grow to the amount $C(1 + r)$. However, the government will collect tax on the interest income, so her after-tax wealth is only $C(1 + r) - rCt$, where t is the tax rate. This can be written as $C(1 + r(1 - t))$, where $r(1 - t)$ is the after-tax rate of return on savings.

Suppose instead the individual decides to buy a physical asset, like a car, that he will use to earn income through a personal business. In this case the amount C is spent on the car, and an amount R shows up as income some time later. However, even though the investor earns total income R from the use of his automobile in the second period, he does not have to pay tax on this full amount. Instead he is allowed to deduct the cost of buying the car from income before calculating tax, so that after-tax wealth is $R - t(R - C)$.

This system treats people who invest in physical assets the same way it treats people who put their money in the bank. In each case tax is payable only on the extra earnings from the use of the amount C. It follows that if the total return from making the physical investment is higher, i.e., $R > C(1 + r)$, the after-tax income to the individual making the decision to invest is also higher. In this sense we can expect the right decisions to be made – people subject to taxation will still invest when they should and keep their money in the bank when they should.

Note that the tax system could achieve the same effect through a subsidy to the cost of investing, rather than by allowing a deduction from the returns. This might be preferred when individuals find it difficult to raise the money to pay for the investment up front. Suppose we subsidize the investment by the amount S when it is made, but now we tax the benefits fully when they are received. The investment now costs only $(C-S)$, but the after-tax return is only $R(1 - t)$. To ensure efficient decisions we want to choose the subsidy S so that the after-tax returns are equal whenever the total returns are equal. A bit of algebra reveals we should choose S such that

$$S = (tC)/(1 + r(1 - t))$$

Not surprisingly, the proper subsidy is equivalent to the present discounted value of the tax deduction that would be received under the usual scheme. To an investor that was short of money, however, the subsidy scheme might make the investment opportunity much more accessible.

Now let us look at the case of post-secondary education. The algebra here gets a bit more complicated, and the reader is referred to Carmichael 1999 for the full treatment. Suppose a person with a high school diploma would earn the amount w(h) during his first four years after high school graduation and w(a) thereafter. Going to university increases earnings after university graduation by the amount R. Individuals are taxed at the average rate t(1) if their wages are low (w(h) or w(a)), but we assume the marginal rate on higher earnings, denoted by t(2), is larger. To attend university he must pay four years' full-cost tuition T, as well as moving and other incidental expenses M.[2] Suppose we give him a non-taxable subsidy S to help defray these costs. Remember that for the purpose of this analysis T is the full cost of tuition, such as would be charged by a private school. (T – S) is the payment made by the student.

We want to find the subsidy S such that whenever the overall benefit (including taxes paid to the government) of attending university is equal to the overall benefit of entering the labour force right out of high school, the after-tax benefits are the same as well. This is the same principle used in calculating the tax treatment for investments in physical capital in the simple model above. A (fair) bit of algebra reveals that the subsidy

$$S = t(2) \, (T + M + w(h)) \, / \, (1 + r(1 - t(2))) - w(h)t(1)$$

will do the trick.

This expression looks complicated, but it is not that difficult to interpret. The numerator of the first term includes the out-of-pocket costs of university (T + M) plus the opportunity cost w(h), multiplied by the marginal tax rate faced by a university graduate. The entire first term is therefore just the present value of the tax deduction that would be enjoyed by graduates if they could deduct the full cost of their investment (including the opportunity cost) from subsequent earnings. This part of the subsidy is calculated exactly as it was in the simple physical-investment case above. However the opportunity cost is itself subject to tax at the rate t(1). In other words, by taxing the opportunity cost of an education, the government already provides an implicit subsidy to students (i.e., it makes attending university financially more attractive). The second term in the expression corrects for this implicit subsidy.

The reader is referred to Carmichael 1999 for further discussion and a series of illustrative examples based on recent Canadian earnings data. There are two points to be made here, however. First, if the government wants to maximize accessibility and at the same time run an efficient tax system, it makes no sense whatsoever to allow students to carry forward their tuition costs so as to deduct them against future income. Students should get no tuition tax deduction at all, but should receive the present value of this benefit as a subsidy to the full cost of their education.

Second, with a steeply progressive tax system the calculated value of this subsidy is often substantial. As a quick example, consider a high school graduate able to earn $10.00 per hour. Over a 2000-hour year he would earn $20,000, and might pay about 10% of that in income tax. Suppose a university degree would place him in the highest marginal tax bracket (say 45% of his income earned over $20,000). To be conservative we set the discount rate at 50%, since these earnings are some years off. Suppose the full cost of tuition and moving expenses (but not living expenses) is $15,000. Then the subsidy works out to $10,353. The student should pay only $4647 in tuition.

One issue with this method of determining the optimal subsidy for a university student is that those students who expect to earn the most (and therefore be in the highest tax bracket) should get the highest subsidy. Indeed a degree that does not increase future income should not be subsidized at all – it should be subject to a surcharge of $w(h)t(1)$. It would be more equitable to offer the same subsidy to all students, in much the same way that the tax system now grants non-refundable tax credits that are worth the same amount to people regardless of their tax bracket. Nonetheless, it seems clear that this subsidy should be substantial, even though the analysis has ignored any public benefits to the education of society's brightest minds.

Are Current Subsidy Levels Too Low?[3]

At the present time subsidies are applied in different amounts to all programs, and the levels are substantial. Can we determine if they are too high or low? One way to address this issue is by looking at enrolments.

Somewhat fewer than 25% of Canadian high school graduates go on to take a university degree. If we consider the rate of return to a university degree, this would seem to be too small a number: more students should be going to university. Estimates of the private rate of return in Canada and elsewhere regularly top 10%, as revealed in the accompanying table.[4] As well, money is not the only benefit correlated with educational status. University graduates also enjoy better health (Kenkel 1991) and spend less time in jail (Lochner and Moretti 2001). In addition, there appear to be some external benefits to having an educated population. Higher education is linked to participation in community affairs, the democratic process, and volunteer work (Bynner and Egerton 2000). In the United States, low-skilled workers earn higher

Table 1   Private Rates of Return to University Education in the OECD

	Men	Women
Canada	8.7	9.9
Denmark	11.5	11.1
France	14.3	15.4
Germany	9.1	8.4
Italy	6.5	8.4
Japan	7.9	7.2
Netherlands	12.1	12.5
Sweden	11.4	10.8
United Kingdom	18.5	16.1
United States	14.9	14.7
Unweighted average	11.7	11.8

wages if they live in a city that has a higher proportion of university graduates (Moretti 2004). This could be due to complementarities in production among workers, as examined by Johnson (1984). Finally, the effect of higher education on economic growth seems to be positive, although estimates are imprecise (Bassanini and Scarpetta 2001).

Given these benefits, it would seem that more and more people should be taking advantage of the opportunity to go to university. However, the numbers above are average monetary returns for those who attend. They do not reflect the expected returns for those individuals who do not attend now but would attend if the system were expanded.

While we have all heard stories of university graduates driving taxis, explicit data on the returns to education for a marginal applicant are hard to find. In one interesting study, Ockert (2003) examined a unique data set from Sweden. In 1982, university applicants were centrally ranked and admission was granted to those with the highest qualifications. A number of students at the bottom of the 'acceptable' category were considered equally qualified. These students were randomly assigned admission to the fixed number of places remaining after all the higher-ranking applicants were placed. Tuition was free. Ockert had information on each applicant's qualifications and labour-market history up to 1996. In his sample, the rate of return to an acceptance letter was actually negative: most marginal applicants would have earned more money had they not been admitted to university, even though the overall average rate of return to a degree was positive.

Although these data are hardly conclusive, it is certainly clear that some university graduates earn much more than others, so that the average rate of return to a university education will be significantly higher than the marginal return. It also seems likely that the social benefit of educating an academically marginal student may be fairly small. If this is the case, the university system should not necessarily aim to bring in more students. It may be true that certain students who could benefit are not able to attend, but it may also be true that some students who are attending would have been better off if they had gone straight to work or into the college system.[5]

Overall, one inescapable conclusion from these data is that those who attend and graduate from university are an elite group. Graduates earn higher incomes, enjoy better health, live longer, and boast higher social status than non-graduates, at least partly due to their experience in university. Unfortunately, the fact that not everyone can enjoy these benefits may not just reflect a lack of access. Some people lack the ability to do well at school, and simply will not benefit from a university education.

Student advocates and others argue that accessibility should be enhanced through larger public subsidies to post-secondary education. But even though the optimal subsidy on pure efficiency grounds may be substantial, there is no evidence that it is too low since there is no current evidence that students with marginal grades would be better off attending university. As well, there is no equity case for further subsidies to university students at the expense of taxpayers, given the relatively privileged lifetime experience that university students can expect to enjoy.

The case for a larger subsidy depends on our concern for those students who have the ability to benefit from attending university, but who cannot do so now for lack of money. The problem is particularly acute at this time due to the very real possibility that tuition rates will be increasing in the future. Universities need more funding, and given current political realities it seems inevitable that any increase in funding will have to come from increased tuition. In this context there is great need for a mechanism that could allow for an increase in student tuition fees and at the same time could transparently maintain or improve accessibility.

Student Loan Programs

Currently in Canada the problem of accessibility is addressed with scholarships and bursaries for poorer students and with student loan programs. Student loans clearly help many students to attend university, but some students graduate with high levels of debt. It has been argued that such debt, perhaps because its anticipated nominal value is higher than anything in the student's pre-university experience, will deter enrolment even though it may turn out to be manageable relative to post-graduation income. The empirical importance of this factor has yet to be established (Finnie and Laporte 2003), but the argument retains some power in public discussions. A second argument is that the obligation[DM]Paying off a debt is more than just a desire, no? to pay off a debt will deter some students from entering occupations that have large public benefits but are less lucrative. Examples might include social work and family medicine. If poorer students are more likely to enter these occupations in the first place because of their pre-university experience, the problem will be exacerbated.[6] It is also clear that if Canadians decide that the non-monetary returns to a university degree should be available to everyone, then a loan program will not improve access to those who want to attend purely for these benefits.

An income-contingent student loan program, such as the one in place in Australia (Chapman 1997) would seem to mitigate these issues, but perhaps not completely. Under such a system, debt payments are geared to income, but the debt persists as a potential claim on future income until it is repaid. Whether this is enough to alleviate 'debt aversion' is again an open question; it may depend on the individual. The present value of the obligation is the same for all students, but those who earn less after graduation will take longer to pay off the obligation, and pay more interest in total.

Since it is inevitable that some students will not earn a significant income after graduation, governments must provide banks with a subsidy in order get them to offer student loans. It follows that all student loan programs, income-contingent or not, are inequitable because they are not designed to break even. Students who never pay off their debts are subsidized by taxpayers, including many who did not go to university and whose children will never attend. Of course it is always possible to mitigate this inequity by introducing other taxes or subsidies, but the program itself introduces a new subsidy to the more privileged.

The Graduate Tax

There is a program that would, in principle, provide universal access to university without requiring a public subsidy. The earliest version of this idea is probably that of Friedman and Kuznets (1945), who argued that students should consider selling an equity share in their education. This would mean that a student would accept money while in school and pay it back later, but rather than principal plus interest the payment would be a percentage of future income. A version of this idea was tried out by Yale University in the 1970s,[7] and a modified version is still in place at the Yale Law School.[8]

Default turned out to be a major problem with Yale's program. Even though Yale could require participants to allow it to get information on their income from the Internal Revenue Service, it still had to face the problem of collecting payment. According to West (1976), this was the most critical issue.

The problem of default is related to the fact that individuals are not allowed to sell their human capital. This would amount to slavery, or indentured servitude at best, both of which are illegal. The government, however, has no trouble forcing people to hand over part of their annual income through taxation. Since most university graduates take part in the above-ground economy, the government should be able to determine their income for the year. This has led several authors to suggest a version of the equity plan where the government provides the equity and then collects the return through a 'graduate tax.' Early references include Merrett (1967) and Glennerster, Merrett, and Wilson (1968), while much more recently Poutvaara (2003) has proposed such a tax for the European Community.

To aid exposition, the rest of this section discusses the graduate tax in the context of a specific example. Suppose that the current direct public subsidy to education were held constant and that the student's share of tuition for university arts and sciences programs were increased to $10,000 per year. Given recent government cutbacks, this would restore the overall quality of service to about the levels of 1990.[9] Total tuition costs to the student over four years would be $40,000.

One feature of a graduate tax would be a cutoff salary below which no graduate would pay any tax. In the simplest case, gross earnings above this rate would be taxed at a fixed percentage. Suppose we set a cutoff salary of $35,000, which is close to the average salary of an arts or

Plan 1

Discount rate		3% per year
Earnings growth		3% per year
Tuition	4 years at $10,000	$40,000
Grad Tax payments last		35 years

Payment Formula: P(t) = (Y(t) − $35,000)*(0.9)

Starting income		PDV of payment stream
$25,000	no payments for 12 years	$14,330.48
$35,000		$40,534.71
$45,000		$72,034.71

sciences graduate two years after graduation.[10] If we assume real income growth of 3% as well as a discount rate of 3%, then a 9% tax rate on income over $35,000 will raise, in present discounted value, the sum of $40,534.71 over the next 35 years. Someone who starts working at $45,000 under the same assumptions will pay $72,034.71 in present discounted value. Someone who starts at $25,000 will pay nothing for the first 12 years, and the present discounted value of all subsequent payments is only $14,330.48. These figures appear in the next table (Plan 1).

There are many details to consider. First, the cutoff income would have to be adjusted for inflation on an ongoing basis. Universities, for their part, cannot wait 35 years to be paid in full for the services they provide to students. The only way this system could be at all useful is if the federal government paid universities up front in return for the right to levy a tax on students.[11] This might require new deficit financing on the part of the government, but such debt would be backed by growth in Canada's human capital, an asset the government is in a unique position to appropriate.[12]

The calculation of a 'break even' tax rate would be a complicated task in practice, and it would take us beyond the scope of this paper to attempt a more precise calculation. In actual fact, salaries for university graduates grow at a much faster rate than 3% in the early years of a career,[13] which might substantially reduce the required tax rate. If the cutoff income were reduced to $30,000, then a tax rate of just over 7% is enough to break even on a graduate who starts at $35,000. So it might be reasonable to think that the rate could be kept below 10%, or 0.25% per $1000 advanced.

These calculations are based on the huge assumption that all students will be required to participate in the program.[14] In practice, if participation is voluntary, a serious problem of adverse selection can be expected to arise. Those students who expect to do well and whose families can afford the direct cost will likely opt out of the program, since this would be less costly by far. There is another problem of adverse selection as well: given that the up-front cost of university would have fallen, some young people with very weak intentions to study and low expected future income might even decide to enter university without intending to graduate.[15] The risk of this behaviour would be even higher if the program were expanded to cover some of students' living expenses.

The latter problem can be handled as it is now – by requiring students to show academic promise in order to be admitted and in order to continue. As mentioned earlier, there is no strong evidence that the overall number of students attending university is too low. We will always need to restrict accessibility on the basis of academic promise in order to ensure that the students who attend university are able to benefit from the experience.

The former issue is more problematic. The Yale Tuition Postponement Option partially addressed it by allowing participants to cease making payments once their accumulated total exceeded 150% of the advanced amount, plus interest. Nonetheless, participation rates remained below 40%, which may explain why the tax rate under the plan was so high: 0.4% per $1000 advanced. (This would be equivalent to a tax rate of 16% in the example above.)

The easiest way to encourage high-income students to participate in a voluntary plan would be to increase the price of opting out. So let us continue to suppose that tuition for an arts or sciences program is $10,000 per year. The government would pay this entire amount for anyone who joins the graduate tax program. However, anyone who opted out of the graduate tax program would have to pay $15,000 per year. In principle, there could be partial participation, whereby every $1500 advanced toward tuition payments would lead to a tax of 0.25% (say) on income in excess of $35,000. However, for every $1500 'advanced' to the student for tuition, the university would receive only $1000 from the government.

After graduation, participants could stop making payments once their total equalled 150% of the actual cost: $60,000 plus interest for

Plan 2

Discount rate		3% per year
Earnings growth		3% per year
Tuition	4 years at $15,000	$60,000
Grad Tax payments last		35 years

Payment Formula: $P(t) = (Y(t) - \$35,000)*(0.9)$

   for □ $P(t)/(1 + r)$ ^t □ $60,000

Starting income		PDV of payment stream
$25,000	no payments for 12 years	$14,330.48
$35,000		$40,534.71
$45,000	no payments after 30 years	$60,000

someone who participated fully. The average graduate would continue to pay the tax over her lifetime, and in present value would still expect to pay about $40,000. This means that there should be a tax rate at which this plan would break even. Those graduates who earn more than average would still subsidize those who do not. The details of a graduate tax scheme with a more-expensive opting-out option are summarized in the accompanying table (Plan 2). Note that under the assumptions above, opting out of the plan costs $60,000 up front, while participation leads to a cost of at most $60,000 in present value. Thus participation rates should be very high. Those people who cannot make the calculation and do opt out will provide a nice subsidy to the university.

One remaining problem is that the plan might begin to resemble a loan again, given the fixed opt-out level of $60,000. Since students' perceptions are at the heart of the debt-aversion issue, this may lead to some of the same problems, even though payments are labelled as extra taxes rather than loan repayments. One way to prevent this without discouraging the participation of people who expect to earn high incomes would be to redesign the tax rates so that people earning very high incomes after graduation would pay at a lower rate. For example, under Plan 1 above, if someone starts at a salary of $45,000 and pays 9% of income in excess of $35,000, she pays a total of $72,034.71 in present value. If we assume instead that she pays 9% of the first $50,000 of income in excess of $35,000, and a fixed amount of $4500 per year if her income rises above $85,000, then the total payment in present value falls to $63,118.33. The total payment by the 'average' student who starts at $35,000 falls from $40,534.71 to $39,649.89. Again, it seems likely that the plan could be designed to break even, although a great deal more effort and data would be needed to determine the appropriate tax rates.

The fact that the program is run by the government through the tax system avoids the problem of default that plagued the Yale Tuition Postponement Option. The fact remains that some students may skip payment by emigrating. But this is also a problem for a student loan program, and indeed it is a problem for any student support program. In principle, it is solved by requiring graduates to pay up before they leave. In practice, some people will escape, and perhaps this cannot always be prevented. In the end, some of the extra money paid by more successful students will subsidize others' escape.

To be most successful, the program should be run at the federal level. This would at least avoid problems due to inter-provincial migration. However, post-secondary education is a provincial responsibility. One can only hope that the federal government and the provinces could manage these political issues. It is also possible that the system would be too expensive to administer. This seems unlikely, however, given Australia's experience in running its income-contingent loan scheme through the tax system.

Finally, one aspect of the current system that this paper has not adequately discussed is the student support available through university and private bursaries and federal programs such as the Millennium Foundation bursaries. These programs attempt to identify students in financial need and provide them with direct support. Direct bursaries are also a major factor at selective colleges in the United States.

Under a bursary system, just as with a graduate tax, richer students pay a higher price for the same education received by their poorer colleagues. The difference between bursaries and a graduate tax is the way they define 'richer' and 'poorer.' Eligibility for bursaries is determined by the income and wealth of the student and her family at the time she attends university. Under a graduate tax, the student is treated as a single individual; his wealth is determined by actual post-graduation earnings. This has the advantage that identification is automatic; students can avoid the remarkably invasive and detailed family income reports required by selective US schools.

Nonetheless, if a graduate tax program were to be implemented in Canada, the bursary money currently available could be used to remove the last remaining barriers to accessibility. For example, bursaries could easily cover the living expenses of those qualified students who are in acute financial need.

Conclusion

A graduate tax has some distinct advantages over the current student loan system, and some advantages over an Income Contingent Student Loan system. First, it is more equitable, in that it does not require a subsidy from general taxpayers to make it solvent. Students who go on to earn high incomes would subsidize those who do not. Second, the program can enhance the accessibility and the quality of university education. Without increasing the current public subsidy to education, governments would be able to offer students four years of tuition-free studies. These students could receive an education at the level of quality provided in 1990 – before the long series of cutbacks began. In return, they would agree to a lifetime increase in taxes, albeit a manageable one as well as an equitable one given the advantages they would enjoy as university graduates. A graduate tax would not impose any constraints on the careers they might choose; if anything, there would be a mild encouragement to choose low-salaried occupations that provide public benefits. Overall, the financial risk of attending university is reduced.

The idea of a graduate tax has been around for at least 30 years. To my knowledge, it has yet to be implemented in any jurisdiction. This may mean that the political and practical difficulties are just too great. Nonetheless, even if it is never implemented, public discussion of a graduate tax may help to advance the debate over post-secondary funding within Canada.

It is puzzling that the Canadian Association of University Teachers (CAUT) and other left-wing voices in the university system remain adamantly opposed to tuition increases. The evidence, some of which this study has referred to, makes it abundantly clear that subsidies to tuition are regressive – they transfer wealth to the middle and upper classes, or to people who will soon enter the middle and upper classes. University graduates are a privileged group in Canada.

Some argue that many students who have the ability to benefit from university cannot afford to pay tuition. Bursary programs help, but students do not always know about them and may not think to apply. Loan programs lead to post-graduation debt, which some students find frightening. The only way to ensure access for everyone, it is argued, is to keep tuition as low as possible. Those who make this argument appear to deny or ignore the regressive distributional nature of this policy, just as they deny the existence of other means to guarantee accessibility.

Underlying this attitude is, I believe, a deeper issue. Many academics believe in an ideal of social justice and want to see themselves as contributing to the public good. They have a vision of the university as an egalitarian public space, accessible to anyone who wants to learn. Yet one of the roles of the university is to take individuals who are already blessed with ability, give them the additional advantage of further education, and then identify them so as to ease their passage into the upper echelons of the capitalist world. For an academic to acknowledge the regressive nature of tuition subsidies would require her to accept her own complicity in this elite-making process.

Student advocates seem to have a more practical agenda. Of course it is not surprising that they oppose increases in tuition, since the extra money will come from them. The public argument, however, is based on the effect that high tuition rates will have on accessibility. But then we must ask why programs such as the income-contingent student loan are opposed. On cannot avoid the suspicion that it is precisely because they improve accessibility. The fear is that if access to the system can be guaranteed, the political decision to raise student fees will be made that much easier.

A graduate tax would make university as accessible as any program of tuition subsidies. Students need not be charged tuition at all, nor would they need to apply for any kind of support, nor be frightened by the prospect of debt. Access to university could be based entirely on academic potential. The tax would even reduce the financial risk of attending university by charging more to those students whose degree has particularly high economic value and less to others. If a public discussion of the graduate tax can be started, it will be interesting to see what CAUT and other voices from the left have to say about it.

In the end, public policy choices toward funding the university system must be based on the broad concerns of efficiency, accessibility, and equity, while acknowledging the system's very real need for more resources. A graduate tax has the potential to help us achieve all of these goals.

Notes

* Department of Economics, Queen's University. This paper encorporates material from 'Restructuring the University System: What Level of Public Support?' *Canadian Public Policy* 25:1 (January 1999), 133–40, and 'How Best to Fund Post-Secondary Education: A Graduate Tax?' presented at the John Deutsch Institute conference 'Higher Education in Canada,' 13–14 February 2004, forthcoming in that conference volume and in the working paper series of the Millennium Foundation. I would like to thank Sean Junor and Derek McKee for comments, and the Social Sciences and Humanities Research Council of Canada for its financial support for this project.

1 This material is based on Carmichael 1999.

2 Living expenses must be paid whether the student goes to university or not, and are therefore not relevant for determination of an optimal subsidy.

3 This section and what follows are based on Carmichael 2004.

4 The table is taken from Blondal, Field, and Girouard 2002.

5 The statement is certainly true *ex post*, given that there are always students who do not make it through their first year.

6 These criticisms of a loan system have been made for many years. Merrett (1967: 292–3) states: 'Certainly working class children have little or no experience of financial manoeuvres ... They especially would be unwilling to saddle themselves with future debts, to indenture themselves. The resulting bias on entry into higher education to the sons and daughters of the wealthy ... would lead to a form of social ossification with obvious moral and technical disadvantages. Second, the penalties will be great for those people who after graduation either enter professions which, although of great importance to the community, do not receive such recognition in terms of salary payments, or enter professions in which the risk of low incomes is very significant, such as the writing of poetry.'

7 Nerlove (1975) and West (1976) both discuss the Yale Tuition Postponement Option. Participants agreed to pay Yale 0.4% of their gross income over a 35-year period per $1000 advanced to them. In practice, since there was an upper limit on the amount that would have to be paid back, the scheme shared some attributes of an income-contingent loan system. However, to 'buy out' of the plan, the graduate would have to pay back 150% of the initial allocation, plus interest.

8 This is called the Career Options Assistance Program. The plan is designed to allow graduates to take on lower-paying jobs without fear of bankruptcy due to high loan payments. This plan is closer to a pure income-contingent loan plan, and is subsidized by Yale University's endowment funds.

9 This was the conclusion of a committee set up to study the requirements

for a quality undergraduate education in the Arts and Science Faculty at Queen's University. The report is available (April 2004) at http:// www.queensu.ca/artsci/internal/quality/pdf/A&SQuality_draft _rept010825.pdf

10 See Finnie 1999 for a trove of data on the earnings of university graduates two and five years after graduation.

11 It is also clear that if the government did not pay up front, universities could not rely on it to separate the income from this tax and dutifully send it to them. Funding would be set according to political priorities and health care would win, as usual.

12 Indeed there is nothing to prevent the government from making a market in these claims. This would have the advantage of creating an asset owned by the government to offset the up-front payments made to students.

13 The data in Finnie 1999 suggest that the average growth rate in real earnings between the second and fifth years after graduation is at least 5% per year.

14 In contrast, current demands by some students and faculty for increases in funding and zero tuition would force all taxpayers to participate.

15 Students who do not graduate should be subject to the tax based on the amount of support they have received, but they may not earn enough income to repay these costs.

References

Barr, N. 1993. 'Alternative Funding Resources for Higher Education.' *Economic Journal* 107: 418, 718–28.

Bassanini, S., and S. Scarpetta. 2001. 'Does Human Capital Matter for Growth in OECD Countries? Evidence from Pooled Mean-group Estimates.' Economics Department working paper 282, OECD, Paris.

Black, S.E., P.J. Devereux, and K.G. Salvanes. 2003. 'Why the Apple Doesn't Fall Far: Understanding Intergenerational Transmission of Human Capital.' Discussion paper no. 926, IZA, Bonn.

Blondal, S., S. Field, and N. Girouard. 2002. 'Investment in Human Capital Through Upper-Secondary and Tertiary Education.' OECD Economic Studies no. 34, 41–89.

Bynner, J., and M. Egerton. 2000. 'The Social Benefits of Higher Education: Insights Using Longitudinal Data.' Discussion paper, Centre for Longitudinal Studies, Institute of Education, London.

Carmichael, H.L. 1999. 'Restructuring the University System: What Level of Public Support?' *Canadian Public Policy* 25:1, 133–40.

– 2004. 'How Best to Fund Post-Secondary Education: A Graduate Tax?' Paper prepared for the John Deutsch Institute conference 'Higher Education in Canada,' 13–14 February 2004, Queen's University.

Chapman, B. 1997. 'Conceptual Issues and the Australian Experience with

Income Contingent Charges for Higher Education.' *Economic Journal* 107:442, 738–51.

Finnie, R. 1999. 'Fields of Plenty, Fields of Lean: Earnings of University Graduates in Canada.' Discussion paper R-99-13E.a, Human Resources Development Canada, Ottawa.

Finnie, R., and C. Laporte. 2003. 'Student Loans and Access to Post-secondary Education: Evidence from the New Post-secondary Education Survey.' Discussion paper, Statistics Canada, Analytical Studies Branch, Ottawa.

Friedman, M., and S. Kuznets. 1945. *Income from Individual Professional Practice.* Cambridge, Mass.: National Bureau of Economic Research.

Glennerster, Howard, S. Merrett, and G. Wilson. 1968. 'A Graduate Tax. *Journal of Higher Education*, 1:1, 26–38.

Greenaway, D., and M. Haynes. 2003. 'Funding Higher Education in the UK: The Role of Fees and Loans.' *Economic Journal* 113:485, 150–66.

Johnson, G.E. 1984. 'Subsidies for Higher Education.' *Journal of Labor Economics* 2:3, 303–18.

Kenkel, D.S. 1991. 'Health Behavior, Health Knowledge, and Schooling.' *Journal of Political Economy* 99:2, 287–305.

Lochner, L., and E. Moretti. 2001. 'The Effect of Education on Crime: Evidence from Prison Inmates, Arrests, and Self Reports.' Discussion paper 8605, National Bureau of Economic Research, Cambridge, Mass.

Merrett, S. 1967. 'Student Finance in Higher Education.' *Economic Journal*, 77:306, 288–302.

Moretti, E. 2004. 'Estimating the Social Return to Higher Education from Longitudinal and Repeated Cross Sectional Data.' *Journal of Econometrics* 121: 1–2, 175–212.

Nerlove, M. 1975. 'Some Problems in the Use of Income Contingent Loans for the Finance of Higher Education. *Journal of Political Economy* 83:1, 157–83.

Ockert, B. 2003. 'What's the Value of an Acceptance Letter? Using College Applicants to Estimate the Return to Education.' Discussion paper, IFAU – Office of Labor Market Policy Evaluation, Uppsala, Sweden.

Poutvaara, P. 2003. 'Educating Europe.' Discussion paper, Center for Business and Education Research, Copenhagen.

Turkheimer, E. 2000. 'Three Laws of Behavior Genetics and What They Mean.' *Current Directions in Psychological Science* 9:5, 160–4.

West, E. 1976. 'The Yale Tuition Postponement Plan in the Mid-Seventies.' *Higher Education* 5, 169–75.